W9-CSX-169

International Accounting

A Global Perspective

M. Zafar Iqbal

California Polytechnic State University

Trini U. Melcher

California State University-San Marcos

Amin A. Elmallah

California State University-Sacramento

SOUTH-WESTERN College Publishing

An International Thomson Publishing Company

Accounting Team Director: Mary H. Draper
Sponsoring Editor: David L. Shaut
Developmental Editor: Leslie A. Kauffman
Production Editor: Peggy A. Williams
Production Services: Robert W. Hill
Cover Designer: Paul Neff
Cover photo: ©PhotoDisc
Marketing Manager: Steven W. Hazelwood

HF
5626
.I66
1997

Copyright © 1997
by South-Western College Publishing

ALL RIGHTS RESERVED
The text of this publication, or any part thereof, may not be reproduced or transmitted in any form or by any
means, electronic or mechanical, including photocopying, recording, storage in an informational retrieval
system, or otherwise, without the prior written permission of the publisher.

ISBN: 0-538-83739-X

2 3 4 5 6 7 8 9 MT 4 3 2 1 0 9 8 7

Printed in the United States of America

I(T)P
International Thomson Publishing
South-Western College Publishing is an ITP Company. The ITP trademark is used under license.

Library of Congress Cataloging-in-Publication Data

Iqbal, M. Zafar.
    International accounting : a global perspective / M. Zafar Iqbal,
Trini U. Melcher.
        p.   cm.
    Includes index.
    ISBN 0-538-83739-X
    1. Accounting--Standards. 2. Financial statements--Standards.
3. Comparative accounting. 4. International business enterprises-
-Accounting.   I. Melcher, Trini U., 1931-   . II. Title.
HF5626.I66 1996
657'.96--dc20
                                                         96-7313
                                                           CIP

In loving memory of my brother

Waheed Ul Zafar

M. Zafar Iqbal

Preface

International Accounting: A Global Perspective focuses on the issues in international accounting in today's global business world. The text offers a unique approach: It has a global perspective, is free from Western cultural bias, and has a multinational orientation. This enhances objective discussion of international accounting issues.

Some of the evidence showing breadth of coverage includes: Three separate chapters (Chapters 8, 9, and 10) devoted to international managerial accounting issues, one chapter on developing countries (Chapter 13), one chapter on Eastern Europe (Chapter 14), a special section containing a complete set of Imperial Chemical Industries reports, and a comprehensive glossary of terms. The same 11 countries are used throughout the book for discussion of comparative practices. Care was taken in selecting the 11 countries to ensure representation of diversified practices in different areas of the world.

International Accounting: A Global Perspective is a current and comprehensive text, suitable for an upper-division undergraduate course or a graduate level course. With its global orientation, it is suitable for adoption worldwide.

Features of the Text

The textbook contents are current and include a description of emerging trends in international accounting. Students and faculty should find the text lucid, succinct, and accurate. Some of the special features are outlined below.

Global perspective. The book has a truly global perspective. The authors feel that an international accounting textbook should be free from any country, regional, or cultural bias.

Currency of contents. The material is up to date and includes the most recent developments in international accounting. Some examples are:

- Agreement between the International Accounting Standards Committee and the International Organization of Securities to develop standards for listing of securities worldwide
- International Monetary Fund's guidelines for voluntary disclosures
- Singapore's newly acquired status as a developed economy
- North American Free Trade Agreement
- European Union
- Asia Pacific Economic Cooperation
- Technology alliances
- Modern approaches to cost controls in global operations
- Expanded discussion of Asia and the Pacific Rim.

By the year 2000 the economies of East Asia are expected to equal that of the U.S., and total about four-fifths of the European Union. This important, and often overlooked, region is discussed in depth in Chapters 1 and 13.

Clear writing style. Discussion is substantive yet succinct. Presentations are organized to lead the student from basic to advanced levels step by step. Key points are emphasized after the discussion.

Real-life applications of concepts. Actual events are brought into discussion to reinforce students' understanding of the concepts. Numerous examples and financial statements from actual companies are incorporated in each of the chapters.

Focus on developing countries and Eastern Europe. Chapters 13 and 14 discuss the unique problems and challenges of developing countries and Eastern European countries respectively.

Comparative practices in selected countries. Throughout the book, the same 11 countries, from different regions of the world, are used for comparison of practices. This provides the students an opportunity to learn the important accounting practices in the 11 countries.

Impact of advances in technology. Among the unique features of this book is a discussion of how advancements in information technology affect environmental factors and accounting practices globally.

End-of-chapter materials. These include:

- **Note to Students.** This innovative and unique feature will help the student keep current on the chapter topics by using listed sources of information. Other information contained in many of the notes should make the student aware of the career opportunities in emerging accounting areas.
- **Chapter Summary.**
- **Questions for Discussion.**
- **Exercises/Problems.**
- **Cases.** Each chapter has at least one end-of-chapter case and several have more than one.
- **Footnotes and References.** This text includes extensive footnotes and chapter bibliographies. This should be helpful for several reasons:
    - ✓ Many undergraduate students are only vaguely aware of international accounting literature. Simply scanning these listings should increase their awareness of the context of international accounting and international business.
    - ✓ The text is intended for use in graduate as well as undergraduate courses. The references will help in pursuing the topics in greater depth, especially in graduate courses.
    - ✓ Some instructors may not have significant international experience but are interested in teaching the international accounting course. Additional readings will help them feel comfortable in the classroom, and also help them broaden their own knowledge base.

The references include classic materials such as Sweeney's dissertation on general price-level-adjusted accounting, statements by standard-setting bodies such as the International Accounting Standards Committee and the Financial Accounting Standards Board, and current developments from sources such as *Business Week, The Wall Street Journal,* and the *Economist.*

Chapter Descriptions

Chapter 1: Introduction to International Accounting. Chapter 1 lays the foundation of the text by discussing the importance of the global economy. The chapter develops a model of environmental influences on accounting and a definition of international accounting.

Chapter 2: Internationalization of Accounting Standards. Chapter 2 contains a discussion of the differences between standardization and harmonization. It reviews the harmonization efforts being undertaken at various levels in the world.

Chapter 3: Financial Reporting Disclosures. Chapter 3 examines the existing disclosure practices and the issues related to measurement and disclosure. The chapter includes discussion of reserves disclosures, segment disclosures, and social impact disclosures. Examples of value-added statements from actual companies are provided in the chapter.

Chapter 4: Setting Accounting Standards in Selected Countries. Chapter 4 describes and compares the standard setting process in the selected 11 countries and current standards for certain important areas.

Chapter 5: Accounting for Changing Prices. Chapter 5 deals with issues from both accounting and economic standpoints. The chapter contains a discussion and examples of constant monetary unit restatement and current value accounting. Gearing adjustments are explained within the context of current value accounting. The chapter includes a comparison of current practices in the featured 11 countries.

Chapter 6: Foreign Currency. Chapter 6 discusses foreign currency transactions, forward exchange contracts, and common methods for foreign currency translation. The four common translation methods are analyzed and compared. It also describes the current practices in the featured 11 countries.

Chapter 7: Specific Reporting Issues. Chapter 7 focuses on business combinations and consolidations, intangible assets, research and development, leases, and pension and post-retirement benefits. The chapter compares existing practices in the selected 11 countries in each of these areas.

Chapter 8: Managerial Accounting Issues: Strategic Planning and Control. Chapter 8 is the first of the three chapters on managerial accounting topics. The chapter covers strategic planning with special attention to cultural considerations. Control systems are discussed with emphasis given to the selection of performance criteria for international subsidiaries. The last section ties in information systems, technological advances, and compatibility with international accounting standards.

Chapter 9: Budgeting, Product Costing, and Foreign Exchange Risk Management. Chapter 9 includes a step by step development of a master budget and a discussion of capital budgeting. Product costing and cost control approaches are described. Cost control approaches discussed include restructuring, activity-based costing, activity-based management, total quality management, just-in-time, kaizen, target costing, and worldwide manufacturing locations. Foreign exchange risk management is discussed within the context of foreign currency risk exposure, transaction risk exposure, translation risk exposure, and economic exposure.

Chapter 10: Transfer Pricing and International Taxation. Chapter 10 discusses various approaches for transfer pricing and also examines international taxation issues.

Chapter 11: International Financial Statement Analysis. Chapter 11 contains a section dealing with problems in the availability of financial information such as reliability of data, timeliness, language and terminology, different currencies, and different formats of financial statements. Financial statement analysis is divided into international financial ratio analysis and trend analysis. Limitations of analysis are also discussed. A special appendix contains a complete set of annual reports for Imperial Chemical Industries.

Chapter 12: Auditing Issues for Global Operations. Chapter 12 deals with auditing in its two dimensions: internal and external. Six models of an internal audit organization structure are presented. The chapter also includes a discussion of the Foreign Corrupt Practices Act. External auditing in the international environment is discussed within the framework of various countries and regions. "True and fair view" is contrasted with "present fairly." The chapter includes a description of the existing independent audit environments in the featured 11 countries.

Chapter 13: Developing Countries: The Emerging World Economic Order. Chapter 13 describes both the challenges and the opportunities in developing countries. Special emphasis is placed on the importance of the role of accounting in developing countries, especially due to large expenditures on infrastructure projects.

Chapter 14: Eastern European Countries. Chapter 14 includes a discussion of socialist accounting. This chapter focuses on financial statement practices and trends in four of the Eastern European countries, namely Hungary, Poland, the Czech Republic, and Russia.

Supplements

The comprehensive package includes three supplements: *Solutions Manual* and a combination *Test Bank* and *Instructor's Manual,* all written by the textbook authors. The instructor's manual should be especially helpful to instructors with little or no teaching or practical international experience. It contains many helpful hints and side comments, as well as chapter outlines and teaching transparency masters.

It is vital that supplements receive as much attention as the text itself. For example, a solutions manual full of errors can greatly reduce the usefulness of a first-rate textbook. Since the authors of the textbook have written the supplements, the accuracy and cohesiveness of the package is ensured. The authors would like to thank Cheryl Fulkerson, University of Texas—San Antonio, for verifying the accuracy of the solutions manual and test bank.

Acknowledgments

Many individuals provided assistance and feedback throughout the writing and development stages of this text. We especially thank the following faculty for their insightful reviews of the manuscript:

Cheryl L. Fulkerson
University of Texas—San Antonio

George O. Gamble
University of Houston

William T. Geary
The College of William and Mary

Abo-El-Yazeed T. Habib
Mankato State University

Clayton A. Hock
Miami University

Carol Olson Houston
San Diego State University

Jai S. Kang
San Francisco State University

Felix Pomeranz
Florida International University

Lawrence Sundby
St. Cloud State University

Appreciation and gratitude are due to Leslie Kauffman, Mary Draper, and Peggy Williams at South-Western College Publishing. It has been a pleasure working with them. Their assistance and guidance were invaluable in bringing the project to its successful culmination. Their professionalism is exemplary.

Our friends and families also contributed greatly to this project. The authors would like to offer the following personal notes of appreciation:

My wife Patrice Iqbal and my good friend Professor Robert W. Hill played critical roles in the development of this book. Their hard work and long hours made a notable difference in the quality of this book. They deserve special thanks and acknowledgment. I am truly thankful to my mother, Mrs. Ghulam Fatima Sharif, for her support. She has always been a source of strength to me.

My father, Dr. Mohammad Sharif, was an exemplary role model. He personified personal ethics, work ethics, and intellectual curiosity.

I have been fortunate to have had several mentors. They have provided me with encouragement, guidance, and assistance throughout my professional career: Donald E. Kieso (Northern Illinois University), Robert H. Raymond and Thomas D. Hubbard (University of Nebraska—Lincoln), Charles T. Horngren (Stanford University), and Kenneth D. Walters (University of Washington). I owe them a tremendous debt of gratitude.

M. Zafar Iqbal
July 1996

I wish to thank Michael Melcher and Jocelyn Gutierrez for their suggestions, and Lynn Dugan for her help in typing parts of the drafts of manuscript.

I also wish to express appreciation to the California State University Advanced and International Accounting students who provided evaluative comments.

Any teaching and research initiative requires the steadfast support, patience, and encouragement of family members. Thus, I would like to express appreciation to Teresa Melcher, Michael Melcher, and Jocelyn Gutierrez.

Trini U. Melcher
July 1996

Brief Contents

Contents

Chapter 3

Financial Reporting Disclosures   69

Chapter 4

Setting Accounting Standards in Selected Countries   107

Chapter 5

Accounting for Changing Prices   139

Chapter 6
Foreign Currency   169

Chapter 7
Specific Reporting Issues   204

Chapter 8
Managerial Accounting Issues:
Strategic Planning and Control   236

Chapter 11
International Financial Statement Analysis   355

Chapter 12

Auditing Issues for Global Operations   476

Chapter 13
Developing Countries: The Emerging World Economic Order   530

Chapter 14
Eastern European Countries   555

Chapter 1

Introduction to International Accounting

Accounting provides information that can be used in making economic decisions. It is a service activity and exists only to serve decision makers. The decision makers use both qualitative and quantitative information from various sources. Accounting provides quantitative information that is primarily financial in nature.[1]

Perhaps the most familiar form of an economic entity is a business organization. In order for the accountant to meet the information needs of decision makers, the information provided should aid in making "reasoned" choices among alternative uses of scarce resources in the conduct of business and economic activities.[2]

The linkage between decision makers and accounting is shown in Figure 1–1. It shows (1) the information needs of decision makers, as perceived by the accountant and (2) the communication of accounting information to the decision makers. This information is provided by the accountant in the form of reports—the final output of an accounting system. The reports are based on collecting and processing data from economic events of the entity.

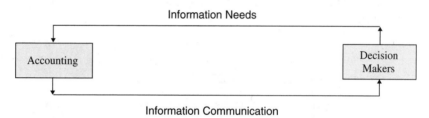

Figure 1–1   Relationship Between Accounting and Decision Making

Why Study International Accounting?

From a student's perspective, the major reason for studying accounting is to develop competencies in collecting and processing data from economic activities and communicating the information, through reports, to the decision makers. This leads us to an important and noteworthy point. *Since the environments in which an economic entity operates are dynamic, the accounting profession must remain current to be useful. Only then can it serve the information needs of decision makers in ever-changing business environments.* We live in

---

[1] *Statement of the Accounting Principles Board No. 4,* "Basic Concepts and Accounting Principles Underlying Financial Statements of Business Enterprises" (New York: American Institute of Certified Public Accountants, 1970), par. 40.

[2] *Statement of Financial Accounting Concepts No. 1,* "Objectives of Financial Reporting by Business Enterprises" (Stamford, Conn.: Financial Accounting Standards Board, 1978), par. 9.

an age in which the economy is fast becoming global. Natural, human, and financial resources often can be shifted from one part of the world to another part conveniently, efficiently, and at great speed. International accounting provides pertinent information to decision makers in this age of a global economy, helping them make resource allocation decisions that maximize the benefit to humankind.

For this reason, it is important to study international accounting. Otherwise, in this age of international operations and worldwide markets there would be an information vacuum, resulting in less than optimal economic decisions. The end result would be misallocation of economic resources worldwide.

Definition of International Accounting

International accounting is defined as *accounting for international transactions, comparisons of accounting principles in different countries, and harmonization of diverse accounting standards worldwide.* This definition encompasses the operational needs of the accountant in financial, managerial, tax, auditing, and other areas of accounting. Additionally, it takes into account broader conceptual issues involving contrasts between accounting standards of different countries as well as harmonization of diverse accounting practices throughout the world.

The Age of the Global Economy

Many powerful trends toward a global economy are evident. The North American Free Trade Agreement (NAFTA) is a free trade agreement among Canada, Mexico, and the U.S. Other countries may join NAFTA at a later stage. The European Union (EU) is already a reality. The demise of the communist economic system in the former U.S.S.R. and Eastern European countries has provided opportunities and challenges for their entry into the free market global economy. An important development accomplished in late 1993 was the conclusion of a revised General Agreement on Tariffs and Trade (GATT) by 117 nations. GATT's intent is to expand international trade. It will reduce tariffs and other international trade obstacles and barriers. As of January 1995, GATT had 124 member countries.

Another interesting and significant phenomenon is the emergence of the economies of Asia, particularly the Pacific Rim, as economic powers. The Pacific Rim and the trading blocs are discussed in greater detail in later sections of this chapter.

An increase in international trade, facilitating the movement of goods and services worldwide, improves the efficiency of resource usage. Each country then specializes in producing those goods and services that it can generate efficiently, and it exchanges what it produces for the products made more efficiently in other countries. This should result in raising the standard of living in all countries involved in international trade. Increased competition also forces firms to be more efficient.

International Business

International business, or international trade, transcends national boundaries. It includes all commercial transactions resulting in flows of goods, services, or financial resources from country to country. International trade has been steadily growing in importance and is currently estimated to be 7 trillion U.S. dollars.

The United States is the largest exporter in the world. U.S. merchandise exports alone (excluding exports of services) support 7.2 million jobs for U.S. workers. A new National Export Strategy was announced by the Clinton administration in late 1993. The plan notes that continued growth of exports is essential for the creation of new jobs in the U.S. The goal is to exceed $1 trillion in exports and thereby create 6 million more jobs for U.S. workers by the turn of the century. This illustrates how important international trade can be to a country's economy.

Several factors have helped accelerate globalization of economies. Standardization of products and production processes, technological advances in information technology, improved transportation, and sophisticated distribution systems are all major contributors. The recent privatization of public sector enterprises worldwide and economic reforms in developing countries are also important factors.

Blurring Boundaries

In this age of international markets and global operations, it is sometimes difficult to identify the country of origin of a product or a company.

> It looks like a trade world turned upside down: The Commerce Department rules that an American company unfairly dumped electric typewriters in the United States—injuring a Japanese company.
>
> Outrageous? Not really, in a world of multinational companies.
>
> The Japanese company is Brother USA, a subsidiary of Brother Industries of Nagoya, Japan. But it makes all the electric typewriters it sells in the United States at a plant employing 600 Americans in Bartlett, Tenn.
>
> The American company is Smith Corona of New Canaan, Conn. Asked about the irony of being sued by the Japanese for dumping in the United States, company spokeswoman Patricia Cornell said, "Several people have pointed that out."
>
> But Smith Corona imports most of the typewriters it sells here from a wholly owned subsidiary in Singapore. And Cornell said the company is closing its only U.S. typewriter-making plant, in Cortland, N.Y., laying off 775 Americans and moving the operation to Mexico.
>
> To add to the multinational mix, nearly half of Smith Corona (47.6 percent) is owned by a British conglomerate, Hanson PLC.

The ruling this week, in a case dating from the Bush administration, should not surprise the new Democratic leaders. Robert Reich, secretary of labor and close economic adviser to President Clinton, wrote in the latest issue of the Harvard Business School magazine:

"In the global enterprise the bonds between company and country. . . are rapidly eroding. Today corporate decisions about production and location are driven by the dictates of global competition, not by national allegiance."[3]

"Hey, this says 'Made in Japan.' "

Drawing by Stevenson; © 1992 The New Yorker Magazine, Inc.

Dependencies on International Trade

The dependency of many well-known companies on international trade can be determined by reviewing a few facts. Eighty percent of Coca-Cola's and 70 percent of Gillette Co.'s sales are from international trade. In 1991, 80 percent of Boeing's orders came from overseas. One of the explanations given by IBM executives for the company's poor performance in recent years is that the company has been hurt by economic slumps in Europe and Asia (especially Japan). This is not surprising because two-thirds of IBM's revenues are derived from international sales. Since 1987, General Electric's revenues from outside the U.S. have increased at an annual rate of 30 percent and now contribute 40 percent of the company's total sales. With this trend, "the day is not far off when the company that helped electrify

[3] "Typewriter dumping case: Which firm is 'American?'" San Luis Obispo *Telegram Tribune,* 4 February 1993, p. B-4.

America will earn more money outside its borders than inside."[4] According to Vice-Chairman Paolo Fresco of GE, "Being national doesn't pay."

This dependency on international business is not confined to large corporations. Tens of thousands of small businesses are involved in exporting or importing. Seventy-five percent of U.S. firms that export have fewer than 100 employees.[5]

The Reasons for Going International

A recent survey by Deloitte Touche Tohmatsu International entitled *Why Companies Go International: International Strategy of Middle Market Companies* summarizes information on the international strategy of 400 medium-size companies in twenty developed countries. Frequently stated reasons for engaging in international operations are given below.[6]

Reason	Percentage
Growth opportunities	84%
Less dependence on domestic economy	39
Customer demand	34
Lower costs	24

The survey also identified problems most often encountered by companies that had decided to go international. The main problems noted by U.S. and Canadian companies are presented below.

Problem Identified	Eastern Europe	Rest of the World
Obtaining information	33%	24%
Financing	31	18
Poor ownership rights	19	11
Uncertain legislative and business environment	56	26
Administrative formalities	25	34
Currency restrictions	28	16
Taxation	11	24

Interestingly, one-fourth of the surveyed companies had discontinued overseas operations during the past five years. Major reasons for quitting included:

- Failure of expected marketing opportunities to materialize.
- Operational failures.
- Problems with business partners.
- Political conflicts.
- Difficulties in making collections.

[4] Tim Smart, Pete Engardio, and Geri Smith, "GE's Brave New World," *Business Week,* 8 November 1993, p. 67.

[5] Jeff Madura, *International Financial Management,* 4th ed. (St. Paul: West Publishing Co., 1995), p. 4.

[6] "Companies Surveyed on Going Global," *Deloitte & Touche Review,* 5 October 1992, pp. 1-2.

Findings of the above survey are consistent with generally recognized reasons for involvement of a company in international business. Those reasons are discussed next.

1. Theory of comparative advantage. According to this classical economic theory, each country should produce only those goods and services that it can produce with relative efficiency. Such goods and services should be exported to other countries. In return, a country should import goods and services that can be produced with relative efficiency in other countries. Taking advantage of the opportunities to sell abroad is the major reason for expansion in international trade. This advantage would not be realized in the absence of specialization, which results from comparative advantage.

> Multinational business has generally increased over time. Part of this growth is due to the increasing realization that specialization by countries can increase production efficiency. Some countries, such as Japan and the United States, have a technology advantage, while countries such as Jamaica, Mexico, and South Korea have an advantage in the cost of basic labor. Since these advantages cannot be easily transported, countries tend to use their advantages to specialize in the production of goods that can be produced with relative efficiency. This explains why countries such as Japan and the U.S. are large producers of computer components, while countries such as Jamaica and Mexico are large producers of agricultural and handmade goods.
>
> Specialization in some products may result in no production of other products, so that trade between countries is essential. This is the argument made by the classical **theory of comparative advantage.** Due to comparative advantages, it is understandable why firms are able to penetrate foreign markets. Many of the Virgin Islands rely completely on international trade for most products, while they specialize in tourism. While the production of some goods is possible on these islands, there is more efficiency in the specialization of tourism. That is, the islands are better off using some revenues earned from tourism to import products than attempting to produce all the products that they need.[7]

The concept of comparative advantage has come under some criticism in recent years because it explains only the export-import dimension of international business. Multinationals—corporations with global operations—are not merely engaged in large volumes of imports and exports. Their worldwide operations include manufacturing, financing, investment, and many other types of activities. Also the theory of comparative advantage assumes that factors of production (e.g., labor and capital) are constant for a country. This assumption has also been challenged on the basis that in this age of high technology, factors of production are often quite mobile. A company engaged in international trade may be able to relocate its operations with relative ease by shifting factors of production to the desired location.

Comparative hourly manufacturing labor costs in fifteen countries for 1993 are shown in Figure 1–2.

---

[7] Madura, p. 9.

Source: Morgan Stanley

Figure 1–2   Hourly Manufacturing Labor Costs

The above comparison indicates that countries such as Indonesia and China have a comparative advantage over countries such as France and Japan in this particular factor of production.

The theory of comparative advantage has its limitations. Clearly, it cannot fully explain all of the dimensions of international business. However, this does not necessarily lead to the conclusion that the theory is invalid. The concept of comparative advantage can and does partially explain the expansion of international trade. When coupled with **product cycle theory** (explained later), the theory of comparative advantage also explains why firms enter international markets in the first place.

2. Imperfect market theory. The second reason for having international operations is to gain access to factors of production. The factors of production may include cheap labor, labor with some special skills, availability of raw materials, etc.

> . . . the real world suffers from **imperfect market** conditions where factors of production are somewhat immobile. There are costs and often restrictions related to the transfer of labor and other resources used for production. There may also be restrictions on funds and other resources transferred among countries. Because markets for the various resources used in production are "imperfect," firms often capitalize on a foreign country's resources. Imperfect markets provide an incentive for firms to seek out foreign opportunities.[8]

[8] Madura, p. 10.

It is clear from the above statement that the assertion by some that factors of production are no longer fixed for a country is exaggerated. There is indeed more mobility but by no means total mobility of factors of production.

3. Product cycle theory. Product cycle theory was mentioned earlier during our discussion of the theory of comparative advantage. According to product cycle theory, a firm starts selling first in the domestic market because it has an important advantage—access to information about its customers and competition. Later, any demand for the company's product in foreign markets is satisfied first by exporting. *Exporting is typically the entry point in international trade for most firms.* Subsequently, the company may decide to locate parts of its operations abroad.

> As time passes, the firm may feel the only way to retain its advantage over competition in foreign countries is to produce the product in foreign markets, thereby reducing its transportation costs. Over time, the competition in the foreign markets may increase as other producers become more familiar with the firm's product. Thus, the firm may develop strategies to prolong the foreign demand for its product. A common approach is to attempt differentiating the product so that other competitors cannot offer exactly the same product.[9]

According to product cycle theory, there is a progression from home markets to international markets, *with exports being the entry point to international markets* as stated earlier.

4. Technology transfer and strategic alliances. A company may engage in international business because it desires to obtain access to advanced technologies developed in different parts of the world. Conversely, a company may be willing to share its advanced technology with companies or governments in other parts of the world to gain access to their markets. Though not new, this phenomenon has become increasingly important in recent years. It has also raised some interesting issues, such as intellectual property rights.

Many technological alliances have been formed and others are being formed to share knowledge for mutual benefit. In global markets, time is often more important than cost. To compete in dynamic global markets, an organization should be able to swiftly produce and distribute products in demand. This means that the organization must have the flexibility to respond quickly to competitive conditions. Corning Inc. puts together technological alliances with other companies to develop and sell new products faster. Corning Inc. has 19 alliances, accounting for approximately 13 percent of its earnings in 1992. An ever-increasing number of companies are entering strategic alliances to share technology. Examples include American Telephone and Telegraph Co.'s alliance with Japan's Matsushita Electric Industrial Co. for the Safari notebook computer project and MCI Communication Corporation's alliances with approximately 100 companies to work jointly on large projects.[10] IBM and Hitachi have entered into technology and licensing agreements to share mainframe computer technology. NEC Corporation of Tokyo and Samsung Electronics of South Korea have formed a joint

---

[9] *Ibid.*

[10] John A. Byrne, Richard Brandt and Otis Port, "The Virtual Corporation," *Business Week,* 8 February 1993, p. 100.

venture to develop advanced computer chips. In Indonesia, GE has set up GE Technology Indonesia to enter into joint ventures in its technology transfer schemes. Interestingly, GE had set up an office in Vietnam to make technology deals in anticipation of the end of the U.S. trade embargo.[11] As we know now, GE's anticipation was correct. On February 3, 1994 President Clinton lifted the trade embargo that was imposed against Vietnam in 1964. This allows GE and other U.S. businesses to participate fully in the fast-growing Vietnamese market. Exhibit 1–1 lists a few specific examples of strategic alliances in Asia.

Exhibit 1–1	Key High-Tech Ventures in Asia		
Country	**Multinational**	**Local Entity**	**Product/Technology**
Hong Kong	GEC–Marconi	Varitronix	LCDs
Korea	Honda	Daewoo Motors	Automobiles
	Hitachi	Goldstar	Semiconductors
Malaysia	Intel	Subsidiary	Chip design
	Matsushita	Subsidiary	TV design
Singapore	Glaxo	Government	Brain drugs
	Apple	Government	Software
Taiwan	Philips	Government	Semiconductors
	Motorola	Cal-Comp	Pocket secretaries

Source: *Business Week*, 7 December 1992, p. 132.

Types of International Involvement

A company can conduct international business by choosing from many different types of activities and levels of involvement. We will now discuss the various levels of involvement and types of activities.

International companies—exporters. A company that exports its products or services overseas is classified as an international corporation.[12] The company may be a direct exporter, an indirect exporter, or both. Being a direct exporter requires the company to have its own marketing operations at various locations worldwide. This includes its own sales staff, channels of distribution, collections, etc. A direct exporter assumes greater risks and costs than an indirect exporter, but also has more control over the marketing of its products in world markets. With successful marketing strategies, the direct exporter may enjoy growth in profits and market share. An indirect exporter sells its product to domestic buyers who subsequently sell it in international markets. Alternately, an indirect exporter may retain an intermediary to identify potential buyers in other countries. Indirect exporting is the less

---

[11] Smart, *et al.,* p. 68.

[12] KPMG, "Blurring Boundaries," *World,* vol. 27, no. 2, 1993, pp. 42-46.

expensive of the two alternatives, at least in the beginning. A company may be a direct exporter to some countries and an indirect exporter to others.

One of the best known international corporations is The Boeing Company. It makes airplanes in Seattle, its home base, and sells them throughout the world.

Strategic alliance. A company may collaborate with companies in other countries to share rights and responsibilities as well as revenues and expenses. In some countries, alliances may be the answer to prevalent political and cultural biases against "foreign" companies. Exhibit 1–2 shows some of the common types of strategic alliances.

Exhibit 1–2   Common Types of Strategic Alliances

Strategic alliances can be formed for a variety of reasons. Some of the more common are described below:

In a **research collaboration,** two or more companies participate in a defined research program and benefit from the results. Research costs can be funded entirely by one of the parties, shared equally by the parties, or shared according to some other agreed-upon proportion.

A **licensing program** is another form of alliance. Proprietary information, such as patent rights or expertise, is licensed by the owner (licensor) to another party (licensee). Compensation paid to the licensor usually includes license issuance fees, milestone payments, and/or royalties.

In a **copromotion deal,** a product is promoted jointly by two companies under the same brand name and marketing plan. Generally the manufacturing company handles receivables, inventory, and so on and pays a commission to the copromotor. Compensation is almost always based on the product sales level.

Other types of strategic alliances include joint ventures, comarketing deals, production collaborations, equity investments, and outsourcing arrangements. The terms of a strategic alliance are defined in a written agreement between the parties.

Source: Greg L. Cellini, *Management Accounting*, June 1993, pp. 56-59.

Joint ventures that involve technology alliance can create a "win-win" situation by providing mutual benefit to all of the collaborators, as discussed earlier. Organización Mabe, an appliance maker in Mexico, is a good example of a successful joint venture. Mabe is half Mexican-owned while the other half is owned by General Electric. Through this partnership Mabe has access to GE's worldwide purchasing power and its advanced technology, while GE benefits from low-cost labor and Mexico's fast-growing appliance market.[13]

---

[13] Geri Smith, "This Venture Is Cooking with Gas," *Business Week,* 8 November 1993, p. 70.

Multinational corporations. A company that considers the globe as a single marketplace is a multinational corporation. To capitalize on international business opportunities, a multinational corporation has worldwide product development, purchasing, manufacturing, marketing and financial operations. Such companies are active players in international trade and international investments. It is important to note that *a corporation becomes multinational because of management's global vision.* Some other terms are also used to describe what we have referred to as a multinational corporation (MNC). Two of those terms are **multinational enterprise** (MNE) and **transnational corporation** (TNC). The latter term is favored by the United Nations.

Perhaps the best-known example of a multinational company is Coca-Cola, which has operations in over 160 countries. Many companies often considered American are in fact multinationals, deriving over half their revenues from sales outside the U.S. Examples include Exxon, Colgate Palmolive, Dow Chemical, Coca-Cola, IBM, American Brands, and Gillette.

MNCs have been a significant driving force in the development of international accounting. Their interest in international accounting extends beyond the esoteric, theoretical issues. The complexity of their operations and the diversity of their transactions demand solutions to many recording and reporting issues not pertinent to purely domestic companies.

A recent report of the United Nations Conference on Trade Development discusses the continuing expansion and influence of multinational (transnational) corporations. Some excerpts of the report are presented below.[14]

- TNCs are a powerful force for binding national economies together. Through complex corporate strategies and intricate network structures, TNCs engage in international production characterized by a sophisticated intrafirm division of labor for each corporate function. As a result, about one-third of the world's private sector productive assets are under the common governance of TNCs.

- The growing influence of TNCs can be seen in the increase in foreign direct investment (FDI) and the growth in the number of TNCs and their foreign affiliates. By the early 1990s there were 37,000 TNCs in the world, with over 170,000 foreign affiliates. The TNC universe is highly concentrated in terms of the share of foreign assets controlled by the largest firms. Roughly 1 percent of parent TNCs own half of the FDI stock or total affiliate assets.

- FDI in the 1980s was increasingly concentrated within the European Community, Japan, and the United States. In the early 1990s, however, FDI flows to developed countries declined, while those to developing countries increased, especially in Asia and Latin America and the Caribbean. This shift was in response to rapid economic growth and fewer restrictions. The information is summarized in Exhibit 1–3 for the period 1987 to 1992.

---

[14] "Report Notes: TNCs' Role in Integration of Global Economy," *Deloitte & Touche Review,* 23 August 1993, pp. 3-4.

Exhibit 1–3	Inflows and Outflows of Foreign Direct Investment—Billions of Dollars					
	1987	**1988**	**1989**	**1990**	**1991**	**1992**
Developed countries:						
Inflows	$109	$132	$167	$172	$108	$ 86
Outflows	132	162	203	225	177	145
Developing economies:						
Inflows	25	30	29	31	39	48
Outflows	2	6	10	9	5	5

Inflows of foreign direct investments in developing countries were approximately $67 billion in 1993 and reached a record $79 billion in 1994. The estimated amount for 1995 is $85 billion. According to a recent survey of Global 1000 companies by Ernst & Young, 80 percent of these companies hold investments in emerging markets, and an additional 4 percent plan to invest within the next five years.[15]

The strategies of TNCs increasingly involve more complex forms of worldwide economic integration. This new approach is made possible by huge improvements in communications and information technologies, which allow TNCs to coordinate a growing number of activities in a widening array of locations.

Major Trading Blocs and the Pacific Rim Region

A discussion of international accounting and international business would not be complete without consideration of two recent important developments, i.e., major trading blocs and the emergence of the Pacific Rim region as an economic power. These developments are important enough to have received the personal involvement and attention of many heads of state of developed countries. It has been asserted by some economic and political commentators that the final outcome in the case of trading blocs has had direct impact on the effectiveness of some of the national leaders involved. For example, the passage of the North American Free Trade Agreement (NAFTA) by the U.S. Congress was considered to be an important personal and political victory for President Clinton. It is also widely believed that had the Maastricht Treaty been rejected in the U.K. (its ratification was necessary for formation of the European Union) the political leadership of Prime Minister John Major would have suffered.

Major Trading Blocs

European Union (EU). European Community nations became a single market on January 1, 1993. The EU originally linked 12 nations of Western Europe by eliminating tariff and

---

[15] "What's Ahead with Global Investors?" *Management Accounting*, January 1995, p. 21.

custom restrictions. Three additional members (Austria, Finland, and Sweden) were authorized to join the EU on January 1, 1995. The 15 nations in the EU include:

Austria	Finland	Great Britain	Italy	Portugal
Belgium	France	Greece	Luxembourg	Spain
Denmark	Germany	Ireland	Netherlands	Sweden

In June 1994, Russia signed a trade and cooperation agreement with the EU. This agreement is an important economic development both for Russia and the EU. In the past, Russia had difficulties in selling its raw materials to the West. The agreement ends import restrictions on most Russian goods and is expected to result in a substantial growth in Russia's exports to the EU countries. In 1993, approximately half of Russia's total exports ($17.9 billion) were purchased by EU countries. The agreement encourages Western investment in the Russian economy, makes it easier for EU businesses to operate in Russia, and will gradually open up Russia to European banks. The main points of this far-reaching accord include:

- Removal of quotas and other restrictions on Russian exports to the EU except for certain textile and steel products.
- Provision for consultation before increasing tariffs on each other's products.
- Declaration of support by the EU for Russia's efforts to join the General Agreement on Tariffs and Trade.

The agreement also includes a provision for a meeting of the Russian president with the presidents of the EU countries and its executive agency twice a year.

The absence of trade barriers is likely to make companies in the EU more competitive in international trade. Consumers would benefit because of lower prices resulting from increased competition among firms in the EU countries. Companies may ship goods to other member nations without often costly and time-consuming border checks. Consumers in each of the EU nations can generally purchase goods and services for personal use in the other member nations without having to pay export or import duties. A citizen of an EU nation may seek and accept employment, or live in any of the other member nations. Regulatory restrictions still remain on some industries such as airlines and telecommunications. Removal of some of these restrictions is planned for the future.

Most of the steps taken in the formation of the EU have so far been toward economic integration. Monetary integration (i.e., a single European currency) is not expected to be realized before the end of the century. An independent European Central Bank will then be established. At present, corporate money transfers may flow freely from one country to another within the EU. Individuals, however, must pay a fee for currency transfers.

North American Free Trade Agreement (NAFTA). This agreement became effective January 1, 1994. Presently, the membership consists of Canada, Mexico, and the U.S. Other countries are expected to join later, beginning with Chile. By eliminating trade barriers among the three member nations, NAFTA creates a single market of over 375 million consumers and over $6 trillion in annual output.

The major objective of NAFTA is to create an open market in the three member countries. Side agreements were also signed regarding treatment of labor and environmental concerns. To provide access to markets in the three member nations, all export taxes, import licenses, duties, quotas, and other restrictions (with a few exceptions) were eliminated. Tariffs on most goods were either eliminated immediately on the effective date, or are planned to be phased out over five or ten years. On politically or economically sensitive goods (e.g., U.S. textiles) the phase-out period will be fifteen years. Fifty percent of tariffs between the U.S. and Mexico are eliminated immediately and 65 percent will be eliminated by 1999.

During the first six months after the implementation of NAFTA, U.S. exports to Mexico increased by 17 percent and to Canada by 10 percent. U.S. imports from these two countries increased by 21 percent and 10 percent respectively for the same period.

The Pacific Rim Region

The Pacific Rim region is the fastest growing economic region in the world. Japan and some other Pacific Rim countries have emerged as economic powers, while others are fast joining their league. Interestingly, Pacific Rim countries are not rich in natural resources. Their productivity is primarily attributable to their focus on activities that add value. They manufacture and export quality goods that have won approval in global markets because consumers perceive them as "good value" products. The companies of the Pacific Rim region have been so successful in international trade that many of their management practices and production techniques are now being emulated by their competitors in other parts of the world, including the U.S. and Western Europe. Some of those concepts include an emphasis on quality, automation and the use of advanced technology, a teamwork approach, cellular manufacturing, just-in-time purchasing, just-in-time production, and flexible manufacturing systems, to name a few.

Government policies in these countries encourage and foster business growth. In many Pacific Rim countries, governments play a cooperative, silent partner role in facilitating all forms of commercial activity—especially international trade. "The intricate arrangement of back-scratching between business and government" is the way an observer described this relationship in Japan.[16] Some have identified culture as the critical factor for productivity:

> . . . perhaps the most important reason for the cohesiveness and efficiency of these Asian countries is their unique culture, known as Confucius Capitalism, which encompasses 2,500 years of Chinese values now called neo-Confucianism, a mixture of Buddhist and Confucian doctrines. Under the neo-Confucianism philosophy, people should seek their own moral self-development while fulfilling their social duties, thereby emphasizing the importance of education. The disciplined surge of Japan's Meiji modernization owed much to the teachings of Confucianism. Thus, a Confucius code of ethics combined with the Buddhist ideas of divine compassion and sacrifice of earthly desires emerged as

---

[16] Rudi Dornbusch, "Japan's Closed Markets: How to Open Them Now," *Business Week,* 19 July 1993, p. 14

Asian culture. Therefore, what makes these economies grow are Confucius-Buddhist values.[17]

Pacific Rim economies, especially the Asian-Pacific economies, are the fastest growing in the world. Rates of real growth in domestic products for twelve Asian-Pacific countries for 1993 are shown in Exhibit 1–4.

Exhibit 1–4	Real Growth in Domestic Products		
Country	**Rate**	**Country**	**Rate**
Philippines	3.0%	Taiwan	7.3%
Japan	3.1	South Korea	7.9
Australia	3.5	Thailand	7.9
Hong Kong	5.8	Malaysia	8.0
Singapore	6.0	New Zealand	2.8
Indonesia	6.2	China	9.5

Average = 5.9%

Source: U.S. Department of Commerce, Massachusetts Institute of Social and Economic Research, Asia Foundation.

In 1992, U.S. exports to Asia amounted to $120 billion and provided jobs for over 2 million American workers.

The advent of a sizable middle class in many of the Asian-Pacific countries is also noteworthy. India has the largest middle class of any single country in the world, numbering 300 million. Approximately half of the people in Singapore, Hong Kong, Taiwan, and South Korea can be classified as an upwardly mobile middle class, while 20 percent of the population in Thailand, Indonesia, and Malaysia approach this economic status. The new buying power of the Pacific Rim consumers, with its creation of huge new markets, has not gone unnoticed in other parts of the world.

South Korea, Taiwan, Hong Kong, and Singapore, often called the Four Tigers of Asia, as well as other Asian-Pacific nations, are developing high technology industries through technology transfers from industrialized countries. Multinational companies are playing a critical role in this phenomenon.

> Rather than merely setting up assembly plants, [multinationals] are forging strategic alliances with Asian partners, working much more closely with local suppliers to improve their capabilities, and sharing more sophisticated work, including product design, directly with their local employees.

[17] Dhia D. AlHashim and Jeffrey S. Arpan, *International Dimensions of Accounting,* 3d. ed. (Boston: PWS-Kent Publishing Company, 1992), p. 34. Also see, Louis Kraar, "Asia 2000" *Fortune,* 5 October 1992, p. 113.

The result is a giant transfer of technology, with U.S. companies leading the charge. Asians are getting technology that would have taken billions of dollars and an entire generation to develop on their own.[18]

As a result of this access to technology, Singapore manufactures over 50 percent of the hard disk drives in the world, and Malaysia is one of the biggest exporters of computer chips.

Many of the countries within the Pacific Rim region are collaborating with each other for mutual benefit. Indonesia, Malaysia, Singapore, the Philippines, Thailand, and Brunei have formed the Association of Southeast Asian Nations. In January 1992, the six countries agreed to remove tariff barriers over the next 15 years. A good example of the application of the theory of comparative advantage is found in economic integration of what is called Asia's growth triangle: Singapore, Malaysia, and Indonesia. The three countries are taking advantage of their comparative strengths:

> Singapore brings capital, links with international markets, management expertise, and technology. Indonesia and Malaysia provide what Singapore lacks: competitively priced labor and land. Over the past few years Singapore, host to over 3,000 international companies, has encouraged more than 500 of them to move labor-intensive operations into neighboring Malaysia and Indonesia. Thomson Consumer Electronics of France, for example, makes components in Malaysia and Indonesia that go into TV sets assembled in its highly automated plant in Singapore.[19]

The export pattern in the Asia-Pacific region has changed during recent years because of huge growth in the intra-Asian trade.

> Economic growth in the Asia-Pacific region has been fueled by increasing regional economic linkages and intraregional integration. As a result, the pattern of trade and investment of the Asia-Pacific developing countries has changed profoundly over the past decade. North America was Asia's main export market during the early 1980s. However, by 1986 Asia had become its own most important and fastest-expanding export market. In 1990, intra-Asian exports totaled about $300 billion compared with Asia's export of $206 billion to North America and $157 billion to Europe. Trade between the developing countries, totaling $145 billion, accounted for almost one-third of their total exports in 1990. Three-quarters of these exports were in manufactured products. Will the expansion of intra-Asian trade and investment continue as rapidly as in the recent past? There are good reasons to expect it will, despite the economic slowdown in Japan. As long as Asian countries continue to liberalize their economies and maintain high levels of investment, intra-Asian trade will continue to outpace growth in the other major export markets, principally North America and Europe.[20]

---

[18] Robert Neff, Bruce Einhorn, Neil Gross, Pete Engardio, and Laxmi Nakarmi, "Multinationals Have a Tiger by the Tail," *Business Week,* 7 December 1992, p. 131.

[19] Louis Kraar, "Asia's Hot New Growth Triangle," *Fortune,* 5 October 1992, p. 136.

[20] Kimimasa Tarumizu, "Global Perspectives," *Journal of Accountancy,* January 1993, p. 66.

San Francisco Declaration. In September 1992 representatives from 20 Pacific Rim nations held a conference in San Francisco. The meeting resulted in the signing of the San Francisco Declaration. Five key goals of the declaration are:

- Removal of barriers to trade, investment, and the flow of technology.
- Nondiscriminatory commercial access for outside economies.
- Strengthening efforts to keep the Pacific Rim region and the global economic system open.
- Adherence to the principles of the General Agreement on Tariffs and Trade.
- Accommodation of subregional trade pacts.

Unlike a treaty that binds the parties, a declaration lacks an enforcement provision. It can, however, be influential by getting commitment from the signatories. The declaration is unique because it combines an informal regional trading strategy with a commitment to global openness. *This concept of trade and investment is called open regionalism.*

Asia-Pacific Economic Cooperation (APEC). APEC is a new organization committed to the trade and investment concept of open regionalism. The organization has 18 member countries, as listed below.

Australia	Indonesia	Philippines
Brunei	Japan	Singapore
Canada	Malaysia	South Korea
Chile	Mexico	Taiwan
China	New Zealand	Thailand
Hong Kong	Papua New Guinea	U.S.

APEC countries account for 40 percent of the world's population, over half of its $12 trillion economy, and more than 40 percent of world trade.

U.S. President Clinton hosted the first APEC summit in Seattle in November 1993. The two-day summit followed a conference of the foreign and economic ministers of the organization. The foreign ministers strongly urged the European Union to make concessions to remove obstacles to reach a new GATT agreement. President Clinton and others have acknowledged that this pressure on Europe, and its timing, provided the needed momentum that resulted in a new GATT accord soon afterwards.

The second APEC summit was held in Jakarta, Indonesia in November 1994. The leaders of the APEC countries reached consensus that the developed economies among their members should remove trade and investment barriers by the year 2010, and that the remaining members would do the same by the year 2020.

International Accounting—Operational and Conceptual Issues

Earlier in this chapter we briefly discussed the reasons why international accounting is an important subject. We also defined international accounting as accounting for international transactions, comparisons of accounting principles in different countries, and harmonization of diverse accounting standards worldwide. This definition takes into account both operational and conceptual issues that have arisen from the global economy.

Challenges Facing International Accounting

International business has progressed beyond the import-export type of activities. Because of the nature of the global economy, more economic interdependencies exist between countries now than ever before in human history. Two developments are especially noteworthy.

- Global operations of MNCs cover a wide spectrum and include product development, production, and marketing. Technology alliances, resulting in technology transfers, are becoming an increasingly important factor in global operations.
- Global capital markets have provided opportunities for investors and borrowers to engage in financing activities worldwide. Advances in telecommunications, electronic transfers, and deregulation now enable investors and borrowers to engage in financial transactions on a real-time basis in international capital markets without any delays due to geographic distances.

The two developments described above have widened the scope of international accounting beyond traditional topics. This is not to imply that the traditional topics are no longer important. In fact, due to the magnitude of international trade and international investments, they have gained increased significance. Some of these topics are listed below.

- Foreign currency transactions
- Foreign currency translations
- Taxation of international operations
- Consolidation of financial statements of foreign subsidiaries and affiliates
- General purchasing power adjustment of financial statements
- Foreign exchange risk management
- Multinational transfer pricing
- Comparative disclosure requirements

Many new and broader issues beg for resolution because they are at the very core of international accounting, i.e., provision of timely information to decision makers worldwide. Some of those challenges are discussed next.

1. Skills and competencies of accountants. The era of the global economy requires additional skills in professional accountants that were perhaps not critical previously. These can be labeled "people skills"—cultural sensitivity and appreciation of cultural diversity. This means that new professionals should have been exposed to multicultural experiences and possess a global perspective.

2. Understanding the cross-functional linkages. It is no longer enough, if it ever was, merely to be proficient in accounting techniques, procedures, and application of standards. Today's accountants need to develop competencies that enable them to view a business in terms of integrated functions. The real value of accounting is in providing information that deals with how various courses of actions affect all parts of a business. Let us look at an example. In analyzing the proposal for automating a certain part of the manufacturing operation, the accountant should take into consideration not just the differential in production costs but also other factors such as employee morale, the quality of products with and without automation, flexibility in manufacturing, and the ability to produce and export swiftly—before the competitors seize a lion's share of the market. This is beyond the traditional role of accountants and involves many "soft" areas where judgment has as much of a role to play as the numbers. The number and variety of these judgmental factors is far more than in the past—and continues to increase.

3. Financial analysis and comparability. Another major challenge facing international accounting is the noncomparability of financial statements of different countries, and the resultant problems in doing financial analysis. At least three factors contribute to the problem.

- Accounting transactions are measured and reported differently in different countries. No two national accounting systems are identical. Differences in measurement and reporting practices, therefore, make it difficult to compare financial statements from different countries. Financial ratios using numbers from such reports are inherently not comparable. This topic is discussed in Chapter 11.
- Business culture and business practices vary from country to country. In some countries, such as Japan, financing is mostly done through debt, while in other countries, such as the U.K., the major source of financing is from equity holders. How can the debt to equity ratio of a Japanese operation be compared with a British operation? Would such a comparison provide the necessary insights to users?
- Terminology is a problem for accounting throughout the world. In some languages, no terms exist to describe certain items. At the extreme, there may be no term for accounting. Additionally, even among English-speaking countries the same term may carry different meanings. For example, "turnover" has an entirely different meaning in the U.S. than in the U.K. Terminology differences are evident from a cursory review of the balance sheets of AT&T and ICI contained in Chapter 11. Both companies are based in English-speaking countries, namely the U.S. and the U.K., respectively.

4. Global information system development. Worldwide operations require a global information system. This system should meet management's needs for financial reporting, strategic planning, short-term planning, organizing, controlling, and decision making. This is one of the major challenges facing international accounting. The development of such a system to serve the multiple and varied needs of management in managing global operations is a complex undertaking. In addition to the usual complications in developing a domestic information system are other factors such as national differences in accounting standards, monetary units, tax laws, restrictions on currency movements outside the country, and general price level changes (especially in hyperinflationary economies). But perhaps the most difficult factor is the varying level of uncertainty across the globe.

The factors described above give some idea of the challenges faced by accounting in the international arena. Resolution of these operational and conceptual issues must be found by taking into account major environmental influences on accounting.

Environmental Influences on Accounting

As we mentioned at the beginning of this chapter, accounting is a service activity. Financial reports, its end product, provide information for economic decision making. Environments differ among countries. Consequently, the types of decisions that need to be made are also different. This explains why there are as many accounting systems as there are countries. Since accounting provides information for making decisions in a unique environment, the accounting systems are necessarily *environment-specific*. For our discussion, we will focus on five major environmental influences:

1. Economic system
2. Political system
3. Legal system
4. Educational system
5. Religion

These major environmental influences play key roles in the formation of societal or cultural values. Economic, legal, and political systems affect each other. The educational system can be a force to counter, reinforce, or modify influences of the economic, political, and legal systems. Since religion is a matter of faith, it is shown separately. The influence of religion as an environmental factor varies from country to country. In many parts of the world, especially in the Middle East, it is perhaps the most powerful of the environmental influences. All five of the environmental influences mentioned above play a major role in forming societal values. The societal values then affect the accounting profession's values. The accounting system of a country is influenced by the shared values of the accounting professionals. In turn, information from the accounting system affects the economic, political, legal, and educational systems as illustrated in Figure 1-3.

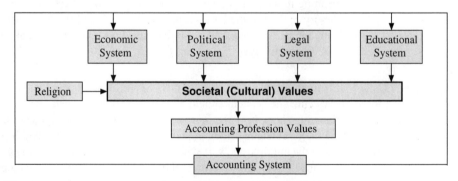

Figure 1–3   Environmental Influences on Accounting

We will now take a closer look at some of these environmental influences to see how they eventually affect accounting.

1. The economic system. The accounting system of a country that has a highly industrialized, high-technology economy would be different from the accounting system of a country that has primarily an agrarian economy. Intangibles (e.g., copyrights and brand names) have much more importance in a country with a developed economy than one that has a subsistence-level economy.

Concentration of ownership versus dispersion of ownership patterns influence the need for and extent of disclosures. Generally, if ownership is broad, there would be a need for greater and varied disclosures to meet the needs of the investors.

The source of financing is also an important consideration regarding the orientation of accounting reports and disclosures. If debt is the major source of financing, then most of the information can be furnished directly to the lenders, instead of being disclosed publicly. Accounting reports, as a result, would be creditor-oriented and their contents would be more specific to meet the needs of lenders.

The tax laws of a country have an impact on income measurement. In many countries (e.g., Japan, Germany, and France), income for tax purposes is the same as for financial reporting. In such cases the accounting system is synchronized with the tax laws. In other countries (e.g., the U.S. and the U.K.), income for tax purposes is computed differently from income for financial reports. The accounting systems in such countries are relatively independent and are not confined by provisions of the tax laws.

Finally, if the economy of a country is highly inflationary, the accounting system will need to adjust historical-cost based financial statements to reflect the impact of inflation. In extreme cases, there may be a departure to a non-historical-cost based measurement.

2. The political system. The political system of a country is an influential factor because its philosophy and objectives determine broad economic policies such as centrally-planned versus market-driven economies and private versus public ownership of property.

There is a close link between political stability and economic stability; they usually go hand in hand. Development of accounting is facilitated if the country does not go through frequent changes in the economic system brought on by political instability and turmoil. Business and economic stability are requisites for accounting development. Ernst & Young's survey of the Global 1000 companies discovered that political instability is considered to be *the major barrier* to investment in a country. Fifty-three percent cited political instability as a major barrier while 36 percent stated that it is somewhat of a barrier. Next in line are financial risk, legal infrastructure, bureaucracy, exchange controls, and commercial infrastructure.[21]

3. The legal system. In many countries, including some Western European countries, the legal system has a direct impact on accounting. Laws contain detailed accounting regulations specifying comprehensive accounting rules and procedures. In such countries, accounting

---

[21] "What's Ahead with Global Investors?" *Management Accounting,* January 1995, p. 21.

is directly dependent on legislative requirements because the government determines and enforces these requirements.

4. The educational system. The educational system and level of literacy impacts the accounting system of a country in two ways. Well-educated users of accounting information can understand sophisticated accounting information. Also, accountants in a country with high educational standards are usually well trained and have good competencies and skills. In sum, educational backgrounds of both users and preparers of accounting information strongly affect the development and sophistication of a country's accounting system.

5. Religion. Religion, in the broad sense of the term, affects basic accounting concepts. In some countries (e.g., Pakistan), the ideas of "profit" or "income" may run counter to widely held religious beliefs. In others, including Pakistan, "interest" may be a problem. The likely result is difficulty in presenting and communicating accounting information.

International Agents for Change in Accounting

In the last section we described environmental influences on accounting. They may be viewed as the factors that are overwhelmingly national. Accounting is a dynamic discipline. In this age of a global economy and worldwide communications there is increasing pressure for change from international forces. In most cases, international influences result in greater harmonization. In other cases, this pressure may cause disclosure of more information. We will now describe eight of the major international influences.

1. Trading blocs. Economic integration necessitates greater harmonization of accounting standards of the member countries. *Harmonization means that different accounting standards may be used in individual countries as long as they are not in conceptual conflict with each other, i.e., they can be reconciled.* Making possible the comparison of international financial information is the major benefit of harmonization. The EU issues **directives,** which are binding on member nations. The directives provide the framework within which the member countries may exercise flexibility in applying national accounting and auditing standards. The EU has legal authority to enforce its directives in the 15 member nations.

In the case of NAFTA, it is too early to observe any impact on the accounting and auditing practices in the three member countries. It is expected, however, that the increase in trade among the member countries will lead to greater uniformity of accounting standards. The major impact is expected to be on accounting standards and practices in Mexico. Environmental accounting is currently receiving attention for many reasons, including the concerns raised during NAFTA negotiations. A pact was signed between the U.S. and Mexico to address environmental issues. This was done to provide assurances to critics of NAFTA that Mexico will enforce its antipollution laws and protect its environment after it merges with Canada and the U.S. to form an integrated economic bloc.

2. International governmental organizations. International governmental organizations have been making efforts to harmonize international accounting standards. Most notable are the United Nations (UN) and the Organization for Economic Cooperation and Develoment (OECD).

The UN has been instrumental in the formation of many organizations that provide economic resources to developing countries and facilitate world trade. These include the International Monetary Fund, the World Bank Group, GATT, and the UN Conference on Trade and Development. The United Nations Commission on Transnational Corporations is involved in many activities to promote international trade, including development of accounting standards and accounting education in Africa and Russia.

The OECD, formed in 1960, is an influential organization. Its membership consists of 25 countries, most of which are highly industrialized. For this reason, the OECD is sometimes referred to as "the club for rich industrial nations." Headquartered in Paris, it promotes worldwide economic development in general, and economic growth and stability of its member countries in particular. The work of OECD focuses primarily on providing financial accounting and reporting guidelines to multinational corporations for disclosures to host countries. The countries listed below are members of the OECD.[22]

Australia	Finland	Ireland	Netherlands	Sweden
Austria	France	Italy	New Zealand	Switzerland
Belgium	Germany	Japan	Norway	Turkey
Canada	Greece	Luxembourg	Portugal	U.K.
Denmark	Iceland	Mexico	Spain	U.S.

3. Professional organizations. The two most influential international professional organizations are the International Accounting Standards Committee (IASC) and the International Federation of Accountants (IFAC). The IASC and the IFAC are engaged in efforts to harmonize accounting and auditing standards, respectively. Although their standards are nonbinding on member nations, they are gaining increasing acceptance, especially in developing countries. In some countries, IASC standards are automatically adopted as national accounting standards.

4. Global capital markets. Global capital markets enable the investors and borrowers to engage in financial transactions worldwide. The regulatory agencies have minimum requirements for listing securities. This requires that companies wishing to transact business in global capital markets provide accounting information to comply with the disclosure requirements of the regulatory agencies. This is illustrated by the following example.

> Since 1989, more than 200 companies from Europe, Asia, and other regions have obtained U.S. listings and sold nearly $76 billion worth of stocks and bonds. But German issuers, unwilling to bring their secretive accounting practices into

---

[22] Mexico, the first member nation from Latin America, was admitted in 1994. While announcing Mexico's admission into the OECD, the President of Mexico declared that Mexico was entering "one of the most important economic organizations in the world." Also in 1994, the OECD and Russia agreed to a "protocol of cooperation." The Czech Republic, Hungary, Poland, Russia, and Slovakia are expected to become members within the next few years.

conformity with the Securities & Exchange Commission's more open standards, refused to join. Then, last autumn, as currency turmoil and worries over the cost of German unification roiled European bourses, Liener [chief financial officer of Daimler, a Germany-based multinational] contacted SEC Chairman Richard C. Breeden. It was time, the CFO argued, for Daimler to open its books and get into the U.S. More and more a global manufacturer, Daimler, says Liener, "can no longer afford to ignore the world's most prominent capital market."

Daimler has already revealed $2.45 billion in secret reserves, will soon disclose profits more frequently, and will value inventories, pension obligations, and foreign-exchange transactions more along U.S. lines. Daimler now expects to list shares in Singapore and Shanghai, speeding plans to raise $1.2 billion on global markets next year. Opening up can be painful, but that's the price of playing in the majors these days.[23]

The International Organization of Securities Commission (IOSCO), a private organization of securities markets regulators, is promoting the integration of securities markets world-wide.

5. Multinational corporations. The operations of MNCs have a great impact on the local economy, employment, and environment. With their major influences the pressure comes from host countries for greater disclosure and accountability. Accounting provides most of the quantitative information to meet such needs.

6. Technological advances. The changes brought on by technological advances affect all aspects of business—manufacturing, financing, distribution, purchasing, etc. Advances in information and communications technology have had a major impact on accounting because the collection and processing of data can be done much faster and at a much lower cost than was possible before. Consequently, accounting can provide more information on a timely basis.

7. Worldwide political developments and trends. The former U.S.S.R. and many East European countries are switching from centrally planned economic systems to open markets. This necessitates adopting new accounting systems that are appropriate for recording and reporting transactions in the new economic systems.

An interesting trend that has developed in recent years is privatization. Many of the enterprises that used to be operated by the public sector have been privatized. This appears to be a worldwide trend, and exists in industrialized as well as developing countries. This puts more demands on accounting in these countries and in some cases could increase the countries' speed of development.

8. Management accounting—relevance regained. In accounting, perhaps the biggest beneficiary of the global economy is the management accounting area. A few years ago many

---

[23] William Glassgall, "Daimler-Benz Opens Up," *Business Week,* 12 April 1993, p. 82.

asserted that management accounting had lost its relevance because it had been in a dormant state for at least fifty years. However, due to fierce competition in international markets, companies were forced to become "lean and mean." Managerial accounting analysis has been quite helpful in making businesses more productive and efficient. A comparison of the current managerial accounting literature and textbooks with those published only a few years ago will convince anyone that managerial accounting has become a current, relevant, and sophisticated area of accounting. The contents of managerial accounting courses now typically include topics such as just-in-time purchasing/production, flexible manufacturing systems, costing of quality programs, crossfunctional integration of information, activity-based costing and management, target costing, and computer-integrated manufacturing, to name a few. Managerial accounting could be used as an example to illustrate how good concepts borrowed from different parts of the world can be implemented to improve quality, increase ability to respond quickly to market changes, and provide better value to the customer.

Note to Students

First, the authors congratulate you for studying this exciting area of accounting. As you already know from the first chapter, it is a dynamic area filling an important need in this age of worldwide operations, a global economy, and international capital markets. We encourage you to become an active participant, rather than being just an observer. The best way to get on the "fast career track" is to gain international professional experience yourself. For international companies this experience is considered essential, always appearing among the top items on the list of required qualifications. Presidents and CEOs of many companies, including Coca-Cola, Merck & Co., GM, Ford, and Chrysler, have been selected primarily due to their international experience.

To prepare for a foreign assignment, take foreign-language lessons and related courses to develop greater cultural understanding and appreciation. If possible, spend time as an exchange student or take an internship abroad. After you start work, take advantage of international training programs if available in your company, or seek an overseas assignment.

To keep abreast of new developments, regularly read at least one international business periodical such as the *Asian Wall Street Journal,* the *Financial Times,* the *Economist,* the *Far Eastern Economic Review,* or *Business Week.* The large accounting firms, especially the "Big Six," have publications dealing with specific countries and specific international topics.

The National Trade Data Bank (NTDB) of the U.S. Department of Commerce is compiled by 15 U.S. government agencies. It contains the latest census data on U.S. imports and exports by commodity and country, the complete *CIA World Factbook,* current market research, the *Foreign Traders Index,* and many other data series. NTDB is available at over 800 U.S. federal depository libraries. It also can be purchased on CD-ROM.

The Center for International Financial Analysis & Research, Inc. (CIFAR) publishes the *Global Company Handbook* and the *Global Company News Digest.* The *Handbook* is also available as Cfarbase on CD-ROM, magnetic tape, or PC diskettes. It has fundamental financial data on 15,000 companies from 50 countries worldwide.

Worldscope/Disclosure has two databases: *Global* and *Emerging Markets.* For more information on these databases, see the Note to Students at the end of Chapter 11.

The Global Opportunities State Committee of the California Society of Certified Public Accountants has developed a *Global Opportunities Resource.* This is an annotated bibliography covering all aspects of international business. The lead author of this text is a member of the Global Opportunities State Committee.

Chapter Summary

- The study of international accounting is important since it provides relevant information to decision makers in an age of international trade and global capital markets.

- International trade is now a source of over one-half of the revenues of many large companies.

- Many companies have developed international marketing strategies to expand their international operations in the future.

- The reasons for international business can be explained by the theory of comparative advantage, the imperfect market theory, the product cycle theory, and technology transfer.

- The types of international involvement by companies include exports (direct and indirect), strategic alliances, and multinational operations.

- The European Union (EU) and the North American Free Trade Agreement (NAFTA) are the two major trading blocs.

- The Pacific Rim region is the fastest-growing economic region in the world. Economic growth in the Asian-Pacific countries of the region is at a higher rate than that of the other countries in the region.

- The Asia-Pacific Economic Cooperation is an 18-member organization committed to open regionalism. Though relatively new, it is already influential.

- International accounting faces many challenges including competency requirements for accountants and some identified gaps in the body of knowledge.

- A study of environmental influences is the necessary first step in explaining the accounting system of a nation. The important environmental influences include the economic system, the political system, the legal system, the educational system, and religion.

- International factors are influencing accounting and auditing standards and practices throughout the world.

Questions for Discussion

1. Why is the study of international accounting more important than it may have been a few decades ago?

2. Give examples of trends toward a global economy. Why might the development of a global economy be beneficial?

3. "Removing barriers to foreign trade will cost our country jobs." Give arguments on both sides of this question.

4. What type of difficulties might arise in defining and enforcing a policy of boycotting "foreign-made" goods?

5. Why might a company choose to engage in international operations? What problems might such a company encounter?

6. List three theoretical reasons for a company to become involved (or not involved) in international business. *Briefly* explain each theory.

7. Explain the difference between a direct and an indirect exporter. Can a single company be both?

8. In terms of international trade, what is a "joint venture"? Give an example—if possible, one not listed in the text.

9. Can you identify any significant differences between the terms "multinational corporation," "multinational enterprise," and "transnational corporation"?

10. Look for trends or other significant patterns in the chart reflecting inflows and outflows of foreign direct investment. What do you see? Would it help to know if the information presented is or is not adjusted for the effects of inflation?

11. Why would a trading bloc be formed? List the two trading blocs discussed in the chapter.

12. Would it make sense for a country to be a member of more than one trading bloc? If this were to happen, then what might follow? (This is a "thinking" rather than a "reciting" question. You won't find an answer in the text, but it's a good idea to think on your own now and then.)

13. Contrast "Confucius capitalism" with what might be called "classical" or "Western" capitalism. Does one appear to have a longer-term view than the other?

14. List the "Four Tigers of Asia" and the three countries making up "Asia's growth triangle." Why are these countries showing such rapid real growth in domestic product? What Asian country, not a member of either group, grew faster in 1993?

15. What is APEC? What are its main objectives? List at least six of its member countries.

16. List three of the five goals of the San Francisco Declaration.

17. What is meant by open regionalism?

18. Are EU directives binding on the member nations?

19. List four challenges facing the accounting profession in coping with the special needs of international accounting.

20. The text identifies five major environmental influences on accounting. How does each affect accounting?

21. The text identifies eight international agents for change in accounting. Identify one or two as particularly important and defend your choice.

22. Discuss the impact of technology on international business and international accounting.

23. Discuss the current state of management accounting. Is there a lesson to be learned from how it regained its relevance?

24. What is your understanding of crossfunctional business relationships? Why is it important for the accountant to understand them?

25. "Harmonization means the same accounting standards throughout the world." Do you agree? Discuss.

26. Name the two most influential international professional organizations influencing accounting. Which of the two is focusing on harmonization of accounting standards?

27. Do global capital markets have any effect on the disclosures made by the listing companies? If so, how?

Case: Comparative Advantage

The following statement was made by Sir James Goldsmith before the U.S. Senate Commerce Committee on November 15, 1994:

> The principal theoretician of free trade was David Ricardo, a British economist of the early nineteenth century. He believed in two interrelated concepts: specialization and comparative advantage. . . . But these ideas are not valid in today's world. Why?
>
> During the past few years, 4 billion people have suddenly entered the world economy. They include the populations of China, India, Vietnam, Bangladesh, and the countries that were part of the Soviet empire, among others. These populations are growing fast; in thirty-five years, that 4 billion is forecast to expand to over 6.5 billion. These nations have very high levels of unemployment and those people who do find jobs offer their labor for a tiny fraction of the pay earned by workers in the developed world. . . .
>
> Until recently, these 4 billion people were separated from our economy by their political systems, primarily Communist or Socialist, and because of a lack of technology and of capital. Today all that has changed. Their political systems have been transformed, technology can be transferred instantaneously anywhere

in the world on a microchip, and capital is free to be invested wherever the anticipated yields are highest.

The principle of global free trade is that anything can be manufactured anywhere in the world to be sold anywhere else. That means that these new entrants into the world economy are in direct competition with the workforces of developed countries. They have become part of the same global labor market. Our economies, therefore, will be subjected to a completely new type of competition.

It must surely be a mistake to adopt an economic policy which makes you rich if you eliminate your national workforce and transfer production abroad, and which bankrupts you if you continue to employ your own people.

Required: Critique the above statement. Among others, address the following issues:

(1) Do you think that population growth in these countries will continue at the rate indicated by the forecasts? Discuss.
(2) Discuss the points mentioned in the statements contained in the third paragraph. Do you agree?
(3) Based on recent developments, is the theory of comparative advantage obsolete? Discuss.
(4) What policy recommendations would you offer to address the concerns raised in the last paragraph?

Please be specific whenever possible. Present pros and cons when an issue has no clear solution.

References

Accounting Principles Board. *Statement of the Accounting Principles Board No. 4.* "Basic Concepts and Accounting Principles Underlying Financial Statements of Business Enterprises." New York: American Institute of Certified Public Accountants, 1970.

AlHashim, Dhia D., and Jeffrey S. Arpan. *International Dimensions of Accounting,* 3d ed. Boston: PWS-Kent Publishing Company, 1992.

American Accounting Association. *Accounting and Culture.* Sarasota, Fla.: American Accounting Association, 1987.

Byrne, John A., Richard Brandt, and Otis Port. "The Virtual Corporation." *Business Week,* 8 February 1993, pp. 98-102.

Cellini, Greg L. "Strategic Alliances in the '90s." *Management Accounting,* June 1993, pp. 56-59.

"Companies Surveyed on Going International." *Deloitte & Touche Review,* 5 October 1992, pp. 1-2.

Conover, Teresa L., Stephen Salter, and John E. Price. "International Accounting Education: A Comparison of Course Syllabi and CFO Preferences." *Issues in Accounting Education,* fall 1994, pp. 259-270.

Dornbusch, Rudi. "Japan's Closed Markets: How to Open Them Now." *Business Week,* 19 July 1993, p. 14.

Eng, Paul M., and Laxmi Nakarmi. "Made in the U.S.A. ...by Hyundai." *Business Week,* 26 October 1992, p. 96.

Glassgall, William. "Daimler Benz Opens Up." *Business Week,* 12 April 1993, p. 82.

Iqbal, M. Zafar. "Market Expansion Challenges Smaller Practice Units." *The Ohio CPA Journal,* April 1994, pp. 41-42.

Israeloff, Robert L. "Positioning a Firm for International Opportunities." *Journal of Accountancy,* February 1993, pp. 46-48, 50.

Koretz, Gene. "A Trading Region Comes of Age in the Pacific." *Business Week,* 17 May 1993, p. 26.

KPMG Peat Marwick. "Blurring Boundaries." *World,* vol. 27, no. 2 (1993), pp. 44-46.

Kraar, Louis. "Asia 2000." *Fortune,* 5 October 1992, pp. 111-113.

———. "Asia's Hot New Growth Triangle." *Fortune,* 5 October 1992, pp. 136-138, 142.

———. "Korea Goes for Quality." *Fortune,* 18 April 1994, pp. 153-158.

Madura, Jeff. *International Financial Management,* 4th ed. St. Paul: West Publishing Co., 1995.

Murray, Mark F. *International Business.* New York: American Institute of Certified Public Accountants, 1993.

Neff, Robert, Bruce Einhorn, Neil Gross, Pete Engardio, and Laxmi Nakarmi. "Multinationals Have a Tiger by the Tail." *Business Week,* 7 December 1992, pp. 131-133.

"Report Notes: TNCs' Role in Integration of Global Economy." *Deloitte & Touche Review,* 23 August 1993, pp. 3-4.

Rosenzweig, Philip. "Why is Managing in the United States so Difficult for European Firms?" *European Management Journal,* March 1994, pp. 31-38.

Sack, Robert J., James R. Boatsman, Robert S. Fell, Jack L. Krogstad, Spencer J. Martin, and Marcia S. Niles. "Mountaintop Issues: From the Perspective of the SEC." *Accounting Horizons,* March 1995, pp. 79-86.

Slipkowsky, John N. "Is Japan the Key to Our Future?" *Management Accounting,* August 1993, pp. 27-30.

Smart, Tim, Pete Engardio, and Geri Smith. "GE's Brave New World." *Business Week,* 8 November 1993, p. 67.

Smith, Geri. "This Venture Is Cooking with Gas." *Business Week,* 8 November 1993, p. 70.

Statement of Financial Accounting Concepts No. 1. "Objectives of Financial Reporting by Business Enterprises." Stamford, Conn.: Financial Accounting Standards Board, 1978.

Sundby, Larry, and Bradley Schwieger. "EC, EZ?" *Journal of Accountancy,* March 1992, pp. 71-76. [Author's note: "EC" stands for Economic Community. The name of this organization was later changed to "EU," which stands for Economic Union.]

Tarumizu, Kimimasa. "Global Perspectives." *Journal of Accountancy,* January 1993, p. 66.

Taxation in North America: The North American Free Trade Agreement. New York: Deloitte Touche Tohmatsu International, 1995.

Why Companies Go International. Brussels, Belgium: Deloitte Touche Tohmatsu International, 1992.

Wills, Stefan, and Kevin Barham. "Being an International Manager." *European Management Journal,* March 1994, pp. 49-58.

Wyatt, Arthur R. "Seeking Credibility in a Global Economy." *New Accountant,* September 1992, pp. 4-6, 51-52.

Zahra, Shaker, and Galal Elhagrasey. "Strategic Management of International Joint Ventures." *European Management Journal,* March 1994, pp. 83-93.

Chapter 2

Internationalization of Accounting Standards

The first chapter established the framework and the need for international accounting. We have entered the age of a global economy and many forces are rapidly broadening its scope.

In Chapter 4, we will discuss the setting of national accounting principles in 11 different countries. As we know, accounting standards (principles) are the rules that govern measuring and recording economic activities and reporting accounting information to users. The terms **rules, principles,** and **standards** will be used interchangeably in this chapter.

This chapter addresses the equally important subject of the internationalization of accounting standards and the setting of global, as compared to national, standards. It presents the efforts of various constituents who are involved in the development of global accounting standards. Global accounting standards are in addition to, not in place of, national standards developed by each country. The terms **global, international,** and **universal** will be used interchangeably in this chapter.

The call for international accounting standards is not new. What is new is the many political and economic developments since 1989. These events are likely to accelerate the flow of trade and capital among nations and to increase the role of multinational corporations. Exhibit 2–1 lists some of the major political and economic events that we all have witnessed in recent years. Very few were accurately predicted and their impact on world trade and business is not yet fully understood.

Need for International Standards

The previous chapter demonstrated the need for accounting information by showing the relationship between decision making and information. Good decisions are based on relevant and timely information about available choices. In the conduct of international business, accounting information is needed to make good decisions. A transnational level of business activities creates demand for internationalizing accounting standards. International accounting supports the growth of worldwide economies and facilitates transacting business across national boundaries.

> . . . world growth is not a zero-sum proposition. Since the postwar recovery began in 1950, average annual growth, globally, has been 3.5%, while the value of trade in real terms has grown 6.5% a year. For every $100 billion more in goods that are traded around, the world growth is pushed $10 billion to $20 billion higher than it otherwise would be.[1]

---

[1] Karen Pennar, "The Global Economy Needs Bridges—Not Walls," *Business Week,* 2 August 1993, p. 60.

Exhibit 2–1   Recent Major Political and Economic Events

Political

- End of the cold war and the beginning of cooperation between the two former enemies, the U.S. and Russia.
- Collapse of communism and the former Soviet Union resulting in the recognition of 15 new states that were in the U.S.S.R.
- Creation of the Commonwealth of Independent States, consisting of 11 former Soviet republics.
- Reunification of Germany.
- Emerging democracies in the countries of Eastern Europe and the end of their domination by the former Soviet Union.
- Emerging democracies in parts of Latin America, Asia, and Africa.
- New active role for the UN to mediate and resolve regional conflicts.

Economic

- Signing of the new General Agreement on Tariffs and Trade (GATT) in December 1993.
- Ratification of GATT by the EU, U.S., and Japan in 1994. This was necessary for its implementation.
- Ratification of the North American Free Trade Agreement (NAFTA) by Canada, Mexico, and the U.S.
- The European Community became the European Union (EU) at the beginning of 1994. The union is making progress toward a European common currency and banking system.
- Approval for the admission of three new members (Austria, Finland, and Sweden) to the EU effective January 1, 1995.
- Movement toward privatization of former government-owned enterprises in Russia, Eastern Europe, Western Europe, Latin America, Asia, and Africa.
- Emergence of joint ventures and other forms of strategic alliances, and Western acquisition of business enterprises in Russia and Eastern Europe.
- Movement in the U.S. to strengthen economic ties with Pacific Rim nations.
- Signs of economic recovery after years of recession in the U.S. and Western Europe.

The flow of goods, capital, and resources across national boundaries and the conduct of business in more than one country require accounting standards that are not country-specific. Many variables, e.g., foreign currencies, different inflation rates, and the need for consolidation, are promoting the internationalization of accounting standards.

One of the early calls to internationalize accounting standards came from a prominent European executive, the president of Royal Dutch Petroleum Company, in 1979.

> Financial information is a form of a language. And if the language of financial information is to be put to use, so that investment and credit decisions can more readily be taken, it should not only be intelligible, it should also be comparable.

International differences in accounting standards should be narrowed. Although this may seem to be an impossible chasm, it can be achieved—if enough countries are willing.[2]

A recent survey of institutional investors, companies, underwriters, and regulators identified the following accounting issues as the most troublesome to understand and reconcile among various countries:[3]

- Accounting for goodwill
- Deferred taxes
- Inventory valuation
- Depreciation methods
- Discretionary reserves
- Fixed asset valuation
- Pensions
- Foreign currency transactions and translations
- Leases
- Financial statement consolidations
- Financial disclosure requirements

Different accounting treatment of any or all of the above areas makes it difficult to analyze and compare financial statements. That is why there is growing support for international accounting standards.

An international set of accounting standards would allow a more level playing field because income statements and balance sheet ratios would become more consistent between competing companies. It also would help alleviate the pressure on the SEC to allow foreign filers in the U.S. capital markets.[4]

The above call for international accounting standards is echoed by another prominent accountant, Arthur R. Wyatt, past president of the International Accounting Standards Committee. According to Wyatt, "The linkage of worldwide capital markets is one of the driving forces behind the movement toward a single set of accounting rules."[5]

Standardization versus Harmonization

Comparability of accounting information is vital to international trade and investment. The question is how to achieve comparability. *Standardization* of accounting rules would ensure full comparability.

---

[2] D. De Bryjne, "Global Standards: A Tower of Babel?" *Financial Executive,* February 1980, pp. 30-39.

[3] Nancy Anderson, "The Globalization of GAAP," *Management Accounting,* August 1993, pp. 52-54.

[4] *Ibid.*

[5] Arthur R. Wyatt and Joseph F. Yospe, "Wake-up Call to American Business: International Accounting Standards Are on the Way," *Journal of Accountancy,* July 1993, pp. 80-85.

Many, however, doubt the feasibility of complete standardization of accounting rules. Specific needs linked with national needs make national accounting standards necessary. As a solution, the concept of *harmonization* has gained widespread popularity. Harmonization of accounting standards means that the differences among nations should be kept at a minimum. Alternative accounting rules or practices may exist in different countries as long as they are "in harmony" with each other and can be reconciled. Harmonization may also mean that a group of nations agrees on a similar set of accounting standards but requires that any departure must be disclosed and reconciled with acceptable standards. Harmonization may additionally mean that financial information is prepared under national as well as international accounting standards. In such a case, the difference is reconciled to inform the user of the impact of different accounting standards on accounting information.

The remainder of this chapter addresses the efforts to harmonize accounting standards among nations. Harmonization efforts will be discussed at international and regional levels, along with recent developments.

International Efforts

To be successful, efforts to harmonize accounting standards need an international base to ensure wide acceptance and implementation. Such efforts would require taking into consideration the views of national standard-setting bodies. Given the diversity existing among national standard-setting bodies, the task of harmonization is obviously challenging.

International harmonization efforts are divided between bodies that represent governments and bodies that represent the accounting profession or other interested groups. In this section we discuss the harmonization efforts of the following:

- The International Accounting Standards Committee (IASC)—representing the accounting profession
- The United Nations (UN)—representing member states (governments)
- The Organization for Economic Cooperation and Development (OECD)—representing governments of member nations
- Other international efforts

There is another active international group representing the accounting profession—the International Federation of Accountants (IFAC)—that has actively encouraged harmonization for many years. Recently, however, the IFAC has focused its attention on establishing international auditing standards and dealing with issues in education, ethics, and management accounting. The structure and work of the IFAC will be presented in Chapter 12.

International Accounting Standards Committee

The IASC is the most active international body with the responsibility to promulgate international accounting standards. These standards are meant to apply to all business environments regardless of the size or type of business activity. The IASC is the only setter of international standards with a clearly stated due process to propose, study, and ultimately issue such standards.

The IASC was established in 1973 as a result of an agreement between the professional accounting organizations of ten countries.[6] As of April 1995, the IASC membership consisted of 110 professional accounting organizations from 82 countries. The member organizations include one million accountants worldwide.

The stated objectives of the IASC are:

- To formulate and publish accounting standards for use in the presentation of financial statements and to promote their worldwide acceptance.
- To work for the improvement and harmonization of accounting standards and procedures relating to the presentation of financial statements.

IASC activities are funded by contributions from member professional accounting organizations, other organizations serving on the IASC board, multinational companies, financial institutions, accounting firms, other organizations, and the sale of IASC publications. There is no funding from governments or intergovernmental organizations.

IASC activities and statements are administered and issued by the IASC board. The Board consists of 17 members, of which 13 members represent professional accounting organizations and the remaining 4 members are from organizations interested in international financial reporting.

IASC standards are issued by its Board, but the detailed investigation of any accounting issue is done by a steering committee. Each steering committee is chaired by a Board representative, and includes representatives from professional accounting organizations, other organizations represented on the Board, and the consultative group.

IASC consultative group. To expand the representation of organizations interested in financial reporting, the IASC has established an international consultative group. The group includes representatives of users and preparers of financial statements, standard-setting bodies, and observers from intergovernmental organizations. This group meets regularly with the Board to discuss policies, principles, and issues relevant to IASC work. The following organizations are members of the consultative group:

- Federation Internationale des Bourses de Valeurs
- International Association of Financial Executives Institutes
- International Chamber of Commerce
- International Confederation of Free Trade Unions and World Confederation of Labor
- International Organization of Securities Commission
- International Banking Association

---

[6] These charter organizations were from Australia, Canada, France, Germany, Ireland, Japan, Mexico, the Netherlands, the U.K., and the U.S.

- International Bar Association
- International Finance Corporation
- The World Bank
- U.S. Financial Accounting Standards Board
- European Commission
- The International Assets Valuation Standards Committee
- Organization for Economic Cooperation and Development (observer)
- UN Transnational Corporations and Management Division (observer)

IASC steering committees include representatives from the consultative group.

Development of international accounting standards. Any member of the IASC or any other interested party may submit suggestions for new accounting standard topics. If accepted by the Board, a steering committee for that topic is set up to deal with it. The committee examines and reviews the accounting issues associated with the topic, the relationship between the topic and the *IASC Framework for the Preparation and Presentation of Financial Statements,* any relevant national and regional standards, the views of member bodies and other interested groups, and the views of prominent individuals on a worldwide basis.

The IASC has established the following procedures, or due process, to develop international standards.

- The steering committee considers the issues involved and develops a **point outline.**
- A **draft statement of principles** is prepared after the Board comments on the point outline.
- The steering committee submits to the Board a **final statement of principles** after its review of the comments on the draft statement.
- After Board approval, the final statement of principles serves as the basis for the preparation of an **exposure draft.** The exposure draft is published after its approval by at least two-thirds of the Board. Interested parties have six months to submit comments on the exposure draft.
- The steering committee prepares a **draft international accounting standard** after its review of comments on the exposure draft.
- The draft international accounting standard is reviewed by the Board and is finally published as an **international accounting standard** (IAS), after any revisions and with the approval of at least three-quarters of the Board.

Figure 2–1 summarizes the above process and its major outcomes.

International accounting standards. Since its creation in 1973, the IASC has issued the following as of August 1995:

- Thirty-two international accounting standards (IASs).
- Revisions of 11 previously issued standards as a result of the Comparability/ Improvement Project.

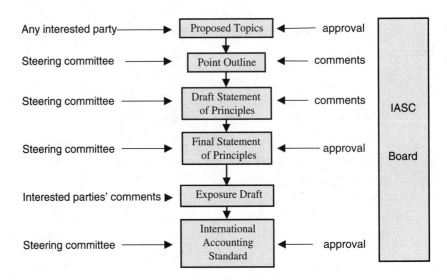

Figure 2-1   Development of IASC International Accounting Standards

- *Exposure Draft E49* dealing with income taxes, to revise *IAS 12*.
- *Exposure Draft E50* dealing with intangible assets.
- *Framework for the Preparation and Presentation of Financial Statements.*

A complete list of the above items is presented in Appendix 2A.

Some standards address both disclosure and measurement issues while others address income measurement and balance sheet valuation at the same time. These standards are widely applicable to multinational as well as domestic business entities.

The IASC Board has also issued a *Framework for the Preparation and Presentation of Financial Statements.* As discussed earlier, this framework guides IASC steering committees in their development of international standards. The framework objectives are:

- Assisting the IASC Board in the development of international standards and in its review of existing standards.
- Assisting the Board in promoting harmonization of accounting standards and procedures relative to the preparation and presentation of financial statements.

The Framework provides a basis for the reduction of the number of alternative accounting treatments permitted under existing IASC standards. The Framework is not in itself a standard and does not give authoritative or clear expression of the IASC position on alternative accounting treatments.

IASC comparability project. Many had expressed concerns over the several alternative treatments allowed under the IASs. In response, the IASC Board decided in 1987 to give high priority to the reduction or elimination of alternative accounting treatments in existing standards. On January 1, 1989, the IASC issued *Exposure Draft 32 (E32),* "Comparability of Financial Statements." *E32* dealt with 29 accounting issues for which free choice of accounting treatment existed. All interested parties were invited to submit comments on the exposure draft.

The IASC Board reconsidered each one of the 29 issues along with comments submitted by interested parties. The Board issued a *Statement of Intent on the Comparability of Financial Statements* in June 1990. This statement declared that of the 29 *E32* proposals:

- Twenty-one should be incorporated in revised international standards without substantive changes.
- Three should have substantive changes.
- Five should be deferred for future consideration.

The implementation of the proposals in the *Statement of Intent* provided the IASC with an opportunity to make revisions to improve the comparability of financial statements. The IASC Board issued 11 revised international accounting standards and an exposure draft to revise *IAS 12*, "Income Taxes ." A list of the 11 revised standards appears in Exhibit 2–2. All these were issued in December 1993, and all have a January 1, 1995 effective date, except for *IAS 7*, which was effective January 1, 1994.

Exhibit 2–2	Revised International Accounting Standards		
IAS Number	Topic	IAS Number	Topic
Disclosure standards		9	Research and Development Costs
7	Cash Flow Statements	11	Construction Contracts
8	Net Profit or Loss for the Period.	16	Property, Plant, and Equipment
	Fundamental Errors and	18	Revenue Recognition
	Changes in Accounting Policies	21	The Effects of Changes in
19	Retirement Benefit Costs		Foreign Exchange Rates
Measurement Standards		22	Business Combinations
2	Inventories	23	Borrowing Costs

Current and future IASC projects. The IASC Board is attempting to gain greater support from national and international preparers and users of financial statements. It is concurrently working with the U.S. Financial Accounting Standards Board on the earnings per share project, has gained support from the International Organization of Securities Commissions, and has expanded its work on behalf of developing nations. Current IASC projects include:

- Review of *IAS 12*, "Income Taxes," for which the Board has published *E49*.
- Issuance of *E50*, "Intangible Assets."
- Initiation of a new project on the *Financial Needs of Developing and Newly Industrialized Countries*.

The last item above would be relevant to a great many countries.

The United Nations

One of the four stated purposes of the United Nations (UN) is to promote international cooperation in solving international problems of economic, social, cultural, or humanitarian characteristics.

UN Economic and Social Council. The UN Economic and Social Council (Council) is empowered to make or initiate studies with respect to international economic matters and make recommendations on such matters to UN members. In 1974, the Council established the Commission on Transnational Corporations (Commission). The Commission was established as a result of a UN study. The report of the study, issued in 1974, noted the lack of information about the activities of multinational corporations and the absence of comparability of multinational corporate reports. The report also recommended the formation of a group of experts under the direction of the Commission to consider the development of international accounting and reporting standards. This recommendation was approved by both the Commission and the Council. In 1976, the UN Secretary General appointed a Group of Experts on International Standards of Accounting and Reporting.

International accounting standards efforts. The Group of Experts on International Standards of Accounting and Reporting consisted of 14 members. The group issued its findings in 1977 in a four-part report titled *International Standards of Accounting and Reporting for Transnational Corporations.* This report included a list of financial and nonfinancial items that should be disclosed by multinational corporations to host governments. Many of the financial items related to information included in the statement of financial position (balance sheet) and the statement of results of operation (income statement). Much of the nonfinancial information related to corporate social responsibility, labor policies, employment, and corporate environmental impact.

The Commission considered the Group of Experts report in 1978. The report was not adopted, partly because the members of the Group of Experts were not representing their respective governments. The Commission recommended to the Council that an intergovernmental group be established to consider international standards of accounting and reporting. The Council approved the Commission's recommendation in 1979. Thirty-four government representatives were appointed to serve on a new group called the Ad Hoc Intergovernmental Working Group of Experts on International Standards of Accounting and Reporting.

The Ad Hoc Group met during 1980 and 1981 but experienced major difficulty in reaching agreement on key issues such as:

- Financial information disclosure by individual enterprises within a group of companies.
- The objectives of financial information.
- Segment accounting information.
- Accounting valuation.

The Ad Hoc Group concluded its work by recommending establishment of an Intergovernmental Working Group of Experts on International Standards of Accounting and Reporting

(ISAR). In 1982, the ISAR group was established to focus on the development of international standards of accounting and reporting. The ISAR Group is composed of 34 elected members representing governments from around the globe.[7] The group meets annually to discuss important accounting issues. An annual report of session discussions has been published under the title *International Accounting and Reporting Issues: 19xx Review* since 1984.

The 1993 session dealt with accounting education and accounting qualification issues. ISAR members agreed that accounting education is lagging behind the globalization of the world economy and called for a global accounting qualification process. Exhibit 2–3 lists issues discussed by ISAR during its 1991 and 1992 sessions.

Following the 1991 session, the Council approved the ISAR recommendation to renew its mandate and to extend its duration from three to five years.

Exhibit 2–3   International Standards of Accounting and Reporting—1991 and 1992 Sessions

1991 session issues

- Reports on current developments at the global and national levels in the field of accounting and reporting by transnational corporations (TNC)
- Accounting for and by joint ventures
- Accounting for environmental protection measures
- Accounting and reporting during and after the transition from public to private enterprises
- Organization of accounting profession and the role and qualification of auditors

1992 session issues

- Reports on current developments at the global and national levels in the field of accounting and reporting by transnational corporations (TNC)
- An international survey of environmental information disclosure by TNCs
- Accounting problems arising during privatization
- Accountancy development in Francophone Africa and in Central and Eastern Europe
- Harmonizing national accounting standards

Organization for Economic Cooperation and Development

The Organization for Economic Cooperation and Development (OECD) was formed in 1960 and has 25 government members. Though the OECD has limited international membership, the world's largest multinational corporations are based in OECD member countries, as shown in Exhibit 2–4.

---

[7] The group members are elected based on the principle of equitable geographic distribution; that is, all world regions are represented.

Exhibit 2–4	National Distribution of Major Multinational Corporations		
*United States	150	*Netherlands	6
*Japan	61	South Korea	4
*United Kingdom	46	*Belgium	3
*Germany	30	*Spain	3
*France	23	*Norway	2
*Sweden	15	South Africa	2
*Canada	13	India	1
*Australia	9	*Luxembourg	1
*Switzerland	9	*New Zealand	1
*Finland	7	Taiwan	1
*Italy	6	Venezuela	1

*OECD member countries

Source: This distribution is based on Fortune 500 global corporations.

The objectives of the OECD are to enhance economic growth and development in member nations, to promote international trade among members, and to serve as an information clearinghouse for its members. The organization serves as a forum for member countries to share vital economic information, discuss issues of mutual concern, and attempt to provide solutions to common problems. The OECD's efforts to harmonize international accounting standards are only a part of the organization's focus on economic growth and development. A valuable contribution of the OECD is its surveys of accounting practices in member countries and its assessment of diversity or conformity of such practices.

Additional OECD efforts include formation of an Ad Hoc Working Group on Accounting Standards. The Group surveyed efforts toward the harmonization of accounting standards and the comparability of financial information. The Group charge includes:

- Supporting existing efforts by international, regional, and national bodies to improve harmonization of accounting standards.
- Providing technical clarification of the terms included in Disclosure of Information Guidelines.
- Functioning as a forum for the exchange of views on UN efforts on accounting and reporting standards.

The Group began to address pertinent technical accounting issues, conduct practice surveys, hold conferences on harmonization of accounting standards, and issue reports dealing with the technical aspects of accounting issues. Examples of the Series on Accounting Standard Harmonization are listed in Exhibit 2–5.

Other International Efforts

Many other international organizations and entities are also involved in the process of harmonizing accounting standards. Among these are:

Exhibit 2–5	Series on Accounting Standard Harmonization
No. 1	Foreign Currency Translation
No. 2	Consolidation Policies in OECD Countries
No. 3	Relationship between Taxation and Financial Reporting and Income Tax Accounting
No. 4	Operating Results of Insurance Companies: Current Practices in OECD Countries
No. 5	Consolidated Financial Statements

Source: Organization for Economic Cooperation and Development

- *Multinational corporations that are major users of international accounting standards.* Multinational corporations are concerned with the cost versus the benefits of an added layer of international standards. Their support for harmonization efforts is vital to its success. Exhibit 2–4 showed the distribution of major multinational corporations by country.
- *International accounting firms, which are also users of international standards.* Their job is to provide accounting and auditing services to clients. International accounting standards enhance the reliance users can place on their services.
- *International trade unions and organizations concerned with the activities of multinational corporations.* The trade union groups include the World Confederation of Labor, the International Confederation of Free Trade Unions, and the European Trade Union Confederation. These groups participate in the activities of the IASC, ISAR, and OECD.
- *International Organization of Securities Commissions* (IOSCO). IOSCO is interested in listing foreign stocks on national stock exchanges. Its endorsement of the efforts to harmonize accounting and auditing standards carries much weight in global capital markets. In July 1995, the IOSCO and the IASC reached an agreement to work together to achieve harmonization of accounting standards. According to the agreement, the IASC will revise its standards to the satisfaction of the IOSCO by mid-1999. Companies preparing their financial statements according to the IASC standards then will be able to list their securities on any of the world's capital markets. The IOSCO is a member of the IASC's consultative group.

Regional Efforts

This section presents the efforts of leading regional efforts to harmonize accounting standards and covers the:

- European Union
- North American Free Trade Agreement
- Other regional efforts

Their impact on standardization of major laws and regulations is expected to increase with more business activities.

European Union

The European Community became the European Union (EU) on January 1, 1994. This powerful regional alliance was established by the Treaty of Rome in 1957. The Treaty of Rome was signed by six European nations: Belgium, France, Germany, Italy, Luxembourg, and the Netherlands. In 1973 Denmark, Ireland, and the United Kingdom joined the common market. Greece joined in 1981, followed by Portugal and Spain in 1986. Austria, Finland, and Sweden became members on January 1, 1995, creating a 15-nation trading bloc.

EU countries felt that business activities should not be confined to their national borders. Stakeholders would benefit from harmonization of laws and regulations governing the free flow of goods, services, capital, and resources within the member countries. This process involved:

- The elimination of national custom duties and other barriers to the free movement of goods and services.
- The standardization of tariffs and trade restrictions with non-member nations.
- The unification of economic and industrial policies by creating a uniform economic environment in the EU. This includes the harmonization of fiscal, monetary, tax, and corporate laws. It also includes harmonization of accounting standards.
- The ultimate creation of political union and harmonization of social, cultural, and political policies within the EU and between EU members and other nations.

Development of EU standards. The European Union functions through the activities of its Commission. The Commission establishes standardization and harmonization of corporate and accounting rules through the issuance of Directives and Regulations. *EU Directives must be incorporated into the laws of member nations. Regulations are laws applicable to all members without the need for national legislation by member countries.* Exhibit 2–6 lists EU Directives and Regulations relative to corporate law and EU accounting standards. The Fourth and Seventh Directives deal exclusively with accounting issues and standards, and are discussed in detail in this chapter.

The process of setting EU directives is somewhat similar to the process used by other standard-setting bodies such as the International Accounting Standards Committee presented earlier in this chapter. The EU Commission selects a project for consideration and requests an **expert report.** This is followed by the preparation of a **discussion document** that is examined by the Commission working group and other interested parties. A **draft directive** is then prepared for consideration by the European Parliament and the Union Economic and Social Committee. Based on comments received, a **proposed directive** is considered by the Union Council of Ministers. *Adoption of a proposed directive or regulation requires a unanimous vote of the Council.* As stated earlier, member nations must then incorporate the Directive into their laws and regulations.

The EU is currently working with other standard-setting bodies to coordinate its harmonization efforts, and is a member of the IASC consultative group. An Accounting Advisory Forum, composed of preparers and users of financial information, was formed as a consultative group to the EU Commission on its standard harmonization efforts.

Exhibit 2–6   EU Directives and Regulations Relevant to Corporate Accounting

Directives

Directive	Topic	Draft Date	Adoption Date
First	Publication of accounts	1964	1968
Second	Separation of private from public companies, minimum capital, limitation on distribution	1970, 1972	1976
Third	Mergers	1970, 1973, 1975	1978
Fourth	Annual accounts format and rules and presentation rules	1971, 1974	1978
Fifth	Structure, management, and audits of companies	1972, 1983	—
Sixth	De-mergers, spin-offs	1978	1982
Seventh	Consolidated accounts, including associated companies	1976, 1978	1983
Eighth	Qualification and work of auditors	1978	1984
Ninth	Links between public company groups (pre-draft)	—	—
Tenth	International mergers of public companies	1985	—
Eleventh	Branch disclosures	1986	1989
Twelfth	Single-member companies	1988	1989
Thirteenth	Mergers and takeovers	1989	—

Regulations

Item	Topic	Draft Date	Adoption Date
European Company Statute	European company subject to EU laws	1970, 1975, 1989	—
European Economic Interests Grouping	Business form for multi-national joint ventures	1973, 1978	1985

The Fourth Directive. The EU Fourth Directive contains comprehensive accounting rules. It covers financial statements, their contents, methods of presentation, valuation methods, and disclosure of information. The Directive was adopted in 1978 and implemented in national accounting regulations by EU members in 1991. EU member countries have leeway in implementing and incorporating the Directive in their national accounting regulations. As such, the Directive serves as a model or benchmark for all member nations. Member countries may require more information than what is required under the Directive. They may require different reporting disclosures and measurement rules based on size or other corporate characteristics. Thus, implementation of the Directive may differ among member countries.

The Directive provides a broadly defined structure of financial information classification and presentation. It requires a balance sheet, an income statement, and notes to financial statements. Financial statements are to present a "true and fair view" (discussed in a later section) of the company's results of operations and its financial position.

The Directive allows either a horizontal or vertical presentation of the balance sheet and income statement. A third modified balance sheet format for the vertical form is also allowed, subject to providing detailed information in the notes to financial statements. The horizontal balance sheet is similar to the format used in the U.S. However, items are presented in reverse order of liquidity, for example, listing fixed assets ahead of current assets. The vertical format shows the amount of shareholders' equity by deducting each liability classification from its related asset classification. Appendix 2D shows the detailed contents of the horizontal balance sheet. Exhibits 2–7 and 2–8 show abbreviated horizontal and vertical balance sheet formats, respectively.

The income statement offers four choices among horizontal or vertical formats, or a classification of expenses by function or nature. The horizontal format shows turnover (sales revenue) added to all other sources of income on the left side, while ordinary and extraordinary charges (expenses) are presented on the right side of the statement. The vertical format shows the profit or loss on ordinary activities after subtracting all charges (expenses) from turnover. Extraordinary profit or loss is shown after offsetting extraordinary charges against extraordinary income. The statement concludes with profit or loss for the fiscal year. Exhibits 2–9 and 2–10 show abbreviated horizontal and vertical income statement formats, respectively. Appendix 2D shows the detailed horizontal and vertical format of the income statement.

The Fourth Directive allows another format of vertical income statement based on the type of expenditure. In this format, turnover (sales revenue) is adjusted by the changes in finished goods and work in process stocks (inventory) and then added to other operating income. Operating expenses charged against income are classified into raw material, staff, depreciation, and other operating charges. Nonoperating income and charges, taxes, and extraordinary income and charges are then included in the statement to produce the profit or loss for the financial year. As stated earlier, *the Fourth Directive allows four income statement formats: horizontal or vertical, and natural or functional classification of expenses.*

True and fair view. An important feature of the Fourth Directive is the adoption of the concept of a *true and fair view*. This is a British concept of what financial statements ought to convey. The concept was not widely applied in continental Europe prior to its inclusion in the Fourth Directive. The implementation of the true and fair view concept means that

**Exhibit 2–7   EU Fourth Directive
Horizontal Balance Sheet**

XYZ Company, Balance Sheet, December 31, 19xx

Stockholders' Equity and Liabilities	Assets
A. Capital and reserves called 　　Called-up share capital 　　Share premium account 　　Revaluation reserve 　　Other reserves 　　Profit and loss account	A. Called-up share capital not paid 　　　*[stock subscriptions receivable]* B. Fixed assets: 　　Intangible assets 　　Tangible assets 　　Investments *[long term]*
B. Provisions for liabilities 　　and charges	C. Current assets: 　　Stocks *[inventories]* 　　Debtors *[receivables]*
C. Creditors *[payables]*	Investments 　　Cash
D. Accrued and deferred income	D. Prepayments and accrued income

---

**Exhibit 2–8   EU Fourth Directive
Vertical Balance Sheet**

XYZ Company, Balance Sheet, December 31, 19xx

A. Called-up share capital not paid

B. Fixed assets:
　　Intangible assets
　　Tangible assets
　　Investments

C. Current assets:
　　Stocks
　　Debtors
　　Investments
　　Cash

D. Prepayments and accrued income

E. Creditors due within one year

F. Net current assets (liabilities): C + D - E

G. Total assets less current liabilities: A + B + C + D - E   (or A + B + F)

H. Creditors due after more than one year

I. Provisions for liabilities and charges

J. Accruals and deferred income

K. Capital and reserves

**Exhibit 2–9   EU Fourth Directive
Horizontal Profit and Loss Account**

XYZ Company, Income Statement, Year 19xx

Charges	**Income**
Cost of sales	Turnover
Distribution costs	Other operating income
Administrative expenses	Income from shares in
Investment write-off	group companies
Interest payable and	Income from other fixed asset
similar charges	investments
Tax on profit or loss on	Other interest receivable and
ordinary activities	similar income

Profit or loss on ordinary activities	**Profit or loss on ordinary activities**
Extraordinary charges	Extraordinary income
Tax on extraordinary profit or loss	**Profit or loss for the financial year**
Other taxes not shown under above items	
Profit or loss for the financial year	

**Exhibit 2–10   EU Fourth Directive
Vertical Profit and Loss Account**

XYZ Company, Income Statement, Year 19xx

Turnover
Cost of sales
Gross profit or loss
Distribution cost
Administrative expenses
Other operating income
Income from shares in group companies
Income from shares in related companies
Income from other fixed asset investments
Other interest receivable and similar income
Investment write-off
Interest payable and similar charges
Tax on profit or loss on ordinary activities
Profit or loss on ordinary activities
Extraordinary income
Extraordinary charges
Tax on extraordinary profit or loss
Other taxes not shown under above items
Profit or loss for the financial year

companies may be required to disclose additional or different information. Each country determines, based on its own circumstances, how its corporations should comply with the true and fair view concept.

The Seventh Directive. The Seventh Directive was first drafted in 1976, revised in 1978, and adopted by the EU commission in 1983. The Directive addresses consolidated financial statement issues. Member nations are given many choices as to how to incorporate its provisions into their company laws.

A key element of this Directive is the definition of the "group" for which consolidation is required. The German view focuses on effective management control and share ownership. The British view focuses on share ownership and legal control. The Seventh Directive adopted the British view, but also allows other control criteria to be applied on an optional basis by member countries. Legal control exists when the parent company has:

- A majority of voting rights or control over a majority of voting rights based on an agreement with other shareholders.
- A control contract agreement giving it the right of dominant influence over another entity.
- The right to appoint the majority of the entity's board of directors.

The Directive provides these guidelines for preparation of consolidated accounts (financial statements):[8]

- Consolidated accounts include the consolidated balance sheet, the consolidated profit and loss account (income statement), and the notes on the accounts (financial statements).
- Clear preparation of the consolidated accounts should be in accordance with the Directive.
- Additional information is required if the application of the Directive is not sufficient to give a true and fair view.
- If the application of specified provisions, in exceptional cases, is incompatible with the true and fair view, departure from that provision is allowed in order to give a true and fair view.
- Member countries may require or permit other information disclosures in the consolidated accounts, in addition to required disclosure under this Directive.

The Seventh Directive is a major development toward harmonization of accounting practices in EU countries. Many European countries did not have any legal requirement for consolidated statements. Prior to the Directive, Germany required consolidation only of domestic subsidiaries. France did not have any requirement for consolidated statements. The Seventh Directive requires worldwide consolidation regardless of the location of the parent company. It also requires that assets purchased through acquisition be measured at fair value. The segment disclosure requirement includes sales by line of business and geographical location.

---

[8] Section 2, Article 16.

Other EU Directives drafted or adopted include:

- Eighth Directive on the qualification and work of auditors.
- Tenth Directive on international mergers of public companies.
- Eleventh Directive on disclosure relating to branches.
- Thirteenth Directive on mergers.
- Directive on interim reporting by listed companies—1982.
- Directive on accounts of banks—1986.
- Draft directive on accounts of insurance companies—1991.

North American Free Trade Agreement—and Beyond

The previous section presented the EU efforts to harmonize accounting standards in member states. The European Union progressed through many stages of economic integration since the Treaty of Rome was signed in 1957. A trade agreement was signed in 1993 between Canada, Mexico, and the U.S. to create a common market. Will NAFTA follow the footsteps of the EU and achieve the same progress to unify the economies of its member countries? It is too early to tell. However, NAFTA has the potential to achieve what the EU countries were able to do.

Many economic, political, social, and historical factors have contributed to increased trade and economic cooperation between the three nations. The initial proposal to negotiate a free trade agreement came from the U.S. in 1989. Private free trade talks began in 1990. Various advisory committees representing governments, business, and the public were formed to provide input to trade negotiators. In 1991, the U.S. Congress granted the government "fast track" authority to complete the free trade talks. This allowed the U.S. government to pursue trade negotiations without much legislative debate. In August 1992, the 2,000-plus page agreement was finalized by negotiators. In late 1992, the NAFTA document and two accompanying agreements were signed by government representatives and were ready for legislative approval. By the end of 1993, NAFTA had won legislative approval in Canada, Mexico, and the U.S.

NAFTA calls for phasing out duties on most goods and services produced in the three countries. It also calls for free movement of professionals—accountants included—within the three countries. A licensed U.S. CPA would eventually be allowed to practice in Canada and Mexico. NAFTA has these objectives:

- Eliminate barriers to trade and facilitate cross-border movement of goods and services between the member nations.
- Promote conditions of fair competition in the free trade area.
- Increase investment opportunities in the three countries.
- Provide adequate and effective protection and enforcement of intellectual property rights in each member country.
- Establish a framework for further cooperation to expand and enhance the benefits of the agreement.

NAFTA would improve access to the market for goods produced in the three countries. All tariffs are to be eliminated on goods originating in Canada, Mexico, and the U.S. either immediately (effective January 1, 1994) or in 5 or 10 equal annual stages. Rules of origin define which goods would be eligible for this preferential treatment. Goods are grouped into four categories, each with a specified date for the elimination of tariffs.

The agreement provides that within two years from the signing date citizenship or permanent residency requirements for licensing or certification of professional service providers will be eliminated. Member countries are required to encourage relevant bodies to develop mutually acceptable standards for licensing and certification of professional service providers. This is an important step toward harmonization of accounting and auditing practices in the three countries, and will also have significant impact on accounting education.

NAFTA is administered by a Commission, similar to the EU. Committees are established for each area. For example, there is a Committee for Financial Services. It is not yet clear how the Commission or the committees will perform their duties.

At the Summit of the Americas meeting held in December 1994, leaders of 34 North and South American countries agreed to work toward a free trade agreement. This would create the largest free trade area in the world, with more than 850 million people and gross domestic product of $13 trillion. If agreement is reached, it is expected to go into effect by the year 2005.[9]

Other Regional Efforts

There are several other regional economic efforts, some of which are new while others are longstanding. As these agreements move toward economic integration, the need to harmonize accounting standards will become inevitable. Some regional organizations—the Arab League, for example—have a blueprint for a harmonized system of accounting for its members. The Arab League has had an organized association of its accountants and auditors for many years: the Arab Society of Certified Accountants. Some progress has been made, especially in establishing accounting standards in countries such as Kuwait, the United Arab Emirates, and Jordan. Exhibit 2–11 includes examples of some non-Pacific Rim trade and economic agreements. Some of these efforts have passed the stage of a regional focus and have begun to focus their efforts on increased international trade. Economic cooperation among the countries in the Pacific Rim region was discussed in Chapter 1.

Recent Developments

National efforts to harmonize accounting standards across national boundaries are as important as regional and international efforts. In many cases, national standard-setting bodies are key players in harmonizing their national standards with international standards, e.g., the International Accounting Standards promulgated by the IASC. The IASC has no power to enforce its standards. It relies on member organizations to implement its harmonization efforts at the national level.

---

[9] "A Free Trade Agreement for the Americas," *Deloitte & Touche Review,* 26 December 1994, p. 4.

> **Exhibit 2–11   Regional Economic and Trade Agreements**
>
> - Community of Sovereign States. Members are Russia, Ukraine, and Byelorussia. Other former Soviet Republics are invited to join.
> - Economic Cooperation of the Black Sea. Members are Azerbaijan, Armenia, Bulgaria, Georgia, Romania, Russia, Turkey, and Ukraine.
> - Baltic Council. Members are Norway and nine countries with borders on the Baltic Sea.
> - Central American Common Market. Members are Guatemala, Honduras, El Salvador, Nicaragua, and Costa Rica.
> - Andean Pact. Members are Bolivia, Colombia, Ecuador, Peru, and Venezuela. The countries plan a free trade area.
> - Arab League. The 21-member league has had an economic cooperation and free trade pact for years. Subgroups are also forming their own free trade areas such as the Maghreb Arab Union (Mauritania, Morocco, Algeria, Tunisia, and Libya).
> - Economic Cooperation Organization. Members are Kazakhstan, Azerbaijan, Kyrgyzstan, Tajikistan, Turkmenistan, Uzbekistan, Afghanistan, Iran, Pakistan, and Turkey.

National efforts to harmonize accounting standards include the following:

- National stock exchanges are considering requirements for multiple listing and foreign corporate listing. Consideration is given to compliance with IASC standards or to reconcile and disclose financial information prepared under home country and listing country standards.
- In many countries, national accounting standard-setters have adopted the International Accounting Standards and published them as their own national standards. For example, this is the case for Singapore, Zimbabwe, and Kuwait.
- In many cases, the national standards of one country are influenced by the standards of another country. Canadian standards, for example, are influenced by U.S. and U.K. standards. Recently, there has been noticeable U.S. influence on Japanese standards. Another example is the influence of Egyptian accounting standards on the standards of many Arab and African countries.

A more active role in the standard-setting process by professional accounting organizations in many countries, especially in Southeast Asia, Eastern Europe, and North Africa, is expected. Reexamination of the recent political and economic events listed in Exhibit 2–1 supports this conclusion. When professional accounting organizations have primary responsibility for setting national accounting standards, the result should be the sharing of ideas, discussion of issues and matters of mutual concern, and perhaps joint projects to find solutions to common problems. Such a process should lead to greater coordination and ultimately result in a reconciling mechanism that achieves harmonization of accounting standards worldwide.

Appendix 2A International Accounting Standards Committee Publications through August 1995

Standards

IAS 1	Disclosure of Accounting Policies
IAS 2	Inventories
IAS 3	Superseded by IAS 27
IAS 4	Depreciation Accounting
IAS 5	Information to be Disclosed in Financial Statements
IAS 6	Superseded by IAS 15
IAS 7	Cash Flow Statements
IAS 8	Net Profit or Loss for the Period, Fundamental Errors and Changes in Accounting Policies
IAS 9	Research and Development Costs
IAS 10	Contingencies and Events Occurring After the Balance Sheet Date
IAS 11	Construction Contracts
IAS 12	Accounting for Taxes on Income
IAS 13	Presentation of Current Assets and Current Liabilities
IAS 14	Reporting Financial Information by Segment
IAS 15	Information Reflecting the Effects of Changing Prices
IAS 16	Property, Plant, and Equipment
IAS 17	Accounting for Leases
IAS 18	Revenue
IAS 19	Retirement Benefit Costs
IAS 20	Accounting for Government Grants and Disclosure of Government Assistance
IAS 21	The Effects of Changes in Foreign Exchange Rates
IAS 22	Business Combinations
IAS 23	Borrowing Costs
IAS 24	Related Party Disclosures
IAS 25	Accounting for Investments
IAS 26	Accounting and Reporting by Retirement Benefits Plans
IAS 27	Consolidated Financial Statements and Accounting for Investments in Subsidiaries
IAS 28	Accounting for Investments in Associates
IAS 29	Financial Reporting in Hyperinflationary Economies
IAS 30	Disclosures in the Financial Statements of Banks and Similar Financial Institutions
IAS 31	Financial Reporting of Interests in Joint Ventures
IAS 32	Financial Instruments: Disclosure and Presentation

Framework

Framework for the Preparation and Presentation of Financial Statements

Statement of Intent

Comparability of Financial Statements

Proposed Revised International Accounting Standard

Exposure Draft E49 Income Taxes

Proposed New International Accounting Standard

Exposure Draft E50 Intangible Assets

Appendix 2B   IASC Constitution

Name and Objectives

1. The name of the organization shall be the International Accounting Standards Committee (IASC).

2. The objectives of IASC are:

   (a) To formulate and publish in the public interest accounting standards to be observed in the presentation of financial statements and to promote their worldwide acceptance and observance.

   (b) To work generally for the improvement and harmonisation of regulations, accounting standards and procedures relating to the presentation of financial statements.

Membership

3. As from 1 January 1984 membership of the International Accounting Standards Committee shall consist of all professional accountancy bodies that are members of the International Federation of Accountants (IFAC). Until 1 January 1984 membership shall be as laid down in the previous Constitution.

The Board

4. The business of the Committee shall be conducted by a Board of up to 17 members consisting of:

   (a) up to thirteen countries as nominated and appointed by the Council of IFAC that shall be represented by representatives from the professional accountancy bodies that are members of IFAC in these countries (in this Constitution the term 'country' shall include two or more countries that may be nominated to accept jointly a single seat on the Board), and

   (b) up to four organisations co-opted under clause 12(a).

5. (a) The term of appointment to the Board of a Member selected under clause 4(a) shall be no more than five years. A retiring Board Member shall be eligible for reappointment. The first appointments under clause 4(a) shall be as of 1 January 1983.

   (b) The term of appointment to the Board of a Member selected under clause 4(b) shall be determined by the Board at the time of appointment.

6. The professional accountancy bodies referred to in clause 4(a) and the organisations co-opted under clause 12(a) may nominate not more than two representatives from their Board Member country or their organisation to serve on the Board. The nominated representatives from each country or organisation may be accompanied at meetings of the Board by a staff observer.

7. The representatives on the Board and the persons nominated to carry out particular assignments or to join steering committees/working parties/groups shall not regard themselves as representing sectional interests but shall be guided by the need to act in the public interest.

8. The President of IFAC, or his designate, accompanied by not more than one technical adviser, shall be entitled to attend meetings of the Board of IASC, be entitled to the privilege of the floor, but shall not be entitled to vote.

9. A report on its work shall be prepared by the Board each year and sent to the professional accountancy bodies and organisations which are represented on the Board and to the Council of IFAC for dissemination to member bodies.

Chairman

10. The Board shall be presided over by a Chairman elected for a term of two-and-a-half years by the Members of the Board from among their number. The Chairman shall not be eligible for re-election. The member country providing the Chairman shall be entitled to a further representative.

Voting

11. Each country represented on the Board and each organisation co-opted under clause 12(a) shall have one vote which may be taken by a show of hands or by written ballot. Except where otherwise provided either in this Constitution or in the Operating Procedures, decisions shall be taken on a simple majority of the Board.

Responsibilities and Powers

12. The Board shall have the power to:

    (a) invite up to four organisations having an interest in financial reporting to be represented on the Board;

    (b) remove from membership of the Board any country or any organisation co-opted under clause 12(a) whose contribution is more than one year in arrears or which fails to be represented at two successive Board meetings.

    (c) publish documents relating to international accounting issues for discussion and comment provided a majority of the Board votes in favour of publication;

    (d) issue documents in the form of exposure drafts for comment (including amendments to existing Standards) in the name of the International Accounting Standards Committee provided at least two-thirds of the Board votes in favour of publication;

    (e) Issue International Accounting Standards provided that at least three-quarters of the Board votes in favour of publication;

(f) establish operating procedures so long as they are not inconsistent with the provisions of this Constitution;

(g) enter into discussions, negotiations or associations with outside bodies and generally promote the worldwide improvement and harmonisation of accounting standards.

*Issue of Discussion Documents,
Exposure Drafts, and Standards*

13. (a) Discussion documents and exposure drafts shall be distributed by the Board to all Member Bodies. A suitable period shall be allowed for respondents to submit comments.

(b) Dissenting opinions will not be included in any exposure drafts or standards promulgated by the Board.

(c) Exposure drafts and standards may be distributed to such governments, standard-setting bodies, stock exchanges, regulatory and other agencies, and individuals as the Board may determine.

(d) The approved text of any exposure draft or standard shall be that published by IASC in the English language. The Board shall give authority to the individual participating bodies to prepare translations of the approved text of exposure drafts and standards. These translations should indicate the name of the accountancy body that prepared the translation and that it is a translation of the approved text. The responsibility for and cost of translating, publishing, and distributing copies in any country shall be borne by the professional body(ies) of the country concerned.

Financial Arrangements

14. (a) An annual budget for the ensuing calendar year shall be prepared by the Board each year and sent to the accountancy bodies and organisations which are represented on the Board, and to the Council of IFAC.

(b) IFAC shall contribute 5% of the budget of IASC in January and 5% in July of each year to defray the costs of participation in Steering Committees by member bodies not represented on the Board of IASC. The remainder of the budget of IASC shall be borne by the members of the Board, except that the Council of IFAC may decide to reimburse wholly or in part the share of the budget charged to one or more Board members.

(c) The countries or organisations represented on the Board shall contribute on 1st January and 1st July each year a sum in such proportions as shall be decided by a three-quarters vote of the Board. Unless otherwise agreed, members of the Board shall contribute equally to the annual budget. Members who are represented on the Board for part only of a calendar year shall contribute a pro rata proportion calculated by reference to the period of their representation on the Board in that year. All Board member contributions shall be billed and collected by IASC.

(d) The Committee shall reimburse the traveling, hotel, and incidental expenses of attendance at Board meetings by one representative from each country or organisation represented on the Board. In addition, the Chairman shall be reimbursed for expenses incurred in attending Board meetings and otherwise on behalf of IASC.

(e) The Board shall determine in its operating procedures what other expenses shall be a charge against the revenues of the Committee.

(f) The Board shall annually prepare financial statements and submit them for audit and send copies thereof to the professional accountancy bodies and organisations which are represented on the Board and to the Council of IFAC for dissemination to the member bodies.

Meetings

15. Meetings of the Board shall be held at such times and in such places as the members of the Board may mutually agree.

16. In conjunction with the General Assembly of IFAC a meeting of the members of IASC shall be held during or immediately prior to each International Congress of Accountants at the location chosen for the congress.

Administrative Office

17. The location of the administrative office of the International Accounting Standards Committee shall be London, England.

Amendments to Constitution

18. Amendments to this Constitution shall be discussed with the Council of IFAC and shall require a three-quarters majority of the Board and approval by the membership as expressed by a simple majority of those voting.

Source: International Accounting Standards Committee.

Appendix 2C   Members of the International Accounting Standards Committee

Australia (2)	Iceland	Paraguay
Austria (2)	India (2)	Peru
Bahamas	Indonesia	Philippines
Bahrain	Iraq	Poland
Bangladesh (2)	Ireland (2)	Portugal
Barbados	Israel	Saudi Arabia
Belgium (2)	Italy (2)	Singapore
Bolivia	Jamaica	South Africa
Botswana	Japan	Spain
Brazil	Jordan (2)	Sri Lanka
Canada (3)	Kenya	Sudan
Chile	Korea	Swaziland
Colombia	Kuwait	Sweden (2)
Croatia	Lebanon (2)	Switzerland
Cyprus	Lesotho	Syria
Czech Republic	Liberia	Taiwan
Denmark (2)	Libya	Tanzania (2)
Dominican Republic	Luxembourg	Thailand
Ecuador	Malawi	Trinidad
Egypt	Malaysia (2)	Tunisia
Fiji	Malta	Turkey
Finland	Mexico	United Kingdom (5)
France (2)	Netherlands	Uruguay
Germany (2)	New Zealand	U.S. (4)
Ghana	Nigeria	Zambia
Greece (2)	Norway (2)	Zimbabwe
Hong Kong	Pakistan (2)	
Hungary	Panama (2)	

Data as of April 1995. Numbers in parentheses indicate the
number of accounting organizations from a given country.

Source: International Accounting Standards Committee.

Appendix 2D   Balance Sheet and Income Statement Format: EU 4th Directive

Section 3
Layout of the Balance Sheet
Article 8

For the presentation of the balance sheet, the Member States shall prescribe one or both of the layouts prescribed by Articles 9 and 10. If a Member State prescribes both, it may allow companies to choose between them.

Article 9
Assets

A. Subscribed capital unpaid of which there has been called (unless national law provides that called-up capital be shown under 'Liabilities.' In that case, the part of the capital called but not yet paid must appear as an asset either under A or under D(II)(5)).

B. Formation expenses as defined by national law, and in so far as national law permits their being shown as an asset. National law may also provide for formation expenses to be shown as the first item under 'intangible assets.'

C. Fixed assets
 I. Intangible assets
   1. Costs of research and development, in so far as national law permits their being shown as assets.
   2. Concessions, patents, licenses, trade marks, and similar rights and assets, if they were:
     (a) acquired for valuable consideration and need not be shown under C(I)(3); or
     (b) created by the undertaking itself, in so far as national law permits their being shown as assets.
   3. Goodwill, to the extent that it was acquired for valuable consideration.
   4. Payments on account.
 II. Tangible assets
   1. Land and buildings.
   2. Plant and machinery.
   3. Other fixtures and fittings, tools, and equipment.
   4. Payments on account and tangible assets in course of construction.
 III. Financial assets
   1. Shares in affiliated undertakings.
   2. Loans to affiliated undertakings.
   3. Participating interests.
   4. Loans to undertakings with which the company is linked by virtue of participating interests.
   5. Investments held as fixed assets.

   6. Other loans.
   7. Own shares (with an indication of their nominal value or, in the absence of a nominal value, their accounting par value) to the extent that national law permits their being shown in the balance sheet.

D. Current assets
 I. Stocks
   1. Raw materials and consumables.
   2. Work in progress.
   3. Finished goods and goods for resale.
   4. Payments on account.
 II. Debtors (amounts becoming due and payable after more than one year must be shown separately for each item).
   1. Trade debtors.
   2. Amounts owed by affiliated undertakings.
   3. Amounts owed by undertakings with which the company is linked by virtue of participating interests.
   4. Other debtors.
   5. Subscribed capital called but not paid (unless national law provides that called-up capital be shown as an asset under A).
   6. Prepayments and accrued income (unless national law provides for such items to be shown as an asset under E).
 III. Investments
   1. Shares in affiliated undertakings.
   2. Own shares (with an indication of their nominal value or, in the absence of a nominal value, their accounting par value) to the extent that national law permits their being shown in the balance sheet.
   3. Other investments.
 IV. Cash at bank and in hand.

E. Prepayments and accrued income (unless national law provides for such items to be shown as an asset under D(II)(6)).

F. Loss for the financial year (unless national law provides for it to be shown under A(VI) under liabilities).

Liabilities

A. Capital and reserves
 I. Subscribed capital (unless national law provides for called-up capital to be shown under this item. In that case, the amounts of subscribed capital and paid-up capital must be shown separately).
 II. Share premium account.

III. Revaluation reserve.

IV. Reserves.

   1. Legal reserve, in so far as national law requires such a reserve.

   2. Reserve for own shares, in so far as national law requires such a reserve, without prejudice to Article 11(1)(b) of Directive 77/91/EEC.

   3. Reserves provided for by the articles of association.

   4. Other reserves.

V. Profit or loss brought forward.

VI. Profit or loss for the financial year (unless national law requires that this item be shown under F under 'assets' or under E under 'liabilities').

B. Provisions for liabilities and charges

   1. Provisions for pensions and similar obligations.

   2. Provisions for taxation.

   3. Other provisions.

C. Creditors (amounts becoming due and payable within one year and amounts becoming due and payable after more than one year must be shown separately for each item and for the aggregate of these items).

   1. Debenture loans, showing convertible loans separately.

   2. Amounts owed to credit institutions.

   3. Payments received on account of orders in so far as they are not shown separately as deductions from stocks.

   4. Trade creditors.

   5. Bills of exchange payable.

   6. Amounts owed to affiliated undertakings.

   7. Amounts owed to undertakings with which the company is linked by virtue of participating interests.

   8. Other creditors including tax and social security.

   9. Accruals and deferred income (unless national law provides for such items to be shown under D under 'liabilities').

D. Accruals and deferred income (unless national law provides for such items to be shown under C(9) under 'Liabilities').

E. Profit for the financial year. (unless national law provides for it to be shown under A(VI) under 'Liabilities').

Section 5
Layout of the Profit and Loss Account
Article 22

For the presentation of the profit and loss account, the Member States shall prescribe one or more of the layouts provided for in Articles 23 to 26. If a Member State prescribes more than one layout, it may allow companies to choose from among them.

Article 23

1. Net turnover.
2. Variation.
3. Work performed by the undertaking for its own purposes and capitalized.
4. Other operating income.
5. (a) Raw materials and consumables.
   (b) Other external charges.
6. Staff costs:
   (a) Wages and salaries.
   (b) Social security costs with a separate indication of those relating to pensions.
7. (a) Value adjustments in respect of formation expenses and tangible and intangible fixed assets.
   (b) Value adjustments in respect of current assets, to the extent that they exceed the amount of value adjustments which are normal in the undertaking concerned.
8. Other operating charges.
9. Income from participating interests, with a separate indication of that derived from affiliated undertakings.
10. Income from other investments and loans forming part of the fixed assets, with a separate indication of that derived from affiliated undertakings.
11. Other interest receivable and similar income, with a separate indication of that derived from affiliated undertakings.
12. Value adjustments in respect of financial assets and of investments held as current assets.
13. Interest payable and similar charges, with a separate indication of those concerning affiliated undertakings.
14. Tax on profit or loss on ordinary activities.
15. Profit or loss on ordinary activities after taxation.
16. Extraordinary income.
17. Extraordinary charges.
18. Extraordinary profit or loss.
19. Tax on extraordinary profit or loss.
20. Other taxes not shown under the above items.
21. Profit or loss for the financial year.

Article 24

A. Charges

1. Reduction in stocks of finished goods and in work in progress.
2. (a) Raw materials and consumables.
   (b) Other current charges.
3. Staff costs.
   (a) Wages and salaries.
   (b) Social security costs, with a separate indication of those relating to pensions.

4. (a) Value adjustments in respect of formation expenses and of tangible and intangible fiscal assets.

   (b) Value adjustments in respect of current
   assets, to the extent that they exceed the
   amount of value adjustments which are
   normal in the undertaking concerned.

5. Other operating charges.

6. Value adjustments in respect of financial assets and of investments held as current assets.

7. Interest payable and similar charges, with a
   separate indication of those concerning affiliated undertakings.

8. Tax on profit or loss on ordinary activities.

9. Profit or loss on ordinary activities after taxation.

10. Extraordinary charges.

11. Tax on extraordinary profit or loss.

12. Other taxes not shown under the above items.

13. Profit or loss for the financial year.

B. Income

1. Net turnover.

2. Increase in stocks of finished goods and in
   work in progress.

3. Work performed by the undertaking for its
   own purposes and capitalized.

4. Other operating income.

5. Income from participating interests, with a
   separate indication of that derived from affiliated undertakings.

6. Income from other investments and loans
   forming part of the fixed assets, with a separate indication of that derived from affiliated
   undertakings.

7. Other interest receivable and similar income
   with a separate indication of that derived
   from affiliated undertakings.

8. Profit or loss on ordinary activities after taxation.

9. Extraordinary income.

10. Profit or loss for the financial year.

Article 25

1. Net turnover.

2. Cost of sales (including value adjustments).

3. Gross profit or loss.

4. Distribution costs (including value adjustments).

5. Administrative expenses (including value
   adjustments).

6. Other operating income.

7. Income from participating interests, with a
   separate indication of that derived from affiliated undertakings.

8. Income from other investments and loans
   forming part of the fixed assets, with a separate indication of that derived from affiliated
   undertakings.

9. Other interest receivable and similar income,
   with a separate indication of that derived
   from affiliated undertakings.

10. Value adjustments in respect of financial
    assets and of investments held as current
    assets.

11. Interest payable and similar charges with a
    separate indication of those concerning af-
    filiated undertakings.

12. Tax on profit or loss on ordinary activities.

13. Profit or loss on ordinary activities after taxa-
    tion.

14. Extraordinary charges.

15. Extraordinary charges.

16. Extraordinary profit or loss.

17. Tax on extraordinary profit or loss.

18. Other taxes not shown under the above
    items.

19. Profit or loss for the financial year.

Article 26

A. Charges

1. Cost of sales (including value adjustment).

2. Distribution costs (including value adjustments).

3. Administrative expenses (including value
   adjustments).

4. Value adjustments in respect of financial
   assets and of investments held as current
   assets.

5. Interest payable and similar charges, with a
   separate indication of those concerning affiliated undertakings.

6. Tax on profit or loss on ordinary activities.

7. Profit or loss on ordinary activities after taxation.

8. Extraordinary charges.

9. Tax on extraordinary profit or loss.

10. Profit or loss, for the financial year.

B. Income

1. Net turnover.

2. Other operating income.

3. Income from participating interests, with a
   separate indication of that derived from affiliated undertakings.

4. Income from other investments and loans
   forming part of the fixed assets, with a separate indication of that derived from affiliated
   undertakings.

5. Other interest receivable and similar income,
   with a separate indication of that derived
   from affiliated undertakings.

6. Profit or loss on ordinary activities after taxation.

7. Extraordinary income.

8. Profit or loss for the financial year.

Source:EU Secretariat, *Fourth Directive*, EU, Brussels.

Note to Students

You have been introduced to the work of many international and regional organizations and trading blocs including the United Nations, the European Union, and the North American Free Trade Agreement. What is perhaps new to many of you is the UN involvement in the development of accounting and financial reporting guidelines. This is evidence of the importance of the study of international accounting and the role played by accounting in the social and economic development of all countries.

Multinational corporations must follow the accounting standards of their own countries. They may also be required to reconcile their financial statements with other accounting standards when they list on foreign stock exchanges. Imagine the costs involved in meeting such requirements.

The appendices at the end of the chapter provide you with valuable information. You may wish to do the following:

- Compare the IASC with any of the national accounting standard-setters you are familiar with.
- Regroup the countries listed in Appendix 2C by continent.
- Assess the information content of vertical versus horizontal income statements and balance sheets.

A global economy, with all its implications, is a reality. This has a direct effect on your future job opportunities and the knowledge required to be a successful professional. For example, note how NAFTA is likely to substantially increase the market for accounting services. Taking advantage of the new opportunities will require knowledge and understanding of the world around you. Good luck, and proceed to learn about specific international accounting issues in the remainder of this text.

Chapter Summary

- Recent political and economic events may accelerate the need for and development of international accounting standards.
- International trade and investment require accounting standards that are not country-specific.
- Harmonization of accounting standards reduces the differences between national standards and improves the comparability of financial statements.
- Worldwide harmonization efforts are classified into international, regional, and national efforts.
- The International Accounting Standards Committee is one of the leading organizations in the efforts to harmonize accounting standards.
- Since its creation in 1973, the IASC has issued 32 standards, numerous exposure drafts, and a framework for the preparation and presentation of financial statements.

- The IASC standards cover measurement, recording, and disclosure issues dealing with the preparation of financial reports.

- The Intergovernmental Working Group of Experts on International Standards of Accounting and Reporting (ISAR) is the UN body involved in harmonization efforts. The Group meets annually and issues an annual report.

- The Organization for Economic Cooperation and Development issues financial reporting guidelines for multinational corporations focusing on disclosure of information by MNCs.

- The European Union is the leading trading bloc in the efforts to harmonize accounting standards among its member countries.

- The Fourth and Seventh EU Directives address the preparation and consolidation of financial statements.

- Canada, Mexico, and the U.S. are members of the North American Free Trade Agreement. It is too early to assess NAFTA's impact on international accounting standards.

- National efforts to harmonize accounting standards are equally important and should be encouraged. The ultimate success of worldwide harmonization efforts will depend on their acceptance by setters of national accounting standards.

Questions for Discussion

1. Review the definition of international accounting presented in Chapter 1. Critically examine the meaning of international accounting standards in light of that definition.

2. How do major world political and economic events influence the need for and development of accounting standards?

3. What is the impact of diversity of national accounting standards on the developers and users of financial information? How does diversity affect the operation of multinational corporations?

4. Compare standardization with harmonization of accounting standards. Should accounting standards be standardized or harmonized worldwide? Discuss.

5. What international organizations are involved in harmonization efforts?

6. Describe the International Accounting Standards Committee's efforts to harmonize accounting standards to date. Be specific.

7. Describe and assess the standard-setting process used by the IASC.

8. Describe and explain the organization structure of the IASC.

9. Why did the IASC undertake the comparability project? What is the long-run significance of this project?

10. What were the outcomes of the IASC comparability project?

11. The accounting standard-setters in the U.S. and U.K. have gone through major organizational changes in the last 40 years. Do you think that the IASC may have to go through similar changes? Express your ideas, drawing on the chapter material, historical precedent, and your own knowledge and experience.

12. What is the main role of the UN in harmonizing worldwide accounting standards?

13. What is the main role of the OECD in harmonizing worldwide accounting standards?

14. Compare and evaluate the harmonization efforts of the IASC, the UN, and the OECD.

15. What is the main thrust of EU efforts to harmonize accounting standards?

16. Examine and evaluate the objectives of the Fourth Directive.

17. Examine and evaluate the objectives of the Seventh Directive.

18. Compare and evaluate EU versus IASC harmonization efforts.

19. Assess the likely impact of the North American Free Trade Agreement on accounting standards.

20. Critically examine the impact of regional economic and trade agreements on the efforts to establish international accounting standards.

21. Japan is not currently a member of any regional trading bloc. Does this affect the development of accounting standards in Japan? If yes, how?

22. Compare and evaluate regional and international efforts to harmonize accounting standards.

23. "National efforts to harmonize accounting standards across national boundaries are as important as international and regional efforts." Comment on this statement.

24. (Appendix 2A) Revised *IAS 7* requires a cash flow statement instead of a statement of changes in financial position. Can you suggest possible reasons for this change? [You may need to consult an intermediate accounting text, or the discussions contained in *FASB Statement No. 95* and *IAS 7*.]

25. (Appendix 2C) Classify the countries listed in Appendix 2C into three groups: highly industrialized countries, emerging industrialized countries, and developing countries. Compare your answers with your classmates' answers and discuss reasons behind any differences.

26. (Appendix 2D) What is the significance of providing alternative formats of the balance sheet and the income statement in the Fourth Directive? Compare the horizontal and vertical balance sheet formats.

Exercises/Problems

2-1 The International Commerce Union (ICU) has provided you with the following financial information for 19x4 (000):

Inventories	DM 16,100	Accounts payable	DM 14,300
Long-term investment	8,100	Other liabilities	2,800
Intangible assets	6,200	Property, plant, and equipment	43,500
Long-term liabilities	12,600	Accounts receivable	8,400
Issued capital	8,600	Other receivables	500
Capital reserve	?	Short-term investment	200
Dividends	2,000	Prepaid expenses	700
Turnover	109,000	Cost of materials and expenses	98,200
Bank deposits	6,800	Bonds payable	30,000
Profit and loss account (beginning balance)	5,000		

Required: Prepare a horizontal balance sheet for ICU.

2-2   Refer to 2-1 above.

Required: Prepare a vertical balance sheet for ICU.

2-3   Refer to 2-1 above. ICU expects that next year's sales will increase, costs will decrease, and overall worldwide operations will show a major improvement. ICU also expects dividends to triple, and owners' equity to increase by 50%.

Required: What is the estimated income (ignore taxes) for next year?

2-4   A U.S. multinational company issued the following income statement for 1993. The statement was prepared in accordance with U.S. accounting standards. The company also provided you with adjusted values in accordance with IASC standards and EU directives.

USMNC Income Statement, 1993 (US$000)

	U.S. Standards	Adjustment to IASC Standards	Adjustment to EU Standards
Sales revenue (turnover)	$19,500	None	None
Cost of sales	10,700	$11,200	$13,100
Gross profit	8,800	?	?
Operating expenses	4,900	4,300	5,200
Operating income	3,900	?	?
Taxes	1,200	1,350	150
Extraordinary gain (loss)	600	(600)	(400)
Net income for the year	$3,300	?	?

Select the best available answer:

1. What is the operating income under IASC standards?
   a. $1,200   d. $8,300
   b. $3,900   e. None of the above
   c. $4,000

2. What is the operating income under EU standards?
   a. $3,900   d. $4,000
   b. $8,100   e. None of the above
   c. $1,200

3. What is the net income under IASC standards?
   a. $1,550   d. $2,050
   b. $1,200   e. None of the above
   c. $5,000

4. What is the net income under EU standards?
   a. $1,550   d. $650
   b. $1,200   e. None of the above
   c. $950

5. A review of the above financial information indicates that:
   a. U.S. and IASC standards are similar.
   b. U.S. and IASC standards are different.
   c. Disclosure of the above information is generally not costly.
   d. The above disclosures are required by IASC.
   e. None of the above.

6. A review of the above financial information indicates that:
   a. U.S. and EU standards are similar.
   b. U.S. and EU standards are different.
   c. The above disclosures are required by the fourth Directive.
   d. The above disclosures are required by the U.S.'s SEC.
   e. None of the above.

7. A review of the above financial information indicates that:
   a. IASC and EU standards are different.
   b. The UN requires the above disclosures.
   c. IASC and EU standards are similar.
   d. IASC standards are superior to EU standards.
   e. None of the above.

2-5 Select the best available answer:

1. The European Union accounting standards are called:
   a. Guidelines.
   b. Reporting issues.
   c. Directives.
   d. International Accounting Standards.

2. The International Accounting Standards Committee pronouncements are called:
   a. Directives.
   b. Accounting and reporting issues.
   c. International Accounting Standards.
   d. Opinions.

3. The policy-making body of the International Accounting Standards Committee is called the:

    a. Commission.

    b. Council of Ministers.

    c. Board.

    d. Cabinet.

4. The Organization for Economic Cooperation and Development efforts are mainly to:

    a. Issue international accounting standards.

    b. Advise member governments on auditing standards.

    c. Prepare guidelines for financial disclosure by MNCs.

    d. Require environmental disclosures.

5. The UN accounting policy-making body is called the:

    a. Financial Accounting Standards Board.

    b. Consultative Group.

    c. Intergovernmental Working Group of Experts for International Standards of Accounting and Reporting.

    d. Council of Ministers.

Case: Why Don't We All Speak Japanese or English?

The following statement was made by a participant at the International Financial Reporting Forum to debate the IASC's Comparability Project:

> I am a user but not a sophisticated user. It seems to me that like things ought to look alike and different things should look different, no matter where they exist. There was an article a little over a year ago in *Management Accounting,* where professors from Rider College took a set of identical circumstances and prepared financial statements as they would appear in four countries. The lowest net income number was ten and that was in Germany. You can add as many zeros as makes you feel comfortable. The highest was 260 and that was in the U.K. Twenty-six times bigger. Now how can financial statements be useful when they show those differences? The U.S. and Australia were in-between, with the U.S. closer to Germany and Australia closer to the U.K. There must be a better way. When you go to a foreign country and do not speak the language, you can get an interpreter and you can analyze, you can spend a lot of money and a lot of time. It would be a great deal easier if we all spoke the same language.
>
> Mr. Cairns and I were in Japan a few weeks ago making presentations to the Ministries of Finance and Justice. We had to use interpreters and it took about three times as long to convey our message to them and their reactions back to us. Why don't we all speak Japanese or English? What we are shooting for here is a common language to make international financial traffic more efficient. We have erected trade barriers in each of our countries through non-comparable financial reporting. It is as clearly a trade barrier as other trade barriers you see. It is a matter of culture and habit rather than a matter of reason. Reason says we ought to be accounting in the same way.[10]

---

[10] School of Accounting, University of Southern California, *An Analysis of the Implications of the IASC's Comparability Project* (Los Angeles: University of Southern California, 1990), pp. 42-43.

Required:
(1) Discuss the issues raised in the above statement. What are the pros or cons of the suggested approach?
(2) Discuss other relevant issues besides the ones raised in the above statement.
(3) Aside from any merits, do you think the suggested approach is a practical one? Discuss.

References

Accounting and Financial Reporting in the European Community. Chicago: Arthur Andersen & Co., January 1993.

Agami, Abdel M. "NAFTA and Harmonization of Accounting." *Multinational Business Review,* spring 1995, pp. 1-7.

Anderson, Nancy. "The Globalization GAAP." *Management Accounting,* August 1993, pp. 52-54.

Anguiera, Marla Alfonso. "Harmonizing the World's Accounting." *New Accountant,* September 1989.

Beresford, D. "Internationalization of Accounting Standards." *Accounting Horizons,* December 1990, pp. 99-107.

Chandler, Roy A. "The International Harmonization of Accounting: In Search of Influence." *The International Journal of Accounting,* vol. 27, no. 3 (1992), pp. 222-233.

Cheney, Glenn A. "Can Accounting Keep Up?" *New Accountant,* September 1993, pp. 22-24.

Cook, T. E., and R. S. Wallace. "Financial Disclosure Regulation and Its Environment: A Review and Further Analysis." *Journal of Accounting and Public Policy* (1990), pp. 79-110.

Corbridge, Curtis L., Walter W. Austin, and David J. Lemak. "Germany's Accrual Accounting Practices." *Management Accounting,* August 1993, pp. 45-47.

Cushing, Robert G., et al. (eds.). *The Challenge of NAFTA.* Austin: The University of Texas, 1993.

EC Commission. *Fourth Council Directive for Coordination of National Legislation Regarding the Annual Accounts for Limited Liability Companies.* Brussels: EC, 1978.

———. *Seventh Council Directive on Consolidated Accounts.* Brussels: EC, 1983.

Fleming, P. D. "The Growing Importance of International Accounting Standards." *Journal of Accountancy,* September 1991, pp. 100-106.

Forker, John, and Margaret Greenwood. "European Harmonization and the True and Fair View: The Case of Long-Term Contracts in the U.K." *The European Accounting Review,* vol. 4, no. 1, (1995), pp. 1-31.

Garrod, Neil, and Isabel Sieringhaus. "European Union Accounting Harmonization: The Case of Leased Assets in the United Kingdom and Germany." *The European Accounting Review,* vol. 4, no. 1 (1995), pp. 155-164.

Goeltz, Richard K. "International Harmonization: The Impossible (and Unnecessary?) Dream." *Accounting Horizons,* March 1991, pp. 85-88.

Grove, Hugh D., and John D. Bazley. "Disclosure Strategies for Harmonization of International Accounting Standards." *The International Journal of Accounting,* vol. 28, no. 2 (1993), pp. 116-128.

Haller, Axel. "The Relationship of Financial and Tax Accounting in Germany: A Major Reason for Accounting Disharmony in Europe." *The International Journal of Accounting,* vol. 27, no. 4 (1992), pp. 310-323.

Harris, Trevor S. *International Accounting Standards versus US-GAAP Reporting.* Cincinnati, Ohio: South-Western Publishing Company, 1995.

Hopwood, Anthony G. "Some Reflections on 'The Harmonization of Accounting Within the EU.'" *The European Accounting Review,* vol. 3, no. 2 (1994), pp. 241-253.

International Accounting Standards. London: International Accounting Standards Committee, 1995.

International Investment and Multinational Enterprises. Paris: Organization for Economic Cooperation and Development, 1979 (originally published in 1976).

Moulin, Donald J., and Morton B. Solomon, "Practical Means of Promoting Common International Standards." *CPA Journal,* December 1989, pp. 38-40.

Nobes, Christopher W., and Robert H. Parker (eds.). *Comparative International Accounting,* 3d ed. Englewood Cliffs, N.J.: Prentice Hall International, 1991.

Norris, Floyd. "In Accounting, Truth Can Be Very Scary." *New York Times,* 11 April 1993.

Purvis, S. E. C., Helen Garnon, and Michael A. Diamond. "The IASC and Its Comparability Project: Prerequisites for Success." *Accounting Horizons,* June 1991, pp. 25-44.

Regulation of the International Securities Market, Policy Statement of the United States Securities and Exchange Commission. New York: Securities and Exchange Commission, November 1988.

School of Accounting, University of Southern California. *An Analysis of the Implications of the IASC's Comparability Project.* Los Angeles: University of Southern California, 1990.

Scott, G., and P. Trobert. *Eighty-eight International Accounting Problems in Rank Order of Importance, A Delphi Evaluation.* Sarasota, Fla.: American Accounting Association, 1980.

Sundby, Larry, and Bradley Schwieger. "EC, EZ?" *Journal of Accountancy,* March 1992, pp. 71-76.

Theunisse, Hilda. "Financial Reporting in EC Countries." *The European Accounting Review,* vol. 3, no. 1 (1994), pp. 143-162.

Thorell, Per, and Geoffrey Whittington. "The Harmonization of Accounting Within the EU: Problems, Perspectives and Strategies." *The European Accounting Review,* vol. 3, no. 2 (1994) pp. 215-239.

United Nations Intergovernmental Working Group of Experts on International Standards of Accounting and Reporting. *Conclusions on Accounting and Reporting by Transnational Corporations.* New York: United Nations, 1988.

————. *International Accounting and Reporting Issues: 1986 Review.* New York: United Nations, 1986.

————. *International Standards of Accounting and Reporting.* New York: United Nations, 1977.

Van Hulle, K., and K. U. Leuven. "Harmonization of Accounting Standards in the EC: Is It the Beginning or Is It the End?" *The European Accounting Review,* vol. 2, no. 2 (1993), pp. 387-396.

Wallace, R. S. Olusegun. "Survival Strategies of a Global Organization: The Case of the International Accounting Standards Committee." *Accounting Horizons,* June 1990, pp. 1-22.

World Bank. *World Development Report.* London: Oxford University Press, 1989.

Wyatt, Arthur R. "An Era of Harmonization." *Journal of International Financial Management and Accounting,* spring 1992, pp. 63-68.

————. "Seeking Credibility in a Global Economy." *New Accountant,* September 1992, pp. 4-6, 51-52.

Wyatt, Arthur R., and Joseph Yospe, "Wake-up Call to American Business: International Accounting Standards Are on the Way." *Journal of Accountancy,* July 1993, pp. 80-85.

Zeff, Stephen A. "International Accounting Principles and Auditing Standards." *The European Accounting Review,* vol. 2, no. 2 (1993), pp. 403-410.

Chapter 3

Financial Reporting Disclosures

In this chapter we will discuss a variety of issues relating to financial reporting disclosures and current disclosure practices and trends. The term **financial reporting disclosures** is broad and encompasses many types of disclosure such as:

- Disclosures within the financial statements.
- Disclosures made as supplements to financial statements.
- Required disclosures.
- Voluntary disclosures.
- Disclosures expressed in monetary terms.
- Disclosures in nonmonetary terms.
- Quantitative disclosures.
- Nonquantitative disclosures that are in a narrative format.

The scope and extent of financial reporting disclosures have widened considerably in recent years. This trend is expected to continue because of the accelerating movement toward globalization of trade and investments. Also, the international environments in which a company operates may contribute to increased disclosures. For example, the heightened awareness of environmental concerns among the public at large or the increased power of labor unions can have a direct impact on the scope and extent of disclosures made about a company's performance in these areas.

The Evolving Disclosure Process

It is widely acknowledged that a corporation's accountability extends to parties beyond investors and creditors for two reasons. First, society entrusts the corporation to manage scarce resources, making it accountable to society. A corporation should provide information to enable members of society to assess its performance in managing and protecting scarce resources. Second, the corporation's operations affect the quality of life and standard of living of individuals who may be neither investors nor creditors. Such individuals should be able to have access to information so that they may review, assess, and influence the activities of the corporation. This wider concept of corporate responsibility has been recognized for decades. The users of financial reports thus include varied groups such as suppliers, customers, employees, workers' unions, regulatory agencies, and people residing in areas where the corporation's operations are located.

The area of financial reporting disclosures is still evolving. At least two issues remain unresolved. First, there is no commonly accepted framework for providing information to users who are neither investors nor creditors. These users are hard to identify and their number and demands for disclosures apparently are increasing. The other issue is that, unlike most of the costs of disclosures, the benefits of disclosures are difficult, if not impossible, to trace in most cases. The diversity of user groups and how each of the user groups benefits from disclosures pose monumental identification and measurement problems.

Socio-Economic Reasons for Financial Reporting Disclosures

Disclosures are made to provide information to decision makers so that they can make informed decisions. Conceptually, there are two major socio-economic reasons for disclosures.

- To minimize risks to capital providers so that they can weigh the predicted returns of each alternative against the associated risks.
- To inform individuals and groups who are affected by the activities and operations of corporations in their quality of life and standard of living. The purpose is to enable them to influence corporate actions if they so desire after reviewing the financial reporting disclosures.

Next we will look at the main motivational factors for corporations to make financial reporting disclosures.

Motivational Factors for Corporations

There are several practical motivational factors for corporations to make financial reporting disclosures.

Internationalization of capital markets. As discussed in Chapter 1, global capital markets are already a reality. Corporations are now able to raise capital from sources in different parts of the world. Regulatory agencies set the minimum disclosure requirements for the companies listed on stock exchanges. Corporations may choose to voluntarily disclose additional information for self-interest. The corporation may be able to obtain capital at lower cost by reducing uncertainty and associated risks to the capital providers by a combination of required and voluntary disclosures.

A byproduct of the globalization of capital markets is the increasing awareness among regulators in many countries for the need to streamline and toughen the regulatory disclosure requirements. For example, Japan established a securities oversight commission in 1992. According to its chairman, "The Securities and Exchange Surveillance Commission was created to help establish fair and transparent securities markets."[1] The governor of the Reserve Bank of India, which is responsible for supervising and regulating the Indian financial industry, recently commented that the Reserve Bank of India "should be given more teeth to help ensure the safety and soundness of the financial system and bring about greater transparency and accountability in operations."[2]

---

[1] "Japanese Launch New Commission," *San Francisco Chronicle,* 21 July 1992, p. B2.

[2] "RBI Seeks More Teeth for Greater Transparency," *India West,* 18 February 1994, p. 14.

Global capital markets are such powerful sources of capital that some companies that had decided in the past against listing their securities in international stock exchanges have now shifted their position in this matter. Typically, the disclosures required by the important international stock exchanges exceed disclosures traditionally made by such companies. A case in point is Daimler-Benz. In order to list its shares on the New York Stock Exchange, the company agreed to value inventories, pension obligations, and foreign exchange transactions on a basis consistent with U.S. accounting standards and also agreed to publish its financial statements more frequently. Gerhard Liener, Chief Financial Officer of Daimler, stated that the company "can no longer afford to ignore the world's most prominent capital market."[3]

Statutory and legal requirements. In some countries, e.g., Germany and Japan, statutory and legal requirements prescribe the accounting treatment of transactions. In such countries, company law and taxation systems are the most important influences on accounting. Significant impact of MNCs on a nation's social, economic, and ecological environments has resulted in the enactment of many new statutes and laws in recent years requiring additional disclosures.

Accounting profession requirements. In most countries where the accounting profession has advanced to a mature state, e.g., Canada, U.S., and U.K., financial reporting disclosure requirements are determined by the profession. The accounting profession in such countries is quite influential. The standard-setting process includes open deliberations, and diverse interest groups are given opportunities to provide input.

Internationalization has compelled the accounting profession in such countries to address some issues that previously had not received much attention. Segment reporting, consolidation, and foreign currency exchange are just a few examples. *Moreover, additional disclosures are being required to enhance comparability of financial statements that are prepared using generally accepted accounting principles of different countries.*

Powerful special interest groups. Some groups may be able to require a corporation to make special disclosures due to their influence and power. For example, a labor union may successfully negotiate special disclosures on matters such as safety conditions, work-related injuries, and classification of employees by age, sex, etc.

Voluntary disclosures. Corporations may make voluntary disclosures when benefits are expected with little or no risk of adverse effects. Some of the reasons for voluntary disclosures are presented below:

- Educating the users of financial reports regarding operating conditions, future prospects, reasons for certain corporate actions, etc.
- Image building may generate goodwill for future economic benefits. Examples include disclosures of expenditures made beyond the minimum environmental regulation requirements, scholarship funds for minority college students, and

---

[3] "Daimler-Benz Opens Up," *Business Week,* 12 April 1993, p. 82.

    training programs for local managers to prepare them for higher-level management positions.

- Avoidance of potential governmental regulation or control. The corporation may make voluntary disclosures in self-interest if there is a risk that non-disclosures may result in governmental regulations or control. The purpose is to forestall any future governmental action that may have potential adverse effects. In such cases, just enough information may be disclosed to "let the steam out" of an issue. The extent of such voluntary disclosures is a matter of judgment.
- Lower cost of capital. Voluntary disclosures are above and beyond what is required by regulators. A corporation competing with other MNCs in global capital markets may find it advantageous to voluntarily provide additional disclosures. Everything else being equal, capital providers would choose company A over companies B and C if they perceive company A to carry lower risk. This perception of lower risk may be a direct result of voluntary disclosures made by company A to remove or reduce uncertainties about its future prospects.

Firms that operate in global capital markets tend to exceed required minimums in providing financial disclosures; that is, companies raising funds internationally are voluntarily disclosing more financial information than required. If it is the competition for investment funds that is propelling this practice, then a number of the financial disclosures observed in annual reports are market driven rather than regulation determined. Therefore, companies should look beyond requirements in formulating their disclosure policies. Investors are apparently demanding additional information and companies can be expected to respond to their demands in order to compete successfully for investment funds.[4]

Costs Versus Benefits Criterion

As mentioned earlier, identification of users and the information they need are necessary for deciding on the types of disclosure to be made and the extent of detail provided. We have noted that identity of the user groups is not always clear. Because of the presence of multiple users with varying information needs for a variety of decisions, there is always a question regarding the "right balance" in providing information to the users. No worldwide consensus exists on this issue.

The above issue is raised here to remind us that accounting information is not free. Accounting systems are economic goods. They cost money, just like bread and milk.[5] Using the cost-benefit approach as the primary criterion to choose an accounting system requires comparing costs with the benefits of alternative accounting systems.

The total costs of financial reporting disclosures, however, are not limited to the monetary costs of installing and maintaining an accounting system for accumulating, processing, and

---

[4] G. K. Meek, D. S. Coldwell, and D. S. Peavey, "Corporate Financial Disclosure: A Global Assessment," in F. Choi (ed.), *Handbook of International Accounting* (New York: John Wiley & Sons, Inc., 1991), pp. 22.27–22.28.

[5] Charles T. Horngren, George Foster, and Srikant M. Datar, *Cost Accounting: A Managerial Emphasis,* 8th ed., (Englewood Cliffs, N.J.: Prentice Hall, 1994) p. 10.

reporting financial information. They also include other costs that are difficult, if not impossible, to quantify. *The common thread among this group of costs is that the information obtained through disclosures may be used for making decisions that are not in the best interest of the corporation providing the information.* In other words, the decision makers' goals may be incongruent with the goals of the corporation. For example:

- Competitors may obtain a competitive advantage.
- Workers' unions may use the information to make costly demands.
- Regulatory agencies may use the information to increase regulation.
- Plaintiffs may use the information to substantiate their legal claims against the corporation.

It is often claimed by corporate operating and financial officers that extensive disclosures erode their competitive advantage. Interestingly, there is no evidence to support this assertion. One may, in fact, make a case that the free flow of information is a prerequisite to an efficient market economy. It is difficult to visualize the existence of a free market economy with firms competing aggressively against each other without an extensive information flow. Disclosures stimulate and encourage competition. This leads to streamlining of corporate operations in order to survive in the competitive environment. Consumers are the ultimate beneficiaries. Internationalization of trade and investments and the emergence of global markets is expected to increase competition as well as the need for information.

Special Measurement and Disclosure Issues in Financial Reporting

Recording economic transactions in the accounting system (**measurement**) precedes preparation of the financial statements (**disclosure**). At the time of recording, monetary values are assigned to economic transactions. The accounting standards of a country provide the rules regarding the assignment of monetary value for recording purposes. Just as accounting standards differ from country to country, so also does the recording of the same type of economic transactions. Therefore, financial reports and disclosures, due to their reliance on accounting records, are directly affected by the manner in which the economic transactions were initially recorded. Measurement and disclosure are interconnected.

Next we will look at some examples of worldwide diversity in this area. Our objective is to develop an appreciation of how the same type of economic transactions may be recorded differently because accounting principles differ worldwide.

Diversity in Measurement

The accounting standards of a country provide guidelines for recording economic transactions. Within the framework they provide an answer to the question: What accounts are to be debited and credited, and for what amounts? We will focus on certain accounting aspects of inventories and review how accounting standards of 11 countries have a variety of treatments, as shown in Exhibit 3–1.

Exhibit 3–1   Inventories—Accounting Differences

Country	"Market" in Lower of Cost or Market	LIFO Allowed	LIFO Common in Usage
Australia	Net realizable value	No	N/A*
Brazil	Replacement cost	Yes	No
Canada	Replacement cost or net realizable value	Yes	No
France	Net realizable value	No	N/A
Germany	Replacement cost	Yes	No
Japan	Replacement cost	Yes	Yes
Mexico	Realizable value	Yes	Yes
Netherlands	Replacement cost	Yes	Yes
Nigeria	Net realizable value	No	N/A
U.K.	Net realizable value	Yes	No
U.S.	Replacement cost	Yes	Yes

*N/A: Not applicable

We will use two examples to illustrate how the information in Exhibit 3–1 affects information in financial reports.

Example   Universal Enterprises is a major merchandising company based in the U.S. The company uses FIFO. The following information is pertinent regarding Universal's inventory.

	(000) Units	Unit Cost	(000) Total Cost
Beginning inventory	100	$10	$ 1,000
Purchases	1,000	12	12,000
Goods available for sale	1,100		$ 13,000

Ending inventory, 50 units		
Net realizable value		$ 550
Replacement cost		$ 650

Using the applicable U.S. accounting principles shown in Exhibit 3–1, "market" is generally considered to be replacement cost while applying lower of cost or market.

The historical cost basis of ending inventory is determined using

FIFO (50×12)   = $600
Replacement cost (given) =   650

Therefore, ending inventory will be shown in the amount of $600, the lower of historical cost using FIFO ($600) and market (replacement cost, $650).

Example   Using the same information as in the previous example, but assuming that U.S. accounting standards have been changed to define "market" as net realizable value instead of replacement cost, the value of ending inventory then would be:

Historical cost basis using FIFO (50 × $12)   = $600
Net realizable value (given)   =   550

The ending inventory will be shown at $550, which is the lower of the two amounts above. The income statement will be charged an additional expense of $50 resulting from marking down ending inventory from $600 to $550.

Exhibit 3–2 shows how treatment of selected items varies among the 11 countries.

Exhibit 3–2	Selected Items—Accounting Differences		
Country	Write-up of Fixed Assets	Interest Capitalization for Asset Construction	Capitalization of Research and Development
Australia	Yes	Yes	Yes in certain cases
Brazil	Yes	No	Yes in certain cases
Canada	No	Yes	Yes in certain cases
France	Yes	Yes	Yes in certain cases
Germany	No	Yes	No
Japan	No	No	Yes in certain cases
Mexico	Yes	Yes	No
Netherlands	Yes in certain cases	Yes	Yes in certain cases
Nigeria	Yes in certain cases	Yes	Yes in certain cases
U.K.	Yes	Yes	Yes in certain cases
U.S.	No	Yes	No

Role of Reserves

Reserves are used commonly in many countries for a variety of reasons. In Japan and many continental European countries, accounting is creditor oriented. Primary users of financial reports are banks since they are the major source of funds for a corporation—rather than the stockholders. Naturally, accounting standards in those countries were established to ensure that creditors' interests would be protected. This has resulted in a conservative accounting practice called the **prudence concept.** Laws in these countries, e.g., Germany, Switzerland, Sweden, and Japan, permit undervaluation of assets and overstatement of expenses and liabilities. For example, in Germany, if a loss is *possible* and reasonable it must be recorded. This contrasts with the U.S. practice of recognizing a potential loss only if it is *probable*. We will next discuss the role of reserves in accomplishing conservative accounting treatments to provide added protection to creditors.

Note: All of the reserves discussed are **equity reserves** and appear in the stockholders' equity section of the balance sheet.

Expense liability reserves. One of the purposes of using reserves is to achieve income smoothing or to show a steady growth in income from year to year. Reserves used for this purpose are generally called **expense liability reserves**. In a highly profitable year, the company transfers a portion of its income into an expense liability reserve, thus understating actual income for that year. The firm moves an amount from the reserve to income in a later year when actual income is low, thereby overstating actual income for that year. This phenomenon has been called **income smoothing**, **income leveling**, and **earnings flexibility**. The use of reserves to transfer income between periods is done by a majority of firms in Austria, Spain, Korea, Australia, and Switzerland.[6]

> Clearly, in countries where income smoothing is practiced to a significant degree, the income statements of the firm are less meaningful for financial analysis, particularly when movement of funds into and out of reserves is not disclosed. In fact, in a number of countries the actual existence of reserves is not even disclosed. These undisclosed reserves are called "hidden" or "silent" reserves.[7]

In 1993, when Daimler-Benz decided to list on the New York Stock Exchange, it disclosed four billion marks ($2.45 billion) in hidden reserves.[8]

Example   In 1996 the actual income of Dutch Company was 56 million guilders, showing an above average increase from the previous year. The reported income for 1995 was 50 million guilders. Dutch Company likes to show an 8 percent annual growth in reported income.

The actual income is 6 million guilders greater than the previous year's income. If the company is to report an annual increase of 8 percent in income, the reported income should be 50 million $\times$ 108% = 54 million guilders. The amount to be credited to an expense liability reserve is 2 million guilders (56 million guilders actual income less 54 million guilders, for reporting, as computed above). The entry to accomplish this is shown below.

Current period expenses	2,000,000	
Reserve for future liability		2,000,000

In a year when the reverse is true, the entry for transferring the amount out of the reserve would debit the reserve account and credit an expense account as shown in the next example.

Example   In 1997 the actual income of Dutch Company was 57.32 million guilders. Since the reported income in 1996 was 54 million guilders, the company would like to report 108% $\times$ 54 million guilders = 58.32 million guilders income in 1997. This requires transferring 1 million guilders from the reserve to income.

---

[6] Dhia D. AlHashim and J. S. Arpan, *International Dimensions of Accounting,* 3d ed. (Boston: PWS-Kent Company, 1992), pp. 86-87.

[7] *Ibid.,* p. 87.

[8] *Annual Report 1993* (Stuttgart, Germany: Daimler-Benz, 1994), p. 73.

| Reserve for future liability . . . . | 1,000,000 | |
| Current period expenses . . . . | | 1,000,000 |

An expense liability reserve is one of many types of reserves. We next discuss other commonly used reserves.

Statutory (legal) reserves. Several countries legally require that companies maintain statutory reserves (also called legal reserves). These reserves are to provide additional protection to creditors. The amounts transferred to the legal reserve are not available for dividends. Usually the legal requirements specify a certain percentage of income that should be credited to a legal reserve. For example, in Italy 5 percent of profit is transferred to the legal reserve until the reserve balance equals 20 percent of share capital (paid in capital). In France the requirement calls for accumulation of 5 percent of net income in legal reserve until the reserve equals 10 percent of share capital.

Example   Hamburg Co.'s income for the current year is 100 million German marks. The legal reserve requirement is to transfer 10 percent of the income into a legal reserve. The entry to transfer is shown below.

Income summary.	100,000,000	
Legal reserve		10,000,000
Retained earnings		90,000,000

General reserve.   Another reserve quite common in usage is called the general reserve. This reserve normally serves the same purpose as an appropriation of retained earnings; i.e., it temporarily restricts the maximum amount that can be declared for dividends.

Example   Directors of Australian Manufacturing Company vote to transfer $5 million from retained earnings to a general reserve. The purpose is to make the amount unavailable for dividends. The entry to record this transaction follows.

| Retained earnings. | 5,000,000 | |
| General reserve . . . . | | 5,000,000 |

In a few countries a general reserve is also used for income smoothing. Accounting procedures for this are similar to those discussed earlier for expense liability reserves.

Revaluation reserve.   In some countries, notably the U.K., France, Italy, and the Netherlands, valuing fixed assets at appraised value or replacement value is prevalent. This is done by upward adjustment of the asset and correspondingly recording an equal amount in a revaluation reserve. Subsequently, the asset is depreciated at the increased value, thus resulting in a higher depreciation charge. The incremental depreciation may be charged directly to a revaluation reserve or to income, depending on accounting standards and tax laws of the country.

Example   Upwar Dajust Company marks up depreciable assets for 100,000 francs. The company uses the straight line method of depreciation assuming no salvage value and a 10-year useful life. Incremental depreciation resulting from the write-up is charged directly to the revaluation reserve. The following entry records the revaluation.

Equipment-value adjustment 100,000
    Revaluation reserve   100,000

Annual depreciation on the revaluation part only is recorded as shown below.

Revaluation reserve 10,000
    Accumulated depreciation-
    value adjustment   10,000

Example   This example is based on the same facts as the preceding example except we assume that the incremental depreciation is charged against income. The entry to record revaluation will be identical to the first entry in the preceding example. The entry for depreciation will be as shown below.

Depreciation expense-value adjustment 10,000
    Accumulated depreciation-
    value adjustment   10,000

Note: In the previous example, the amount of depreciation expense charged against income was based on historical cost of the asset and was not affected by upward revaluation. In the current example, the amount of depreciation expense charged against income is based on the marked up value of the asset. Therefore, the income statement reflects incremental depreciation resulting from revaluation.

The last entry required under this method is to adjust the revaluation reserve as shown below.

Revaluation reserve 10,000
    Retained earnings   10,000

Perceptions Based on the Method of Disclosure

Recent research suggests that different disclosure methods result in different user perceptions. A study compared the effects of two methods of disclosing an obligation: **balance sheet recognition** versus **footnote disclosure**. Commercial lenders were surveyed to determine whether the disclosure method affected their perceptions of the item. It was discovered that the commercial lenders were more likely to perceive the obligation as a form of debt when it was recognized as a balance sheet liability than when disclosed in the footnotes accompanying the financial statements. The researchers concluded that the method of disclosing, i.e., balance sheet recognition versus supplemental disclosure, is an important issue that must be considered in the formulation of accounting standards.[9]

It is not correct to conclude that uniform accounting standards lead to uniform disclosures. Accounting standards normally provide a *range of acceptability,* as opposed to prescribing

[9] R. M. Harper Jr., W. G. Mister, and J. R. Strawser, "The Effect of Recognition versus Disclosure of Unfunded Postretirement Benefits on Lenders' Perceptions of Debt," *Accounting Horizons,* September 1991, pp. 50-56.

one "right" disclosure method. Empirical evidence suggests that within one country there can be a variety of ways companies make disclosures. A recent study comparing goodwill disclosures by 621 publicly traded firms in the U.S. demonstrated that the firms varied substantially in their goodwill-related asset and expense disclosures. The authors of the study concluded that for this reason investors cannot easily identify the financial statement effects of current goodwill accounting rules for a substantial number of firms with material goodwill.[10]

Disclosure Approaches of Multinationals

A multinational company has to decide on the disclosure mode for reporting in different countries. Since there are no required international reporting standards to provide guidance, MNCs have tried a variety of approaches to communicate information to the audiences abroad. We will discuss six of these approaches.

1. Compliance with local requirements. Most countries in the world (the U.S. being a notable exception) accept financial reports prepared according to the accounting principles of the reporting entity's base country. This is the most convenient and the least costly way for MNCs to fulfill their legal reporting requirements. No special effort is made to assist the users in understanding and interpreting the financial reports.

2. Translation into the local language. A slight improvement over the first approach is to translate the text part of financial reports into the local language. It is common for many MNCs to publish their reports in several languages in addition to the languages of their base countries. Bayer publishes its annual report in English, French, and German. A shorter report is published in English, French, German, Italian, Japanese, and Spanish.

3. Translation into the local currency and language. Besides translating the text portion of the financial reports into the local language, many companies also translate the monetary amounts into the local currency. Usually, the exchange rate effective at year-end is used to translate all of the monetary amounts. Toyota uses this approach for its U.S. audience.

4. Provision of information on accounting standards used. A few multinational companies provide information on the accounting principles that were used for the preparation of financial reports. This approach recognizes the reality of different accounting standards throughout the world and attempts to help the reader by providing an explanation of the accounting standards on which financial reports are based.

5. Selective restatements. A few companies provide partial restatements of their reports. For example, a Swedish-based multinational may restate its income amount according to Australian accounting principles for its Australian readers. The Australian readers can correctly assume that the restated income amount is comparable to incomes of other companies using Australian accounting standards. Selective restatements partially solve the

---

[10] L. Duvall, R. Jennings, J. Robinson, and R. Thompson II, "Can Investors Unravel the Effects of Goodwill Accounting?" *Accounting Horizons,* June 1992, pp. 1-14.

problems created by diversity in accounting standards throughout the world. Examples of companies using this approach include Daimler-Benz and Hafslund Nycomed.

6. Secondary statements. Secondary statements are a complete set of financial statements including accompanying notes prepared according to accounting standards of another country. In addition, the independent auditors express an opinion on secondary statements using auditing standards of that country. These statements are prepared specifically for users in another country and attempt to enhance understanding and usefulness for the target audience. They have been issued mostly by Japanese multinationals for North American users. The issuing companies include Hitachi, Toshiba, and Honda.

Analysis of the six approaches. As we move from the first approach to the last one, it becomes clear that each succeeding approach indicates a higher level of effort on the part of an MNC to reach out to its financial statement users.

The first approach, compliance with local requirements, does not create any extra disclosure burden for the MNC. No special efforts are made to help users abroad.

Translating either the text part of financial reports into the local language or both the text and the monetary amounts may provide limited assistance to some users. It is questionable, however, if these approaches are noteworthy improvements over the first approach in terms of the users' ability to understand the reports and interpret them. Granted that, for example, a British user who does not understand the Dutch language would not be able to read the financial reports of a Dutch-based multinational in the Dutch language and currency. But would the usefulness of the financial reports be improved if the text were translated into the English language? Would the usefulness be further enhanced if the currency portion were translated from guilders into British pounds using the year-end exchange rate? These types of translations fail to make adjustments and accommodations for differences in accounting standards, terminology, the local currency's relative stability, and business customs. Particularly troublesome is the translation of currency using the year-end exchange rates, called **convenience translation.**

The next approach entails providing information on accounting standards used for preparation of financial statements. This information may be useful if *both* of the following criteria are satisfied:

- The company thoroughly describes and explains its accounting policies, standards, and methods used.
- The users have the technical knowledge to reconcile differences in amounts resulting from different accounting principles.

Based on the above criteria, it is safe to say that this approach has limited usefulness in terms of the number of users it would potentially benefit.

Selective restatements are an improvement over any of the approaches analyzed so far. Selected amounts are restated using local accounting principles and are, therefore, comparable to corresponding items in other companies. The main limitation of this approach is that it can be misleading if financial ratios are computed by using a combination of restated and non-restated amounts.

Example   A Dutch-based multinational restates its sales ($1,000,000) and income ($120,000) for U.S. users. However, no balance sheet items are restated. The total of assets on the balance sheet is $15,000,000 (non-restated).

$$\text{Profit margin} \quad = \quad \frac{120,000}{1,000,000} \quad = \quad 12\%$$

If a user is interested in computing profit margin, it can be done because both income and sales amounts are restated. However, if the reader is interested in computing return on investment, it would not be possible because total assets are not restated. *Restated and non-restated amounts should not be combined to perform ratio analysis.*

The secondary statements approach uses the accounting principles of another country for the preparation of financial statements with the objective that it will enhance understandability and usefulness for the target audience. This approach, though clearly preferable to any of the first five approaches, has two main drawbacks. The obvious one is the *cost.* This approach is usually quite costly, involving preparation as well as auditing costs. In addition, the approach cannot compensate for the *differences in operating environments* in different countries as discussed in Chapter 1. The interpretation of financial reports, even if the reports are translated to local accounting principles, may be difficult because business customs differ from country to country. *National business customs leave an imprint on the primary financial statements that cannot be duplicated in secondary statements.* This has been eloquently stated by Lowe in discussing Japanese consolidated financial statements using U.S. accounting principles.

> The notion of control through direct or indirect majority share ownership and the presence of a holding company or a dominant parent company are foreign concepts to the typical Japanese executive. Share ownership is generally regarded as of minor significance in the forming and maintaining of corporate groups. Consequently, American practices of consolidation tend to group Japanese corporations in a manner contrary to their normal functioning. Such practices tend to break up the complex and dynamic reality of the natural groups into American-type corporate groups attempting to portray an American perspective to something uniquely Japanese.
>
> Japanese consolidated statements patterned after American standards have survived only because foreign users have been largely unaware of their inappropriate focus and innocent misrepresentation.
>
> Many of the most important firms affecting the future fortunes of the group are not even represented in these statements.
>
> Consequently, its [Japan's] unique business organizational environment often makes its consolidated financial reports less rather than more useful to readers.[11]

---

[11] Howard D. Lowe, "Shortcomings of Japanese Consolidated Financial Statements," *Accounting Horizons,* September 1990, pp. 8-9.

The problem can be alleviated by providing, along with secondary statements, a discussion of important and unique cultural traditions affecting business customs of the country. This reminds us again that in this age of a global economy it is becoming increasingly important to learn about other cultures to do our jobs effectively.

Specific Disclosures: Issues and Practices

In the absence of required worldwide disclosure standards, the type and quality of disclosures made by companies vary from country to country and from company to company. In this section we will look at some specific disclosure issues and also discuss important emerging practices. To appreciate the complexity of the problem faced by an MNC in deciding on the degree of disclosure, let us note these important issues:

- There are multiple users with multiple needs.
- Users in different countries have varying levels of education directly affecting their ability to comprehend and interpret sophisticated financial information. Efforts are required to ensure that the disclosed information is not misinterpreted.
- The sheer size of a typical MNC generates information of mind-boggling volume. A decision must be made as to what and how much should be disclosed from the mass of data.
- Information originates from different operating environments and from different parts of the world. Disclosure in some cases may embarrass or anger the local government or population, resulting in adverse effects on the MNC. Balancing potential risks of political/governmental sanctions and backlash from cultural sensitivities against the need for disclosure is a necessity.
- A balance must be struck between legitimate needs of users for decision-making information against the possibility that disclosures may be misused by others.
- Economic costs of disclosure and its cost effectiveness in conditions where many user groups cannot be identified and benefits cannot be traced requires exercise of a high degree of judgment.

It should be clear from the above points that deciding what to disclose, how much to disclose, and how to disclose it is not a simple endeavor. It requires weighing and balancing many opposing factors. In the end one can only hope that the final mix will serve appropriate needs of users.

Segment Disclosures

Consolidated financial statements, in spite of their obvious advantages, have a major drawback. The aggregation of all segments of the business into one overall economic entity makes it impossible for the users to assess the company's dependencies on individual business segments. Segment information is needed to identify trends of growth, profitability, and risks associated with each segment. A variety of risks may be associated with individual segments, e.g., volatile fluctuation in the value of currencies, high inflation rates or hyper-inflation, social unrest, political turmoil, and instability of governments in countries where segments have operations. The process of consolidation produces reports that may not reveal these conditions.

Before we discuss segment reporting, we should address the question: What is a segment? Unfortunately, there is no easy answer to this question because the term is defined in many different ways worldwide.

U.S. requirements. Theoretically, the U.S. appears to have the most elaborate requirements for segment reporting. Its FASB identifies four types of business segments: foreign operations, export sales, industry lines, and major customers. According to the FASB, any foreign operation meeting *either one of the two criteria* below is a segment.[12]

- Foreign operations whose revenue from sales to unaffiliated customers is 10 percent or more of the consolidated revenue, *or*
- The identifiable assets of foreign operations are 10 percent or more of consolidated assets.

In addition, the combined sales to unaffiliated customers in all reportable segments should be at least 75 percent of the total sales to unaffiliated customers by the company as a whole. The FASB requires companies to disclose revenue, operating profit or loss, and identifiable assets for their foreign operations in the annual financial statements if the above criteria are met. Though the criteria seem specific at first glance, the FASB leaves it to the company to determine what countries or group of countries would appropriately constitute a geographic segment. This has resulted in the companies keeping their geographic segment disclosures on a broad, aggregated basis.

The U.S. Securities and Exchange Commission has conformed its earlier lines-of-business reporting requirements to the segment reporting guidelines specified by the FASB.[13]

International Accounting Standards Committee. *International Accounting Standard 14,* "Reporting Financial Information by Segment," requires that companies whose securities are publicly traded and other "economically significant" enterprises present certain information for each significant industry segment and geographic area of operation. The information disclosures required are similar to those of *SFAS No. 14.*[14] One notable difference between the two standards is that FASB disclosures are optional for nonpublic companies, whereas IASC disclosures are required for economically significant nonpublic companies. *IAS 14* does not include specific definitions of an industry or geographic segment. It is left to the management's judgment to determine the segments for reporting.[15]

---

[12] *Statement of Financial Accounting Standards No. 14,* "Financial Reporting for Segments of a Business Enterprise" (Stamford, Conn.: Financial Accounting Standards Board, December 1976).

[13] *Accounting Series Release No. 236,* "Industry Segment Reporting: Adoption of Disclosure Regulation and Amendments of Disclosure Forms and Rules" (Washington, D.C., Securities and Exchange Commission, December 1977).

[14] *International Accounting Standard 14,* "Reporting Financial Information by Segment" (London: International Accounting Standards Committee, 1994).

[15] *Ibid.,* par. 12.

United Nations. As discussed in Chapter 2, the United Nations Economic and Social Council created an Intergovernmental Working Group of Experts on International Standards of Accounting and Reporting (ISAR) in 1982. The ISAR does not establish accounting standards but instead holds annual forums for discussion of international accounting issues. In 1988, the ISAR published a report that includes a section on industry and geographic segments. The recommendations include the following:

- Only significant segments should be separately reported.
- Industry segments and geographical area segments are determined by each enterprise. Some of the factors to be considered for industry segment include the nature of the products and services, risk and growth of the products and services, and the profitability and nature of markets. For determination of geographical area segments these factors, among others, are listed for consideration: physical location of operations, proximity of operations, and existing conditions in each area.
- The required disclosures for both industry and geographical segments include external sales, operating profits, identifiable assets, internal transfers, transfer pricing policies, and number of employees.[16]

European Union. EU's Fourth Directive specifies certain minimum disclosure requirements for segment reporting. Those include the following:

- Sales to outsiders broken down by identifiable categories (segments) of activity (industry) and geographical markets.
- The average number of employees by the segments.

The Directive allows companies to omit disclosure of sales revenue by segments if disclosure would harm the company, provided that the omission is disclosed in notes.[17]

Organization for Economic Cooperation and Development. In 1976, the OECD issued guidelines for multinational enterprises that included recommendations regarding segment disclosures for the multinational companies operating in OECD member countries. These guidelines call for the following disclosures:[18]

- The geographical areas (group of countries or individual countries as determined to be appropriate by each enterprise for its particular circumstances) where operations are carried out.
- The income and sales revenue by geographical areas and sales in the major lines of business.

---

[16] United Nations, Intergovernmental Working Group of Experts on International Standards of Accounting and Reporting, *Conclusions on Accounting and Reporting by Transnational Corporations* (New York: United Nations, 1988), pp. 19-20.

[17] *Fourth Council Directive for Coordination of National Legislation,* "Regarding the Annual Accounts of Limited Liability Companies" (Brussels: European Community, 1978), Articles 43 and 45.

[18] *International Investment and Multinational Enterprises* (Paris: Organization for Economic Cooperation and Development, 1976), pp. 14-15.

- Significant new capital investment by geographical area and, as far as practicable, by major lines of business.
- The average number of employees in each geographical area.
- Transfer pricing policies.

In 1987, ten years after recommending those guidelines, the OECD published results of a survey on adoption of the guidelines by 184 large MNCs from 12 member countries. The study found that overall disclosure of segment financial data was unsatisfactory for the reasons described below:

> In several areas such as sales, operating results, average number of employees and new capital investment, the reluctance of a considerable number of companies to provide segment information by line of business and/or geographical area is one of the main reasons why the results cannot be considered satisfactory.[19]

The study especially noted the lack of quality in geographical disclosures. Disclosures of sales and income by geographical area were found to be either altogether absent or reported in very broad terms: for example, domestic and foreign.[20] In 1990, the OECD published another report to provide further guidance on segment reporting to multinational companies operating in the member countries.[21] This report does not contain any new recommendations. Instead, it discusses the major issues relating to segment reporting disclosures. Obviously, the OECD considers segment reporting to be an important area that is in need of significant improvements.

Status of segment disclosures. At present, segment reporting is still at an experimental stage. There is a lack of uniformity in reporting because companies, in the absence of explicit criteria, are left to make arbitrary decisions as to what constitutes a segment. As noted by the OECD, aggregation of operations in broad geographical segments is prevalent among multinationals.

Another report comparing the disclosure requirements and practices in 14 countries with highly developed capital markets was published by IOSCO in 1991. This report also concluded that there is significant variation in the requirements and practices in this area. The report also found that with the exception of revenue disclosure there are no common disclosure requirements for foreign operations among the participating countries.[22] Results of the IOSCO survey are shown in Exhibit 3–3. The disclosure requirements in Exhibit 3–3 include the requirements of both accounting standards and of securities laws and regulations.

---

[19] Organization for Economic Cooperation and Development, Working Group on Accounting Standards, *Disclosure of Information by Multinational Enterprises: Survey of the Application of the OECD Guidelines* (Paris: Organization for Economic Cooperation and Development, 1987), p. 8.

[20] *Ibid.*, p. 9.

[21] *Segmented Financial Information* (Paris: Organization for Economic Cooperation and Development, 1990).

[22] *Comparative Analysis of Disclosure Regimes* (Quebec: International Organization of Securities Commissions, 1991), p. 4.

Exhibit 3–3   Disclosure for Each Industry Segment

Country	Revenue	Operating Profit or Loss	Identifiable Assets	Discussion of Unusual Segment Performance
Australia	Required	Required	Required	Required
Belgium	Required	—	—	—
Canada	Required	Required	Required	Required
France	Required	Required	—	Customary
Germany	Required	—	—	Required
Hong Kong	Required	Required	Required	—
Italy	Required	—	—	—
Japan	Required	Required	—	Required
Luxembourg	Required	—	—	—
Netherlands	Required	—	—	—
Spain	Required	—	—	Required
Switzerland	Customary	—	Customary	—
U.K.	Required	Required	Required	Customary
U.S.	Required	Required	Required	Required
European Union	Required	—	—	—

Source: International Organization of Securities Commissions, *Comparative Analysis of Disclosure Regimes* (Quebec: IOSCO, 1991), page 17 (adapted).

A review of accounting literature reveals that in developed countries disclosure of sales revenue for industry and geographic segments is the most prevalent requirement. A smaller number of countries also require disclosure of profits by industry and geographic segments. In a number of countries, the segment disclosures may be omitted if the corporate management considers them to be harmful to the company's competitive position. Pressures to disclose segment information will probably increase as demands for more information are made by investors, creditors, and security market regulators.

Social Impact Disclosures

Social impact disclosures include many different types. These may be required to make management accountable for its actions, in exchange for the freedom to manage scarce economic resources. Many companies also make voluntary disclosures to enhance the enterprise's image as a socially responsible corporate citizen. We will look at disclosures in three categories: employees, value added activities, and environmental concerns. We should note that orientation of social impact disclosures is heavily influenced by specific societal concerns in a country. We will discuss the pertinent issues and also review current practices and requirements.

Employees. Human resource disclosure requirements have received the greatest attention in the social impact reporting area. Annual reports of companies from most countries routinely contain information on employees. The level of specificity and detail, however, vary considerably. This can be attributed to societal conditions and pressures in a country. For example, in the U.S. the disclosures focus on equal employment opportunities for underrepresented groups, while in Germany the disclosures emphasize working and safety conditions and employee training. Even though this area has received more attention than any other area of social impact reporting, the general purpose disclosure requirements are still quite limited.

At the international level, perhaps the U.N. has been in the forefront in recommending extensive disclosures in this area. The U.N. recommends disclosures of the number of employees for the company and by segments (geographic, and line of business). It also recommends that corporate policies regarding recognition of labor unions and labor relations be disclosed.[23] The OECD recommends disclosure of the number of employees in each geographical segment. The European Union's Fourth Directive and Seventh Directive have similar requirements. They require information on the average number of employees, a breakdown of the number of employees by "category," and a breakdown of employee costs. The Directives do not define what constitutes a category (segment).

At the national level, perhaps the most extensive disclosures are required in France. **Bilan Social** (social report) contains mainly employee-related information covering topics such as pay structure, hiring policies, health and safety conditions, training, and industrial relations. In practice, the most common disclosure to be found is the number of employees. Otherwise, reporting in this area is still at the early stages of development.

Value added activities. Value added reporting is a recent development. Value added statements show the value added to acquired materials and services by various groups in the company.

Value added = Total revenue − Cost of goods, materials, and services purchased externally.

Value added statements of Dyno Industries and Hafslund Nycomed are shown in Exhibits 3–4 and 3–5, respectively.

The purpose of value added statements is to show, in financial terms, the contributions made by many participating groups in the creation of wealth in a company. Value added statements are prepared primarily in European countries, especially Germany, Sweden, the U.K., Norway, and France, where they are required as part of **Bilan Social**.

At the international level, there are no formal recommendations or requirements regarding value added statements except by the U.N., which recommends disclosure of value added information. Since there are no requirements at the international or national level (except France), there is considerable diversity in value added disclosures. Overall, the extent of disclosure is quite low and, when made, such disclosures are supplementary to the financial reports.

---

[23] United Nations Center on Transnational Corporations, *Conclusions on Accounting and Reporting by Transnational Corporations* (New York: United Nations, 1988).

Exhibit 3–4   Value Added Statement—Dyno Industries

A value added statement is based on the traditional statement of income and shows the value added in a company by labour, capital and technology, and how this value added is distributed among the various interest groups in the community.

The gross value added by the company's own operations is calculated by subtracting the cost of purchased goods and services from the gross operating income. Depreciation (the reduction in the value of production equipment resulting from a year's wear and tear) must be similarly deducted from the gross value added to arrive at the net value added.

Financial income, i.e., the income from making capital available to others, for instance in the form of shares or bank deposits, and net other income, for instance from the sale of fixed assets, provides Dyno with extra value for distribution. The Corporation has also received government grants, which must be included

in the total value added to be distributed among the four interest groups: employees, providers of capital, government and local authorities, and Dyno itself.

VALUE ADDED STATEMENT

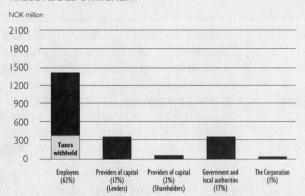

VALUE ADDED:

NOK million	1992	1991
Gross operating income	**7,480.2**	7,724.0
– cost of purchased goods and services	**4,905.8**	5,143.5
Gross value added		
from operations	**2,574.4**	2,580.5
– ordinary depreciation	**465.8**	515.7
Net value added		
from operations	**2,108.6**	2,064.8
+ Financial income	**213.0**	156.7
+ Share in earnings of		
associated companies	**7.2**	-23.5
Value added		
from operations	**2,328.8**	2,198.0
+ Government grants	**7.4**	6.5
Total value added available		
for sharing and retention	**2,336.2**	2,204.5

ALLOCATION OF VALUE ADDED

NOK million	%	1992	1991
To employees			
Gross wages and benefits	62	**1,459.8**	1,431.3
(whereof tax)		**-361.4**	-363.9
To providers of capital			
Interest on borrowing	17	**388.8**	380.7
Dividends to shareholders			
and minority interests	2	**49.6**	53.7
To government and			
local authorities			
Taxes on income and capital	3	**79.5**	91.0
Other taxes and levies	14	**327.1**	337.3
To the Corporation			
Retained for future earnings	1	**31.4**	-89.5
The value added applied	100	**2,336.2**	2,204.5

Source: Dyno Industries, *Annual Report 1992,* p. 30.

Exhibit 3–5   Value Added Statement—Hafslund Nycomed AS

The value added statement shows the added value created within the corporation through the commitments of labour, capital, and technology, and how these values are distributed among those who have contributed to their creation.

The values added are distributed to the employees, as wages and social benefits for their labour; to capital investors, as interest (lenders) and dividends (shareholders); to the central and local government, as corporate and excise taxes; and a portion is retained by Hafslund Nycomed AS for security and the creation of new value.

The gross value added from operations is obtained by subtracting the total cost of goods sold from the corporation's total operating revenues. Ordinary depreciation, which represents the diminution in value of production equipment/technology, is subtracted from the gross value added to yield the net value added.

CREATED VALUES

NOK million	1992	1991
Total operating revenues	5,843	5,510
– Consumption of purchased goods/services	2,432	2,361
Gross value added	3,411	3,149
– Ordinary depreciation	501	557
Net value added	2,910	2,592
+ Financial income	183	89
+/– Minority interests	(2)	28
Extraordinary items	(80)	–
Values for distribution	**3,011**	**2,710**

DISTRIBUTION OF VALUES

NOK million	1992	1991
EMPLOYEES		
Gross wages and social benefits	1,034	891
(Including income taxes)	268	254
CAPITAL INVESTORS		
Interest	332	388
Dividends	215	152
CENTRAL AND LOCAL GOVERNMENT		
Corporate and excise taxes	640	617
CORPORATION		
Retained in the Corporation	790	662
TOTAL	**3,011**	**2,710**

DISTRIBUTION OF VALUE ADDED
1991

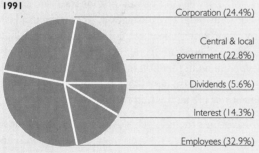

Corporation (24.4%)

Central & local government (22.8%)

Dividends (5.6%)

Interest (14.3%)

Employees (32.9%)

DISTRIBUTION OF VALUE ADDED
1992

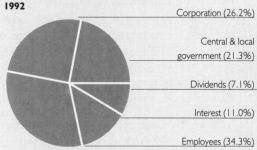

Corporation (26.2%)

Central & local government (21.3%)

Dividends (7.1%)

Interest (11.0%)

Employees (34.3%)

Source: Hafslund Nycomed AS, *1992 Annual Report*, p. 42.

Environmental concerns. Environmental concerns have been receiving considerable attention for many reasons, including increasing public awareness, tougher governmental laws and regulations, and well-known environmental disasters in recent years. For example, Union Carbide's chemical leak in Bhopal (India) in 1984 caused approximately 4,000 deaths and 200,000 injuries. The investors are especially interested in this disclosure area because environmental cleanups required of a company directly affect corporate earnings.

In spite of the acknowledged importance of this disclosure area, only a few requirements exist worldwide and disclosures (when made) tend to be descriptive. At the international level, the U.N. recommends disclosure of the measures undertaken by a company to promote a cleaner environment and to reduce risks of harm to the environment. Interestingly, the U.N. guidelines also recommend environmental audits and risk assessments by companies.[24]

The World Bank, the largest intergovernmental lending agency, and its sister institution, the International Monetary Fund, have been giving attention to the environment during their annual meetings. Specifically, they are laying plans to meet the goals set out at the 1992 Earth Summit. It is estimated that $70 billion in new aid will be needed by developing countries to fund a major global cleanup plan.

Environmental concerns have been expressed for nearly every Eastern European country. The problem is so immense in that region that, according to studies, it is threatening economies and the welfare of all of the countries. According to one estimate, just cutting sulfur dioxide emissions by 60 to 80 percent would cost about $10 billion annually.

At the national level, there are presently very few countries that have specific requirements for environmental disclosures. However, it is expected that disclosure requirements will increase rapidly because of environmental concerns. Even in the absence of widespread disclosure requirements, an increasing number of corporations such as General Motors and Imperial Chemical Industries are making voluntary environmental disclosures. The notable trend during recent years has been to provide more detailed information. According to a 1994 survey of 1,300 major U.S. companies by Price Waterhouse, the companies have begun to issue annual environmental reports in response to pressure from many fronts. Interestingly, 73 percent of respondents had an environmental audit function in 1994, up from 40 percent in 1992. The Price Waterhouse report on the survey also noted that although no preparation standards exist in the U.S., several organizations are addressing them.[25]

The countries requiring environmental disclosures include Norway, the U.S., and France. Norway requires the board of directors' report to include information on emission levels and measures taken or planned to clean up the environment. The Securities and Exchange Commission of the U.S. requires disclosure of contingent environmental liabilities. The Commission's staff has been looking closely over the past several years at the adequacy of

---

[24] United Nations Commission on Transnational Corporations, *Information Disclosure Relating to Environmental Measures* (New York: United Nations, 1990), p. 6.

[25] Price Waterhouse LLP, *Progress on the Environmental Challenge—A Survey of Corporate America's Environmental Accounting and Management* (New York: Price Waterhouse LLP, 1994), pp. 5-35.

environmental disclosures. The SEC regularly receives information from the U.S. Environmental Protection Agency on companies that have past, present, or potential problems in compliance with environmental laws.[26] France recently revised its penal code, effective March 1, 1994, to make corporations accountable for endangering others. The code includes provisions dealing with "environmental terrorism," including willful pollution.

Even though not required, comprehensive environmental disclosures are quite commonly found in the financial reports of companies based in the U.K., Switzerland, Germany, and most Scandinavian countries.

In order to strengthen corporate compliance with environmental laws and to instill sensitivity to the environment in personnel, management might do the following:

- In the mission statement, include an environmentally responsible position.
- Develop a detailed policy document on how to prevent, detect, and correct environmental problems.
- Conduct environmental audits periodically to ensure compliance with corporate policies.
- Include the environmental area in the criteria used to evaluate managers. This can provide a powerful incentive to managers.
- Consider developing a systematic method of disclosing corporate donations and other efforts to support educational, environmental, and other organizations engaged in activities to make progress in environmental cleanup, renewal of natural resources, and development of alternate, cleaner technologies.

International Accounting Standards Committee

The International Accounting Standards Committee (IASC) is the only private organization engaged in setting international accounting standards. As discussed in Chapter 2, the IASC addressed the issue of harmonization of accounting standards through its Comparability/Improvements project initiated in 1987. The expressed purpose of the project was to reduce the number of choices of accounting treatments. In 1989 the IASC issued *Exposure Draft 32,* "Comparability of Financial Statements," containing proposed changes to IASs. In 1990, the "Statement of Intent on the Comparability of Statements," describing the IASC's decisions based on comment letters on the proposals in *E32,* was released. The IASC issued the revised IASs in December 1993.

Critics have pointed out for many years that different national accounting standards are not conducive to international capital market efficiency. Completion of the Comparability/Improvements project is a significant step toward harmonization of accounting standards. Many countries either adopt IASs as national standards or use them as the basis for developing national requirements. In developing countries, the tendency is to adopt or adapt IASs. It is

---

[26] "Environmental Disclosure: Recent Developments," *Deloitte & Touche Review,* 13 July 1992, pp. 1-2.

especially true of the countries that are or have been members of the British Common-wealth.[27] In addition, the London and Hong Kong stock exchanges allow foreign issuers to comply with their listing requirements by presenting financial statements prepared using IASs. Increased competition in international capital markets may force all countries to follow the lead of these two stock exchanges. Nevertheless, the agreement between the IASC and the IOSCO, as mentioned in Chapter 2, is expected to result in acceptance of IASs in 1999 for listing in capital markets worldwide.[28] We will next review three IASs that are especially relevant to this chapter.

IAS 1: Disclosure of Accounting Policies

IAS 1 deals with the disclosure of all significant accounting policies used in preparation of financial statements.[29] *Going concern, consistency, and accrual are fundamental accounting assumptions.* Where fundamental accounting assumptions are followed in financial statements, disclosure of such assumptions is not required. If a fundamental accounting assumption is not followed, that fact should be disclosed together with the reasons.

- Prudence, substance over form, and materiality should govern the selection and application of accounting policies.
- Financial statements should include clear and concise disclosure of all the significant accounting policies that have been used.
- The disclosure of the significant accounting policies used should be an integral part of the financial statements. The policies should normally be disclosed in one place.
- Wrong or inappropriate treatment of items in balance sheets, income statements or profit and loss accounts, or other statements is not rectified either by disclosure of accounting policies used or by notes or explanatory material.
- Financial statements should show corresponding figures for the preceding period.
- A change in an accounting policy that has a material effect in the current period or may have a material effect in subsequent periods should be disclosed together with the reasons. The effect of the change should, if material, be disclosed and quantified.

IAS 5: Information to be Disclosed in Financial Statements

IAS 5 sets the standards of minimum disclosure of information in the financial statements. The required financial statements include a balance sheet, an income statement, notes, and other statements and explanatory material that are identified as part of the financial statements. It requires that all necessary material information be disclosed to make financial statements clear and understandable. *IAS 5* also requires supplementary information disclo-

---

[27] S. E. C. Purvis, H. Gernon, and M. A. Diamond, "The IASC and Its Comparability Project: Prerequisites for Success," *Accounting Horizons,* June 1991, pp. 28-29.

[28] Arthur R. Wyatt and J. F. Yospe, "Wake-up Call to American Business: International Accounting Standards are on the Way," *Journal of Accountancy,* July, 1993, p. 82.

[29] *IAS 1,* "Disclosure of Accounting Policies" (London: International Accounting Standards Committee, 1994).

sures if necessary. The standard specifies itemized disclosures in the balance sheet and income statement.[30]

IAS 18: Revenue Recognition

This statement deals with the basis of recognition of revenue in the income statement arising in the course of ordinary activities of the enterprise from: sales of goods, rendering of services, and use by others of the enterprise resources yielding interest, royalties, and dividends. [31]

- Revenue from the sale of goods should be recognized when all of the following conditions have been satisfied:
  - (a) the enterprise has transferred to the buyer the significant risks and rewards of ownership of the goods;
  - (b) the enterprise retains neither continuing managerial involvement to the degree usually associated with ownership nor effective control over the goods sold;
  - (c) the amount of revenue can be measured reliably;
  - (d) it is probable that the economic benefits associated with the transaction will flow to the enterprise; and
  - (e) the costs incurred or to be incurred in respect of the transaction can be measured reliably.
- When the outcome of a transaction involving the rendering of services can be estimated reliably, revenue associated with the transaction should be recognized by reference to the stage of completion of the transaction at the balance sheet date. The outcome of a transaction can be estimated reliably when all of the following conditions are satisfied:
  - (a) the amount of revenue can be measured reliably;
  - (b) it is probable that the economic benefits associated with the transaction will flow to the enterprise;
  - (c) the stage of completion of the transaction at the balance sheet date can be measured reliably; and
  - (d) the costs incurred for the transaction and the costs to complete the transaction can be measured reliably.
- An enterprise should disclose:
  - (a) the accounting policies adopted for the recognition of revenue, including the methods adopted to determine the stage of completion of transactions involving the rendering of services;
  - (b) the amount of each significant category of revenue recognized during the period, including revenue arising from;
    - (i) the sale of goods;
    - (ii) the rendering of services;
    - (iii) interest;

---

[30] IAS 5, "Information to be Disclosed in Financial Statements" (London: International Accounting Standards Committee, 1994).

[31] IAS 18, "Revenue Recognition" (London: International Accounting Standards Committee, 1994).

(iv) royalties;

(v) dividends; and

(c) the amount of revenue arising from exchanges of goods or services included in each significant category of revenue.

The disclosure requirements of *IAS 18* include the disclosures required by *IAS 10,* "Contingencies and Events Occurring after the Balance Sheet Date." These include contingent gains and contingent losses arising from items such as warranty costs, claims, penalties, or possible losses.

Appendix 3A   Summary of the (U.S.) SEC's Disclosure Requirements—Regulation S-K

Financial statements

Consolidated

Separate (parent and/or significant subsidiaries)

Schedules

10-Q type interim financial statements

Brief description of business

101 Description of business:

(a) general development of business

(b) financial information about industry segments

(c) narrative description of business

(d) financial information about foreign and domestic operations and export sales

102 Description of property

103 Legal proceedings

201 Market price of and dividends on the registrant's common equity & related stockholder matters

202 Description of registrant's securities

301 Selected financial data

302 Supplemental financial data

303 Management's discussion and analysis of financial condition and results of operations

304 Disagreements with accountants on accounting and financial disclosure

Identification of directors and executive officers

Submission of matters to a vote of security holders

401 Directors and executive officers

402 Executive compensation

403 Security ownership of certain beneficial owners and management

404 Certain relationships and related transactions

501 Forepart of registration statement and outside front cover page of prospectus

502 Inside front and outside back cover pages of prospectus

Source: United States Securities and Exchange Commission, Washington, D.C.

Appendix 3B   Selected Information Requirements of the (U.S.) SEC's Regulation S-X

Article 3 – General Instructions as to Financial Statements

Rule 3-01 Consolidated balance sheets

3-02 Consolidated statements of income and changes in financial position

3-03 Instructions to income statement requirements

3-04 Changes in other stockholders' equity

3-09 Separate financial statements of subsidiaries not consolidated and 50 percent or less owned persons

3-10 Financial statements of guarantors and affiliates whose securities collateralize an issue registered or being registered

3-11 Financial statements of an inactive registrant

3-12 Age of financial statements at effective date of registration statement or at mailing date of proxy statement

3-13 Filing of other financial statements in certain cases

3-14 Special instructions for real estate operations to be acquired

3-15 Special provision as to real estate investment trusts

3-16 Reorganization of registrant

3-17 Financial statements of natural persons

Article 3A – Consolidated and Combined Financial Statements

Article 4 – Rules of General Application

Article 5 – Commercial and Industrial Companies

Article 12 – Form and Content of Schedules

12-07 Accumulated depreciation, depletion, and amortization of
        property, plant, and equipment
12-08 Guarantees of securities of other issuers
12-09 Valuation and qualifying accounts
12-10 Short-term borrowings
12-11 Supplementary income statement information

Source: United States Securities and Exchange Commission, Washington, D.C.

Note to Students

There is a common misconception that financial reports contain only required disclosures. As we have seen in this chapter, corporations often develop and present new types of voluntary disclosures. Value added disclosures are an example of such a contribution by corporate entities. As a professional, you should keep the main purpose of accounting—providing information to decision makers—foremost. You are not confined by accounting standards and regulatory requirements to accomplish this purpose. In fact, you are in a position to go beyond the minimum requirements and develop new ways to communicate information to your target audience.

Accounting is dynamic because it is always attempting to meet the information needs of users. Sometimes, as we discussed above, the members of the profession identify the need and develop methods to communicate new information. Other times, the need is identified by parties outside the profession.

Environmental accounting is an emerging area of specialization in accounting. According to Robert Half International Inc., public accounting clients are increasingly asking for environmental accounting specialists. At the XIV World Congress of Accountants, one session was devoted to addressing environmental accounting issues. Accountants have an important role to play in the protection of our environment, as they do in solving many other problems confronting our global community.

Chapter Summary

- Financial reporting disclosures include many types of disclosures and, for a variety of reasons, the trend is toward more disclosures.

- A corporation is held accountable to investors and creditors as well as society at large. The latter accountability concept arises from entrusting a corporation to manage scarce resources and also from its ability to influence lifestyles of parties other than capital providers.

- Several motivational factors prompt corporations to make financial reporting disclosures. Corporations make voluntary as well as required disclosures.

- Total costs of financial disclosures include both monetary and non-monetary costs.

- Disclosures are directly affected by how economic transactions are recorded (measured). There is a diversity in the measurement process worldwide.

- Reserves are used primarily to provide additional protection to creditors.

- The method of disclosure affects perceptions of users of financial reports.

- Lack of disclosure uniformity exists even when companies are using the same accounting standards.

- Multinationals use many disclosure approaches ranging from compliance with local requirements to preparation of secondary statements.

- Segment disclosures are necessary to observe trend patterns in important segments of a multinational.

- Social impact disclosures are heavily influenced by societal concerns in a country, with human resource disclosures receiving the most attention.

- The IASC Comparability/Improvements project was started in 1987 and completed in 1993.

- Three IASs, *IAS 1, IAS 5,* and *IAS 18,* are especially relevant to financial reporting disclosures.

Questions for Discussion

1. Give at least four types of disclosures included in financial reporting.

2. What are some of the reasons for the trend toward more disclosures?

3. What are the two issues that remain unresolved in the area of financial reporting?

4. What are the conceptual socio-economic reasons for financial reporting disclosures?

5. Corporations disclose only what they are required to disclose. Do you agree? Explain.

6. List at least three motivational factors for corporations to make financial reporting disclosures.

7. Why do firms that operate in global capital markets tend to exceed minimum financial disclosure requirements?

8. What is the commonality among the costs of providing disclosures that are difficult or impossible to quantify?

9. "Extensive disclosure hurts our company's competitive position." Do you agree? Discuss.

10. How are financial reports affected by the measurement process?

11. What is meant by the prudence concept?

12. How is income smoothing or a steady growth rate in income accomplished by using an expense liability reserve?

13. "Uniform accounting standards would lead to uniform disclosures." Do you agree? Discuss.

14. There are six multinational disclosure approaches discussed in the chapter. Can you name four of those?

15. Distinguish between selective restatements and secondary statements.

16. Discuss the pros and cons of selective restatements.

17. What are the two drawbacks of the secondary statements approach?

18. Describe at least three issues that make the decision on the degree (extent) of disclosure a complex one.

19. What is the major drawback of consolidated financial statements?

20. "Both *IAS 14* and *SFAS No. 14* apply to public and nonpublic companies." Do you agree? Explain.

21. Discuss the UN segment disclosure recommendations.

22. What are the OECD segment disclosure recommendations?

23. In discussion of social impact disclosures, three types of disclosures were mentioned: employees, value added activities, and environmental concerns. What type of disclosure has received the most attention?

24. "Value added = Total revenues – Cost of goods sold." Do you agree? Explain.

25. Name at least two countries where value added reports are commonly prepared.

26. "Because of its importance, the environmental disclosures area is at an advanced state of development." Do you agree? Explain.

27. Three countries require environmental disclosures. Can you name two of them?

28. *IAS 1* deals with the disclosure of all significant accounting policies used in preparation of financial statements but does not require disclosure of fundamental accounting assumptions. Why?

29. Does *IAS 5* specify itemized disclosure? If so, can you name those financial statements?

30. "*IAS 18* deals with revenue recognition from all activities of an enterprise." Do you agree? Explain.

Exercises/Problems

3-1   Anderson Company is a major company based in Atascadero, U.S. The company uses LIFO. The following information is available regarding Anderson's inventory.

	Units	Unit Cost
Beginning inventory	500	$15
Purchases	10,000	17

Ending inventory has 700 units, which can be sold for $10,000. However, if sold, Anderson will have to pay the freight expenses in the amount of $200. The replacement cost of ending inventory is $11,200.

Required: Determine the value of ending inventory using U.S. accounting standards.

3-2 Refer to the information in 3-1, but assume that U.S. accounting standards for inventory valuation are now the same as those of U.K. Determine the value of ending inventory using the newly assumed accounting standards.

3-3 In 1995, the actual income of Kim Company in Korea was 75 million won. Kim Company likes to show an annual growth of 10 percent in earnings. The reported income in 1994, the previous year, was 60 million won. Kim Company uses an expense liability reserve.

Required: Make an appropriate entry for the transfer into or out of expense liability reserve to achieve the desired income amount for reporting.

3-4 Refer to 3-3 above. The actual income of Kim Company was only 70 million won in 1996.

Required: Make an appropriate entry for the transfer into or out of expense liability reserve to achieve the desired income amount for reporting.

3-5 Many companies in Europe include a value added statement in their annual reports. Companies in other countries, Australia for example, are also disclosing value added information. Some feel that companies in other countries will soon follow this practice and that value added statements may become another worldwide disclosure. The value added statement for Waheed International for 19x4 follows:

Turnover (sales revenues)		£ 14,800
Other income (nonoperating income)		600
		15,400
Acquired resources (purchases 60%;		
depreciation 20%; other service expenses 20%)		8,800
Value added		6,600
Distribution of value added:		
Employees: Wages and salaries	£ 3,200	
Creditors: Interest expense	1,200	
Government: Income tax	800	
Shareholders: Dividends	400	5,600
Retained for future investment		£ 1,000

Required:
(1) Prepare a traditional income statement based on the above information, using the vertical format.
(2) Comment on the differences between the two statements.
(3) What are the benefits of the value added statement?

3-6 Pierre Company has share capital in the amount of F80 million. The income for 1996 is in the amount of F6 million. Pierre is subject to the legal reserve requirements in France.

Required: Make the entry to close out the income summary account assuming:
(1) The balance in the legal reserve is F8.0 million.
(2) The balance in the legal reserve is F7.0 million.
(3) The balance in the legal reserve is F7.9 million.

3-7   The directors of Foster Company in Australia vote to transfer $3 million to the general reserve to make this amount unavailable for dividends.

Required: Make the appropriate entry to record the above transaction.

3-8   Thompson Company, a U.K. based multinational, has decided to make an upward adjustment of depreciable assets in the amount of £500,000. The company uses the straight line depreciation method, assumes no salvage value, and assumes a five-year useful life.

Required: Make the entries for
(1) Upward adjustment of assets.
(2) Annual depreciation assuming:
    (a) incremental depreciation is charged to the revaluation reserve.
    (b) incremental depreciation is charged against income.
(3) Refer to Requirement (2) above. In which case, (a) or (b), is the depreciation expense in the income statement based on historical cost?
(4) Make the appropriate entry to adjust the revaluation reserve when the incremental depreciation is charged against income.

3-9   Prepare a succinct analysis of the six disclosure approaches of multinationals. Limit your analysis to approximately 200 words.

3-10   Compare the segment disclosure requirements of *IAS 14* and the FASB's *SFAS No. 14*.

3-11   Describe the OECD guidelines on segment disclosures.

3-12   Selected information for the Global Company is presented below (US$ million) for 1996.

Region	Sales Revenue	Identifiable Assets
Central America	$1,900	$1,000
North America	225	200
Western Europe	725	175
Corporate level	-	375
Consolidated	$2,850	$1,750

Required: Identify Global's foreign segments using the percentage criteria in the FASB's *SFAS No. 14* for sales revenue and identifiable assets.

3-13   The authors have made five recommendations regarding corporate compliance with environmental laws (see p. 91).

Required: List those recommendations. Can you make other recommendations that might be helpful in this area?

3-14   The traditional income statement of Sharif International for the year ended March 31, 1996
appears below in rupees.

		Rs. 000s
Sales	90,000	
Cost of goods sold (all purchased from outside companies)	60,000	
Gross profit		30,000
Salaries and retirement benefits	15,000	
Rent expense	3,000	
Auditing and legal services	1,000	
Interest expense	2,000	21,000
Income before taxes		9,000
Provision for income taxes		4,000
Net income		5,000

Dividends declared and paid during the year amounted to Rs. 1,500,000

Required: Transform Sharif International's traditional income statement to a value added
statement.

3-15   Given below is Patrice Inc.'s income statement:

Patrice Inc.
Statement of Income
For the Year Ended December 31, 1995

		$ 000s
Sales	$ 3,975	
Cost of goods sold	2,830	
Gross profit		$ 1,145
Salaries, wages, and employment-related expenses	650	
Rent expense	47	
Outside consulting fees	53	
Interest expense	17	767
Income before taxes		378
Provision for income taxes		179
Net income		199

Notes: 1. All goods sold were purchased from outside suppliers.
          2. Dividends declared and paid during 1995 amounted to $100,000.

Required: Prepare a value added statement from the above income statement.

Case: Management Control Systems and the Environment[32]

ICI, a multinational chemical company with its head office in London, publishes a section in its Annual Report on "Safety, Health, and the Environment." It now also publishes a separate Environmental Report that is sent to its shareholders.

(1) Details of environment-related expenditures. For instance, at ICI's Huddersfield plant, a new boiler plant was constructed using "novel technology for capturing sulfur dioxide. The result has been a halving of sulphur dioxide emissions in the flue gases." ICI stated that all major new projects it undertakes now are assessed for their impact on the environment at all stages in their development. Environmental expenditures, total revenues, and net earnings of ICI were reported to be:

Environmental expenditures (billions)	19x2	19x3	19x4
Capital equipment related	0.081	0.132	0.164
Operating related	0.194	0.187	0.197
Revenues (billions)	12.906	12.488	12.061
Net earnings (billions)	0.919	0.789	0.565

(2) Number of fines and prosecutions for noncompliance with environmental laws and regulations:

19x2	19x3	19x4
36	26	21

(3) Total waste emissions to land, air, and water (in millions of tons):

	19x2	19x3	19x4
Nonhazardous	5.334	5.205	4.817
Hazardous	0.678	0.475	0.350
	6.012	5.680	5.167

(4) Number of reportable accidents per 100,000 working hours:

19x2	19x3	19x4
0.28	0.23	0.18

Required:

(1) Why might ICI send an *Environmental Report* to its shareholders in addition to sending its *Annual Report?*

(2) One commentator argued that ICI's *Environmental Report* should not have been sent to shareholders with its *Annual Report.* His argument was: "The financial information in the Annual Report is objective and audited by KPMG Peat Marwick. Information about safety, health, and the environment is subjective and nonaudited. I object

[32] Horngren, Charles T., George Foster, and Srikant M. Datar, *Cost Accounting: A Managerial Emphasis,* 8th ed., (c) 1994, pp. 490-491. Reprinted by permission of Prentice Hall, Upper Saddle River, N.J.

to this pandering to the greenies. We should not waste ICI money responding to every social pressure group." How would you respond to this commentator?

(3) Should the data in items 2 (fines), 3 (emissions), and 4 (accidents) be included in a management control system, or should a management control system focus only on financial/internal information? Explain.

(4) What problems might arise in ICI determining what amount of its expenditures are related to "safety, health, or the environment"?

(5) Comment on trends in ICI's data reported in this question. Does an increase in environment-related expenditures mean an improvement in environmental performance?

References

Cairns, David. "What is the Future of Mutual Recognition of Financial Statements and Is Comparability Really Necessary?" *The European Accounting Review,* vol. 3, no. 2 (1994), pp. 343-352.

Comparative Analysis of Disclosure Regimes. Quebec: International Organization of Securities Commissions, 1991.

Deppe, Larry A. "Disaggregated Information: Time to Reconsider." *Journal of Accountancy,* December 1994, pp. 65-68, 70.

Duvall, L., R. Jennings, J. Robinson, and R. Thompson II. "Can Investors Unravel the Effects of Goodwill Accounting?" *Accounting Horizons,* June 1992, pp. 1-14.

Emmanuel, Clive, and Neil Garrod. "Segmental Reporting in the U.K. How Does *SSAP 25* Stand Up to International Comparison?" *The European Accounting Review,* vol. 3, no. 3 (1994), pp. 547-562.

"Environmental Disclosure: Recent Developments." *Deloitte & Touche Review,* 13 July 1992, pp. 1-2.

Ewer, Sid R., Jon R. Nance, and Sarah J. Hamlin. "Accounting for Tomorrow's Pollution Control." *Journal of Accountancy,* July 1992, pp. 69-74.

Fourth Council Directive for Coordination of National Legislation. "Regarding the Annual Accounts of Limited Liability Companies." Brussels: European Community, 1978.

Gumbel, Peter, and Greg Steinmetz. "German Firms Shift to More-Open Accounting." *Wall Street Journal,* 15 March 1995, pp. C1, C10.

Haller, Axel, and Peter Park. "Regulation and Practice of Segmental Reporting in Germany." *The European Accounting Review,* vol. 3, no. 3 (1994), pp. 563-580.

Harper, R. M. Jr., W. G. Mister, and J. R. Strawser. "The Effect of Recognition Versus Disclosure of Unfunded Postretirement Benefits on Lenders' Perceptions of Debt." *Accounting Horizons,* September 1991, pp. 50-56.

Horngren, Charles T., George Foster, and Srikant M. Datar. *Cost Accounting: A Managerial Emphasis.* 8th ed. Englewood Cliffs, N.J.: Prentice Hall, 1994.

International Accounting Standard 1. "Disclosure of Accounting Policies." London: International Accounting Standards Committee, 1994.

International Accounting Standard 5. "Information to be Disclosed in Financial Statements." London: International Accounting Standards Committee, 1994.

International Accounting Standard 14. "Reporting Financial Information by Segment." London: International Accounting Standards Committee, 1994.

International Accounting Standard 18. "Revenue Recognition." London: International Accounting Standards Committee, 1994.

International Investment and Multinational Enterprises. Paris: Organization for Economic Cooperation and Development, 1979 (originally published in 1976).

Lowe, Howard D. "Shortcomings of Japanese Consolidated Financial Statements," *Accounting Horizons,* September 1990, pp. 1-9.

Meek, G. K., D. S. Coldwell, and D. S. Peavey. "Corporate Financial Disclosure: A Global Assessment," in F. Choi (ed.), *Handbook of International Accounting.* New York: John Wiley & Sons, Inc., 1991, pp. 22.1-22.30.

Organization for Economic Cooperation and Development, Working Group Accounting Standards. *Disclosure of Information by Multinational Enterprises: Survey of the Application of the OECD Guidelines.* Paris: Organization for Economic Cooperation and Development, 1987.

Progress on the Environmental Challenge—A Survey of Corporate America's Environmental Accounting and Management. New York: Price Waterhouse, 1994.

Purvis, S. E. C., Helen Gernon, and Michael A. Diamond. "The IASC and Its Comparability Project: Prerequisites for Success," *Accounting Horizons,* June 1991, pp. 25-44.

Sack, Robert J., James R. Boatsman, Robert S. Fell, Jack L. Krogstad, Spencer J. Martin, and Marcia S. Niles. "American Accounting Association's Securities and Exchange Commission Liaison Committee." *Accounting Horizons,* vol. 9, no. 1 (March 1995), pp. 79-86.

Securities and Exchange Commission. *Accounting Series Release No. 236.* "Industry Segment Reporting: Adoption of Disclosure Regulation and Amendments of Disclosure Forms and Rules," Washington, D.C.: U.S. Government Printing Office, December 1977.

Segmented Financial Information. Paris: Organization for Economic Cooperation and Development, 1990.

Statement of Financial Accounting Standards No. 14. "Financial Reporting for Segments of a Business Enterprise." Stamford, Conn.: Financial Accounting Standards Board, December 1976.

United Nations Center on Transnational Corporations. *Conclusions on Accounting and Reporting by Transnational Corporations.* New York: United Nations, 1988.

————. *Information Disclosure Relating to Environmental Measures.* New York: United Nations, 1990.

United Nations Intergovernmental Working Group of Experts on International Standards of Accounting and Reporting. *Conclusions on Accounting and Reporting by Transnational Corporations.* New York: United Nations, 1988.

Wyatt, Arthur R., and Joseph Yospe. "Wake-up Call to American Business: International Accounting Standards Are on the Way," *Journal of Accountancy,* July 1993, pp. 80-85.

Chapter 4

Setting Accounting Standards in Selected Countries

While accounting is often called the language of business, its meaning varies from country to country. Just as U.S. accounting standards conform to the perceived needs of U.S. business, accounting standards abroad reflect varying conceptions of the role accounting plays in the economy. Whereas a *contador publico* in Mexico City considers the stockholder the primary user of financial statements, an accountant in Dusseldorf gears financial statements to tax authorities. How are accounting standards determined in different countries? What are the implications of different accounting standards? These are some of the issues discussed in this chapter.

As the twenty-first century draws near, nations are becoming increasingly integrated economically. Harvard Business School accounting professor David Hawkins states that accounting in emerging markets is a potential mine field.[1] For example, the North American Free Trade Agreement among Canada, Mexico, and the U.S. is an important trade alliance. As Kurt P. Ramin, partner with Coopers & Lybrand, states:

> Because NAFTA will increase trade activities between the United States, Mexico, Canada and other countries, at Coopers & Lybrand we'll increase staff exchanges between our Mexican and U.S. firms. For instance, about 15 or 20 people in our offices in Houston and other locations close to the border will work closely with our Mexican offices.

> We also plan to implement sophisticated training programs. One example is audit procedure training, since we'll be using the same audit approach. Also, the United States and Mexico recently agreed on a double taxation treaty for the first time, so we have to train a lot of people in that area, too.[2]

Eastern Europe presents an interesting laboratory for accounting standards. The change from a planned economy to a market-based economy requires the development of an accounting framework and an accounting profession to meet information needs for economic decision making. In a planned economy, the objective of accounting is to assist in monitoring economic plans. A market-based economy, however, requires information about a company's financial performance, financial position, and cash flows. Countries in Eastern Europe and Asia are moving at different speeds due to political uncertainties. Cultural considerations also bear on how quickly profit-oriented reporting systems will be implemented. These are challenging and fascinating times for the accounting profession.

---

[1] As quoted by Roula Khalaf, "Free Style Accounting," *Forbes*, 1 March 1993, pp. 102-103.

[2] Kurt P. Ramin, "Where We Stand in Mexico," *Financial Executive*, March/April 1993, p. 19.

Businesses that hope to profit from international trade must understand the nuances of varying accounting standards. Today's international accountants are attempting to translate the accounting practices of various nations into a common dialect and thereby assist businesses in becoming active players in the international trade arena.

Sources of Diversity

As discussed in Chapter 1, accounting standards are heavily influenced by a nation's internal environment. An important factor in the way a nation sets its accounting standards is the degree of government involvement in the economy. All economies lie somewhere between the two extremes of total state control and a completely free-market system. This continuum is illustrated in Figure 4–1 below.

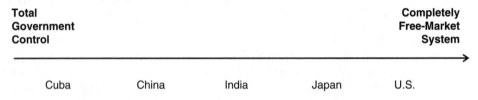

Figure 4–1 Government Involvement in Economy

In countries with relatively few publicly-owned corporations and mostly state-controlled markets, the government usually takes a decisive role in promulgating accounting standards. In contrast, in countries with large corporations that have widely dispersed ownership, accounting standard setting is often handled by the profession itself.

Since different approaches to standard setting arise from different perceptions of what constitutes useful accounting information, the diversity of approaches yields dramatically different accounting standards worldwide. Following are some examples of the important sources of diversity.

The Balance Sheet Versus the Income Statement

Accounting standards tend to be oriented toward users of accounting information. For example, if banks are the main capital providers, then standards will emphasize the balance sheet, since bank authorities must evaluate the degree of short-term and long-term liquidity of an entity. Banks need to know whether an entity can pay its debts.

In contrast, where stockholders are the main source of corporate capital, a corporation's earnings are quite an important indicator of its success. Therefore, the income statement is crucial.

Disclosure

Chapter 3 discussed this topic at length. Companies in some European countries tend to disclose less information than U.S. companies. As discussed in Chapter 3, reserves are sometimes set up to smooth out earnings. Sometimes statutes dictate that part of income should be transferred to a reserve for additional protection of creditors.

Consolidated Statements

Consolidated statements present the financial information of the parent company and its subsidiaries as if they constitute one economic entity. Consolidated statements are not required in many countries. In the U.S., consolidated statements were common near the turn of the century. This did not happen in the United Kingdom until the 1930s. In the rest of continental Europe, consolidated statements were a post-war phenomenon. The accounting standard requiring consolidation was not issued in Japan until 1975. Approximately 25 countries now require consolidated statements.

Goodwill Accounting

Goodwill is the amount paid for above-normal profits. Accounting for goodwill varies worldwide depending on the country. Goodwill can be written off immediately or over as many as 40 years, as shown in Exhibit 4–1.

Exhibit 4–1 Purchased Goodwill Accounting		
Country	**Amortization**	**Immediate Write-off**
Australia	Yes – 20 years maximum	No
Brazil	Yes	No
Canada	Yes – 40 years maximum	No
France	Yes	Yes*
Germany	Yes	Yes*
Japan	Yes – 5 years maximum	No
Mexico	Yes	Yes
Netherlands	Yes – 10 years maximum	No
Nigeria	Yes	Yes
U.K.	Yes	Yes**
U.S.	Yes – 40 years maximum	No

*Restricted to goodwill on consolidation.
**Directly to equity without passing through income statement.

Research Expenditures

Research expenditures account for additional diversity in accounting standards worldwide. Exhibit 4–2 shows how standards differ in 11 countries.

This chapter describes the accounting standard-setting process and some general rules followed in the preparation of financial statements for these 11 countries. Chapter 11 includes many examples of actual financial statements from companies based in different countries.

Exhibit 4–2	Research Expenditures Accounting		
	Maximum	**Immediate Write-off**	
Country	**Amortization Period**	**Allowed**	**Required**
Australia	Not specified	Yes	
Brazil	10 years	Yes	
Canada	Not applicable		Yes
France	5 years	Yes	
Germany	Not specified	Yes	
Japan	5 years	Yes	
Mexico	Not applicable		Yes
Netherlands	5 or 10 years	Yes	
Nigeria	Not applicable		Yes
U.K.	Not applicable		Yes
U.S.	Not applicable		Yes

Standard-Setting and Reporting Practices in Selected Countries

Australia

Standard setting. Accounting standards in Australia are derived from the Corporations Law and Regulations, the Annual Reporting Acts, the Australian Accounting Standards, standards issued by the Australian Accounting Standards Board, and the Accounting Guidance Releases (AGRs). The Corporations Law and Regulations regulate companies in Australia and set forth disclosure requirements for corporations. The Annual Reporting Acts set out general accounting requirements for public sector entities. The Australian Accounting Standards (AASs) are issued by the Australian Accounting Research Foundation (AARF) on behalf of the Institute of Chartered Accountants in Australia and the Australian Society of Certified Practicing Accountants. Directors and auditors who are members of these organizations are required to comply with the AASs. Accounting standards issued by the Australian Accounting Standards Board (AASBs) are incorporated in the Corporation Law. Accounting Guidance Releases are issued by the AARF. They are designed either to give interpretation of certain standards or to deal with new issues.

Financial statements. The Corporations Law dictates the format of the balance sheet, income statement, and statement of cash flows. The statements and notes are required to give the reader a "true and fair view" of the results of operation and the financial position. Hence, the directors' report signed by two directors and the auditor's report indicating the truth and fairness of the financial information must accompany the financial statements.

Consolidation. Financial statements must be prepared in a single consolidated set; if this is not done, the reason for not doing so and the extent to which group accounts are affected by intercompany balances and transactions must be disclosed. Any company listed on the Australian Stock Exchange must submit consolidated financial statements.

Segment information. Companies with "material" segments should disclose segmental information. A material segment is defined as one whose revenue, profits, or assets represent more than 10 percent of the total revenue, profits, or assets of the company or a group of companies. When segments constitute at least 75 percent of the total revenue, expenses, and assets, they should be separately identified. When a segment constitutes at least 90 percent of revenue, profits, and assets, it may be identified as a single entity. These criteria for material segments are very similar to the U.S. standards. Comparability of financial information between companies should also be a consideration in the determination of material segments. Both geographical and industrial segment disclosures are required.

Normally, segment information does not include interest expense and interest income, although they are used as reconciling items between the individual segment amounts and the total figures reported. Items such as equity accounting entries and extraordinary items and income tax figures are also not part of segment disclosure information.

Brazil

Standard setting. Brazilian Corporate Law applies to all companies organized as Sociedade Anonima (SA). Investors may dispose of their interest in SAs more easily than their interests in a Ltda. The Securities Exchange Commission, Commissao de Valores Mobiliarios (CVM), is responsible for accounting standards for the companies that are publicly traded. The Brazilian Accountants' Institute, Instituto Brasileiro de Contadores (IBRACON), issues and codifies accounting standards. If these standards are approved by the CVM they are binding on all publicly traded companies. Generally accepted practices become the standards where no codified standard is issued by the CVM or IBRACON.

The primary basis for measurement is historical cost. Since Brazil has undergone hyperinflation, historical cost is adjusted for current purchasing power. This is accomplished by adjusting nonmonetary assets and stockholders' equity. Legislation determines the index that is used. The effect of this adjustment is reflected in income for the year. Fixed assets can be adjusted for appraisal increases according to corporate law.

In Brazilian accounting, the notion of "a going concern" is assumed. Financial statements are prepared on the accrual basis. The principles of conservatism, materiality, and consistency are considered important in the preparation of financial statements.

Financial statements. Financial statements are accompanied by the administrative council's report, which contains comments on these statements. A balance sheet, income statement, statement of changes in shareholders' equity, statement of changes in financial position, and the accompanying notes comprise the contents of these statements. The basic format is dictated by corporate law. The income statement includes operating and nonoperating items as well as an adjustment for the effects of inflation.

Most Brazilian companies, including the subsidiaries of multinational corporations, are organized as Limitadadas (Ltda). These are the limited liability companies whose owners are liable for the full amount of the company's legal capital until it has been paid. These companies generally adopt accounting principles in order to comply with tax laws. Thus, financial statements may not conform to generally accepted accounting principles.

Consolidation. Consolidation is required when companies are publicly traded and investment in subsidiaries represents more than 30 percent of their net worth. The 30 percent is taken on balances using the equity basis of accounting. Although preparation of consolidated statements is a requirement for publicly traded companies, there are some exceptions: If control of the subsidiary is temporary; the subsidiary is under receivership; or if consolidation would be misleading, for example, if the subsidiaries are in dissimilar businesses.

Segment information. There are no specific disclosure requirements in this area. Corporate Law does, however, require the Administrative Council to publish a report outlining lines of business and major actions during the year. The CVM gives guidance on segment information. Some of the required disclosures include products, services, and the volume and amount of sales during the past two years.

Canada

Standard setting. Authoritative pronouncements, accounting literature, and acceptable practices constitute GAAP in Canada. The Canadian Institute of Chartered Accountants (CICA) issues the standards. They appear as recommendations in the CICA Handbook. When there is no formal guidance, the profession resorts to less formal guidance by the CICA as well as generally accepted practices. Canadian GAAP is probably the closest to U.S. GAAP of any of our 11 countries.

Financial statements. Financial statements normally include a balance sheet, an income statement, a statement of retained earnings, a statement of changes in financial position, and explanatory notes.

Financial statements are prepared in accordance with the historical cost basis. The going concern assumption is made in the preparation of financial statements unless evidence indicates otherwise. Consistency is also viewed as important in financial statements. The same accounting principles are followed from period to period unless there is good reason to change to another principle. Accrual basis accounting is employed, and the effect of transactions is reflected in the financial statements when they occur.

Consolidation. A company with one or more subsidiaries is required to prepare consolidated financial statements when the subsidiaries are considered controlled enterprises. The ability to control a subsidiary is indicated by the parent company's continuing power to determine its strategic operating, investing, and financing policies without the cooperation of others. Generally, a percentage of ownership that enables the parent company to elect a majority of the board of directors is evidence of the ability to control. In some situations, such as severe statutory restrictions or plans to dispose of the subsidiary in the near future, consolidation is not required despite majority ownership.

Segment information. Public companies as well as life insurance companies are required to disclose segment information. Reportable segments are by industry and by geographical markets. Disclosures for each reportable segment include outside sales, intersegment sales, operating income or loss, and total carrying value of identifiable assets.

France

Standard setting. Two bodies are responsible for accounting standards in France. They are the Institute of Public Accountants and Authorized Accountants (Ordre des Experts Comptables et des Comptables Agrees) and the Stock Exchange Commission (Commission des Operations de Bourse). The first organization assists members in the application of accounting legislation and regulations by providing guidelines and interpretations. The latter organization publishes recommendations and opinions in efforts to encourage companies and their auditors to follow sound accounting and auditing practices.

Generally accepted accounting principles are set forth in the following sources:

- Business Code (Code de Commerce).
- General Accounting Plan (Plan Comptable General). This is a chart of accounts that must be followed by all manufacturing and commercial entities. The accounting plan is based on the Fourth Directive of the European Union.

Financial statements. In France, the financial statements include the balance sheet, income statement, and notes to the statements. Multipurpose financial statements are not the rule. Rather, accounting regulations dictate that the information to be included in the notes should vary with the size of business. A statement of changes in financial position is not required.

Basic accounting concepts followed in the preparation of financial statements include the going concern, the accrual basis, the historical cost convention, the consistency principle, and the principle of prudence (conservatism). Two principles not currently included in French accounting are substance over form and materiality. Thus, in France, form generally prevails over substance.

Consolidation. Consolidated statements in France are prepared to conform with international accounting standards. Individual company statements, on the other hand, follow to a great degree the tax requirements. National legislation and regulatory French accounting standards are derived from national legislation and regulatory texts. They are further supplemented by authoritative pronouncements. All subsidiaries are required to be consolidated. There are exceptions, however:

- Subsidiaries in which there is temporary control.
- Subsidiaries whose operations are so dissimilar to the parent's that the presentation would not be meaningful.
- Subsidiaries whose assets are seriously and permanently impaired.

Segment information. Information on net sales by industry as well as geographical information is required. In cases where supplying this information would hurt the company economically, a note to the statements should state this fact. However, public companies must present quarterly consolidated sales by segment. Judgment must be used in defining what constitutes a segment because French law does not give any guidelines or criteria. A segment would be considered significant if it represents more than 10 percent of sales, operating income, and assets.

Germany

Standard setting. German accounting principles and standards have their origin in the German Commercial Code, generally accepted accounting practices, tax court rulings, pronouncements of the German Institute of Certified Public Accountants, and the German Stock Corporation Law. The strongest influence on generally accepted accounting principles in Germany is the German Stock Corporation Law of 1965 and its revision in 1987 to comply with provisions of the EU Directives.

Financial statements. Companies are required to present a balance sheet, income statement, and notes to the statements. A statement of retained earnings and statement of changes in cash or changes in financial position are not required.

The Commercial Code also requires large and medium-sized companies and limited liability companies to supplement financial statements with an annual management report. In addition to the company's economic progress and position, the report must cover events subsequent to the balance sheet. The disclosures include expected developments in the company and its markets. This report must be provided to shareholders, and must be published in the German Federal Gazette or filed with the local Commercial Register.

Basic accounting concepts include the going concern, the historical cost basis, and the accrual concepts. In addition, the prudence concept must also be followed. The prudence concept provides for disclosure of all anticipated risks and losses up to the balance sheet date, and recognition of unrealized profits is prohibited. In any measuring process, the principle of individual valuation must be followed. An application of this principle is the prohibition of netting assets against liabilities. There are no specific foreign-currency translation requirements.

Consolidation. In Germany, a company is required to present consolidated financial statements and a group management report no later than five months after the balance sheet date if any one of the following conditions exist:

- It owns controlling interest (voting interest).
- In the capacity as a shareholder it has the right to nominate or dismiss the majority of the officers of the subsidiary.
- It has consummated an agreement as to its controlling influence.

Excluded from consolidation are subsidiaries dissimilar in nature, those that are relatively insignificant in the group in terms of income, net assets, etc., those in which the parent's controlling interest might be in jeopardy, subsidiaries in which the parent's shares are held only for resale, or cases where there are lengthy delays in obtaining information for consolidated statements.

Segment information. The Commercial Code requires disclosures of sales by industry and by geographically defined markets.

Japan

Standard setting. Generally accepted accounting standards in Japan have their foundation in legal provisions, authoritative pronouncements, accounting literature, and accepted practice. Accounting standards dictated by legal provisions and authoritative pronouncements are as follows:

- Income Tax Law *(Zeiko).* Income tax law covers the determination of taxable income. All expenses and writedowns for tax purposes must also be included for reporting purposes.
- *Financial Accounting Standards for Business Enterprises.* The Business Accounting Deliberation Council (BADC) formulates and issues these standards. The BADC is an advisory body to the Ministry of Finance. The standards issued include general standards, income statement standards, and balance sheet standards.
- Pronouncements of the Audit Committee of the Japanese Institute of Certified Public Accountants.

Financial statements. Joint stock companies (known as Kabushiki Kaishas), according to the Commercial Code, must include a balance sheet, an income statement, the business report, proposed retained earnings appropriations, and supporting schedules. The Securities and Exchange Law also requires cash flow statements for publicly traded companies.

These statements do not need to be prepared on a comparative basis. In addition, the balance sheet, income statement (with a schedule of costs of good manufactured), statement of appropriation of retaining earnings, and supporting schedules must be filed with the Ministry of Finance. For filing purposes, comparative statements are required and Ministry of Finance ordinances prescribe terminology and methods of preparation of financial statements.

The objective of financial statements in Japan is to protect the creditors and current investors. The following is noteworthy:

> Japan yesterday established a securities watchdog commission to ensure fairness in stock markets and prevent a reoccurrence of the financial scandals that rocked the country's financial industry last summer. . . .

> The new committee is modeled on the U.S. Securities and Exchange Commission. But critics say it will have less autonomy and fewer inspectors than its American counterpart.[3]

Thus, disclosures dealing with dividend availability, creditworthiness, and earnings per share are of paramount importance. A company's financial position and results of operations must be in compliance with the law and the company's articles of incorporation. In most cases, financial statements are prepared using the historical cost basis. The accrual basis of accounting is employed.

---

[3] "Japanese Launch New Commission," *San Francisco Chronicle,* 21 July 1992, p. B2.

Consolidation. Securities and Exchange Law (SEL) is the set of requirements that applies to companies that have raised over 100 million yen publicly and are either listed on stock exchanges or traded in over-the-counter markets. Companies falling under the SEL must prepare a consolidated balance sheet, income statement, and statement of surplus. Companies are required to disclose the accounting policies used in consolidation.

Segment information. Listed companies must provide segment information on industry segments, segments by domestic and overseas location, and overseas sales.

Mexico

Standard setting. In Mexico, the Mexican Institute of Public Accountants is the standard-setting body. There are four categories of standards: generally accepted accounting principles, generally accepted auditing standards, code of ethics, and continuing professional standards. The Institute has created specific commissions for each of the four major categories.

Certain regulated industries, such as banks that are owned by the government, may follow special accounting treatment and thus may depart from the generally accepted accounting principles.

The Commission of Accounting Principles of the Mexican Institute of Public Accountants adheres to the entity concept as well as the principles of realization,[4] historical cost, going concern, materiality, consistency, and adequate disclosure. Inflation accounting has been addressed recently.

The Mexican Institute of Public Accountants also has a code of professional ethics that covers a great array of topics. Media advertising, for example, is prohibited by the code of professional ethics.

Financial statements. The basic financial statements include a balance sheet, an income statement, a statement of changes in shareholders' equity, and a statement of changes in financial position based on cash flows, as well as the accompanying notes. These statements are prepared on a comparative basis. There is an account representing the excess (deficiency) due to the difference between current cost and holding gains in inventory and fixed assets. The index used is the national consumer price index (NCR).

Consolidation. If a parent has direct or indirect control equal to or more than 50 percent of the participating stock, these subsidiaries must be consolidated. Exceptions from this requirement occur in cases of subsidiaries where:

- Control is temporary.
- Businesses are dissimilar.
- Parent control is limited.
- They are in bankruptcy.

---

[4] Realization refers to the situation where services have been substantially performed and cash, a receivable, or some other asset that can be objectively measured has been received.

Segment information. No requirements exist for segment-related disclosures. As a result, Mexican companies do not disclose segment information.

Netherlands

Standard setting. An act of Parliament forms the basis for annual reports of companies in Title 9 of the Civil Code. Title 9 also provides flexibility to comply with the Fourth Directive of the European Union. A committee, the Council for Annual Reporting, is working on a draft of generally accepted accounting principles. This group consists of users, preparers, and auditors of financial statements.

Financial statements. Title 9 outlines the accounting concepts to be followed in the preparation of financial statements. The most important concept is that the financial statements provide "insight" in making decisions regarding an entity's financial position and results of operations. Information on solvency and liquidity, to the extent possible, should also be provided. Required financial statements include a balance sheet, income statement, and the accompanying notes.

Requirements of the Civil Code include using the matching concept as well as the realization, going concern, accrual, and prudence concepts. The historical cost basis is allowed for valuation purposes. However, for inventories, tangible, financial, and fixed assets, current value is also allowed.

Consolidation. Title 9 requires that all group companies and the parent company should be consolidated. Group companies are defined as subsidiaries and participating interests. Exceptions with regard to the consolidation requirement are:

- Difference in activities.
- If the group companies in total are insignificant.
- If financial data cannot be obtained or there is delay in obtaining same.
- If group companies are going to be disposed of.

Segment information. Segment disclosures are required if sales of a business or a geographical segment exceed 10 percent of the total net sales.

Nigeria

Standard setting. The Nigerian Accounting Standards Board (NASB) issues Statement of the Accountancy Standards (SASs). NASB standards are based on International Accounting Standards. Where no accounting standards have been issued by NASB, the original International Accounting Standards apply.

Financial statements. All public companies are required to prepare a balance sheet, an income statement, a statement of changes in financial position, a five-year financial summary, and explanatory notes. The financial statements must also include a statement of accounting policies, the auditor's report, and the directors' report.

Financial statements are prepared using historical cost and accrual accounting. Comparability between companies is enhanced by consistency of accounting principles from one year to the next. Substance over legal form prevails and requires professional judgment.

Consolidation. All subsidiaries must be consolidated with these exceptions:

- Equity increases will not accrue to the parent (the cost method is then used).
- Control is temporary.
- Control is seriously impaired (the cost method should be used).
- The operations of the subsidiary are so dissimilar that including them would not provide useful information. (The equity method for the investment would then be used.)

Segment information. Currently, no Nigerian reporting standard exists on segment disclosures, and *International Accounting Standard 14* is followed. The Companies and Allied Matters Act of 1990 requires disclosures of sales and profit by industry segments.

United Kingdom

Standard setting. The Financial Council Limited provides support to its operational bodies: the Accounting Standards Board (ASB) and the Financial Reporting Review Panel. The ASB promulgates and issues accounting standards. These standards are to be followed unless there are good reasons for departing from them. Generally accepted accounting principles stem from the following:

- Valuation requirements, accounting for consolidations, disclosure requirements, and format of financial statements are covered by the Companies Act of 1985, as amended in 1989.
- *Financial Reporting Standards* (FRSs) issued by the ASB.
- *Statements of Standard Accounting Practice* (SSAPs). SSAPs were issued by the Accounting Standards Committee (ASC) before the ASB was formed. The Accounting Standards Committee was replaced by the ASB.
- *Statements of Recommended Practice* (SORPs) issued by the ASC. These are used when no specific guidelines exist for a specialized area.
- Approved SORPs issued by specialized industries and approved by the ASB.
- The U.K.'s International Stock Exchange's Continuing Obligations cover disclosure requirements for companies listed on the Stock Exchange.
- Technical releases such as those issued by ASB.

Unlike the U.S., where the SEC has the authority to set detailed rules for financial statements, no such legal power exists in the United Kingdom. There are certain laws and established practices that must be followed, but by and large corporate directors in the U.K. have considerable discretion.

Financial statements. Required financial statements include a profit and loss account (income statement), a balance sheet, a cash flow statement (for large companies), a statement of total recognized gains and losses, a statement of accounting policies, and accompanying notes. Financial statements are generally based on historical cost except in specific situations where the Companies Act allows use of either current cost or market value.

Consolidation. Consolidation is required for all subsidiaries, partnerships, and limited companies. Control is the key criterion rather than legal ownership. Exceptions to consolidated statements are:

- The investment in the subsidiary is not material. However, if two subsidiaries exist, the total investment should be considered in applying the materiality criterion.
- Restrictions are such that the parent company cannot exercise control.
- Subsidiary information cannot be obtained.
- The subsidiary is for resale.
- The operations of the subsidiary(ies) are so dissimilar that including them would not convey a true and fair view.

Segment information. Segment reporting is required. The directors determine the segments according to appropriate categories of lines of business and geographical areas. The required disclosures include sales and profit or loss of each segment. Disclosure requirements for public companies and large private companies are more extensive and also include disclosure of net assets, income before tax, extraordinary items, interest, etc. Public companies are defined by the Companies Act as those with a minimum initial authorized share capital of £50,000 and at least 25 percent of the shares must have been paid up. Large private companies are those that meet certain specifications for income, total assets, and average number of employees. The criteria for income and assets are adjusted periodically for inflation.

United States

Standard setting. The U.S. Congress has given the Securities and Exchange Commission (SEC) responsibility for establishing generally accepted accounting principles (GAAP) for companies whose stock is publicly traded. The SEC has, in turn, largely delegated this responsibility to the accounting profession.

1. The *Financial Accounting Standards Board* (FASB) is the main body responsible for promulgating accounting standards in the U.S. It was established in 1973 as a replacement for the Accounting Principles Board. The FASB is composed of seven members. The Financial Accounting Foundation oversees the FASB's operations and provides its funding.

The FASB follows due process procedures in establishing accounting principles. These procedures include:

- Creating a task force to define a problem.
- Issuing a discussion memorandum.
- Scheduling a public hearing.
- Analyzing comments received.

- Making a decision as to issuance of a standard. If a standard is to be issued, preparing and circulating an exposure draft.
- Scheduling another public hearing.
- Approving (or disapproving) the exposure draft. If approved by at least five of seven board members, a new standard is issued.

Pronouncements of the FASB include:

- *Statements of Financial Accounting Concepts.* These are fundamental concepts on which accounting and reporting standards are based.
- *Statements of Financial Accounting Standards.* These are the major pronouncements issued by the FASB, and are the primary basis for GAAP.

2. The *Governmental Accounting Standards Board* (GASB) was created in 1984. GASB's responsibility is to establish accounting principles for municipal and state government bodies, hospitals, universities, and other not-for-profit entities. The Financial Accounting Foundation oversees the operations and financing of the GASB.

3. The *American Institute of Certified Public Accountants* (AICPA) is an organization of certified public accountants. It is influential in the development of accounting principles and practices. Before the FASB was formed in 1973, the AICPA exerted influence through the Committee on Accounting Procedure (1939-1959) and the Accounting Principles Board (1959-1973). With the creation of the FASB, the AICPA formed the Accounting Standards Executive Committee (AcSEC) which issues *Statements of Position* on matters not covered by the FASB.

Financial statements. The required set of financial statements consists of a balance sheet, a statement of income and retained earnings, a statement of cash flows, a statement of changes in stockholders' equity, and notes to the statements. Comparative financial data is generally provided, and SEC rules require comparative statements for more than one year for publicly traded companies.

Consolidation. Consolidated financial statements are required when a parent has a controlling interest in the voting stock of one or more other entities. Exceptions to the requirement for consolidated statements occur when control is temporary (such as when the parent intends to divest itself of a subsidiary), when a subsidiary is in bankruptcy or in receivership, or when restrictions cast doubt on the parent's ability to control a subsidiary.

Segment information. A reportable industry segment is defined as one where a segment's revenue is 10 percent or more of the combined revenues of all industry segments, where a segment's assets constitute 10 percent or more of total identifiable assets of all industry segments, or where operating profit or loss is 10 percent or more (in absolute terms) of total operating profit of all industry segments that did not incur an operating loss. The segments reported should account for at least 75 percent of combined revenue from sales to unaffiliated customers of all industry segments. For each reportable industry segment, the major disclosures include sales to outside customers, intersegment sales or transfers, operating profit or loss, and identifiable assets.

Foreign operations. In addition to industry segment information, disclosures are required for operations located outside the home country. These disclosures include revenue, operating profit or loss, and identifiable assets for foreign operations. The disclosures must be made if either the foreign operations generate sales revenue from unaffiliated customers that is 10 percent or more of consolidated sales revenue, or the identifiable assets of foreign operations are 10 percent or more of consolidated total assets. If operations are located in more than one geographical area outside the home country, the disclosures must be made for each geographical area with sales to outside customers of 10 percent or more of consolidated sales.

Export sales. Revenue from export sales (from the home country) to unaffiliated customers must be reported separately if the amount is 10 percent or more of consolidated sales revenue.

Major customers. Disclosures on each major customer contributing 10 percent or more to the company's total revenue are also required. In such cases, the amount of revenue from each major customer and the industry segment or segments that make the sales must be disclosed.

Exhibits 4–3, 4–4, and 4–5 summarize the elements of financial statements, the segment disclosure requirements, and the basic accounting concepts and conventions, respectively, for the 11 countries we have discussed above.

Exhibit 4–3   Elements of Financial Statements

Country	Balance Sheet	Income Statement	Statement of Funds/Cash Flow
Australia	R	R	R
Brazil	R	R	R
Canada	R	R	R
France	R	R	O
Germany	R	R	O
Japan	R	R	P
Mexico	R	R	R
Netherlands	R	R	O
Nigeria	R	R	R
U.K.	R	R	L
U.S.	R	R	R

R = Required
P = Required for publicly traded companies
L = Required for large companies
O = Optional

Exhibit 4–4 Segment Disclosure Requirements

| | Required Segment Disclosures | |
Country	Geographical	Industry
Australia	R	R
Brazil	O	O
Canada	R	R
France	R	R
Germany	R	R
Japan	R	R
Mexico	O	O
Netherlands	R	R
Nigeria	R	R
U.K.	R	R
U.S.	R	R

R = Required
O = Optional

Exhibit 4–5 Basic Accounting Concepts and Conventions

Country	Cost	Accrual	Going Concern	Legal Form vs. Substance
Australia	HR	Required	Required	Substance
Brazil	HP	Required	Required	Substance
Canada	HC	Required	Required	Substance
France	HR	Required	Required	Legal form
Germany	HC	Required	Required	Both
Japan	HC	Required	Required	Both
Mexico	CC/HP	Required	Required	Substance
Netherlands	HR	Required	Required	Substance
Nigeria	HR	Required	Required	Substance
U.K.	HR	Required	Required	Substance
U.S.	HC	Required	Required	Substance

CC = Current cost
HC = Historical cost
HP = Historical cost with price-level adjustments
HR = Historical cost with revaluation option

Note to Students

To keep abreast of standard setting and related developments around the world, it is useful to read professional journals such as *The International Journal of Accounting Education and Research*. Also, some of the popular financial journals such as *Forbes* and *The Wall Street Journal* carry items on changes in accounting standards. Some practitioner journals such as the *Journal of Accountancy* carry feature articles as well as news items dealing with international accounting practices. Major public accounting firms publish a series of guides dealing with accounting standards and business issues in various countries. Many also publish newsletters to provide timely information on new developments in accounting standards.

Chapter Summary

- This chapter explored the accounting standard-setting process in 11 countries. Because of different environments, diversity in standard setting is apparent.

- In spite of differences in the form and content of financial statements, however, there are many similarities.

- All of the 11 countries require a balance sheet and income statement.

- Nine of the 11 countries require geographic and industry segment disclosures.

- The countries examined have generally reached similar understandings on issues of historical cost, consistency, materiality, and going concern.

Questions for Discussion

1. Why is there a need for accounting standards?

2. What factors influence a nation's accounting standards?

3. Who are generally the primary users of financial statements in countries where a private entity issues accounting standards?

4. Why is it useful to understand the standard-setting process in different countries?

5. What are consolidated financial statements?

6. How is the format of financial statements determined in Australia?

7. Describe the standard-setting process in Brazil.

8. Brazil has undergone very high inflation. How is this reflected in financial statements?

9. Name two widely used principles not currently included in French accounting.

10. What is the basic characteristic of individual, nonconsolidated company statements in France?

11. What are the segment reporting requirements in Germany?

12. Why is consistency important in financial statements?

13. What is the main objective of financial statements in Japan?

14. The terms "taxable income" and "financial reporting income" are used in the U.S. Is there such a difference in Japan? Explain.

15. What are the basic financial statements in Mexico? What is the excess (deficiency) account?

16. What is the most important concept stressed in financial statements in the Netherlands?

17. Explain the segment reporting requirements in Nigeria.

18. What financial statements are generally required in the United Kingdom?

19. What are the segment disclosure requirements in the United Kingdom?

20. The Financial Accounting Standards Board in the U.S. follows a due-process model in developing standards. Outline this due-process model.

21. What is the scope of GASB responsibility in the United States?

Exercises/Problems

4-1   Assume that Taimur Corporation bought a machine for 210,000 guilders on January 3, 1995. The machine has an estimated useful life of 10 years with no salvage value. The machine has a current cost of 300,000 guilders.

Required:
(1) Using straight line depreciation on an average cost basis, compute depreciation using the historical cost model.
(2) Compute depreciation using the current cost model.

4-2   The Latif Company in Australia has four industry segments, A, B, C, and D. The revenue from the segments for the past year amounted to:

Segment	Revenue
A	$ 4,000,000
B	3,000,000
C	500,000
D	2,500,000

Required: Identify the segments that qualify as "material" segments.

4-3   Daimler-Benz became the first German company to be listed on a U.S. stock exchange. This occurred after a long stalemate between Daimler-Benz and the U.S. Securities and Exchange Commission over compliance with U.S. accounting standards. The two parties finally struck a compromise in which Daimler-Benz agreed to conform in substance to U.S. accounting standards. Critics of the SEC maintain that U.S. accounting rules deter foreign companies from listing their shares in the U.S. Defenders of the SEC argue that the U.S. has the best accounting rules in the world and that U.S. standards should not be lowered. [Hint: This question draws on material from the first four chapters, the arguments presented in Case Study 1 in Chapter 12, and from general business and accounting concepts.]

Required:

(1) Present arguments supporting the SEC position.

(2) Present arguments opposing the SEC position.

4-4 The 10 largest Japanese companies reported return on investment of 4 percent in 1990 while the largest U.S. companies reported a 5.9 percent return. But the Japanese companies really didn't do that badly. [Hint: Look at the Tanaguchi case at the end of this chapter.]

Required: Explain how this probably happened.

4-5 The following statement appeared in a recent accounting journal: "If goodwill was a person, she/he would probably stand trial around the world on numerous counts of complicity in undesirable or criminal acts."[5]

Required: Discuss the possible meanings of this statement. [Hint: Read the article to fully understand the main point of the statement.]

4-6 A Dutch company changed its accounting principles in 1971, 1981, and 1989. The profit figures surrounding the years of accounting principle changes appear below in guilders:

	1968	1969	1970	Old 1971	New 1971	1972
Net income	450	520	430	250	350	700

	1978	1979	1980	Old 1981	New 1981	1982
Net income	646	550	330	340	365	450

	1986	1987	1988	Old 1989	New 1989	1990
Net income	900	860	750	600	799	(850)

In addition, the following key information is available:

	1971	1989	1990
Number of employees	380,000	305,000	275,000
Sales	Fl 20,000	Fl 60,000	Fl 55,000
Net income	350	799	(850)
Shareholders' interest	6,800	17,000	12,000
Borrowed capital	14,200	35,000	38,000

Required: Provide possible explanations for the changes in accounting principles.

---

[5] L. Kirkham and J. Arnold, "Goodwill Accounting in the UK," *The European Accounting Review,* vol. 1, no. 2, p. 421.

4-7   Faisal Company, a U.S. entity, has industry segments, A, B, C, and D. During the year, the sales revenue of each segment was as follows (in millions of U.S. dollars):

Segment	Sales Revenue
A	150
B	980
C	590
D	100

Required: Identify the reportable industry segments according to U.S. GAAP, using only the sales revenue criterion. State the basis for your selections.

Case: Tanaguchi Corporation — Identifying Differences between U.S. and Japanese GAAP

ABSTRACT: This case examines the effects of differences in accounting principles between the United States and Japan on financial statements and financial statement ratios. It also illustrates the impact of different economic, strategic, institutional, and cultural factors on interpretations of profitability and risk. It places particular emphasis on the relation between financial and tax reporting, and the importance in Japan of operating through corporate groups, or keiretsu.[6]

Dave Ando and Yoshi Yashima, recent business school graduates, work as research security analysts for a mutual fund specializing in international equity investments. Based on several strategy meetings, senior managers of the fund decided to invest in the machine tool industry. One international company under consideration is Tanaguchi Corporation, a Japanese manufacturer of machine tools. As staff analysts assigned to perform fundamental analysis on all new investment options, Ando and Yashima obtain a copy of Tanaguchi Corporation's unconsolidated financial statements and set out to calculate their usual spreadsheet of financial statement ratios. Exhibit 4–6 presents the results of their efforts. As a basis for comparison, Exhibit 4–6 also presents the median ratios for U.S. machine tool companies for a comparable year. The following conversation ensues.

Dave: Tanaguchi Corporation does not appear to be as profitable as comparable U.S. firms. Its operating margin and rate of return on assets are significantly less than the median ratios for U.S. machine tool operators. Its rate of return on common equity is only slightly less than its U.S. counterparts, but this is at the expense of assuming much more financial leverage and therefore risk. Most of this leverage is in the form of short-term borrowing. You can see this in its higher total liabilities to total assets ratio combined with its lower long-term debt ratio. This short-term borrowing and higher risk are also evidenced by the lower current and quick ratios. Finally, Tanaguchi Corporation's shares are selling at a higher multiple of net income and stockholders' equity than are those of U.S. machine tool companies. I can't see how we can justify paying more for a company that is less profitable and more risky than

[6] Paul R. Brown and Clyde P. Stickney, "Instructional Case: Tanaguchi Corporation," *Issues in Accounting Education,* vol. 7, no. 1, spring 1992, pp. 57-68 (abridged).

comparable U.S. companies. It doesn't seem to me that it is worth exploring this investment possibility any further.

Yoshi: You may be right, Dave. However, I wonder if we are not comparing apples and oranges. As a Japanese company, Tanaguchi Corporation operates in an entirely different institutional and cultural environment than U.S. machine tool companies. Furthermore, it prepares its financial statements in accordance with Japanese generally accepted accounting principles (GAAP), which differ from those in the U.S.

Dave: Well, I think we need to explore this further. I recall seeing a report on an associate's desk comparing U.S. and Japanese accounting principles. I will get a copy for us (Exhibit 4–10).

Required: Using the report comparing U.S. and Japanese accounting principles (Exhibit 4–10) and Tanaguchi Corporation's financial statements and notes (Exhibits 4–7 through 4–9), identify the most important differences between U.S. and Japanese GAAP. Consider both the differences in acceptable methods and in the methods commonly used. For each major difference, indicate the likely effect (increase, decrease, or no effect) on

(1) net income,
(2) total assets, and
(3) the ratio of liabilities divided by stockholders' equity

resulting from converting Tanaguchi's financial statements to U.S. GAAP.

Exhibit 4–6   Comparative Financial Ratio Analysis for Tanaguchi Corporation and U.S. Machine Tool Companies

	Tanaguchi Corporation	Median ratio for U.S. Machine Tool Companies[a]
Profitability ratios		
Operating margin after taxes (before interest expense and related tax effects)	2.8%	3.3%
Total assets turnover	1.5	1.8
= Return on assets	4.2%	5.9%
Common's share of operating earnings[b]	.83	.91
Capital structure leverage[c]	3.8	2.6
= Return on common equity[d]	133.0%	139.0%
Operating margin analysis		
Sales	100.0%	100.0%
Other revenue/sales	.4	—
Cost of goods sold/sales	(73.2)	(69.3)
Selling and administrative/sales	(21.0)	(25.8)
Income taxes/sales	(3.4)	(1.6)
Operating margin (excluding interest and related tax effects)	2.8%	3.3%
Asset turnover analysis		
Receivable turnover	5.1	6.9
Inventory turnover	6.3	5.2
Fixed asset turnover	7.5	7.0
Risk analysis		
Current ratio	1.1	1.6
Quick ratio	.7	.9
Total liabilities/total assets	73.8%	61.1%
Long-term debt/total assets	4.7%	16.1%
Long-term debt/stockholders' equity	17.9%	43.2%
Times interest covered	5.8	3.1
Market price ratios (per common share)		
Market price/net income	45.0	5.7
Market price/stockholders' equity	5.7	1.2

[a] Source: Robert Morris Associates, *Annual Statement Studies* (except price-earnings ratio).
[b] Common's share of operating earnings net income to common/operating income after taxes (before interest expense and related tax effects).
[c] Capital structure leverage = average total assets/average common stockholders' equity.
[d] The amounts for return on common equity may not be precisely equal to the product of return on assets, common's share of operating earnings, and capital structure leverage due to rounding.

Exhibit 4–7 Unconsolidated Balance Sheet—Tanaguchi Corporation

	(in billions of yen) March 31	
Assets	Year 4	Year 5
Current assets		
Cash	¥ 30	¥ 27
Marketable securities (Note 1)	20	25
Notes and accounts receivable (Note 2):		
Trade notes and accounts	200	210
Affiliated company	30	45
Allowance for doubtful accounts	(5)	(7)
Inventories (Note 3)	130	150
Other current assets	25	30
Total current assets	¥ 430	¥ 480
Investments		
Investment in and loans to affiliated companies (Note 4)	¥ 110	¥ 140
Investments in other companies (Note 5)	60	60
Total investments	¥ 170	¥ 200
Property, plant, and equipment (Note 6)		
Land	¥ 25	¥ 25
Buildings	110	130
Machinery and equipment	155	180
Less: Depreciation to date	(140)	(165)
Total property, plant, and equipment	¥ 150	¥ 170
Total assets	¥ 750	¥ 850
Liabilities and Stockholders' Equity		
Current liabilities		
Short-term bank loans	¥ 185	¥ 200
Notes and accounts payable:		
Trade notes and accounts	140	164
Affiliated company	25	20
Other current liabilities	40	50
Total current liabilities	¥ 390	¥ 434
Long-term liabilities		
Bonds payable (Note 7)	¥ 20	¥ 20
Convertible debt	20	20
Retirement and severance allowance (Note 8)	122	153
Total long-term liabilities	¥ 162	¥ 193
Stockholders' equity		
Common stock, ¥ 10 par value	¥ 15	¥ 15
Capital surplus	40	40
Legal reserve (Note 9)	16	17
Retained earnings (Note 9)	127	151
Total stockholders' equity	¥ 198	¥ 223
Total liabilities and stockholders' equity	¥ 750	¥ 850

Exhibit 4–8   Unconsolidated Statement of Income and Retained Earnings —Tanaguchi Corporation

	(in billions of yen) Fiscal Year 5
Revenues	
Sales (Note 10)	¥ 1,200
Interest and dividends (Note 11)	5
Total revenues	¥ 1,205
Expenses	
Cost of goods sold	¥ 878
Selling and administrative	252
Interest	13
Total expenses	¥ 1,143
Income before income taxes	¥ 62
Income taxes (Note 12)	(34)
Net income	¥ 28
Retained earnings	
Balance, beginning of fiscal year 5	¥ 127
Net income	28
Deductions:	
Cash dividends	(3)
Transfer to legal reserve (Note 9)	(1)
Balance, end of fiscal year 5	¥ 151

Exhibit 4–9   Notes to Financial Statements (continued on next page)

Note 1: Marketable securities. Marketable securities appear on the balance sheet at acquisition cost.

Note 2: Accounts receivable. Accounts and notes receivable are noninterest bearing. Within 15 days of sales on open account, customers typically sign noninterest-bearing, single-payment notes. Customers usually pay these notes within 60 to 180 days after signing. When Tanaguchi Corporation needs cash, it discounts these notes with Menji Bank. Tanaguchi Corporation remains contingently liable in the event customers do not pay these notes at maturity. Receivables from (and payable to) affiliated company are with Takahashi Corporation (see Note 4) and are noninterest bearing.

Note 3: Inventories. Inventories appear on the balance sheet at lower of cost or market. The measurement of acquisition cost uses a weighted average cost flow assumption.

Note 4: Investments and loans to affiliated companies. Intercorporate investments appear on the balance sheet at acquisition cost. The balances in this account at the end of Year 4 and Year 5 comprise the following:

	Year 4	Year 5
Investments in Tanaka Corporation (25%)	¥ 15	¥ 15
Investment in Takahashi Corporation (80%)	70	70
Loans to Takahashi Corporation	25	55
	¥ 110	¥ 140

Exhibit 4–9   Notes to Financial Statements (concluded)

Note 5: Investments in other companies. Other investments represent ownership shares of less than 20 percent and appear at acquisition cost.

Note 6: Property, plant, and equipment. Fixed assets appear on the balance sheet at acquisition cost. The firm capitalizes expenditures that increase the service lives of fixed assets, while it expenses immediately expenditures that maintain the originally expected useful lives. It computes depreciation using the declining balance method. Depreciable lives for buildings are 30 to 40 years and for machinery and equipment are 6 to 10 years.

Note 7: Bonds payable. Bonds payable comprises two bond issues as follows:

	Year 4	Year 5
12% semi-annual, 10¥ billion face value bonds, with interest payable on March 31 and September 30 and the principal payable at maturity on March 31, Year 20; the bonds were initially priced on the market to yield 10%, compounded semi-annually	¥ 11.50	¥ 11.45
8% semi-annual, ¥ 10 billion face value bonds, with interest payable on March 31 and September 30 and the principal payable at maturity on March 31, Year 22; the bonds were initially priced on the market to yield 10%, compounded semi-annually	8.50	8.55
	¥ 20.00	¥ 20.00

Note 8: Retirement and severance allowance. The firm provides amounts as a charge against income each year for estimated retirement and severance benefits but does not fund these amounts until it makes actual payments to former employees.

Note 9: Legal reserve and retained earnings. The firm reduces retained earnings and increases the legal reserve account for a specified percentage of dividends paid during the year. The following plan for appropriation of retained earnings was approved by shareholders at the annual meeting held on June 29, Year 5:

Transfer to legal reserve	¥ (1)
Cash dividend	(3)
Directors' and statutory auditors' bonuses	(1)
Elimination of special tax reserve relating to sale of equipment	1

Note 10: Sales revenue. The firm recognizes revenues from sales of machine tools at the time of delivery. Reported sales for Year 5 are net of a provision for doubtful accounts of ¥ 50 billion.

Note 11: Interest and dividend revenue. Interest and dividend revenue includes ¥ 1.5 billion from loans to Takahashi Corporation, an unconsolidated subsidiary.

Note 12: Income tax expenses. The firm computes income taxes based on a statutory tax rate of 55 percent for Year 5.

Exhibit 4–10   Comparison of U.S. and Japanese GAAP (page 1 of 5)

1. Standard-setting process

U.S.   The U.S. Congress has the legal authority to prescribe acceptable accounting principles, but it has delegated that authority to the Securities and Exchange Commission (SEC). The SEC has stated that it will recognize pronouncements of the Financial Accounting Standards Board (FASB), a private-sector entity, as the primary vehicle for specifying generally accepted accounting standards.

Japan   The Japanese Diet has the legal authority to prescribe acceptable accounting principles. All Japanese corporations (both publicly and privately held) must periodically issue financial statements to their stockholders following provisions of the Japanese Commercial Code. This Code is promulgated by the Diet. The financial statements follow strict legal entity concepts.

Publicly listed corporations in Japan must also file financial statements with the Securities Division of the Ministry of Finance following accounting principles promulgated by the Diet in the Securities and Exchange Law. The Diet, through the Ministry of Finance, obtains advice on accounting principles from the Business Advisory Deliberations Council (BADC), a body composed of representatives from business, the accounting profession, and personnel from the Ministry of Finance. The BADC has no authority on its own to set acceptable accounting principles. The financial statements filed with the Securities Division of the Ministry of Finance tend to follow economic entity concepts, with intercorporate investments either accounted for using the equity method or consolidated.

All Japanese corporations file income tax returns with the Taxation Division of the Ministry of Finance. The accounting principles followed in preparing tax returns mirror closely those used in preparing financial statements for stockholders under the Japanese Commercial Code. The Minister of Finance will sometimes need to reconcile conflicting preferences of the Securities Division (desiring financial information better reflecting economic reality) and the Taxation Division (desiring to raise adequate tax revenues to run the government).

2. Principal financial statements

U.S.   Balance sheet, income statement, statement of cash flows.

Japan   Balance sheet, income statement, proposal for appropriation of profit or disposition of loss. The financial statements filed with the Ministry of Finance contain some supplemental information on cash flows.

3. Income statement

U.S.   Accrual basis.

Japan   Accrual basis.

4. Revenue recognition

U.S.   Generally at time of sale; percentage-of-completion method usually required on long-term contracts; installment and cost-recovery-first methods permitted when there is high uncertainty regarding cash collectibility.

Exhibit 4–10   Comparison of U.S. and Japanese GAAP (page 2 of 5)

Japan   Generally at time of sale; percentage-of-completion method permitted on long-term contracts; installment method common when collection period exceeds two years regardless of degree of uncertainty of cash collectibility.

5. Uncollectible accounts

U.S.   Allowance method.

Japan   Allowance method.

6. Inventories and cost of goods sold

U.S.   Inventories valued at lower of cost or market. Cost determined by FIFO, LIFO, weighted average, or standard cost. Most firms use FIFO, LIFO, or a combination of the two.

Japan   Inventories valued at lower of cost or market. Cost determined by specific identification, FIFO, LIFO, weighted average, or standard cost. Most firms use weighted average or specific identification.

7. Fixed assets and depreciation expense

U.S.   Fixed assets valued at acquisition cost. Depreciation computed using straight line, declining balance, and sum-of-the-years'-digits methods. Permanent declines in value are recognized. Most firms use straight line for financial reporting and an accelerated method for tax reporting.

Japan   Fixed assets valued at acquisition cost. Depreciation computed using straight line, declining balance, and sum-of-the-years'-digits methods. Permanent declines in value are recognized. Most firms use a declining method for financial and tax reporting.

8. Intangible assets and amortization expense

U.S.   Internally developed intangibles expensed when expenditures are made. Externally purchased intangibles capitalized as assets and amortized over expected useful life (not to exceed 40 years). Goodwill cannot be amortized for tax purposes.

Japan   The cost of intangibles (both internally developed and externally purchased) can be expensed when incurred or capitalized and amortized over the period allowed for tax purposes (generally 5 to 20 years). Goodwill is amortized over 5 years. Some intangibles (e.g., property rights) are not amortized.

9. Liabilities related to estimated expenses
   (warranties, vacation pay, employee bonuses)

U.S.   Estimated amount recognized as an expense and as a liability. Actual expenditures are charged against the liability.

Japan   Estimated amount recognized as an expense and as a liability. Actual expenditures are charged against the liability. Annual bonuses paid to members of the Board of Directors and to the Commercial Code auditors are not considered expenses, but a distribution of profits. Consequently, such bonuses are charged against retained earnings.

Exhibit 4–10   Comparison of U.S. and Japanese GAAP (page 3 of 5)

10. Liabilities related to employee retirement and severance benefits

U.S.   Liability recognized for unfunded accumulated benefits.

Japan   Severance benefits more common than pension benefits. An estimated amount is recognized each period as an expense and as a liability for financial reporting. The maximum liability recognized equals 40 percent of the amount payable if all eligible employees were terminated currently. There is wide variability in the amount recognized. Benefits are deducted for tax purposes only when actual payments are made to severed employees. Such benefits are seldom funded beforehand.

11. Liabilities related to income taxes

U.S.   Income tax expense based on book income amounts. Deferred tax expense and deferred tax liability recognized for temporary (timing) differences between book and taxable income.

Japan   Income tax expense based on taxable income amounts. Deferred tax accounting not practiced. In consolidated statements submitted to the Ministry of Finance by listed companies (see No. 18), deferred tax accounting is permitted.

12. Noninterest-bearing notes

U.S.   Notes stated at present value of future cash flows and interest recognized over term of the note.

Japan   Notes stated at face amount and no interest recognized over term of the note. Commonly used as a substitute for Accounts Payable.

13. Bond discount or premium

U.S.   Subtracted from or added to the face value of the bond and reported among liabilities on the balance sheet. Amortized over the life of the bond as an adjustment to interest expense.

Japan   Bond discount usually included among intangible assets and amortized over the life of the bonds. Bond discount and premium may also be subtracted from or added to face value of bonds on the balance sheet and amortized as an adjustment of interest expense over the life of the bonds.

14. Leases

U.S.   Distinction made between operating leases (not capitalized) and capital leases (capitalized).

Japan   All leases treated as operating leases.

15. Legal reserve (part of shareholders' equity)

U.S.   Not applicable.

Japan   When dividends are declared and paid, unappropriated retained earnings and cash are reduced by the amount of the dividend. In addition, unappropriated retained earnings are reduced and the legal reserve account is increased by a percentage of this dividend, usually 10 percent, until such time as the legal

---

Exhibit 4–10   Comparison of U.S. and Japanese GAAP (page 4 of 5)

reserve equals 25 percent of stated capital. The effect of the latter entry is to capitalize a portion of retained earnings to make it part of permanent capital.

16. Appropriations of retained earnings

U.S.   Not a common practice in the U.S. Appropriations have no legal status when they do appear.

Japan   Stockholders must approve, each year, the proposal for appropriation of profit or disposition of loss. Four items commonly appear: dividend declarations, annual bonuses for directors and Commercial Code auditors, transfers to legal reserves, and changes in reserves.

The income tax law permits certain costs to be deducted earlier for tax than for financial reporting and permits certain gains to be recognized later for tax than for financial reporting. To obtain these tax benefits, the tax law requires that these items be reflected on the company's books. The pretax effect of these timing differences do not appear on the income statement. Instead, an entry is made decreasing unappropriated retained earnings and increasing special retained earnings reserves (a form of appropriated retained earnings). When the timing difference reverses, the above entry is reversed. The tax effects of these timing differences do appear on the income statement, however. In the year that the timing difference originates, income tax expense and income tax payable are reduced by the tax effect of the timing difference. When the timing difference reverses, income tax expense and income tax payable are increased by a corresponding amount.

17. Treasury stock

U.S.   Shown at acquisition cost as a subtraction from total shareholders' equity. No income recognized from treasury stock transactions.

Japan   Reacquired shares are either cancelled immediately or shown as a current asset on the balance sheet. Dividends "received" on treasury shares are included in income.

18. Investments in securities

A. Marketable securities (current asset)

U.S.   Lower of cost or market method.

Japan   Reported at acquisition cost, unless price declines are considered permanent, in which case lower of cost or market.

B. Investments (noncurrent asset)

U.S.   Accounting depends on ownership: Less than 20%, lower of cost or market; 20% to 50%, equity method; greater than 50%, consolidated.

Japan   The principal financial statements are those of the parent company only (that is, unconsolidated statements). Intercorporate investments are carried at acquisition cost. Listed companies must provide consolidated financial statements as supplements to the principal statements in filings to the Ministry of Finance. The accounting for investments in securities in these supplementary statements is essentially the same as in the U.S.

Exhibit 4–10 Comparison of U.S. and Japanese GAAP (page 5 of 5)

19. Corporate acquisitions
U.S.   Purchase method or pooling of interests method.

Japan   Purchase method.

20. Foreign currency translation
U.S.   The translation method depends on whether the foreign unit operates as a self-contained entity (all-current method) or as an extension of the U.S. parent (monetary/nonmonetary method).

Japan   For branches, the monetary/nonmonetary translation method is used, with any translation adjustment flowing through income. For subsidiaries, current monetary items are translated using the current rate, other balance sheet items use the historical rate, and the translation adjustment is part of shareholders' equity.

21. Segment reporting
U.S.   Segment information (sales, operating income, assets) disclosed by industry segment, geographical location, and type of customer.

Japan   Beginning in 1990, sales data by segment (industry, geographical location) are required. No disclosure by type of customer.

Sources: The Japanese Institute of Certified Public Accountants, *Corporate Disclosure in Japan* (July 1987); KPMG Peat Marwick, *Comparison of Japanese and U.S. Reporting and Financial Practices* (1989).

References

Accounting Comparisons UK/Europe—I. London: Coopers & Lybrand Deloitte, 1990.

AlHashim, Dhia D., and Jeffrey S. Arpan. *International Dimensions of Accounting.* 3d ed. Boston: PWS-Kent Publishing Company, 1992.

Anderson, Nancy. "The Globalization GAAP." *Management Accounting,* August 1993, pp. 52-54.

Brazil: International Tax and Business Guide. New York: Deloitte Touche Tohmatsu International, 1993.

Canada: International Tax and Business Guide. New York: Deloitte Touche Tohmatsu International, 1994.

Coopers & Lybrand. *The Accounting Profession in Nigeria.* New York: American Institute of Certified Public Accountants, 1993.

———. *International Accounting Summaries.* 2d. ed. New York: John Wiley & Sons, Inc., 1993.

Corbridge, Curtis L., Walter W. Austin, and David J. Lemak. "Germany's Accrual Accounting Practices." *Management Accounting,* August 1993, pp. 45-47.

Galaz, Gomez-Mortin, Chavero, Yamazaki, S. C., and Deloitte & Touche. *The Accounting Profession in Mexico.* 2d ed., rev. New York: American Institute of Certified Public Accountants, 1992.

Gumbel, Peter, and Greg Steinmetz. "German Firms Shift to More-Open Accounting." *Wall Street Journal,* 15 March 1995, pp. C1, C10.

Guy Barbier & Associés. *The Accounting Profession in France.* 2d ed., rev. New York: American Institute of Certified Public Accountants, 1992.

Haried, A., L. Haried, and R. Smith. *Advanced Accounting.* New York: John Wiley & Sons, Inc., 1991.

International Accounting Standard 27. "Consolidated Financial Statements and Accounting for Investment in Subsidiaries." London: International Accounting Standards Committee, 1994.

Khalaf, Roula. "Free Style Accounting." *Forbes,* 1 March 1993, pp. 102-103.

Lee, Tom. "Mark to Market: The U.K. Experience." *Journal of Accountancy,* September 1994, pp. 84-86, 88.

Mortensen, Roger. "Accounting for Business Combinations in the Global Economy: Purchase, Pooling, or ———?" *Journal of Accounting Education,* winter 1994, pp. 81-87.

Purvis, S. E. C., Helen Gernon, and Michael A. Diamond. "The IASC and Its Comparability Project: Prerequisites for Success." *Accounting Horizons,* June 1991, pp. 25-44.

Ramin, Kurt P. "Where We Stand in Mexico." *Financial Executive,* March/April, 1993, p. 19.

Saudagaran, S., and M. Solomon. "Worldwide Regulatory Disclosure Requirements," in F. Choi (ed.), *Handbook of International Accounting.* New York: John Wiley & Sons, Inc., 1991.

Statement of Accounting Standards No. 1. "Disclosure of Accounting Policies." Lagos, Nigeria: Nigerian Accounting Standards Board, 1984.

Statement of Accounting Standards No. 2. "Information to be Disclosed in Financial Statements." Lagos, Nigeria: Nigerian Accounting Standards Board, 1984.

Statement of Financial Accounting Concepts No. 1. "Objectives of Financial Reporting by Business Enterprises." Stamford, Conn.: Financial Accounting Standards Board, 1978.

Statement of Financial Accounting Concepts No. 6. "Elements of Financial Statements." Stamford, Conn.: Financial Accounting Standards Board, December 1985, pp. ix-x.

Statement of Financial Accounting Standards No. 14. "Financial Reporting for Segments of a Business Enterprise." Stamford, Conn.: Financial Accounting Standards Board, 1976.

Statement of Financial Accounting Standards No. 94. "Consolidation of All Majority-Owned Subsidiaries." Stamford, Conn.: Financial Accounting Standards Board, 1987.

Survey of International Accounting Practices. Chicago: Arthur Andersen & Co. 1991.

United Kingdom: International Tax and Business Guide. New York: Deloitte Touche Tohmatsu International, 1995.

Chapter 5

Accounting for Changing Prices

We assume in accounting theory that the monetary unit is stable over time, inflation does not exist, and a dollar, a yen, or a franc is worth the same today as it was many years ago. This assumption is important for the historical cost model. Of course, this is not the case in reality, especially in most of the developing countries. In Brazil, for example, the inflation rate in 1991 was an amazing 1,800 percent.

In light of the realities faced by many economies today, the historical cost model has been criticized for failing to take economic factors into account. Critics argue that failure to consider general or specific price changes makes comparability among statements difficult.

General Versus Specific Price Indexes

General Price Index

A **general price index** is constructed by taking the prices of a "basket" of goods and averaging them at a certain point in time. This average is then compared with the average price of those same goods at some base period. We can thus estimate the amount of inflation or deflation. In the United States, a widely used index is the Consumer Price Index for all Urban Consumers.

Example Exhibit 5–1 illustrates the construction of a general price index. To keep it simple, the basket consists of only five goods and their respective prices in the years 1995 and 1990. Prices for this group of consumer goods increased an average of 24 percent. However, while prices of four of the items increased, the price of plastic wrap actually decreased by 16 percent. A general price index incorporates the collective change in prices of a group of items rather than the change in price of a single item.

Exhibit 5–1	Construction of a General Price Index		
Item	**1995**	**1990**	**Change (%)**
Margarine (16 oz.)	$ 1.00	$ 0.90	+11
Plastic wrap (one roll)	1.60	1.90	-16
Milk (half gallon)	1.50	1.20	+25
Fish (1 lb.)	3.00	1.75	+71
Bread (loaf)	1.27	1.00	+27
	$ 8.37	$ 6.75	
Price index (1990 base year)	124*	100	

*100 × ($8.37 ÷ $6.75) = 124

Specific Price Index

The price of a specific good may or may not be affected by changes in general price levels. It may depend mostly on its supply and demand. In the United States, while prices of most goods have risen in recent years, prices of personal computers have decreased. A **specific price index** shows the price changes for a specific good or service over time. One way to determine the specific price for a good is to ascertain the current cost of that item or, alternatively, what it would cost to replace. For example, the cost of a building may require the use of a construction index. One would have to approximate the cost of labor, materials, and overhead in order to approximate the replacement cost of a building. Many specific indexes are published by industry groups.

Valuation Problems with Changing Prices

As mentioned in the introduction to this chapter, prices are assumed to be stable under the historical cost model. The central flaw in this model, however, is that it combines monetary units of different dimensions. Monetary units at different times have different purchasing power; when these units are combined, financial statements are distorted.

Example   Assume machine A was purchased five years ago and machine B was purchased today, each at a cost of $5,000. The machinery account balance would be $10,000. However, since the dollar buys only half of what it bought five years ago, the $10,000 balance in the machinery account is misleading.

Now suppose that the machinery is depreciated by applying a 10 percent annual rate to the $10,000. The annual depreciation is $1,000. Of this amount, $500 applies to machine A and $500 applies to machine B. However, these are dollars of different dimensions. Though easy to compute, the amount is meaningless. We are referring to two pieces of equipment that were purchased when the dollar had different values. When we try to match revenue with expenses, the problem arises again—the $500 depreciation expense in each case relates to a different purchasing power.

The accounting profession has been struggling with the problem of changing prices for many decades. The German economy had extremely high inflation rates in the 1920s. After World War II, increasing prices caused financial reporting problems in the U.S. In recent years inflation has been moderate in most industrialized economies, while high inflation rates have been common in developing countries. According to the International Monetary Fund (IMF), global prices rose at the rate of 23.3 percent in 1994. However, this average figure hides the fact that the rate of inflation in industrialized countries is much lower than the global average, while in developing countries the rate is much higher. This is depicted in Figure 5–1.

An analysis by the IMF from 1991 through 1994 reveals contrasting trends. During this period consumer price inflation dropped from a 4.2 percent annual rate to 2.6 percent in the U.S., and from 5.6 percent to 0.2 percent in Canada. During the same four-year period, inflation rates doubled in two regions: Latin America and Africa. This is because central banks in industrialized countries have used monetary policy to curb inflation by limiting money-supply growth. The major concern of central banks in most developing countries, however, is to finance economic development projects or provide resources for operating public sector enterprises.[1] Not all developing countries have high inflation. Over the past decade many fast-developing countries such as Singapore, Malaysia, Taiwan, and Thailand have managed to achieve spectacular economic development with low inflation and high savings rates.

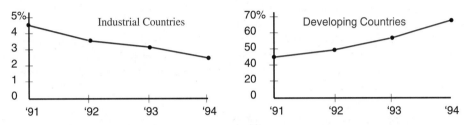

Source: *Business Week,* 8 May 1995, p. 28. Data from International Monetary Fund.

Figure 5-1   Inflation: Thriving in the Third World

Not all developing countries have high inflation. Over the past decade many fast-developing countries such as Singapore, Malaysia, Taiwan, and Thailand have managed to achieve spectacular economic development with low inflation and high savings rates.

Tight monetary policy, resulting in high interest rates, is effective in controlling inflation. At the same time, it fuels consumer demand for goods and services. This has two potential consequences. First, rising consumer demand may increase imports. Second, the strong currency (due to the low inflation rate) puts the country at a relative disadvantage in exporting its goods. The combined effect of the two can create a trade deficit for the country. This dilemma is currently being faced by countries such as Taiwan and Israel. Figure 5–2 depicts the potential consequences of a tight monetary policy.

Figure 5-2   Potential Impact of Tight Monetary Policy

The ever-present challenge is to find a balance between acceptable levels of inflation while maintaining economic growth and competitiveness in world markets.

---

[1]   Christopher Farrell, "Inflation's Uneven Spread," *Business Week,* 8 May 1995, p. 28.

Monetary Items

A **monetary item** is either cash or another asset or liability that will be received or paid out in a fixed number of monetary units. In a balance sheet restated for changes in the general purchasing power of the monetary unit, monetary items are included based on their current amounts.

During an inflationary period, a holder of monetary assets experiences a holding loss because such assets, representing a fixed number of monetary units, will have less purchasing power in the future. A debtor owing monetary liabilities will have a gain through making payment in a fixed number of monetary units of lesser purchasing power. In an income statement adjusted for price level changes, the gain or loss from holding monetary items appears as a monetary gain or loss.

Nonmonetary Items

A **nonmonetary item** is one that does not represent a claim to, or for, a specified number of monetary units. Examples of nonmonetary items include inventory, equipment, land, common stock, and retained earnings. In price-level adjusted financial statements, nonmonetary items are adjusted for changes in *general* purchasing power. Exhibit 5–2 shows how the historical cost of land in nominal dollars would be restated in constant dollars, denoted C$ in this chapter. Note that these constant-dollar amounts are still a form of historical cost; the C$ 200,000 amount in the 12/31/99 column is simply the original $100,000 cost at 12/31/79 adjusted to reflect a doubling in the general price level over the twenty-year period since the land was acquired.[2]

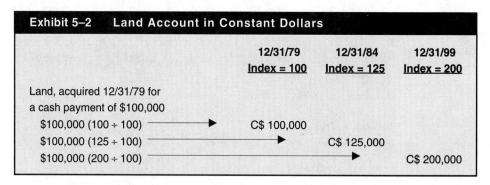

For students, salary levels provide an example that is closer to home. Assume that starting salaries for accounting graduates five years ago averaged $26,000 per year. You are told that average for current graduates is $30,000. At first, this sounds like an improvement. But is it? Not if we find that there was 25 percent inflation during this period. In today's terms,

---

[2] For simplicity in this example, the base period index has been assumed to be 100, making it easy to see that the adjustment ratio at 12/31/99, (200 ÷ 100), reflects a doubling of the general price level. More typically, the indexes are less convenient; a current index of 180.4 and a base index of 90.2 also reflects the same doubling. In general, the adjustment ratio is the current index divided by the base index. Multiplying the historical cost by this ratio yields the historical cost expressed in current dollars.

$26,000 would mean $26,000 \times (125 \div 100) = $32,500, $2,500 *less* than it was five years ago.[3]

Constant Monetary Unit Restatement

Constant monetary unit restatement is a general term for restating financial statements for changes in purchasing power of the monetary unit. In the United Kingdom, accountants use the term **current purchasing power accounting**. In the United States, accountants refer to **constant dollar accounting** or **general price-level accounting**. The rest of this section contains a brief summary of the steps involved in constant unit restatement. The subsequent section provides a comprehensive example.[4]

Balance Sheet

The starting point for the restatement process is usually the balance sheet. The basic steps are as follows:

- Identify assets and equities as either monetary or nonmonetary.
- Extend monetary items at their face (nominal) amounts.
- Adjust nonmonetary items for changes in purchasing power since their acquisition.
- Roll-forward prior year balances. If price-level adjusted statements were prepared for the previous year, all balances to be used for comparison with the current year must be rolled forward, i.e., expressed in terms of current-year price levels. So if there was 10 percent inflation, all balances in all prior-year statements would be multiplied by 110 percent.

Income Statement

The income statement is normally adjusted after the balance sheet, since cost of goods sold uses the adjusted inventory balances and depreciation is based on adjusted plant and equipment amounts. The basic idea is that events are adjusted from the price levels in effect at the time they occurred to year-end levels.

- Identify and adjust material items using the price indexes in effect at the date each item was acquired.
- Compute depreciation based on adjusted historical cost.
- Adjust items that can be assumed to occur evenly throughout the year, such as sales and purchases, using an average index.

---

[3] Adjustments for inflation are made so that amounts are expressed in current dollars. Restatement in terms of purchasing power at some prior date *could* be done. But we all tend to think in terms of today's purchasing power, and rarely is there a basis for selecting a particular prior date.

[4] This summary of steps and the following comprehensive example assume that the unadjusted financial statements are expressed in the parent company currency, and that the price indices used are drawn from the parent company's country. There are significant issues as to whether adjustments for inflation should be made in subsidiary statements *before* translation (using the foreign country's price-level index) or *after* translation (using the parent country's price level index). Discussion of these issues is beyond the scope of this text.

- Compute cost of goods sold, using the price-level adjusted beginning and ending inventories developed when adjusting the balance sheet and the adjusted purchases amount from the preceding step.
- Calculate the purchasing power gain or loss from holding monetary items.

Illustration of Constant Monetary Unit Restatement

Exhibit 5–3 (page 145) shows comparative balance sheets for December 31, 1995 and December 31, 1994 for Osaka Corporation. The income statement for the year ended December 31, 1995 is shown in Exhibit 5–4 (page 146). *Both statements are in nominal dollars.* In the following illustration we will be preparing a price-level adjusted balance sheet for December 31, 1995, and a price-level adjusted income statement for the year 1995. The assumed indexes for consumer prices at pertinent dates are in Exhibit 5–5 (page 146).

Restatement of Balance Sheet

Exhibit 5–6 (page 147) shows the restated balance sheet for Osaka Corporation at December 31, 1995.

Monetary items. *Cash, accounts receivable, and all payables* are monetary items. Thus, they are extended to the constant-dollar balance sheet at the face amount because that is what Osaka Corporation will receive or pay out.

Nonmonetary items. *Inventories* have to be adjusted to reflect the change in purchasing power. To do this requires knowing when the goods were purchased. Ending inventories are assumed to have been acquired evenly throughout the last quarter of the year.

Property, plant, and equipment requires breaking apart these accounts according to the acquisition dates.

Common stock and additional paid-in capital are adjusted using the index in the year the capital stock was sold.

Retained earnings is the difference between the restated assets and all other restated equities. In restating, it is a "plug" figure.

Restatement of Income Statement

Exhibit 5–7 (page 148) shows the 1995 income statement of Osaka Corporation restated to constant dollars.

Items with specific dates. Equipment purchased in 1989 with an original cost of $15,000 and accumulated depreciation at date of sale of $5,000 was sold in June 1995 for $5,000. The loss on sale of equipment was restated as follows:

Selling price: $5,000 × (150 ÷ 138)	C$ 5,435
Less book value ($15,000 − 5,000) × (150 ÷ 107)	14,019
Constant dollar loss on sale	C$ 8,584

Exhibit 5–3   Comparative Balance Sheets (Nominal Dollars)

Osaka Corporation
Comparative Balance Sheets
December 31, 1995 and 1994

	1995	1994
Assets		
Current assets:		
Cash	$ 30,000	$ 10,000
Accounts receivable (net)	100,000	90,000
Inventories (FIFO)	120,000	100,000
Total current assets	250,000	200,000
Property, plant, and equipment:		
Land	100,000	100,000
Building (net of accumulated depreciation)	200,000	220,000
Equipment (net of accumulated depreciation)	130,000	120,000
Total property, plant, and equipment	430,000	440,000
Total assets	$ 680,000	$ 640,000
Equities		
Current liabilities:		
Accounts payable	$ 100,000	$ 50,000
Salaries payable	50,000	70,000
Total current liabilities	150,000	120,000
Bonds payable	300,000	300,000
Total liabilities	450,000	420,000
Stockholders' equity:		
Common stock ($1 par value, 100,000 shares issued & outstanding)	100,000	100,000
Additional paid-in capital	20,000	20,000
Retained earnings	110,000	100,000
Total stockholders' equity	230,000	220,000
Total liabilities and stockholders' equity	$ 680,000	$ 640,000

Depreciation. Details of the depreciation restatement appear in Exhibit 5–7. Note that the $28,571 adjusted depreciation on the building represents the portion of original cost, expressed in current purchasing power, that is charged to expense in the current year.

Items spread throughout the year. Revenues, selling and administrative expenses, interest expense, and income tax expense are assumed to have occurred evenly throughout the year. Accordingly, these items are adjusted to year-end dollars using the average price index for the year.

Exhibit 5–4	Income Statement (Nominal Dollars)

Osaka Corporation
Income Statement
for the Year Ended December 31, 1995

Revenues		$ 530,000
Expenses:		
Cost of goods sold	$ 360,000	
Selling and administrative	60,000	
Depreciation	30,000	
Interest	30,000	
Loss on sale of equipment	5,000	
Income taxes	15,000	500,000
Net income		$ 30,000

Exhibit 5–5	Index of Consumer Prices at Various Dates

Date	Index	Date	Index
January 1985 (corporation formed and land purchased)	100	January 1995	130
		February 1995	132
Average for the year 1986 (building constructed)	*105.0*	March 1995	134
		April 1995	135
April 1989 (equipment purchased)	107	May 1995 (equipment purchased)	136
		June 1995 (equipment sold)	138
November 1992 (equipment purchased)	115	July 1995	139
		August 1995	141
October 1994	120	September 1995	144
November 1994	122	October 1995	146
December 1994	125	November 1995	148
		December 1995	150
Average for 4th quarter 1994 (beginning inventory acquired)	*122.3*	*Average for 1995*	*139.4*
		Average for 4th quarter 1995 (ending inventory acquired)	*148.0*

Cost of goods sold. The calculation of constant dollar cost of goods sold, shown in Exhibit 5–8 (page 148), is based on the assumptions that beginning and ending inventories were acquired at the average price levels in effect during the last quarters of 1994 and 1995, respectively. Purchases are assumed to have been acquired at the average price level in effect throughout the 1995 year.

Purchasing power gain or loss. Purchasing power gains or losses arise from holding monetary items during times when the general purchasing power of the unit changes. Exhibit

Exhibit 5–6   Restatement of Balance Sheet to Constant Dollars

Osaka Corporation
Restatement of Balance Sheet from Nominal to Constant Dollars
December 31, 1995

	Nominal Dollars	Ratio	Constant Dollars
Assets			
Current assets:			
Cash	$ 30,000	150/150	C$ 30,000
Accounts receivable (net)	100,000	150/150	100,000
Inventories	120,000	Exhibit 5–8	121,622
Total current assets	250,000		251,622
Property, plant, and equipment:			
Land	100,000	150/100	150,000
Building (net)	200,000	150/105	285,714
Equipment (net)			
1989 purchase	76,000	150/107	106,542
1992 purchase	25,000	150/115	32,609
1995 purchase	29,000	150/136	31,985
Total property, plant, and equipment	430,000		606,850
Total assets	$ 680,000		C$ 858,472
Equities			
Current liabilities:			
Accounts payable	$ 100,000	150/150	C$ 100,000
Salaries payable	50,000	150/150	50,000
Total current liabilities	150,000		150,000
Bonds payable	300,000	150/150	300,000
Total liabilities	450,000		450,000
Stockholders' equity:			
Common stock ($1 par value, 100,000			
shares issued and outstanding)	100,000	150/100	150,000
Additional paid-in capital	20,000	150/100	30,000
Retained earnings	110,000	Plug	228,472
Total stockholders' equity	230,000		408,472
Total equities	$ 680,000		C$ 858,472

Exhibit 5–7　Restatement of Income Statement to Constant Dollars

Osaka Corporation
Restatement of Income Statement from Nominal to Constant Dollars
for the Year Ended December 31, 1995

	Nominal Dollars	Ratio	Constant Dollars
Revenues	$ 530,000	150/139.4	C$ 570,301
Expenses:			
Cost of goods sold	360,000	Exhibit 5–8	409,922
Selling and administrative	60,000	150/139.4	64,562
Depreciation:			
1986 building acquisition	20,000	150/105	28,571
1989 acquisitions	4,000	150/107	5,607
1992 acquisition	5,000	150/115	6,522
1995 acquisition	1,000	150/136	1,103
Interest	30,000	150/139.4	32,281
Loss on sale of equipment	5,000	See text	8,584
Income taxes	15,000	150/139.4	16,141
Total expenses	500,000		573,293
Income (loss) before purchasing power gain or loss			(2,992)
Purchasing power gain on net monetary position		Exhibit 5–9	63,231
Net income	$ 30,000		C$ 60,239

Exhibit 5–8　Restatement of Cost of Goods Sold to Constant Dollars

Osaka Corporation
Restatement of Cost of Goods Sold from Nominal to Constant Dollars
for the Year Ended December 31, 1995

	Nominal Dollars	Ratio	Constant Dollars
Beginning inventories	$ 100,000	150/122.3	C$ 122,649
Purchases	380,000	150/139.4	408,895
Available for sale	480,000		531,544
Less ending inventories	120,000	150/148	121,622
Cost of goods sold	$ 360,000		C$ 409,922

5–9 displays the computation of, in this case, a purchasing power gain. Osaka Corporation paid $20,000 in dividends at the end of 1995.

Exhibit 5–9	Purchasing Power Gain or Loss

Osaka Corporation
Calculation of Purchasing Power Gain or Loss
for the Year Ended December 31, 1995

	Nominal Dollars	Ratio	Constant Dollars
Net monetary position, January 1, 1995*	$ (320,000)	150/125	C$(384,000)
Increases in net monetary assets from:			
Sales	530,000	150/139.4	570,301
Sale of equipment	5,000	See text	5,435
	535,000		575,736
Decreases in net monetary assets from:			
Purchases of inventories	380,000	150/139.4	408,895
Selling & administrative expenses	60,000	150/139.4	64,562
Interest expense	30,000	150/139.4	32,281
Income taxes	15,000	150/139.4	16,141
Dividend payments	20,000	150/150.0	20,000
Equipment purchase	30,000	150/136.0	33,088
	535,000		574,967
Net monetary position, December 31, 1995	$ (320,000)		C$ (383,231)
Less: *nominal-dollar* net monetary position, December 31, 1995			(320,000)
Purchasing power gain			C$ 63,231
*Monetary assets:			
Cash and accounts receivable (net)	$ 100,000		
Monetary liabilities:			
Accounts payable, salaries payable, and bonds payable	(420,000)		
Net monetary position	$ (320,000)		

Osaka Corporation had a purchasing power gain for 1995 because the company owed more than it was owed during a time of rising prices. *This means paying net debt with cheaper dollars*. Gain is computed as follows:

- Determine the net monetary position at the beginning of the year.
- Analyze all transactions that affect monetary items and restate each of those using the appropriate index. For example, in the case of sales, cash and receivables are increased thus increasing monetary assets.

- Add or subtract the adjusted amounts to arrive at the constant dollar net monetary position.
- The difference between the year-end net monetary positions in nominal versus constant dollars is the purchasing power gain or loss.

Evaluation of Constant Monetary Unit Accounting

Although constant monetary unit accounting provides comparative information on the effect of inflation across firms, inflation affects firms differently. The degree of inflation is a function of the composition of assets and equities. Highly leveraged firms experience monetary gains during inflationary times.

Constant monetary unit financial statements are not designed to provide information on specific prices of goods and services. In order to have this type of information, it is necessary to use current value accounting.

Constant monetary unit accounting has been used commonly in South America for many years. The current trend, however, appears to be toward adoption of a current value approach. For example, Argentina used to require general price-level adjustment. A resolution now requires use of current value accounting for periods beginning on or after January 1, 1993. Exhibit 5–10 contains the note from the 1993 consolidated annual report of Teléfonos De México S.A. de C.V. dealing with adjustments for changing prices.

Current Value Accounting

The terms **current value accounting** or **current cost accounting** include all valuation systems designed to express specific prices. Current value financial statements show the effects of changes in prices of individual items. There are various definitions of current value based on either input prices or output prices. Replacement cost is an input price type of measurement, whereas current value at which assets could be sold is an example of an output price or exit measurement. The procedures for reflecting input or output prices are the same.

Cash and accounts receivable are generally stated at their cash or cash equivalent value. Other assets are adjusted, as necessary, to reflect their current value. In some cases, particularly with regard to fixed assets, a specific price index to approximate a form of current value may be employed. Alternately, independent market appraisals or an assignment of current value by the board of directors may be used. Most current liabilities will be shown at the face amount. Long-term debt will require a present value calculation. The excess of current value of assets over current value of liabilities equals stockholders' equity. Amounts in the income statement are restated to approximate their current value.

Gearing Adjustments

Many current value accounting models incorporate a gearing adjustment. The **gearing adjustment**, made in the income statement, relates to the effect of inflation. Though different

Exhibit 5–10   Teléfonos De México Inflation Adjustments

Recognition of the effects of inflation on financial information

The Company recognizes the effects of inflation on financial information as required by Mexican Accounting Principles Bulletin B-10 ("Accounting Recognition of the Effects of Inflation on Financial Information"), as amended. Consequently, the amounts shown in the financial statements and in these notes are expressed in Mexican new pesos with purchasing power at the date of the latest financial statements presented (December 31, 1993). The December 31, 1993 restatement factor applied to the financial statements at December 31, 1992 was 8.01%.

Property, plant and equipment and construction in progress are restated using the specific-cost method. Depreciation is calculated on the restated investment at the beginning of the year using the retirement and replacement method.

Inventories are valued at average cost and restated on the basis of specific costs. Capital accounts, premium on the sale of shares, and retained earnings were re-

stated using adjustment factors based on the Mexican national consumer price index (NCPI).

The excess or deficit from restatement of stockholders' equity consists of the accumulated monetary position loss at the time the provisions of Bulletin B-10 were first applied (NPs. 3,125,587 at December 31, 1993) and of the result of holding nonmonetary assets, which represents the net difference between restatement by the specific-cost method and restatement based on the NCPI.

The monetary effect represents the impact of inflation on monetary assets and liabilities. The net monetary effect for each year is included in the statement of income as a part of the integral cost of financing.

Source: Teléfonos De México S.A. de C.V., *Annual Report 1993*, pp. 58-59.

current value accounting models have their own version of the gearing adjustment, the basic idea is the same.

This adjustment recognizes that it is not necessary to make the current cost adjustments for operating assets to the extent that they are financed by creditors. When average borrowings are greater than average monetary assets, the stockholders are in a favorable position during inflationary economic conditions. Expressed differently, the loss of an entity's creditors due to eroding purchasing power of monetary unit is a gain to the stockholders. Therefore, income is increased by making a gearing credit. In situations where the amount of average monetary assets is greater than average borrowing, a gearing charge is made to income statement, thereby reducing the income amount.

The amounts for gearing adjustment are computed by multiplying the ratio of average borrowing to average operating assets with the current value adjustments such as for current cost of goods sold, and current cost of depreciation:

$$\text{Gearing adjustment} \quad = \quad \frac{\text{Average borrowing}}{\text{Average operating assets}} \quad \times \quad \begin{array}{l} \text{Total current value adjustments} \\ \text{made (for cost of goods sold,} \\ \text{depreciation, etc.)} \end{array}$$

A gearing adjustment thereby takes into account the effect of inflation while applying a current value accounting model.[5]

Evaluation of Current Value Accounting

Although current value accounting can provide relevant information for coping with changing prices, there are arguments against its use:

- Determining current cost is inherently subjective.
- In some cases, current costs may be difficult to calculate if the product is not commonly sold.
- Purchasing power gains or losses often are not recognized in current value models.
- There is no consensus regarding treatment of holding gains or losses. Should they appear in the income statement or should they be entered directly into stockholders' equity in the balance sheet? The chosen treatment may have a significant effect on the reported earnings of the company.

Many countries in Europe and Asia allow historical cost with optional current value revaluation. Very few countries require exclusive use of current cost accounting.

Exhibits 5–11 and 5–12 show examples of current value accounting disclosures for U.K.-based ICI and Norway-based Dyno, respectively.

Inflation Accounting in Selected Countries

Although inflation accounting has been discussed in the accounting literature for over 50 years, it did not gain momentum in Western countries until the 1970s and 1980s. In the 1980s the real issue appeared to be not whether to use inflation accounting but how to accomplish it. In this section, we will review how selected countries cope with inflation in financial reports.

Australia

Much literature has been produced in Australia on inflation accounting. R. J. Chambers, who has advocated the realizable value of assets, and R. S. Gynther, who has espoused current cost accounting, have made significant contributions.

---

[5] M. Zafar Iqbal, *Comparison of the Alternatives Proposed in Selected Countries to Cope with the Impact of Changing Prices on Published Financial Statements,* Ph.D. diss. (Lincoln, Nebr.: University of Nebraska, 1979), pp. 78-92.

Exhibit 5–11　ICI Current Value Revaluations

	Land and buildings		Plant and equipment	
	1994	1993	1994	1993
Revalued assets included in tangible fixed assets	£m	£m	£m	£m
At revalued amount	104	102	127	129
Depreciation	41	37	112	112
Net book value	63	65	15	17
At historical cost	57	57	129	130
Depreciation	31	31	120	119
Net book value	26	26	9	11

Source: ICI, *1994 Annual Report and Accounts*, p. 22.

Exhibit 5–12　Dyno Current Value Revaluations

PROPERTY, PLANT AND EQUIPMENT

Property, plant and equipment are entered on the Balance Sheet at original purchase cost, plus revaluation, and less straight-line depreciation. The rates for calculating straight-line depreciation have been determined on the basis of an evaluation of the individual fixed asset's economic lifetime. Profits made on the sale of fixed assets are entered as operating income, and losses as operating expenses.

NOK million	Buildings	Land
Cost as of 1 Jan 1993	1,134.0	258.1
Revaluations as of 1 Jan 1993	92.2	149.8
Investments in 1993	116.4	45.6
New companies	23.6	3.2
Disposals in 1993	-49.5	-49.3
Transfers in 1993	8.8	-1.4
Foreign currency translation	17.7	2.8
Balance as of 31 Dec 1993	1,343.2	408.8

Source: Dyno, *Annual Report 1993*, pp. 17 and 21.

The Australian Accounting Standards Committee (AASC), which used to issue exposure drafts for the Institute of Chartered Accountants in Australia, and the Australian Society of Accountants issued several proposals on inflation accounting. Although there was a lot of debate on the subject, most Australian accountants preferred the current value accounting proposal. A draft standard was issued in 1981 on current cost accounting (CCA). The objective was to have Australian companies supply current cost information on a supplementary basis, with the the goal being that eventually CCA would become the principal basis for financial reporting. There were strong objections to the implementation of CCA information. Because of these objections, the draft standard was issued as the less authoritative "Current Cost Accounting," *Statement of Accounting Practice 1*. This statement encourages issuance of current cost information in the form of supplementary financial statements. This information should include an income statement, a balance sheet, a statement of changes in shareholders' equity, and explanatory notes. Alternately, companies may use current cost as the basis for primary statements. In such cases, historical-cost based supplementary statements are required.

Only a few companies incorporate CCA information in Australia. The years of research and debate have had little impact on accounting practice.

Brazil

Brazil is among the Latin American countries that have experienced high inflation. Accountants have been making adjustments for inflation since the 1950s. To curb inflation, the Brazilian government introduced a new currency called the real on July 1, 1994. The real is backed by the Central Bank's foreign exchange reserves, and is anchored to the U.S. dollar. To ease inflationary pressures, the Brazilian government has also discontinued the long-standing practice of indexing wages and other transactions.

The Brazilian Corporate Law requires companies to adjust fixed assets, accumulated depreciation, investments, deferred charges, and stockholders' equity for general price-level changes by using an index published by the government. The inflation adjustments on the balance sheet are carried to appropriate parts of the income statement.

The Securities Exchange Commission requires that all listed companies prepare and publish a complete set of comparative *primary* financial statements in constant monetary unit. The set of financial statements includes a balance sheet, an income statement, a statement of changes in shareholders' equity, a statement of changes in financial position, and notes to financial statements. Brazil is one of the few countries in the world that requires inflation accounting adjustments in primary financial statements.

Canada

Canadian accounting and financial reporting practices are often influenced by the United States. Canadian experience in implementing inflation accounting closely parallels the U.S. experience. In 1982 Canada adopted a standard that was very similar to the standard in effect in the U.S. at that time. Subsequently, the requirements of the standard were abolished.

The Canadian Institute of Chartered Accountants recommends supplementary disclosures. Some of these voluntary disclosures relate to general price-level changes, while others are on current value basis.

France

A recommendation was made in 1976 that companies listed on the stock exchange should provide supplementary financial statements using general price-level accounting. Although it was a government-sponsored committee that made the recommendation, the French government did not accept its proposal.

There are no statutory requirements in France for disclosure of information in the inflation accounting area. French statutes allow revaluation of property, plant and equipment, and investments to current value. In practice this is rarely done by French companies since the unrealized gains are taxable, although depreciation on revalued basis is deductible for tax purpose. The adjustment, if made, must be transferred to a revaluation reserve account in stockholders' equity.

Germany

The German Institute of Certified Public Accountants recommends that the effect of inflation on profit be shown in supplementary statements. This should be done by restating cost of goods sold and depreciation to their replacement costs. As in France, the low rate of inflation coupled with a lack of tax incentives has resulted in firms not providing such information.

Japan

The Business Accounting Deliberation Council issued a report titled "Disclosure of Financial Information for Changing Price Level Accounting," which stated that it was not necessary to require information on changing prices from Japanese corporations. This conclusion is understandable since inflation in Japan has been relatively low. Japanese companies adhere strictly to historical cost basis.

Mexico

Because of severe inflation, Mexican accounting principles require that all companies adjust their financial statements. Companies may use either constant monetary unit method or current replacement cost method for inflation adjustments. For application of the constant monetary unit method, the National Consumer Price Index, published by the Bank of Mexico, is used. Current replacement cost method may be applied only to restate inventories and fixed assets. The Securities Exchange Commission, however, requires that all public companies use only current replacement cost for revaluation of inventories and fixed assets. Unlisted companies may use either method as long as the same method is applied to an item on a consistent basis.

The gain or loss on net monetary position is included in the income statement as a separate item. In the case of companies using current replacement cost, the gain or loss from holding nonmonetary assets appears in stockholders' equity. Mexico, like Brazil, is among the very few countries in the world requiring inflation-adjusted primary financial statements.

Netherlands

Current value accounting has been used in the Netherlands, albeit by few companies, since the 1920s. Dutch law allows financial statements on either current value basis, or on historical basis with supplementary current value information in notes. The current value, when used, is often the replacement value. The law does not allow revaluation of intangible assets or current assets other than inventories. The EU Fourth Directive, enacted in December 1983, was responsible for new company legislation stating that corporate bodies could value tangible fixed assets and inventories on a current cost basis.

Relatively few companies use current value basis for primary financial reporting. Philips Electronics N.V. was the best known of all the Netherlands-based companies using current value basis for primary financial reporting. However, Philips discontinued the practice several years ago.

Nigeria

Financial statements are prepared in accordance with historical cost. There is no statutory requirement to disclose the effects of inflation. If fixed assets are adjusted to reflect current value, the revaluation basis is disclosed.

United Kingdom

Statement of Standard Accounting Practice 16 was issued in 1980 which required current cost accounting either in supplementary statements or in the primary statements with historical cost also as a requirement.[6] As in many other countries, the requirement was abandoned in 1988 because of the falling inflation rates and lack of support from business entities. Companies Act 1985 allows revaluation of certain assets. Companies may revalue their assets using either current value method or constant monetary unit approach. The majority of companies issue modified historical cost statements, using historical cost basis with revaluation of fixed assets.

United States

The accounting profession has had an ongoing debate about incorporating some type of inflation adjustments into the financial statements for many decades. The 1960s and 1970s were replete with research on different ways to accomplish this goal. Many researchers advocated some form of current value, while others favored general price-level (constant dollar) restatement of financial statements. The FASB circulated an exposure draft in 1974 proposing constant dollar adjustments. The exposure draft came under heavy criticism.

In 1976, the SEC took the initiative by requiring supplementary disclosures of the replacement cost of inventory, cost of sales, and certain long-lived assets.[7] The constant dollar exposure draft was withdrawn by the FASB. Instead, it issued *SFAS No. 33* in 1979 requiring general purchasing power information as well as current value information on supplementary basis from certain large companies.[8] A few years later, however, it was decided to rescind *SFAS No. 33,* and the Financial Accounting Standards Board issued *SFAS No. 89,* officially removing its disclosure requirement.[9]

---

[6] Accounting Standards Committee, "Current Cost Accounting," *Statement of Accounting Practice No. 16* (London: Institute of Chartered Accountants in England and Wales, 1980).

[7] Securities and Exchange Commission, "Disclosure of Certain Replacement Cost Data," *Accounting Series Release No. 190* (Washington, D.C.: U.S. Government Printing Office, 1976).

[8] *Statement of Financial Accounting Standards No. 33,* "Financial Reporting and Changing Prices" (Stamford, Conn.: Financial Accounting Standards Board, 1979)

[9] *Statement of Financial Accounting Standards No. 89,* "Financial Reporting and Changing Prices" (Stamford, Conn.: Financial Accounting Standards Board, 1986).

It would be erroneous to infer from the above discussion that the U.S. requires the use of historical cost basis. The valuation basis required by the U.S. generally accepted accounting principles can best be described as hybrid, or modified historical cost. For example, *SFAS No. 115* requires valuation at current value (mark-to-market) for equity securities with a readily determinable market value and for debt securities not intended to be held to maturity.[10]

IASC and Inflation Accounting

The IASC accepted the reality that there were different schools of thought on accounting for inflation. In 1981, it issued *IAS 15,* which *recommends* that the following information should be disclosed by large public companies:[11]

- The amounts of the adjustment to or the adjusted amount of depreciation of property, plant, and equipment.
- The amount of the adjustment to or the adjusted amount of cost of sales.
- The adjustments to monetary items.
- The overall effect on income.
- The current cost of property, plant, and equipment and inventories if the current cost method is used.
- The methods used to calculate the information as well as the type of indices used.

The IASC issued *IAS 29,* "Financial Reporting in Hyperinflationary Economies," in 1989. It *requires* that financial statements of a company reporting in a currency of a hyperinflationary economy be restated at balance sheet date for general purchasing power changes.[12] This applies whether statements were based on historical cost or current value.

Although *IAS 29* does not indicate a specific rate characterizing a hyperinflationary economy, it does give some guidelines:

- The population prefers nonmonetary assets or a relatively stable foreign currency over local currency.
- Sales and purchases on credit incorporate amounts for expected losses in purchasing power even for relatively short credit periods.
- Interest rates, prices, and wages are tied to a price index.
- The cumulative inflation rate for three years is approaching or exceeds 100 percent.

IAS 29 applies to *primary* financial statements. The gain or loss on the net monetary position should be included in net income and separately disclosed.

---

[10] *Statement of Financial Accounting Standards No. 115,* "Accounting for Certain Investments in Debt and Equity Securities" (Norwalk, Conn.: Financial Accounting Standards Board, 1993).

[11] *International Accounting Standard 15,* "Information Reflecting the Effects of Changing Prices" (London: International Accounting Standards Committee, 1981).

[12] *International Accounting Standard 29,* "Financial Reporting in Hyperinflationary Economies" (London: International Accounting Standards Committee, 1989).

Concluding Observations

Two observations can be made regarding inflation accounting.

First, accounting for changing prices becomes hotly debated in industrialized countries when they experience high rates of inflation. When inflation rates go down, interest in this topic drops correspondingly.

Second, the question of how to deal with inflation has been studied for a long time—but never resolved. Some of the references listed at the end of this chapter make interesting reading, not only because of their incisiveness but also because they present strong but diverse arguments both for and against the proposed solutions.

Note to Students

If you want to keep current on worldwide inflation rates, there is no better way than reading the popular financial press. These periodicals provide a barometer for inflation rates throughout the world.

Today, debates about inflation have apparently come to a standstill in the industrialized countries, and many requirements for supplementary financial statements accounting for inflation have been rescinded. This "calm after the storm" is the result of apparent control over inflation.

Developing countries generally continue to have high inflation rates. Their dilemma is to find a balance between acceptable rates of inflation and the desired levels of economic growth. Their challenge is to be able to spend on economic development projects while keeping inflation under control.

Accounting students need to develop a conceptual foundation of inflation accounting to be prepared for future developments. To increase conceptual understanding, you may want to read some of the references at the end of the chapter. We especially recommend Henry Sweeney's *Stabilized Accounting,* an accounting classic on general price-level adjustments.

Chapter Summary

- The 1970s and 1980s was a time of substantial experimentation in accounting systems trying to cope with the inflation problem. This occurred after much research had been done on the subject.
- The reason for the experimentation was the high level of inflation during those two decades.
- Hyperinflation still abounds in many developing countries.
- Inflation rates in industrialized countries have been below 5 percent in recent years.

- Generally, the inflation adjustments have been made using two types of accounting systems: the *constant monetary* unit approach and the *current value* approach.
- Constant monetary unit accounting merely restates historical-cost-based financial statements using a general price index.
- Current value accounting adjusts the financial statements for specific price changes.
- The gearing adjustments are incorporated in many current value accounting models.
- The gearing adjustments recognize that in an inflationary economy it is not necessary to make current cost adjustments for the portion of operating assets financed by creditors.
- Many countries, especially in Europe, accept the current value revaluation option.
- Constant monetary unit accounting adjustments have traditionally been a common practice in many South American countries.
- Brazil and Mexico are among the very few countries in the world requiring that *primary* financial statements be adjusted for changing prices.
- Canadian experience in implementing inflation accounting is similar to the U.S. experience.
- IASC's *IAS 15* deals with information disclosures related to changing prices.
- *IAS 29* provides disclosure standards for companies reporting in currencies of hyperinflationary economies.

Questions for Discussion

1. What is inflation? If you hold cash during an inflationary period, what is the effect?

2. What are the merits of restating financial statements by using general price-level indexes?

3. What is a monetary item? A nonmonetary item? Give examples of each.

4. What are the deficiencies of historical statements in a country such as Brazil?

5. How is a fixed asset restated for changes in price levels? How about the related depreciation expense and accumulated depreciation?

6. What is the current status of *SFAS No. 33* in the United States?

7. What is a net monetary gain or loss?

8. In what financial statement does a monetary gain or loss appear?

9. Indicate whether the following are monetary or nonmonetary items:

   a. Stocks held as investments.

   b. Bonds held as investments.

   c. Merchandise inventory.

   d. Preferred stock.

   e. Sales revenue.

10. If prices are steadily rising, indicate whether the following produces a purchasing power gain, loss, or neither:

   a. Maintaining a balance in a checking account.

   b. Depreciating an asset.

   c. Additional paid-in capital on preferred stock.

11. What are specific price indices?

12. What is an input price? An output price?

13. When and why are countries likely to introduce "inflation accounting"?

14. What is the purpose for making a gearing adjustment? How is it accomplished?

15. Discuss *IAS 15* guidelines.

16. Under what conditions is an economy considered hyperinflationary according to *IAS 29*?

17. In what type of economy is *IAS 29* applicable? What are its major requirements?

18. In coping with the inflation problem, what is the general practice in South American countries? What appears to be the current trend?

19. How does Mexico deal with the inflation problem in financial statements?

20. Compare the experience with *SFAS No. 33* in the U.S. with the United Kingdom's experience with *SSAP No. 16*.

21. Discuss the Netherlands' accounting approach to the inflation problem.

Exercises/Problems

5-1   Select the best available answer:

   1. The inherent flaw of historical cost basis is that it:
      a. Misstates monetary items
      b. Fails to match revenue with expenses
      c. Combines monetary units of different dimensions
      d. Shows equipment at the same book value as a number of years ago
      e. b and c

   2. Purchasing power gains or losses arise from:
      a. Fluctuations in the exchange rate
      b. Changes in the stock market
      c. Holding monetary items during a period when the general purchasing power of the monetary unit changes
      d. Holding nonmonetary items during a period when the general purchasing power of the monetary unit changes
      e. None of the above

3. Monetary items include all of the following except:
   a. Cash
   b. Accounts receivable
   c. Inventories
   d. Bonds payable
   e. None of the above are monetary items

5-2 Select the best available answer:

1. This country's Business Accounting Deliberation Council stated that it was not necessary to require changing price level accounting:
   a. Nigeria
   b. Japan
   c. Germany
   d. Canada
   e. None of the above

2. Accounting approaches for changing prices include:
   a. The current value approach
   b. The historical cost approach
   c. The general price-level adjustments approach
   d. a and b
   e. a and c

3. Nonmonetary items include:
   a. Inventory
   b. Equipment
   c. Retained earnings
   d. All of the above
   e. None of the above

5-3 Select the best available answer:

1. Equipment was purchased at a time when the specific index was 150. Today, the specific index is 200, and the current purchase price of the same equipment is $6,000. The cost of the equipment when purchased was about:
   a. $4,500
   b. $8,000
   c. $1,500
   d. $3,000
   e. None of the above

2. A change in a general price index from 120 to 180 during a period shows that purchasing power has declined by:
   a. 60 percent
   b. 50 percent
   c. 33 1/3 percent
   d. 180 percent
   e. None of the above

3. Which of the following is a nonmonetary item?
   a. Inventory.
   b. Notes payable
   c. Notes receivable
   d. Prepaid expense
   e. None of the above
4. During a period of inflation, a purchasing power loss results from holding:
   a. Nonmonetary assets
   b. Nonmonetary liabilities
   c. Monetary assets
   d. Monetary liabilities
   e. None of the above

5-4   Kumar Co. purchased a new machine on January 1, 1995, for 500,000 francs. The machine is depreciated using the straight-line method and a 10-year life. Assume estimated salvage value is zero. The general price level index was 200.0 on January 1, 1995, and 225 on December 31, 1995. The average index for 1995 was 215.

Required: Calculate the amount of depreciation for 1995 and the book value of the machine on December 31, 1995 using historical costs restated for the general price-level changes.

5-5   Peterson Company began business in 1980 when the general price index was 80. At that time, the company acquired all of its plant assets. Sales, purchases, and operating expenses occur evenly throughout a year. At the end of 1996, Peterson's comparative balance sheets in Swiss francs showed:

	December 31	
	1995	**1996**
Monetary assets	Fr. 300,000	Fr. 280,000
Monetary liabilities	320,000	315,000
Other assets	240,000	300,000
Other liabilities	80,000	115,000

Other data for 1996:	
Sales	270,000
Beginning inventory (FIFO basis)	70,000
Purchases of merchandise	170,000
Ending inventory (FIFO basis)	95,000
Depreciation expense	20,000
Other operating expenses and taxes	70,000
Dividends paid at the end of 1996	45,000

Price index information:	
Beginning of operations	80
Beginning of 1996	120
Average index during 1996	122
End of 1996	124

Required:

(1) Calculate Peterson's purchasing power gain or loss for 1996.

(2) Prepare Peterson's income statement on a constant monetary unit basis.

5-6   Selected information from Lieber's financial statements follows:

	1995	**1996**
Building (acquired in 1992)	DM 300,000	DM 300,000
Accumulated depreciation	60,000	80,000
Land (acquired in 1992)	100,000	100,000

Price index information:	
Average for 1992	90
December 31, 1995	135
December 31, 1996	150
Average for 1996	140

Required:

(1) Calculate depreciation expense in constant marks for 1996.

(2) Calculate the book value of the building at December 31, 1996 in constant marks.

(3) Determine the amount for land in constant marks in the December 31, 1996 balance sheet.

5-7   Zaki and Safee Inc. reported the following financial information for its first year of operations:

Zaki and Safee Inc.
Income Statement
For the Year Ended December 31, 1996

Sales	$350,000
Cost of goods sold	200,000
Gross margin	150,000
Operating expenses	70,000
Net income	$ 80,000

Zaki and Safee Inc.
Balance Sheet
December 31, 1996

Assets		**Liabilities and Stockholders' Equity**	
Cash	$ 50,000	Liabilities	$100,000
Inventory	100,000	Stockholders' equity	300,000
Fixed assets (net)	250,000	Total liabilities and	
Total assets	$400,000	stockholders' equity	$400,000

Current cost information for 1996 is as follows:

Sales	$350,000	Cash	$ 50,000
Cost of goods sold	230,000	Inventory	120,000
Operating expenses	70,000	Fixed assets	275,000

Required: Compute Zaki and Safee Inc.'s net income on a current cost basis. Assume that holding gain or loss appears in current cost basis income statement.

5-8   The income statement for 1996 and balance sheet on December 31, 1996 for Shahruz Pinole Co. appear below:

Shahruz Pinole Co.

Income Statement

For the Year Ended December 31, 1996

Sales	$400,000
Cost of sales	250,000
Gross profit	150,000
Operating expenses	50,000
Net income	$100,000

Shahruz Pinole Co.

Balance Sheet

December 31, 1996

Assets		Liabilities and Stockholders' Equity	
Cash	$ 70,000	Notes payable	$ 30,000
Accounts receivable (net)	50,000	Accounts payable	60,000
Inventory	80,000	Paid-in capital	410,000
Land	500,000	Retained earnings	200,000
		Total liabilities and	
Total assets	$700,000	stockholders' equity	$700,000

Additional information:
1. The general price indexes for selected dates are given below:

January 1, 1993	105
June 30, 1995	120
December 31, 1996	140
Average for 1996	130

2. The company was founded on January 1, 1993. All capital stock was issued at that time.
3. One-half of the land was acquired on January 1, 1993. The other one-half was acquired on June 30, 1995.
4. The purchasing power loss for 1996 is $10,000.
5. Ending inventory consists of units purchased uniformly in 1996.
6. There was no beginning inventory for 1996. Cost of sales consists of the units purchased uniformly throughout 1996.

Required:
(1) Prepare a constant dollar income statement for Shahruz Pinole Co. for the year ended December 31, 1996.
(2) Prepare a constant dollar balance sheet for Shahruz Pinole Co. on December 31, 1996. (Hint: Retained earnings is a balancing item.)

5-9   Sattar N.V. is preparing a constant monetary unit balance sheet. The average general price index for the year was 150, and at the year-end it was 155. Historical cost basis amounts in selected accounts, and the corresponding index when the amount was recorded, are shown below:

	Amount	Index
Accounts receivable (net)	Fl. 20,000	155
Machinery	100,000	125
Accumulated depreciation on machinery	30,000	125
Patent (net)	10,000	130
Accounts payable	25,000	155
Bonds payable	75,000	120
Common stock	80,000	100

Required: Restate the historical cost basis amounts for preparing the constant-guilder balance sheet for Sattar N.V.

5-10   Z. H. Mudh Company is preparing a constant monetary unit income statement for the year ended December 31, 1997. The average price index for the year was 150. The price index at the year-end was 160. Amounts in selected accounts and the corresponding index when the amount was recorded are shown below:

	Amount	Index
Sales revenue	$200,000	150
Cost of goods sold	90,000	140
Depreciation expense	30,000	?
Salaries expense	40,000	150
Interest expense	15,000	?

The depreciation expense was for equipment that was purchased when the index was 130. Interest expense is on bonds payable, issued at par when the index was 120. The tax rate is 30 percent. Taxes and interest are paid evenly throughout the year. The purchasing power gain on net monetary position for 1997 was $5,000.

Required: Prepare a constant dollar income statement.

5-11   Lindberg Company's monetary liabilities exceeded its monetary assets by $10,000 on January 1, 1996. The following events occurred during 1996:

1. Made cash sales of $300,000 uniformly during the year.
2. Paid salaries of $90,000 uniformly during the year.
3. Sold investment in Farhan, Iman & Laraib Corporation stock for $50,000 at the end of September.
4. Issued 2,000 shares of common stock at $20 per share at the end of June.
5. At the end of 1996: Purchased equipment for $120,000 cash, paid income taxes of $40,000, and paid dividends of $10,000.

The general price index for 1996 was as follows:

Beginning of year	120	End of 3rd quarter	128
End of 1st quarter	122	End of 4th quarter	132
End of 2nd quarter	124	Average for year	126

Required: Compute Lindberg Company's purchasing power gain or loss for 1996.

Case: Accounting for Changing Prices

Carols Rodriguez S.A. started manufacturing operations in 1950. The company has been continuously experiencing growth in its sales and manufacturing activities. Recently, a new controller, Ms. Shiza, was hired. She feels that historical cost financial statements do not provide adequate information to the users for informed decisions. After consideration of various proposals for supplementary financial information to be included in the 1996 annual report, she has decided to present a balance sheet as of December 31, 1996, and an income statement for 1996, both restated for general price-level changes.

Required:
(1) Distinguish between financial statements restated for general price-level changes and current value financial statements.
(2) Distinguish between monetary and nonmonetary items.
(3) Describe the steps Ms. Shiza should follow in preparing the supplementary constant monetary unit statements.
(4) Identify the similarities and differences between the unadjusted historical cost financial statements and constant monetary unit financial statements.
(5) Can the 1996 supplementary statements be presented for comparative purposes in 1997 without adjustment? Explain.

References

Accounting Principles Board. *APB Statement No. 3.* "Financial Statements Restated for General Price-Level Changes." New York: American Institute of Certified Public Accountants, 1969.

Accounting Standards Committee. *Statement of Accounting Practice No. 16.* "Current Cost Accounting." London: Institute of Chartered Accountants in England and Wales, 1980.

Coopers & Lybrand. *The Accounting Profession in Nigeria.* New York: American Institute of Certified Public Accountants, 1993.

————. *International Accounting Summaries.* 2d ed. New York: John Wiley & Sons, Inc., 1993.

Dyno Industrier A.S. *Annual Report 1993.* Oslo, Norway: Dyno, 1994.

Farrell, Christopher. "Inflation's Uneven Spread." *Business Week,* 8 May 1995, p. 28.

Financial Reporting and Changing Prices: A Survey of Preparers' Views and Practices. New York: Arthur Young and Company, 1981.

Galaz, Gomez Mortin, Chavero, Yamazaki, S.C., and Deloitte & Touche. *The Accounting Profession in Mexico.* 2d ed., rev. New York: American Institute of Certified Public Accountants. 1992.

Gerboth, Dale L., and Robert W. Berliner. "FASB Statement No. 33, 'The Great Experiment.' " *Journal of Accountancy,* May 1980, pp. 48-54.

Gibson, R. W. "Accounting for Monetary Items Under CCA." *Accounting and Business Research,* fall 1981, pp. 281-90.

Guy Barbier & Associés. *The Auditing Profession in France.* 2d ed., rev. New York: American Institute of Certified Public Accountants, 1992.

Imperial Chemical Industries PLC. *1994 Annual Report and Accounts.* London: ICI, 1995.

Inflation Accounting Steering Group. *Guidance Manual on Current Cost Accounting.* London: Institute of Chartered Accountants in England and Wales, 1976.

International Accounting Standard 15. "Information Reflecting the Effects of Changing Prices." London: International Accounting Standards Committee, 1981.

International Accounting Standard 29. "Financial Reporting in Hyperinflationary Economies." London: International Accounting Standards Committee, 1989.

Iqbal, M. Zafar. "Comparison of the Alternatives Proposed in Selected Countries to Cope with the Impact of Changing Prices on Published Financial Statements." Ph.D. diss., University of Nebraska, 1979.

————. "Development of Inflation Accounting Standards in the United States." *Industrial Accountant* (Pakistan), October-December 1981, pp. 31-33.

————. "Reporting the Impact of Changing Prices in Great Britain." *Accounting for Inflation.* Englewood Cliffs, N.J.: Prentice-Hall, 1981, pp. 153-163.

————. "Reporting the Impact of Changing Prices in New Zealand." *Accounting for Inflation.* Englewood Cliffs, N.J.: Prentice-Hall, 1981, pp. 174-181.

KPMG Century Audit Corporation. *The Accounting Profession in Japan.* 2d ed., rev. New York: American Institute of Certified Public Accountants, 1992.

Moret Ernst & Young. *The Accounting Profession in the Netherlands.* 2d ed., rev. New York: American Institute of Certified Public Accountants, 1991.

Raymond, Robert H., M. Zafar Iqbal, and Eldon L. Schafer. "The Gearing (Leverage) Adjustment: A Historical and Comparative Analysis." *The International Journal of Accounting,* vol. 17 (fall 1982), pp. 139-157.

Rosenfield, Paul. "The Confusion Between General Price-Level Restatement and Current Value Accounting." *Journal of Accountancy,* October 1972, pp. 63-68.

Securities and Exchange Commission. *Accounting Series Release No. 190.* "Disclosure of Certain Replacement Cost Data." Washington, D.C.: U.S. Government Printing Office, 1976.

Shriver, Keith A. "An Empirical Examination of the Potential Measurement Error in Current Cost Data." *Accounting Review,* January 1987, pp. 79-96.

Statement of Financial Accounting Standards No. 33. "Financial Reporting and Changing Prices." Stamford, Conn.: Financial Accounting Standards Board, 1979.

Statement of Financial Accounting Standards No. 89. "Financial Reporting and Changing Prices." Stamford, Conn.: Financial Accounting Standards Board, 1986.

Statement of Financial Accounting Standard No. 115. "Accounting for Certain Investments in Debt and Equity Securities." Norwalk, Conn.: Financial Accounting Standards Board, 1993.

"Submission on the Report of the Committee of Inquiry into Inflation Accounting." *Accountants Journal* (New Zealand), May 1977, pp. 153-56.

Sweeney, Henry W. *Stabilized Accounting.* New York: Holt, Reinhart & Winston, 1964. Originally published by Harper in 1936.

Teléfonos De México S.A. de C.V. *Annual Report 1993.* Cuauhtémoc, Mexico: TELMEX, 1994.

Westwick, C.A. "The Lesson to be Learned from the Development of Inflation Accounting in the U.K." *Accounting and Business Research,* autumn 1980, p. 356-364.

Chapter 6

Foreign Currency

There is a major difference between a company doing business internationally and a company whose business is confined within its national boundaries. The multinational company is involved in international activities: international operations and international investments. This increases the number as well as the complexity of its transactions. The financial reporting system of a company involved in international activities is inherently more complex due to this fact, and more diverse due to different information needs of multiple users throughout the world.

A major factor contributing to the complexity of financial reporting is that different currencies are involved in international activities. Each country has its own currency and currency laws and regulations. All transactions involving assets, liabilities, equity, revenues, and expenses are recorded by the subsidiaries in the currency of the country in which they are located. The question is: How can total amounts for the multinational company for a period be determined when multiple currencies are involved? This requires that different currencies be converted to one currency. Let us assume that a multinational company's headquarters are in the Netherlands, and that it has subsidiaries in the U.S., Mexico, Spain, South Korea, Austria, and Indonesia. This means that before the consolidated statements can be prepared, all the account balances in the local currency of the U.S. (dollar), Mexico (peso), Spain (peseta), South Korea (won), Austria (schilling), and Indonesia (rupiah) will have to be converted to guilders, the currency of the Netherlands.

On the surface, the problem appears to have an easy solution: convert the local currency of each country to guilders by using the exchange rate for the currency. An **exchange rate** is the amount of one currency needed to obtain one unit of another currency. The problem is quite complex, however, because exchange rates are seldom stable.[1]

Exchange Rates

The **conversion value** of a currency is the equivalent amount of another currency at a given exchange rate. As the exchange rate changes, so does the conversion value of a foreign currency. Therefore, exchange rate changes have a direct effect on the amounts in the consolidated reports that show income and financial position of the multinational company. Clearly, the greater the exchange rate fluctuations, the greater the impact on the consolidated financial statements.

Changes in values of different currencies, as reflected by the changes in exchange rates, result from several factors. One of the important factors is a country's *rate of inflation.* Currency of a country with a high inflation rate will depreciate in value when compared with the currency of a country with a low inflation rate. With a high inflation rate, a country's

---

[1] The authors gratefully acknowledge the assistance of Professor Earl Keller in the preparation of parts of this chapter.

currency has declining power to purchase everything—including another country's currency.

Another important reason for exchange rate fluctuations is the nature of a country's *balance of payments.* A country whose exports exceed imports will run a balance of payments surplus. This surplus appreciates the value of its currency. Of course, a country with a balance of payments deficit will experience a decline in the value of its currency.

Interest rates in a country also play an important role in the exchange rate of its currency. Investors from other countries purchase the currency of a country that has high interest rates, thus earning more interest. This increases the demand for the currency, resulting in appreciation of its value. The appreciation of the German mark is attributed to this factor, as stated in the following:

> Generally speaking, countries with high interest rates are able to attract more capital than can countries with low interest rates. In Germany, rates have been steadily rising while those in the U.S. have been falling, causing investors to sell off dollars in favor of marks. Although this gap has existed for months, fears broke out last week that the rift could widen if the U.S. were forced to again lower rates to spur the recovery and Germany had to raise rates to damp an overheating money supply.[2]

Many of the environmental factors, discussed in Chapter 1, also have a direct impact on the exchange rate changes of a country. Especially important are the *political system, economic system,* and the *degree of political stability.*

Changes in exchange rates result in exchange gains and losses. These gains and losses can be classified as realized or unrealized.

Exchange Gains and Losses

Exchange gains or losses may be realized or unrealized. **Realized gains or losses** are gains or losses that are actually incurred. These result from the *exchange* of one currency for another. These gains and losses are from foreign currency *transactions.* **Foreign currency transactions** are transactions denominated in a currency other than the reporting currency of the entity:

> The 30% fall in the lira has been a huge boon for the Vatican. That's because most of its expenses are incurred in lira, while most receipts come in dollars and German marks from wealthy Catholic communities in the U.S. and Germany. Last year, the Holy See's budget deficit was only $3.4 million, compared with $87.5 million the year before. It has also brought in Nomura Securities Inc. and Merrill Lynch & Co., among others, to sharpen up portfolio management.[3]

---

[2] Rick Wartzman, "Dollar's Fall Raises Broad Questions on Causes, Outlook for U.S. Markets," *The Wall Street Journal,* 26 August 1992, p. A2.

[3] "Lira Falls, Vatican Smiles," *Business Week,* 19 July 1993, p. 45.

In the case of **unrealized gains or losses**, no exchange of currency takes place. These unrealized gains or losses result from a **foreign currency translation**, which is a translation of amounts in accounts of subsidiaries recorded in a foreign currency to the currency used for consolidated financial statements.

Foreign Currency Transactions

As noted earlier, realized exchange gains and losses may result from foreign currency transactions. Such transactions require future settlements in a foreign currency.[4] Since exchange rates fluctuate, the result of exchange rate changes from the date the transaction was recorded to the date when the transaction is settled results in transaction gains or losses.

Example A Pakistani firm buys equipment from a U.S. firm for $1 million when the exchange rate is $1.00 = 25.00 rupees. The transaction is recorded:

Equipment..........................	25,000,000	
Accounts payable................		25,000,000
($1 million @ Rs. 25.00)		

The Pakistani firm settles the account after 30 days when the exchange rate is $1.00 = Rs. 28.00. Therefore, to pay off the liability, Rs. 28,000,000 will be required to obtain $1 million. This results in a transaction loss to the Pakistani firm in the amount of Rs. 3 million:

1,000,000 × (28 - 25) = <u>3,000,000</u>

The above can be summarized in the following manner:

Transaction Gain or Loss = Difference between exchange rate on transaction recording date and exchange rate on settlement date × Amount owed in foreign currency units

How should the transaction loss be recorded by the Pakistani firm on the settlement date? There are two approaches—the *one-transaction* and the *two-transaction*.

One-Transaction Approach

Under the **one-transaction approach**, the final settlement would be shown as an adjustment to the equipment account:

Accounts payable	25,000,000	
Equipment..........................	3,000,000	
Cash..........................		28,000,000
($1 million @ Rs. 28.00)		

Under the one-transaction approach, the transaction is not considered to be completed until the final settlement. Any transaction gain or loss will be reflected on the settlement date in

---

[4] *Statement of Financial Accounting Standards No. 52,* "Foreign Currency Translation" (Stamford, Conn.: Financial Accounting Standards Board, 1981), par. 15.

an adjustment to the value of the resource acquired. In the example above, the foreign exchange rate change required Rs. 3 million more than originally recorded. The cost of the equipment is, therefore, increased by the amount of this loss. In sum, a foreign exchange loss would result in recording of a higher cost for the resource acquired through an upward adjustment that is made on the settlement date. Had the situation been the reverse, the foreign exchange gain would have resulted in a downward adjustment of the equipment since it would not have cost as many rupees to obtain $1 million on the settlement date as originally recorded.

Note: No exchange gain or loss is recorded in the one-transaction approach.

Two-Transaction Approach

Under the **two-transaction approach**, there are two separate and distinct transactions. Purchase of the equipment is recorded in the same manner as in the one-transaction approach:

Equipment	25,000,000	
Accounts payable		25,000,000
($1 million @ Rs. 25.00)		

Under the two-transaction approach, no adjustment to the equipment account is made at the settlement date. Instead, any gains or losses are separately recorded as gains or losses from exchange rate changes. In this example, the following entry records the cash settlement and recognizes the exchange loss of Rs. 3,000,000:

Accounts payable.....................	25,000,000	
Loss on foreign exchange	3,000,000	
Cash		28,000,000
($1 million @ Rs. 28.00)		

Which of the two approaches is preferable? There is no consensus on this issue. Both approaches are practiced in different parts of the world. In some countries one of the approaches is specifically required. In other countries, it is left to the managers to choose. In the U.S., any gains or losses from foreign exchange transactions must be recorded in accordance with the two-transaction approach and shown immediately in the income statement as normal operating items.[5]

Supporters of the two-transaction approach point out that the import transaction and the method of settlement involve two separate decisions. Since exchange gains and losses result from the settlement method, they should be recorded separately; assumption of foreign currency exchange risk by selecting settlement in the future should not have any effect on the recorded cost of imported or exported assets. Recording loss or gain separately gives recognition to the fact that there is an economic effect in assuming the risk of exchange rate changes. There is merit to the above argument and perhaps for this reason the popularity of the two-transaction approach is increasing worldwide.

---

[5] *Statement of Financial Accounting Standards No. 52* (Stamford, Conn.: Financial Accounting Standard Board, 1981).

Forward Exchange Contracts

A firm may plan to protect itself from potential losses from exchange rate changes. This can be done by entering into a forward exchange contract. A **forward exchange contract** is an agreement to buy (or sell) a foreign currency in the future at a fixed rate called a **forward rate**. In this age of advanced telecommunications, efficient and well-established foreign exchange markets exist for all major currencies. Forward exchange contracts usually cover 30-day, 90-day, or 180-day periods (see Exhibit 6–1).

Exhibit 6–1   Sample Exchange Rates

EXCHANGE RATES
Friday, July 21, 1995

The New York foreign exchange selling rates below apply to trading among banks in amounts of $1 million and more, as quoted at 3 p.m. Eastern time by Bankers Trust Co., Dow Jones Telerate, Inc. and other sources. Retail transactions provide fewer units of foreign currency per dollar.

Country	U.S. $ equiv. Fri	U.S. $ equiv. Thu	Currency per U.S. $ Fri	Currency per U.S. $ Thu
Argentina (Peso)	1.0001	1.0005	.9999	.9995
Australia (Dollar)	.7353	.7345	1.3601	1.3616
Austria (Schilling)	.1026	.1030	9.7445	9.7045
Bahrain (Dinar)	2.6525	2.6525	.3770	.3770
Belgium (Franc)	.03506	.03519	28.519	28.418
Brazil (Real)	1.0718	1.0775	.9331	.9281
Britain (Pound)	1.5944	1.5953	.6272	.6268
30-Day Forward	1.5934	1.5942	.6276	.6273
90-Day Forward	1.5910	1.5918	.6285	.6282
180-Day Forward	1.5865	1.5873	.6303	.6300
Canada (Dollar)	.7352	.7343	1.3602	1.3619
30-Day Forward	.7352	.7333	1.3601	1.3638
90-Day Forward	.7343	.7322	1.3619	1.3657
180-Day Forward	.7324	.7303	1.3653	1.3693
Chile (Peso)	.002637	.002646	379.20	377.95
China (Renminbi)	.1205	.1205	8.3002	8.3004
Colombia (Peso)	.001118	.001118	894.40	894.20
Czech. Rep. (Koruna)	....	....	....	....
Commercial rate	.03852	.03867	25.963	25.863
Denmark (Krone)	.1854	.1859	5.3935	5.3805
Ecuador (Sucre)	....	....	....	....
Floating rate	.0003888	.0003887	2572.00	2573.00
Finland (Markka)	.2367	.2374	4.2256	4.2130
France (Franc)	.2075	.2081	4.8183	4.8065
30-Day Forward	.2073	.2078	4.8249	4.8119
90-Day Forward	.2071	.2077	4.8282	4.8152
180-Day Forward	.2070	.2075	4.8314	4.8187
Germany (Mark)	.7218	.7241	1.3854	1.3810
30-Day Forward	.7226	.7243	1.3839	1.3807
90-Day Forward	.7242	.7259	1.3809	1.3777
180-Day Forward	.7265	.7282	1.3765	1.3733
Greece (Drachma)	.004446	.004448	224.94	224.83
Hong Kong (Dollar)	.1293	.1293	7.7368	7.7362
Hungary (Forint)	.007901	.007926	126.56	126.16
India (Rupee)	.03188	.03188	31.370	31.370
Indonesia (Rupiah)	.0004480	.0004482	2232.00	2231.00
Ireland (Punt)	1.6420	1.6436	.6090	.6084
Israel (Shekel)	.3394	.3397	2.9467	2.9441
Italy (Lira)	.0006238	.0006211	1603.00	1610.00
Japan (Yen)	.01130	.01134	88.480	88.140
30-Day Forward	.01135	.01140	88.068	87.717
90-Day Forward	.01145	.01150	87.325	86.975
180-Day Forward	.01160	.01164	86.235	85.880
Jordan (Dinar)	1.4368	1.4368	.6960	.6960
Kuwait (Dinar)	3.3311	3.3350	.3002	.2998
Lebanon (Pound)	.0006180	.0006180	1618.00	1618.00
Malasia (Ringgit)	.4084	.4082	2.4485	2.4498
Malta (Lira)	2.8727	2.8729	.3481	.3481
Mexico (Peso)	....	....	....	....
Floating rate	.1641	.1630	6.0950	6.1350
Netherlands (Guilder)	.6441	.6460	1.555225	1.5479
New Zealand (Dollar)	.6751	.6759	1.4814	1.4796
Norway (Krone)	.1623	.1627	6.1625	6.1460
Pakistan (Rupee)	.03209	.03209	31.159	31.159
Peru (new Sol)	.4495	.4494	2.2245	2.2250
Philippines (Peso)	.03933	.03926	25.425	25.470
Poland (Zloty)	.4211	.4211	2.3750	2.3750
Portugal (Escudo)	.006865	.006879	145.66	145.37
Saudi Arabia (Riyal)	.2666	.2666	3.7507	3.7407
Singapore (Dollar)	.7149	.7147	1.3988	1.3992
Slovak Rep. (Koruna)	.03425	.03416	29.200	29.275
South Africa (Rand)	.2745	.2748	3.6427	3.6389
South Korea (Won)	.001323	.001322	755.85	756.45
Spain (Peseta)	.008377	.008404	119.37	118.98
Sweden (Krona)	.1398	.1391	7.1530	7.1875
Switzerland (Franc)	.8659	.8687	1.1549	1.1512
30-Day Forward	.8681	.8711	1.1520	1.1480
90-Day Forward	.8724	.8757	1.1462	1.1419
180-Day Forward	.8782	.8815	1.1387	1.1344
Taiwan (Dollar)	.03787	.03791	26.408	26.375
Thailand (Baht)	.04036	.04036	24.780	24.780
Turkey (Lira)	.00002245	.00002252	44551.50	44401.50
United Arab (Dirham)	.2723	.2723	3.6728	3.6728
Uruguay (New Peso)	....	....	....	....
Financial	.1560	.1560	6.4100	6.4100
Venezuela (Bolivar)	.005890	.005890	169.79	169.78
SDR	1.5549	1.5591	.6431	.6414
ECU	1.3371	1.3390	....	....

Special Drawing Rights (SDR) are based on exchange rates for the U.S., German, British, French, and Japanese currencies. Source: International Monetary Fund.

European Currency Unit (ECU) is based on a basket of community currencies.

Source: *The Wall Street Journal*, 24 July 1995, p. C6

In our example, the Pakistani firm could have avoided the loss from the exchange rate change by entering into a 30-day forward exchange contract to buy one million dollars at the forward rate of $1.00 = Rs. 25.00. By doing so, the firm would have protected itself from any potential future exchange loss.

While a forward exchange contract enables a firm to avoid a potential future loss, it may also result in forgoing a potential future gain. For example, if the Pakistani firm had entered into a forward exchange contract at the rate of $1.00 = Rs. 25.00 and the rate on the settlement date is $1.00 = Rs. 23.00, the Pakistani firm would miss the opportunity to make a gain of Rs. 2,000,000. Had the Pakistani firm purchased one million dollars at the spot rate on the settlement date, it would have spent only Rs. 23,000,000. A **spot rate** is the rate quoted for *current* currency transactions.

The topic, "managing foreign exchange risk," is discussed in greater detail in *Chapter 9: Budgeting, Product Costing, and Foreign Exchange Risk Management.*

Foreign Currency Translation

Unlike foreign exchange transactions, **foreign currency translation** does not involve actual currency exchanges. The foreign currency translation gains and losses result from restatement of all foreign subsidiary accounts for consolidation in the parent company's financial statements. The translation is necessary because adding the amounts expressed in many different currencies will not provide a meaningful total. For example, we cannot add British pounds, Canadian dollars, Indonesian rupiahs, and Swiss francs and arrive at a total that is meaningful.

If foreign exchange rates were static, the currency translation process would be no more than a simple arithmetical exercise. However, as previously mentioned, exchange rates are seldom stable—let alone static. This is what makes foreign exchange translation a complex technical topic.

Companies with international operations prepare consolidated financial statements for a variety of uses and users. Four of the common methods used to translate amounts from different foreign currencies to the domestic or functional currency (to be defined later) are described next. Comparison and analysis of the four methods will be done in the next section of this chapter.

Current Rate Method

The **current rate method** is the simplest and easiest to use of all the translation methods. All assets and all liabilities are translated at the current exchange rate—the rate at the balance sheet date. Paid-in capital accounts are translated at the applicable historical rates. Dividends are translated at the exchange rate on the date of declaration. Gains or losses from translation are included in the accumulated translation adjustment account in the stockholders' equity. On the income statement, all revenue and expense items are translated at the weighted average exchange rate for the period.

Example   It is assumed for this illustration that:

1. The French franc is the local currency of the subsidiary and the U.S. dollar is the currency of its parent company.
2. The subsidiary's inventories are stated at cost. The inventory at December 31, 19x2 was acquired when the exchange rate was $0.11. Inventory on hand on December 31, 19x1 was acquired when the exchange rate was $0.16.

3. Property, plant, and equipment was acquired in prior years when the exchange rate was $0.16, except for equipment costing 300,000 francs that was acquired late in December 19x2 when the exchange rate was $0.11. No depreciation was recorded for 19x2 on this equipment purchased in December 19x2.

4. Sales, purchases, and operating expenses all occurred uniformly throughout the year 19x2.

5. The common stock was issued when the exchange rate was $0.16.

6. The December 31, 19x1 translated retained earnings balance was $217,000.

7. The cumulative translation adjustment at December 31, 19x1 was a negative $22,000.

8. Relevant exchange rates are:

Current rate (C) at December 31, 19x1 .. $0.15
Average rate (A) for 19x2........................ 0.12
Current rate (C) at December 31, 19x2 .. 0.10
Historical rate (H) ....Depends on acquisition date

Exhibits 6–2 and 6–3 show the translated income statement and translated balance sheet respectively according to the current rate method.

The plug figure of ($179,000) shown in Exhibit 6-3 is the accumulated translation adjustment. This represents all the translation gains and losses of the past periods as well as the current period taken together.

Current-Noncurrent Method

Under the **current-noncurrent method**, balance sheet items classified as "current" are translated at the current exchange rate on the balance sheet date and items classified as

Exhibit 6–2	Translated Income Statement Using the Current Rate Method		

French Subsidiary
Income Statement
For The Year Ended December 31, 19X2

	Francs	Rate	Dollars
Sales	10,000,000	A .12	1,200,000
Expenses			
Cost of goods sold:			
Beginning inventory	1,500,000		
+Purchases	+6,000,000		
- Ending inventory	−2,000,000		
	5,500,000	A .12	660,000
Depreciation expense	200,000	A .12	24,000
Operating expense	3,300,000	A .12	396,000
Income tax expense	400,000	A .12	48,000
Total expenses	9,400,000		1,128,000
Net income	600,000	To balance sheet	72,000

Exhibit 6–3   Translated Balance Sheet Using the Current Rate Method

French Subsidiary
Balance Sheet
December 31, 19X2

	Francs	Rate		Dollars
Assets:				
Cash	200,000	C	.10	20,000
Accounts receivable, net	1,000,000	C	.10	100,000
Inventory	2,000,000	C	.10	200,000
Property, plant, and equipment	6,300,000	C	.10	630,000
Accumulated depreciation	(500,000)	C	.10	(50,000)
Total assets	9,000,000			900,000
Liabilities and owners' equity:				
Accounts payable	2,500,000	C	.10	250,000
Income tax payable	200,000	C	.10	20,000
Long-term debt	2,800,000	C	.10	280,000
Total liabilities	5,500,000			550,000
Common stock	1,500,000	H	.16	240,000
Retained earnings:				
Beginning balance	1,400,000	Given		217,000
Net income	600,000	From inc. stmt.		72,000
Cumulative translation adjustment		Plug		(179,000)
Total owners' equity	3,500,000			350,000
Total liabilities and owners' equity	9,000,000			900,000

"noncurrent" are translated at appropriate historical rates. Therefore, all current assets and current liabilities are translated at the exchange rate at the balance sheet date. All noncurrent assets and noncurrent liabilities are translated at the historical exchange rates in effect when those items were acquired or incurred.

In the current-noncurrent method, income statement items—revenue and all expenses except depreciation and amortization of noncurrent assets—are translated at a weighted average exchange rate. The depreciation and amortization expenses of noncurrent assets are translated at their appropriate historical rates.

Monetary-Nonmonetary Method

The **monetary-nonmonetary method** emphasizes monetary-nonmonetary classification for the translation. On the balance sheet, monetary items are translated at the current exchange rate on the balance sheet date and nonmonetary items are translated at their historical exchange rates. Monetary items are all assets and liabilities expressed in fixed amounts of currency. Examples of monetary assets include cash and receivables (current and noncurrent). Assets such as prepaid insurance, inventory, fixed assets, etc. do not fit the definition of monetary items and are considered nonmonetary. Since liabilities almost always are stated in fixed units of currency, they are considered monetary. However, if the amount of a liability is not fixed, then it would be considered a nonmonetary item. Examples of nonmonetary liabilities include items such as warranties on products sold and advances on sales contracts.[6]

Income statement items with the exception of cost of goods sold and depreciation and amortization of noncurrent assets are translated at a weighted average exchange rate for the period. Cost of goods sold and depreciation and amortization expenses of noncurrent assets are translated at the appropriate historical rates.

Temporal Method

Under the **temporal method**, currency translation is viewed as a restatement of the financial statements. The foreign currency amounts are translated at the exchange rates in effect at the dates when those items were measured in the foreign currency. This results in the following:

- Cash, receivables, and payables are translated at the current rate on the balance sheet date.
- All remaining assets, liabilities, and capital stock are translated at the historical exchange rates that were in effect when those assets were acquired, liabilities were incurred, and capital was contributed.[7] (This assumes use of the historical cost basis.)
- Most revenues and expenses are translated at a weighted average rate for the period. Cost of goods sold, depreciation expense, and amortization expense are translated at the appropriate historical exchange rates.
- All transaction gains and losses are taken directly to the income statement and, therefore, affect income reported for the period.

Example It is assumed for this illustration that:

- The French franc is the local currency of the subsidiary and the U.S. dollar is the currency of its parent company.
- The subsidiary's inventories are stated at cost. The inventory on hand at December 31, 19x2 was acquired when the exchange rate was $0.11. Inventory on hand on December 31, 19x1 was acquired when the exchange rate was $0.16.
- Property, plant, and equipment was all acquired in prior years when the exchange rate was $0.16, except for equipment costing 300,000 francs that was acquired late in December 19x2 when the exchange rate was $0.11. No depreciation was recorded in 19x2 on this equipment purchased in December 19x2.
- Sales, purchases, and operating expenses all occurred uniformly throughout 19x2.
- The common stock was issued when the exchange rate was $0.16.
- The December 31, 19x1 translated retained earnings balance was $260,000.

[6] *Statement of Financial Accounting Standards No. 33* (Stamford, Conn.: Financial Accounting Standard Board, 1979), Appendix D.

[7] If current value accounting is used, assets and liabilities are carried at their current value in foreign currency. The temporal method would then require them to be translated at the current exchange rate.

- Relevant exchange rates are:

Current rate at December 31, 19x1	$0.15
Average rate for 19x2.............................	0.12
Current rate at December 31, 19x2	0.10

Exhibits 6–4 and 6–5 show the translated income statement and translated balance sheet according to the temporal method.

Comparison and Analysis

The current rate method is the only method of translation among the four discussed that originated outside the U.S. It was proposed by the Institute of Chartered Accountants in England and Wales in 1968.[8] In 1970, The Institute of Chartered Accountants of Scotland declared the current method to be the only acceptable method of translation.[9] This is the easiest of all the methods to apply and is attractive due to its simplicity. The current rate method merely restates the foreign currency financial statements into the reporting currency. Accounting principles used by the foreign subsidiary are not changed for translation. This gives recognition to the fact that the foreign subsidiary operates in an environment different from the one in which the parent company operates. The original financial ratios in the foreign currency are also unaffected by current method translation because the account balances in the foreign currency are multiplied by a constant rate. In essence, this method preserves the flavor of the local environment of the foreign subsidiary. *The current rate method is the most popular translation method in practice worldwide.*

The current-noncurrent method of foreign currency translation is based on the balance sheet classification of items as current or noncurrent. This classification is not relevant for the purpose of translation.[10] Also, as noted by Professor Hepworth, the lack of association of foreign exchange gains and losses with income from international operations distorts reported earnings.[11]

The monetary-nonmonetary method is also based on the balance sheet classification of various items. The classification in this case is on the basis of the monetary and nonmonetary nature of each item. The reason given earlier for the shortcomings of the current-noncurrent method also applies to the monetary-nonmonetary method: Balance sheet classification of an item is not necessarily a relevant basis for the translation method. A translation method that depends solely on a monetary-nonmonetary distinction would be unsatisfactory for the purpose of translation.[12] An additional problem arises when a foreign subsidiary states its

[8] *The Accounting Treatment of Major Changes in the Sterling Parity of Overseas Currencies* (London: Institute of Chartered Accountants in England and Wales, 1968), par. 14.

[9] Institute of Chartered Accountants of Scotland, "Treatment in Company Accounts of Changes in the Exchange Rates of International Currencies," *The Accountant's Magazine,* September 1970, pp. 415-423.

[10] *Research Report No. 36, Management Accounting Problems in Foreign Operations* (New York: National Association of Accountants, 1960), p. 17.

[11] Samuel R. Hepworth, *Reporting Foreign Operations* (Ann Arbor, Mich.: Bureau of Business Research, University of Michigan, 1956).

[12] *Statement of Financial Accounting Standards No. 8*, "Accounting for the Translation of Foreign Currency Transactions and Foreign Currency Financial Statements" (Stamford, Conn.: Financial Accounting Standard Board, 1975), pp. 58-59.

Exhibit 6–4   Translated Income Statement Using the Temporal Method

French Subsidiary
Income Statement
For The Year Ended December 31, 19X2

	Francs	Rate		Dollars
Sales	10,000,000	A	.12	1,200,000
Expenses				
Cost of goods sold:				
Beginning inventory	1,500,000	H	.16	240,000
+Purchases	+6,000,000	A	.12	+720,000
- Ending inventory	-2,000,000	H	.11	-220,000
	5,500,000			740,000
Depreciation expense	200,000	H	.16	32,000
Operating expense	3,300,000	A	.12	396,000
Income tax expense	400,000	A	.12	48,000
Total expenses	9,400,000			1,216,000
Income before translation gain	600,000			-16,000
Translation gain		Plug		219,000
Net income		From bal. sheet		203,000

Exhibit 6–5   Translated Balance Sheet Using the Temporal Method

French Subsidiary
Balance Sheet
December 31, 19X2

	Francs	Rate		Dollars
Assets:				
Cash	200,000	C	.10	20,000
Accounts receivable, net	1,000,000	C	.10	100,000
Inventory	2,000,000	H	.11	220,000
Property, plant, and equipment	6,000,000	H	.16	960,000
Property, plant, and equipment	300,000	H	.11	33,000
Accumulated depreciation	(500,000)	H	.16	(80,000)
Total assets	9,000,000			1,253,000
Liabilities and owners' equity:				
Accounts payable	2,500,000	C	.10	250,000
Income tax payable	200,000	C	.10	20,000
Long-term debt	2,800,000	C	.10	280,000
Total liabilities	5,500,000			550,000
Common stock	1,500,000	H	.16	240,000
Retained earnings:				
Beginning balance	1,400,000	Given		260,000
Net income	600,000	Plug		203,000
Total owners' equity	3,500,000			703,000
Total liabilities and owners' equity	9,000,000			1,253,000

nonmonetary assets on a basis other than historical cost. For example, let us assume that a foreign subsidiary states its fixed assets at replacement cost. Under the monetary-nonmonetary method, the historical exchange rate would be applied to the non-historical (replacement) cost of the fixed assets for translation. The resulting figure after translation would have a questionable information value at best, and would probably be misleading.

The temporal method has some attractive features. It retains the original measurement bases of the items in the foreign currency, since it uses the exchange rates in effect at the dates when the measurements in foreign currency amounts were made. The objective is to translate assets and liabilities in a manner that will keep their measurement base at the dates of original transactions.[13] The temporal method is adaptable to any basis of measurement (e.g., historical cost, replacement cost, market value, etc). When the temporal method is used to translate historical cost measurements in foreign currency, the results obtained are the same as under the monetary-nonmonetary method. However, under the current cost, the discounted cash flow, or any other non-historical cost basis, the temporal method and the monetary-nonmonetary method would show different results. The temporal method merely converts the foreign currency accounts and does not change the accounting standards (principles) used by the foreign subsidiary.

If current value accounting is used, assets and liabilities are carried at their current value in the foreign currency. The temporal method would then require that they be translated at current rates.

Exhibit 6–6 shows the translation exchange rate used in each of the translation methods for selected balance sheet and income statement items. None of the translation methods is perfect for all situations. Therefore, the selection of a translation method is an important decision. Different translation methods, if applied to the same set of financial statements of a subsidiary, would show different results. A subsidiary showing income before translation may show a loss after translation due to a translation loss. Conversely, a subsidiary with a loss before translation may show income after translation due to the translation gain. Clearly, translation methods also affect reporting of balance sheet items.

Practices in Selected Countries

So far we have discussed two approaches for recording foreign currency transactions and four methods of foreign currency translation. On the basis of this foundation, we will now take a closer look at the comparative practices in eleven countries. A review of the practices in these countries makes us appreciate the fact that different approaches are used in different countries. In addition, often modifications are made to the basic models as discussed in this chapter. These adaptations are usually made either to address issues specific to the country or to accommodate concerns of various constituents with conflicting interests. The latter, unfortunately, often results in a standard for practice that is the result of a compromise and may not necessarily be conceptually sound.

[13] Leonard Lorensen, *Reporting Foreign Operations of U.S. Companies in U.S. Dollars* (New York: American Institute of Certified Public Accountants, 1972).

| Exhibit 6–6 | Exchange Rates Used in Various Translation Methods for Selected Balance Sheet and Income Statement Items |

	Exchange Rate for Translation			
	Current Rate Method	Current-Noncurrent Method	Monetary-Nonmonetary Method	Temporal Method
Cash	C	C	C	C
Current receivables	C	C	C	C
Inventory (at cost)	C	C	H	H
Long-term receivables	C	H	C	C
Long-term investments (cost)	C	H	H	H
Property, plant, and equipment	C	H	H	H
Intangible assets (long-term)	C	H	H	H
Current liabilities	C	C	C	C
Long-term debt	C	H	C	C
Paid-in capital	H	H	*H	H
Retained earnings	B	B	B	B
Revenues	A	A	A	A
Cost of goods sold	A	A	H	H
Depreciation expense	A	H	H	H
Amortization expense	A	H	H	H

A = Average exchange rate for the current period
C = Current exchange rate at balance sheet date
H = Historical exchange rate
B = Balancing (residual or plug) figure

*Assumes no nonconvertible preferred stock

In this chapter, until now, we have not specifically used the term **hedging**. To protect themselves against risks associated with foreign exchange fluctuations, managers may decide to take certain measures referred to as **hedging strategies**. There are numerous financial instruments available for implementation of hedging strategies. Forward exchange contracts, discussed briefly earlier in the chapter, are one of the commonly used instruments in hedging strategies. The topic of managing foreign exchange risk is discussed in *Chapter 9: Budgeting, Product Costing, and Foreign Exchange Risk Management.* To compare practices in selected countries, the above explanation of hedging should suffice.

Many countries distinguish between integrated and self-sustaining foreign operations. An **integrated foreign operation** is one whose economic activities have a direct impact on the reporting (parent) entity. Such a foreign entity is financially and/or operationally dependent on its parent company. On the other hand, a **self-sustaining foreign operation** is one whose activities generally have no direct impact on the reporting entity's operations. Typically, the funds generated by a self-sustaining foreign operation are adequate to meet its operational and financing needs. Also, such foreign operations usually have fewer dealings and less operational interdependency with the parent than do the integrated foreign operations.

Exhibits 6–7 through 6–9 show the foreign currency translation practices of Bayer Group, Toyota, and Teléfonos De México respectively.

Australia

In Australia, if a foreign operation is integrated with the reporting entity, its accounts are translated using the temporal method. Foreign exchange gains or losses are included in the net income of the current period.

Financial statements of a self-sustaining foreign operation are translated using the current rate method. Any exchange gain or loss is taken directly to adjust the foreign currency translation reserve in stockholders' equity.

Foreign currency transactions are recorded using the two-transaction approach.

The disclosure requirements include:

- Translation method(s) used.
- Total transaction gain or loss in the current period income statement.
- Changes in the foreign currency translation reserve.
- Foreign currency exposure/hedging strategies.

Brazil

The Brazilian Accountants Institute (IBRACON) issues pronouncements of accounting principles. After these pronouncements are approved by the Securities Exchange Commission (CVM) they become mandatory for publicly traded companies.

The Brazilian statement dealing with foreign currency standards, issued by IBRACON and approved by CVM, classifies foreign operations into two types. Each type requires application of a different procedure as described below.

The first type includes operations in countries with "hard" currencies, or countries with "soft" currencies but with an effective system for adjustment of financial statements for effects of inflation.[14] For such countries, the current rate method is required.

The second type of foreign operations is in countries with "soft" currencies, high inflation rates, and no existing system to make adequate inflation adjustments. For operations under such conditions the Brazilian inflation accounting system is used for all nonmonetary items in the balance sheet except inventories.[15]

All exchange gains or losses are included in current period income.

Disclosure of the method(s) used for translation of foreign currency statements is required in a note to the financial statements.

---

[14] No definition is provided for "hard" and "soft" currencies, but hard currencies are easily convertible to other national currencies. Examples include the U.S. dollar, British pound, German mark, and Japanese yen.

[15] *Investments in Foreign Operations and Criteria for Conversion of Financial Statements in Other Currencies to Local Currency* (IBRACON, 1986).

Exhibit 6–7   Bayer Group Foreign Currency Translation

BAYER GROUP
CONSOLIDATED BALANCE SHEETS (Partial)
(DM million)

Stockholders' Equity and Liabilities

Stockholders' equity	1994	1993
Capital stock of Bayer AG	3,465	3,354
Capital reserves of Bayer AG	4,915	4,672
Retained earnings	8,118	9,086
Net income	1,970	1,327
Translation differences	(1,866)	(664)
Minority interests in consolidated subsidiaries	453	431
	17,055	**18,206**
Provisions		
Provisions for pensions and similar commitments	8,451	7,650
Other provisions	4,825	4,091
	13,276	**11,741**
Other liabilities		
Financial obligations	6,276	5,264
Trade accounts payable	2,407	2,085
Miscellaneous liabilities	3,113	2,767
	11,796	**10,116**
Deferred income	**236**	**108**
	42,363	**40,171**

Foreign currency translation

In the individual consolidated companies' statements, foreign currency receivables and payables that are not hedged are translated either at the rate at which they were initially recorded or at the closing rate, whichever yields the lower amount for payables. Foreign currency receivables and payables that are hedged by means of forward exchange contracts are translated at the hedged rates.

The majority of foreign consolidated companies are to be regarded as foreign entities since they are financially, economically and organizationally autonomous. Their functional currencies are thus the respective local currencies. The assets and liabilities of these companies are translated at closing rates, income and expense items at the average rates for the year.

Where, in exceptional cases, the operations of a foreign company are integral to those of Bayer AG, the functional currency is the German mark. A temporal translation method is therefore used that is recognized in income. Property, plant and equipment, intangible assets, investments in affiliated companies and other securities included in investments are translated at the average exchange rate in the year of addition, along with the relevant amortization, depreciation and write-downs. All other balance sheet items are translated at the closing rate. Income and expense items (except amortization, depreciation and write-downs) are translated at the average rate for the year.

As in the past, companies operating in hyperinflationary economies prepare hard-currency statements. Accordingly their statements are, in effect, translated by the temporal method described above.

Exchange differences arising from the translation of foreign companies' balance sheets are shown in a separate stockholders' equity item. In case of divestiture, the respective exchange differences are reversed and recognized in income.

Source: Bayer, *Annual Report 1994,* p. 49 and p. 57.

**Exhibit 6–8   Toyota Motor Corporation and Consolidated
                  Subsidiaries Foreign Currency Translation**

Consolidated Balance Sheets (Partial)

Toyota Motor Corporation and Consolidated Subsidiaries

June 30, 1994 and 1993

	Millions of yen	
ASSETS	**1994**	1993
Current Assets:		
Cash and cash equivalents	¥ 944,879	¥1,054,251
Short-term investments	762,181	384,258
Trade notes and accounts receivable	1,044,232	1,092,039
Inventories	399,242	391,186
Other	1,592,999	1,649,883
Less: allowance for doubtful receivables	(45,654)	(41,863)
Total current assets	4,697,879	4,529,754
Investments and Other Assets:		
Investments in securities	917,512	876,445
Investments in unconsolidated subsidiaries and affiliates	922,269	843,828
Long-term loans	362,293	444,538
Other	46,107	90,263
Less: allowance for doubtful receivables	(9,714)	(10,199)
Total investments and other assets	2,238,467	2,244,875
Property, Plant and Equipment:		
Land	517,698	513,183
Buildings and structures	1,250,872	1,216,452
Machinery and equipment	4,282,436	3,900,106
Construction in progress	59,329	115,353
Less: accumulated depreciation	(3,477,347)	(3,181,346)
Net property, plant and equipment	2,632,988	2,563,748
Translation Adjustments	88,304	76,040
Total Assets	¥9,657,638	¥9,414,417

Foreign currency translation

Accounts of overseas consolidated subsidiaries have been translated into yen at the rate of exchange prevailing at the end of the fiscal year used in consolidating the accounts of each company.

Source: Toyota, *Annual Report 1994,* p. 34 and p. 40.

Exhibit 6–9   Teléfonos De México S.A. de C.V.
Foreign Exchange Differences

Consolidated Statements of Income
(Thousands of Mexican new pesos with purchasing power at December 31, 1993)

	Year ended December 31	
	1993	1992
Operating revenues:		
Long-distance service:		
International	NPs. **4,849,817**	NPs. 4,745,910
Domestic	**8,294,563**	7,772,517
Local service	**10,528,765**	9,102,152
Other	**928,415**	742,519
	24,601,560	22,363,098
Operating expenses:		
Salaries and related costs	**5,783,780**	5,307,171
Depreciation	**2,908,681**	2,373,735
Maintenance and other expenses	**3,488,182**	3,002,856
Telephone service tax	**2,139,048**	1,973,440
	14,319,691	12,657,202
Operating income	**10,281,869**	9,705,896
Integral cost of financing:		
Interest income	(**1,434,560**)	(1,543,859)
Interest expense	**929,959**	1,009,213
Exchange (gain) loss	(**32,578**)	64,270
Monetary effect	(**28,062**)	(251,402)
	(**565,241**)	(721,778)
Income before income tax and		
employee profit sharing	**10,847,110**	10,427,674
Provisions for:		
Income tax	**1,197,716**	1,199,049
Employee profit sharing	**646,301**	614,670
	1,844,017	1,813,719
Net income	NPs. **9,003,093**	NPs. 8,613,955

Exchange differences

Transactions in foreign currency are recorded at the prevailing exchange rate at the time
of the related transaction. Foreign currency denominated assets and liabilities are
translated at the prevailing exchange rate at the balance sheet date. Exchange
differences are applied directly to income of the year.

Source: Teléfonos De México S.A. de C.V., *Annual Report 1993,* p. 52 and p. 59.

Canada

The financial statements of integrated foreign operations are translated according to the temporal method. Exchange gains or losses for integrated foreign operations are shown in the income statement immediately, except those arising from long-term monetary items. Exchange adjustments for long-term monetary items are deferred and amortized over the remaining life of the related item.

The financial statements of self-sustaining foreign operations are required to be translated under the current rate method. Exchange gains or losses are accumulated as a separate item in the stockholders' equity section in the translation adjustment account.[16]

For foreign currency transactions, the two-transaction approach is required. However, gains or losses on long-term monetary assets and liabilities are deferred and amortized.

Disclosure of methods of amortization for deferred exchange gains or losses is required. Any material changes in the translation adjustment account in stockholders' equity should be disclosed.

France

The financial statements of an integrated foreign operation are translated using the temporal method. Foreign exchange gains and losses are shown immediately in the income statement.

The current rate method is required for the translation of financial statements of a self-sustaining foreign operation. The foreign exchange gains or losses are reported as a separate item in shareholders' equity.

For foreign currency transactions, unrealized foreign exchange losses are shown immediately in the statutory (non-consolidated) income statement, while unrealized gains are not recorded. The companies are, however, allowed to include both unrealized gains and unrealized losses in consolidated income statements.

Listed companies with significant involvement in foreign currency markets are required to include an analysis of management's sensitivity to exchange fluctuations, i.e., hedging strategies. Methods used to translate the financial statements of foreign subsidiaries should be disclosed in the notes accompanying the consolidated financial statements.

Germany

There are no specific requirements for the translation of foreign currency financial statements in German law or accounting principles. In practice, either the current rate method or the temporal method is used for translation of financial statements of foreign operations. The translation method selected usually determines the treatment of foreign exchange gains or losses. If the temporal method is used, exchange adjustments are generally recognized in the income statement. In cases when the current rate method is used, the exchange gains or losses

---

[16] *CICA Handbook* (Toronto: Canadian Institute of Chartered Accountants, December 1983), Section 1650.

are usually included in the stockholders' equity. Interestingly, the amounts of exchange gains or losses are not normally shown separately in financial statements.

No distinction is made between integrated foreign operation and self-sustaining foreign operation for translation purposes. In spite of the non-existence of any statutory or professional accounting requirements for foreign currency translation methods, consistency in the use of a translation method and its disclosure are required.

Foreign currency transactions are generally recorded according to the two-transaction approach. However, foreign exchange losses are immediately recognized, but foreign exchange gains are deferred until the date of settlement. This is in accordance with the prudence concept.

Japan

Financial statements of all foreign operations are translated using the modified temporal method. The departure from the pure temporal method is in translation of long-term monetary assets and liabilities. They are translated at the exchange rate in effect when the asset was acquired or the liability was incurred. Accumulated foreign exchange translation gains or losses from foreign subsidiaries are shown as an asset or liability in a translation adjustment account on the balance sheet. In the case of divisions or branches, translation adjustments are reported in the income statement of the current period. Disclosure of the translation method used is required.[17]

The Japanese generally use the two-transaction approach for foreign currency transactions, except when transactions with a fixed yen amount are involved. For these transactions, gains or losses are deferred until the date of settlement.

Mexico

There are no published statements of comprehensive professional standards or statutory requirements relating to foreign currency translation. The treatment of specific items is addressed in various accounting statements. In such cases, the current rate method is generally required.

Where there are no required Mexican accounting principles, often *Statement of Financial Accounting Standards No. 52* (United States) is relied upon in practice. However, practices vary widely since *SFAS No. 52* is not mandatory.

Netherlands

Accounting principles in the Netherlands are developed with a business economic approach rather than a legalistic statutory approach. The Dutch Commercial Code requires that accounting be based on sound business practice. It is not surprising that the Dutch accounting profession develops accounting principles to respond to dynamic economic conditions.

[17] Business Accounting Deliberation Council, *Accounting Standards for Foreign Currency Translation*, (Tokyo: Japanese Institute of Certified Public Accountants, 1976).

Financial statements of integrated foreign operations are translated according to the current rate method if the entity uses current value accounting. If the financial statements are on historical cost basis, then the temporal method is used. All gains or losses from translation are included in net income of the current period.

Financial statements of a self-sustaining operation are translated using the current rate method and resulting gains or losses are transferred directly to a reserve account in the shareholders' equity.

The two-transaction approach is used for foreign currency transactions.

Disclosures of the foreign currency translation methods used and the treatment of foreign exchange gains or losses are required.

Nigeria

Nigeria was one of the thirteen countries appointed to the IASC board for a five-year term starting January 1, 1983. Accounting standards are issued by the Nigerian Accounting Standards Board, which issues *Statements of Accountancy Standards* (SASs). For those reporting situations where an SAS has not been issued, the provisions of the relevant International Accounting Standard of the IASC are used. The Nigerian Accounting Standards Board's *SAS No. 7* deals with foreign currency.

Financial statements of integrated foreign operations are translated using the temporal method. Most exchange gains and losses are included in the determination of income of the current period.

Financial statements of self-sustaining foreign operations are translated according to the current rate method. Translation gains or losses are accumulated separately in a translation adjustment account in the shareholders' equity.

The treatment of exchange gains or losses on foreign-currency-denominated transactions depends on their nature. Such gains and losses are included in income determination, except when they arise from long-term monetary items. In the latter situation, they are deferred and amortized over the life of the item.

Any material changes in the translation adjustment account during the period are required to be disclosed. The amount of exchange gains or losses included in income, however, need not be separately disclosed.[18]

United Kingdom

Financial statements of integrated foreign operations are translated using the temporal method. Gains or losses arising from translation are shown on the income statement of the current period.

---

[18] Coopers and Lybrand, *International Accounting Summaries,* 2d ed. (New York: John Wiley & Sons, Inc., 1993).

Financial statements of self-sustaining foreign operations are translated according to the current rate method. Gains or losses from translation are recorded as adjustments to reserves in the stockholders' equity. A great majority of companies in the U.K. use the current rate method.

Disclosures are required to be made of:

- Translation methods used.
- Amount of translation gains or losses taken to stockholders' equity during current period.
- Amount of translation gains or losses included to determine income of the current period.
- Net movement on reserves attributable to exchange differences.

Foreign-currency-denominated transactions are recorded using the two-transaction approach. All gains or losses are reflected in net income of the current period.

United States

The term *functional currency* is basic to the understanding and application of U.S. foreign currency standards. According to *SFAS No. 52*, the **functional currency** of an entity is the currency of the primary environment in which the entity operates.[19] For a more in-depth discussion of functional currency, refer to Appendix 6A.

An integrated foreign operation has the U.S. dollar as its functional currency. The temporal method is used for translation of financial statements of an integrated foreign operation. The amount of translation gains or losses are included in current period income.

Financial statements of self-sustaining foreign operations (the functional currency is other than the U.S. dollar) are translated using the current rate method. Translation gains or losses are shown as a separate part of shareholders' equity.

For foreign currency transactions, the two-transaction approach is used. There are two exceptions to this requirement: When the exchange adjustments relate to certain intercompany transactions that are of a long-term nature, and when foreign currency transactions are intended to offset other exchange gains or losses that would normally be reported in the income statement.

Financial statement disclosures include:

- Total transaction gain or loss included in determining income for the current period.
- An analysis of changes during the period in shareholders' equity arising from translation adjustments.
- Any material rate changes that occur after the balance sheet date.

SFAS No. 52 is discussed in Appendix 6A.

[19] *SFAS No. 52*, p. 76.

IASC Standard 21: The Effects of Changes in Foreign Exchange Rates

IAS 21 deals with foreign currency.[20] First issued in 1983, the standard was revised in 1993.

For integrated foreign operations, *IAS 21* requires that the financial statements be translated using the temporal method. Translation gains or losses are included in current period income.

The standard requires the current rate method for translation of self-sustaining foreign operations. The translation gains or losses are transferred to reserves and reported in shareholders' equity. Income statement items of a self-sustaining foreign operation should be translated either at the actual rates or the average rate for the period, and the gains and losses are taken to a separate section of the shareholders' equity.

The disclosure requirements include:

- An analysis of the impact of the translation adjustment on related parts of stockholders' equity and income statement.
- Methods used for translation.

IAS 21 recommends the two-transaction approach in general. The revised *IAS 21* requires that the financial statements of foreign subsidiaries operating in hyperinflationary economies must be restated in accordance with *IAS 29*, prior to translation.

Exhibit 6–10 summarizes the foreign currency translation requirements in the eleven countries and the revised *IAS 21*.

Appendix 6A   Discussion of SFAS No. 52

Translation and Remeasurement

Statement of Financial Accounting Standards No. 52, titled "Foreign Currency Translation," is the current authoritative pronouncement on this topic in the U.S. *SFAS No. 52* recognizes a local company perspective. The method of conversion depends on the functional currency of the foreign operation. Functional currency is the currency of the primary economic environment in which the foreign entity operates. Generally, it would mean that the foreign entity generates and expends cash in the functional currency.[21] Other guidelines provided by the Financial Accounting Standards Board to determine a firm's functional currency of the firm, in addition to cash flows, are summarized below.

- If the sale price of the foreign entity's products is determined by worldwide competition rather than the local market, then the functional currency may be the parent's currency.

---

[20] *International Accounting Standard 21,* "The Effects of Changes in Foreign Exchange Rates" (London: International Accounting Standards Committee, 1983) and the revisions approved in November 1993 under the Comparability/Improvements Project.

[21] *SFAS No. 52,* Appendix A.

Exhibit 6–10   Foreign Currency Translation Comparison

| | Treatment of Exchange Differences | | |
| | Foreign Currency Transactions* | | Self-sustaining Foreign Operations* |
Country/Organization	Short-term Monetary Items	Long-term Monetary Items	
IASC	I	I	R
Australia	I	I	R
Brazil	I	I	I
Canada	I	D	R
France	GD, I	GD, I	R
Germany	GD, I	GD	NS
Japan	I	I	D
Mexico	I	I	NS
Netherlands	I	I	R
Nigeria	I	D	R
United Kingdom	I	I	R
United States	I	I	R

*Some countries, such as the United States, refer to the "functional currency" of operations. For the purpose of this matrix, it has been assumed that for "Foreign currency transactions," the functional currency is the reporting currency. For "Self-sustaining foreign operations," the functional currency is the local currency.

D   Deferral of exchange differences permitted or required.
GD   Exchange gains deferred; losses recognized in income (except to the extent of previously deferred gains).
I   Exchange differences recognized in income.
R   Exchange differences taken to reserves.
NS   No treatment specified.

Source: Coopers & Lybrand, *Foreign Currency Translation and Hedging,* 1994, p. 205 (adapted).

- If costs for the entity's product are primarily local costs, then the functional currency may be the foreign entity's local currency.
- If the sales market is mostly in the parent's country or sales are denominated in the parent's currency, then the functional currency may be the parent's currency.
- If financing is denominated in the foreign entity's local currency, then the functional currency may be the foreign entity's local currency.[22]

The *SFAS No. 52* requirements are designed to reflect in consolidated financial statements the financial results and relationships of individual consolidated entities as measured in their primary, i.e., functional currency.[23]

The above discussion may be summarized in the following manner:

[22] Jay M. Smith and K. Fred Skousen, *Intermediate Accounting,* 11th ed. (Cincinnati, Ohio: South-Western Publishing Co., 1992), p. 1022.

[23] *SFAS No. 52,* par. 70.

- If the subsidiary is relatively self-sustaining and its operations are confined to the foreign country in which it is located, then the local currency would be the functional currency. For example, if the subsidiary of a U.S. pharmaceutical firm manufactures and distributes its products in Thailand, then the functional currency of the Thai subsidiary will be the local currency, the baht, and not the U.S. dollar, the currency of its parent company.
- If operations of a foreign subsidiary are integrated with the parent company, the functional currency would be the parent company's currency. For example, an Indonesian operation assembles the parts received from its U.S. parent company and returns the product to the U.S. parent for distribution. The functional currency of the Indonesian subsidiary is the U.S. dollar and not the Indonesian rupiah.

In a highly inflationary economy, *SFAS 52* requires use of the reporting currency as the functional currency. A highly inflationary economy is defined as one that has cumulative inflation of approximately 100 percent or more over a three-year period.

If the foreign subsidiary's accounts are kept in a foreign currency that is also judged to be its functional currency, its financial statements are *translated* to the U.S. dollars using the current rate method. Translation gains and losses are disclosed separately in consolidated equity.

If the U.S. dollar is deemed to be the functional currency, a foreign subsidiary's financial statements are *remeasured* using the temporal method. In such a case, all translation gains and losses are included in current period net income.[24]

Foreign Currency Transactions

SFAS No. 52 defines a foreign currency transaction as a transaction requiring settlement in a foreign currency.[25]

The rules for foreign currency transactions in *SFAS No. 52* are shown below.

- At the date the transaction is recognized, each asset, liability, revenue, expense, gain or loss arising from the transaction shall be measured and recorded in the functional currency of the recording entity by use of the exchange rate in effect at that date.
- At each balance sheet date, recorded balances that are denominated in a currency other than the functional currency of the recording entity shall be adjusted to reflect the current exchange rate.[26]

In essence, *SFAS No. 52* requires the two-transaction approach for foreign currency transactions. There are two exceptions to this requirement. The first involves intercompany transactions of a long-term nature. The second exception applies when the foreign currency

[24] *Ibid.,* par. 15.

[25] Note the terminology *translated* and *remeasured* as used in *SFAS No. 52.*

[26] *Ibid.,* par. 16.

transactions are intended to offset exchange gains or losses that otherwise would be reported in the income statement.

Appendix Summary

Exchange rates have a direct impact on conversion of the financial statements of a foreign operation into U.S. dollars. According to *SFAS No. 52,* the method of conversion depends on the foreign entity's functional currency. If the functional currency is the U.S. dollar, the financial statements are *remeasured* using the temporal method. If the functional currency is the foreign operation's local currency, the financial statements are *translated* using the current rate method.

SFAS No. 52 requires the two-transaction approach for foreign currency transactions.

Appendix 6B   Selected Currencies

Country	Currency	Country	Currency
Angola	Kwanza	Ghana	Cedi
Argentina	Peso	Greece	Drachma
Australia	Dollar	Hong Kong	Dollar
Austria	Schilling	Hungary	Forint
Azerbaijan	Manat	Iceland	Krona
Bahamas	Dollar	India	Rupee
Bahrain	Dinar	Indonesia	Rupiah
Bangladesh	Taka	Iran	Rial
Belgium	Franc	Ireland	Punt
Bermuda	Dollar	Israel	Shekel
Bolivia	Boliviano	Italy	Lira
Botswana	Pula	Jamaica	Dollar
Brazil	Real	Japan	Yen
Brunei Darussalam	Dollar	Jordan	Dinar
Cambodia	Riel	Kenya	Shilling
Canada	Dollar	Korea (South)	Won
Chile	Peso	Kuwait	Dinar
China	Yuan	Lebanon	Pound
Colombia	Peso	Luxembourg	Franc
Costa Rica	Colon	Malaysia	Ringgit
Cyprus	Pound	Malta	Lira
Czech Republic	Koruna	Mexico	Peso
Denmark	Krone	Morocco	Dirham
Dominican Republic	Peso	Netherlands	Guilder
Ecuador	Sucre	New Zealand	Dollar
Egypt	Pound	Nigeria	Naira
El Salvador	Colon	Norway	Krone
Fiji	Dollar	Pakistan	Rupee
Finland	Markka	Papua New Guinea	Kina
France	Franc	Paraguay	Guaraní
Germany	Deutsche Mark	Peru	Sol

Philippines	Peso	Taiwan	Dollar
Poland	Zloty	Tanzania	Shilling
Portugal	Escudo	Thailand	Baht
Puerto Rico	U.S. Dollar	Tunisia	Dinar
Qatar	Riyal	Turkey.	Lira
Russian	Ruble	Uganda	Shilling
Saudi Arabia	Riyal	United Arab Emirates	Dirham
Singapore	Dollar	United Kingdom	Pound
Slovak Republic.	Koruna	United States	Dollar
South Africa	Rand	Uruguay	Peso
Spain	Peseta	Venezuela.	Bolivar
Swaziland	Lilangeni	Vietnam.	Dong
Sweden	Krona	Western Samoa	Tala
Switzerland	Franc	Yemen	Riyal
Syria.	Pound	Zimbabwe.	Dollar

Note to Students

To keep up with current developments affecting the value of currencies of various countries, you should regularly read a business newspaper or a business news magazine such as *The Wall Street Journal, Financial Times, The Asian Wall Street Journal,* and *Business Week.* At a minimum, you should read the business section of a large city newspaper.

To keep current with the national and IASC standards, regularly read at least one accounting journal. Many accounting journals, especially those oriented toward practitioners, have articles and news items on both national as well as IASC standards. Examples include *Journal of Accountancy, The Accountant's Magazine, Journal of Accounting Auditing and Finance, IASC News, Journal of International Financial Management and Accounting, Abacus*, and *Journal of International Accounting.*

To get an in-depth understanding of generally accepted accounting principles in a specific country, study the authoritative pronouncements. It is also helpful to review sets of financial statements of actual companies showing applications of the standards to get a clearer understanding.

Chapter Summary

- One of the complexities in financial reporting of companies involved in international activities (operations and investment) is caused by different currencies.

- Foreign currency transactions and foreign currency translation require that before consolidated financial statements can be prepared, approaches and methods must be selected to record exchange rate adjustments.

- For foreign currency transactions two approaches may be used: the one-transaction approach or the two-transaction approach. The latter is more popular in practice worldwide.

- The four basic methods for translating financial statements in a foreign currency are the current rate method, the current-noncurrent method, the monetary-nonmonetary method, and the temporal method.

- A review of practices in various countries reveals that the translation method selected usually depends on whether a foreign operation is considered to be integrated with the parent company or viewed as a self-sustaining (self-contained) entity.

- Various modifications are made by individual countries while adopting a translation method. Therefore, it is necessary to take a close look at the specific country's reporting standards relating to accounting treatment of foreign currencies.

Questions for Discussion

1. Define foreign currency transaction.

2. What are the two approaches to recording foreign currency transactions?

3. What is the underlying logic for using the two-transaction approach as opposed to the one-transaction approach for foreign currency transactions?

4. What are the advantages and disadvantages of using the one-transaction approach versus the two-transaction approach in accounting for foreign currency transaction gains and losses?

5. Do you prefer the one-transaction approach or the two-transaction approach to foreign currency transactions? Explain the reasons for your position.

6. How are foreign currency transactions generally accounted for under *IAS 21*?

7. Can a firm take measures to eliminate the risks associated with foreign currency transactions due to exchange rate fluctuations? Explain.

8. What is a forward exchange contract?

9. What are the two key features of a forward exchange contract?

10. Refer to the sample exchange rates shown in Exhibit 6–1. Did the market, at the date shown, expect the British pound to increase, decrease, or stay the same relative to the dollar over the next few months?

11. What is the main difference between a transaction gain or loss and a translation gain or loss?

12. What does it mean to translate the financial statements of a foreign operation? Why is it done?

13. What does it mean to translate a financial statement item at the historical rate? the current rate?

14. What is meant by an integrated foreign operation? a self-sustaining foreign operation?

15. Explain and evaluate the current-noncurrent method of foreign currency translation.

16. Explain and evaluate the monetary-nonmonetary method of foreign currency translation.

17. List similarities and differences between the current-noncurrent method and the monetary-nonmonetary method.

18. Discuss the temporal method of foreign currency translation.

19. Contrast between the results of translation using the temporal method when foreign operation financial statements are prepared according to historical cost basis vs. current value basis.

20. Discuss the current rate method of foreign currency translation.

21. Which of the four translation methods discussed in the chapter recognizes the different operating environment of a foreign operation?

22. Since foreign currency translation merely involves conversion of a foreign currency balance to another currency by using the appropriate exchange rate, why is it such a complex topic?

23. Describe the main similarities and differences in the current-noncurrent, monetary-nonmonetary, temporal, and current rate methods of translating items on a foreign currency balance sheet.

24. Answer Question 23 for a foreign currency income statement.

25. (Appendix 6A) Explain the concept of functional currency as used in *SFAS No. 52*.

26. (Appendix 6A) Identify the primary factor in determining a firm's functional currency. What other factors can influence the determination of the firm's functional currency?

27. (Appendix 6A) Explain the terms *translation* and *remeasurement* as used in *SFAS No. 52*, "Foreign Currency Translation."

28. (Appendix 6A) Describe the essential features of *SFAS No. 52*, "Foreign Currency Translation."

Exercises/Problems

6-1   Schmidt Imports, a German corporation, purchased merchandise on May 1 on 30-day open account in the sum of 60,000 Dutch guilders from Netherlands Exports. On May 1, the rate of exchange was 1 Dutch guilder = 0.90 German mark.

On May 31, Schmidt Imports purchased a draft in the sum of 60,000 Dutch guilders for payment to Netherlands Exports at the cost of 50,000 German marks.

Required:
(1) Using the one-transaction approach, what entries are to be recorded on the books of Schmidt Imports:
   a. on May 1.
   b. on May 31.
   Show computations.
(2) Do requirement (1) using the two-transaction approach. Show computations.

6-2 California Surfboards, a U.S. corporation, sold merchandise on March 1 on 30-day open account in the sum of 100,000 Argentine pesos to the Juan Importers. The rate for the Argentine peso on March 1 was 1 U.S. dollar = 1.05 Argentine pesos. On April 1, the Juan Importers paid its account by remitting 100,000 Argentine pesos to California Surfboards. The rate on April 1 was 1 U.S. dollar = 1.10 Argentine peso.

Required:
(1) Using the one-transaction approach, state what entries are to be recorded by California Surfboards:
   a. on March 1.
   b. on April 1.
   Show computations.
(2) Complete requirement (1) above, this time using the two-transaction approach. Show computations.

6-3 On July 15, Wallis Enterprises, a calendar-year U.S. manufacturer, purchased 100 million yen worth of parts from the Yokoyama Company paying 20 percent down, the balance to be paid in three months. Interest at the annual rate of 10 percent is payable on the unpaid foreign currency balance. The exchange rate on July 15 was $1.00 = ¥125. On October 15, the exchange rate was $1.00 = ¥110.

Required: Prepare journal entries in U.S. dollars to record the incurrence and settlement of this foreign currency transaction assuming:
(1) a single-transaction approach.
(2) a two-transaction approach.

6-4 Cheng Corporation is the Taiwanese subsidiary of Excel International, a Canadian manufacturer. Cheng's balance sheet is shown below. The current exchange rate is Canadian $.05 = NT$1 (20 Taiwanese dollars to the Canadian dollar). The historical exchange rate is Canadian $.04 = NT$1 (25 Taiwanese dollars to the Canadian dollar).

Balance Sheet of Cheng Corporation (000,000's)

Assets		Liabilities and Shareholders' Equity	
Cash	$ 10,000	Accounts payable	$ 20,000
Accounts receivable	20,000	Long-term liabilities	30,000
Inventories (cost = 30,000)	25,000		
Fixed assets (net)	50,000	Shareholders' equity	55,000
Total	$105,000	Total	$105,000

All accounts are in Taiwanese dollars. Inventories are carried at lower of cost or market.

Required: Translate the Taiwanese dollar balance sheet of Cheng Corporation into Canadian dollars using the current rate method.

6-5 Based on the information in Exercise 6-4, translate Cheng Corporation's balance sheet using the temporal method.

6-6   Based on the information in Exercise 6-4, translate Cheng Corporation's balance sheet using the current-noncurrent method.

6-7   Based on the information in Exercise 6-4, translate Cheng Corporation's balance sheet using the monetary-nonmonetary method.

6-8   Waheed Inc., has a foreign subsidiary that needs to be translated into Canadian dollars. The financial statements are as follows:

Balance Sheet
December 31, I9x1

	Local Currency (LC)	
Cash	LC	150,000
Accounts receivable		225,000
Merchandise inventory		60,000
Fixed assets (net)		400,000
	LC	835,000
Current liabilities	LC	200,000
Long-term debt		250,000
Common stock		310,000
Retained earnings		75,000
	LC	835,000

Statement of Income and Retained Earnings
for the Year Ended December 31, I9x1

	Local Currency (LC)	
Sales	LC	600,000
Cost of goods sold		250,000
Gross profit		350,000
Depreciation expense		55,000
Other expense		105,000
Total expenses		160,000
Income before tax		190,000
Income tax		90,000
Net income		100,000
Retained earnings 1/1/19x1		20,000
Dividends		-45,000
Retained earnings 12/31/19x1	LC	75,000

The following are exchange rates per unit of LC:

At 12/31/19x1 . . . . $1.40
When fixed assets were acquired, long-term
debt incurred, and capital stock sold. 1.80
Average for 19x1. . . . . 1.50

At 7/1/19x1	1.60
At 10/1/19x1	1.65
For 19x1 beginning inventory	1.70
For 19x1 ending inventory.................	1.55

Additional information:

Revenues, expenses, and inventory purchases were incurred uniformly during the year.

Dividends were paid in equal amounts on 7/1 and 10/1.

The retained earnings balance 1/1/19x1 was Canadian $15,000.

Beginning inventory was LC 50,000 and ending inventory was LC 60,000.

Required:

(1) Translate the financial statements using the current rate method.

(2) Translate the financial statements using the temporal method.

6-9 Identify the four foreign currency translation methods discussed in this chapter with regard to the translation of the items below. Use these abbreviations:

> H - Historical rate
> C - Current rate
> A - Average rate
> B - Balancing figure

a. Cash

b. Accounts receivable

c. Inventory (at cost)

d. Long-term receivables

e. Long-term investments

f. Property, plant, and equipment

g. Long-term intangible assets

h. Accounts payable

i. Long-term debt

j. Paid-in capital

k. Retained earnings

l. Sales revenue

m. Cost of goods sold

n. Depreciation expense

o. Amortization expense

6-10

Appendix 6A

For each of the following foreign financial statement items, indicate whether current, average, or historical exchange rates would be used to translate them into U.S. dollars under *SFAS No. 52*. Assume that the foreign currency is the functional currency for this foreign operation.

a. Cash

b. Merchandise inventories

c. Accounts receivable

d. Fixed assets

e. Accounts payable

f. Long-term debt

g. Revenue from sales

h. Depreciation expense

i. Amortization expense

6-11

Appendix 6A

For each of the following financial statement items, indicate what exchange rate under *SFAS No. 52* should be used to translate foreign currency amounts into the U.S. dollar. Use H for the historical rate, C for the current rate, and A for the average rate. Assume that the foreign currency is the functional currency for this foreign operation.

a. Sales revenue

b. Depreciation expense

c. Accounts receivable

d. Long-term notes receivable

e. Long-term bonds payable

f. Prepaid insurance

g. Goodwill

h. Salaries expense

i. Plant, property, and equipment

j. Cash

k. Accounts payable

l. Income taxes expense

m. Inventories

6-12

Appendix 6A

Amti Megabuck Corporation's subsidiary in Bombay has fixed assets valued at 10,000,000 rupees (Rs). Of these, one-quarter was acquired four years ago when the exchange rate was Rs 20 = $1.00. The balance was acquired two years ago when the exchange rate was Rs 25 = $1.00. Fixed assets are being depreciated using the straight-line method with an estimated useful life of 10 years. Relevant exchange rates for the current year are:

Year-end rate: Rs 30 = $1.00

Average rate: Rs 28 = $1.00

Required:

(1) Conforming to *SFAS No. 52,* calculate the Indian subsidiary's depreciation expense for the current year assuming the rupee is the functional currency.

(2) Repeat (1) above assuming the U.S. dollar is the functional currency.

Case: Translation of Foreign Currency Financial Statements

You have just graduated from a university and started your first accounting job with Canadian International Limited, a multinational corporation based in Canada.

On your third day at the job, the chief accountant walked into your office and said, "We just received the financial statements of our new French Subsidiary. I am still undecided as to what translation method to use. Could you please translate the balance sheet and the income statement from French francs to Canadian dollars using the current rate method and the temporal method. Then let us discuss which method would be appropriate to use." He gave you the information and left. You were pleased to receive this assignment, as you had taken the international accounting course in your senior year. You started reviewing the information the chief accountant had left with you. The information is reproduced below.

French Subsidiary
Balance Sheet
December 31, 1996

Cash		F 500,000
Accounts receivable		2,000,000
Inventory		1,500,000
Land		2,000,000
Buildings and equipment	F10,000,000	
Less: Accumulated depreciation	1,000,000	9,000,000
Total assets		F15,000,000
Accounts payable		F2,500,000
Other current liabilities		1,000,000
Long-term debt		5,500,000
		9,000,000
Paid-in capital		5,000,000
Retained earnings January 1, 1996	0	
Plus: Net income	1,500,000	
Less: Dividends	500,000	
Retained earnings December 31, 1996		1,000,000
Total liabilities and stockholders' equity		F15,000,000

French Subsidiary
Income Statement
For the Year Ended December 31, 1996

Sales		F12,000,000
Cost of sales:		
Inventory January 1, 1996		
Purchases	F8,500,000	
Inventory December 31, 1996	(1,500,000)	
Cost of sales		7,000,000
Gross margin		5,000,000
Depreciation expense		1,000,000
Other operating expenses		2,000,000
Income tax expense		500,000
Net income		F 1,500,000

Other information:
1. French Subsidiary started its operations at the beginning of January 1996.
2. The exchange rate on December 31, 1996 was $1.00 = F4.50.

3. The ending inventory was purchased when the exchange rate was $1.00 = F4.65.
4. The land and equipment were purchased when the exchange rate was $1.00 = F4.45.
5. The common stock was issued when the exchange rate was $1.00 = F4.45.
6. The dividends were paid when the exchange rate was $1.00 = F4.60.
7. The average exchange rate for 1996 was $1.00 = F4.55.

Required:
(1) Translate French Subsidiary's balance sheet and income statement from francs into dollars using the current rate method.
(2) Do requirement (1) using the temporal method.
(3) Compare the two foreign currency methods. Which of the two methods do you prefer? Explain.
(4) Records of French Subsidiary are kept in French currency. How would you determine whether or not to translate the financial statements into Canadian dollars, the reporting currency. Would you use the current rate method or the temporal method?

References

AASB 1012. "Foreign Currency Translation." Sydney: Australian Accounting Standards Board, 1988.

Accounting Standards Committee. *Statement of Standard Accounting Practice No. 20.* "Foreign Currency Translation." London: Institute of Chartered Accountants in England and Wales, 1983.

Australian Accounting Standard 20. "Foreign Currency Translation." Sydney: Australian Accounting Research Foundation, 1987.

Business Accounting Deliberation Council. *Accounting Standards for Foreign Currency Translation.* Tokyo: Japanese Institute of Certified Public Accountants, 1976.

Center for International Financial Analysis and Research, Inc. *International Accounting and Auditing Trends.* vol. 1. Princeton, N.J.: Center for International Financial Analysis and Research, Inc., 1990.

Coopers & Lybrand. *International Accounting Summaries.* 2d ed. New York: John Wiley & Sons.

"Foreign Currency Translation." *CICA Handbook.* Toronto: Canadian Institute of Chartered Accountants, 1983.

Foreign Currency Translation and Hedging. New York: Coopers & Lybrand, 1994.

Guy Barbier & Associés. *The Auditing Profession in France.* 2d ed., rev. New York: American Institute of Certified Public Accountants, 1992.

Halsey, G. B., R. C. Wilkins, and C. C. Woods, III. "The Fundamental Financial Instrument Approach." *Journal of Accountancy,* November 1989, pp. 71-78.

Hepworth, Samuel. *Reporting Foreign Operations.* Ann Arbor, Mich.: Bureau of Business Research, University of Michigan, 1956.

International Accounting Standard 21. "The Effects of Changes in Foreign Exchange Rates." London: International Accounting Standards Committee, 1983. Revised in 1993.

KPMG Century Audit Corporation. *The Accounting Profession in Japan.* 2d ed., rev. New York: American Institute of Certified Public Accountants, 1992.

Lorenson, Leonard. *Accounting Research Study No. 12.* "Reporting Foreign Operations of U.S. Companies in U.S. Dollars." New York: American Institute of Certified Public Accountants, 1972.

Statement of Financial Accounting Standards No. 8. "Accounting for the Translation of Foreign Currency Transactions and Foreign Currency Financial Statements." Stamford, Conn.: Financial Accounting Standards Board, 1975.

Statement of Financial Accounting Standards No. 52. "Foreign Currency Translation." Stamford, Conn.: Financial Accounting Standards Board, 1981.

Stewart, J. E. "The Challenges of Hedge Accounting." *Journal of Accountancy,* November 1989, pp. 48-60.

A Survey and Analysis of Standards and Practices on Accounting for Foreign Currency. Wilton, Conn.: Deloitte & Touche, 1991.

Tonkin. D. J., and L. Skerratt (eds.). *Financial Reporting 1988-1989: A Survey of UK Reporting Practice.* London: Institute of Chartered Accountants in England and Wales, 1989.

"Treatment in Company Accounts of Changes in the Exchange Rates of International Currencies." *The Accountant's Magazine,* September 1970, pp. 415-423.

Veazey, Richard E., and Suk H. Kim. "Translation of Foreign Currency Operations: SFAS No. 52." *Journal of World Business,* winter 1982, pp. 17-22.

Chapter 7

Specific Reporting Issues

The theory and practice of international accounting contains a number of important technical issues. For example, the issue of inflation effects addressed in Chapter 5 has dramatic implications for international accounting. Another critical topic is transfer pricing. However, since it is not feasible to devote a complete chapter to each technical issue affecting international accounting, we will limit our discussion to some of the more important reporting issues and how they are treated in selected countries.

Included in this chapter are discussions of the following specific reporting issues:

- Business Combinations and Consolidations
- Intangible Assets
- Leases
- Pensions and Post-Retirement Benefits

This chapter will also examine the implications of the *European Union Seventh Directive* on accounting for consolidations.

Business Combinations and Consolidations

Companies seek growth. They may grow slowly or some may accomplish growth seemingly overnight. Growth can result from internal or external strategies.

Internal expansion is achieved by introducing new product lines, services, or capacity. Some companies have expanded their production opportunities by establishing *maquiladoras*[1] in Mexico. Setting up such "off-shore" facilities has enabled them to access the U.S. market while establishing a strong base in Mexico.

External expansion, on the other hand, is when one company acquires one or more companies. The parent company could acquire a supplier to reduce its costs of production or acquire a rival to reduce competition for customers.

There are times in the economic histories of countries when the "urge to merge" is especially popular. In the United States, for example, merger mania swept the country in the 1960s as many prosperous firms tried to dominate their industries. Other periods of increased merger activity were the 1980s and the early 1990s. Small companies had a difficult time surviving; one way to compete was to combine with other companies. However, merger activities may lead to adverse effects. Companies may lose valuable talent. Reduced research and development activities in the wake of the merger may result in loss of competitive position over time.

---

[1] "Maquiladora" refers to the system of production of goods by global corporations in border cities in northern Mexico. It offers lower costs compared with the United States and Canada, and was created by the Mexican government in 1965 to deal with population pressure and unemployment.

Types of Business Combinations

Let us look at the different types of business combinations. *The fundamental basis of business combinations is to control.* This is accomplished by acquiring assets or acquiring over 50 percent of the voting stock of another entity.

Where net assets are acquired, the combination is legally a statutory merger or a statutory consolidation. In the **statutory merger**, shown in Figure 7–1, one company acquires the net assets of another company or companies. For example, Company A acquires the net assets of Companies B and C. Companies B and C go out of existence and the only company that survives is Company A. In effecting a statutory merger, Company A may issue stock to stockholders of Companies B and C or could pay cash, or issue bonds, preferred stock, common stock, or a combination thereof.

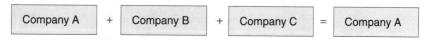

Figure 7–1 **Statutory Merger: Company A acquires company B and company C; companies B and C go out of existence**

In a **statutory consolidation**, shown in Figure 7–2, the transaction consists of acquiring the net assets of another company or companies. However, in this situation, a brand new company is created. Company D is created to take over the net assets of Companies A, B, and C. Companies A, B, and C go out of existence and the stockholders of Companies A, B, and C, are given consideration that can take the form of cash, debt, preferred or common stock, or a combination of cash, debt or capital stock.

Figure 7–2 **Statutory Consolidation: A brand new company, company D, takes over the net assets of companies A, B, and C; companies A, B, and C go out of existence**

A combination where control is achieved by acquisition of voting stock is considered a **parent/subsidiary relationship**. The important point here is that control is achieved by acquiring more than 50 percent of a company's voting stock. The company acquiring the stock is called the **parent**; the company whose stock is acquired is the **subsidiary**. In this type of business combination, both parent and subsidiary continue to exist as separate legal entities and maintain their own financial records and statements. For external reporting, combined statements or consolidated financial statements are issued.

A parent/subsidiary form of combination may have certain advantages over the statutory merger or statutory consolidation. First, there is no need to acquire all the voting stock. This makes it less expensive than a net asset acquisition. Second, there is less risk, since the maximum liability is limited to the investment in the subsidiary. Finally, there may be tax advantages in acquiring stock rather than net assets.

Pooling of Interests and Purchase Methods

In the previous section we considered the business combination from the legal viewpoint. However, there are also accounting issues. The two methods used for effecting a business combination from an accounting stance are the **purchase method** and the **pooling of interests method**. With the purchase method, there is a change in accountability. An asset is acquired and fair market value is used to record the acquisition. In the case of a pooling of interests, there is no change in accountability. Thus, book values are used. The pooling and purchase methods apply to all business combinations—statutory merger, statutory consolidation, and parent/subsidiary combinations. The main characteristics of purchase and pooling are as follows:

- *Purchase method.* The acquired entity's assets and equities are combined at fair market value. Goodwill is created to the extent that cost exceeds the fair market value of the identifiable assets of the unit acquired.
- *Pooling of interests method.* The acquired entity's assets and equities are combined at book value. No goodwill is created in a pooling of interests.

In either case, the parent company's own assets and equities are included in the combination at book value.

International perspectives. Pooling of interests accounting is rare. Australia prohibits its use. Mexico accounts for business combinations using purchase accounting. France lists its assets and liabilities at agreed upon prices according to the purchase agreement. Brazil, Canada, and Nigeria only use the pooling of interests method when the acquiring company cannot be identified. In Japan, mergers that are consummated by an exchange of shares between the acquired company and the acquiring company are treated as poolings of interests. Germany and the U.K. consider pooling acceptable if certain criteria are met. While the Netherlands is silent on the issue, it has used pooling to present a "true and fair view" of certain business combinations.

In the U.S., both the pooling of interests and the purchase methods are generally accepted accounting principles. However, before the pooling of interests method can be used, certain criteria have to be met. They are:

- At least 90 percent of the outstanding voting common stock of one company must be exchanged for voting common stock of the other company.
- The combination must be effected in one transaction.
- The two companies must have been autonomous for a period of two years prior to the initiation of the plan and voting rights of the stockholders in the resulting combined company must be neither restricted nor deprived for a period of time. In addition, there are restrictions on the amount of cash consideration that is paid.

Goodwill

In a combination accounted for using the purchase method, the acquiring company records the transaction at its cost. If cash is given, the cost is the cash paid. If debt securities are given, then it is necessary to determine the present value of those securities in order to determine the cost of the combination. In those cases where capital stock is ʃ necessary to use either the fair market value of the capital stock given or the fair marƙᴄᴄ of the assets received, whichever is more readily determinable.

Once cost is determined, it must be allocated to the identifiable assets. Any excess of cost over the sum of the identifiable assets (including intangibles) less liabilities is recorded as goodwill. To illustrate, suppose that on January 1, 1995, Paz Company, a Mexican company, acquired the assets and assumed the liabilities of Solis Company in a merger by giving one of its 15 peso par value common shares to the former stockholders of Solis Company for every five shares of the 5 peso par value common shares they held. Assume further that this combination is to be accounted for as a purchase. Paz Company stock has a fair value of 45 pesos. Balance sheets for Paz Company and Solis Company (along with pertinent fair value) on January 1, 1995 are as shown in Exhibit 7–1.

Exhibit 7–1   Pre-Merger Balance Sheet Data

January 1, 1995
(Pesos)

	Paz Company Book Value	Solis Company Book Value	Fair Value
Cash and receivables	Ps 50,000	Ps 10,000	Ps 10,000
Inventories	100,000	50,000	50,000
Other assets	450,000	170,000	210,000
Total assets	Ps 600,000	Ps 230,000	
Current liabilities	Ps 25,000	Ps 40,000	40,000
Common stock (15 par value)	375,000		
Common stock (5 par value)		150,000	
Retained earnings	200,000	40,000	
Total liabilities and stockholders' equity	Ps 600,000	Ps 230,000	

To record the exchange of stock for the net assets of Solis Company, Paz Company would make the following entry:

Cash and receivables	10,000	
Inventories.	50,000	
Other assets	210,000	
Goodwill.	40,000	
Current liabilities.		40,000
Common stock (6,000 x 15).		90,000
Excess over par value		180,000

Because the business combination is a merger, Solis Company ceases to exist as a legal entity. Under the purchase method, the cost of the net assets of Solis is equal to the fair value

(6,000 shares times 45 pesos or 270,000 pesos) of the shares given in exchange. Common Stock is credited for 6,000 shares times the par value of 15 pesos and the remainder is credited to Excess over Par Value. Individual assets acquired and liabilities assumed are recorded at their fair values. After all identifiable assets and liabilities are recorded, an excess over fair value of 40,000 pesos results and is recorded as goodwill.

Exhibit 7–2 presents the balance sheet of Paz Company after the acquisition of the net assets of Solis Company.

Exhibit 7–2	Paz Company Balance Sheet after Acquisition of Solis Net Assets		
	Paz Company		
	Balance Sheet		
	January 1, 1995		
	(pesos)		
Cash and receivables	Ps 60,000	Current liabilities	Ps 65,000
Inventories	150,000	Common stock (15 par value)	465,000
Other assets	660,000	Excess over par value	180,000
Goodwill	40,000	Retained earnings	200,000
		Total liabilities and	
Total assets	Ps 910,000	stockholders' equity	Ps 910,000

Consolidated Financial Statements

Consolidated financial statements are the statements prepared by the parent company that essentially portray the financial position and results of operations of the parent and its subsidiaries as though they were one economic unit. We know that the parent and its subsidiaries are distinct legal entities and keep their individual books and records. However, it is important to give stockholders a "single company" view of the parent and its subsidiaries. Since the parent company and its subsidiaries are considered a single entity, transactions within the affiliated group must be eliminated. For example, intercompany receivables and payables are eliminated to avoid double counting assets and liabilities. Similarly, intercompany profits on assets sold from one member of the affiliated group to another are eliminated since an entity cannot profit from transactions with itself.

Basic to the preparation of consolidated statements is the elimination of the investment account and the subsidiary's equity. The investment account represents the parent's investment in the net assets of the subsidiary. Thus, the investment account and the subsidiary's equity account are reciprocal. Because the subsidiary's assets and liabilities are combined with the parent's assets and liabilities, the investment account must be eliminated so that there is no double counting. In other words, the subsidiary's net assets are in fact substituted for the investment account. It is important to emphasize that the elimination entries are made on the workpapers. The individual books and records of the parent and its subsidiaries remain intact.

We can illustrate the process of creating a consolidated balance sheet with three different examples where P Company has acquired stock of S Company. The illustrations are based on the balance sheets for P Company and S Company at December 31, 1995, shown in Exhibit 7–3.

| Exhibit 7–3 | Balance Sheets for P Company and S Company |

P Company
Balance Sheet (unconsolidated)
December 31, 1995

Assets		Liabilities and Equity	
Cash	$140,000	Accounts payable	$ 30,000
Accounts receivable	50,000	Long-term debt	200,000
Other assets	545,000	Total liabilities	230,000
		Common stock (no par value)	400,000
		Retained earnings	105,000
		Total stockholders' equity	505,000
		Total liabilities and	
Total assets	$735,000	stockholders' equity	$735,000

S Company
Balance Sheet
December 31, 1995

Assets		Equity	
Cash	$ 30,000	Common stock	$100,000
Other assets	70,000		
Total assets	$100,000	Total equity	$100,000

Example 1   *Cost of parent company's investment equal to book value of subsidiary's stock acquired. 100 percent of subsidiary's stock acquired.*

Assume that on January 1, 1996, S Company had 1,000 shares of $10 par value stock. P Company acquires all of the shares of stock of S Company for $100,000 in cash. After this transaction, P Company has $40,000 remaining in Cash, and an Investment in S Company of $100,000. Workpapers are the first step in the preparation of consolidated financial statements. These consolidated workpapers are used as a tool for accumulating data. The workpapers may require adjusting and elimination entries. Adjusting entries may be needed to correct some of the subsidiary's accounts. Elimination entries are necessary to cancel the effects of intercompany transactions.

Exhibit 7–4 illustrates a workpaper for the preparation of a consolidated balance sheet for P Company on January 1, 1996.

Exhibit 7–4   Consolidated Balance Sheet Workpaper
100%-Owned Subsidiary

Consolidated Balance Sheet Workpaper
P Company and Subsidiary
January 1, 1996

	P Company	S Company	Eliminations Debit	Eliminations Credit	Consolidated Balance Sheet
Cash	$ 40,000	$ 30,000			$ 70,000
Accounts receivable	50,000				50,000
Other assets	545,000	70,000			615,000
Investment in S	100,000			(A) $100,000	0
	$735,000	$100,000			$735,000
Accounts payable	$ 30,000				$ 30,000
Long-term debt	200,000				200,000
Common stock	400,000	$100,000	(A)$100,000		400,000
Retained earnings	105,000				105,000
	$735,000	$100,000	$100,000	$100,000	$735,000

The workpaper entry to eliminate the investment account against S Company's stockholders' equity in general journal form is as follows:

| Common stock . . . . | 100,000 | |
| Investment in S Company . . . . | | 100,000 |

Note that the assets of the subsidiary were substituted for the Investment in S Company of $100,000 and that the $100,000 common stock of S Company has been eliminated. This leaves the consolidated stockholders' equity the same as the parent company stockholders' equity. The elimination entries are made only on the workpaper; the individual records of P Company and S Company are not changed.

Example 2   *Cost of parent company's investment equal to book value of subsidiary's stock acquired. Less than 100 percent of subsidiary's stock acquired.*

Assume that on January 1, 1996, S Company had 1,000 shares of $10 par value stock. P Company acquires 700 shares of stock in S Company for $70,000 in cash. After this transaction, P Company has $70,000 remaining in cash and an Investment in S Company account of $70,000. The workpaper appears in Exhibit 7–5.

The workpaper entry is:

| Common stock . . . . | 70,000 | |
| Investment in S Company . . . . | | 70,000 |

Exhibit 7–5   Consolidated Balance Sheet Workpaper
Minority Interest, but No Goodwill

Consolidated Balance Sheet Workpaper
P Company and Subsidiary
January 1, 1996

	P Company	S Company	Eliminations Debit	Eliminations Credit	Consolidated Balance Sheet
Cash	$ 70,000	$ 30,000			$100,000
Accounts receivable	50,000				50,000
Other assets	545,000	70,000			615,000
Investment in S	70,000			(A) $70,000	0
	$735,000	$100,000			$765,000
Accounts payable	$ 30,000				$ 30,000
Long-term debt	200,000				200,000
Common stock, P	400,000				400,000
Common stock, S		$100,000	(A) 70,000		30,000M
Retained earnings	105,000				105,000
	$735,000	$100,000	$70,000	$70,000	$765,000

M=Minority interest

Note that the assets of the subsidiary again were substituted for the investment on the parent company's books. Also note that the consolidated stockholders' equity is still the same as the parent stockholders' equity. The minority interest appears at $30,000 because the parent's share of $70,000 (70% of $100,000, the stockholders' equity of S Company) has been eliminated.

Again remember that elimination entries are made only on the workpaper. The individual records of P Company and S Company remain intact.

Example 3   *Cost of parent company's investment exceeds book value of subsidiary's stock acquired. Less than 100 percent of subsidiary's stock acquired.*

Assume that on January 1, 1996, P Company acquired 70 percent of the shares of S Company for $75,000. P Company then has $65,000 remaining in cash and an investment in S Company of $75,000. Note that the $75,000 represents $5,000 more than 70 percent of the $100,000 S Company stockholders' equity. If the excess is not attributable to any identifiable assets, P Company has paid $5,000 for goodwill. A workpaper for a consolidated balance sheet on January 1, 1996 appears in Exhibit 7–6.

The workpaper entry is:

Common stock - S Company	70,000	
Goodwill.	5,000	
Investment in S Company		75,000

**Exhibit 7–6   Consolidated Balance Sheet Workpaper
Both Minority Interest and Goodwill**

Consolidated Balance Sheet Workpaper
P Company and Subsidiary
January 1, 1996

	P Company	S Company	Eliminations Debit	Eliminations Credit	Consolidated Balance Sheet
Cash	$ 65,000	$ 30,000			$ 95,000
Accounts receivable	50,000				50,000
Other assets	545,000	70,000			615,000
Investment in S	75,000			(A) $75,000	0
Goodwill			(A) $ 5,000		5,000
	$735,000	$100,000			$765,000
Accounts payable	$ 30,000				$ 30,000
Long-term debt	200,000				200,000
Common stock, P	400,000				400,000
Common stock, S		$100,000	(A) 70,000		30,000M
Retained earnings	$105,000				105,000
	$735,000	$100,000	$75,000	$75,000	$765,000

M=Minority interest

Note the differences between Exhibit 7–5 and Exhibit 7–6. In the first exhibit, Cash is greater because it took less cash to acquire S Company stock. In Exhibit 7–6, Goodwill appears in the consolidated balance sheet column.

The term **unconsolidated financials** merely means that the parent company would issue its single company financial statements. This occurs when the parent and its subsidiaries are in such dissimilar businesses that presenting consolidated statements would not give the correct picture. Also, if the parent does not have effective control (for example, the subsidiary is prevented from directing dividends to the parent by government restrictions), then consolidated statements are not appropriate.

Consolidation Procedures In Selected Countries

Financial statement consolidation practices vary worldwide. There is no consensus on what constitutes a consolidated entity. The importance given to consolidated statements, as opposed to parent company statements, also varies from country to country.

Australia. Presentation of consolidated financial statements is required based on control rather than a specific percentage of ownership. No exception is made for temporary control or dissimilar activities. The purchase method is required, with cost based on fair value.

Brazil. In Brazil, financial institutions are required to consolidate all subsidiaries. Nonfinancial institutions are carried using the equity method and are considered as permanent assets in the parent's consolidated balance sheet. The major test for determining whether controlled subsidiaries should be consolidated is the significance test. To be significant the investment's value must exceed 30 percent of the stockholders' equity of the parent company.

Canada. Consolidating financial statements in Canada is straightforward. It involves combining the assets, liabilities, and results of operations of the parent and its subsidiaries. Intercompany gains and losses are, of course, eliminated.

Both the pooling of interests method and the purchase method are acceptable for business combinations in Canada. However, the pooling of interests method may be used only when it is not possible to identify the acquirer in the business combination. Thus, pooling of interests is uncommon in Canadian financial statements.

France. No French company is permitted to raise funds publicly without consolidated financial statements. To comply with the *EU Seventh Directive,* French law requires publicly related companies to prepare consolidated statements.

In France, there are two categories of consolidation: full consolidation and proportional consolidation.

- **Full consolidation** is the consolidation of dependent companies. Dependent companies are those companies under long-term control. Control derives from: (a) holding a majority of voting rights. (b) Power to appoint more than half of the supervisory, management, or administrative organization. A presumption of power is assumed when 40 percent of voting stock is held. (c) The ability to exercise control.

- **Proportional consolidation** or **proportionate consolidation** is a vehicle used for joint ventures. In this type of consolidation, the percentage of shares held is applied to each line of the balance sheet and income statement.

The purchase method is the only method accepted. However, any purchase is assumed to have occurred as of the beginning of the accounting year.

Germany. Under current German practice, consolidated financial statements are required for domestic and foreign subsidiaries if any of the following are exceeded:

	Consolidation Basis	**Combined Basis**
Balance sheet total	DM 39 million	DM 47 million
Annual sales value	DM 80 million	DM 96 million
Number of employees	500	500

The parent company can determine whether to use the consolidation limits or the combined bases limits.

Japan. Pooling of interests is rare in Japan. Companies usually follow the purchase method of accounting for effecting business combinations. However, consolidated statements are still considered to be supplementary statements.

Mexico. In Mexico the determination of purchase vs. pooling accounting has to do with whether the majority of the shareholders of the acquired company retain an interest in the surviving company. If this situation exists, the pooling method should be used. In cases where a Mexican company owns more than 50 percent of another company, the subsidiary normally should be consolidated.

Comisión Nacional de Valores requires companies listed on the "Bolsa," the Mexican Stock Exchange, to produce consolidated financial statements.

Investments in unconsolidated subsidiaries must be presented on the lower of equity value or net realizable value in the consolidated financial statements.

Netherlands. The approach for business combinations in the Netherlands is consistent with the *EU Seventh Directive.* Purchase accounting is followed for the formation of business combinations. Typical consolidation of a parent and subsidiaries is followed. In those cases where subsidiaries are not consolidated, the equity method is followed.

Nigeria. All subsidiaries are normally consolidated based on control. Control is defined as ownership of over 50 percent of a subsidiary's voting shares and the right to elect a majority of the board of directors. Exceptions are made when increases in equity are not likely to benefit the parent, control is temporary or seriously impaired, or the subsidiary is so different that its inclusion would not be helpful. The purchase method is used except when an acquirer can not be identified, in which case the pooling of interests method is used.

United Kingdom. Consolidated statements are required based on control rather than legal ownership. Exceptions to this requirement include materiality, impairment of control, temporary ownership, or differences in activities. Acquisition accounting (purchase) is used in most cases, with merger accounting (pooling of interests) provided for in specific cases. **Merger relief**, an exemption from accounting for the premium on shares used to acquire a subsidiary, is available by law.

United States. Consolidated statements are required based on ownership of a majority voting interest, with exceptions for temporary or impaired control. Pooling of interests accounting is required if specific criteria are met, otherwise purchase accounting is mandatory. Fairly detailed supplemental disclosures are also required, as shown in APB *Opinion Nos. 16, 17,* and *18; SFAS No. 94, FASB Interpretation No. 35;* and *SEC Regulation S-X.*

European Union's Seventh Directive

As mentioned in Chapters 1 and 2, EU directives and regulations are legally binding throughout the EU. However, each member state must adapt this legislation to comply with its own national laws. The directive imposes minimum legislation and the individual country may add additional requirements where appropriate.

The Seventh Directive covers consolidated statements. Before its adoption in 1983, deliberations were held on whether the U.K. approach of ownership holdings and legal rights was preferable to the German approach of effective management control in determining what constituted a "group." A compromise was made allowing the member nations to add control criteria other than ownership holdings to define a group.

What this directive has accomplished is to make consolidation of all foreign subsidiaries a reality. Equity accounting for associated corporations and line-of-business reporting are covered by the directive. However, there are options such as omitting a subsidiary if it is in a dissimilar type of business, excluding financial holding corporations, and exempting small groups. Another important option is allowing pooling and proportional consolidation, including criteria for goodwill accounting.

This directive has been a major attempt to improve comparability of financial statements of member nations. Although it does offer flexibility and some members have been slow in implementing the directive, it appears to have improved the communication of accounting information. Exhibits 7–7 through 7–9 present consolidation practices of AT&T (U.S.-based), Bayer AG (Germany-based), and Renault (France-based) respectively.

Intangible Assets

With the growth of business combinations worldwide, particularly in the 1990s, it is important to consider the accounting for intangibles. An intangible such as a patent can be the most important asset to an entity. Included in the category of intangibles are such assets as goodwill, patents, franchises, and research and development.

Goodwill

Goodwill arises in a purchase type of transaction where the acquiring company pays more than the fair value of the identifiable assets or more that the fair value of the common stock of the subsidiary. In effect, it is the consideration given for above-normal earning power of the company being acquired.

Thus, there is a difference of opinion over which periods the cost of the goodwill benefits the acquiring company. Should goodwill be written off against stockholders' equity immediately or should it be amortized over some stated period? The underlying rationale for keeping goodwill as an asset is that in a successful business, goodwill will continue because the economic benefits will accrue to the entity over its life—assumed to be indefinite.

Those of the opinion that goodwill should be amortized argue that the goodwill that has been purchased has a limited life, and that its cost should be written off over some period of time, in conformity with the accrual concept. This approach is followed in the United States, where goodwill is amortized over a period not to exceed 40 years.

Another school of thought argues that goodwill should be written off immediately against stockholders' equity. Goodwill is not separate from the business as a whole. In other words, it is not separately realizable and thus should be written off against equity. Another argument

Exhibit 7–7   Consolidation Practice—AT&T

Consolidation

Ownership of affiliates	Accounting method
More than 50%	Fully consolidated
20% to 50%	Equity method
Less than 20%	Cost method

The fiscal year of essentially all AT&T operations ends December 31.

Source: AT&T, *1994 Annual Report,* p. 33.

Exhibit 7–8   Consolidation Practice—Bayer AG

Companies consolidated

The financial statements of the Bayer Group include Bayer AG and 31 German and 141 foreign consolidated subsidiaries in which Bayer AG, directly or indirectly, has a majority of the voting rights or which are under its uniform control.

Four joint ventures in which Bayer AG holds a 50 percent interest are included by proportionate consolidation. These companies account for DM 936 million of the income and DM 886 million of the expenses shown in the income statement, DM 303 million of noncurrent assets, DM 400 million of current assets, DM 121 million of financial obligations, and DM 298 million of the remaining liabilities.

A further nine subsidiaries and two associated companies are included by the equity method.

The number of fully consolidated companies has risen by nine from the previous year. The number of companies included by proportionate consolidation has increased by two.

Excluded from consolidation are 117 subsidiaries and 38 associated companies that in aggregate are of minor importance to the net worth, financial position, and earnings of the Bayer Group, as well as four companies that exist for social purposes. Total sales of the excluded subsidiaries are equivalent to 1 percent of Group sales.

Source: Bayer AG, *Annual Report 1994,* p. 55.

Exhibit 7–9   Consolidation Practice—Renault

PRINCIPLES OF CONSOLIDATION

The consolidated financial statements include the financial statements of all the significant companies controlled directly or indirectly by the Group.

Significant companies in which the Group has a material influence are accounted for by the equity method, except for joint-venture companies, which are consolidated on a proportional basis.

All material intercompany transactions and unrealized internal profits are eliminated.

Source: Renault, *Financial Position 1993,* p. 12.

is that the expense arising from amortization of goodwill hinders comparability and thus should be omitted from the income statement.

Accounting for goodwill is diverse among the countries of the world. In certain countries, goodwill is charged against equity immediately. In other countries, the time frame for maximum amortization is much longer. Exhibit 7–10 shows how our selected group of countries account for goodwill.

Exhibit 7–10	Accounting for Goodwill			
	Immediate Expensing	**Charged to Equity**	**Maximum Amortization**	**Straight-line Amortization**
Australia	No	No	20 yrs.	Yes
Brazil	No	No	No maximum	Yes
Canada	No	No	40	Yes
France	No	Rare	20	Yes
Germany	No	Yes	5	Yes
Japan:				
Legal merger	Yes	No	5	Yes
Consolidation	No	No	5	Yes
Netherlands	Yes	Yes	No maximum	Yes
Mexico	No	No	20 yrs.*	Yes
Nigeria	No	No	Estimated life	Yes
United Kingdom	No	Yes	N/A	N/A
United States	No	No	40	Yes

N/A = Not applicable
*In Mexico, maximum amortization period for negative goodwill is five years.

If the cost of a business combination is less than the sum of the fair values of its identifiable assets, the difference can be viewed as negative goodwill. Practices to account for negative goodwill are diverse. In Australia, Canada, and the U.S. this requires reduction in certain acquired assets. Negative goodwill is credited to equity in the Netherlands and the U.K.

Research and Development

The term **research and development costs** refers to the direct and indirect outlays for developing new products including techniques and processes. This category is usually divided into pure research, applied research, and development.

Accounting for research and development costs may consist of systematic amortization or direct write-off. The justification for systematic amortization is that this expenditure will benefit current and future periods and falls in line with the accrual concept. Proponents of the direct write-off method defend their position on the grounds that it is very difficult to estimate the periods benefited by the expenditure. They argue that the write-off would be just an arbitrary allocation.

As with goodwill, practices differ throughout the world. However, the trend is toward the prudence approach. Even the United States has taken that posture. Previously, research and development costs were capitalized and then amortized. However, companies were managing their profits though amortization. To correct this situation, the FASB adopted *SFAS No. 2*, "Accounting for Research and Development Costs," requiring companies to treat research and development costs as period costs.

Leases

Leases are important means to finance acquisition of property or of rights to use property in both domestic and international operations. A **lease** is a contract between a lessor and a lessee that gives the lessee the right to use specific property owned by the lessor, for a given time period, in exchange for cash or other consideration—typically a commitment to make future cash payments. In some cases, it is taken for granted that the property will be returned to the lessor at the end of the lease term. In other cases, the property is expected to remain with the lessee. In still other cases, eventual disposition of the property may be subject to option, or may be negotiated during or at the termination of the lease.

Accounting for Leases

Leases cover a wide range of possibilities. A company might acquire a few minutes of time on a supercomputer under a "lease" agreement, or it might in substance acquire the supercomputer outright under an agreement also called a "lease." Possible accounting treatments have important consequences for income, assets, and liabilities.

Rental. In some cases the lessor retains not only legal title, but most of the risks and rewards of ownership. Examples are day-to-day auto rentals or month-to-month apartment rentals. The lessee may be responsible for unusual wear and tear but the ultimate resale value is the concern of the lessor. Such leases are often called **rentals**. The lessor shows the property as a long-term asset, records periodic depreciation, rent revenue as received or accrued, and profit or loss on disposition of the asset. The lessee records rent expense, but has no asset, records no depreciation, and has no concern with gain or loss on asset disposition.

Sale and purchase. At the other extreme, the lease transfers all risks and rewards of ownership from the lessor to the lessee and is in substance a *sale* by the lessor and a *purchase* by the lessee. If such an arrangement is accounted for as a sale, the lessor records revenue and cost of sales at the inception of the lease (date of sale), thereby recognizing profit or loss. To the extent that the lessor provides financing, a long-term receivable results. The lessor records the compensation for this financing as interest revenue, just as for any long-term receivable. The lessee records purchase of an asset, periodic depreciation, interest expense on any long-term liability, and (eventually) gain or loss on disposition of the asset.

Accounting problems. The above two extremes—rental versus sale and purchase—are relatively straightforward in concept. But practical formulation and application of lease accounting rules involves ambiguity and arbitrariness. Reasons for these problems include:

- *Lack of clear-cut distinctions.* Leases cover the entire range from rental to sale with few clear-cut distinctions. This makes it difficult to set classification criteria.
- *Form versus substance.* The legal form and economic substance may differ. In particular, legal title is of little or no significance in identifying the economic substance of a lease. Legal title may be retained by a lessor as an aid to enforcing payment—just as it is retained by a seller under a contract of sale.
- *Rule-pushing.* Parties to a lease may tailor its terms to produce a desired result under accounting rules. For example, the same lease can sometimes be treated as a sale by the lessor and a rental by the lessee, with neither party showing an asset.

Motivation. Earlier we noted that the accounting treatment of leases has important financial statement consequences. These consequences affect not only lessor and lessee, but also independent accountants attesting to the financial statements.

- *Lessor.* Treatment of a lease as a sale means "front-end" recognition of profit-the difference between cost and the selling price. In addition, if the lessor provides financing, interest revenue is mostly recognized in the early years. Management is often under pressure to show current year profits; hence, treatment as a sale is likely to be preferred.
- *Lessee.* Treatment of a lease as a rental arrangement rather than a purchase makes assets available for use without showing a liability on the lessee's books. This makes the debt to equity ratio appear more favorable, and can improve the lessee's borrowing position. In addition, it is less complicated to record monthly rental payments than to account for a fixed asset and a long-term liability.
- *Independent accountants.* Accountants attesting to the fairness of the lessor's financial statements can be embarrassed or even held financially liable if a lessor's profitable "sales" turn out to have no substance, and recorded revenue turns out to be non-existent. The lessee's accountants, and the accounting profession as a whole, face problems if important obligations are inadequately disclosed.

Operating versus Capital Leases

While application of accounting treatments differs widely in different countries, the following possible treatments and their associated terminology are sufficiently accepted to form a useful classification scheme. In the examples in this section, we use broad terms such as liability, revenue, and expense rather than the specific terminology of any one country. In the interest of simplicity, we ignore recurring items such as maintenance and taxes, which can be paid by either lessor or lessee.

Operating leases. Leases referred to above as rentals are commonly called **operating leases** as to both lessor and lessee.

Example   Lessor Company purchases a bulldozer from Bilal Tractor on 1/1/91 at a price of $80,000. Lessor leases (rents) the machine to Lessee Company for $3,000 per month, and depreciates it over an 8-year term with no estimated residual value. On 1/1/99, Lessor sells the used bulldozer for $5,000.

Lessor Company entries, operating lease

Jan. 1, 1991	Asset (equipment held for lease)	80,000	
	Cash		80,000
	To record acquisition of bulldozer.		
Jan. 31, 1991	Cash	3,000	
	Rent revenue		3,000
	To record rent for a typical month.		
Dec. 31, 1991	Depreciation expense	10,000	
	Accum. deprec., asset		10,000
	To record depreciation for year.		
Jan. 1, 1999	Cash	5,000	
	Accum. deprec., asset	80,000	
	Asset (equipment held for lease)		80,000
	Gain on sale of asset		5,000
	To record sale of fully-depreciated asset.		

With an operating lease, the lessor's profit, if any, emerges gradually over time as the excess of revenues and gain over expenses.

Lessee Company entries, operating lease

Jan. 31, 1991	Rent expense	3,000	
	Cash		3,000
	To record rent for a typical month.		

Under an operating lease, the lessee shows rent expense, but no asset and liability, and no depreciation expense or interest expense.

Capital leases. Leases treated as a sale by the lessor to the lessee are commonly known as **capital leases**. For the lessor, capital leases are further broken down as sales-type leases where a dealer's or manufacturer's profit or loss is a basic part of the transaction, or **financing leases** where the lessor provides financing and earns interest revenue but earns no profit on the sale.[2]

Example   *Capital lease.* Lessor Company purchases a bulldozer from Bilal Tractor on 12/31/90 at a price of $80,000. Lessor then leases the machine to Lessee Company for a payment of $2,000, plus $1,586 at the end of each month for a fixed term of 100 months, based on a price of $102,000 and an implicit interest rate of 12 percent. Title to the bulldozer passes to Lessee at the end of the lease term. Lessee depreciates the machine over a 10-year term with no estimated residual value. On 12/31/00 Lessee sells the used bulldozer for $5,000. In the broad sense of the term, this is a capital lease for both parties. Since Lessor is acting to earn a dealer's profit, the lease will be classified as a **sales-type lease** for the lessor.

---

[2]   Another lease type, the leveraged lease, is primarily used to obtain tax benefits. This topic, dependent on a country's tax laws, will not be discussed here.

Lessor Company, sales-type lease

Dec. 31, 1990	Asset (inventory)	80,000	
	Cash		80,000
	To record acquisition of bulldozer.		

Dec. 31, 1990	Cash	2,000	
	Receivable	158,600	
	Cost of goods sold	80,000	
	Discount on receivable		58,600
	Sales		102,000
	Asset (inventory)		80,000
	To record lease of bulldozer as		
	a sales-type lease.		

Jan. 31, 1991	Cash	1,586	
	Receivable		1,586
	To record receipt of monthly payment.		

Jan. 31, 1991	Discount on receivable	1,000	
	Interest revenue		1,000
	To record interest for first month.		
	(12% ÷ 12) × $100,000 = $1,000		

Note that Lessor Company is acting as a dealer, recording a sale just as under a contract of sale. Lessor recognizes the dealer's profit immediately, and accounts for the receivable just as it would for any long-term receivable.[3]

Lessee Company, capital lease

Dec. 31, 1990	Asset (bulldozer)	102,000	
	Cash		2,000
	Payable (obligation under lease)		100,000
	To record leased asset and related obligation.		

Jan. 31, 1991	Interest expense	1,000	
	Payable (obligation under lease)	586	
	Cash		1,586
	To record January payment and interest.		

Dec. 31, 1991	Depreciation expense	10,200	
	Accumulated depreciation, bulldozer		10,200
	To record depreciation for 1991.		

Dec. 31, 2000	Cash	5,000	
	Accumulated depreciation, bulldozer	100,000	
	Asset (bulldozer)		100,000
	Gain on sale of asset		5,000
	To record sale of bulldozer.		

[3] Terminology will differ from one country to another. The receivable, shown above as a gross $158,600 less $58,600 discount, could be shown at $100,000 and accounted for on a net basis; this would not affect the substance of the transaction.

In a lease treated as a capital lease, the lessee is in roughly the same position as an outright purchaser.

Direct-financing lease. In a direct-financing lease, the lessor provides financing only, and assumes financial risks but does not assume inventory risk. In the above example, the direct-financing lessor (usually a bank or leasing company) pays the manufacturer or dealer the sales price ($102,000 above) and then collects the cash payments from the lessee. The dealer (in this case not a lessor) is paid by the lessor and records the sale as above. The lessor records the remaining entries dealing with cash receipts and interest revenue. The lessee's accounting remains the same.

The accounting differences among different countries, and the complexities of lease accounting, arise more from the determination as to *when* a particular method is applicable. Once this is decided, the *how* problem is less difficult.

Accounting for Leases in Selected Countries

Lease accounting is certainly not uniform in the international scene. The operating lease convention tends to be more common outside the United States. Leveraged leases are rare in the accounting principles of the 11 countries selected for comparison.

Australia. A noncurrent asset and a corresponding noncurrent liability should be set up for a finance lease on the books of the lessee. Accounting for finance leases on the books of the lessor is the reciprocal of what the lessee does. For a sales-type lease, the lessor recognizes profit immediately and after that accounts for the lease as a finance lease, i.e., each payment received consists of interest income and a reduction of principal. Accounting for operating leases is straightforward. The lessor records each payment received as income and the lessee shows the payment as expense. Exhibit 7–11 shows the accounting treatment of leases by Foster Brewing, an Australia-based multinational company.

Exhibit 7–11   Leasing Practice—Foster Brewing

Leasing

   Where an asset is acquired by means of finance lease, the present value of the minimum lease payments is recognised as an asset at the beginning of the lease term and amortized on a straight line basis so as to write the asset off over its estimated useful life. The liability in respect of capitalised leases is reduced by the principal component of each lease payment and the interest component is expenses.

   Leases classified as operating leases are not capitalised and lease rental payments are charged against profits as incurred.

Source: Foster Brewing Group Limited, *Annual Report 1994*, p. 31.

Brazil. Accounting standards treat all leases as operating regardless of the economic substance. For lessors, only public companies and financial institutions in the leasing business are required to consider the substance of the lease. In general for these lessors, there is a tendency toward more capitalization.

Canada. Leasing principles consider the accounting treatment based on the risks and rewards of ownership related to the leased property. Leases that essentially transfer risks and rewards are treated as capital leases. All others are considered operating leases.

France. In statutory financial statements, all leases are treated as operating leases. Finance leases may be treated as capital leases in consolidated statements.

Germany. Whether risks and rewards are transferred determines the classification of a lease as a finance lease or an operating lease. Complex tax rules determine the accounting for each finance lease.

Japan. Capital leases are rare. Arrangements usually are structured as installment sales or as operating leases.

Mexico. Leases are considered capital (finance) leases if they transfer the rewards and benefits of ownership to lessees.

Netherlands. Guidance from U.K. and U.S. accounting principles form the basis for determination of capital leases. All other leases are considered operating leases.

Nigeria. Rules for classifying leases as either finance or operating do not exist. However, if the lease period is 75 percent or more of the economic life of the leased period, or if the present value of the lease payments equals 90 percent or more of the fair market value of the lease amount, the lease is *normally* classified as a financing lease. Leases of land and buildings are usually treated as operating leases.

United Kingdom. If the present value of the minimum lease payments equals or exceeds the fair market value of the leased property, or if a bargain purchase option exists, a lease is classified as a capital lease.

United States. Leasing in the U.S. has become so complex that several accounting pronouncements have been issued. The main pronouncement addressing lease accounting is *SFAS No. 13,* "Accounting for Leases."

In the U.S., if a lease meets any one of the following four criteria, the lease is a capital lease to the lessee:

- The lease transfers ownership of the leased asset to the lessee by the end of the lease term.
- The lease contains a bargain purchase option.
- The lease term is equal to 75 percent or more of the remaining estimated life of the leased asset at the lease inception.
- The present value of the minimum lease payments at the inception of the lease is at least 90 percent of the market value of the leased asset at that time.

For a lessor, the above four criteria still apply. In addition, to qualify as a capital lease the collectibility of lease payments must be reasonably assured, and there can be no important uncertainties to future costs to be incurred by the lessor. If a lease is classified as a capital lease for the lessor, it is a sales-type lease if the lessor is a manufacturer or dealer (i.e., is subject to inventory risk and is trying to make a profit) or as a financing lease if the lessor's objective is only to earn interest by providing financing.

Lease accounting in the U.S. is very detailed compared with the rest of the world. However, this is not the only area of accounting where accounting principles are detailed. The next special issue—pensions—also has some very specific requirements.

Pensions and Post-Retirement Benefits

In international business, accounting for pensions and post-retirement benefits is even more complex than for leases. Many companies have established pension plans to pay retirement benefits to their employees. There are two basic types of pension plans: the defined contribution plan and the defined benefit plan. **Defined contribution plans** present no real accounting problems since the assets in the pension fund determine the amount of retirement benefits. The employer makes the following entry for the annual contribution to the pension fund:

Pension Expense	xxx,xxx	
Cash		xxx,xxx

In a **defined benefit plan**, as the name implies, the benefits to be received in the future are specified. Usually, the benefits are a function of the number of years an employee has been employed and the amount of salary that has been earned during employment. The difficult problem is determining the annual contribution amounts and pension expense. Factors such as projected future salary levels, employee turnover, employee life expectancy, and pension fund performance (in generating income from its investments) affect the calculation. Actuaries have the expertise to make these calculations.

When a defined benefit plan is established, there is immediately a past service cost associated with the plan. Past service cost occurs because employees are given credit for past years of service. Typically, this amount is very large and firms must devise a plan for installment funding. In addition to the funding issue, there is also an accounting problem. Since the purpose of adopting a plan is to affect future recruitment, retention, and performance of employees, the past service cost is allocated over the current and future periods—the periods benefited.

There often are amendments to a pension plan after it is established. Again, actuarial calculations enter into the modifications of the pension expense and the fund contributions. Another problem that can arise is that the obligation may be underfunded. In other words, the accumulated pension retirement benefits may exceed the pension fund assets. In this situation, it is reasonable to set up a liability for the amount of underfunding.

Pension and Other Post-Retirement Benefits
Accounting in Selected Countries

In most of the 11 countries selected for comparison, the cash approach to pension accounting is generally followed, i.e., contributions are expensed as they are made. The U.S. is the only country that requires an annual determination of the annual discount rate based upon current market conditions. The actuarial present value of benefits, pension expense, and employer's pension obligation is computed using such a rate. This tends to lead to more volatility in pension expense and consequently net income when there are fluctuations in interest rates. Because of this volatility, the FASB in *SFAS No. 87,* "Employers' Accounting for Pensions," requires that a firm use the corridor method. Essentially, the **corridor method** sets lower and upper limits on pension expense. Since the U.S. has the most detailed and restrictive requirements for pensions, this section begins with a short narrative on pension accounting in the U.S.

APB Opinion No. 8, "Accounting for the Cost of Pension Plans," was the first attempt by the U.S. accounting profession to deal with the topic of pensions. This opinion was later superseded by *SFAS No. 87* and by *SFAS No. 106. SFAS No. 87* has two main requirements:

- The cost of the plan must relate directly to the terms of the plan.
- Employers must recognize a liability for the underfunded portion of the plan.

According to *SFAS No. 87,* the principal components of pension expense are:

- Service cost.
- Interest cost.
- Actual return on plan assets.
- Amortization of *prior service cost.*[4]
- Gain or loss to the extent recognized.
- Amortization of transition asset or liability.[5]

SFAS No. 106 requires use of accrual accounting for post-retirement benefits other than pensions and is effective for fiscal years beginning after December 15, 1992. Post-retirement benefits include pensions, health, and other welfare benefits. This statement applies to all employers who have more than 500 employees under their U.S. plans.

The following briefly describes pension accounting in our selected countries.

Australia. An exposure draft (ED 53) entitled "Accounting for Employee Entitlements," issued in 1991 by the AARF, sets forth proposed standards for pensions. In a defined benefit plan, the liability and asset should be set up on the difference between the present value of accrued employees' benefits at the balance sheet and the net market value of the pension plan's assets. Accrued benefits consist of the present value of future wage and salary levels.

---

[4] Prior service cost is really past service pension cost plus any amendments to the plan. Past service pension cost was a term used in *APB No. 8* and refers to pension benefits attributable to services rendered before the inception of the plan.

[5] Employers of all plans are required to comply with *SFAS No. 87* for years beginning after December 15, 1986. In bridging the gap between *APB No. 8* and *SFAS No. 87,* a transition asset or liability may be created.

The discount rate used is a risk-adjusted market rate. Pension expense would be equal to the contributions made plus or minus changes in the pension plan liability for the period.

Brazil. Company-sponsored pension plans are not common. For defined benefit plans, the actuarially determined contribution required to fund the plan is considered a reasonable basis for recording pension expense. However, pension expense is sometimes based on the cash contribution.

Canada. Expense for the periods under a defined contribution plan is based on contributions made. For a defined benefit plan, the past service pension cost and changes therein should be deferred and amortized over the current and future periods. The accrued benefit method should be used for determining the cost of benefits based on salary projections. Differences between pension expense and cash payments result either in a liability or a deferred charge in the balance sheet.

France. For the most part, government agencies administer employee retirement plans: contributions made by employers are later distributed to retirees. Essentially, employers operate on a cash basis, with contributions charged to expense as they are made. No requirement exists for recognizing future pension commitments. A few companies provide supplemental benefits. In such cases companies expense contributions when made, although an actuarial method may be used in recording pension liabilities.

Germany. German tax law limits the amounts employers can contribute to an autonomous pension fund. Social security-type programs are a legal requirement in Germany. Pension funds are funded through insurance companies hence, employers need only accrue liabilities for unpaid premiums.

Mexico. Pensions are accounted for based on the types of benefits. Only contributions to a trust are tax deductible. Past service pension costs must be reasonably applied to future years.

Japan. Employee pension plans have generally consisted of the lump-sum payment variety. Amounts have been a function of rate of pay and length of time in service. Since the government generally takes care of pensions, Japanese companies normally do not provide other types of post-retirement benefits. When companies do provide plans, they are usually funded through financial institutions.

Netherlands. Most plans are defined benefit plans. Plans are regulated in the Act on pension and saving funds. The main provision of this Act is that employee vested amounts must be reinsured with a life insurance company that is independent from the employer or placed in a pension fund that is also independent from the employer. There are two methods of calculating pension liabilities: static and dynamic. Under the **static method**, liabilities may not mesh with contributions or lump-sum premiums. In other words, they are related to the years of service of the employee. Under the **dynamic method**, the liabilities are related to annual wages. The dynamic method is somewhat of a smoothing device that may not be related to the contributions made. Any charges for pensions are part of operating results. However, any changes or prior service cost are either extraordinary items on the income statement or are charged directly to equity.

Nigeria. No accounting standards for pensions exist. For companies that have set up pensions, *IAS 19,* "Retirement Benefit Costs," is used. Further disclosures are not required.

United Kingdom. The authority for pension accounting is found in *SSAP 24,* which sets forth the measurement and disclosure requirements. Basically, there are two types of plans: defined benefit and defined contribution. *SSAP 24* states that pension costs are related to current and future pensionable earnings based on actuarial assumptions. When there are changes in the plan such as changes in actuarial methods, etc., the actuary determines over which periods these should be written off.

United States. The discussion of U.S. pension accounting is at the start of this section.

Exhibits 7–12 and 7–13 describe the post-retirement benefits practices of AT&T and Renault respectively.

Exhibit 7–12   Post-retirement Benefits Practice—AT&T

Postretirement Benefits

We adopted Statement of Financial Accounting Standards (SFAS) No. 106, "Employers' Accounting for Postretirement Benefits Other Than Pensions," effective January 1, 1993. This standard requires us to accrue estimated future retiree benefits during the years employees are working and accumulating these benefits. Previously, we expensed health care benefits as claims were incurred, and life insurance benefits as plans were funded.

We also reimburse the divested regional Bell companies for a portion of their costs to provide health care benefits, increases in pensions and other benefits to predivestiture retirees under the terms of the Divestiture Plan of Reorganization. Through 1992 we expensed these reimbursements as incurred.

We recorded a one-time pretax charge for the unfunded portions of these liabilities of $11,317 million ($7,023 million or $4.54 per share after taxes). Apart from these cumulative effects on prior years of the accounting change, our change in accounting had no material effect on net income and it does not affect cash flows.

Source: AT&T, *1994 Annual Report,* p. 34.

Exhibit 7–13   Post-retirement Benefits Practice—Renault

PENSIONS AND OTHER POST RETIREMENT BENEFITS

The cost of pensions and other post retirement benefits (medical expenses for retired persons, other insurance premium contributions) is provided for progressively as entitlements are earned by employees. Entitlements are determined at each period end in line with the seniority of personnel and the likelihood of presence in the company at the date of retirement or at the minimum age required to be eligible in the case where certain entitlements are irrevocably vested prior to such date. The computation is based on an actuarial method integrating employees' prospects of changes in wages, age at retirement and the profitability of long-term investments. The effects of changes in these assumptions are only recognized where they lead to a revaluation of the provision for an amount over 10%; they are then spread over the remaining working lives of active employees.

Source: Renault, *Financial Position 1993,* p. 14.

Note to Students

This chapter has been devoted to selected reporting issues. Knowing about current practices in different parts of the world lets us see the need for improvement. For example, practices regarding leases and pensions have been evolving. It is important for you, the student of accounting, to understand the evolutionary process of accounting. In the future, you may help to resolve today's unsolved accounting problems.

Being aware of international markets and how accounting, the language of business, provides users information for decision making in the global scene, the student can appreciate the significance of international financial reporting issues. We live in an exciting era. It will be even more exciting for those who are studying accounting presently because they will see how indispensable accounting is in the international world of business. Accounting does not just work in a vacuum; it is a useful tool that will help the countries of the world in their efforts to make goods, services, capital, and people mobile. It is important for the student to become immersed in all the relevant subjects, including finance, marketing, sociology, political science, and anthropology, that help us understand how the global economy works.

Chapter Summary

- This chapter has presented selected reporting issues and shown how these issues are being addressed.

- The accounting profession has wrestled with these important and difficult reporting issues for a long time.

- As the world becomes smaller and the movement toward a global economy accelerates, there is a need to provide more and better information to users of financial information.

- As business becomes more complex and dynamic, accounting must adapt to maintain its usefulness.

- Legislation such as the EU directives has made a difference by enhancing financial statement comparability.

- Advances in accounting are made by continued dialogue among members of the profession, those in positions of power, users of information, and others willing to accept the challenges that arise in this fast-paced world of international business.

- The issues addressed in this chapter are complex and will continue to be debated in the future.

Questions for Discussion

1. What is internal expansion?

2. Compare and contrast internal and external expansion.

3. Distinguish between a statutory merger and a statutory consolidation.

4. How is control of a company achieved?

5. Contrast and compare the pooling of interests method with the purchase method.

6. How does goodwill arise in a business combination?

7. How prevalent is the use of the pooling of interests method in the world?

8. Before a pooling of interests can occur in the U. S., what criteria must be met?

9. Brazil, Canada, and Nigeria can use pooling of interests in only one isolated situation. What is it?

10. What are consolidated financial statements?

11. Why are the investment account and the subsidiary's equity eliminated in the preparation of consolidated statements? Where are the elimination entries made?

12. What is an unconsolidated subsidiary?

13. How do nonfinancing types of investments appear in a Brazilian consolidated balance sheet?

14. What are the two categories of consolidation in France?

15. What authoritative pronouncements does the Netherlands follow with respect to pooling of interests?

16. What is the rationale for systematic write-off of research and development costs?

17. What is the difference between a capital lease and an operating lease?

18. What criteria do Germany and Japan follow in lease accounting?

19. What is common practice for lease accounting in Mexico?

20. What accounting approach is most common for pensions in the 11 countries covered in this chapter?

21. Who administers most of the pension retirement plans in France?

22. Can you think of situations where it would make economic sense *not* to amortize goodwill?

23. What guidelines are followed by Nigerian companies that have set up pension plans?

24. What topic is covered in the Seventh Directive?

25. In a high-technology environment, intangible assets become increasingly more important. Do you agree? Explain.

Exercises/Problems

7-1   On January 1, 1995, Wakamatsu Corporation purchased 100 percent of the common stock of Shigao by issuing 40,000 shares of its ¥40 common stock with a market value of ¥60. The equity sections of the two company's balance sheets on 12/31/94 were:

	Wakamatsu	**Shigao**
Common stock	¥ 700,000	¥600,000
Paid-in surplus	280,000	90,000
Surplus	320,000	210,000
	¥1,300,000	¥900,000

Required:
(1) Prepare the journal entry on Wakamatsu Corporation's books to record the purchase of Shigao Company.
(2) Prepare the elimination entry required for a consolidated balance sheet.

7-2   On January 1, 1996, Aámer Company purchased a 70 percent interest in Wong Company for $650,000, at which time Wong Company had retained earnings of $250,000 and capital stock of $300,000. Any difference between cost and book value was attributable to goodwill with a remaining useful life of 20 years. Aámer and Wong reported net incomes from their independent operations of $300,000 and $200,000 respectively.

Required: Prepare an analysis to determine consolidated net income for the year ended December 31, 1996.

7-3   On January 1, 1996, Swazy Company purchased a 75 percent interest in Shaukat Company for 300,000 French francs. On this date, Shaukat Company had common stock of F75,000 and retained earnings of F200,000. Shaukat Company's equipment on the date of Swazy Company's purchase had a book value of F200,000 and a fair value of F300,000.

Required: Prepare the December 31 consolidated financial statements workpaper entries for 1996.

7-4   The balance sheets of Penman Company and Saen Company as of January 1, 1996 are presented below in Dutch guilders.

	Penman	**Saen**
Plant and equipment (net)	Fl. 4,800,000	Fl. 1,000,000
Inventories	2,500,000	250,000
Receivables	800,000	300,000
Cash	600,000	250,000
Total assets	Fl. 8,700,000	Fl. 1,800,000
Share capital	Fl. 4,500,000	Fl. 1,000,000
Share premium	500,000	0
Other reserves	2,200,000	400,000
Liabilities	1,500,000	400,000
Total equities	Fl. 8,700,000	Fl. 1,800,000

On that date, the two companies agreed to merge. To effect the merger, Penman Company agreed to exchange 10,000 unissued shares of its common stock for all of the outstanding shares of Saen Company. The total par value of 10,000 shares of Penman common stock is Fl. 1,500,000 and their total market value is Fl. 1,700,000. The fair market values of Saen

Company's assets and liabilities are equal to their book values with the exception of plant and equipment, which have an estimated fair market value of 1,200,000 guilders.

Required: Prepare a balance sheet for Penman Company immediately after the merger under the assumptions that:
(1) The merger is treated as a purchase.
(2) The merger is treated as a pooling of interests.

7-5   In 1996, the Datar Corporation incurred research and development costs as follows (amounts are expressed in Nigerian nairas):

Materials and equipment	₦ 230,000
Labor	200,000
Indirect costs	100,000
Total	₦ 530,000

These costs relate to a product that will be marketed in 1996. The costs should be recovered by December 31, 2000.

Required:
(1) What is the amount of research and development costs that should be expensed in 1996?
(2) Included in the above costs is 100,000 nairas for equipment that can be used on other research projects. Estimated useful life of the equipment is four years, and it was acquired at the beginning of 1996. What is the amount of research and development costs that should be expensed in 1996 under these assumptions? Datar uses the straight-line method of depreciation.

7-6   Pierre Company leases a large specialized machine to the Francois Company at a total rental of 1,800,000 French francs, payable in five annual installments in the following declining pattern: 25 percent for the first two years, 20 percent in the third year, and 15 percent in each of the last two years. The lease begins January 1, 1996. In addition to the rent, Pierre is required to pay annual costs of F15,000 to cover repairs, maintenance, and insurance. The lease qualifies as an operating lease for reporting purposes. Pierre incurred initial direct costs of F15,000 in obtaining the lease. The machine cost Pierre F3,100,000 to build and has an estimated life of 10 years with an estimated residual value of F100,000. Pierre uses straight-line depreciation. Both companies report on a calendar-year basis.

Required:
(1) Prepare appropriate journal entries on Pierre's books for the years 1996 and 2000 related to the lease.
(2) Prepare appropriate journal entries on Francois' books for the years 1996 and 2000 related to the lease.

7-7   In 1996, Melker Inc., a U.S.-based company, entered into a lease for a new oil press. The lease states that annual payments will be made for five years. The payments are to be made in advance on January 1 of each year. At the end of the five-year period, Melker may purchase the oil press. The estimated economic life of the equipment is 12 years. Melker uses the calendar year for reporting purposes and uses straight-line depreciation for other equipment. The following additional information about the lease is available:

Annual lease payments	$ 110,000
Purchase option price	$ 40,000
Estimated fair market value of oil press after 5 years	$ 100,000
Incremental borrowing rate	10 percent
Date of first lease payment	Jan. 1, 1996

Required:
(1) Compute the amount to be capitalized as an asset for the lease of the oil press.
(2) Prepare a schedule showing the computation of the interest expense for each period.
(3) Give the journal entries that would be made on Melker's books for each of the first two years of the lease.
(4) Assume that the purchase option is exercised at the end of the lease. Give the journal entry to record the exercise of the option by Melker.

7-8 The balance sheets of two Canadian companies, P Company and S Company, as of January 1, 1996 are presented below.

	P	S
Cash	$ 1,200,000	$ 500,000
Receivables	1,600,000	500,000
Inventories	5,000,000	400,000
Plant and equipment (net)	9,600,000	2,000,000
Total assets	$17,400,000	$3,400,000
Payables	$ 3,000,000	$1,000,000
Paid-in capital	9,000,000	2,000,000
Retained earnings	5,400,000	400,000
Total liabilities and stockholders' equity	$17,400,000	$3,400,000

The two companies effect a merger whereby P Company exchanged its capital stock for all the outstanding shares of S Company. Shares of S Company were exchanged at a ratio of one share of P for every two shares of S. Market values per share were P $100 and S $200, respectively. The fair values of S Company's assets and liabilities are equal to their book values except plant and equipment, which have an estimated fair value of $2,500,000.

Required: Prepare a balance sheet immediately after the merger using the pooling of interests method.

Case: Goodwill Forever?

The following item summarizes a proposal by the U.K.'s Accounting Standards Board:[6]

> The Accounting Standards Board's proposals on accounting for goodwill are a triumph of diplomacy as well as intellectual ingenuity. The ASB's style has hitherto been somewhat confrontational, but the new rules are designed to please those who prepare accounts—namely companies—and those who use them, chiefly investors.
>
> Amazingly, given the passions which goodwill accounting provokes, the proposals are likely to meet with widespread approval. This is despite the fact that companies' favoured way of dealing with the substance—writing it off against reserves—is set to be outlawed. The reason is that companies will not be obliged to write goodwill off against earnings over an arbitrary number of years. They may do this if they want, but in practice big companies will opt to leave the goodwill on the balance sheet, testing it from year to year to see whether there has been any diminution in its value. Sensibly, companies will be able to keep brands and other intangibles on the balance sheet, subject to similar tests.
>
> If the proposals are adopted, the quality of accounts will be doubly improved. Goodwill will be visible in the accounts, not written off and forgotten. Furthermore, the tests on the value of goodwill seem rigorous and yet not unduly complicated, and will prove a useful discipline for managers. They will however add to the pressures on auditors, who will be forced to exercise judgment where they may have preferred clear-cut guidelines.

Required:
(1) Discuss reasons supporting amortization of goodwill.
(2) Discuss reasons against amortization of goodwill.
(3) What alternative do you prefer based on the points made in (1) and (2)? Explain.
(4) Can the arguments supporting or against goodwill amortization be extended to other intangibles? Explain. Include examples in your analysis.

---

[6] "Goodwill," *Financial Times,* 15 June 1995, p. 14.

References

Arthur Andersen & Co. *Accounting for Business Combinations, Goodwill and other Intangibles.* Chicago: Arthur Andersen & Co., 1991.

Australia: International Tax and Business Guide. New York: Deloitte Touche Tohmatsu International, 1994.

Brazil: International Tax and Business Guide. New York: Deloitte Touche Tohmatsu International, 1993.

Canada: International Tax and Business Guide. New York: Deloitte Touche Tohmatsu International, 1994.

Coopers & Lybrand. *International Accounting Summaries.* 2d ed. New York: John Wiley & Sons, Inc., 1993.

————. *The Accounting Profession in Nigeria.* New York: American Institute of Certified Public Accountants, 1993.

Doing Business in Australia: Information Guide. New York: Price Waterhouse, 1993.

Doing Business in Brazil: Information Guide. New York: Price Waterhouse, 1991.

Doing Business in Canada: Information Guide. New York: Price Waterhouse, 1994.

Doing Business in France: Information Guide. New York: Price Waterhouse, 1993 and 1994 Supplement.

Doing Business in Germany: Information Guide. New York: Price Waterhouse, 1994.

Doing Business in Japan: Information Guide. New York: Price Waterhouse, 1993.

Doing Business in Mexico: Information Guide. New York: Price Waterhouse, 1993.

Doing Business in Netherlands: Information Guide. New York: Price Waterhouse, 1990 and 1993 Supplement.

Doing Business in Nigeria: Information Guide. New York: Price Waterhouse, 1994.

Doing Business in United States: Information Guide. New York: Price Waterhouse, 1992 and 1993 Supplement.

France: International Tax and Business Guide. New York: Deloitte Touche Tohmatsu International, 1993.

Galaz, Gomez Mortin, Chavero, Yamazaki, S. C., and Deloitte & Touche. *The Accounting Profession in Mexico.* 2d ed., rev. New York: American Institute of Certified Public Accountants, 1992.

Garrod, Neil, and Isabel Sieringhaus. "European Union Accounting Harmonization: The Case of Leased Assets in the United Kingdom and Germany." *The European Accounting Review,* vol. 4, no. 1 (1995), pp. 155-164.

Germany: International Tax and Business Guide. New York: Deloitte Touche Tohmatsu International, 1995.

Guy Barbier & Associés. *The Accounting Profession in France.* 2d ed., rev. New York: American Institute of Certified Public Accountants, 1992.

Japan: International Tax and Business Guide. New York: Deloitte Touche Tohmatsu International, 1994.

Kieso, Donald E., and Jerry J. Weygandt. *Intermediate Accounting.* 8th ed. New York: John Wiley & Sons, Inc., 1995.

KPMG Century Audit Corporation. *The Accounting Profession in Japan.* 2d ed., rev. New York: American Institute of Certified Public Accountants, 1992.

Mexico: International Tax and Business Guide. New York: Deloitte Touche Tohmatsu International, 1995.

Moret Ernst & Young. *The Accounting Profession in the Netherlands.* 2d ed., rev. New York: American Institute of Certified Public Accountants, 1991.

Netherlands: International Tax and Business Guide. New York: Deloitte Touche Tohmatsu International, 1994.

Nobes, Christopher W., and Robert H. Parker (eds.). *Comparative International Accounting.* Englewood Cliffs, N.J.: Prentice Hall, 1991.

Oldham, K. Michael. *Accounting Systems and Practice in Europe.* Brookfield, Vermont: Gower Publishing Company, 1987.

Prince, D. D. *EEC Directives on Company Law and Financial Markets.* Oxford: Clarendon Press, 1991.

Schoonderbeck, Jan W. "Setting Accounting Standards in the Netherlands." *The European Accounting Review.* vol. 3, no. 1 (1994), pp. 132-142.

A Survey and Analysis of Consolidation/Equity Accounting Practices. New York: Price Waterhouse, 1991.

A Survey and Analysis of Standards and Practices on Accounting for Leases. New York: Ernst & Young, 1991.

A Survey and Analysis of Standards and Practices on Employer's Accounting for Pensions. New York: Coopers & Lybrand, 1991.

United Kingdom: International Tax and Business Guide. New York: Deloitte Touche Tohmatsu International, 1995.

United States: International Tax and Business Guide. New York: Deloitte Touche Tohmatsu International, 1994.

Zeff, Stephen A., and Bala G. Dharan. *Readings and Notes on Financial Accounting.* New York: McGraw-Hill, Inc., 1994.

Chapter 8

Managerial Accounting Issues: Strategic Planning and Control

The accounting system within any organization may be viewed as consisting of financial accounting and managerial accounting. The distinction between the two is based on the primary users of information. **Managerial accounting** information is used by managers and others within the organization to *plan* and *control* activities of the organization and to *make decisions*. **Financial accounting** information is primarily for users outside the organization. The main focus of this chapter is on international managerial accounting issues related to strategic planning and control.

International Managerial Accounting

Managerial accounting concerns itself with the provision of information that is primarily for internal users. The information is for three broad purposes:[1]

- *Policy formulation, strategic planning, and tactical planning.* **Nonroutine reports** are prepared for the purpose of providing information to managers to assist them formulate policies, prepare strategic plans, and prepare tactical (operational) plans. Strategic planning is discussed in detail in a later section. Tactical plans, or operational plans, are the plans designed to implement strategic plans. Typically, tactical plans are for a part of the organization, cover a time period shorter than strategic plans, and are implemented by middle and lower level managers.

- *Planning activities and controlling operations.* **Routine reporting** enables managers to plan activities and control operations. A performance report, comparing actual performance against budgetary goals, is an example of such a report. The trend is toward preparation of reports that are more frequent, and more nonfinancial in nature. For example, a shift manager may receive a daily report that contains data on the total number of units produced, tons of raw materials used, number of labor hours used, and the number of defective units produced.

- *Resource allocation and pricing decisions.* **Special purpose reports** prepared by managerial accountants help managers make resource allocation and pricing decisions. Such reports are usually based on costs versus benefits analysis of various alternatives. Increasingly, the trend is toward inclusion of more nonfinancial and nonquantitative information to enhance their usefulness. Pertinent information on quality, response time, and channels of distribution may be presented to the management along with financial figures for each alternative. Examples of such

---

[1] Charles T. Horngren, George Foster, and Srikant M. Datar, *Cost Accounting—A Managerial Emphasis* (Englewood Cliffs, N.J.: Prentice Hall, 1994), p. 4.

reports include whether to make or buy a part and whether to accept or reject a special order (at below-normal selling price).

The complexity of international operations places additional demands on managerial accounting as discussed in subsequent sections of this chapter.

Strategic Planning

According to W. Edwards Deming, acknowledged by many to be the father of the quality movement, there must be a clear goal or long-range plan to stay in business. **Strategic planning** is the process of deciding on the goals of the organization, and the strategies for attaining these goals.[2] A **strategic plan** integrates an organization's major goals, policies, and action sequences into a cohesive whole.[3] It helps an organization allocate its resources, to capitalize on its strengths, to take advantage of projected changes in the environments, and to be competitive. Strategic planning is not new to the corporate scene. It has been practiced by domestic corporations for many years, especially in industrialized countries. However, not enough attention has been given to strategic planning for international operations.

Multinational corporations make choices while formulating their international business strategies. They must answer questions such as:

- In which countries should the company expand or curtail its operations?
- What should be the scope of operations in a new country? Should it be a sales operation? A manufacturing operation? Both?
- Should the entry in a new country be in the form of a joint venture or should it be as a wholly-owned subsidiary?

The strategic planning process of a multinational corporation takes into account the internal as well as external environmental factors of a company. Prediction of external environmental factors is difficult even within the boundaries of one nation. The task is inherently more complex where many countries are involved. This explains the reluctance exhibited by many multinational corporations to rush into business ventures in the former Soviet republics and many East European countries. They have discovered that legal and political conditions in those countries are often too fluid to predict.

Complexities in Developing Global Business Strategies

Multinational corporations must deal with numerous variables while developing a global business strategy.

Economic and legal environments differ from country to country. Each country has its own business regulatory framework, tax system, financial reporting requirements, inflation rates, and currency with fluctuating exchange rates.

---

[2] Robert N. Anthony, *The Management Control Function* (Boston: The Harvard Business School Press, 1988), p. 30.

[3] James Brian Quinn, *Strategies for Change* (Homewood, Ill.: Richard D. Irwin, Inc., 1980), p. 7.

Political environments are different worldwide. Often the political system has a direct impact on the business operations. Governments in some countries do not allow foreign-based companies to form certain types of business organizations. Many Middle Eastern countries require that a local citizen must be a partner in the business venture of a foreign-based company. Lack of political stability increases the political risk for foreign-based enterprises, as does the abrupt change in governmental policies in countries that do not have a long-standing tradition of free market economy. Regional conflicts may impair movements of goods and services.

Labor considerations are different for each country. In some countries, for example Germany, labor unions are quite powerful. Labor laws may have an impact on the ability of a multinational company to hire and terminate workers. Some countries, for example Egypt and India, have strict laws that make it difficult to lay off workers. Labor productivity and the availability of skilled workforce vary in different parts of the world.

Language and cultural differences may create problems in communicating strategies and plans. Some cultures make the acceptance of planning difficult due to a cultural sense of fatalism regarding the future. The degree of reliance on trust and on long-standing traditions also varies among cultures.

Nature of Information

The formulation of a strategic plan is a time consuming process, often taking one or two years. According to Anthony, "In the classroom, strategic problems can be analyzed by assuming cause/effect relationships, but in the real world, knowledge of these relationships is likely to be so uncertain that use of sophisticated analytical tools is often not worth the effort."[4] In strategic planning, the information reflects an attempt to predict the future and, therefore, is inherently imprecise.

The information for strategic planning is mostly from the external environment. The nature of strategic planning makes it impossible to foresee all the information needed. Therefore, it is not possible to design an information system that can provide all the information for strategic planning. This explains why strategic planning is so time consuming. Information, mostly about the external environment, has to be collected and analyzed during the strategic planning process. Strategic planners may be able to make some use of the data stored in the database of an information system. However, due to the unique information requirements of strategic planning, the data must be rearranged to be useful.[5]

Relationship with the budget. A budget is a formal plan usually expressed in monetary terms and usually for a period of one year. The budget, therefore, is a short-range plan. When an organization has a strategic plan, the budget is essentially to make detailed plans to implement the strategy for the period involved. It is critical that the goals in the budget be consistent with the strategic plan.

---

[4] Anthony, The Management Control Function, p. 46.

[5] Ibid., pp. 50-52.

Environmental Considerations

As mentioned above, most of the information for strategic planning is external in nature. Stability and complexity of environments vary from country to country. The economies of Sweden and Germany are relatively stable. They remain strong free market economies. The environments of some countries are quite dynamic. France's policies on socialism versus private enterprise are noticeably affected by each election. The greater the degree of environmental instability in a country, the more difficult it is to predict environmental conditions.[6]

The environments also differ in terms of their complexity. Japanese and Indian managers, for example, are subject to norms and values that are far more complex than are U.S. managers.[7]

Cultural Considerations

Before discussing cultural considerations, an important point needs to be made: National boundaries and cultural boundaries often do not coincide.[8] Cultural patterns in California are much different than those in, say, Alabama. The culture in the northern part of Italy is more similar to Switzerland than it is to the southern part of Italy. Quebec's culture is different than that of any other province in Canada. Cultural diversity can be a source of synergy in a multinational organization. Therefore, by adopting a multinational strategy an organization can become more than a sum of its parts. Operations in one cultural setting can benefit from operations in other cultural settings by gaining a better understanding of how the world works.[9]

Culture and individual behavior. Individual behavior varies across cultures. A large-scale study based on 116,000 responses from workers in 40 countries identified cultural differences that can be grouped in four dimensions.[10]

- **Power distance** reflects the extent of inequality between superiors and subordinates. In a **high-power-distance culture**, a person at a higher position in the organizational hierarchy makes the decision and the employees at the lower levels simply follow the instructions. In a **low-power-distance culture**, employees perceive few power differences and follow a superior's instructions only when either they agree or feel threatened.

---

[6] Warren J. Keegan, Global Marketing Management, 4th ed. (Englewood Cliffs, N.J.: Prentice-Hall, 1989), p. 682.

[7] Gregory Moorhead and Ricky W. Griffin, Organizational Behavior, 2d ed. (Boston, Mass.: Houghton Mifflin Company, 1989), p. 682.

[8] Nancy J. Adler, Robert Doctor, and S. Gordon Redding. "From the Atlantic to the Pacific Century: Cross Cultural Management Review." Journal of Management (summer 1986), pp. 295-318.

[9] Tamotsu Yamaguchi, "The Challenge of Internationalization." Academy of Management Executive (February 1988), pp. 33-36.

[10] Geert H. Hofstede, Culture's Consequences: International Differences in Work Related Values (Beverly Hills, Calif.: Sage Publications, 1980).

Among the high-power-distance countries are Spain, France, Japan, Singapore, Mexico, Brazil, and Indonesia. The examples of cultures with a low-power-distance include the U.S., Israel, Austria, Denmark, Ireland, Norway, Germany, and New Zealand.

- **Individualism** is a state in which the employee attaches higher importance to personal and family interests than to the organization. **Collectivism** is the feeling that interests of the organization should have top priority.

  The employees in a culture that values individualism usually assess situations in terms of how decisions will affect them personally and professionally. The people in cultures characterized by collectivism put the needs of the organization first and, therefore, organizational interests take higher priority. The most individualistic cultures include the U.S., Australia, the U.K., the Netherlands, Canada, and New Zealand. Cultures characterized by a very high degree of collectivism include Colombia, Pakistan, Taiwan, Peru, Singapore, Japan, Mexico, Greece, and Hong Kong.

- **Uncertainty avoidance** is the extent to which uncertainty is avoided in a culture. A culture with a high level of uncertainty avoidance gives importance to employment stability and a low level of stress.

  Employees in Denmark, the U.S., Canada, Norway, Singapore, Hong Kong, and Australia tolerate a high level of uncertainty. Uncertainty avoidance is high among employees in Israel, Austria, Japan, Italy, Argentina, Peru, France, and Belgium.

- **Masculinity** is the relative importance of the qualities associated with men such as assertiveness and materialism. **Femininity** is characterized by quality of life and nurturing. Masculine societies define male-female roles more rigidly than do the societies with a high degree of femininity. Highly masculine cultures include Japan and Austria, while the highly feminine societies include Norway, Sweden, Denmark, and Finland.

Cross-cultural considerations are important in the strategic planning process as well as in the design of control systems. To cope with the challenges posed by cultural environments in different parts of the world, it is necessary that a multinational company adapt to different cultures where it conducts business. Cultural variations have a direct impact on how managers and employees in different parts of the world make and accept decisions, how they view their professional careers in comparison with personal and family interests, and what motivates them.

Business managers of multinationals are increasingly becoming aware of cultural implications. A recent survey of 150 senior executives of Fortune 1000 companies by Deloitte & Touche LLP indicated that the executives feel that "Globalization is more than international business—it is a complete, conceptual evolution."[11] The executives stated that as companies expand globally, the primary challenge they face is the cultural barrier, followed by

---

[11] "Global Expansion Not Deterred by Falling Dollar," Deloitte & Touche Review, 10 July 1995, p. 3.

economic barriers and trade and political barriers. They also stated that when management makes the decision to expand overseas, the keys to success are:[12]

- Building a local presence.
- Modifying products and services to suit local cultures.
- Using technology effectively.
- Employing local staff to run foreign operations.

Immigrants to the base country of a multinational company are often valuable resources for bridging cultural gaps and fostering cultural understanding. The following example illustrates the important role played by the immigrants from India to the U.S. in helping U.S.-based multinationals establish business operations in India.[13]

> . . . U.S. émigrés often return to head operations for such companies as GE Capital, McKinsey, and AT & T. They often end up explaining Indians and Americans to each other. "My role is to provide a cultural interpretation," says Kartar Singh, senior vice-president of Cogentrix Inc. in Charlotte, N.C. Singh now spends much of his time helping Cogentrix build a $1.5 billion power plant in Mangalore.

Local presence often makes it easier to receive acceptance from local culture. Texas Instruments has effectively used the strategy of local presence. Before its global strategy, Texas Instruments was almost forced out of the market by competition. Now Texas Instruments has fabrication plants in more countries than any other chip manufacturer, and other chip makers are following Texas Instrument's practice. Local presence enables a company to tap market growth wherever it occurs.[14]

Risk Management

Risk management is the identification of threats and the design of an approach to their containment. It is a major concern of strategic planners. Economic and business information is vital to the preparation of strategic plans. Such information includes economic development indicators, information about banking and credit availability, employment data, and demographical statistics. Such information may either not be available, or if available may not be accurate or current. This highlights the need for strategic planning. The lack of information should not derail the strategic planning process. Planning becomes even more important when the level of risk is high.

Multinational corporations make choices when preparing their international business strategy. An enterprise with a well-articulated strategic plan should:[15]

[12] Ibid., p. 4.

[13] Joyce Barnathan, Sharon Moshavi, Heidi Dawley, Sunita Wadekar Bhargava, and Helen Chang, "Passage Back to India: Expatriates Seek a Motherlode in the Motherland," Business Week, 17 July 1995, p. 45.

[14] Peter Burrows, Linda Bernier, and Pete Engardio, "Texas Instruments' Global Chip Payoff: The Company Is Ready to Cash in on the Biggest Bonanza in High-tech History." Business Week, 7 August 1995, p. 64.

[15] Samuel C. Certo and J. Paul Peter, Strategic Management—Concepts and Applications (Burr Ridge, Ill.: Richard D. Irwin, Inc., 1995), p. 6.

- Set a clear direction.
- Know its strengths and weaknesses compared with its competitors.
- Devote its hard-won resources to projects that employ its set of core competencies, the primary skills within the organization.
- Identify factors in the political and social environment that require careful monitoring.
- Recognize which competitor actions need critical attention.

Each strategic choice presents its own set of opportunities and associated risks. A strategist might steer a company away from operating in a certain country because of inherent political risks. An integral part of strategic planning is to determine the degree of risk a company is willing to take in making a strategic choice. The degree of risk inherent in a strategic choice may be a function of many variables, some of which are:[16]

- *Risk of value loss.* In evaluating a strategic choice, the planners must take into account that the total value of the resources invested in the implementation of its strategic plan creates the risk that those resources may lose their value partially or in total. This potential loss may occur because of internal events such as chronic inadequate availability of qualified personnel in a country where operations were started. The loss of value may also result from changes in external environment. For example, there may be a downward shift in the sales volume of cigarettes because of local government's concerted efforts to educate the population about health hazards from consuming tobacco products.
- *Risk and length of time.* The longer the time period, the higher the probability of exposure to risk involving value loss. Moreover, with a very long time horizon, there is a possibility that the rate of return demanded by the investors may be so high that it may make it difficult, if not impossible, to attract investment funds.
- *Risk and the proportion of resources committed.* This risk is a function of the proportion of the total resources being committed to the implementation of a strategic plan. The success or failure of a plan involving investment of a substantial portion of the total resources available to an enterprise can have drastic and far-reaching consequences for the management and investors.

Risk reduction. A firm may adopt various risk reduction mechanisms. These include forming joint ventures or alliances to spread the risk. An extreme case is formation of a virtual organization. In a virtual organization, various enterprises join forces to take advantage of their respective strengths to collectively work on a project. As soon as the project is completed, the participants go their separate ways. A classic example of an industry where virtual organizations are the norm is the movie-making industry.

Another risk reduction mechanism is establishing geographically dispersed international operations. Chevron was forced to abandon its operations in Sudan about a decade ago, due

---

[16] Tony Morden, Business Strategy and Planning: Text and Cases (Berkshire, England: McGraw-Hill Book Company Europe, 1993), pp. 214-216.

to anarchy, after the company had already invested nearly $1 billion. Chevron has a policy in place now requiring that no single country should account for more than 25 percent of the company's annual investment abroad.

A third risk reduction mechanism is to avoid head-on competition with companies that have resources of such a high magnitude at their disposal that they can create insurmountable obstacles. Such competitors may have the ability and willingness to outspend others for as long a time period as necessary to keep or increase their own market share. "If you don't have a competitive advantage, don't compete," advises John F. Welch Jr., CEO and chairman of General Electric Company.[17]

Competitiveness and Quality

The strength of competition is an influential factor in strategic planning for global operations. According to a recent survey of the U.S. senior executives of Fortune 1000 companies, global competition has moved to the top of the list of the issues considered to be most important.[18]

The impact of competition on strategic planning can be illustrated by using Chevron Corporation's example. Chevron, the U.S.'s third largest oil and gas company, shifted its focus from domestic to global operations in order to become competitive. Watching "big playing fields opening up all around the world" finally persuaded Chevron it couldn't rely on the "very restrictive set of opportunities here in the U.S.," stated David O'Reilly, vice president of strategic planning. Chevron's strategic shift is explained by its chairman Kenneth Derr: "Growth opportunities for international oil companies have never been greater."[19]

The strategic plan must take into account the fact that competitive forces are an especially important variable in international markets when the competitors are well established and resourceful. Chevron, for example, faces stiff competition from Exxon Corporation and Royal Dutch/Shell Group, both with greater financial resources and more diversified worldwide interests.[20] To be competitive, a business must have customer focus. It is widely acknowledged that quality is the most important of the competitive weapons.

> Businesses know that to survive and build long-term competitive advantage they must focus on fundamentals. This begins with a strategic look at customer needs: what does the customer want? What is the value of the business's products or services? How well do they meet these needs, compared with the competition? Answering these questions, the business can uncover its potential sources of competitive advantage and develop a plan to tap them.

[17] Greg Goldin, "A Hardhead's 'Soft Values': John F. Welch Jr." Worldbusiness, spring 1995, p. 40.

[18] "Global Expansion Not Deterred by Falling Dollar," Deloitte & Touche Review, 10 July 1995, p. 3.

[19] Andy Pasztor, "Global Search: Chevron Is Plunging Into Foreign Projects to Build Oil Reserves," Wall Street Journal, 24 February 1994, p. 1.

[20] Ibid.

To implement this plan, the business must then conduct a strategic review and where necessary re-engineer its core business processes, redesign its products and renovate its production methods. In each area, the business must assess its ability to satisfy customers.

In its core processes the business should aim to outperform its rivals in five key areas: quality, time, cost, innovation and customer service.[21]

Quality standards and quality awards. There are several international and national quality standards. The International Standards Organization's Standard 9000 Series specifies the methods by which a system can be implemented to ensure that all specified quality performance requirements are fully met. The Malcolm Baldrige National Quality Award has been presented annually since 1988 to the companies in the U.S. that have excelled in quality. The award, presented by the President of the U.S., may be given up to two companies in each of three categories: manufacturing, service, and small businesses.

The Deming Prize, established by the Japanese Union of Scientists and Engineers, is the most honored quality award in Japan. Requirements for the Deming Prize include, perhaps, the most demanding auditing process.

Other quality standards and models include the British Standard 7850 Guide to TQM, the British Quality Award, the European Quality Award, and the Marketing Quality Assurance (MQA) Specifications. Exxon Chemical International Marketing B.V. was the first organization to receive registration to MQA in 1991. Exxon Chemical achieved registration in seven European offices located at Brussels, Cologne, Madrid, Milan, Paris, Rotterdam, and Southampton. AT&T has the high distinction of winning three Baldrige Awards (no other company has won more than one) and a Deming Prize.

The European Quality Award, mentioned in the last paragraph was established by the European Foundation for Quality Management. The award emphasizes customer satisfaction, employee satisfaction and impact on society.[22]

Role of Accounting

Strategic planning deals with vision for a direction of the organization.[23] The role of information is central to the strategic planning process. Accountants are important players in this process because they have the expertise to perform various types of analyses that can be helpful in managing resources to develop competitive advantage. The analyses necessary during the strategic planning process include those of customers, markets, and competitors. Market share leadership requires, among other things, cost management and quality.

---

[21] International Review (New York: Coopers & Lybrand, 1994), p. 21.

[22] John S. Oakland, Total Quality Management: The Route to Improving Performance. 2d ed. (Oxford, England: Butterworth Heinemann Ltd., 1993), pp. 148-151.

[23] Michael D. Akers and Grover L. Porter, "Strategic Planning At Five World Class Companies," Management Accounting, July 1995, p. 24.

Accountants also play an important role in developing projections as financial expressions of the strategy. The strategic plans become a mechanism for resource allocation. Once plans are implemented, accountants provide tools to measure goal achievement. By analysis, accountants also ensure that there is integration of annual, tactical, and strategic plans.

Accountants' expertise in financial statement analysis is invaluable during the strategic planning process. By analyzing the competitors' financial statements, accountants provide important insights into the competitors. This is a significant contribution to the process.

Control Systems

The previous section discussed strategic planning. This section presents control concepts and considerations for multinational corporations in designing an effective control system.

A **control system** compares the actual performance (results) with planned performance (goals) so that management may take appropriate action when necessary. A control system includes both internal and external information.

In addition to formal control systems, informal control methods play an important role in multinational companies. The main informal control method is to transfer an executive from one international operation to another with explicit or implicit understanding about expected performance. Another informal control method is to hold meetings between parent company executives and subsidiary executives, usually at a subsidiary location. Annual meetings of executives from international operations also provide an opportunity to informally assess performance and to exchange information.

Cultural differences necessitate adaptation of control measures to each country's cultural environment. Different currencies, languages, communication styles, and levels of technological development are but a few of the issues facing multinational corporations while designing and implementing control measures across national boundaries.

Languages and national currencies need special mention. A subsidiary in a new country might mean another language in which strategic plans, budgets, and reports are written. In some countries, India for example, there are many different languages and each has many dialects. Some technical words may be difficult or impossible to translate into the local language. Different national currencies and their fluctuating exchange rates affect every aspect of a multinational corporation including control. A material change in the exchange rate may render the business plan unrealistic. The problem is compounded when a multinational company has subsidiaries in many countries and each of those subsidiaries in turn is involved in business transactions in many countries. Unexpected or sudden restrictions on transfer of foreign currencies by local governments may constrain the subsidiary's ability to implement its plans.

Centralization versus Decentralization

An important consideration in the design of a control system is the multinational company's philosophy regarding the extent to which it delegates decision-making authority to managements of subsidiaries. Decentralized multinational organizations give managements of the subsidiaries considerable independence of action. Centralized multinational organizations retain to a great extent the authority to make decisions at parent company headquarters. Centralization and decentralization are a matter of degree. No organization can possibly be fully centralized or fully decentralized.

All other things being equal, the greater the physical distance between the multinational company headquarters and an international operation, the more autonomous the international operation will be. Physical distance in international operations often makes travel and communications costly and time consuming. This often leads to greater delegation of authority to local management. Another important reason is that local managers have more knowledge about local conditions. They should be in a position to make decisions quickly and take timely actions, especially if the local environment is not very stable.

The current trend is clearly toward greater decentralization. Chevron Corporation, for example, is moving toward less central control. Most of the well-known multinational companies are highly decentralized, with each subsidiary enjoying a high degree of autonomy. The examples include Unilever, Imperial Chemical Industries, Royal Dutch Shell, Philips, Procter & Gamble, 3M, Ford, and General Motors. Still, a few multinationals maintain a high degree of centralization. They include Nikon, Sony, and Matsushita.

Performance Evaluation

A key step in the control process is performance evaluation. It is important not to limit the performance evaluation information to either formal reports or to financial results:[24]

> Information about what has actually happened comes to the manager's attention both from formal reports and also from informal sources. The informal sources include conversations, memoranda, meetings, and personal observations. Since informal information is not governed by the disciplines that are built into a formal reporting system, its validity varies. Thus, the bias of the originator or other sources of inaccuracy needs to be taken into account. When this is done, informal information can be extremely important. Formal reports alone are an inadequate basis for control.

> An important control principle is that the formal performance reports should contain no surprises. Important news should be conveyed to interested parties informally, as soon as feasible, and in any event prior to submission of formal reports.

> Since a management control system is built around a financial budget, there is a natural tendency to structure performance reports so that they correspond to the budget and to emphasize the correspondence between actual and budget in evaluating performance. This may result in an overemphasis on the financial

---

[24] Anthony, The Management Control Function, p. 95.

results. Because measures to nonfinancial, and especially nonquantitative, performance may be difficult to make, these aspects of performance may be given less weight than they should be. Overemphasis or misuse of these measures can have dysfunctional consequences.

A research report issued by The Conference Board, based on a study conducted through an international group of corporations, institutional investors, and advisors explores the use of new performance measures to better manage business.

The study found that purely financial, traditional accounting-based performance measures lack predictive behavior, reward the wrong behavior, and give inadequate consideration to hard-to-quantify resources such as intellectual capital.

The study group concluded that nonfinancial "key" performance measures should be used to capture not only the value of existing assets, but also the potential for future performance. Typical key measures include:

- Quality of output.
- Customer satisfaction/retention.
- Employee training.
- Research and development investment and productivity.
- New product development.
- Market growth/success.
- Environmental competitiveness.

The key measures are intended to augment (not replace) traditional financial performance measures. The study recommended that three critical factors be observed while choosing performance measures:

- Do not mistake data for information.
- You are what you measure.
- What gets measured gets managed.

By tying key measures to the strategic vision of the company, there is assurance that as the vision changes so do the performance measures.[25]

Measures of performance for workers. Business and accounting literature has very little information on the measures of performance used in different cultures to assess an individual's contributions. Most often we must resort to inferences such as: Workers in a culture that puts a premium on individualism would tend to have performance measures that evaluate the individual's own contributions, while a culture dominated by collectivism would use performance measures to assess an individual's performance in terms of what he/she contributes to the group effort.

---

[25] Deloitte & Touche LLP, "Challenging Traditional Measures of Performance," *Deloitte & Touche Review,* 7 August 1995, pp. 1-2.

Performance Evaluation of a Subsidiary

Performance evaluation of a subsidiary is an assessment of how the subsidiary carries out corporate strategy. A subsidiary's performance is measured, and reports of its performance are prepared. These reports compare actual performance with planned performance. This comparison may result either in a corrective action, or a revision of the plans.[26] Conceptually, performance evaluation of foreign subsidiaries is similar to that of domestic operations. However, performance evaluation of foreign subsidiaries, by necessity, includes additional features to take into account those factors that are not present in domestic operations. Examples of such factors are different inflation rates and varying foreign currency exchange rates. The information from the evaluation process is used to direct management's attention to the areas in need of improvement. An effective performance evaluation system should have the following elements:

- Performance evaluation criteria.
- Measurement of actual performance.
- Performance evaluation reports.

Performance Evaluation Criteria

Performance evaluation criteria should include both financial and nonfinancial measurements. Each performance evaluation criterion poses unique measurement and information-gathering problems. Criteria to evaluate performance should be specific to the subsidiary. A cost center is evaluated differently from a profit center. A new subsidiary may be exempted from meeting certain performance standards until it is fully established. For example, newly established operations in the former Soviet republics are more concerned with survival and testing the local market than with making a profit during the early years of operation. Also, some criteria may not be applicable in a given operating environment. For example, cash flow from a subsidiary to the parent company is not a useful criterion for a subsidiary located in a country with tight foreign currency control. Employee benefits and employee satisfaction are important components of the evaluation system in some countries, while these factors are less important elsewhere.

Exhibits 8-1 and 8-2 list examples of financial and nonfinancial performance evaluation criteria respectively. A key point to remember while selecting evaluation criteria is that performance will be judged against the criteria chosen. Therefore, different evaluation criteria motivate managers differently. A good guideline is to use multiple criteria so that managers are motivated to improve performance in all areas considered important by the top management.

Relevant issues for criteria selection.   Three important issues must be considered while choosing performance criteria for international subsidiaries:

1.   Goals and objectives often differ among international subsidiaries and thus uniform performance criteria for all subsidiaries would not be appropriate. A foreign sub-

---

[26] Anthony, The Management Control Function, p. 125.

Exhibit 8–1   Performance Evaluation—Financial Criteria

Profitability ratios relative to resources or revenues
- Return on investment
- Return on stockholders' equity
- Return on sales (profit margin)
- Gross profit ratio

Target amount relative to key performance area
- Sales revenues
- Operating income
- Net income
- Residual income
- Total production cost
- Labor cost
- Research and development cost
- Investment in new technology cost

Cash flow from subsidiaries
- Cash flow amount expressed in the foreign currency
- Cash flow amount expressed in the parent company's currency
- Changes in cash flow over time

Budget comparisons
- Budgeted vs. actual sales
- Budgeted vs. actual profit
- Budgeted vs. actual costs
- Cost, revenue, and volume variances

Exhibit 8–2   Performance Evaluation—Nonfinancial Criteria

- Percent growth in sales volume
- Market share
- Asset turnover
- Inventory turnover
- New plants and plant expansions
- New products and product innovations
- Customer service
- Employee benefits and employee relations
- Community and social service
- Relations with government and local constituents
- Environmental concerns
- Labor productivity
- New manufacturing systems
- Manufacturing cycle efficiency
- Throughput time
- Delivery cycle time

sidiary may be established to manufacture a component for other subsidiaries. Another subsidiary may be formed to take advantage of certain advanced technology in the host country. Yet a third subsidiary may be established to take advantage of tax incentives granted by the local government. Exhibit 8-3 shows examples of different corporate objectives and related performance evaluation criteria.

Exhibit 8–3 Examples of Corporate Objectives and Evaluation Criteria	
Corporate Objectives	**Performance Evaluation Criteria**
Market objectives:	
Open new markets	Market share and penetration
Presence in market	Sales volume
Manufacturing objectives:	
Productivity and efficiency	Cost reduction and cost savings
Production of components	Components volume produced
Raw material sourcing	Cost of raw material
Capacity management	Overhead cost per unit of output
Advanced manufacturing technology	New manufacturing processes used
Financial objectives:	
Profitable investment	Return on investment; residual income
Short-term investment recovery	Cash flow to parent company
Customer service objectives:	
Customer service	Number of customer complaints
Product quality	Warranty costs

2. Environmental factors differ among countries and change over time within the same country. The evaluation criteria should take into account different local environments. A multinational corporation may find it easier to produce and sell a product in one country than in another country, depending on protectionist policies of local governments.

   Local operating environments often change over a period of time. The evaluation standards should be reviewed and adjusted periodically, if necessary, to account for changes in local operating environments. In many developing countries consumer goods used to be subjected to high tariffs to discourage their importation. Many of the same countries now allow importation of consumer goods at favorable terms.

3. Many foreign subsidiaries face conditions and requirements that are not within their control. This should be taken into account while selecting performance evaluation criteria. For example:

   - Price controls may be imposed by local governments, requiring that all price increases be approved by a government agency in advance.

- Employment laws may require that compensation to workers be linked to seniority rather than performance.
- Foreign-based multinational corporations may not be allowed to own land, thus having to lease facilities at high rents.
- The parent company policies or the government in the parent company's base country may impose controls. For example, there may be restrictions on transfer of technology, capital spending, and payments to local government officials.

Subsidiary management should participate in setting performance criteria. Many multinational corporations express performance standards as a range rather than as a fixed number. This is especially desirable for a newly formed subsidiary. Preferably, the amounts should be expressed in the local currency. If translated amounts are to be used, the exchange rate for translation should be specified.

Two well-known performance evaluation criteria are return on investment and residual income.

Return on investment. Return on investment (ROI) incorporates the investment base and profits to assess performance. Higher ROI means better performance.

$$\text{Return on investment} = \text{Investment turnover} \times \text{Profit margin}$$

$$= \frac{\text{Revenue}}{\text{Investment}} \times \frac{\text{Profit}}{\text{Revenue}} = \frac{\text{Profit}}{\text{Investment}}$$

As shown above, there are two components of ROI: Investment turnover and profit margin. Investment turnover expresses the subsidiary's ability to turn over invested capital into revenue. Profit margin is a ratio of profit to sales revenues. The two components delineate that ROI can be improved by higher sales, lower cost, or lower invested capital. The management can decide on the "best mix" to improve ROI by examining available alternatives. For example, sales revenues could be improved by increasing selling prices, increasing sales volume, or increasing both. These alternative courses of action direct management's attention to available options.

Concentrating only on the short-term profitability is one of the "deadly diseases" for businesses in the view of W. Edwards Deming.[27] It undermines quality and productivity. An inherent danger of using ROI as a sole criterion to measure performance is that it may motivate managers to emphasize the short-run at the cost of long-run profitability. This is especially true when the investment base used in ROI computations is net historical cost of assets. The older and more greatly depreciated the assets, the higher the ROI. In fact, it may be possible to show higher ROI, due to lower net investment base resulting from depreciation, even when income has declined from one period to the next. This is illustrated in the following example.

[27] W. Edwards Deming, Out of the Crisis (Cambridge, Mass.: MIT Press, 1986).

Example

	Year 1	**Year 2**
Revenue	DM 10,000	DM 9,900
Depreciation expense	1,000	1,000
Other expenses	6,018	6,000
Profit	DM 2,982	DM 2,900
Investment (gross)	DM 30,000	DM 30,000
Less: accumulated depreciation	9,000	10,000
Investment (net)	DM 21,000	DM 20,000
Return on investment	$\frac{2,982}{21,000} = 14.2\%$	$\frac{2,900}{20,000} = 14.5\%$

When ROI is used as a performance measure, the investment base used in ROI calculations should preferably be either gross amount (historical cost) or current replacement cost. ROI should be used in combination with other performance evaluation criteria. Otherwise managers may have no incentive to invest in technologically advanced assets. It is important to make such investments to produce quality products that can withstand competitive pressures of the global markets.

Residual income. Residual income (RI) expresses performance in the form of a profit amount that is left after the cost of invested capital has been subtracted.

Residual income = Income – Imputed interest on invested capital

The goal is to maximize residual income while meeting other performance criteria. Senior management must decide in advance on the imputed interest rate to be used for computing the cost of invested capital. It is conceptually desirable to use different rates for different subsidiaries to reflect varying levels of risks.

An inherent advantage of the residual income approach is that it focuses on maximization of a monetary amount rather than a percentage, as is the case with ROI. Managers are then motivated to make any investment that will increase the residual income amount, even if the ROI drops from its present level.

Example

	Without Additional Investment	**With Additional Investment**
Income:		
Revenues	DM 6,000,000	DM 6,500,000
Expenses	4,000,000	4,220,000
Profit	2,000,000	2,280,000
Cost of capital:		
10% of DM 10,000,000	1,000,000	
10% of DM 12,000,000 (after additional investment)		1,200,000
Residual income	DM 1,000,000	DM 1,080,000

Return on investment $\qquad$ $\dfrac{2,000,000}{10,000,000} = 20.0\%$ $\qquad$ $\dfrac{2,280,000}{12,000,000} = 19.0\%$

As shown in this example, if the performance criterion is residual income, the manager is likely to make additional investment of DM 2,000,000. This will increase the residual income by DM 80,000. Any investment whose return is higher than cost of capital will increase residual income. However, the manager is not likely to make the additional investment if the performance criterion is return on investment, since the additional investment will cause a drop in ROI from 20 percent to 19 percent.

In spite of this conceptual appeal of the residual income approach, it is not nearly as common in practice as ROI.

Performance criteria commonly used. The principle measure used for marketing performance is share of market. Share of market information in larger markets is usually obtained from independent commercial marketing audit services. It is a valuable measure because it provides a comparison with the competitors in the same markets.

The most common measure of financial performance in international operations is return on investment.[28] Applying such financial measurement is complicated, however, for operations in different countries. The comparison must take into account different currencies, different rates of inflation, and different tax laws, all of which contribute to this complexity. In the final analysis, comparing the financial performance of operations in different countries is difficult and somewhat subjective.

A recent study of multinationals included their performance criteria. The information on four of the companies is summarized in Exhibit 8-4.

Measurement of Actual Performance

International subsidiary investment may be defined variously as total assets available, operating assets, total assets less current liabilities, or parent company equity. Income may also be defined in different ways as operating income, income before taxes, income before interest and taxes, or net income. Valuation of individual assets (assigning a monetary value to an asset) may be based on historical cost, current replacement cost, or disposal value. A depreciable asset has a gross value or a net value (after deducting accumulated depreciation). A decision should be made as to how the investment and the income are to be defined, and how the assets are to be valued. Valuation bases for assets differ among accounting rules of different countries.

International subsidiaries pose these additional measurement challenges: Changes in foreign exchange rates, varying inflation rates, and cross-border transfer pricing.

- Fluctuation in exchange rates would affect the computation of performance measurement. An ROI based on the subsidiary's own currency would differ from one based on the parent company's currency. A change in the exchange rate will affect

[28] Certo and Peter, Strategic Management, pp. 184 and 186.

Exhibit 8–4	Performance Criteria	
Multinational	**Financial Criteria**	**Non-financial Criteria**
Johnson Controls, Inc.	Cost management	Market share Quality Product development and innovation
Coors Brewing Company	Return on equity Price/value rating Sales volume Growth/profitability	Growth in international markets Quality Product innovation Employee relations
Xerox Corporation	Return on investment	Market share Quality Employee motivation
3M Company	Return on investment Earnings per share Cost management	Market share Quality Employee relations

Source: Adapted from Michael D. Akers and Grover L. Porter, "Strategic Planning at Five World-Class Companies," *Management Accounting*, July 1995, pp. 24-31.

the ROI computation. For example, if current assets are translated at the current exchange rate, unfavorable changes in the exchange rate will result in a lower value assigned to current assets when measured in the parent company's currency. A decision should be made regarding the exchange rate to be used if the foreign currency amounts are to be translated. As mentioned in an earlier section, it is desirable to use the amounts expressed in local currency to avoid the complexities related to exchange rate fluctuations.

- Unless adjusted, subsidiaries in countries with hyperinflation or high inflation rates will show more favorable ROIs than those in countries with lower inflation rates. It is recommended that the computations of ROIs be adjusted for inflation to reflect performance more accurately. Restating historical costs for inflation by using a general price index is discussed in Chapter 5.

- Different transfer-pricing systems are discussed in Chapter 10. A given transfer-price system affects reported performance of both the buying subsidiary and the selling subsidiary.

Performance Evaluation Reports

A variance is the difference between actual performance and planned performance. Managerial and cost accounting textbooks discuss the information value and describe the calculations of price, efficiency, production volume, sales, and other types of variances. According to Anthony:[29]

[29] Anthony, The Management Control Function, p. 133.

Although textbooks have described the calculations of these variances for years, few formal reporting systems identify any but the most obvious ones, and many systems do not identify any. With the computation power of computers, calculations for most variances can be made routinely and quickly.

Anthony further states, "I do not understand why managers do not require the identification of many textbook variances that seem to me to be important."[30]

Subsidiary performance versus management performance. It is important to separate subsidiary performance from management performance. The key is to distinguish between the factors within the subsidiary management control and the factors beyond its control. As earlier sections have discussed, both local conditions as well as policies of the parent company affect a subsidiary's reported performance.

To the extent possible, an international subsidiary's performance should be adjusted to reflect what is within the control of subsidiary management. The effects of uncontrollable factors should be isolated. Though conceptually attractive, such a distinction is often hard to make in practice. For example, a subsidiary manager may not control an item directly but may have significant indirect control over it through his/her actions.

The main objective of performance evaluation is to motivate people to improve their performance over time, and to do their best to achieve organizational goals. It is, therefore, imperative that managers have a clear understanding of the goals and have the appropriate level of autonomy. Only then can they make the decisions that reflect their true performance.

Information Systems in the Age of Global Economy

Accounting has undoubtedly acquired greater significance with multinational operations and global economy. The following statement delineates the information storage and retrieval aspect of an accounting system:[31]

> Accounting comes into its own with the rise of the corporate economy and large-scale business enterprise—the rapid spread of joint stock companies which began in the nineteenth century. . . . At the same time, in larger-scale business firms, the information storage and retrieval aspect of accounting became even more important than it had been before.

Often, the emphasis is placed on financial statements only, without due recognition being given to the accounting records. The value of accounting records is made forcefully by Professor Yuji Ijiri:[32]

> The economy may suffer somewhat without financial statements, but should there be a blackout on accounting records, the whole economy will collapse in

---

[30] Ibid.

[31] Basil Yamey, "Accounting in History," The European Accounting Review, vol. 3, no. 2 (1994), p. 380.

[32] As quoted by Yamey, Ibid., p. 375.

a matter of weeks, if not days. . . . Lack of records will also let irresponsible behavior proliferate, quickly destroying the fabric of the economy.

Though it is important that accountants be active participants in the design of the information system, the extent of their actual involvement varies from country to country. For several decades, Scandinavian countries have used the participatory design approach. In the participatory design approach, all users must take an active, involved role in the development of the information system.

By getting involved in system design, accountants benefit in numerous ways. Accountants' input during the participatory design process ensures that the system will be better suited to their needs, thus enabling them to provide service effectively and efficiently. Also, by being involved in the information system design they can provide valuable advice to the system experts in areas such as cost accounting, internal control, and data communication.[33] The need for active involvement is confirmed by the results of a recent Conference Board report based on a survey of 251 chief financial officers (CFOs) and other senior finance officers in North American and European companies. According to the report, a detached finance function (including accounting) does not respond to the new imperative to execute flexible, worldwide product and customer strategies. According to the report, global competition forces CFOs to focus on:

- Reducing the cost of the finance function. Planned actions to reduce costs include centralization and automation of accounting, developing shared financial services by consolidating transactions to attain economies of scale, and reducing costly errors by improving the quality of input.
- Reorienting their staff to serving and sharing control with line managers. Global competition has caused many CFOs to encourage finance and accounting personnel to learn more about the business in order to deliver value-added services to line managers.
- Taking a lead role in formulating and implementing global strategy. Interestingly, 80 percent of the respondents reported that their companies are centralizing global strategy, and a majority indicated that the finance function (including accounting) is leading the process. Within this mission, CFOs' top two priorities will remain the same: budgeting/planning and acquisitions/divestments.[34]

According to the findings of another recent survey, globalization will affect information systems on a wide scale. Eighty-four percent of the companies with international operations plan further integration of their international systems over the next two years. The majority (59 percent) of these multinational companies have no integration or very little integration today. Only 21 percent of the respondents felt that international integration is not important or not very important.[35]

---

[33] William M. Baker, "Shedding the Bean Counter Image: Become An Active Participant in Information System Design," Management Accounting, October 1994, p. 30.

[34] "Role of Finance Function is Changing in Global Firms," Deloitte & Touche Review, 17 October 1994, pp. 1-2.

[35] Leading Trends in Information Services (Wilton, Conn.: Deloitte Touche Tohmatsu International, 1995), p. 29.

Cultural Considerations

An information system provides control measures that attempt to motivate—and motivation is concerned with human behavior. Since multinational companies operate in multiple societies, each with its own culture, designing a system that will influence human behavior in the desired manner requires cultural awareness. This is a prerequisite for a successful system. Otherwise, there may be undesirable consequences:[36]

> If the damage to cultural values is substantial, the members of the culture will find ways to retaliate. They withhold their cooperation, resort to foot-dragging, and use other subtle ways to make the changes not worth having. The resulting lowered morale is one of the prices paid by managers who choose to ignore the social consequences of the intended changes.

Impact of Technological Advances

The advances in telecommunications and computing technologies have been phenomenal during the last few years. The problem faced by accountants and business executives in multinational companies today is not the lack of technology. Rather, the problem is choosing the technology that will best meet their needs. An often-encountered impediment to adoption of advanced technology is long-standing business practices:[37]

> Does your legal department let you accept a contract that has been sent by electronic mail? Can your employees fill out their expense forms on PCs, then get them approved and filed electronically? Does inflation flow freely throughout your organization to wherever it's needed, rather than up and down the hierarchy? Can customers dial into your computers to check the status of orders—instead of playing phone tag with somebody in your sales department? Is your company saving money by electronically linking up with a dozen suppliers in a just-in-time inventory network?
>
> The answer is probably: Not yet. And it isn't because the telecommunications world hasn't dreamed up enough products and services.

"The technology is here," observes an expert. "The problem is not with the technology, but with the corporate processes. Companies must fundamentally change the way they do business and that's hard."[38] Hard though it may be, the fact is that more and more companies are using networking technology to speed up internal processes and to transact business. Besides speed and cost-savings, networking provides flexibility:[39]

---

[36] Joseph M. Juran, Juran on Quality by Design: The New Steps for Planning Quality into Goods and Services (New York: The Free Press, 1992), p. 433.

[37] Catherine Arnst, "The Networked Corporation: Linking Up Is Hard To Do—But It's A Necessity," Business Week, 26 June 1995, p. 86.

[38] Ibid., p. 87.

[39] Ibid.

A networked corporation can do business anywhere, anytime, getting a jump on competitors that still conduct business the old fashioned way. And it no longer matters where your best and brightest talent resides: Sweden's L.M. Ericsson has 17,000 engineers in 40 research centers located in 20 countries around the world, all linked to one network. Development teams in Australia and England work together on the same design, then zip off the final blueprint to a factory in China.

The impact of technology advances on globalization, and their dramatic effect on a multinational's operations are summarized by John F. Smith, Jr., Chief Executive Officer and President of General Motors:[40]

The major driver of change for General Motors today is the same as for most companies: it's globalization. Advances in technology and communication are making the "small world" a reality, and the world will only get smaller and smaller in coming years. The real growth markets of the twenty-first century are outside North America and Western Europe, and it is easier than ever for global companies to manufacture virtually any product in virtually any region. This trend toward global integration should be viewed as an opportunity—not a problem.

Just because the network technology allows sharing of information does not mean that it will happen automatically. Management of the company must be willing to share information with others. It may mean loss of some control by management, but it is necessary to derive the maximum benefit from networking.

Software considerations. To be effective in their jobs, accountants in a multinational corporation must be aware of international accounting issues such as reporting requirements, consolidation, value-added taxes, and intercompany transactions. Properly configured accounting software can be very helpful because it eliminates costly unreconciled differences and can handle multicurrency and intercompany transactions:[41]

In multinational companies, resolving issues associated with intercompany processing, fluctuating exchange rates, transfer pricing, and tax laws make the balancing problem a true balancing act without the right software.

A more cost-effective, accurate, and responsible alternative is to implement at each company and division standardized accounting procedures that are based on a single accounting software system. The key to making this solution work is in selecting software designed with multinational, multicurrency, multilingual applications in mind.

A comprehensive accounting manual that contains charts of accounts and standard practices and procedures can be very helpful for ease of consolidation, auditing, and communication.

---

[40] 1994 Annual Report (Detroit, Mich.: General Motors Corporation, 1995), p. 1.

[41] Michael O'Brien, "Going Global: What to Look for in Financial Software," Management Accounting, April 1995, p. 59.

Coca-Cola has developed such a manual for its worldwide operations.[42] Exhibit 8-5 contains important considerations for selecting a multinational accounting software system.

Exhibit 8–5 Key Features for Multinational Accounting Software

1. Choose a single system designed and developed for multinational use.
2. Look for an international, single-version system that supports a single set of books in multiple languages. This enables each user to access the system by using a preferred language.
3. Users in a multinational operation should be able to post intercompany entries effortlessly across different charts of accounts, different closing calendars, and different currencies.
4. The system should have the ability to process the foreign currency transactions in its own value, and also have the capability to perform the conversion to "base" currency in accordance with GAAP while retaining the foreign value dimension.
5. The software system should provide tables that enable users to define average, month-end, spot, and forward currency exchange rates. These defined rates should be available at a transaction level.
6. The system should incorporate international banking procedures. It should allow for payment output methods such as drafts, electronic data interchange, and checks. The system should support various address formats for check and accounts receivable processing.
7. Tax handling in the system should be tax table driven. As tax laws and tax rates change, the user should be able to make the needed changes without having to modify the software.
8. The software vendor should be using industry standard tools to support languages, graphic user interface, and hardware.
9. The system should have treasury management features. A user should be able to view a cash account in its native currency. For example, an account in British pounds should be available to view in British pounds even if the user accesses the account in German marks. Currency forecasting is enhanced when a user can forecast currency position by netting out the activity in accounts receivable and accounts payable based on anticipated due dates.
10. The vendor's support organization should be familiar with multinational accounting issues. More importantly, the same level of support should be available worldwide.

Source: Adapted from Michael O'Brien, "Going Global: What to Look for in Financial Software," *Management Accounting*, April 1995, p. 60.

---

[42] Andrew L. Nodar, "Coca-Cola Writes An Accounting Procedures Manual," Management Accounting, October 1986, pp. 52-53.

It is important to distribute the adopted software package to all operating entities of the multinational company to ensure uniformity, integrity, and accuracy of the accounting information.

Education. The development and installation of a workable system is no small endeavor. The time required is rarely less than one year, and five years or more are frequently needed in sizable organizations.[43] A total and integrated system provides not only the summary information on key elements that will be used by the top management, but it also provides detailed information to meet specific needs of individual responsibility centers.

To ensure that operating managers use the system to its fullest capability, a comprehensive education program is imperative. "The preparation of manuals, explanations, sample reports, and other written material is a necessary part of the education process, but it is not the most important part. The important part is to explain to managers how the new system can help them do a better job."[44]

Information System Compatibility with International Accounting Standards

The primary focus of this chapter is on managerial functions of strategic planning and control. However, a total and integrated information system not only serves the information needs of internal users but also provides data that are necessary for external reporting.

Trends and recent developments clearly indicate that the International Accounting Standard Committee's standards are gaining wider acceptance. The German government recently announced that it will accept the use of IASC's International Accounting Standards (IASs) for Germany-based multinational companies that are seeking listings on foreign security exchanges. Many countries, especially developing countries, have already adopted IASs as their national accounting principles. The World Bank encourages use of IASs in accounting for the projects financed by the organization.[45] Some countries, for example China, use the IASs for regulation of their joint ventures. Multinational companies are also increasingly adopting IASs. Renault (France-based), Ciba-Geigy Limited Group (Switzerland-based), Shanghai Petrochemical (China-based) and Anglo American Corporation (South Africa-based) are just a few examples. The London Stock Exchange and Hong Kong Stock Exchange both accept the International Accounting Standards for listing.

The IOSCO, an influential international organization of securities industry regulators, had been working with the IASC since 1988 in an attempt to agree on a core of IASs that the IOSCO could endorse for capital markets worldwide. On July 11, 1995 it was announced in

---

[43] Anthony, The Management Control Function, p. 139.

[44] Ibid., p. 140.

[45] Anne J. Rich, "Understanding Global Standards," *Management Accounting*, April 1995, p. 51.

Paris that an agreement had been reached between the IASC and IOSCO. According to the agreement, by mid-1999 companies preparing their financial statements according to IASC standards will be able to list their shares on any of the world's capital markets. This will require the IASC to revise its IASs to the satisfaction of IOSCO. The chairman of the IOSCO technical committee stated, "IOSCO is committed to working with the IASC to ensure a successful completion of the work on a timely basis."[46] Sir Bryan Carsberg, IASC secretary general, added, "The world is becoming a global market place and one can't refuse to recognize that."[47] The implications of this development for the accounting system of a multinational company are profound. It would be highly desirable, and probably necessary, to ensure that the accounting system generates information that is needed to prepare financial statements in conformity with IASs.

The International Accounting Standards Committee recently released a Draft Statement of Principles, "Presentation of Financial Statements." It contains proposals that, when implemented, will make financial statements more comparable and make the information within them more accessible. The proposals intend to improve both the structure and content of financial statements.

Note to Students

In this chapter you have been presented with important managerial accounting issues related to strategic planning, control, and information systems. Information about multinational companies and their international activities is available in major periodicals. Articles about multinational corporations include news about their strategies, plans, new investments or divestments, pricing, and profitability. Articles on such topics frequently appear in *The Wall Street Journal, Financial Times, Business Week, Forbes, Fortune,* and *The Economist.*

However, an important but often overlooked source of information is the management discussion and analysis section of a company's annual report. This section often contains a wealth of information on a company's strategies, plans, markets, products, and policies. For example, Toyota's 1994 annual report has an extensive discussion about Toyota's cost management strategies and how it saved $1.5 billion during the previous year by effective cost management. The following statement from the annual report expresses Toyota's approach eloquently (page 1):

> . . . We are taking our destiny into our own hands. We can't change the world. But we can change ourselves. We can adapt our cost structure to market realities. And we can target products aggressively at the most vigorous sectors of demand. In short, that's what we are doing. "Taking our destiny into our own hands"—not a bad idea! Jack Welch Jr., CEO and Chairman of GE puts it even more bluntly, "Control your destiny, or someone else will."

---

[46] Jim Kelly and Richard Lapper, "Plan for Global Accounting Standards," Financial Times, 12 July 1995, p. 4.

[47] Ibid.

Chapter Summary

- Strategic planning focuses on the development of the multinational corporation's overall objectives.

- Environmental factors affect the development of global business strategy.

- Each strategy has different implications for corporate constituents and for the managerial accounting function.

- Multinational corporations face unique and complex issues in designing their control systems.

- Problems encountered in the design of a global control system include diversity among nations with respect to culture, languages, and national currencies.

- A control system may work well in one country but not in another.

- The backbone of control systems is reporting on performance.

- Performance evaluation of international operations is similar in concept to the evaluation of domestic business activities but must take local operating conditions into account.

- Performance evaluation criteria include both financial and nonfinancial measurements. A multicriteria evaluation system helps avoid dysfunctional decision making.

- Return on investment and market share are commonly used criteria to evaluate the performance of international subsidiaries.

- Different goals require different performance evaluation criteria.

- It is important to distinguish between the performance of a subsidiary and the performance of its management.

- Technological advances are having a profound impact on multinational corporations.

- Accountants should be actively involved in the design of an information system.

- The IASC's International Accounting Standards are receiving wider acceptance.

Questions for Discussion

1. Compare financial accounting with managerial accounting.

2. Give examples of the unique features of multinational corporations that increase demands on the managerial accounting function.

3. Define strategic planning.

4. Give examples of external and internal conditions addressed in the strategic planning process.

5. Why should management accountants be involved in strategic planning of multinational corporations?

6. What are the advantages and disadvantages of employing Japanese-educated management accountants in international subsidiaries of Japanese multinational corporations?

7. What is meant by a control system and how does this differ from strategic planning?

8. List the types of environmental factors that are considered in designing multinational corporations' control systems.

9. "One would expect multinational corporations to prefer to design one uniform control system for domestic and international operations." Do you agree or disagree? Why?

10. What are the major considerations while designing a control system?

11. Why is it important to address information system issues when designing a multinational control system?

12. Give three examples each of financial and nonfinancial performance evaluation criteria.

13. Compare return on investment with residual income.

14. What are the issues facing multinational corporations in computing ROI and RI for their international subsidiaries?

15. Discuss some of the issues that should be addressed in selecting performance evaluation criteria for international subsidiaries.

16. Why is it important to distinguish between the performance of an international subsidiary and the performance of its management?

17. The chapter included the following statement by Professor Robert N. Anthony: "I do not understand why managers do not require the identification of many textbook variances that seem to me to be important." Comment on the statement.

18. Multinational corporations commonly use return on investment to evaluate the performance of international operations. Can you think of any reasons for this practice?

19. How may an international subsidiary improve its performance under the return on investment criterion?

20. How may an international subsidiary improve its performance under the residual income criterion?

21. In your opinion, are people from diverse cultures more alike or more different? Explain.

22. The United States limits the exportation of high technology equipment to some countries. Do you agree or disagree with such a policy? Give reasons.

23. What are the advantages and disadvantages of transferring managers to various international locations?

24. Contrast cultural dimensions of:
   a. masculinity and femininity.
   b. individualism and collectivism.

25. Give two examples each of countries with the cultural dimension of

   a. High tolerance of uncertainty.
   b. Low tolerance of uncertainty.

26. Give two examples each of countries with the cultural dimension of

   a. High-power-distance.
   b. Low-power-distance.

27. Compare centralization with decentralization philosophy of management.

28. Describe the essence of the recent agreement between the IASC and the IOSCO.

Exercises/Problems

8-1 A French multinational corporation plans to establish a business operation in Russia. You, as a management consultant, are asked to prepare a country report for use in planning the new venture. Your report should include information about each of the following areas:

   a. Culture   f . Local markets
   b. Economy   g. Labor laws
   c. Tax system   h. Balance of payments
   d. Currency   i. Local accounting standards
   e. Competition

   Required: For each area, state the type or category of information that should be included in your report.

8-2 Toyota Corporation's entry into the U.S. market began with the sale of a few cars and trucks in 1957. Toyota Sales, U.S.A. was established that year to market its product in North America. Since the 1970s, the company has adopted a new strategy for the U.S. market, which has included:

   • Establishment of jointly owned research and testing facilities in the U.S.
   • Expansion of information-gathering activities about U.S. markets and consumers.
   • Establishment of a joint venture with General Motors to produce GM and Toyota cars.
   • Sourcing auto parts and products in the U.S.

   Required: Research Toyota's current strategy with regard to the U.S. market relative to each of the following factors:
   (1) Location of manufacturing plants.
   (2) Sourcing raw material and components.
   (3) Financing.
   (4) Labor force.
   (5) Middle-management personnel.

8-3 Refer to the information provided in Problem 8-2. Explain the implications of the new strategy for each of the following constituents:

   a. The Japanese government.

    b. U.S. labor unions.

    c. Other Japanese auto manufacturers.

    d. U.S. auto buyers.

    e. U.S. manufacturers of auto parts and components.

8-4 Refer to the information given in Problem 8-2. Assume that Toyota Corporation continued the 1957 strategy of limiting its U.S. operation to its fully-owned Toyota Sales, U.S.A. subsidiary. Explain how the old and new strategies affect each of the following managerial accounting functions:

    a. Performance evaluation.

    b. Control systems.

    c. Budgeting.

8-5 Khalid Inc., a subsidiary of a Pakistani multinational corporation operating in the U.S., provides you with the following performance information for 19x4. The information is denominated in U.S. dollars and also in Pakistani rupees (Rs). The dollar-denominated information was translated using different exchange rates, based on the nature of items being reported (e.g., depreciation expense and investment amounts were translated using relevant historical exchange rates).

Khalid Inc.
Selected Data for 19x4

Sales revenues	$ 25,000	Rs 622,500
Costs and expenses	22,500	580,500
Operating income	$ 2,500	Rs 42,000
Investment (assets)	$ 10,000	Rs 264,000

Required:

(1) Compute return on investment using dollar- and rupee- denominated information.

(2) Compute residual income using dollar- and rupee- denominated information. Assume the imputed interest rate for computing the cost of invested capital is 8 percent.

(3) Evaluate and comment on the performance of Khalid Inc. based on the analysis in Parts (1) and (2).

8-6 The information provided below is for two foreign investments of a U.S. multinational corporation. The weighted average cost of capital for the U.S. corporation is 12 percent.

	Canadian Subsidiary	Egyptian Joint Venture
Years in business	26	2
Line of business	Manufacturing	Retailing
Parent company equity	Wholly owned	49%
Functional currency	Canadian $	Egyptian pound (£)
Net assets in the operation	$ 62 million	£ 17.5 million
Operating income	$ 15 million	£ 1.5 million

Required:

(1) Compute residual income (RI) for each subsidiary, using corporate cost of capital.

(2) Discuss and comment on the use of RI as an appropriate performance evaluation criterion for the two subsidiaries.

8-7 Given below are the summary balance sheet and income statement of the French subsidiary of Cody and Ryan Cerf International.

Balance Sheet (F,000)		Income Statement (F,000)	
Current assets	F10,500	Sales	F36,000
Long term operating assets	16,000	Cost of goods sold	18,000
Other long term assets	8,500	Gross margin	18,000
Total assets	F35,000	Operating expenses	8,500
		Non-operating expenses	3,000
Current liabilities	14,500	Income before taxes	6,500
Long term liabilities	2,500	Income tax expense	2,500
Stockholders' equity	18,000	Net income	F 4,000
Total liabilities and			
stockholders' equity	F35,000		

Required: Calculate the return on investment (ROI) and residual income (RI) for the French subsidiary. Document your calculations for each of the above measures. What two components make up ROI?

8-8 Nawaz UAE Ltd. has three divisions. Selected financial information (in millions of dirhams) for 1995 and 1996 follow:

Division	Operating Income 1995	1996	Revenues 1995	1996	Investment 1995	1996
A	Dh 1,000	Dh 1,200	Dh 5,000	Dh 5,400	Dh 4,500	Dh 4,800
B	150	175	7,500	8,000	3,500	4,000
C	250	300	2,000	2,200	3,000	3,500

Required:

(1) Calculate the 1995 ROI for each division. Explain the differences in their ROI.

(2) Calculate the 1996 ROI for each division.

(3) Ahmed, Manager of Division A, is considering a proposal to invest Dh 250 million in advanced technology equipment. The estimated increment to 1997 operating income would be Dh 40 million. Would adoption of a residual income measure motivate Ahmed to accept the investment proposal? Would Ahmed be motivated to invest in the advanced technology equipment if ROI is the measure of performance? Nawaz UAE Ltd. has a 12 percent cost of capital requirement for each division.

8-9 Select five countries other than those mentioned in the Chapter during discussion of culture and individual behavior. Rank them for the four cultural dimensions (power distance, individualism, uncertainty avoidance, and masculinity) from high to low. Support your ranking by providing reasons.

Case: Ameripill Company

The purpose of this case is to illustrate numerous issues involved in evaluating international subsidiary performance using accounting information. In particular, the case demonstrates how performance evaluation impacts decision making at the subsidiary level. Case facts are based on an extensive set of interviews both at the parent and international subsidiary levels. The importance of considering global implications when designing and using accounting-based international subsidiary performance evaluation systems is highlighted. The case can also be used to integrate tax and regulatory issues into the performance evaluation setting and to make links between organizational design and performance evaluation.[48]

Overview of Ameripill Company's International Organization

Located in Bartow, Alabama, the Pharmaceutical Division of Ameripill Company ranks among the top fifteen drug companies in the world. The Pharmaceutical Division is divided into three worldwide operating units with a vice president in charge of each: North American, Europe, and the rest of the world including South America, Africa, and Asia. The European Vice President, Gene Roget, views Europe and one strategic unit with many markets. He thinks strategically about market share, product innovation, acquisitions, and financial success. Organizationally, he works closely with Collen Stein, Pharmaceutical Vice President of Finance. Stein has recently combined the international and U.S. domestic finance groups. The international subsidiary financial analysis activities are concentrated in one unit under Stein called International and Domestic Financial Services. An abbreviated organization chart for the company is shown in Exhibit 8–6. Except for the international general managers and the Puerto Rico and The Hague manufacturing managers, all executives are based in Bartow.

Important and explicit responsibilities of Stein are to develop financial policies, make measurement decisions, and monitor results to optimize Ameripill's pharmaceutical profit levels. On an international level, this becomes an extraordinarily complex task. Included are direct and indirect responsibilities to:

- Design a financial performance evaluation system to encourage general managers in specific countries to maximize their contribution to corporate earnings.
- Help maximize companywide gross margin from pharmaceutical sales through effective marketing, product strategies, and increased market shares.
- Minimize the companywide tax liability through international transfer pricing.
- Coordinate country-by-country pricing strategies to maximize total sales dollars and global gross margin. This includes decisions to market or not market a specific drug in a specific country.

[48] Susan F. Haka, Barbara A. Lamberton, and Harold M. Sollenberger, "International Subsidiary Performance Evaluation: The Case of the Ameripill Company," Issues in Accounting Education, spring 1994, pp. 168-179.

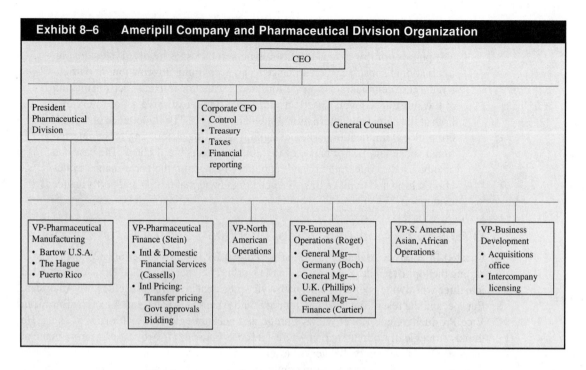

Exhibit 8–6   Ameripill Company and Pharmaceutical Division Organization

- Obtain approvals for marketing drugs and for prices in each country, since most non-U.S. countries control pharmaceutical prices, as well as access to their markets.
- Minimize production cost by selecting optimal manufacturing locations, while balancing in-country requirements and production loading.
- Maximize cash flows to Bartow and minimize nontransferable cash balances, exposure risk due to currency exchange fluctuations, and transfer penalties.
- Develop financing strategies to help acquire other companies and to create intercorporate relationships that will contribute to company sales, to market share, and directly to profits.
- Create capital and legal structures to optimize financial, operating, legal, and political needs, avoid operating losses, and protect company investments in non-U.S. countries.

The staffs to accomplish these responsibilities are divided among Stein, the corporate CFO's office, and certain other units reporting to Stein. Coordination occurs through a working group called the International Profitability Group (IPG) chaired by Olivia Cassells, Director of International and Domestic Financial Services. Group membership includes Cassells; the Corporate Director of Taxes Treasury, and Financial Reporting; the Pharmaceutical Division Managers for International Pricing and Manufacturing Accounting; and representatives from the Vice President of Business Development and the General Counsel offices. This group meets regularly to review problem areas, to recommend courses of action within the finance area, and to communicate possible financial impacts to the executive group.

Stein believes many of the goals and responsibilities listed above are inevitably linked to the international incentive evaluation system created and operated by the staff of International and Domestic Financial Services. Over the past two or three years, several complaints have been lodged with Roget and Stein by the international subsidiaries' general managers (GMs) regarding their incentive scheme. Stein has decided to use the coming year's results to evaluate the effectiveness of the international incentive scheme.

The Profit Measurement System

Ameripill domestic units are evaluated on growth in market share, sales volume, and revenue. Because of the complexities of international markets, the international profit measurement system has three reporting levels—legal entity earnings, responsibility earnings, and global earnings. Legal entity earnings are used for required reporting needs such as for tax and regulatory purposes within each country. Responsibility earnings include import and export sales that country managers can influence, given what is known to them about prices, costs, and transfer prices. Global earnings are a broader corporate view of sales and costs and represent an economic earnings view of each subunit. The global earnings figure is calculated only for the Bartow financial and operations executives. For international subsidiaries, the general managers are evaluated in two ways:

1. Actual results compared to budget focusing on gross margin, ROA, cash flow, and inventory and receivables levels. The evaluation looks at the entire operation using "responsibility earnings" and "earnings before taxes" and is the basis for evaluating and comparing the performances of all international general managers.
2. A management incentive system administered through the International Financial Performance System (IFPS). The IFPS in the bonus system and focuses on a subsidiary's contribution to "global earnings," "earnings before taxes," "responsibility earnings" growth over last year, return on managed assets, inventory levels, and market share performance. IFPS bonuses are based 60 percent on the local unit's results and 40 percent on the region's contribution to "global earnings."

Exhibits 8–7, 8–8, and 8–9 present preliminary results for 1992 and a forecast for 1993 for the United Kingdom, France, and Germany in the format sent to Bartow for early analysis of 1992 performance.

Comments from the Wednesday Meeting

A meeting of the International Profitability Group is planned for Friday, December 11, 1992. It is Wednesday, and Olivia Cassells and Collen Stein are meeting in Bartow to review the agenda and supporting discussion documents that will be sent to each attending member. Cassells has materials from Vice President Roget's office, the directors in the Pharmaceutical Division, and the corporate offices. Cassells is sure that several controversial issues will be raised. Selected items from the agenda include the following:

A. Final financial staff approval of the acquisition of Koblenz Chemie Company.
B. Problems using cash balances in the U.K. and possible production changes at the U.K. subsidiary.

Exhibit 8–7   Financial Results—United Kingdom

International Pharmaceutical Subsidiaries
Financial Summary
(000s omitted)

Country: United Kingdom	Budget '93	Actual '92
Sales	$ 49,960	$ 48,080
Cost of sales	(21,982)	(21,155)
Direct expenses	(14,658)	(14,512)
Other income (expense)	(1,499)	(1,155)
Responsibility earnings	11,821	11,258
Interest income (expense)[1]	(358)	(241)
Exchange gain (loss)[2]	(142)	(338)
Division charges[3]	(1,629)	(1,640)
Earnings before tax	$ 9,692	$ 9,039
Managed assets	$ 84,500	$ 88,860
IFPS goals:		
EBT = 18%	19.4%	18.8%
ROA = 15%	11.5%	10.2%
Responsibility earnings growth = 5%	5.0%	4.8%
Inventory (month's supply) = 1.0 months	2.5 months	3.2 months

[1] Based on locally incurred debt
[2] Based on average 1992 exchange rate ($1.4 per U.K. pound)
[3] Fixed charge negotiated annually between Bartow and the subsidiary

C.   Problems with the IFPS.

D.   Price increase for a product in the French market.

After a quick review of the tentative 1992 international subsidiary results, attention turns to the agenda.

Acquisition of Koblenz Chemie Company. Olivia Cassells begins the Wednesday meeting by discussing a recommendation from the Business Development office and Roget that the Board of Directors acquire Koblenz Chemie Company for 25,000,000 DM ($15.5 million), about eight times earnings. The Koblenz Chemie Co. management has forecast 1993 sales to be 12,000,000 DM ($7.4 million).[49] Cassells notes that the acquisition has several advantages. First, it gives Ameripill access to a key German generic drug market. Koblenz has an 8 percent market share in Germany in its product lines. Second, it provides Ameripill with the opportunity to have a stronger market position in Germany, particularly in the newly opened former East German market. In recent years, Ameripill's German market share has remained at about 2 percent of the total pharmaceutical market. Third, Ameripill can offer Koblenz access to international markets.

---

[49] Assume that the acquisition of the Koblenz business in 1993 will cause the German subsidiary's Sales, Cost of Sales, and Direct Expenses to increase by the same percentage. Other subsidiary income and expenses are not expected to change.

Exhibit 8–8   Financial Results—Germany

International Pharmaceutical Subsidiaries
Financial Summary
(000s omitted)

Country: Germany	Budget '93	Actual '92
Sales	$156,840	$137,440
Cost of sales	(65,872)	(57,995)
Direct expenses	(50,286)	(46,603)
Other income (expense)	(300)	(210)
Responsibility earnings	40,382	32,632
Interest income (expense)[1]	(1,312)	(939)
Exchange gain (loss)[2]	(150)	(210)
Division charges[3]	(4,700)	(4,123)
Earnings before tax	$ 34,220	$ 27,360
Managed assets	$ 73,760	$ 72,900
IFPS goals:		
EBT = 18%	21.8%	19.9%
ROA = 15%	46.4%	37.5%
Responsibility earnings growth = 5%	23.7%	15.6%
Inventory (month's supply) = 1.0 months	1.2 months	1.5 months

[1] Based on locally incurred debt
[2] Based on average 1992 exchange rate ($.62 per German DM)
[3] Fixed charge negotiated annually between Bartow and the subsidiary

---

Stein inquires about inputs from Hans Drossel, Controller of the German subsidiary, about the acquisition. Cassells replies, "I'm not sure Drossel knows about it. Our acquisition guys researched this one. They think that the integration of Koblenz into our German organization shouldn't be a problem since they're located within 50 kilometers of each other." Both Stein and Cassells agree that even though the price seems high given Koblenz's earnings since 1989, Koblenz appears to be a quality operation in all respects. Stein notes, "The Koblenz acquisition seems to be a sure thing. I hear the accounting records are a mess. That's not surprising given that it was a privately owned firm. We'll have some work to do to get it into Ameripill's reporting and cash management systems." Cassells agrees that system compatibility problems exist but goes on to suggest that no problems with final financial approval of the deal are likely to occur.

Cassells reminds Stein that another German issue might be impacted by this acquisition. Due to the rapid changes in the former East Bloc, Business Development has been studying the situation and recommends expanding the sales force and entering the former East German market. Business Development projects this potential market to be $300 million and conservatively estimates that Ameripill could capture 10 percent of this market by the year 2000. Preliminary contacts have been made with former government officials with whom

Exhibit 8–9   Financial Results–France

International Pharmaceutical Subsidiaries
Financial Summary
(000s omitted)

Country: France	Budget '93	Actual '92
Sales	$108,720	$102,560
Cost of sales	(53,414)	(50,254)
Direct expenses	(31,529)	(29,742)
Other income (expense)	(946)	(1,026)
Responsibility earnings	22,831	21,538
Interest income (expense)[1]	(1,033)	(1,047)
Exchange gain (loss)[2]	(272)	(286)
Division charges[3]	(3,263)	(3,077)
Earnings before tax	$ 18,263	$ 17,128
Managed assets	$ 74,220	$ 73,460
IFPS goals:		
EBT = 18%	16.8%	16.7%
ROA = 15%	24.6%	23.3%
Responsibility earnings growth = 5%	6.0%	5.2%
Inventory (month's supply) = 1.0 months	0.9 months	1.1 months

[1] Based on locally incurred debt
[2] Based on average 1992 exchange rate ($.16 per French franc)
[3] Fixed charge negotiated annually between Bartow and the subsidiary

Ameripill has had previous business relationships. Ameripill sales in the entire Eastern Bloc have been very low.

A request, now nearly eight months old, from the German GM to create a sales force in eastern Germany, has been reviewed by Business Development. Cassells says, "Business Development thinks the near-term financial feasibility looks dim but the question of having an Ameripill presence must be discussed. Roget is pressing all of us for a positive response. I hear he has given the okay to the German GM and controller to create a temporary eastern Germany sales force. Roget says it's now or never." Cassells believes these unilateral steps may be premature and may have adverse effects on the German subsidiary's bottom line for 1992 and 1993.

Cash balances in the U.K. and production changes at the U.K. subsidiary.   Item B on the agenda generates more concern. Stein begins by discussing the historical tax problems associated with moving cash between international locations and the U.S. Stein notes that the U.K. subsidiary has generated a sizable cash position. Stein points out that strategies must be created to move cash to the U.S. or other locations where it can be invested profitably. Cassells suggests expanding manufacturing in the U.K. as a way to move the cash surplus without incurring costly penalties. Stein comments, "I thought that the tax law limited our options about transferring cash from the U.K. to the States." Cassells agrees, but suggests,

"We could expand manufacturing and export to other countries, such as Germany, at cost. We may need the cash in Germany to pay for other acquisitions and expansion we see in eastern Germany. Also, we may have more flexibility in transferring cash to the United States."

Cassells and Stein then have a long discussion about implementing the export strategy of moving cash from the U.K. to Germany. Cassells suggests that Smoothkare, a product currently manufactured at The Hague for export to Germany, could be manufactured in the U.K. Cassells remarks, "I'm sure we could easily replace the lost Smoothkare manufacturing volume at The Hague with an equally profitable product." However, a sizeable investment would be required to expand manufacturing capacity in the U.K.

Stein reminds Cassells that the cash problem was becoming worse each day, and a two- to three-year wait would only compound the problem. Stein suggests that perhaps current manufacturing capacity could be converted to produce Smoothkare, which could be transferred to Germany at cost. Stein asks Cassells if she had considered these options.

Cassells responds, "Yes, the U.K. general manager won't be too keen on this idea. He has written a detailed memo to Roget outlining the problems associated with expanding manufacturing in the U.K. (See Exhibit 8–7). First, producing Smoothkare will require us to increase the U.K.'s managed assets to approximately $90 million. Also the U.K. GM complained that, at the current volume, nearly half of his time is spent on production problems. Yet his performance is measured by responsibility earnings and ROA numbers—all sales-based. Also, the pressure to keep working capital low backfires in two ways. Low inventories mean that short, frequent, and expensive batches cause per-unit costs to be well above the Hague's and Puerto Rico's manufacturing unit costs. And since cash can't be moved out without significant tax penalties, large near-cash balances cause total working capital to balloon. I'll bet the U.K. GM will think that expanding manufacturing will divert attention away from marketing and that U.K. profits will tumble. The U.K. GM will see both of these as bad news for evaluating the U.K. subsidiary's responsibility earnings results and for his IFPS evaluation."

Problems with the International Financial Performance System (IFPS). Stein notes the problems associated with moving cash out of the U.K. are related to the incentive scheme—an item next on the agenda. Cassells and Stein begin discussing the IFPS and its impact on international decisions. Cassells points out that several previous complaints had been forwarded from the U.K. GM. The regional Vice President (under Roget) and one of the financial analysis visit each subsidiary three times a year. During the last visit to the U.K., the GM raised several questions about the IFPS and the annual performance review. Cassells relays the essence of these complaints to Stein: "The GM is not clear how the IFPS measurements are calculated. He sees only reports that show his U.K. responsibility earnings in pounds as they come from the U.K. accounting records. He says the ratios used in the budget and the IFPS are seriously distorted by manufacturing operations in the U.K."

Collen Stein asks, "Is the U.K. GM the only subsidiary that is concerned?" Cassells says, "Not really. None of them seems to understand the incentive system or how their bonus is determined. The U.K. GM's complaint is one that we have heard over and over again from GMs. They want to know what 'global earnings' is and how it's calculated."

Stein recalls, "Yes, now that I think about it, Roget has complained to me about the IFPS scheme and even threatened to send each GM the details of how each subsidiary compares to one another. I assumed that the changes we made in '91—which shifted the scheme away from company wide uniformity to more emphasis on individual subsidiary goals—solved these concerns. Maybe the IPG needs to look at this issue and suggest some improvements."

Product pricing in the French market. Cassells and Stein move to the last item on the agenda, the price increase for Saincoeur in France. Saincoeur is a highly successful treatment for heart attack victims, and is sold under other names in all of Ameripill's markets. Stein begins by telling Cassells that he understands that the International Pricing office will recommend raising the price of Saincoeur in France. Its low price in France is causing problems for the rest of the European markets. Cassells suggests two options. First, Ameripill could push hard to get approval for a price increase; second, it could withdraw Saincoeur from the French market to protect prices of the same product in other countries. Roget had reported pricing inquiries and pressure from Italy, the Swiss, and even Germany to reduce the price for the equivalent drug in their markets. The International Pricing office also suggested that, without a quick resolution of the pricing issue, Saincoeur should be with-drawn from the French market.

Stein asks, "Olivia, what kind of price concession would that mean for the other European markets? What's the financial impact?" Cassells notes that Saincoeur is barely profitable at the French price. "If Ameripill isn't careful, our margins for the equivalent products will decline all over the European market." Cassells and Stein decide to review the financial summaries for the product at a later date. However, Cassells concludes by stating, "Clearly, withdrawing from the French market is better than cutting our margin for the rest of Europe. Based on our preliminary reading of the data, the potential damage to Ameripill's total global earnings is as much as 10 times the French's Saincoeur earnings loss."

Meanwhile, Back at the International Subsidiaries

Managers in each subsidiary meet on a regular weekly basis to assess operations, trouble-shoot, and review operating plans. During these weekly meetings, information is exchanged among each subsidiary's management group members. In particular, communications from the parent are typically announced and discussed in these weekly meetings. The following meetings took place within ten days of Cassells' and Stein's Wednesday meeting.

France. In France, the general manager Jacques Cartier, his director of marketing, and his controller are discussing operations and strategies in their weekly meeting. The controller mentions a rumor she heard from the Bartow Financial Analyst who had just been in France for his quarterly visit. The controller comments, "I heard a rumor that the Bartow pricing group is recommending withdrawing Saincoeur from our market. Italy and the Swiss are pressuring Ameripill to match the French price. Bartow is concerned that their margins will suffer all over Europe."

Cartier expresses immediate concern since Saincoeur is 10 percent of France's 1993 sales forecast. Cartier commented, "The French subsidiary currently has problems attaining the corporate goal of 18 percent earnings before tax (EBT). Loss of Saincoeur will make meeting that goal more difficult and reduce our return on assets (ROA) since we lose sales volume without any impact on our investment base. Sales and cost of sales will decrease proportionally, but direct expenses will decrease by only 10 million francs. Other financial accounts will be unaffected. As a result, French bonuses from the IFPS scheme will be reduced." The director of marketing comments, "Americans! I bet that the real financial impact is not that big. What do they care as long as the company overall is making a little more money?"

The controller replies, "I've heard that they are looking at the impact on global earnings. I wish I knew how that was calculated. I have no idea how that is going to impact our bonuses."

United Kingdom. It's Monday in the United Kingdom subsidiary headquarters in Maidenhead near London, and the weekly meeting between the general manager, John Phillips, and the controller, Lee Grant, is about to start. Phillips brings in a fax received late Friday from corporate about expanding manufacturing in Great Britain. The memo requested input from the U.K. General Manager about the possibility of producing Smoothkare and then shipping Smoothkare at a little above cost to Germany. Smoothkare is a prescription drug used to treat skin problems in elderly persons and has been produced solely at The Hague plant for world wide distribution. He points out that corporate is thinking about expanding the U.K. subsidiary's manufacturing capacity.

Phillips wants to persuade corporate to adopt the desired U.K. strategy, whether it is to expand and produce Smoothkare or not. He wonders whether the person who wrote the memo has read any of his reports and memos about IFPS. Grant points out that the U.K. subsidiary already produces several products transferred at close to cost and that those products provide no positive weight in the evaluation process. Phillips wonders if expanding the manufacturing operating would improve the IFPS bonus numbers.

Phillips says, "I don't know; corporate hasn't said too much about timing, but they could implement the expansion fairly quickly. For example, Ameripill could buy that old Worsley manufacturing facility next door and have it operational in less than a year. He adds, still thinking about his communications with Bartow, "You know, I've never seen a report on what our combined sales and manufacturing efforts contribute to Ameripill's profits. There is a basic conflict between its emphasis on sales and our need to sell and manage this factory too." Grant adds, "I've had a number of conversations with Cassells about the incentive scheme. I am not sure that they realize the significance of the problems created by the incentive scheme. For example, the pressure to keep our inventories down and improve our ROA causes us to schedule many short manufacturing runs. As a result, we'll never get our unit costs close to the Hague numbers."

Phillips, now more agitated, states, "I do know, expanding manufacturing to include Smoothkare will not help our earnings, will create more manufacturing problems, and will increase our operating costs—all bad news for us, particularly for our IFPS results. Our asset base will increase, inventories will grow, and we'll need more people to handle the manufacturing. I heard that Germany paid The Hague about 8,500,000 pounds for

Smoothkare this year. They use cost plus 20 percent for a transfer price, I think. We would must use the same transfer price that The Hague used because Bartow guaranteed that price to the German subsidiary for a five-year period. Our manufacturing costs would be at least 15 percent higher than The Hague's if past comparisons hold."

Germany. Hans Drossel, controller of the German subsidiary, schedules lunch with Dr. Joachim Boch, the general manager. Both have been active in building a sales force in the former East German portion of the new Germany. This effort has fortunately begun to at least cover the out-of-pocket costs of building this new staff. Now near the end of 1992, the tentative financial results show strong potential. Boch says, "I didn't think our Eastern sector strategy would pay off as fast as it has. It was risky, with only Roget's informal okay, but I think it's working." Drossel looks at the numbers and adds, "You know, it's the only way to get the growth we need to meet the financial goals we have in our 1993 budget. Right now the eastern German sales forecast is 2,000,000 marks, and the potential could be two or three times that if we had a strong generic drug product line. We just don't have the product lines to get a bigger market share. I think we'll have some explaining to do in our annual financial review when Cassells' people arrive from Bartow."

After looking at the product line sales days, Drossel comments, "Our ability to price Smoothkare just under our main competitor really helped sales and our responsibility earnings. I hope we can get another cost reduction from The Hague plant in 1993." Boch nods his head affirmatively.

Boch then asks Drossel about rumors that Bartow had made a formal decision to enter the former East Bloc markets. "You know, I think our proposal about the Eastern markets must have gotten lost in the mail. Roget says it's being studied by the financial guys—but, come on, isn't eight months' study a little ridiculous? Not only that, but in the meantime, several really profitable small pharmaceutical firms have been gobbled up by the big Swiss drug companies. Where are our people?" Drossel responds, "We seem to be preoccupied with bottom-line results while the Swiss seem to be looking for market share first and let the profits develop later."

Required:
(1) Estimate the impact on in-country IFPS goals of:
  a. United Kingdom: Expanding current manufacturing capacity by acquiring the Worsley plant.
  b. Germany: Acquiring of Koblenz Chemie Co.
  c. France: Withdrawing Saincoeur from the French market.
(2) Discuss potential strategic reactions of the general managers in the United Kingdom, Germany, and France to questions (1) a, (1) b, and (1) c, respectively.
(3) Discuss the strengths and weaknesses of Ameripill's IFPS plan.
(4) Make specific recommendations for changing the IFPS plan. Support your recommendations by citing specific case examples.

References

Agami, Abdel M. "Global Accounting Standards and Competitiveness of U.S. Corporations." *Multinational Business Review,* spring 1993, pp. 38-43.

Aguayo, Rafael. *Dr. Deming: The Man Who Taught the Japanese About Quality.* London: Mercury Books, 1991.

Akers, Michael D., and Grover L. Porter. "Strategic Planning At Five World-Class Companies." *Management Accounting,* July 1995, pp. 24-31.

Ansoff, H. Igor, and E. McDonnell. *Implanting Strategic Management.* Englewood Cliffs, N. J.: Prentice-Hall, 1990.

Anthony, Robert N. *The Management Control Function.* Boston, Mass.: The Harvard Business School Press, 1988.

Appleyard, A. R., N. C. Strong, and P. J. Walton. "Budgetary Control of Foreign Subsidiaries." *Management Accounting* (U.K.), September 1990, pp. 44-45.

Arnst, Catherine. "The Networked Corporation." *Business Week,* 26 June 1995, pp. 86-89.

Bailes, Jack C., and Takayuki Assada. "Empirical Differences Between Japanese and American Budget and Performance Evaluation Systems." *The International Journal of Accounting,* vol. 26, no. 2 (1991), pp. 131-142.

Barnathan, Joyce, Sharon Moshavi, Heidi Dawley, Sunita Wadekar Bhargava, and Helen Chang. "Passage Back to India." *Business Week,* 17 July, 1995, pp. 44-46.

Certo, Samuel C., and J. Paul Peter. *Strategic Management: Concepts and Applications.* 3d ed. Burr Ridge, Ill.: Richard D. Irwin, Inc., 1995.

Chakravarthy, Balaji, and Yves Doz. "Strategy Process Research: Focusing on Corporate Self-Renewal." *Strategic Management Journal,* summer 1992, pp. 5-14.

Crosby, Philip B. *Quality Is Free.* New York: McGraw-Hill Book Company, 1979.

————. *Quality Without Tears.* New York: McGraw-Hill Book Company, 1984.

Deming, W. Edwards. *Japanese Methods for Productivity and Quality.* Washington, D.C.: George Washington University, 1981.

————. *Out of the Crisis.* Cambridge, Mass.: MIT Press, 1986.

————. *Quality, Productivity and Competitive Position.* Cambridge, Mass.: MIT Press, 1982.

Drucker, Peter F. "The Coming of the New Organization." *Harvard Business Review,* January-February 1988, pp. 45-53.

Feigenbaum, Armand V. "America on the Threshold of Quality." *Quality,* January 1990, pp. 16-18.

Grant, R. M. *Contemporary Strategy Analysis.* Oxford, England: Blackwell, 1991.

Horngren, Charles T., George Foster, and Srikant M. Datar. *Cost Accounting: A Managerial Emphasis.* 8th ed. Englewood Cliffs, N.J.: Prentice Hall, 1994.

Howe, W. Stewart. *Corporate Strategy.* London: The Macmillan Press Ltd., 1986.

Iqbal, M. Zafar. "Historical Overview of Developments in Cost and Managerial Accounting." *The Academy of Accounting Historians Working Paper Series,* vol. 2, Richmond, Va.: The Academy of Accounting Historians, 1979, pp. 303-317.

————. "International Dimension in Managerial Accounting." *Management Accounting Campus Report,* spring 1993, p. 3.

————. "ISO 9000: Fact and Fiction." *Journal of Accountancy,* February 1994, p. 67.

Ishikawa, Kaoru. "How to Apply Companywide Quality Control in Foreign Countries." *Quality Progress,* September 1989, pp. 70-74.

————. *Quality Control Circles at Work.* Tokyo: Japanese Union of Scientists and Engineers, 1984.

Johnson, Gerry, and Kevan Scholes. *Exploring Corporate Strategy: Text and Cases.* 3d ed. Hertfordshire, U.K.: Prentice-Hall International (UK) Ltd., 1993.

Juran, Joseph M. *Juran on Quality by Design: The New Steps for Planning Quality into Goods and Services.* New York: The Free Press, 1992.

————. *Juran's New Quality Road Map.* New York: The Free Press, 1991.

————. *Juran's Quality Control Handbook.* 4th ed. New York: McGraw-Hill Book Company, 1988.

Karatsu, Hajime. *An Invitation to QC.* Tokyo: Japanese Union of Scientists and Engineers, 1988.

————. *Mastering the Tools of QC.* Tokyo: Japanese Union of Scientists and Engineers, 1987.

Kaufman, Roger. *Strategic Planning Plus: An Organizational Guide.* London: Sage Publications Ltd., 1992.

Kennedy, P. "Doing Business in the New Eastern Europe: A Risk Profile." *The International Executive,* vol. 31, no. 6 (1990), pp. 7-13.

Kiam, V.K. "Eastern Europe: The New Entrepreneurial Frontier." *The International Executive,* vol. 31, no. 5 (1990), pp. 9-12.

Krishnaiah, P. R., and C. R. Rao. *Handbook of Statistics 7: Quality Control and Reliability.* Amsterdam, Neth.: North-Holland, 1988.

Lascelles, David, and Barrie G. Dale. "Quality Management: The Chief Executive's Perception and Role." *Journal of European Management,* March 1990, pp. 67-75.

Leading Trends in Information Services. Chicago: Deloitte Touche Tohmatsu International, Management Consulting Division, 1995.

Mann, Nancy R. *The Keys to Excellence.* London: Mercury Books, 1990.

Matsushita, K. *Not for Bread Alone.* Kyoto, Japan: PHP Institute, 1984.

Mintzberg, Henry. "The Design School: Reconsidering the Basic Premises of Strategic Management." *Strategic Management Journal,* vol. 11, no. 3 (1990), pp. 171-195.

Morden, Tony. *Business Strategy and Planning: Text and Cases.* Berkshire, England: McGraw-Hill Book Company Europe, 1993.

Mori, Kiyoshi. "Yen and Cents Abroad, Small Business Moves Toward True Internationalization." *Japan Update,* September 1993, pp. 12-13.

Oakland, John S. *Total Quality Management: The Route to Improving Performance.* 2d ed. Oxford, England: Butterworth-Heinemann Ltd., 1993.

O'Brien, Michael. "Going Global: What to Look For in Financial Software." *Management Accounting,* April 1995, pp. 59-60.

Ohno, Taiichi. *Toyota Production System: Beyond Large Scale Production.* Cambridge, Mass.: Productivity Press, 1978.

Ozawa, M. *Total Quality Control and Management.* Tokyo: Japanese Union of Scientists and Engineers, 1988.

Porter, Michael E. Competitive Strategy. New York: The Free Press, 1980.

Quinn, James Brian. *Strategies for Change.* Homewood, Ill.: Richard D. Irwin, Inc., 1980).

Riahi-Belkaoui, Ahmed. *The Cultural Shaping of Accounting.* Westport, Conn.: Quorum Books, 1995.

Rich, Anne J. "Understanding Global Standards." *Management Accounting,* April 1995, pp. 51-54.

Shields, Michael D., Chee W. Chow, Yutaka Kato, and Yu Kakagawa. "Management Accounting Practices in the U.S. and Japan: Comparative Survey Findings and Research Implications." *Journal of International Financial Management and Accounting,* spring 1991, pp. 61-77.

Smith, P. "Organizational Behavior and National Cultures." *British Journal of Management,* vol. 3 (1992), pp. 39-51.

Taguchi, Genichi, and Don Clausing. "Robust Quality." *Harvard Business Review,* January-February 1990, pp. 65-75.

Taylor, Frederick W. *The Principle of Scientific Management.* New York: Harper & Row, 1911.

Trepo, Georges X. "Introduction and Diffusion of Management Tools: The Example of Quality Circles and Total Quality Control." *European Management Journal,* winter 1987, pp. 287-293.

Chapter 9

Budgeting, Product Costing, and Foreign Exchange Risk Management

The previous chapter dealt with strategic planning and control issues that must be addressed by multinational corporations. It also discussed control issues related to design of an information system. This chapter presents *operational aspects* of the framework discussed in Chapter 8: operating budgets, capital budgets, product costing, and foreign exchange risk management.

Budgeting

Budgeting is among the most widely used managerial accounting tools. A **budget** translates corporate plans into financial terms. Organizations use budgets for planning, control, and performance evaluation.

Master Operating Budget

The **master operating budget** summarizes corporate goals for a period of time (normally one year). A good budgeting system includes a budget for each responsibility center in the multinational organization. There are four common types of responsibility centers:

1. A **cost center** is responsible mainly for incurring and controlling costs. Examples of cost centers are purchasing offices, manufacturing plants, and assembly plants located in different parts of the world.

2. A **revenue center** is primarily responsible for generating revenues, e.g., sales offices or service centers in different countries.

3. A **profit center** is responsible for both revenues and costs. An example is an operation responsible for both purchase and sale of goods.

4. An **investment center** is responsible for costs, revenues, profits, and investment in assets. An example is an international operation with responsibility to acquire and sell goods, and to acquire and dispose of its assets.

Major components of a typical master budget are:

- Sales budget.
- Production budgets and cost of sales budgets.
- Marketing and administrative expenses budget.
- Budgeted income statement.

We next discuss issues *multinational corporations* face during budget preparation.

Centralized versus decentralized budgeting systems. Only if the scope of international operations includes limited sales, limited purchases, or minor manufacturing can a multinational corporation maintain a centralized budgeting system. Otherwise, the need for knowledge of local conditions, different currencies, and multiple sourcing dictates a decentralized budgeting system. In some cultures, the concept of planning may not be understood or accepted. Educating and training local managers are prerequisites to effective budgeting systems in such settings.

Sales forecasts. The sales budget is the foundation on which all other budgets are built. Preparation of the sales budget requires:

- *National demographic and economic statistics* such as population, income levels, national growth, economic conditions and trends, and consumer preferences.
- *Company historical data* on sales, prices, level of customer service, the effect of marketing campaigns, etc.
- *An active and knowledgeable sales force with first-hand information about markets, customers, and competitors.*
- *Market research* to obtain information on consumer behavior, market trends, and alternative distribution channels.

In some countries, such information may be readily available, while in others it may be unavailable or unreliable. For example, a developing nation may not have accurate information on per capita income or the impact of inflation on disposable income. Information about competition may also be difficult to obtain—particularly if competition is from local industries protected by government regulations or from public sector enterprises.

Domestic and foreign currencies. Budgets are expressed in the currency unit of the country where operations are located, and are then translated into the parent company's currency. *While financial accounting rules control translation of foreign currency for financial reporting purposes, there are no such limitations on translation for budgets.* However, the multinational company's management should make the decision regarding the exchange rate used to translate budgets.

Changes in foreign currency exchange rates. Unforeseen significant changes in foreign currency exchange rates render the budget unrealistic. The multinational company may impose local sourcing of funds on its subsidiary to avoid the adverse impact of changes in exchange rates. Local sourcing of funds may be costly, thus decreasing the subsidiary's operating profit.

Export/import and flow of funds regulation. Many countries enact regulation to enhance their exports and limit their imports. They also may restrict or prohibit the transfer of hard currency outside the country. A foreign subsidiary's budget may include sourcing raw material from another country. This may turn out to be infeasible because of unexpected changes in export/import regulations or changes in fund transfer regulations.

Global sourcing of factors of production. Global sourcing of factors of production adds uncertainties and necessitates greater coordination. For example, consider a manufacturing plant located in Kenya and owned by a British multinational. The plant relies on raw materials imported from Tanzania, workers from India, Korea, and Taiwan, technology from the U.S., middle managers from Europe, and top management personnel from the U.K. Only with proper planning and consideration of the many uncertainties can a viable budget be developed.

Combined effect of exchange rate changes and global sourcing. When acquisition of factors of production involves multiple currencies, significant changes in relative exchange rates can reduce the reliability of projections. This may require frequent revisions of budgets to make them realistic enough to be useful.

Budget Preparation Process

Now we will focus on the main steps required to prepare an operating budget by working through an example.

Example   The following budgets have been prepared for a French subsidiary of a U.S. multinational corporation for 1999. Exhibit 9–1 shows the sales budget.

Exhibit 9–1	Sales Budget (000)		
	Units	**Selling Price**	**Sales Revenue**
Sales	325	F 80	F 26,000

Exhibit 9–2 shows the production budget in units based on projected sales volume of 325,000 units and a planned increase of 15,000 units in finished goods inventory.

Exhibit 9–2	Production Budget in Units (000)
Sales (Exhibit 9–1)	325
Plus target ending finished goods inventory	27
Total needs	352
Less beginning finished goods inventory	12
Required production	340

The budgeted production volume and data about inputs required for each unit of finished goods enable management accountants to prepare the production cost budget. This budget and supporting data are shown in Exhibit 9–3.

Another schedule, shown as Exhibit 9–4, is prepared for the cost of raw material purchases. Note the assumed inventory increase is 60,000 ounces based on an assumed beginning inventory of 144,000 ounces and a planned ending inventory of 204,000 ounces.

Exhibit 9–5 shows the cost of sales budget, built up from the preceding supporting budgets. The cost of the 12,000 units in beginning inventory of finished goods is F528,000. The cost of the ending inventory of 27,000 units is F1,188,000 using the *average cost method.*

Exhibit 9–3   Production Cost Budget

	Required Input for Production* (000)	Cost per Unit of Input	Total Cost (000)
Raw material: 6 oz. required for each output unit; cost is F1.47 per oz.	2,040 oz.	F 1.47	F 3,000
Labor: Each unit of output requires 0.471 hours at a cost of F50 per hour	160 hrs.	50	8,000
Manufacturing overhead: From overhead budget (not shown)	–	–	4,000
Total production cost			F 15,000

*Total production, 340,000 units (Exhibit 9–2)

Exhibit 9–4   Cost of Raw Material Purchases Budget (000)

Required raw material (Exhibit 9–3)	2,040 oz.
Plus targeted ending raw material inventory	204
Total needs	2,244
Less beginning raw material inventory	144
Required purchases	2,100 oz.
Cost of raw material purchases, F1.47 per oz.	F 3,087

Exhibit 9–5   Cost of Sales Budget (000)

Beginning finished goods inventory	F 528
Total production cost (Exhibit 9–3)	15,000
Cost of goods available for sale	15,528
Less cost of ending finished goods inventory (F44 × 27)	1,188
Cost of sales	F 14,340
Cost per unit of ending finished goods inventory:	
Units in beginning inventory	12,000
Units to be produced	340,000
Units available for sale	352,000
Cost of goods available for sale (from above)	F 15,528
Cost per unit F15,528 ÷ 352 (rounded)	F 44

Exhibit 9–6 shows the combined marketing and administrative expenses budget. Separate budgets could, of course, be developed and presented.

Exhibit 9–6	Marketing and Administrative Expenses Budget (000)	
Marketing expenses:		
Commissions	F 250	
Salaries	1,700	
Advertising	600	
Customer service	450	
Total		F 3,000
Administrative expenses:		
Salaries	750	
Supplies	450	
Miscellaneous expenses	300	
Total		1,500
Total marketing and administrative expenses		F 4,500

Information included in Exhibits 9–1 through 9–6 can now be combined to show the results of planned operations. The budgeted income statement, showing the overall impact of all preceding budgets, appears in Exhibit 9–7.

Exhibit 9–7	Budgeted Income Statement (000)
Sales volume in units	325
Sales revenue (Exhibit 9–1)	F 26,000
Cost of sales (Exhibit 9–5)	14,340
Gross margin	11,660
Marketing and administrative expenses (Exhibit 9–6)	4,500
Operating income	F 7,160

We prepared our exhibits for a one-year period only. In practice, the one-year budget would normally be divided into monthly or quarterly segments.

Capital Budgeting

Capital budgeting includes identifying, evaluating, and planning long-term investments. This section focuses on evaluation of long-term projects for *international investment decisions*. Such decisions involve spending large sums of capital (cash) with significant implications for future corporate performance.

Lack of availability of market and economic indicators needed to predict cash flows tend to increase the risks of foreign investments. Multinational corporations find it necessary, therefore, to consider factors that are usually not relevant for domestic investment decisions.

- *Securing capital for investment projects in other countries may be difficult and costly.* Many banks demand higher interest rates and require costly investment insurance.
- *While making investment analyses, only cash flows that can be repatriated by the parent company should be considered, unless cash flows are earmarked for local reinvestment or dividend payments.*
- *Differing inflation rates, fluctuating foreign exchange rates, and risks inherent in global transfer of capital necessitates the use of methods that take these factors into account.* Discounted cash flow and payback methods are preferable since they readily incorporate these factors.
- *A factor for political risk should be added to the normal economic risk factor for evaluating investments to be made abroad.*

Capital Budgeting Methods

Methods used to evaluate investment projects include discounted cash flow, payback period, and accounting rate of return. These methods require estimates of initial investment, future cash flows from the project, project life, cost of capital, and the desired minimum rate of return on new investment. Application of these methods to domestic or foreign investment requires forecasts of future events and assessments of risks. Risk assessment for international investments is more complicated because of unknown variables in foreign environments.

Net present value. We define the **net present value (NPV) method** as the amount by which the present value of expected net future cash inflows exceeds the initial investment. The rate used to discount future cash flows is normally equal to the corporation's cost of capital plus a risk factor, or is equal to the corporation's required rate of return. Acceptable projects should have a minimum of zero NPV. A positive NPV means that the return from the project exceeds the discount rate. Projects with a negative NPV fall short of the required rate of return.

Example   Belleville, Inc., a U.S.-based multinational corporation, is considering opening a manufacturing plant in Malaysia or Singapore. The Overseas Investment Division of Belleville, Inc. gathered the information shown at the top of the next page about the two prospective plants, expressed in the Malaysian ringgit (R) and the Singapore dollar ($).

We assume no residual value at the end of useful life for either plant. Relevant present value factors are shown in Exhibit 9–8.

The computation of the net present value for each plant *before* taking risk into consideration is shown in Exhibit 9–9.

Both plants show positive net present value and are thus acceptable. The Singapore plant shows a higher net present value and accordingly shows prospects of better financial performance than the Malaysian plant.

	Malaysian Plant (000)	Singapore Plant (000)
Required investment	R 27,100	S$ 20,075
Estimated yearly revenues	14,300	10,600
Annual costs and expenses	8,580	6,350
Project net cash inflows (operating income)	R 5,720	S$ 4,250
Discount rate (cost of capital)	8%	8%
Risk factor	6%	4%
Useful life	8 years	8 years

Exhibit 9–8   Present Value of an Ordinary Annuity of One Monetary Unit

Period (years)	Discount Rate			
	8%	10%	12%	14%
6	4.623	4.355	4.111	3.889
8	5.747	5.335	4.968	4.639
10	6.710	6.145	5.650	5.216

Exhibit 9–9   NPV Analysis before Consideration of Risk (000)

	Malaysian Plant (000)	Singapore Plant (000)
Annual net cash inflows	R 5,720	S$ 4,250
Present value factor (Exhibit 9–8)	5.747	5.747
Present value of net cash inflows	32,873	24,425
Required investment	27,100	20,075
NPV	R 5,773	S$ 4,350
Current exchange rate in US dollars	2.75	1.95
NPV in US dollars	US$ 2,099	US$ 2,231

The computation of NPV for each plant *after* considering the risk factor is shown in Exhibit 9–10. The present value factors now take into account the level of risk in each country.

The analysis indicates that the Malaysian plant is no longer acceptable. It shows a negative net present value of R565,000 or US$205,000. The Singapore plant remains acceptable, showing a positive net present value of $1,039,000 or US$533,000.

Exhibit 9–10 NPV Analysis after Consideration of Risk (000)	Malaysian Plant (000)	Singapore Plant (000)
Annual net cash inflows	R 5,720	S$ 4,250
Present value factor (Exhibit 9–8)	4.639	4.968
Present value of net cash inflows	26,535	21,114
Required investment	27,100	20,075
NPV	R (565)	S$ 1,039
Current exchange rate in U.S. dollars	2.75	1.95
NPV in U.S. dollars	US$ (205)	US$ 533

Payback period. The **payback period (PBP) method** is based on how quickly the investing entity recovers its invested cash. PBP is the time it will take to recover invested cash from projected net cash inflows to be generated by the project.

$$PBP = \frac{\text{Initial cash investment}}{\text{Net cash inflows from project each period}}$$

Example This example shows the application of the payback period method to evaluating Project A versus Project B.

	Project A	Project B
Initial investment (a)	$420,000	$630,000
Estimated annual net cash inflow (b)	$120,000	$140,000
Payback period (a ÷ b)	= 3.5 years	= 4.5 years

Everything else being equal, Project A is preferable to Project B because invested cash is recovered sooner, i.e., 3.5 years versus 4.5 years.

Accounting rate of return. The **accounting rate of return (ARR) method** is based on accounting income as reported in accrual-basis financial statements.

$$ARR = \frac{\text{Annual net cash inflows - Depreciation expense}}{\text{Initial capital investment}}$$

Example This example shows the use of the accounting rate of return method in comparing Project A and B (above), assuming straight-line depreciation. Both projects have a five-year life.

Again Project A appears preferable to Project B because it earns a higher accounting rate of return. Note, however, that with a different set of data it is possible that the PBP method and the ARR method would prefer different projects. In our examples, both methods favored Project A, but this will not always be the case.

	Project A	Project B
Annual net cash inflow	$120,000	$140,000
Depreciation expense	84,000	126,000
Accounting income (a)	$ 36,000	$ 14,000
Initial investment (b)	$420,000	$630,000
ARR (a ÷ b)	= 8.6%	= 2.2%

Application of the payback period and accounting rate of return methods may require adaptation due to the unique nature of foreign investment. This may include:

- Shortening the minimum payback period and raising the minimum required return to account for foreign economic and political risks.
- Accounting for any risk that may be caused by future changes in foreign exchange rates.
- Computing two payback periods and accounting rates of return, one reflecting a *project perspective* and the other reflecting a *parent company perspective.* This is desirable when differences exist between the project's projected cash flows and earnings and the amounts expected to be remitted to the parent company.
- Using after-tax cash-flow and earnings amounts. Foreign investment projects and their earnings face complex tax issues at home and abroad. The amounts used while applying the methods may be adjusted for the impact of tax laws and regulations on cash flows and earnings. This is necessary when the projects considered are in different countries with significantly different tax rates.
- Adjusting for differences in accounting among countries. These differences may affect measurement of income, depreciation, and investment. To make meaningful comparisons, it is necessary to use comparable amounts.

The purpose of the preceding discussion is to highlight key issues facing multinational corporations in evaluating foreign investment projects. Application of capital budgeting methods involves practical and theoretical considerations beyond those presented here.[1]

Economic Risk versus Political Risk

International direct investments by multinational corporations often face high economic and political risks because of lack of knowledge about foreign environments. **Economic risk** is the uncertainty surrounding key elements of the investment process. These elements include projections of initial and subsequent investment, revenues, operating expenses, inflation, useful life, market conditions, and foreign exchange rate movements. With the exception of foreign exchange rate movements, all of these elements are similar to what corporations face

---

[1]   See, for example, Charles T. Horngren, George Foster, and Srikant M. Datar, *Cost Accounting: A Managerial Emphasis,* 8th ed. (Prentice Hall, 1994), Chapters 20 and 21 for an in-depth discussion of capital budgeting methods. See also Alan C. Shapiro, *Multinational Financial Management,* 4th ed. (Allyn & Bacon, 1992), Part IV for a comprehensive discussion of foreign investment analysis.

when making domestic investment decisions. Foreign exchange risk and how it affects multinational operations is presented in a later section of this chapter.

The political risk factor is unique and differs from country to country. *Assessment of political risk may be the most challenging aspect of the multinational corporation's foreign direct investment.* **Political risk** refers to actions and activities of foreign (host) governments directed at multinational corporations. Though becoming rare, extreme measures against multinational corporations by host governments may include nationalization, expropriation, or forced acquisition of corporate assets. More usually, the host governments impose special restrictions on multinational operations such as requiring employment of local managers and workers.

Coping with political risk requires formal and effective strategic planning prior to the decision to invest abroad; it also requires managing risk once it materializes and planning for disinvestment in countries with unacceptable risk levels.

A multinational corporation may develop the internal capability to forecast and manage political risk in countries where it operates or plans to operate. External organizations specializing in political risk assessment and management are also available to provide needed service. Many countries, especially industrialized nations, offer government-sponsored insurance against foreign political risk. For example, the U.S. Overseas Private Investment Corporation provides insurance against political risk to U.S.-based multinational corporations.

Product Costing

Traditional costing methods classify costs of producing and selling goods and services into three categories: manufacturing, marketing, and administrative. Manufacturing cost is usually further classified into direct material, direct labor, and manufacturing overhead. Under absorption costing, all manufacturing costs for a period are assigned to the units produced during that period, and are classified as product costs. Marketing and administrative costs are considered period costs, and are charged against revenues in the period in which they occur. The above framework can be adapted to international business environments to account for multiple sourcing of raw material, different labor costs among nations, and different overhead costs resulting from different operating conditions. Additional issues relevant to the determination of product cost in each country include:

- Labor productivity differs from one country to another. Corporations must balance labor cost with labor productivity in each country.
- Customers in different countries have different expectations for product quality and customer service. Product quality is a major competitive weapon, especially in industrialized nations. Product availability continues to be the main concern in many developing countries.
- Some countries may enjoy relatively low cost of some factors of production. This may be offset by other costs such as regulatory compliance cost, distribution cost, or cost of delays.

- Government regulations may result in different cost behavior in different countries. For example, direct labor cost is considered variable in the U.S. Salary payment requirements in other countries causes direct labor cost to be fixed.
- Foreign exchange rates fluctuate over time, resulting in overcosting or undercosting of materials sourced from outside.

Product Costing as a Competitive Weapon

Individual factors of production are sourced locally or abroad, and are assigned to different product lines. Indirect costs are allocated to different product lines according to the cost allocation base selected. Choice of an inappropriate allocation base results in overcosting some product lines and undercosting others. *If selling prices are based on full absorption cost, overcosting or undercosting affects the competitive position of each product line and may result in unwarranted elimination or expansion of a particular product line.*

Example

Exhibit 9–11 illustrates the above multinational product-costing concept. We assume two products, A and B, produced by two multinational companies, MNC1, and MNC2.

Exhibit 9–11 Multinational Product Costing				
	MNC1		MNC2	
Product	**A**	**B**	**A**	**B**
Selling price per unit	$150	$ 90	$150	$ 90
Direct costs	70	60	70	60
Indirect costs—allocated	40	40	60	20
Total cost per unit	110	100	130	80
Unit profit margin	$ 40	$(10)	$ 20	$ 10

Assume that the two companies' costs are identical, but the MNC1 cost allocation system overcosts product B. Based on the above data, MNC1 might eliminate product B. Such elimination may be ill advised because it would result in no significant reduction of common fixed costs. Since all common fixed costs would now be assigned to product A, product A in turn may lose market share, since its overcosting is likely to lead to overpricing.

If the MNC2 cost allocation system accurately relates to consumption of overhead resources, both products A and B are likely to be appropriately priced and should maintain their competitive position.

Cost and Productivity

In the global market, cost is not the only competitive weapon. Labor productivity is another key element. **Productivity** is output per hour of workers' time. It is a key indicator of an economy's competitiveness. Many factors contribute to productivity and, therefore, to national and corporate competitiveness. Examples of these factors are:

- Employment of high technology.
- Production environment and factory layout.
- Employees' education and training.
- Workers' motivation and performance.
- Employee empowerment.

High labor cost in a country does not necessarily mean a less competitive position. Labor cost should be compared with labor productivity. Let us examine the following example of how cost and productivity combined provide a better indication of competitive position. In the example, Country Z, despite its higher hourly labor cost, has a competitive advantage over Countries X and Y.

	Country		
	X	**Y**	**Z**
Average cost per labor hour	$20	$30	$40
Output units per one hour of labor time	1	2	4
Average cost per unit of output	$20	$15	$10

Example   National competitive advantage based on overall labor productivity and specific industry productivity has been the subject of public interest in most industrialized nations. Figure 9–1 compares German and Japanese industrial productivity with that of the U.S. for nine major industries in 1990.

Another study compared labor wages and labor productivity of Korea, Thailand, Malaysia, and the Philippines with that of the U.S. Its conclusions were that labor costs to produce one unit of output in those countries are closer to the U.S. levels when *both* wages and productivity were taken into account.[2] This is shown in Figure 9–2. Labor unit costs were actually above the U.S. levels in Malaysia and the Philippines due to low productivity despite their low wages.

Cost Control Approaches

Methods to control costs, improve product quality, and swiftly respond to customer needs are requisites for success in the competitive environment of the 1990s. Many companies are realizing that it is impossible to sustain global competitiveness without effective cost management. Some significant corporate cost control approaches are described next.

Downsizing and restructuring.   Many multinational corporations have significantly reduced their workforce, both labor and management, in recent years. Examples include Volkswagen, IBM, AT&T, and General Motors Corporation. Many other corporations are currently faced with this challenge.

Jürgen E. Schrempp, who became chief executive officer of Daimler-Benz in May 1995, will have to cut tens of thousands of jobs. He is likely to close the money-losing Daimler-Benz Industrie unit with sell-offs and transfers of its profitable operations to other divisions.

---

[2]   Gene Koretz, "The Equalizer: Productivity," *Business Week,* 11 September 1995, p. 26.

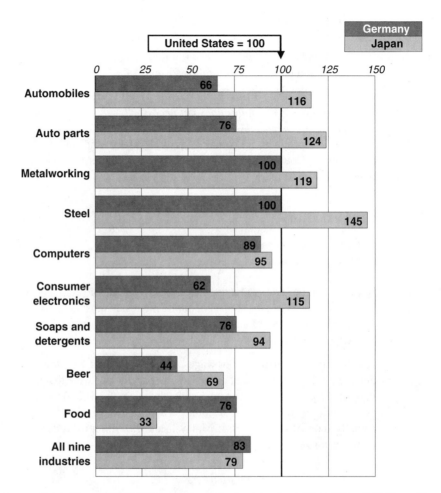

United States = 100

Germany
Japan

	0	25	50	75	100	125	150
Automobiles	Germany: 66 / Japan: 116
Auto parts	Germany: 76 / Japan: 124
Metalworking	Germany: 100 / Japan: 119
Steel	Germany: 100 / Japan: 145
Computers	Germany: 89 / Japan: 95
Consumer electronics	Germany: 62 / Japan: 115
Soaps and detergents	Germany: 76 / Japan: 94
Beer	Germany: 44 / Japan: 69
Food	Germany: 76 / Japan: 33
All nine industries	Germany: 83 / Japan: 79

Source: Sylvia Nasar, "U.S. Still Has an Edge in Productivity, Study Finds," *New York Times,* 22 October 1993.

Figure 9-1   Industrial Productivity in the U.S., Germany, and Japan: Output per Hour Worked in 1990

One of the divisions expected to undergo massive restructuring is Daimler-Benz Aerospace (DASA). Analysts expect that restructuring at DASA alone will result in reduction of up to half of its 40,000 workforce. Schrempp has already cut 40 percent of Daimler's 500 executive jobs at the Stuttgart corporate headquarters.[3]

Activity-based costing and activity-based management.   Activity-based costing is a method of measuring the cost and performance of activities and cost objects. Costs are

---

[3]   John Templeman, "The Shocks for Daimler's New Driver," *Business Week,* 21 August 1995, pp. 38-39.

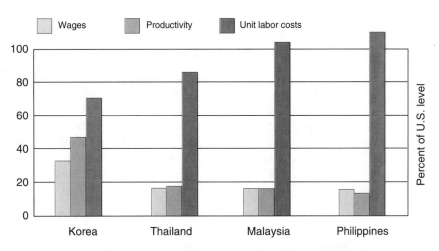

Source: Gene Koretz, "The Equalizer: Productivity," *Business Week,* 11 September 1995, p. 26.

**Figure 9–2   Manufacturing Industry Productivity in the U.S.,
Korea, Thailand, Malaysia, and the Philippines**

assigned to activities based on their use of resources. Then costs of activities are assigned to cost objects based on their use of activities. Activity-based costing recognizes the *causal* relationships of cost drivers to activities. A **cost object** is any customer, product, service, project, or other work unit for which a separate cost measurement is desired. A **cost driver** is any factor that causes a change in the cost of an activity. For example, the quality of parts received by an activity is a determining factor in the work required by that activity. The higher the percentage of defective parts received by an activity, the higher the work required to perform the activity. An activity may have multiple cost drivers associated with it.[4]

Activity-based costing is a powerful tool for accurate costing of products, services, and projects. It assigns costs according to resources used, rather than by some arbitrary allocation method. This is helpful to companies in product strategy, product pricing, and cost reduction in the manufacturing processes. Cost reduction in manufacturing processes is made possible by activity-based costing because it *identifies* cost drivers. By focusing on cost drivers, management can take appropriate steps to reduce costs. These may include using different parts, changing design of the product, or incorporating equipment modifications.

Examples of the companies using ABC include Hewlett-Packard, Tektronix, Zytec Corporation, Dayton Extruded Plastics, and Northern Telecom Limited.

Activity-based management is a discipline that focuses on the management of activities for improving the value received by the customer and the profit achieved by providing this value. This discipline includes cost driver analysis, activity analysis, and performance

---

[4] Peter B.B. Turney, *Common Cents: The ABC Performance Breakthrough* (Portland, Oregon: Cost Technology, 1992), pp. 315-316.

measurement. Activity-based management draws on activity-based costing as its major source of information.[5]

Both cost control and value received by the customer are important:[6]

> When deciding what to measure, it is helpful to think of process measures as covering two broad categories: the value provided to the customer and the efficiency of the process itself. It is important that an organization have performance data from both categories so it can maintain a balance between the interests of the customer and the business. A company that focuses only on meeting customer needs might find itself losing money as a result of inefficient internal operations, while a company focusing solely on internal efficiency may lose customers whose needs are inadequately met.

> Customer "value added" is most easily measured by quantifying the company's ability to meet or exceed key customer needs—measuring such performance attributes as quality, availability and service. Process efficiency is most easily captured by measuring cycle time.

> The relationship between efficiency and cycle time is apparent from the following logic: If customer needs are being met (that is, providing value-added products or services at competitive cost) in shorter and shorter cycle times, then the processes are by definition becoming increasingly efficient. The following are common examples of measures available in each category:

Measures of customer value added:

- Alignment of product-service performance to customer expectations.
- Cost versus the features-benefit received.
- Quality and reliability.
- Service and support provided.
- Recovery from problems.

Measures of cycle time:

- New-product-service development time.
- Time to market.
- Order fulfillment cycle time.
- Performance to schedule.
- Recovery-response time.
- Rework and other nonvalue-added time.

---

[5] James M. Reeve, ed., *Readings & Issues in Cost Management* (Cincinnati, Ohio: South-Western College Publishing, 1995), p. 416.

[6] Kavasseri V. Ramanathan and Douglas S. Schaffer, "How Am I Doing?" *Journal of Accountancy,* May 1995, p. 82.

As the above excerpt demonstrates, cost control has a direct relationship with cycle time: shorter cycle times mean greater efficiency. Turney cites two rules of activity-based management:[7]

- Deploy resources to activities that yield the maximum strategic benefit.
- Improve what matters to the customer.

An increasing number of companies have adopted activity-based management. Examples include Siemens, Tektronix, Black and Decker, AT&T, General Motors, and General Electric.

Total quality management. One of the major outcomes of the pursuit of quality is elimination of the need for a high cost of rework. As mentioned in chapter 8, quality is critical to stay competitive. Adoption of quality standards and quality audits conducted by internal auditors can be effective in ensuring that quality standards are being met, and internal and external failure costs are minimized. **Internal failure costs** are the costs incurred when a defective product is detected *before* it is shipped to customers. **External failure costs** are the costs of a defective product *after* it is shipped to the customer. External failure costs include opportunity costs such as loss of potential future sales. Examples of companies where internal auditors take an active role in total quality management program implementation include ITT London & Edinburgh and Hong Kong Telecommunications Limited.[8]

Just-in-time and Kaizen. Just-in-time is a logistics approach designed to result in minimum inventory and waste during the manufacturing process.[9] Just-in-time has been practiced in Japan for many decades. Through elimination of costly inventory and rework, companies such as Toyota have been able to reduce costs amounting to billions of U.S. dollars.[10]

A cornerstone of the just-in-time approach is Kaizen. **Kaizen** focuses on establishing cost reduction targets for each cost element, product line, organization unit, and manufacturing plant. Cost reduction is achieved through continuous improvement efforts by cross-functional teams.

Daihatsu Motor Co. uses the Kaizen system. Starting from the previous year's actual costs, a cost reduction target is selected for each product. The annual target is converted to monthly cost reduction goals. The cost reduction target rate is normally fixed over time, but may vary based on analysis of the production environment. Exhibit 9-12 shows an annual profit plan based on the Kaizen system. The term "standard variable costs" refers here to actual costs of the preceding period.

---

[7] Turney, *Common Cents,* p. 143.

[8] David Sherick, "ISO's Impact," *Internal Auditor,* June 1995, pp. 30-32.

[9] Callie Berliner and James A. Brimson, eds., *Cost Management for Today's Advanced Manufacturing* (Boston, Mass.: Harvard Business School Press, 1988), p. 241.

[10] Toyota Motor Corporation, *Annual Report 1994* (Toyota City, Japan: Toyota Motor Corporation), pp. 2-11.

Exhibit 9–12 Annual Profit Plan—Daihatsu Motor Co.	
Projected sales revenues	¥ xxxx
Less standard variable costs	xxx
Budgeted contribution margin	xxx
Less cost reduction target	xxx
Adjusted contribution margin	xxx
Less budgeted fixed costs*	xxx
Budgeted operating income	¥ xxx

*No cost reduction targets are established for fixed costs. However, the budgeted amount for each fixed cost element is established after review and analysis of past actual fixed costs.

Source: Adapted from Yasuhiro Monden and John Lee, "How Japanese Auto Maker Reduces Costs," *Management Accounting,* August 1993, pp. 22-26.

Target costing.   **Target costing** is a method that sets cost targets for new products based on market price. The analysis starts with estimated selling price (market-based) and subtracts profits to arrive at target cost:

Sales price (market-based)
Less desired profit (based on a standard return on sales %)
= Target cost

Target costing develops product cost information by working back from market-based pricing and subtracting a standard return on sales percentage to arrive at an allowable cost for new products. This allowable cost establishes a cost reduction target for engineers, motivating them to reduce costs by improving product design, value engineering, and perhaps trade-offs on functionality.[11] Target costing has been widely used in Japan since the early 1970s, and is gaining popularity worldwide. Among the companies using target costing are Toyota, NEC, Epson, Fanuc, Culp Inc., and Mercedes-Benz. The new CEO on Daimler-Benz, parent company of Mercedes-Benz, plans to implement competitive market driven prices throughout Daimler-Benz to make it competitive globally.[12]

Worldwide manufacturing locations.   Many multinational corporations are finding that it is economical to geographically disperse manufacturing facilities. All major Japanese automakers have manufacturing plants in the U.S. Texas Instruments has found it to be advantageous to produce chips at various locations throughout the world. Daimler-Benz plans to invest in new plants in the U.S., France, and China. Mitsubishi has targeted Asia. It has ten joint ventures in fast growing Asian nations, and others in Australia and New

[11] Robert S. Kaplan, ed., *Measures for Manufacturing Excellence* (Boston, Mass.: Harvard Business School Press, 1990), p. 4.

[12] Templeman, "The Shocks for Daimler's New Driver," p. 39.

Zealand.[13] Advances in technology and telecommunications make it feasible in many cases where this would not have been the case a few years back.

Foreign currency exchange rate considerations. Many multinational corporations are taking into account foreign currency risk exposure while making their sales and sourcing plans. This is an effective way to increase revenue and reduce costs. Everything else being equal, it is advantageous to sell in countries with relatively stronger currencies, and to manufacture and purchase in countries with relatively weaker currencies. One of the cost reduction strategies of Daimler-Benz Aerospace is to shift production and parts purchasing into weaker currency areas.[14] This topic is discussed in depth in the next section.

Foreign Exchange Risk Management

Foreign exchange risk management is the management of the risk of loss from currency exchange rate movements on transactions, translation, or remeasurement involving foreign currency. In other words, it represents the actions taken by a company to protect itself against possible future losses arising from future changes in currency exchange rates.

Unlike domestic corporations, multinational business transactions such as cross-border sourcing of raw material and transfer of income across national boundaries are denominated in more than one currency. This exposes multinational corporations to risks associated with unexpected changes in foreign currency exchange rates.

International subsidiaries maintain their assets and liabilities, earn revenues, and pay expenses in local currency. The parent company faces the risk of a decline in the value of the equity in its subsidiary every time the value of the foreign currency depreciates.

The increased importance of international trade and the expansion of the global capital market has brought pressure on many countries to let market forces determine the value of their currencies against other currencies. This has resulted in frequent changes in exchange rates, making it an almost daily occurrence. Many countries have seen their currencies appreciate in value relative to major trading currencies such as the U.S. dollar, while others have seen the value of their currencies decline.

Foreign Currency Risk Exposure

An asset, liability, revenue, or expense account denominated in a foreign currency is exposed to foreign currency risk when that currency's exchange rate changes. In the case of translation, the currency rate changes affect only those accounts that are translated at the current rate; accounts translated at the historical rate are not affected. A foreign subsidiary has a **positive exposure** when it has more current assets than current liabilities. The subsidiary would have a **negative exposure** if it had more current liabilities than current assets.

---

[13] Edith Updike and Laxmi Nakarmi, "A Movable Feast for Mitsubishi," *Business Week,* 28 August 1995, pp. 50-51.

[14] Templeman, "The Shocks for Daimler's New Driver," p. 39.

Consider the following financial position of two foreign subsidiaries, fully owned by a U.S. parent company. The British subsidiary has a positive exposure because its current assets exceed its current liabilities. The French subsidiary has a negative exposure because it is in the reverse situation.

	British Subsidiary (000)	French Subsidiary (000)
Current assets	£ 8,000	F 16,000
Current liabilities	5,500	20,000

The U.S. parent company will experience a translation gain when the value of the British pound appreciates relative to the U.S. dollar or when the value of the French franc declines relative to the U.S. dollar. The U.S. parent company will experience a translation loss when the value of the British pound depreciates relative to the U.S. dollar. The same will happen when the value of the French franc appreciates relative to the U.S. dollar.

Foreign Currency Rate movement	Positive Exposure (CA>CL)	Negative Exposure (CA<CL)
Foreign currency appreciates	Translation gain	Translation loss
Foreign currency depreciates	Translation loss	Translation gain

The exposure to foreign currency risk is not limited to the translation of financial statements. Multinational corporations are also exposed to such risk caused by changes in the exchange rate between their home currency and the currencies of their international subsidiaries. For example, an appreciation in the value of the Japanese yen relative to the U.S. dollar affects the value of the assets, liabilities, and profits of a Japanese multinational's subsidiary operating in the U.S. This appreciation reduces the value of the subsidiary's assets, increases the value of its obligations in the U.S., and reduces the value of its U.S. profit. The cash flow from the subsidiary in the U.S. to its parent company in Japan is reduced because of the appreciation of the yen relative to the U.S. dollar. The same amount of U.S. dollars will now exchange for fewer yen.

Buyers and sellers of foreign goods and services are also exposed to foreign currency risk when the exchange rate changes between the transaction date and the settlement date. The following two sections discuss the transaction risk exposure and translation risk exposure in greater detail.

Transaction Risk Exposure

Foreign currency transactions were explained in Chapter 6. These transactions require settlement in a foreign currency; this has implications for future cash flows. The **transaction risk exposure** is caused by the changes in the exchange rate between the transaction date and the settlement date. Only one of the two parties to the transaction is exposed.

Assume that an Egyptian company buys goods from a U.S. supplier and is required to pay at a later date in U.S. dollars. The Egyptian buyer faces transaction risk exposure while the U.S. supplier does not. If the purchase contract requires payment in Egyptian pounds, the U.S. supplier is the party facing a transaction risk exposure.

Example Exhibit 9–13 shows business transactions entered into by a U.S. subsidiary in Austria during the year. *Note: Transaction exposure exists only when a transaction is denominated in a foreign currency and the settlement date (date of receivables or payables) is different from the date of the transaction.*

Exhibit 9–13	Examples of Transaction Risk Exposure— Austrian Subsidiary of a U.S. Multinational Corporation			
Transaction	**Transaction Date**	**Settlement Date**	**Transaction Exposure**	**Exposed Currency**
Purchase of raw material from Switzerland	February 1	April 1	Yes	Swiss franc
Purchase of parts from local supplier	February 1	March 1	No	—
Purchase of parts from Germany	February 10	April 10	Yes	German mark
Payment to parent company for use of patent	March 1	March 1	No	—
Service contract with a local trucking company	March 1	May 1, July 1	No	—
Sale of equipment in local market	June 1	September 1	No	—
Sale of parts to a U.S. company	June 1	August 1	Yes	U.S. dollar
Sale of equipment to a French company	June 15	September 15	Yes	French franc

A company that faces transaction exposure may choose to do nothing to protect itself against possible future loss. If it chooses to do nothing, and if the foreign currency exchange rate is different at settlement date, the company will experience a gain or loss depending on whether the rate change is favorable or not. The financial markets offer many ways to protect (hedge) against transaction exposure and new ways are being developed. Some of the methods used to hedge against transaction exposure include:

- *Risk shifting.* The buyers/sellers may require that the transaction be denominated in their own currency. Accordingly, the foreign exchange risk exposure shifts to the other party.

- *Currency-risk sharing.* The buyer and seller agree on a base transaction price at a specified exchange rate. The base price remains the same if the exchange rate changes within an agreed-upon range. The two parties share equally the effect of a change in the exchange rate outside the range.
- *Price adjustment.* The parties agree in advance to adjust the transaction price to offset any adverse impact to the exposed party from changes in the exchange rate.
- *Foreign currency forward contract.* A **foreign currency forward contract** is an agreement with a currency trader, e.g., a bank, to deliver in the future one currency for another at an agreed-upon "forward" exchange rate.

Accounting for the first three methods above is straightforward. Accounting for forward foreign exchange contracts, however, is a bit more complex.

Example

Assume that General Motors (GM) sells trucks to a Saudi Arabian buyer on January 15, 19x3. The transaction price is 20 million Saudi riyals (R) payable on April 1, 19x3. The spot exchange rate on January 15 is R1 = $.30. GM faces a transaction risk exposure because any change in the above exchange rate will affect the dollar amount GM receives on April 1. If the future spot rate on April 1 is R1 = $.32, GM will receive $6,400,000, i.e., $400,000 more than it would have received on the transaction date. A drop in the future spot rate to R1 = $.25 means that GM will receive $5,000,000 on April 1, i.e., a loss of $1,000,000. GM may choose to hedge against this type of risk and enter into a forward foreign exchange contract to sell 20 million Saudi riyals on April 1, 19x3 at the forward exchange rate of R1 = $.28. GM is then assured of receiving $5,600,000 from the sale of its trucks by delivering the 20 million Saudi riyals it receives on April 1 to the foreign exchange trader. GM protects or insures itself against undesirable changes in the exchange rate but also gives up the opportunity for potential gain if the rate changes in its favor. This *opportunity gain or loss* and the forecast of future movements in the exchange rates are among the factors considered by GM financial managers when they contemplate entering into a forward foreign exchange contract. Exhibit 9–14 presents examples of forward contract gain or loss based on assumed future spot exchange rates of $.30, $.28, or $.25 for one Saudi riyal. In all cases, GM is assured of receiving $5,600,000 in cash flow from the sale of trucks.

Exhibit 9–14 Forward Contract Gain or Loss				
Future Spot Exchange Rate (April 1)	**Accounts Receivable at Settlement Date**		**Opportunity**	**GM Cash**
	R	**$**	**Gain (Loss)**	**Inflow**
R1 = $.30	20 million	$6.0 million	($400,000)	$5.6 million
R1 = $.28	20 million	$5.6 million	—	$5.6 million
R1 = $.25	20 million	$5.0 million	$600,000	$5.6 million

GM records would show the following journal entries and ledger accounts ($) assuming that the future spot rate on April 1 is R = $0.28.

January 15	**1.** Accounts receivable	6,000,000	
	Sales revenue		6,000,000
	Records sales transaction at the spot rate.		

	1a Forward contract receivable		5,600,000	
	Forward exchange suspense		400,000	
	Forward contract payable			6,000,000
	Memorandum entry (no posting			
	appears in ledger) to record receivables			
	at forward rate and payables at spot rate.			
	2. Deferred foreign exchange expense		400,000	
	Deferred charges			400,000
	Records discount expense to be written			
	off in the future.			
April 1	**3.** Foreign exchange expense		400,000	
	Deferred foreign exchange expense			400,000
	Records foreign exchange expense caused			
	by the difference between the spot rate ($.30)			
	and the forward rate ($.28).			
	4. Cash		5,600,000	
	Deferred charges		400,000	
	Accounts receivable			6,000,000
	Records execution of the forward			
	foreign exchange contract.			

	Accounts Receivable					Sales Revenue		
(1)	6,000,000	6,000,000	(4)				6,000,000	(1)

	Deferred Foreign Exchange Expense					Deferred Charges		
(2)	400,000	400,000	(3)	(4)	400,000		400,000	(2)

	Cash				Foreign Exchange Expense	
(4)	5,600,000		(3)	400,000		

Companies account for transaction risk exposure currency-by-currency. Multinational corporations must decide whether to centralize or decentralize management of transaction risk exposure.

Translation Risk Exposure

Multinational corporations prepare consolidated financial statements reflecting worldwide results of operations, financial position, and cash flows. Chapter 6 presented alternative methods for translating the accounts of foreign subsidiaries into the parent company's currency. *Only accounts that are translated at the current exchange rate are subject to translation risk exposure as the rate changes over time. Accounts translated at the historical exchange rate continue to appear at their constant value in the parent company's currency.* The amount of translation risk exposure depends on the method used to translate foreign financial statements, net asset or net liability position, the direction of the change in the foreign exchange rates, and the magnitude of such change. These factors combined result in a change in the value of a foreign subsidiary's assets and liabilities measured in the parent company's currency.

Chapter 6 presented four financial statement translation methods: the current rate method, the current-noncurrent method, the monetary-nonmonetary method, and the temporal method. We will use the example of the U.S. subsidiary in France presented in Chapter 6 to illustrate accounting measurement of translation risk exposure under each of the four translation methods. This illustration will focus on the translation exposure of the subsidiary's balance sheet. The French subsidiary's balance sheet on December 31, 19x2 is presented below in French francs:

Cash	F 200,000	Accounts payable	F 2,500,000
Accounts receivable	1,000,000	Income tax payable	200,000
Inventories	2,000,000	Long-term debt	2,800,000
Net property, plant,			
and equipment	5,800,000	Stockholders' equity	3,500,000
		Total liabilities and	
Total assets	F 9,000,000	stockholders' equity	F 9,000,000

We will use an exchange rate of F1 = $0.15 to translate the French subsidiary's accounts into U.S. dollars. As discussed earlier, a translation gain or loss occurs when the exchange rate changes. We will assume a devaluation of the French franc to F1=$0.10.

Exhibits 9–15 to 9–18 show the measurement of the balance sheet translation exposure under each of the four translation methods. Each translation method shows a different translation exposure amount, measured in French francs, and a different translation gain (loss) measured in U.S. dollars.

Under the current translation method shown in Exhibit 9–15, the subsidiary net assets (stockholders' equity) of F3,500,000 is exposed. The devaluation of the French franc causes a translation loss of F3,500,000 × .05 = $175,000. Translation loss can also be computed as the difference between balances of stockholders' equity before and after devaluation.

Stockholders' equity balance before devaluation	$525,000
Stockholders' equity balance after devaluation	350,000
Translation loss	$175,000

Under the current-noncurrent translation method shown in Exhibit 9–16, only the net working capital of F500,000 is exposed. The decline in the value of the French franc causes a translation loss to the U.S. parent company of F500,000 × $.05 = $25,000.

Under the monetary-nonmonetary translation method shown in Exhibit 9–17, the monetary assets and liabilities are the only exposed accounts. The French subsidiary has a negative risk exposure because its monetary liabilities (F5,500,000) exceed its monetary assets (F1,200,000). The negative risk exposure of F4,300,000 causes a translation gain of F4,300,000 × $.05 = $215,000.

Exhibit 9–15   Translation Risk Exposure—Current Method

	Balance Sheet in Francs	Translation before Devaluation of Franc (F1=$.15)	Translation after Devaluation of Franc (F1=$.10)
Assets:			
Cash	F 200,000	$ 30,000	$ 20,000
Accounts receivable	1,000,000	150,000	100,000
Inventories	2,000,000	300,000	200,000
Net property, plant, and equipment	5,800,000	870,000	580,000
Total assets	F 9,000,000	$ 1,350,000	$ 900,000
Liabilities and stockholders' equity:			
Accounts payable	F 2,500,000	$ 375,000	$ 250,000
Income tax payable	200,000	30,000	20,000
Long-term debt	2,800,000	420,000	280,000
Stockholders' equity	3,500,000	525,000	350,000
Total liabilities and stockholders' equity	F 9,000,000	$ 1,350,000	$ 900,000
Translation exposure	F 3,500,000		
Translation loss			$ 175,000

Exhibit 9–16   Translation Risk Exposure—Current-Noncurrent Method

	Balance Sheet in Francs	Translation before Devaluation of Franc (F1=$.15)	Translation after Devaluation of Franc (F1=$.10)
Assets:			
Cash	F 200,000	$ 30,000	$ 20,000
Accounts receivable	1,000,000	150,000	100,000
Inventories	2,000,000	300,000	200,000
Net property, plant, and equipment	5,800,000	870,000	870,000
Total assets	F 9,000,000	$ 1,350,000	$ 1,190,000
Liabilities and stockholders' equity:			
Accounts payable	F 2,500,000	$ 375,000	$ 250,000
Income tax payable	200,000	30,000	20,000
Long-term debt	2,800,000	420,000	420,000
Stockholders' equity	3,500,000	525,000	500,000
Total liabilities and stockholders' equity	F 9,000,000	$ 1,350,000	$ 1,190,000
Translation exposure	F 500,000		
Translation loss			$ 25,000

Exhibit 9-17   Translation Risk Exposure—Monetary-Nonmonetary Method

	Balance Sheet in Francs	Translation before Devaluation of Franc (F1=$.15)	Translation after Devaluation of Franc (F1=$.10)
Assets:			
Cash*	F 200,000	$ 30,000	$ 20,000
Accounts receivable*	1,000,000	150,000	100,000
Inventories	2,000,000	300,000	300,000
Net property, plant, and equipment	5,800,000	870,000	870,000
Total assets	F 9,000,000	$ 1,350,000	$ 1,290,000
Liabilities and stockholder's equity:			
Accounts payable*	F 2,500,000	$ 375,000	$ 250,000
Income tax payable*	200,000	30,000	20,000
Long-term debt*	2,800,000	420,000	280,000
Stockholders' equity	3,500,000	525,000	740,000
Total liabilities and stockholders' equity	F 9,000,000	$ 1,350,000	$ 1,290,000
Translation exposure	F 4,300,000		
Translation gain			$ 215,000
*Monetary items			

Exhibit 9-18   Translation Risk Exposure—Temporal Method

	Balance Sheet in Francs	Translation before Devaluation of Franc (F1=$.15)	Translation after Devaluation of Franc (F1=$.10)
Assets:			
Cash	F 200,000	$ 30,000	$ 20,000
Accounts receivable	1,000,000	150,000	100,000
Inventories	2,000,000	300,000	200,000
Net property, plant, and equipment	5,800,000	870,000	870,000
Total assets	F 9,000,000	$ 1,350,000	$ 1,190,000
Liabilities and stockholder's equity:			
Accounts payable	F 2,500,000	$ 375,000	$ 250,000
Income tax payable	200,000	30,000	20,000
Long-term debt	2,800,000	420,000	280,000
Stockholders' equity	3,500,000	525,000	640,000
Total liabilities and stockholders' equity	F 9,000,000	$ 1,350,000	$ 1,190,000
Translation exposure	F 2,300,000		
Translation gain			$ 115,000

Under the temporal translation method shown in Exhibit 9–18, the current assets and total liabilities are exposed. Total liabilities of F5,500,000 exceed the exposed current assets of F3,200,000 by F2,300,000. This negative risk exposure results in a translation gain of $F2,300,000 \times \$.05 = \$115,000$.

The translation risk exposure measured above represents a risk that results from the consolidation of the French subsidiary's foreign currency balance sheet into the parent company accounts measured in U.S. dollars. A depreciation in the value of the French franc and a positive exposure results in a translation loss when there is positive exposure and a translation gain in the case of negative exposure.

Multinational corporations can manage their translation exposure by entering into forward foreign currency contracts. Alternatively, they can adjust the foreign subsidiary fund flows. For example, a positive exposure and a decline in the value of the foreign currency would mean that the parent company should attempt to reduce the foreign currency assets and increase the foreign currency liabilities. A summary of adjusting fund flows between a parent company and its subsidiary is shown below:

Foreign Currency Rate Movement	Net Assets Exposure	Net Liabilities Exposure
Foreign currency appreciates	Increase	Decrease
Foreign currency depreciates	Decrease	Increase

The transaction and translation risk exposures presented are known as **accounting exposures**. Transaction exposure focuses on the outstanding future foreign currency receipts and payments. Translation exposure focuses on the classification of financial statement items in two categories: those affected by changes in the foreign currency rates and those that are not affected. Neither exposure addresses the impact of changes in the exchange rates on future cash flows resulting from operating decisions.

Economic Exposure

Changes in foreign exchange rates affect the competitive position of the company in the world market. **Economic exposure** results from the impact of changes in exchange rates on future cash flows.

A change in exchange rates affects prices of a subsidiary's inputs and outputs in the market, thus affecting its profitability and its future cash flow. A foreign subsidiary that obtains its raw material and labor from its local market will not have its costs affected by changes in the exchange rates. But if it acquires raw material from a foreign market, the cost of raw material will increase every time the subsidiary's local currency depreciates relative to the currency of the country from which it acquires raw material. Sales revenues are affected as well when the subsidiary sells its output in a foreign market. Sales revenues will increase every time the currency of that market appreciates relative to the subsidiary's local currency.

Economic exposure is caused by actual changes in exchange rates between currencies of countries in which the subsidiary operates.

To measure the economic exposure of a U.S. multinational corporation having two subsidiaries in Great Britain, we will assume a change in the British pound exchange rate from £1 = $2.00 to £1 = $1.50.

Exhibit 9–19 shows an example of the results of operations for each subsidiary measured in British pounds and U.S. dollars before depreciation of the value of the pound relative to the dollar. Each subsidiary sells its outputs and acquires its inputs from both countries. Each subsidiary is allocated parent company overhead of $250,000. Each subsidiary shows an operating income of $750,000 and cash flow from operations of $1,000,000.

Exhibit 9–19   Results of Operations, with Exchange Rate of £1 = $2.00

	Subsidiary A			Subsidiary B		
	$	**£**	**Total $**	**$**	**£**	**Total $**
Sales	$4,000,000	£ 500,000	$5,000,000	$1,000,000	£2,000,000	$5,000,000
Operating expenses	1,000,000	1,500,000	4,000,000	3,000,000	500,000	4,000,000
Allocated corporate overhead	250,000	–	250,000	250,000	–	250,000
Operating income			$ 750,000			$ 750,000
Cash flow			$1,000,000			$1,000,000

Exhibit 9–20 shows the effect of depreciation in the exchange rate of £1.00 from $2.00 to $1.50. The competitive position of the two subsidiaries, the reported operating income, and the cash flows have been affected by this. Subsidiary A, which sells more in the U.S. and sources more inputs in Britain, gained from the change in the exchange rate. Its operating income and cash flow have increased to $1,250,000 and $1,500,000 respectively. Subsidiary B, which sells relatively more in Britain and sources less inputs in Britain, finds its operating income disappears as a result of the change in the exchange rate. Its cash flow also drops from $1,000,000 to $250,000.

Exhibit 9–20   Results of Operations, with Exchange Rate of £1 = $1.50

	Subsidiary A			Subsidiary B		
	$	**£**	**Total $**	**$**	**£**	**Total $**
Sales revenue	$4,000,000	£ 500,000	$4,750,000	$1,000,000	£2,000,000	$4,000,000
Operating expenses	1,000,000	1,500,000	325,000	3,000,000	500,000	3,750,000
Allocated corporate overhead	250,000	–	250,000	250,000	–	250,000
Operating income			$1,250,000			$ 0
Cash flow			$1,500,000			$ 250,000

The table below summarizes the effects of a change in the foreign currency exchange rate on a subsidiary's competitive position, operating profit, and cash flows resulting from the depreciation or appreciation of the value of its currency relative to other currencies.

Foreign Currency Rate Movement	Selling More Output to Outside and Sourcing More at Home	Selling Less Output to Outside and Sourcing Less at Home
Subsidiary currency appreciates	Worse	Improved
Subsidiary currency depreciates	Improved	Worse

Managing economic exposure is a complex task for corporations that do business in countries with volatile foreign exchange rates. Methods of managing economic exposure include:

- Locating manufacturing facilities only after taking into account economic exposure.
- Using the portfolio approach. In the **portfolio approach**, the parent company offsets negative exposure in one country with positive exposure in another.
- Flexible planning to take advantage of favorable changes in foreign currency exchange rates.
- Pricing and promotion planning to adjust to changing competitive position in weak currency countries.

Prediction of Foreign Currency Exchange Rate Changes

The measurement of transaction, translation, and economic risk exposures and the management of foreign currency exchange risk discussed above requires the ability to accurately predict changes in exchange rates. Multinational corporations must develop an effective information system that will enable them to track, assess, and predict changes in foreign exchange rates. The system must account for all relevant factors that will most likely cause changes in exchange rates. Some of the important factors that affect the exchange rate between two currencies include:

- The *political and social environments of the countries.* Stable environments have lower risks.
- *Political risk.* Government policies toward multinationals' economic activities and investments. This was discussed in an earlier section.
- *Economic growth.* Rates of economic growth and changes in productivity.
- *Inflation.* Typically, a higher inflation rate in a country adversely affects the exchange rate of its currency relative to the currency of other countries with lower inflation rates.
- *Balance of payments.* A country experiencing a balance of payments problem may devalue its currency in an attempt to improve its balance of trade and payments.

- *Interest rates.* Higher interest rates generate more demand on that country's currency. This results in a higher exchange rate with respect to countries with lower interest rates.

These factors should be considered in the design of a multinational company's information system.

Competitiveness Across Nations

The annual World Competitiveness Report is published jointly since 1980 by the Geneva-based World Economic Forum and the International Institute for Management Development in Lausanne, Switzerland. The report rates national competitiveness according to a complex formula involving 378 different criteria in eight major categories, ranging from a country's government and public attitudes toward business to its management quality and its technological base. The 1995 edition of the report was published recently and includes 48 nations. The United States and Singapore were ranked No. 1 and 2, while Japan slipped to No. 4 in 1995 from No. 3 in 1994. Among the 48 nations included in 1995, Russia is rated last behind Venezuela. Figure 9–3 shows competitiveness rankings of the top 15 nations as reflected in the report.[15] Note that three of the four most competitive nations are Asian.

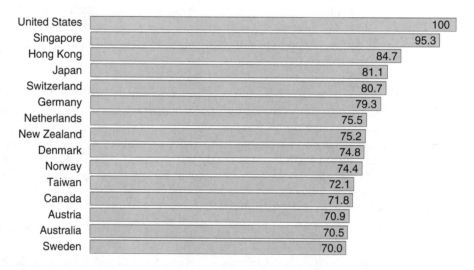

Source: *World Competitiveness Report* (Geneva: World Economic Forum; Lausanne: International Institute for Management Development), as shown in Los Angeles Times, 6 September 1995, p. D1.

Figure 9–3   Economic Competitiveness—Top Fifteen Nations

[15] Tyler Marshall, "U.S. Widens Its Competitiveness Lead, Study Says," *Los Angeles Times,* 6 September 1995, pp. D1 and D11.

Note to Students

You have been presented with four additional managerial accounting topics. They are operating budgets, capital budgeting, product costing, and foreign exchange risk management. Information about foreign exchange is available from every major newspaper. Foreign exchange is a commodity and is traded all over the world. Investors must keep up-to-date knowledge of changes in exchange rates. You may have to do so yourself if you plan a trip abroad. Waiting to acquire foreign exchange at travel time puts your plans at risk if major unfavorable changes in rates occur.

Information about corporate plans for cost reduction, operating strategies, or investment in new plants or locations is available on an almost daily basis in major newspapers. Business and news periodicals such as *Fortune, Forbes, Business Week,* and *The Economist* regularly publish detailed articles on multinational corporate investment and production plans.

Increased global competition has forced many companies to reexamine and reduce their costs. "Rightsizing" is a common business term in the 1990s. Almost every major corporation in the world has announced and implemented workforce reduction plans.

A unique feature of this chapter is how chapter topics correspond to career opportunities. Business graduates—especially those in accounting, finance, and information systems—can get jobs as staff, manager, or analyst in budgeting, product costing, and foreign exchange functions.

Chapter Summary

- The budget preparation process begins with a forecast of sales and culminates with the preparation of projected financial statements.
- Capital budgeting is the process of identifying, evaluating, and planning long-term investments.
- Commonly used capital project evaluation techniques include discounted cash flow, payback period, and accounting rate of return methods.
- Foreign investment analysis must consider both economic and political risks associated with foreign environments.
- Political risk refers to possible actions by host governments that may have negative effects on a multinational's operations.
- Issues in determining product cost include labor productivity, product quality, cost management, foreign government regulations, and changes in foreign exchange rates.
- Accurate costing of goods and services is important for competitive pricing in global markets.
- Productivity levels influence a company's competitive position.
- Global competition has forced multinational corporations to pay more attention to cost controls.

- Assets, liabilities, revenues, and expenses denominated in a foreign currency are exposed to foreign exchange risk.
- Transaction, translation, and economic exposures are related to the payment and receipt of cash, amount of exposed resources, and future cash flows.
- The concept of economic exposure relates to the impact of volatile exchange rates on a company's competitive position.
- Forecasting foreign exchange rates depends on many factors.

Questions for Discussion

1. What are the main purposes of budgeting?

2. Discuss the similarities and differences between strategic planning and budgeting.

3. How does the budget assist in the coordination of the activities among foreign subsidiaries and between the subsidiaries and the parent company?

4. List and define the major components of the master operating budget.

5. Why is it more difficult to forecast sales volumes for multinational corporations?

6. Define each of the following: cost center, profit center, revenue center, and investment center.

7. Contrast centralized versus decentralized budget systems.

8. How do changes in foreign exchange rates affect the budgeting process?

9. Explain how global sourcing of factors of production affects the budgeting process.

10. Explain how foreign exchange controls and cash flow restrictions affect the budgetary process.

11. Define capital budgeting and contrast it with budgeting for operations.

12. List and explain some of the factors that affect foreign investments.

13. List and briefly explain the main investment evaluation methods.

14. What is meant by economic risk?

15. What is meant by political risk?

16. Explain the relationship between risk and required rate of return for foreign investment projects. Would you expect the return required from foreign capital investment to be generally higher, lower, or the same as the return required from domestic capital investment? Why?

17. What are the elements of product costing?

18. Explain how multinational sourcing of factors of production affects product costing.

19. What is meant by cost allocation across national boundaries?

20. Explain how product costing affects global competitiveness.

21. Define, compare, and contrast the following:
    a. Transaction exposure.
    b. Translation exposure.
    c. Economic exposure.

22. A multinational corporation is considering a large sale to a Jordanian company and is willing to collect sales proceeds in Jordanian dinars. Write a memorandum advising the company of issues to consider before entering into a sales agreement.

23. What is meant by foreign exchange risk management?

24. What are foreign currency forward contracts?

25. What conditions are likely to lead a country to devalue its currency?

26. What are the implications of foreign exchange rate changes in the design of a multinational company's information system?

Exercises/Problems

9-1 Sharif Allied Company (SAC) is a subsidiary of a Swedish multinational corporation. SAC expects to sell 216,000 car racks during 19x4. Ending inventory of the racks is kept at a two month's sales volume. Racks are sold evenly throughout the year. Ending inventory for 19x3 was 24,000 racks.

Required: Compute the volume of racks that should be produced during 19x4.

9-2 Refer to the SAC information in Problem 9-1 above. The SAC production manager provided the following estimate of raw material requirements per rack:

Metal sheets	16 ft.
Clasps	4 ea.
Screws	22 ea.
Elbow ends	6 ea.

Production is evenly distributed over the year. Ending inventory is equal to one month's raw material requirements. There was no beginning inventory of metal sheets or elbow ends.

Required:
(1) Compute the quantity of metal sheets that should be purchased during 19x4.
(2) Compute the quantity of elbow ends that should be purchased during 19x4.

9-3 Refer to the SAC information in Problem 9-1 above. SAC's accounting department provided the following information regarding cost of raw material:

Metal sheets	$6.00	per foot
Clasps	1.50	per clasp
Screws	0.40	per screw

Elbow ends   2.50   per elbow

Required:

(1) Compute the purchase cost of metal sheets during 19x4.

(2) Compute the purchase cost of elbow ends during 19x4.

9-4   Rakhshanda SpA is an Italian multinational corporation with plants in four countries and sales operations in twenty-one. The company wants to open a new plant to serve the Americas' spare auto parts market. Management has narrowed the new location to three countries: Brazil, Canada, and Mexico. The International Division of Rakhshanda SpA has provided you with the following information about the three proposed plants in each country's respective currency. Rakhshanda SpA's cost of capital is 8 percent.

	Brazil (reals 000,000)	Canada (dollars 000)	Mexico (pesos 000,000)
Required investment	R 28,200	$ 5,100	Ps 18,600
Annual net cash inflow	R 9,215	$ 1,075	Ps 5,640
Plant useful life	6 years	10 years	8 years
Current exchange rates: 1 Italian Lira	R 4.3	$ 0.0011	Ps 2.8

Required:

(1) Compute the net present value for each plant according to the cost of capital only. Rank the three plants in their order of preference.

(2) Based on your knowledge of the above three countries, you assess the political environment in each. This results in the assignment of the following political risk factors: 8 percent to Mexico, 6 percent to Brazil, and 4 percent to Canada. Compute the net present value for each plant, taking into consideration the assigned risk factor.

(3) Compare and comment on your answers to Parts (1) and (2).

9-5   You have been asked to prepare a capital budgeting analysis for a proposed new plant. Your company, Can Super, Inc. (CSI) has its head office in Hamilton, Canada. CSI is considering opening an assembly plant in North America or Central America. The final four locations being considered are: Austin (U.S.), Mexico City (Mexico), Sacramento (U.S.), and Panama City (Panama). The Financial Forecast Group has provided the following information:

	Austin	Sacramento	Mexico City	Panama City
Required investment	$ 16,500	$ 18,100	$ 12,400	$ 11,500
Annual cash inflow	6,800	7,200	5,100	5,200
Annual cash outflow	4,100	4,300	3,900	3,800
Useful life	10 years	10 years	8 years	8 years

Use straight-line depreciation and assume no salvage value.

Required:

(1) Rank the four proposed plants according to the payback period method.

(2) Rank the four proposed plants according to the accounting rate of return method.

9-6 Medical Instrument Systems (MIS) produces a line of medical instruments. The company is attempting to enter the Japanese market and believes it has an advantage over Japanese competitors, particularly in one product line, medical instrument zooming device (MIZ). MIS has provided you with the following cost information relevant to production of MIZ and its sister product, medical instrument compression device (MIC). Both products are currently sold in the U.S. market. Per unit cost information is given below:

	MIZ	MIC
Direct costs	$1,100	$2,600
Allocated indirect cost	1,800	1,800
Total cost per unit	$2,900	$4,400

Indirect cost (manufacturing overhead) is allocated on the basis of direct labor hours. Manufacturing overhead cost amounted to $3,500,000 in 19x4 while total direct labor hours for both products were 35,000. Each unit of MIZ and MIC required 18 direct labor hours.

A newly hired cost accountant has recommended that for accurate costing the indirect cost allocation should be based on machine hours rather than on direct labor hours. Total machine hours in 19x4 amounted to 17,500 hours.

Required:
(1) Compute the rate for indirect cost allocation based on machine hours.
(2) Assume that each unit of MIZ requires 6 machine hours while each unit of MIC requires 12 machine hours. Compute the total cost per unit for MIZ and MIC.
(3) The average selling price per unit of MIZ in Japan is $2,800. Can MIS compete in the Japanese market?
(4) Discuss the implications of changing the cost allocation base from direct labor hours to machine hours.

9-7 Parvin, Inc., an Egyptian subsidiary of British Manufacturing Ltd., had the following balance sheet on March 31, 19x3:

Assets	(000)	Liabilities and Equity	(000)
Cash	E£ 2,000	Taxes payable, current	E£ 2,500
Short-term investments,		Other current liabilities	23,500
equity securities	1,500		
Accounts receivable	39,000	Long-term loans	25,500
Inventories	26,000	Bonds payable	45,000
Net long-term assets	92,000	Stockholder's equity	64,000
Total	E£160,500	Total	E£160,500

The exchange rate on March 31 was 6 Egyptian pounds (£E) for every British pound (UK£). On April 30, 19x3, the exchange rate changed to £E6.20 = UK£1.00

Required: Compute Parvin's translation exposure under the current-noncurrent translation method. What is Parvin's translation gain (loss) for the month of April?

9-8 Refer to the Parvin, Inc. balance sheet in the previous problem.

Required: Compute Parvin's translation exposure under the monetary-nonmonetary translation method. Assume that the exchange rate on April 30, 19x3 was £E5.60 = UK£1.00. What is the amount of translation gain (loss) for the month of April?

9-9   Canadian Fun, Inc. entered into the following business transactions during 19x3:

a.   Purchased raw material from a Mexican supplier for 8,000,000 pesos on February 1. The purchase agreement calls for payment within 45 days. The exchange rate on February 1 was Canadian $1 = 2,460 pesos.

b.   Purchased parts and components from a U.S. supplier. Delivery of goods and payments occurred on March 1 and June 1. Each shipment had a price of Canadian $250,000. Exchange rates on March 1 and June 1 were Canadian $1 = US$.82 and US$.86 respectively.

c.   Sold equipment to a French company for 6,500,000 francs (F) on March 20. Collection of receivables in francs is scheduled for June 20. The exchange rate on March 20 was F3.8 = Canadian $1.

d.   Granted a loan on March 1 to a newly starting company in the Philippines with the option to convert the loan to equity capital within four months. Otherwise the loan amount of $3,200,000 is to be paid back in pesos on August 1. The exchange rate on March 1 was Canadian $1 = 19.2 pesos.

e.   On May 10, paid Canadian $800,000 to an American software vendor for a new computer system.

f.   Borrowed 12,000,000 Yen on April 1 from a Japanese bank to explore forming an affiliate in that country. The loan and interest are to be paid back after six months. The annual interest rate is 12 percent.

g.   Agreed to send 20 middle managers to attend summer session at Harvard Business School. Total cost of the program is estimated to be $11,500 per person. The session begins on July 15. A deposit of 20 percent of cost is required two months in advance. The remainder is due on the first day of the session. The exchange rate on May 15 was Canadian $1 = US$ 0.86.

h.   Entered into a contract to purchase components from another Canadian company. The contract calls for six shipments beginning May 1 at a cost of Canadian $120,000 per shipment. Each payment is due one month after delivery.

Required:
For each of the above transactions, indicate whether Canadian Fun faces a transaction risk exposure. For each risk exposure, indicate the currency and the amount exposed.

9-10   Refer to Transaction c in Problem 9-9. Canadian Fun decided to hedge against future changes in the exchange rate and entered into a forward contract with Banque de France. The contract forward rate was French F3.9 = Canadian $1.

Required: Record the sales transaction on March 20 and all the entries relating to the forward contract agreement.

9-11   Wheaton Tools is a fully owned Norwegian subsidiary of Minnesota Mining and Manufacturing Co. (MMM). Wheaton Tools produces small tools for sale in Norway. Its budget for 19x3 is shown below. Wheaton Tools is expected to transfer its net cash flow on an annual basis to MMM. Variations from the budget were immaterial. The exchange rate at the time of budget preparation was K5.5=$1. At the end of the year, the exchange rate was K6.2=$1.

	(Norwegian krone 000)
Sales revenue	K 24,000
Cost of sales	13,200
Gross margin	10,800
Operating expenses*	4,400
Income before taxes	6,400
Income tax	1,600
Net income	K 4,800

*Includes 940,000 depreciation expense.

Required:
(1) Compute the net cash flow in krone and in dollars before and after the exchange rate change.
(2) What is the economic impact of the exchange rate change?
(3) What can Wheaton Tools do in the future to manage its risk exposure?

9-12   Select the best available answer:

1. Patel Company expects to sell 200,000 units in the next period and plans to have ending finished goods inventory of 20,000 units. The beginning inventory of finished goods was 40,000 units. During the next period, Patel would need to produce:
   a. 200,000 units.
   b. 220,000 units.
   c. 180,000 units.
   d. None of the above.

2. A sale for 200,000 francs was made by a French company to a Canadian company when the exchange rate was F4.5 = $1.00. The rate changed to F5.0 = $1.00 when the payent is due. The transaction is denominated in francs.
   a. The seller faces a transaction exposure of 200,000 francs.
   b. The seller has a transaction loss of 22,220 francs.
   c. The seller has a transaction gain of 22, 220 francs.
   d. None of the above.

9-13   Maryhill Inc., a Canadian multinational, is trying to decide whether to open a manufacturing plant in Malaysia or Singapore. The cost of capital for Maryhill is 6 percent and the added risk because of the location is 4 percent for Malaysia and 2 percent for Singapore. The table on page 316 shows the expected cash flows related to the project.

Required:
(1) Compute the net present value of each project.
(2) What is your recommendation based on this analysis?[16]

---

[16] D. Cerf, adapted.

	Malaysia (ringgits 000)	Singapore (dollars 000)
Required initial investment	R 19,000	$16,000
Expected annual cash inflow	14,300	10,600
Expected annual cash outflow	10,500	7,200
Useful life of manufacturing plant	8 years	8 years

Present Value of an Ordinary Annuity of One Monetary Unit

Years	6%	8%	10%	12%	14%
6	4.917	4.623	4.355	4.111	3.889
8	6.210	5.747	5.335	4.968	4.639
10	7.360	6.710	6.145	5.650	5.216

Case: Global Petroleum Company

Nooristan was one of the world's fastest growing countries during the 1980s and early 1990s. It had a remarkable 12 percent growth rate measured in terms of gross domestic product. Its democratically elected government—though quite corrupt and often slow to respond because of its bureaucracy—implemented policies that were generally considered business-friendly. As a result, hundreds of foreign-based companies made investments and established production and marketing operations in Nooristan. These firms manufactured wide-ranging consumer goods, provided insurance and banking services, and worked on big government developmental projects. They employed hundreds of thousands of Nooristan citizens. Nooristan also became an important trading partner of many developed countries, supplying them with its natural resources, especially oil, as well as manufactured goods.

In spite of the country's notable economic growth, Nooristan's government faced criticism from a broad spectrum of the population. Intellectuals found that though governmental policies were liberal in the business area, they were quite oppressive when it came to individual liberties such as freedoms of speech, association, and political affiliation. The intellectuals had a sizable following among the students from various universities. The students often went on strike—which usually resulted in violent confrontations with the police. Another source of strong opposition was the religious right. Religious fundamentalists considered the government to be overly concerned about economic and material advancements—often, they claimed, at the cost of losing traditional values. They also felt that Western influence was brought by multinationals and by other facets of international business. In their opinion, Western influence had resulted in the erosion of fundamental spiritual beliefs in the country. In 1996, there were widespread strikes and demonstrations that crippled, and at times halted, almost all business and commercial activities. This fostered additional discontent among the population fueled by shut-down of all means of public transportation, banks, and a shortage of food supplies and gasoline. In September 1996, a military coup overthrew the government. The coup was applauded by a majority of the population, especially by the religious right.

The general who led the coup was installed as the new president. Soon after he took office, he declared that one of his top priorities would be to review all business contracts entered by the former government with "foreign companies". He stated that most of the contracts had been awarded to those companies by corrupt officials in the former government. He asserted that most of those companies were there solely to exploit the human and material resources of Nooristan. To support his assertion, he said that those companies applied lower safety and health standards to their product produced for consumers in Nooristan, while upholding much higher standards in their own country's domestic markets. This, he stated, was evidence of their exploitive attitude and disregard for the welfare of local population.

Soon afterwards, the new government took numerous steps that drastically affected multi-national companies. It started to cancel contracts that were deemed to be not in the best interest of Nooristan. Payments to all multinational companies for the government projects completed or in progress were frozen until it was determined that the amounts billed to the government were "reasonable" and "fair."

Next came nationalization of key industries. These included telecommunication, petro-chemical, construction, and hydroelectric industries. The government also expropriated the assets of Nooristan's 100 largest companies, as measured by their net worth. Almost all of these were wholly owned subsidiaries of multinationals. The industry takeovers were estimated to be worth tens of billions of pound sterling, and involved companies employing approximately 500,000 workers.

One of the most costly expropriation losses reported in the U.K. was by Global Petroleum Company. Global had diversified operations in Nooristan, which included oil drilling, oil refining, pipeline construction, and petrochemicals. These operations were conducted through a wholly owned subsidiary called NoorGlo. By the end of 1996, all of NoorGlo's operations had been taken over by the new government. Global provided detailed information in a note in its 1996 annual report. The note stated that the company intends to recover the loss resulting from its expropriated assets (valued at 1.1 billion pound sterling) by aggressively seeking a remedy from the Nooristan government, both in Nooristan and in the U.K. The company also would continue to demand payments (amounting to 50 million pound sterling) from the Nooristan government for work already completed on projects in accordance with the contractual agreements. The company acknowledged that substantial losses may be involved due to the situation in Nooristan.

Required:
(1) What methods can Global use to analyze the risks associated with the political environment of a country such as Nooristan?
(2) What actions should Global take to minimize its risks after the investment is made?
(3) Discuss the implications of the political situation in Nooristan on its economic growth.
(4) Discuss the likely actions to be taken by the current and potential future investors regarding investments in Nooristan.
(5) What would you do, as a investor from the outside, if you have investments in Nooristan? Provide reasons for your actions.

References

Allen, David. "Financial Management: The Leading Edge of Management Accounting." *Management Accounting,* June 1992, pp. 53-54.

American Institute of Certified Public Accountants. *Derivatives—Current Accounting and Auditing Literature.* New York: American Institute of Certified Public Accountants, 1994.

Anthony, Robert N., John Dearden, and Vijay Govindarajan. *Management Control Systems.* 7th ed. Homewood, Ill.: Irwin, 1992.

Appleyard, A. R., N. C. Strong, and P. J. Walton. "Budgetary Control of Foreign Subsidiaries." *Management Accounting* (U.K.), September 1990, pp. 44-45.

Arthur Andersen & Co., et al. *Survey of International Accounting Practices.* Chicago: Arthur Andersen & Co., 1991.

Bailes, Jack C., and Takayuki Assada. "Empirical Differences Between Japanese and American Budget and Performance Evaluation Systems." *The International Journal of Accounting,* vol. 26, no. 2 (1991), pp. 131-142.

Bavishi, Y.B. "Capital Budgeting Practices in Multinationals." *Management Accounting,* August 1981, pp. 32-35.

Bescos, Pierre-Laurent, and Carla Mendoza. "ABC in France." *Management Accounting,* April 1995, pp. 33-41.

Brausch, John M. "Beyond ABC: Target Costing for Profit Enhancement." *Management Accounting,* November 1994, pp. 45-49.

Center for International Education and Research in Accounting. *Managerial Accounting: An Analysis of Current International Applications.* Urbana, Ill.: Center for International Education and Research in Accounting, University of Illinois, 1984.

Cooper, Robert, and Robert W. Kaplan. *The Design of Cost Management Systems: Text, Cases, and Readings.* Englewood Cliffs, N.J.: Prentice Hall, 1991.

Coopers & Lybrand. *Guide to Financial Instruments.* 3d ed. New York: Coopers & Lybrand, 1994.

Drucker, Peter F. "The Emerging Theory of Manufacturing." *Harvard Business Review,* May-June 1990, pp. 94-102.

Dubina, Daniel E., and David L. Unger. "Derivatives: How to Monitor the Risk." *Outlook,* spring 1995, pp. 24-30.

Dyckman, Thomas R., Harold Bierman, Jr., and Dale C. Morse. *Cost Accounting.* 2d ed. Cincinnati, Ohio: South-Western Publishing Co., 1994.

Gange, Margaret L., and Richard Discenza. "New Product Costing Japanese Style." *CPA Journal,* May 1992, pp. 68-71.

Glasgall, William, and Greg Burns. "Hedging Commandments." *Business Week,* 31 October 1994, pp. 98-99.

Hammer, Lawrence H., William K. Carter, and Milton F. Usry. *Cost Accounting.* 11th ed. Cincinnati, Ohio: South-Western Publishing Co., 1994.

Horngren, Charles T., George Foster, and Srikant M. Datar. *Cost Accounting: A Managerial Emphasis.* 8th ed. Englewood Cliffs, N.J.: Prentice Hall, 1994.

Hosseini, Ahman, and Zabihallah Rezaee. "Impact of SFAS No. 52 and Performance Measures of Multinationals." *The International Journal of Accounting,* vol. 25, no. 1 (1990), pp. 43-52.

Hunt, Daniel V. *Quality in America: How to Implement a Competitive Quality Program.* Homewood, Ill.: Business One Irwin, 1992.

Igual De Montijo, Claire M. "Converting to a Central Financial Database." *Management Accounting,* September 1995, pp. 64-67.

International Accounting Standard 21. "The Effects of Changes in Foreign Exchange Rates." London: International Accounting Standards Committee, 1983. Revised in 1993.

International Accounting Standard 32. "Financial Instruments: Disclosure and Presentation." London: International Accounting Standards Committee, 1995.

Jones, Lou F. "Product Costing at Caterpillar." *Management Accounting,* February 1991, pp. 34-42.

Kaplan, Robert S., ed. *Measures for Manufacturing Excellence.* Boston, Mass.: Harvard Business School Press, 1990.

Kawada, Makota, and Daniel F. Johnson. "Strategic Management Accounting: Why and How." *Management Accounting,* August 1993, pp. 32-38.

Keehn, Silas. "Remember—Central Bankers Are Paid to Worry!" *Economic Perspectives,* July/August 1994, pp. 2-7.

Kraar, Louis. "The Multinationals Get Smarter about Political Risks." *Fortune,* 24 March 1980, pp. 86-100.

Lebas, Michel. "Managerial Accounting in France." *The European Accounting Review,* vol. 3, no. 3 (1994), pp. 471-487.

Lueshman, T.A. "The Exchange Rate Exposure of a Global Competitor." *Journal of International Business Studies,* 2d quarter 1990, pp. 225-242.

Mannino, Paul V., and Ken Milani. "Budgeting for an International Business." *Management Accounting,* February 1992, pp. 36-41.

Molvar, Roger H.D., and James F. Green. "The Question of Derivatives." *Journal of Accountancy,* March 1995, pp. 55-61.

Monden, Yasuhoro, and John Lee. "How a Japanese Auto Maker Reduces Cost." *Management Accounting,* August 1993, pp. 22-26.

Mori, Kiyoshi. "Yen and Cents Abroad, Small Business Moves Toward True Internationalization." *Japan Update,* September 1993, pp. 12-13.

Näsi, Salme. "Development of Cost Accounting in Finland from the Last Century to the 1960s." *The European Accounting Review,* vol. 3, no. 3 (1994), pp. 489-514.

Oblak, D.J., and R. Helm. "Survey and Analysis of Capital Budgeting Methods Used by Multinationals." *Financial Management,* winter 1980, pp. 37-41.

Pflumm, Robert. "Is Mark-to-Market Accounting a Threat to U.S. Competitiveness?" *Management Accounting,* August 1993, pp. 55-57.

Sack, Robert J., James R. Boatsman, Robert S. Fell, Jack L. Krogstad, Spencer J. Martin, and Marcia S. Niles. "Mountaintop Issues: From the Perspective of the SEC." *Accounting Horizons,* March 1995, pp. 30-32.

Shields, Michael D., Chee W. Chow, Yutaka Kato, and Yu Nakagawa. "Management Accounting Practices in the U.S. and Japan: Comparative Survey Findings and Research Implications." *Journal of International Financial Management and Accounting,* spring 1991, pp. 61-77.

Slikpowsky, John N. "Is Japan the Key to Our Future?" *Management Accounting,* August 1992, pp. 27-30.

Statement of Financial Accounting Standards No. 8. "Accounting for the Translation of Foreign Currency Transactions and Foreign Currency Financial Statements." Stamford, Conn.: Financial Accounting Standards Board, 1975.

Statement of Financial Accounting Standards No. 52. "Foreign Currency Translation." Stamford, Conn.: Financial Accounting Standards Board, 1981.

Statement of Financial Accounting Standards No. 119. "Disclosure about Derivative Financial Instruments and Fair Value of Financial Instruments." Norwalk, Conn.: Financial Accounting Standards Board, 1994.

Stewart, J. E. "The Challenges of Hedge Accounting." *Journal of Accountancy,* November 1989, pp. 48-60.

Turney, Peter B. B. *Common Cents: The ABC Performance Breakthrough.* Portland, Oregon: Cost Technology, 1992.

Winograd, Barry N., and Robert H. Herz. "Derivatives: What's an Auditor to Do?" *Journal of Accountancy,* June 1995, pp. 75-80.

Chapter 10

Transfer Pricing and International Taxation

Transfer pricing and international taxation are two highly interrelated issues. Both clearly affect multinational corporations' management decisions regarding the size, type, location, and degree of autonomy of operations in other countries. As will be discussed in this chapter, transfer pricing decisions are heavily influenced by different taxation systems and tax rates in the countries of operation. Pricing of goods and services transferred across national boundaries could be used to shift corporate income to low income-tax-rate nations, hence tax authorities and government agencies in most countries pay close attention to transfer pricing practices to ensure that these practices are not used for tax avoidance. The U.S., for example, specifies which transfer pricing methods are acceptable. The U.S. Internal Revenue Code empowers tax authorities to intervene if unacceptable transfer pricing methods are used.

Different and often complex tax systems are perhaps the second most distinguishing aspect of multinational business operations, after foreign currency. Foreign currency exchange rates frequently change, and so do corporate tax rates. In England, for example, corporate tax rates are set annually as part of the national budget. Countries change their corporate tax rates and systems for a variety of reasons: to generate more revenues, provide incentives for foreign investment, eliminate tax loopholes, or respond to emerging national and international economic conditions.

Transfer Pricing

A **transfer price** is what one segment of a company charges another segment of the *same company* for the transfer of a good or a service. Conceptually, transfer pricing within a multi-division company results from corporate decentralization strategy, with the desire to evaluate accurately the performance of each autonomous (decentralized) division. Transfer of goods and services is common among subsidiaries of multinational corporations. Setting transfer prices among foreign subsidiaries or between the parent company and its foreign subsidiaries raises issues that are not applicable to situations involving only domestic intracompany transfers.

Transfer Pricing Methods

Assume that Divisions A and B are subunits of the same multinational corporation. When Division A sells a product or service to Division B, it would like to receive the highest possible price from Division B. Division B, on the other hand, would like to pay the lowest price. Managers of both divisions are very interested in the price they pay or receive because the reported performance of each division is directly affected by transfer pricing.

In practice, multinational corporations use different transfer pricing approaches. These approaches include market-based, cost-based, and negotiated transfer prices.

Market-based transfer pricing assumes the existence of an outside market for the product (or service) transferred from one subunit to another subunit of the corporation. This market price is often adjusted downward to reflect cost savings from selling internally. The problems with market-based transfer prices are that the product (or service) being transferred may not be identical to others sold in the open market, or the market may not be competitive.

Cost-based transfer pricing has many variations. The lowest cost-based price is the out of pocket or incremental cost to the selling division. This is generally equal to the variable cost of producing and marketing the component or product. Other cost-based prices include variable cost plus markup, full cost, and full cost plus markup. Full cost includes both variable and fixed cost of developing, producing, and marketing the product. It is better to use standard costs to avoid passing inefficiencies of the selling division to the buying division.

Negotiated transfer pricing requires the managers of selling and buying divisions to negotiate a mutually acceptable transfer price. This becomes necessary if, for example, there is no outside market for the product being transferred internally. Obviously if there is no outside market, no market price would be available. Another situation requiring negotiation of a transfer price involves availability of idle capacity in the selling division. When the selling division has idle capacity after meeting outside demand, it would benefit from transferring the product to another division at any price above its incremental cost. How much above the incremental cost? This is where negotiation comes into the picture.

Multinational corporations encounter all of the issues facing domestic companies in the design of a transfer pricing system. Since foreign subsidiaries are separate legal *and* economic entities, additional factors require consideration.

- *Government regulations and restrictions differ widely among countries.* Regulations governing the conduct of specific lines of business are common in many countries. Restrictions may be placed on commodities exported or imported. For example, a thorny trade issue between Japan and the U.S. for many decades has been the exclusion of other countries from the Japanese rice market. Regulations may also cover work force, employee benefits, employment of foreign nationals, and ownership of land.
- *Tax rates applied to corporate income as well as allowable deductions differ significantly from one country to another.* Rates could be as low as 5 percent in one country and as high as 40 percent in another. For example, at present, rates are about 22 percent in Japan and 35 percent in the U.S. In addition, there are likely to be taxes imposed by a country's components, e.g., provinces, states, or even cities.
- *Tariffs and duties are imposed on imports and sometimes on exports in most countries.* This directly affects sourcing and plant location decisions. It was reported, for example, that U.S. trade barriers cost American consumers $19 billion a year by driving up the price of many imported products.

- *Many countries, particularly developing nations, restrict outflows of hard currency.* Some countries have multiple exchange rates with an unfavorable rate for transferring currency outside. Such foreign exchange controls restrict currency movements and limit availability of capital for business activities elsewhere.
- *Different inflation rates among nations affect transfer price determination.* Fear of local currency devaluation because of higher inflation rates triggers a rush to convert local currency into the parent company's currency, or some other stable currency.

The above factors lead to overpricing or underpricing transfers of goods and services across national boundaries. Exhibit 10–1 shows the local conditions under which the parent company or one of its subsidiaries may charge higher or lower transfer prices to a foreign subsidiary. The conditions in the parent company's country would be reversed if goods were transferred from the foreign subsidiary to the parent company.

Exhibit 10–1 Local Conditions for Overpricing or Underpricing Transfers from a Parent to a Foreign Subsidiary	
Overpricing conditions	Underpricing conditions
Higher corporate tax rate	Lower corporate tax rate
Lower tariffs on imports	Higher tariffs on imports
High inflation rate	Low inflation rate
High political and economic risk	Low political and economic risk
Need to transfer capital out of foreign country	Need to keep capital locally for future investment
Short-term investment strategy in the foreign country	Long-term investment strategy in the foreign country
Local market share secure and satisfactory	Competitive position in local markets needs improvement

Objectives of International Transfer Pricing

The transfer pricing system adopted by a multinational corporation is supposed to strike a balance between what could be conflicting sets of objectives. A good system addresses the following (sometimes conflicting) objectives:

- *The achievement of strategic corporate goals.* This means that the overall corporate interest should guide subsidiary decisions, including transfer pricing decisions. Foreign subsidiary management actions are not always in harmony with corporate goals, especially in cases when taking different actions may jeopardize the reported performance of the subsidiary. A given transfer price resulting in higher overall corporate taxes may be a direct consequence of the local manager's interest in reporting the highest possible reported profit for the subsidiary.

- *Freedom for local management to make decisions affecting local performance.* Decision-making freedom is enhanced where foreign subsidiaries are separate legal *and* economic units within the same multinational corporate family. Often this conflicts with what is in the best interest of the company as a whole. No interference, to support the independence of subsidiaries, could result in setting transfer prices not in harmony with corporate goals. Subsidiary A may refuse to sell products to Subsidiary B at a price lower than market price even though the lower price would make a contribution to overall corporate profit.

The above transfer pricing objectives and the local conditions outlined in Exhibit 10–1 show the complexity of determining the "right" transfer price.

Conflicting conditions may exist, making it difficult to set a price advantageous both to the subsidiary and to the company as a whole.

- A foreign country may have lower corporate tax rates *and* lower tariffs and duties on imports. The first condition supports lower transfer prices while the latter supports higher transfer prices. If the foreign subsidiary is a joint venture with the foreign government and the local market is competitive, a transfer price higher than market may alienate the foreign government. The foreign government may also attach great importance to local sourcing of labor and materials.
- A foreign country with a balance of payments deficit tends to limit imports and also to restrict the outflow of hard currency. These conditions may further complicate a multinational's investment strategy. A short-term investment strategy generally favors high transfer prices for goods and services provided to a foreign subsidiary and a quick repatriation of funds to the parent company.
- A foreign country may experience a relatively high inflation rate but at the same time may have a stable political system and few adverse environmental factors. Again, the first condition supports higher transfer prices while the latter supports a lower price for goods and services transferred to the subsidiary.

Conditions in a given country never remain the same. Conditions change over time in response to shifts in environmental factors. For example, policies that discouraged foreign investment in the republics of the former Soviet Union are now virtually abolished and are being replaced with favorable policies. Inflation, taxes, and tariffs and duties may rise or fall, further complicating the task of developing clear transfer pricing guidelines.

Legal Requirements

International transfer pricing has become a subject of concern to many governments in developed as well as developing countries. Transfer pricing policies affect the amount collected by governments from tariffs, duties, and corporate income taxes. In the U.S., for example, Section 482 of the Internal Revenue Code gives the government the right to prevent shifting of revenues or deductions among related taxpayers to exploit differences in tax rates between countries. Preference is given to market price—price based on *arm's length transactions* between unrelated entities. This requires existence of a market for the same or similar products. Two other transfer pricing methods are allowed under the provisions of Section 482. The *resale price method* is based on the buyer's final resale price less the buyer's additional expenses and normal profit margin. The third method is the *cost-plus method,* regarded as the least desirable method. This method is based on the determination of the cost of production and distribution plus a normal profit margin for the seller. The text of Section 482 and its relevance to multinational transfer pricing are presented in more detail in Appendix 10A.

Recommended Transfer Pricing Strategy

Whenever possible, multinational corporations should use a market-based transfer price, i.e., the price used by uncontrolled entities or a derivative of a market price such as the resale price explained above. A market-based pricing strategy is supported by theoretical analysis and also has the following advantages:

- *Legality.* Complies with pricing requirements imposed by governments throughout the world. This clears doubts about the multinational corporation's intention to assume fairly the tax and tariff burdens imposed by local governments.
- *Goal congruence.* Fully addresses the goal congruence issue. Market prices account for the opportunity cost of selling internally instead of selling to outside parties.
- *Equitable treatment.* Ensures equitable evaluation of performance of all subsidiaries involved. Both buyer and seller can readily accept the market forces behind market prices.
- *Simplicity.* A market price based on an arm's length transaction is simple to use and easy to understand.

Illustration: International Transfer Pricing, Taxes, and Tariffs

Let us illustrate how alternative transfer prices are computed and show the impact of different corporate tax rates and import tariffs resulting from changes in the transfer price. Best Shirt, Inc., a U.S. multinational corporation, owns two subsidiaries, one each in Malaysia and the U.S. The Malaysian subsidiary manufactures 100,000 shirts for sale to the U.S. subsidiary. The U.S. subsidiary resells the shirts for $14 each in the U.S. market. The Malaysian subsidiary's cost per shirt is as follows:

Production cost	$3.25
Variable cost (production and marketing)	3.50
Full production and marketing cost	4.05

Market-based transfer pricing. The market price per shirt would be equal to the sales price in the local Malaysian market or the sales price to unrelated companies in the U.S. or in any other country. This sales price would be adjusted for any additional expenses necessary to sell to an unaffiliated party. Let us assume that a Canadian company offers to buy the shirts for $11.50 each. Estimated marketing expenses associated with the sale to the

Canadian company are $3.50 per shirt. Given these conditions, the adjusted market price is $11.50 − $3.50 = $8.00 per shirt.

Cost-based transfer pricing. Cost-based transfer prices would vary depending on the definition of "cost" used to determine the price and the amount of markup. We will look at three examples of cost-based prices.

- A price based on production cost plus 200 percent markup would be $3.25 + ($3.25 × 200%) = <u>$9.75</u> .
- A price based on variable production and marketing costs plus 150 percent markup would be $3.50 + ($3.50 × 150%) = <u>$8.75</u>.
- A price based on full production and marketing costs plus 100 percent markup would be $4.05 + ($4.05 × 100%) = <u>$8.10</u>.

Effect of different transfer prices on net income. The next two exhibits illustrate the effects of different prices on tariffs, income taxes, and net income for Best Shirts, Inc., the Malaysian subsidiary, and the U.S. subsidiary. For simplicity, the illustrations include only the amounts related to the manufacture and sale of 100,000 shirts under the cost structure shown above.

Exhibit 10–2 shows summarized income statement data assuming a transfer price of $5 per shirt. The major income tax burden is in the U.S. where the corporate tax rate is 35 percent compared with 20 percent in Malaysia.

Exhibit 10–2   Effect of Transfer Price of $5 per Shirt

Income Statement Data
Best Shirt, Inc. and Subsidiaries

	Malaysian subsidiary	U.S. subsidiary	Best Shirt, Inc.
Sales revenue	$500,000	$1,400,000	$1,400,000
Cost of goods sold	325,000	500,000	325,000
Import tariffs (15%)	–	75,000	75,000
	325,000	575,000	400,000
Gross profit	175,000	825,000	1,000,000
Marketing and administrative expenses	80,000	425,000	505,000
Operating income	95,000	400,000	495,000
Corporate income taxes (20% and 35%)	19,000	140,000	159,000
Net income	$ 76,000	$ 260,000	$ 336,000
Total taxes and tariffs	$ 19,000	$ 215,000	$ 234,000

Exhibit 10–3 shows the data for the assumed transfer price of $8. This shifts taxable income to Malaysia, where the lower income tax rate more than offsets the increased U.S. tariffs. The net effect is a reduction in combined tariffs and taxes of $15,750 (from $234,000 to $218,250) with a corresponding $15,750 increase in net income.

Exhibit 10–3 Effect of Transfer Price of $8 per Shirt

Income Statement Data
Best Shirt, Inc. and Subsidiaries

	Malaysian subsidiary	U.S. subsidiary	Best Shirt, Inc.
Sales revenue	$800,000	$1,400,000	$1,400,000
Cost of goods sold	325,000	800,000	325,000
Import tariffs (15%)	–	120,000	120,000
	325,000	920,000	445,000
Gross profit	475,000	480,000	955,000
Marketing and administrative expenses	80,000	425,000	505,000
Operating income	395,000	55,000	450,000
Corporate income taxes (20% and 35%)	79,000	19,250	98,250
Net income	$316,000	$ 35,750	$ 351,750
Total taxes and tariffs	$ 79,000	$ 139,250	$ 218,250

Motivation. The Malaysian government would insist that the transfer price not be unrealistically low, since this would reduce its tax revenues. The U.S. government, to protect its revenues, will object to an overly high transfer price. The selling company will tend to prefer a high transfer price and the buying company will want the lowest possible transfer price.

What about the parent company? If we ignore constraints imposed by possible reactions of tax authorities and subsidiary managements, then in this situation the parent would try to shift income to Malaysia to the point where no more tax benefits would be available. The optimum transfer price would be the one that reduces taxable income of the U.S. subsidiary to zero.

International Taxation

Tax issues relevant to transfer pricing were discussed above. Differences in tax rates among nations affect transfer pricing. This section will present other selected taxation issues relevant to multinational corporations. A brief discussion of U.S. taxation of foreign income is included as an example of one country's taxation of foreign operations. Foreign tax regulations affect foreign investment decisions, form of foreign operation, location, financing, and the flow of funds across national boundaries.

There is universal agreement that multinational corporation income from domestic sources should be subject to the same tax that is levied on domestic companies' income. There is less agreement on whether and how to tax foreign income and foreign corporations. There is also less agreement on whether corporate tax should be in the form of direct or indirect taxes, or even whether corporations should be taxed in the first place.

National Tax Systems

Environmental differences among nations account for much of the differences in national tax systems. Even in countries that share similar environmental factors, e.g., Western democracies, tax systems may differ because of different national approaches to raising government revenues.

The territorial and the worldwide approaches. The **territorial approach**, used in Panama and Hong Kong for example, taxes only domestic income. Foreign-source income should be taxed in the country where it is earned. The **worldwide approach**, used in the U.S., subjects both domestic and foreign-source income to taxes.

Allowed deductions. Countries differ in allowing deduction of expenses from revenues to determine taxable income. Examples are the allowed useful life of fixed assets, expensing versus capitalization of research and development costs, and inventory costing methods.

Classic and integrated systems. The **classic system** subjects income to taxes when income is received by the taxable entity. The **integrated system** attempts to eliminate double taxation by taxing corporate income differently depending on whether it is distributed to shareholders or retained internally. Income retained internally is subjected to a higher tax rate. The classic approach is used in the U.S. while the integrated approach is used in Germany.

Direct and indirect taxes. In the U.S., corporate tax is a direct tax on corporate income, while in Europe the value-added tax (VAT), an indirect tax, is the major source of government revenues from corporate tax. The VAT is discussed later in this chapter.

The above differences clearly influence how foreign-source income is taxed. Exhibit 10–4 presents a comparison of the tax treatment of foreign-source income in eleven countries. Exhibit 10–5 shows the different taxation of foreigners and foreign entities in the same countries.

To further illustrate differences in tax systems, major elements of German and U.S. taxation of corporate income are compared in Exhibit 10–6.

Foreign Tax Credit and Tax Treaties

A **foreign tax credit** is a means to avoid double taxation of foreign-source income. For example, in the U.S. credit is given for foreign income taxes paid by foreign subsidiaries.

Exhibit 10–4 Tax Treatment of Foreign-Source Income

Country	Taxation of Foreign-Source Income	Credit for Foreign Taxes Paid
Australia	Income received by residents from foreign sources is exempt from taxation if taxed in the country from which it is derived. Exemption does not apply to dividend, interest, and royalty income from countries with tax treaties.	A credit is available for foreign taxes paid on foreign-source income not exempt from Australian taxes.
Brazil	Resident individuals are taxed on worldwide income. Resident corporations are not taxed on foreign-source income.	For resident individuals a foreign tax credit is available when tax payments are made to countries with which Brazil has a treaty.
Canada	Resident individuals are taxed on worldwide income. Resident corporations are taxed on worldwide income.	A credit is available for taxes paid to countries with which Canada has a treaty.
France	Individual residents of France are taxed on their worldwide income. However, income from personal services in other countries can be excluded from taxation in France. Territorial system that taxes business on profits from France only. A French company can elect to be taxed on its worldwide income, in which case a foreign tax credit is available.	A foreign tax credit is available for income subject to tax in a foreign country.
Germany	Resident individuals are taxed on worldwide income. Resident corporations are taxed on worldwide income.	Foreign credit available. Tax treaties exempt some sources of income.
Japan	Individuals are taxed on worldwide income if they have been a resident continuously for more than five years. Japanese corporations are taxed on their worldwide income.	A foreign tax credit is available. A foreign tax credit is available for taxes paid to a foreign government. As an incentive for investment, a credit is also available for taxes exempted or reduced by the foreign country if a tax treaty permits the credit.
Mexico	Resident individuals are taxed on worldwide income. Resident entities are taxed on worldwide income.	A credit is available for foreign taxes paid.
Netherlands	Resident individuals are taxed on worldwide income. Resident corporations are taxed on worldwide income. Income of foreign subsidiaries is not taxed until distributed to the parent corporation.	A foreign tax credit is available.
Nigeria	Residents are taxed on income from foreign sources if income is brought into or received in Nigeria. Resident companies are taxed on worldwide income.	Limited double taxation relief is available to companies for transactions with nationals of the U.K. and Commonwealth countries.
United Kingdom	Resident corporations are taxed on worldwide income.	A foreign tax credit is available, limited to direct overseas tax payable.
United States	U.S. citizens and residents are taxed on worldwide income. There are provisions to exempt some or all income earned in foreign countries and U.S. possessions. U.S. corporations are taxed on their worldwide income. Income from qualified foreign sales corporations may be exempt.	Taxpayers can either use a credit or deduct the taxes as an expense.

Source: Adapted from Kathleen E. Sinning, *Comparative International Taxation,* American Accounting Association, 1986, pp. 9-11.
Note: Tax rates and policies change frequently. These tables are provided only to illustrate differences among countries, and not for application to actual current situations.

Exhibit 10–5   Taxation of Foreigners and Foreign Entities

Country	Foreigners	Foreign Entities
Australia	Nonresidents are taxed only on Australia-source income at a withholding rate of 30% unless reduced by treaty. Residents for more than half the year are taxed as Australian citizens. The income from sources outside of Australia is exempt if subject to tax in the country in which it was derived.	Nonresident corporations are taxed on Australia-source income. A foreign entity that is resident in a country with which Australia has a treaty is not subject to taxation in Australia unless it has a permanent establishment there. A foreign entity with a permanent establishment in Australia is taxed on income attributable to the permanent establishment.
Brazil	Foreign nationals are subject to the same tax regulations as Brazilian citizens. However, during the first year holders of temporary business visas are subject to tax only on Brazilian income.	Subsidiaries of foreign corporations receive the same tax treatment as domestic companies. Foreign corporations are not normally subject to tax on income from sales to Brazil.
Canada	Nonresidents are taxed only on Canadian-source income at the same rates as residents. Residents are taxed on their worldwide income.	Nonresident corporations are taxed on Canadian-source income at the same rates as resident corporations.
France	Nonresident individuals are taxed only on French-source income. An individual who is a nonresident may be taxed on an amount higher than declared.	Foreign operations in France are taxed as French companies. Branches of foreign corporations carrying out commercial or industrial activities are subject to French taxation. Dividends paid to nonresident corporations are subject to a 25% withholding tax.
Germany	Nonresident individuals are taxed on German-source income at a minimum rate of 25%. Residents are taxed on worldwide income.	Nonresident corporations are taxed only on German-source income. Business profits generated through a German permanent establishment or branch are subject to a 50% tax. Income not connected with a permanent establishment is taxed at 50%. Dividends paid to a foreign parent are subject to a 25% withholding tax.
Japan	Foreign individuals residing in Japan for at least one year are considered residents and are taxed on Japan-source income and foreign-source income remitted to Japan. A foreigner employed in Japan less than one year is taxed 20% on Japan-source income.	Foreign entities are taxed on their Japan-source income. Japanese branches of foreign corporations are generally subject to the same taxes as Japanese corporations. Japan-source dividends, interest, royalty, and rental income are subject to a 20% withholding or less if provided by treaty.
Mexico	Nonresidents are taxed on Mexico-source income. Nonresidents with a permanent establishment in Mexico are taxed on Mexico-source income and on income attributable to the establishment.	Profits of foreign branches in Mexico are taxed at corporate rates. The profits are considered to be distributed currently and are also subject to a 55% withholding tax. Mexican subsidiaries of foreign corporations are subject to withholding on profits actually distributed.

Exhibit 10 - 5   Taxation of Foreigners and Foreign Entities (continued)

Country	Foreigners	Foreign Entities
Netherlands	Nonresident individuals are taxed only on specified sources of income from the Netherlands. Foreign nationals assigned to the Netherlands may deduct 35% of their salaries from taxable income. Nonresident shareholders are subject to a 25% dividends withholding tax.	Dutch branches of foreign corporations are taxed as Dutch corporations. Nonresident corporations are taxed on Netherlands-source income.
Nigeria	Foreigners whose employment income is derived from Nigeria are subject to tax.	Only the Nigerian income of a foreign company is subject to tax.
United Kingdom	Nonresidents are taxed on income from property, employment, and trade carried on in the U.K. Residents employed in the U.K. are taxed on income remitted to them while in the U.K.	Foreign-owned corporations are taxed in the same manner as domestically owned corporations. Any income earned by an agency in the U.K. is taxed in the U.K.
United States	Nonresident aliens are taxed at regular rates on income from U.S. sources that are connected with a trade or business. U.S.-source income not connected with a trade or business is taxed to a nonresident alien at 30% unless a lower rate is set by treaty.	A foreign corporation engaged in a U.S. trade or business is taxed at regular U.S. rates on income from U.S. sources and foreign sources connected with the business. A 30% tax is assessed on U.S.-source income not connected with the business. The rate can be reduced by treaty. A foreign corporation that is not engaged in a U.S. trade or business is taxed only on U.S.-source income at regular U.S. rates.

Source: Adapted from Kathleen E. Sinning, *Comparative International Taxation*, American Accounting Association, 1986, pp. 12-15. *Note: Tax rates and policies change frequently. These tables are provided only to illustrate differences among countries, and not for application to actual current situations.*

When a U.S. subsidiary in Germany, say, pays withholding taxes on dividends distributed to its U.S. parent company, its U.S. parent company is allowed a tax credit equal to the withholding tax paid in Germany.

The U.S. foreign tax credit (FTC) is a dollar-for-dollar reduction in the taxpayer's U.S. tax liability. Tax authorities limit the amount of the FTC allowed to prevent taxpayers from receiving credit against U.S. taxes levied on U.S.-source income. The tax credit for any taxable year is limited to the *lesser* of actual foreign taxes paid or accrued, or the U.S. taxes (before the FTC) on foreign-source taxable income. The FTC limit is computed as shown below:

$$\text{FTC limit} = \text{U.S. taxes before FTC} \times \frac{\text{Foreign-source income}}{\text{Foreign and U.S. income}}$$

Exhibit 10–6   Corporate Taxation: U.S. and Germany

U.S.

Taxes on corporate income

Regular federal income tax, at the following rates:

Taxable income		Tax on	Percentage
Over	Not over	column 1	on excess
$ 0	$ 50,000	$ 0	15%
50,000	75,000	7,500	25
75,000		13,750	34

In addition, a 5% surtax applies on taxable income between $100,000 and $335,000, which results in a maximum surtax of $11,750. This surtax eliminates the benefits of the graduated rates for corporations with taxable income in excess of $335,000. In effect, such corporations are subject to a flat 34% tax. In addition to the regular federal income tax, the following taxes may apply:

Top rate on net capital gains. For tax years beginning on or after July 1, 1987 the tax on long-term capital gains is the same as the tax rates applicable to ordinary income.

Federal alternative minimum tax. An alternative minimum tax (AMT) is imposed equal to 20% of alternative minimum taxable income (AMTI). AMTI is computed by adjusting the corporation's regular taxable income by specified adjustments and "tax preference" items.

Environmental tax. All corporations are liable for an environmental tax of 0.12% of modified alternative minimum taxable income in excess of $2 million.

Personal holding company tax. U.S. corporations and certain foreign corporations that receive substantial "passive income" and are "closely held" maybe subject to personal holding company tax. The tax is 28% of undistributed personal holding company income, and is in addition to the regular tax. A foreign personal holding company is subject only to the regular corporate income tax, but its U.S. shareholders are taxable on their respective shares of the corporations income whether distributed or not.

Germany

Taxes on corporate income

Corporation tax (Körperschaftsteuer).

Germany has introduced an imputation system of corporation tax for business years ending after December 31, 1976. The tax reform act of 1990 brought significant changes, which are in force as from 1990. The new tax rates are as follows:

	Profits earned in	
	Germany	West Berlin
Companies incorporated under German law:		
Profits distributed to stockholders	36%	28.80-32.8%
Undistributed profits	50	38.75-40.0
Foreign corporation branches:		
On total profits	48	35.65-41.4

Municipal trade tax, income element (Gewerbeertagsteuer). Effective rate varies from 11.1% to 20% (except West Berlin, 9.1%) according to municipality. Deductible as an expense for corporation tax.

Net assets tax. 0.6% on 75% of taxable business assets over DM 125,000 per annum. Not deductible as an expense or for corporation tax purposes.

Capital element of municipal trade tax. Approximately 0.5% to 1% per annum on capital as computed for this purpose. Deductible as an expense for corporation tax purposes.

Capital transactions tax. 1% on capital introduced into a business by its stockholders. Deductible as an expense. To be abolished from 1992 onward.

Turnover (added-value) tax. On proceeds of sales and services effected in Germany at 14% (7% on certain transactions). The taxpayer is generally entitled to offset against this tax the amount of such tax charged to him by his suppliers or assessed on imports.

Branch income

Both corporation tax and municipal trade tax on income are imposed on the taxable income of a foreign company's

Exhibit 10–6 Corporate Taxation: U.S. and Germany (continued)

S corporations. Corporations with 35 or fewer share-holders, none of whom can be corporations, that meet certain other requirements may elect to be taxed under Subchapter S. S corporations are taxed in a manner similar to, but not identical with, partnerships and are generally not subject to federal income tax.

State and municipal taxes. The rates vary from state to state and generally range from 1% to 12% (although some states impose no income tax). The most common taxable base is income, which is generally allocated to a state based on a three-factor formula: tangible assets, sales and other receipts, and payroll.

Other taxes

Most states and some cities impose sales or use taxes. Many also impose franchise taxes, which are either supplemental to or in lieu of income taxes. The federal government and many state governments also impose miscellaneous excise taxes on various products at either the manufacture, wholesale, or retail levels.

Branch income

Tax rates on branch profits are the same as on corporate profits. For years beginning after December 31, 1986, the law also imposes a 30% branch level tax on a foreign corporation's U.S. branch earnings and profits for the year that are effectively connected with a U.S. business.

Corporate residence

A corporation organized or created in the United States under the law of the U.S. is a domestic corporation. A domestic corporation is a resident corporation even though it does no business or owns no property in the U.S. A foreign corporation engaged in trade or business within the U.S. is a resident foreign corporation.

German branch. Income received by a German corporation from a foreign source is included in taxable income for corporation tax purposes unless a tax treaty provides for exemption.

Other taxes

Capital gains. Capital gains (and losses) are taxed as ordinary business income for losses. *It is possible to post-pone the taxation of part or all of the gains on certain fixed assets where the gain is offset against the cost of certain replacement items.*

Intercompany dividends. Taxed as normal income for corporation tax purposes, with a tax credit being granted for the full underlying (36%) imputation tax and the 25% withholding tax.

Corporate residence

A corporation is resident in Germany for tax purposes if either its place of incorporation or its place of central management is in Germany. If the corporation is resident by reference to its German central management only, but is incorporated abroad under legislation less stringent than the German rules, the German tax authorities may ignore the corporate form and tax the profits of the entity as though they had been earned by the shareholders directly.

Source: Price Waterhouse, *Corporate Taxes: A Worldwide Summary,* 1991 Edition.
Note: Tax rates and policies change frequently. These tables are provided only to illustrate differences among countries, and not for application to actual current situations.

Example   A U.S. multinational corporation reported taxable income from an Irish subsidiary of $2,000,000 and U.S. income of $4,000,000. The company paid taxes of $800,000 to the government of Ireland. Its U.S. tax liability before FTC was $2,100,000. The FTC claimed by the company is limited to $700,000 as computed below.

$$\text{FTC limit} = \$2,100,000 \times \frac{\$2,000,000}{\$6,000,000} = \$700,000$$

The expansion of international trade and business has prompted many countries to enter into tax treaties to minimize double taxation. The 1980s witnessed a rapid growth in economic and political ties between the U.S. and Egypt. A key component of the expanding economic and trade relationships between the two nations was the signing of a tax treaty in 1980, which became effective in 1981. The treaty's main objectives are the avoidance of double taxation of income and the elimination of obstacles to international trade and investments. Exhibit 10–7 presents the key components of the U.S.- Egypt tax treaty that are relevant to business enterprises.

Exhibit 10–7 U.S. – Egypt Tax Treaty	
Article 1	Taxes covered
Article 2	General definitions of important terms used in the treaty
Article 3	The meaning of fiscal residence in Egypt and the U.S.
Article 4	Source of income
Article 5	The meaning of permanent establishment for a business
Article 6	General rules of taxation
Article 7	Income from real property
Article 8	Business profits
Article 9	Shipping and air transport (profit derived from)
Article 10	Related persons
Article 11	Dividends
Article 12/13	Interest/Royalties
Article 15	Capital gains
Article 25	Relief from double taxation

Tax Incentives

Countries compete to attract foreign investment and foreign capital. They also devise ways to encourage exports of goods and services. *Tax incentives* are among the most effective ways to attract foreign investment and to support exports. A common form of the former is a tax holiday for a given number of years: Foreign investors are exempt from taxes for the holiday period if they fulfill certain conditions, such as investing in a specific industry or employing some quota of native workers.

Tax incentives to encourage exports take many forms. Countries may exempt exported goods from paying taxes such as the value-added tax, or give favorable tax treatment to income earned from exporting goods and services. In the U.S., the **foreign sales corporation** (FSC) is a form of tax incentive designed to encourage exports by U.S. corporations. FSCs must meet certain conditions such as incorporating in a foreign country, performing export functions outside the U.S., and performing substantive economic activities. The income of an FSC is partially exempt from U.S. corporate income tax.

Value-Added Tax

The **value-added tax** (VAT) is a type of indirect corporate tax and is common in Europe. Recently the U.S. state of Michigan enacted a type of value-added tax and the U.S. Government is looking into the value-added concept as a means to generate revenues to fund newly proposed health care reforms.

European countries and the European Union (EU) rely very heavily on the value-added tax to generate income for the European governments and for the EU. The VAT concept is based on assessing tax on each stage of production or business activity that adds value to parts or goods purchased from outside businesses. The difference between VAT and sales taxes is that the sales taxes are computed only at the point of retail sale rather than at each stage of the production or marketing processes.

Example A German manufacturer sells a product to a wholesaler who distributes the product to retailers. The retailers, in turn, sell the product to the public. The value-added tax is levied against the difference between the sale and purchase price of the product at each stage of transferring the product from manufacturing to retailing to the public. Assume a value-added tax rate of 14 percent and the following sales/purchase prices:

	Sales price	Purchase price	Amount subject to VAT	VAT at 14%
Manufacturing*	DM 600	DM 300	DM 300	DM 42
Wholesaling	DM 750	DM 600	DM 150	DM 21
Retailing	DM 850	DM 750	DM 100	DM 14
Total			DM 550	DM 77

*Purchase price is for the purchase of raw material.

Note that the total value added in all stages is DM 550. This amount added to the purchase price of DM 300 paid at the initial stage of manufacturing results in the selling price to the public of DM 850. Total VAT, DM 77, is equal to 14 percent of the total value added of DM 550.

U.S. Taxation of Foreign Income

The U.S. corporate tax system is based on the concept of worldwide income. Income earned by a foreign branch of a U.S. multinational corporation is subject to U.S. tax like any other corporate income. The foreign branch is considered an extension of its U.S. parent company. Income earned by a foreign branch is also subject to tax in the country where the branch operates. U.S. tax rules allow the multinational corporation to deduct foreign-paid taxes to arrive at its taxable income or to claim the foreign tax paid as a credit toward its U.S. tax liability. The latter option is preferred by taxpayers because, as discussed earlier, it allows them to match foreign taxes paid dollar for dollar.

Controlled foreign corporations. As a general rule, income earned by foreign subsidiaries of U.S. multinational corporations is not subject to U.S. tax until it is received in dividends by the parent company. There are few exceptions to this general rule. The most notable exception applies to the **controlled foreign corporation** (CFC). The tax provisions that apply to CFC are known as the **Sub-part F rule**. This rule was introduced to counter the widespread formation of business operations in the "tax-haven" foreign locations. Tax-haven foreign locations are places where U.S. corporations form a paper company for the purpose of shifting income to foreign jurisdictions that have no or low corporate tax rates. The Bahamas, Panama, Liberia, and the Virgin Islands are examples of tax-haven countries.

Let us now look at how it works. A controlled foreign corporation purchases goods produced by U.S. companies at no profit to the seller, and resells them worldwide. Income is shifted from the U.S. to the tax-haven jurisdiction. Sub-part F income is income earned by CFCs and is subject to U.S. tax whether or not it is paid in dividends to the parent company.

Foreign-controlled corporations. Income from investment and businesses earned by a **foreign-controlled corporation** (FCC) in the U.S. is subject to U.S. taxes. Investment income is subject to a flat rate of 30 percent, unless a different rate is part of a tax treaty between the U.S. and another country. Business income earned by foreign-controlled corporations from the conduct of trade or business in the U.S. is subject to normal U.S. corporate tax rates.

Taxes paid by FCCs have been the subject of wide publicity in the U.S. recently. The concern is whether FCCs pay their "fair share" of corporate taxes. This concern is directly related to foreign corporations' transfer pricing policies. Some believe that high prices are charged on the export of parts and components to the U.S. for the purpose of reducing corporate taxable income. Exhibit 10–8 shows the number of tax returns of foreign- and U.S-controlled corporations. In the group of large corporations, 102 foreign-controlled corporations (15 percent) and 362 U.S.-controlled corporations (8 percent) paid less than $100,000 in income taxes in 1989. About 45 percent of large foreign-controlled corporations paid no or minimal taxes, as opposed to 41 percent for U.S.-controlled corporations.

Taxation of Foreign Exchange Gains and Losses

Chapter 6 presented U.S. accounting requirements under *FASB Statement No. 52* for translating foreign currency transactions and financial statements into the parent company's currency. In the U.S., tax determinations are made on the taxpayer's functional currency, the U.S. dollar. An exception is the currency used by a **qualified business unit** (QBU). A QBU is a self-contained foreign business operation. The currency of the QBU is the currency in which the unit keeps accounting records, borrows or lends money, and measures significant

Exhibit 10–8	Number of Returns of Foreign- and U.S.-Controlled Corporations			
	Foreign-controlled corporations		U.S.-controlled corporations	
Companies with assets of $250 million or more	Number of returns	Percent of asset group	Number of returns	Percent of asset group
No tax paid	207	29.9	1,555	33.4
Less than $100,000	102	14.7	362	7.8
$100,000 under $1 million	137	19.8	561	12.1
$1 million or more	247	35.6	2,172	46.7
Total	693	100.0	4,650	100.0
Companies with assets of $100 million or more but less than $250 million				
No tax paid	238	39.5	1,614	34.0
Less than $100,000	88	14.6	467	9.8
$100,000 under $1 million	158	26.2	1,717	36.1
$1 million or more	119	19.7	954	20.1
Total	603	100.0	4,752	100.0

Source: General Accounting Office, *International Taxation—Taxes of Foreign- and U.S.-Controlled Corporations,* GAO/GGD-92-112FS, General Accounting Office, June 1993, p. 5.

revenues and expenses. However, under certain conditions, a QBU may elect to use the dollar as its functional currency. Under U.S. tax rules, foreign currency transactions are accounted for from the two-transaction perspective. Transaction gains or losses are not recognized until the settlement of all relevant receivables or payables.

Example   A U.S. exporter sells equipment to a British buyer for £500,000 on November 15, 19x3 when the exchange rate was £1 = $1.60. Assume that the exchange rate changed at the end of the year, on December 31, 19x3, to £1 = $1.50, and changed again at the settlement date, February 15, 19x4, to £1 = $1.55. The accounting treatment, under *FASB Statement No. 52,* and the tax treatment are as follows:

Under the *accounting treatment,* the original sale is recorded at $800,000 on November 15. On December 31, 19x3, a foreign exchange loss of £500,000   ($1.60 - $1.50) = $50,000 is recorded. On February 15, 19x4, a foreign exchange gain of $25,000 is recorded to reflect the change in the exchange rate between the end of the year and the settlement date.

Under the *tax treatment,* the original transaction would be recorded in the same way as shown above, at $800,000. No gain or loss is recorded until the settlement date. At that date, a foreign exchange loss of $25,000 is recorded to reflect the difference between the accounts receivable of $800,000 and the amount of $775,000 received on February 15, 19x4.

Transaction gains or losses denominated in a currency other than the functional currency are also accounted for under the two-transaction perspective. The foreign exchange gain or loss is accounted for as ordinary income when the foreign currency transaction is settled.

The section on managing foreign exchange risk presented in the previous chapter introduced the concept of a forward foreign currency contract. Under U.S. tax rules, a gain or loss from a forward contract qualifying as a hedge against changes in the foreign exchange rates can be integrated with its related original transaction. The gain or loss is recognized when the original transaction and the forward contract are settled.

Appendix 10A   U.S. Internal Revenue Code–Section 482

Section 482 of the U.S. Internal Revenue Code states:

> *§482. Allocation of income and deductions among taxpayers.* In any case of two or more organizations, trades, or businesses (whether or not incorporated, whether or not organized in the United States, and whether or not affiliated) owned or controlled directly or indirectly by the same interests, the Secretary may distribute, apportion, or allocate gross income, deductions, credits, or allowances between or among such organizations, trades, or businesses, if he determines that such distribution, apportionment, or allocation is necessary in order to prevent evasion of taxes or clearly to reflect the income of any of such organizations, trades, or businesses. In the case of any transfer (or license) of intangible property (within the meaning of section 936(h)(3)(B)), the income with respect to such transfer or license shall be commensurate with the income attributable to the intangible.

Authority is given to the Secretary of the Treasury to prevent a shifting of income or deductions between related parties to take advantage of the differences in national tax rates. As it was explained in the transfer pricing section of the chapter, intracompany transfer of goods and services across national boundaries may be overpriced or underpriced to avoid paying higher taxes.

U.S. tax regulations require that the pricing of intracompany transfers of goods and services be based on an "arm's-length" price. The best example of an arm's-length price is the market price used for the transfer of goods and services between unrelated parties. In essence, Section 482 is an attempt to ensure that intracompany transfers are priced as if the transfers were made between unrelated (uncontrolled) parties. In case of disagreement, Section 482 allows U.S. tax authorities to compute what the transfer price should be. The multinational corporation may dispute this computation by showing why it is unreasonable. Section 482 tax regulations state:

> The purpose of Section 482 is to place a controlled taxpayer on a tax parity with an uncontrolled taxpayer by determining, according to the standards of an uncontrolled taxpayer, the true taxable income from property and business of a controlled taxpayer.

Determination of transfer prices under Section 482 for the sale of tangible property can be done using one of three methods. These are the *comparable uncontrollable price* method, the *resale price* method, and the *cost-plus* method. The U.S. Internal Revenue Service prefers the first over the other two methods.

An arm's-length price under the first method is the price determined from similar transactions between two parties where one or both are not members of the same corporate family. Similar transactions refer to the physical characteristics of the product being transacted. Adjustments are allowed in the price of uncontrolled transactions when reasonable differences exist and can be determined. For example, there can be differences in the shipping and insurance expense portion of the price for which an adjustment can be made. Infrequent or special sales are not considered comparable. The transfer price under this method is equal to the price paid in comparable uncontrolled transactions. The price is adjusted for any reasonable differences between the products or their transaction terms such as additional product packaging or price discount to maintain existing markets.

Comparable uncontrolled prices are not always available. In this case, the next-preferred transfer pricing method is the resale price method. Under this method, the transfer price is determined by deducting from the resale price to an uncontrolled entity an appropriate markup and any reasonable expenses incurred by the reseller. For example, consider the case of Subsidiary A that sells a product to Subsidiary B, both subsidiaries controlled by the same parent company. Subsidiary B incurs additional expenses and resells the product to Company X, which is not controlled by the same parent company. The price for the product that Subsidiary A should charge is computed by using the resale price to Company X after deducting Subsidiary B markup and making other reasonable price adjustments.

Tax regulations allow the use of the resale price method when there are no comparable uncontrolled transactions, the resale is made within a reasonable period of time from the original transfer between controlled entities, and there are no significant product changes made by the reseller.

The third method, cost-plus, is the least preferred of the three methods. As the name implies, and as discussed in the transfer pricing section in the chapter, this method begins with the cost of producing the product. Product cost is determined according to acceptable cost accounting methods. A reasonable gross profit amount, based on a percentage of cost, is added to the cost to compute the transfer price. The gross profit percentage should be derived from transactions between uncontrolled parties.

U.S. tax authorities introduced new transfer pricing guidelines in 1988, allowing a corporation to apply for approval of its transfer prices. A multinational corporation would apply for an "Advanced Determination Ruling," or ADR, to get approval for a parent-subsidiary specific product pricing. The company is required to include justification and detailed financial information in support of the proposed price. The information is considered by tax authorities before an approval is granted. The main advantage is to have a transfer price that is approved in advance.

Appendix 10B   Illustration of U.S. Taxation of Foreign Source Income

As explained earlier, U.S. taxation of foreign-source income depends, in part, on the organizational form of foreign business operations. This illustration[1] is based on the three common forms of foreign business operations: a branch, a subsidiary, or a controlled foreign corporation (CFC). Each of the above is fully owned by one of three different U.S. multinational corporations: USMNC1, USMNC2, and USMNC3. Exhibit 10–9 lists the assumptions underlying this illustration, foreign tax credit computations, and U.S. tax liability calculations for the three multinational corporations. Assumption 8 is necessary for the computation of creditable foreign taxes.

Exhibit 10–9   Assumptions—USMNC1, USMNC2, USMNC3
1. The U.S. tax rate is a flat 35% and U.S. income before taxes and before income from foreign entities is $40 million.
2. The multinational corporations do not file a consolidated U.S. tax return. The effect of filing a consolidated return would be that the income of the branch and of the wholly owned subsidiary would be treated essentially the same. That is, 100% of income would be reported in a U.S. return and the corporation would then get a credit for foreign taxes paid or accrued.
3. The foreign tax rate is a flat 30% of taxable income. Income before taxes for the foreign operation is $10 million.
4. The foreign country is a treaty country that also allows the foreign counterparts to receive a credit for U.S. taxes paid for U.S.-based foreign operations.
5. Gross revenues and cash remittances to U.S. taxpayers are considered the same. The nature of the remittance is different for the subsidiary than that for the branch and the controlled foreign corporation.
6. The difference in the deductions between the subsidiary, the branch, and the CFC are attributable to certain home office expenses that are not deductible in the foreign country unless incurred therein.
7. USMNC3 owns 100% of the controlled foreign corporation.
8. Post-1986 undistributed net income after tax for each foreign subsidiary and the CFC is $22.4 million. Post-1986 net foreign income taxes for each subsidiary and the CFC are $9.6 million.
9. The foreign tax rate on dividends distributed by the subsidiary to the parent company (USMNC1) is 5%.
10. All three U.S. multinational corporations are in the same line of business.

Exhibit 10–10 lists the financial information for the three foreign operations: the branch, the subsidiary, and the CFC. Income taxes paid/accrued to foreign governments are based on a flat tax rate of 30 percent of net income before tax. Foreign withholding on dividends

[1]   The illustration in this appendix is based on an example written by Dr. Stephen R. Crow, Professor of Taxation at California State University, Sacramento. The authors gratefully acknowledge Dr. Crow's contribution.

Exhibit 10–10   Financial Information

Description	Wholly-owned subsidiary USMNC1	Foreign branch USMNC2	Controlled foreign corporation USMNC3
Gross revenue	$10,000,000	$10,000,000	$10,000,000
Deductions	1,000,000	1,000,000	2,000,000
Income before taxes on income	9,000,000	$ 9,000,000	$ 8,000,000
Income taxes paid or accrued (30%)	$ 2,700,000	$ 2,700,000	$ 2,400,000
Sub-part F income	–	–	5,600,000
Cash transfers to U.S.	–	4,000,000	4,000,000
Dividends paid to U.S. shareholder	4,000,000	N/A	0
Taxes withheld on dividends (5%)	200,000	–	–
Ownership percentage	100%	N/A	100%

distributed to USMNC1 by its subsidiary is computed at a rate of 5 percent. Foreign-source income (gross revenue) is $10,000,000 from each foreign entity. USMNC3 is able to claim a $2,000,000 deduction against its CFC gross revenue (see assumption 6 in Exhibit 10–9).

According to the U.S. Internal Revenue Code the method used to compute foreign taxes deemed paid is:

$$\frac{\text{Dividends paid to USMNC1}}{\text{Aggregate post-1986 net income}} \times \text{Aggregate post-1986 foreign income taxes}$$

Using the information in Exhibit 10–11:

$$\frac{C}{A} \times B = \frac{\$4,000,000}{\$22,400,000} \times \$9,600,000 = \$1,714,285$$

We note in Exhibit 10–11, which shows the foreign tax credit computation for USMNC1, that total creditable foreign taxes are the sum of foreign taxes withheld on dividends and the foreign taxes deemed paid. Foreign income included in U.S. income is the total of gross dividends received and foreign taxes deemed paid. U.S. taxable income is the total of foreign income ($5,714,285) and the U.S. income before taxes and before income from foreign entities ($40,000,000). Net U.S. income tax liability is the difference between U.S. taxes and the foreign tax credits of $1,914,285.

Exhibit 10–12 shows the computation of creditable foreign tax for USMNC2, U.S. taxes, and net U.S. income tax liability. The calculation of the USMNC2 credit for foreign taxes is straightforward. It is the same as the amount of foreign taxes paid. Foreign branch operation is considered an extension of the U.S. parent company.

Exhibit 10–11   USMNC1—Foreign Tax Credit
Dividends from Subsidiary, No Sub-part F Income

Item	Description	Amount
A	Aggregate post-1986 income, net of foreign taxes paid	$22,400,000
B	Aggregate post-1986 foreign income taxes paid or accrued, net of prior credits taken	9,600,000
C	Dividends paid to U.S. shareholder USMNC1 in current taxable year	4,000,000
D	Foreign taxes withheld on dividends	$ 200,000
E	Foreign taxes deemed paid by shareholder corporation USMNC1 (C ÷ A) × B	1,714,285
F	Total creditable foreign taxes (D + E)	$ 1,914,285
	Gross dividends received (C)	$ 4,000,000
	Foreign taxes deemed paid (E)	1,714,285
G	Foreign income included in U.S. income (C + E)	$ 5,714,285
	U.S. taxable income (including foreign dividends)	$45,714,285
	U.S. tax at 35%	$16,000,000
	Foreign tax credit (F)	1,914,285
	Net U.S. income tax liability	$14,085,715

Exhibit 10–12   USMNC2—Foreign Tax Credit
Income from Foreign Branch Operation

Item	Description	Amount
A	Branch income (before tax)	$ 9,000,000
B	Foreign taxes paid at 30%	$ 2,700,000
C	Foreign branch income included in U.S. income	$ 9,000,000
D	U.S. income (before inclusion of foreign branch)	40,000,000
E	U.S. taxable income (C + D)	$49,000,000
F	U.S. tax at 35%	$17,150,000
G	Creditable foreign tax (B)	2,700,000
	Net U.S. income tax liability	$14,450,000

Exhibit 10–13 shows the computation of creditable foreign tax for USMNC3, U.S. taxes, and the net U.S. income tax liability.

Exhibit 10–13	USMNC3—Foreign Tax Credit. Affiliate is Controlled Foreign Corporation with Sub-part F Income	
Item	Description	Amount
A	CFC aggregate post-1986 income net of foreign taxes paid	$22,400,000
B	CFC aggregate post-1986 foreign income taxes paid or accrued, net of prior credits taken	9,600,000
C	Subsidiary's foreign income before taxes	8,000,000
D	Foreign taxes paid or accrued on current year's foreign taxable income (30%)	2,400,000
E	Sub-part F income before taxes	8,000,000
F	Pro rata share of Sub-part F income included in U.S. income	8,000,000
G	Creditable foreign taxes $[(E - D) \div A] \times B$	2,400,000
	U.S. taxable income (including Sub-part F income)	$48,000,000
	U.S. tax at 35%	$16,800,000
	Foreign tax credit (G)	2,400,000
	Net U.S. income tax liability	$14,400,000

The equation for creditable foreign tax is:

$$\frac{\text{Sub-part F income before taxes} - \text{Foreign taxes paid}}{\text{Aggregate post-1986 net income}} \times \text{Aggregate post-1986 foreign income taxes}$$

$$= \frac{E - D}{A} \times B = \frac{\$8,000,000 - \$2,400,000}{\$22,400,000} \times \$9,600,000 = \$2,400,000$$

In this illustration, the creditable foreign taxes amount is the same as the amount of foreign taxes paid or accrued on the current year's foreign taxable income. USMNC3's allowed creditable foreign taxes, under the IRC of 1986, is the lesser of foreign taxes paid or creditable foreign taxes. U.S. taxable income is $48,000,000, U.S. taxes are $16,800,000, foreign tax credit allowed is $2,400,000, and net U.S. income tax liability is $14,400,000.

Exhibit 10–14 compares the results shown in Exhibits 10–11, 10–12, and 10–13. USMNC1 enjoys the lowest net U.S. tax liability, followed by USMNC3 and then USMNC2. Income from a foreign branch results in a higher tax liability for its U.S. parent company. Foreign-source income from a foreign subsidiary results in lower tax liability for the parent company. A word of caution: Tax laws and regulations in the U.S. and around the world are complex. Their applications to a specific case requires specialized tax knowledge and experience. The above illustration is meant to present an overview of some of the tax issues relative to the U.S. taxation of foreign-source income.

Exhibit 10–14 Comparative Analysis by Type of Entity			
Description	Wholly-owned subsidiary USMNC1	Foreign branch USMNC2	Controlled foreign corporation USMNC3
Foreign-source income	$ 5,714,285	$ 9,000,000	$ 8,000,000
U.S.-source income	40,000,000	40,000,000	40,000,000
Total for U.S. taxable income	$45,714,285	$49,000,000	$48,000,000
U.S. income tax	$16,000,000	$17,150,000	$16,800,000
Foreign income tax credit	1,914,285	2,700,000	2,400,000
Net U.S. tax liability	$14,085,715	$14,450,000	$14,400,000

Exhibit 10–15 provides a summary of definitions for the items contained in the earlier exhibits for USMNC1, USMNC2, and USMNC3.

Exhibit 10–15 Summary of Relevant Definitions			
Item	Wholly owned subsidiary USMNC1	Foreign branch USMNC2	Controlled foreign corporation USMNC3
A Foreign-source income	Sum of dividends paid to USMNC1 plus foreign taxes deemed paid	Foreign branch income	Sub-part F foreign income before taxes
B U.S.-source income	Assumed	Assumed	Assumed
C Total U.S. taxable income	A + B	A + B	A + B
D U.S. income tax	C × Tax rate	C × Tax rate	C × Tax rate
E Foreign income tax credit	Sum of foreign taxes withheld on dividends plus foreign income taxes deemed paid	Foreign taxes paid	The lesser of creditable foreign taxes or foreign taxes paid or accrued
F Net U.S. taxable income	D – E	D – E	D – E

Note to Students

You have been presented with two important international managerial accounting topics: transfer pricing and taxation. Both issues are technical and complex. Business publications contain many articles on transfer pricing that address international issues and the practices of multinational corporations. *The Wall Street Journal* and other financial periodicals frequently publish articles on international transfer pricing. There are specialized tax services, tax periodicals, and tax cases in every university library. In addition, many well-known accounting periodicals have sections on taxation.

Many issues related to transfer pricing and taxation have been debated recently in the media. Here are some examples:

- Demands for more restrictions on the freedom of multinational corporations to set transfer prices for goods moved across national boundaries.
- Debate as to whether foreign companies pay their "fair share" of U.S. corporate taxes.
- Discussion of reduction of import tariffs to encourage more appropriate transfer pricing for imported goods, with higher corporate income tax collections perhaps compensating for lower import duties.
- Consideration of possible benefits to consumers of tax and trade treaties, such as the recently established North American Free Trade Agreement.

The price you pay for an imported car or television set is based on the transfer prices charged to the importing company. Transfer prices are based on business expenses. Taxes are business expenses. So international transfer pricing and tax policies make you richer or poorer.

Chapter Summary

This chapter presented two important international managerial accounting topics: transfer pricing and taxation. Transfer pricing for goods moved across national boundaries affects reported performance. Taxation is one of the key factors managers must consider in choosing among alternative transfer pricing strategies. Corporate income taxes also influence many managerial decisions and affect cash flows between the parent company and its subsidiaries. A multinational corporation must deal not only with the tax system of its home country but with the systems of all countries in which it transacts business.

- Transfer prices include market-based, cost-based, and negotiated prices.
- A transfer price is what a seller charges a buyer when both are members of the same corporate family.
- Different transfer prices result in different reported operating income and performance for both buyer and seller.
- The market-based transfer price is equal to the price charged by one entity to another unrelated entity based on an "arm's length" transaction.

- There are several possible cost-based transfer prices, depending on the definition of cost in the particular case.

- Cost-based prices are perceived as more objective and are typically based on information provided by the accounting system.

- Many factors influence the choice of transfer pricing methods employed by multinational corporations.

- Taxation, tariffs, government regulations, and cash flow restrictions are among the factors considered in choosing a pricing method.

- Existing national conditions might lead to underpricing or overpricing goods transferred across national boundaries.

- Conditions in a given country can change over time, complicating transfer pricing decisions.

- Market-based transfer prices have several advantages over cost-based transfer prices.

- The tax system of a country is generally the product of its own environment.

- All countries have the right to impose taxes on entities operating within their jurisdictions.

- Tax systems differ depending on the taxation approach used by a country. Different approaches are based on concepts such as territorial, worldwide, classic, and integrated tax systems.

- The foreign tax credit is designed to avoid double taxation of foreign-source income.

- Many countries use tax incentives to attract foreign investment and to encourage exports.

- The value-added tax is based on value added at each stage of production or business activity.

- The U.S. corporate income tax is based on the concept of worldwide income.

- As a general rule, income earned by foreign subsidiaries of U.S. multinational corporations is taxed when it is received in dividends by the parent company.

- The sub-part F rule was introduced in the U.S. Internal Revenue Code to counter the widespread formation of businesses in tax-haven jurisdictions.

- For tax purposes, foreign currency transactions are accounted for from the two-transaction perspective.

Questions for Discussion

1. Explain what is meant by transfer pricing.

2. What are the objectives of a multinational transfer pricing system?

3. What factors are unique to the transfer pricing system of a multinational?

4. What is meant by market-based pricing? Cost-based pricing?

5. How do laws and regulations affect multinational transfer pricing?

6. What is meant by cost-plus price? Negotiated price?

7. What is meant by subsidiary autonomy? How does autonomy as a corporate goal influence the determination of transfer prices?

8. Explain how alternative transfer pricing methods influence the reported performance of subsidiaries engaged in the exchange of goods and services.

9. Discuss how national currency control systems imposed by many developing nations impact the choice of transfer prices.

10. Discuss how tariffs imposed on imports affect the choice of transfer prices.

11. Explain what is meant by underpricing and the conditions that might lead to underpricing.

12. Explain what is meant by overpricing and the conditions that might lead to overpricing.

13. Why do the authors recommend using market-based transfer prices?

14. Why do countries tax corporate income?

15. What is the difference between national taxation and international taxation?

16. Explain what is meant by:
    a. Territorial and worldwide approaches.
    b. Classic and integrated tax systems.

17. What is meant by tax credit?

18. What are some of the key issues that may be part of a tax treaty?

19. What is meant by tax incentives and how do they affect multinational corporations?

20. Define value-added tax and compare it with sales tax.

21. (Appendix 10A) State and explain transfer pricing methods allowed under Section 482 of the U.S. tax system.

22. (Appendix 10B) How is foreign-source income taxed under U.S. rules:
    a. For income from foreign branches?
    b. For income from foreign subsidiaries?

Exercises/Problems

10-1 The Canadian subsidiary of a Dutch multinational corporation sells one half of its output to local buyers and the other half to another subsidiary located in New York. The selling price of $40 per unit is the same for both buyers. Both subsidiaries operate as independent profit centers. It costs the Canadian subsidiary $36 to produce each unit, and 70 percent of the cost is variable. The U.S. subsidiary found out that it can buy the same product from a Brazilian supplier at $32 per unit.

Required: Ignore the implication of any exchange rate changes, taxation, and tariffs.

(1) Should the U.S. subsidiary be allowed to buy from outside? What action is best for the parent company assuming that the Canadian subsidiary has enough capacity to meet internal and external demand?

(2) Would your answer in (1) above be different if the Canadian subsidiary has no excess capacity, i.e., it can get enough orders from outside to utilize its full capacity?

(3) What problems may arise if the parent company forces the Canadian subsidiary to lower its selling price for the U.S. subsidiary to match the $32 per unit selling price of the Brazilian supplier?

10-2   URGlobal (URG) acquired a plant in Poland. The plant has been operating at 55 percent of capacity and efforts to bring it to 75 percent have not been successful. URG expects the plant to operate at 65 percent capacity during 19x4. The price and cost per unit of one of its products, IMFRE, are:

Price	$1,350
Variable costs	720*
Fixed costs	150**

*50 percent direct labor   **Based on 65 percent capacity utilization, or 19,500 units.

URG has another plant in Singapore that uses a component identical to IMFRE. The Singapore plant has been buying the component from an independent supplier at a cost of $950 per unit. However, the supplier has notified the Singapore plant's manager that the price of the component will be $1,000 per unit in the future. The Singapore plant manager thinks that she should be able to acquire IMFRE from Poland for $720, the incremental cost of producing one unit at the Polish plant. The Polish manager has refused, claiming that he must cover his cost ($870) and earn a reasonable profit. The Vice-President for International Business refuses to interfere and suggests the two managers meet to negotiate a price.

Required:

(1) What are the merits of each manager's arguments?

(2) What is the range of possible negotiated prices?

(3) Recommend a reasonable price. Support and document your answer.

(4) Assume now that the Polish manager cannot lay off workers due to local labor laws. What would be your answer to requirement (3) under this assumption?

10-3   Select the best available answer:

1. Which of the following may influence the determination of a transfer price?
   a. Taxation
   b. Tariffs
   c. Both of the above
   d. None of the above

2. A market-based transfer price for goods sold across national boundaries assumes that:
   a. A market-based price is available.
   b. A market-based price should not be adjusted for cost savings due to an internal transfer.
   c. Tax regulations are not relevant.
   d. Accurate product costs cannot be determined.

3. Subsidiary A sells goods to Subsidiary B. Subsidiary B is located in another country that has a lower tax rate. Given a high degree of centralization, this will tend to lead to:
   a. Overpricing.
   b. Underpricing.
   c. A transfer price determined by Subsidiary A.
   d. A transfer price determined by Subsidiary B.
4. The sale of goods by Subsidiary A to Subsidiary B when Subsidiary A is operating at full capacity requires that the transfer price should take into consideration:
   a. Opportunity cost to A.
   b. Opportunity cost to B.
   c. Opportunity cost to both A and B.
   d. Opportunity cost to neither A nor B.

10-4 Dela International, Inc. (DII) is a U.S.-based multinational company. DII plans to open a new branch in one of three locations in separate countries. Initial plans call for selling goods valued at $6,500,000 to the overseas branch. The International Business Operations Division has compiled the following information about the three countries:

	Country A	**Country B**	**Country C**
Estimated sales revenues	$14,200,000	$14,200,000	$14,200,000
Local costs and expenses:			
Variable costs (as percent of sales revenue)	12%	10%	14%
Fixed costs	$2,000,000	$2,500,000	$1,500,000
Import tariffs	6%	8%	10%
Local corporate tax rate	16%	10%	10%
Cash flow to DII (as percent of net income)	70%	60%	80%
Local taxes on distributed cash (as percent			
of distributed cash	5%	5%	5%

Required:
(1) Prepare a projected income statement for each country.
(2) Compute the cash flow to DII from the proposed overseas branch in each country.
(3) The corporate tax rate in the U.S. is 35 percent. What would be DII's U.S. tax liability in each case before taking into account any foreign tax credit?
(4) Assuming that foreign taxes are creditable, compute the DII U.S. net tax liability after the foreign tax credit.
(5) Compute the taxes payable to each of the three countries being considered.
(6) Which branch would be most profitable?

10-5 Refer to the information in the previous problem. Assume that the value of goods of $6,500,000 is based on cost plus 20 percent markup on cost. Therefore, the assumed value of $6,500,000 is 120 percent of the cost.

Required: Assume DII decides to transfer goods at cost rather than $6,500,000. Prepare a projected income statement for each country.

10-6   Patsburg Pleasure International (PPI) is a Netherlands-based multinational corporation. PPI imports components for one of its products from Norway and processes them further to produce its popular bicycle model CBIKEGO. PPI's marketing division sells the product to retail stores throughout Europe. PPI provides you with the following financial information for its business in the Netherlands for 19x4 in guilders (Fl):[2]

Cost of imported components	Fl 5,620,000
Transfer price to marketing division	8,410,000
Sales to retailers	13,560,000

Assume that the value-added tax in the Netherlands is 15 percent.

Required:
(1) Compute the amount of value-added tax.
(2) Assume that the value-added tax is abolished in favor of a 7 percent sales tax. Compute the amount of sales tax.
(3) Compare the value-added tax approach with the sales tax approach.

10-7   A Mexican subsidiary of a Japanese company would like to sell 1,000 units of its product called fredios to a subsidiary in Thailand. The Mexican subsidiary has plenty of excess capacity. The costs of production *per unit* is direct materials 1,000 pesos (Ps), direct labor 5,000 Ps, and variable overhead 500 Ps. Total fixed overhead is 20,000 Ps. The price from another supplier to the subsidiary in Thailand is 15,000 Ps. The price that the fredios is sold to the open market in Mexico is 18,000 Ps.

Required:
(1) If the managers of the Mexican and Thai subsidiaries get together to negotiate a transfer price, what is the range within which they could agree on a price that would be mutually beneficial? Substantiate your answer.
(2) Assume the two managers cannot agree on a price. The manager of the Thailand subsidiary buys fredios from the outside supplier, and the Mexican facility consequently does not produce the 1,000 units. Determine the effect on the income of the Japanese company as a whole.[3]

10-8   (Appendix 10B) Global U.S., Inc. provides you with the following information for 1995:

Dividends received from an overseas subsidiary	$ 2,400,000
Foreign taxes withheld on dividends	100,000
Aggregate post-1986 foreign income taxes paid, net of prior credit taken	12,000,000
Aggregate post-1986 income, net of foreign taxes paid	36,000,000

Required: Compute the amount of the total creditable foreign taxes allowable under the U.S. Internal Revenue Code.

---

[2] The symbol Fl is an abbreviation of "florin," but "guilder" is the term in current use.

[3] Douglas Cerf (adapted).

10-9 (Appendix 10B) Global Trade Enterprises (GTE) is a U.S. multinational corporation with branch offices in 12 foreign countries. GTE reported U.S.-source income of $8.5 million. Seven overseas branches reported total losses of $3.2 million while five branches reported a $1.1 million profit. Assume a U.S. tax rate of 30 percent, and that paid foreign taxes are based on 10 percent of branch income, and these are creditable for U.S. tax purposes.

Required:
(1) Compute U.S. taxable income.
(2) What is the amount of U.S. tax liability before foreign tax credit?
(3) Compute the net U.S. tax liability after foreign tax credit.

10-10 (Appendix 10B) Overseas Production Systems, Inc. has provided you with the following information from its tax planning unit. The worldwide taxable income of Overseas Production Systems including income from the Mexican branch is $22 million.

	Mexican branch (000)
Foreign income before tax	$2,000
Foreign income tax paid	800
Foreign taxes paid on dividends	0
Creditable foreign taxes	800

Required: Assume a U.S. flat corporate tax rate of 32 percent. Compute the amount of the projected U.S. tax liability before foreign tax credits and the amount of net U.S. tax liability.

Case: Vinings International Corporation

The Electronic Division of Vinings International Corporation, a diversified international company headquartered in Atlanta, sells switch-relay boards in the United States and several foreign countries. All divisions are treated as profit centers for performance evaluation purposes. The selling price for these kits is $40 in the United States, where the effective income tax rate is approximately 50 percent. Vinings International Corporation has a 60-percent-owned subsidiary in Chile, which buys substantial quantities of the switch-relay boards from the Electronic Division and sells them to local wholesalers at a price of 20,000 Chilean pesos per unit. The current exchange rate is 250 Chilean pesos to one U.S. dollar. The total cost of the boards delivered to the Chilean port is $30, of which $2 is transportation cost. Chilean tariffs on Electronic Division products are 40 percent on declared value. These duties are paid by the Chilean subsidiary and become part of its cost of inventory. The Chilean customs authorities will not permit the declared value to be less than $30; however, they have no set upper limit. The applicable income tax rate in Chile is 35 percent. There are no other restrictions or taxes affecting the transfer of funds from Chile to the United States.

Required: What declared value would you recommend, as a representative of the:
(1) Electronic Division management.
(2) Chilean subsidiary management.

(3)   Vinings International Corporation headquarters management.

Source: Adapted by Yezdi K. Bhada from Charles T. Horngren, *Cost Accounting: A Managerial Emphasis,* 5th ed. (Englewood Cliffs, N.J.: Prentice-Hall, 1982), p. 658.

References

"Brazil." *International Tax and Business Guide.* New York: Deloitte Touche Tohmatsu International, 1993.

"Corporate and Withholding Tax Rates." *International Tax and Business Guide.* New York: Deloitte Touche Tohmatsu International, 1995.

Corporate Taxes: a Worldwide Summary. New York: Price Waterhouse, 1991.

Crow, Stephen, and Eugene Sauls. "Setting the Right Transfer Price." *Management Accounting.* December 1994, pp. 41-47.

"Documentation Requirements in International Transfer Pricing." *International Tax and Business Guide.* New York: Deloitte Touche Tohmatsu International, 1995.

Doernberg, R.L. *International Taxation in a Nutshell,* 2d ed. St. Paul, Minn.: West Publishing Company, 1993.

Doing Business in Brazil: Information Guide. New York: Price Waterhouse, 1991.

Doing Business in Nigeria: Information Guide. New York: Price Waterhouse, 1994.

Foreign Nationals in the United States: Information Guide. New York: Price Waterhouse, 1994.

Halperin, Robert, and Bin Srinidhi. "U.S. Income Tax Transfer Pricing Rules For Intangibles as Approximations of Arm's Length Pricing." *The Accounting Review,* vol. 71, no. 1 (1996), pp. 61-80.

Hoffman, William, et al. *West's Federal Taxation: Corporations, Partnership, Estates, and Trusts,* 1992 ed. St. Paul, Minn.: West Publishing Co.

International Taxation, Taxes of Foreign and U.S.-controlled Corporations. GAO/GGD-93-112FS. General Accounting Office. U.S. June 1993.

International Taxation, Update Information on Transfer Pricing. GAO/T-GGD-93-16. General Accounting Office. U.S., 25 March 1993.

International Accounting Standard 21. "Effects of Changes in Foreign Exchange Rates." London: International Accounting Standards Committee, 1993.

"IRS Issues Final Transfer Pricing Penalty Regulations," *Deloitte & Touch Review,* 19 February 1996, pp. 5-6.

Jayson, Susan. "OBRA '93: The Good and Bad for Corporate Taxpayers." *Management Accounting,* December 1993, pp. 19-20.

Kelly, Jim. "Leading Companies Face Tougher Tax Line Over Transfer Pricing." *Financial Times,* 17 July, 1995 pp. 1 and 14.

Kilby, John. "Transfer-Pricing Guidelines for Multinational Enterprises and Tax Administrations." *World Tax News,* September 1995, pp. 1-5.

Klingler, John, and James B. Savage. "Deciphering the New Accounting for Income Tax Rules." *Management Accounting,* August 1988, pp. 32-38.

Neumann, Edward. "Transfer Pricing: New Rules and a Flatter Playing Field in 1991." *Business International Money Report,* 7 January 1991, p. 7.

Parks, James T. "A Guide to FASB's Overhaul of Income Tax Accounting." *The Journal of Accountancy,* April 1988, pp. 24-34.

Pratt, James W., Jane O. Burns, and William N. Culsrud. *Corporate, Partnership, Estate, and Gift Taxation,* 1993 ed. Homewood, Ill.: Irwin Taxation Series, 1992.

Sinning, Kathleen C. (ed.). *Comparative International Taxation.* Sarasota, Fla.: American Accounting Association, 1986.

Smith, Carlton M. "Use of Advance Pricing Agreements Enhanced by New Revenue Procedure." *The Journal of Taxation,* June 1991, pp. 374-378.

Stern, Harry L. "The New Statement on Accounting for Income Taxes." *Management Accounting,* April 1988, pp. 56-59.

Stout, David E., and James A. Schweikart. "The Relevance of International Accounting to the Accounting Curriculum: A Comparison of Practitioner and Educator Opinions." *Issues in Accounting Education,* spring 1989, pp. 126-143.

Tang, Roger Y. W. "Transfer Pricing in the 1990s" *Management Accounting,* February 1992, pp. 22-26.

"Taxation in the Asia-Pacific Region." *International Tax and Business Guide. New York: Deloitte Touche Tohmatsu International, 1995.*

"Taxation in Central and South America." *International Tax and Business Guide.* New York: Deloitte Touche Tohmatsu International, 1995.

"Taxation in Eastern Europe." *International Tax and Business Guide.* New York: Deloitte Touche Tohmatsu International, 1995.

"Taxation in North America: The North American Free Trade Agreement." *International Tax and Business Guide.* New York: Deloitte Touche Tohmatsu International, 1995.

"Taxation in Sub-Saharan Africa." *International Tax and Business Guide.* New York: Deloitte Touche Tohmatsu International, 1995.

"Taxation in Western Europe." *International Tax and Business Guide.* New York: Deloitte Touche Tohmatsu International, 1995.

"Thin Capitalization." *International Tax and Business Guide.* New York: Deloitte Touche Tohmatsu International, 1993.

Tomsett, Eric G., and Peter Blackwood. "Documentation Requirements in International Transfer Pricing." *World Tax News,* March 1995, pp. 1-5.

U.S. Citizens Abroad: Information Guide. New York: Price Waterhouse, 1994.

Tomsett, Eric G., Martin McClintock, Otmar Thoemmes, and Reiner Imig. "International Planning Opportunities Through Commissionaire Arrangements." *World Tax News,* July 1995, pp. 1-4.

"Value Added Tax Refunds in Europe." *International Tax and Business Guide.* New York: Deloitte Touche Tohmatsu International, 1994.

Wagenhofer, Alfred. "Transfer Pricing Under Asymmetric Information." *European Accounting Review,* vol. 3, no. 1 (1994), pp. 71-104.

Worldwide Executive Tax Guide and Directory: 1996 Edition. Paris, France: Ernst & Young International, September 1995.

Chapter 11

International Financial Statement Analysis

Financial statement analysis is the conversion of the data in financial statements into useful information. Current trends are making financial statement analysis increasingly important for several reasons. There has been a worldwide movement toward the privatization of public enterprises and the liberalization of trade, investment, and currency policies. This has resulted in a substantial increase in international trade and cross-border investments. Advances in technologies such as information gathering, information processing, and telecommunications has made it feasible to make financial and nonfinancial information available in different parts of the world—on an on-line basis if necessary.

Availability and communication of information is vital for global markets' efficiency. Parties doing business with each other now often live in different countries. They must be able both to access financial information and to understand it to make decisions. Parties making direct or indirect investments or buying or selling products and services in other countries need financial information to transact their business. We will briefly discuss some of the important reasons for an enhanced level of interest in financial statement analysis.

Reasons For International Financial Statement Analysis

There has been a dramatic increase in the activity in international markets. This has necessitated financial statement analysis for the reasons discussed next.

Availability of high returns on investment in other countries. Investors, especially institutional investors, are often attracted by the high returns they can earn in many developing countries in Asia and Latin America. The high rates often cannot be matched by investment opportunities in economically developed countries. Opportunities in developing countries extend beyond investments in the securities of business corporations. They also include securities issued by the governments to meet their capital needs for several reasons. The reasons include planned expenditures on development programs, especially those involving infrastructure projects, and for meeting maturing debt obligations.

Risk diversification. Fund managers are also interested in risk diversification. While individual emerging markets may be volatile, as a group they are not. That is because their business cycles aren't tied to one another's, nor do they move in unison with the industrial world's.[1] Knowledgeable sources agree that it is important to diversify while investing in emerging markets.

Positioning for competitive reasons. Many companies are making direct investments abroad to have a geographic base that will position them to target certain markets. Quite a

---

[1] John Pearson, Joyce Barnathan, Bill Hinchberger, and George Wehrfritz, "Many Third World Players Are Going World-Class," *Business Week,* 12 July 1993, p. 56.

few developing countries already have a sizeable population with disposal income available for spending on consumer goods. Estimates show that currently half of the population in South Korea, Taiwan, Hong Kong, and Singapore is middle class. The percentage for Thailand, Indonesia, Malaysia, and India is approximately 25 percent. This new global middle class is a rich potential market for companies such as General Electric, Levi Strauss, Coca-Cola, Asea Brown Boveri, Alcatel Alsthom, and many others. It is not surprising that many corporations have selected specific countries as their target markets. For example, General Electric has selected India, China, and Mexico as its target markets for future expansion. The consumer demand in these countries as well as many others is projected to grow dramatically in the coming years.

Another competitive reason is provided by the imperfect market theory. According to the imperfect market theory, a main reason for having international operations is to gain access to factors of production. Cheap labor, availability of raw materials, technological knowledge, and managerial expertise are important for companies to remain competitive.

Simultaneous appreciation of investment with currency. When the currency of a country becomes stronger and more valuable relative to other countries, the value of investments made in that country also appreciates. Let us assume that a German citizen makes an investment in South Korea. If the South Korean won appreciates relative to the German mark, it increases the value of the investment. This is attributable to the Korean currency appreciation, independent of the investment's own performance.

Relaxation of equity ownership restrictions. Many countries have implemented economic reforms. These include relaxation or removal of the limits on equity ownership for foreigners. For example, Brazil used to allow foreigners to acquire only up to 40 percent of any Brazilian enterprise; in October 1993, however, the Brazilian government amended this law to permit foreign investors to own 100 percent of any company. Multinational companies are thus able to acquire subsidiaries in those countries, and are in a position to exercise control on their operations to the extent desired. Even a highly decentralized multinational may prefer to have majority ownership in a company via establishing a parent-subsidiary relationship. Such a relationship ensures that the parent company may count on the subsidiary as an integral component of its strategic plan. It provides the subsidiary the direction to align its goals with the parent's worldwide strategy.

Industry and competitor analysis. The companies engaged in global trade and investments often need to analyze financial statements of their competitors and of the leading companies in the industry. This allows them to note important trends and to gain knowledge of their own relative strengths and weaknesses. This is crucial when there are a small number of key players in the market. Many decisions, such as pricing of products and services, are heavily influenced by the competitors' plans, strategies, capacity, product innovation, and development.

Decisions involving business transactions. Financial information is needed to make many decisions in the ordinary course of conducting business. Before extending credit, the suppliers need financial information to assess the creditworthiness of the customer. Financial information is also often helpful in negotiating a mutually agreeable price between the seller and the buyer.

Perceived Problems in the Availability of Financial Information

There are several factors that make it difficult to obtain and use financial information about economic entities in other countries. Some of these problems are simply minor inconveniences. Others are more serious and require attention from the accounting profession, security market regulators, multinationals, and others.

Before we start discussing these problems, it should be noted, however, that the current trend is clearly toward greater availability of financial information. Many existing financial services provide financial information specific to countries and companies. Such information is available in print as well as electronically, the latter sometimes on an on-line basis. Now we focus on some of the issues concerning the availability of financial information in global markets.

Reliability of Data

Many developing countries do not have reliable systems to accumulate data, and in some cases the data collected may be deliberately revised to show a better than actual performance. Unreliability of data is a common problem in many poor countries. The problem, however, seems to be diminishing.

> Still, statistical shenanigans are becoming much less pervasive than before. In much of the world, there are genuinely impressive efforts under way to improve the quality of economic statistics, often with the advice of outside consultants and international agencies. And for good reason. It takes accurate numbers to institute free-market reforms. When rigid command economies crumble and highly decentralized markets take over, governments suddenly need sound data to run their fiscal and monetary policies, says Jan Svejnar, economist at the University of Pittsburgh, and economic adviser to Czech President Vaclav Havel.

> And as foreign investors and multinational corporations expand their presence in developing countries, they require better guideposts on wages, prices, and other critical variables, before committing millions in equity investments or in new factories. "Countries which develop a reputation for not having reliable statistics may pay a price in the international capital markets," says William Sterling, international economist at Merrill Lynch & Co. Adds Carlos Jarque, president of Mexico's National Institute of Statistics, Geography & Informatics (INEGI): In today's world, "we think a country without statistics cannot develop."[2]

---

[2] Christopher Farrell, Joyce Barnathan, and Elisabeth Malkin, "Statistics Can't be Damn Lies any Longer," *Business Week,* 7 November 1994, p. 118.

The above quoted item further states that when free market technocrats gain power in an emerging capitalist country, one of the first things they do is overhaul data collection.

Adequacy of Disclosures

As discussed in Chapter 3, the disclosures made in annual reports vary from country to country. The U.S. generally accepted accounting principles unquestionably have the most comprehensive disclosure requirements. In many other countries, including some industrialized nations, disclosures are usually limited to the legal requirements. Some of the financial statements that are required in most countries are commonly not published in other countries. In Germany, for example, a statement of retained earnings and a statement of cash flows or a statement of changes in financial position are not required. The case is the same in India, Italy, the Netherlands, and many other countries. Exhibit 11–1 displays information regarding EU countries involving the funds flow statement and other selected practices.

Exhibit 11–1 EU Countries' Accounting Treatments

Country	Funds flow statement	Equity method	Revaluation reserves	Reserve account Statutory	General	Hidden
Belgium	No	Rare	Yes	Yes	Yes	Some
Denmark	Yes	Yes	Yes	Yes	Yes	Some
France	Yes	Yes	Yes, countrywide	Yes	Yes	Prohibited
Germany	Rare	Prohibited	No	No	No	No
Greece	No	Rare	Yes, countrywide	Yes	Yes	Some
Ireland	Yes	Rare	Yes	No	No	Prohibited
Italy	Yes	Rare	Yes	Yes	Yes	Some
Luxembourg	Rare	Rare	No	Yes	Yes	Rare
Netherlands	Yes	Yes	Yes	Yes	Yes	Prohibited
Portugal	Rare	Rare	Yes, countrywide	Yes	Yes	Some
Spain	Rare	Rare	Yes, countrywide	Yes	Yes	Some
United Kingdom	Yes	Yes	Yes	No	No	Prohibited

Source: Larry Sundby and Bradley Schwieger, "EC, EZ?" *The Journal of Accountancy*, March 1992, p. 73.

The situation, however, is improving. The global capital markets are forcing those companies that desire to raise capital from cross-border sources to make disclosures that would satisfy the information needs of sophisticated users—security market regulators, financial analysts, and mutual fund managers. The current trend is to make the financial statements contain the information that would be needed by investors, potential investors, creditors, and other parties.

Timeliness of Information

To be useful, the information should be adequate, relevant, accurate, and also *timely*. It is necessary for the users to receive information early enough so that it has not become irrelevant due to obsolescence. Frequently the time lags between the year-ends and the availability of financial information are in months. In many countries the financial statements are commonly published four months or longer after the end of the fiscal year. The delay between the dates of year-end and the auditor's report is shown in Exhibit 11–2 for selected companies. Time lags increase the likelihood that financial statements will be obsolete, and thus useless (or at least less useful) by the time they are published. With the advances in both data collection and information processing technology, including desktop publishing capability, such time lags should shorten in the future.

Exhibit 11–2   Delay Between Year-End and Date of Auditor's Report

Company	Country Base	Date of Year End	Date of Auditor's Report
Bayer	Germany	12-31-94	03-02-95
Daimler-Benz	Germany	12-31-94	03-22-95
Volkswagen AG	Germany	12-31-93	02-23-94
Schering	Germany	12-31-93	03-03-94
Canadian Pacific Limited	Canada	12-31-93	03-11-94
Foster's Brewing Group Ltd.	Australia	06-30-94	09-05-94
Toyota	Japan	06-30-94	09-28-94
General Motors	U.S.	12-31-94	01-30-95
AT&T	U.S.	12-31-94	01-24-95
Dyno	Norway	12-31-93	03-10-94
Orkla	Norway	12-31-93	03-03-94
Hafslund Nycomed	Norway	12-31-92	03-17-93
Reckitt Colman	U.K.	12-31-93	03-24-94
ICI	U.K.	12-31-94	03-06-95
Renault	France	12-31-93	04-13-94
BSN Groupe	France	12-31-92	03-23-92
Rhône-Poulenc	France	12-31-91	02-19-92
Aerospatiale	France	12-31-91	04-03-92
O'okiep Copper	South Africa	12-31-93	03-14-94
Philips	The Netherlands	12-31-94	02-21-95
Scitex	Israel	12-31-94	02-15-95
Teléfonos de México	Mexico	12-31-93	02-25-94

Language and Terminology

Much has been written about the worldwide communication problems posed by different languages. This perceived problem appears to have created no major hurdle in the global economy, for several reasons. English has been widely accepted by business for cross-national transactions, especially in developing countries. Given the current trends, it is conceivable that English will be the language of choice for business communication worldwide.

Terminology differences, even when the same language is used, create varying levels of difficulty. In many cases, terminology differences are no more than a minor inconvenience. Financial analysts and sophisticated investors tend to adapt quickly to terminology differences *when there are no differences in their definition.* To facilitate understanding, computer software is now available that helps one cope with differences between "British English" and "American English." *When the same term has different definitions in different countries, it poses a greater challenge to the analyst.* One would expect that *cash and cash equivalents* would have fairly uniform meaning worldwide. This, however, is not the case as shown in Exhibit 11–3.

Exhibit 11–3   Differences in the Definitions of Cash and Cash Equivalents

	Canada	New Zealand	U.S.	South Africa	U.K.	IASC
Treatment of cash and cash equivalents:						
(a) net of short-term borrowings	x	x				
(b) net of short-term bank borrowings					x	
(c) gross			x*	x*		x
Treatment of equity securities as cash equivalents:						
(a) specifically excluded		x				x**
(b) not specifically included	x		x	x	x	
Specific guidelines on maturity periods for cash equivalents						
(a) yes		x		x		x
(b) no	x		x		x	
Cash flow statement should disclose components of						
(a) cash and cash equivalents	x					x
(b) cash equivalents			x		x	
(c) no disclosure is required		x		x		

*Netting is not mentioned.
**Unless they are in substance cash equivalents.

Source: R.S. Olusegun Wallace and Paul A. Collier, "The 'Cash' in Cash Flow Statements: A Multi-Country Comparison," *Accounting Horizons,* December 1991, p. 48.

Different Currencies

Similar to different terminology, working with unfamiliar currencies requires a bit of adjustment. However, once users become familiar with a foreign currency (in terms of its relative value to the domestic currency), adaptation comes quickly. Most investors and other users of financial statements deal with a limited number of financial statements that are in a foreign currency at one time, anyway. This creates manageability of the currency differences. It would be difficult, and maybe confusing, for even experienced investors and financial analysts if they had to simultaneously use the information in financial statements of, say, 30 unfamiliar currencies at a given time.

Differences in Format of Financial Statements

Financial statement formats are not uniform worldwide. There are many variations involving the order of presentation, the individual items that are grouped in each classification, the extent of netting of different accounts, and even the length of period used for distinction between current and noncurrent items.

In Germany, for example, the order of presentation in the balance sheet is to list fixed assets first and then current assets. The German fixed asset classification includes intangible assets, property, plant, and equipment, and investments. In the U.S., the fixed assets classification is limited to property, plant, and equipment only. Current assets are presented before noncurrent assets in the U.S. The German balance sheet shows the stockholders' equity section first, followed by liabilities. The reverse order is used in the U.S. Exhibits 11–4 and 11–5 present examples of balance sheets of Volkswagen AG (Germany) and AT&T (U.S.).

The order of presentation in the U.K. balance sheet has a unique feature. After the fixed asset classification (which includes intangible assets, tangible assets, and investments) the next order of listing includes current assets, followed by current liabilities. Then a total is shown for total assets less current liabilities. This, of course, precludes listing of current liabilities with noncurrent liabilities. Exhibit 11–6 illustrates the balance sheet of ICI, a U.K. multinational.

Classification of items as "extraordinary" in the income statement differs across countries. Even when the criteria for identifying extraordinary items may appear to be similar, they are interpreted and applied differently. Thus, an item considered extraordinary in one country may not necessarily be identified as such in another country.

Format-related differences in financial statements such as the order of presentation, classification differences, and offsetting practices are typically not a major impediment to the use of financial statements. They are easily reconcilable.

Current Trends in Financial Reporting

As mentioned earlier, the current trends are clearly toward more disclosures in financial reporting. Many external forces are influencing this trend. The major sources of institutional pressure include the IASC, the IFAC, EU, and the IOSCO. The IOSCO especially has had

Exhibit 11–4   Volkswagen Group Balance Sheet

	— DM million —	
Assets	Dec. 31	Dec. 31
	1993	1992
Fixed assets		
Intangible assets	646	631
Tangible assets	23,067	24,050
Financial assets	1,823	2,747
Leasing and rental assets	7,517	7,393
	33,053	**34,821**
Current assets		
Inventories	11,026	9,736
Receivables and other assets	22,517	21,065
Securities	1,119	1,497
Cash on hand, deposits at German Federal Bank,		
and Post Office Bank balances, cash in banks	11,157	7,836
	45,819	**40,134**
Prepaid and deferred charges	**426**	**329**
Balance-sheet total	**79,298**	**75,284**
Stockholders' equity and liabilities		
Stockholders' equity		
Subscribed capital of Volkswagen AG	1,671	1,664
Ordinary shares 1,350		
Non-voting preferred shares 321		
Potential capital 498		
Capital reserve	4,284	4,253
Revenue reserves	5,237	7,547
Net earnings available for distribution	71	71
Minority interest in consolidated subsidiaries	1,003	927
	12,266	**14,462**
Special items with an equity portion	**3,191**	**3,659**
Special item for investment subsidies	**23**	**18**
Provisions	**25,912**	**22,209**
Liabilities	**36,927**	**34,231**
Deferred income	**979**	**705**
Balance-sheet total	**79,298**	**75,284**

Source: Volkswagen AG, *Annual Report 1993,* p. 74.

Exhibit 11–5   AT&T Consolidated Balance Sheets

Dollars in millions (except per share amount)	AT&T and Subsidiaries at December 31 1993	1992
Assets		
Cash and temporary cash investments	$ 532	$ 1,310
Receivables, less allowance of $1,003 and $829		
Accounts receivable	11,933	11,040
Finance receivables	11,370	8,569
Inventories	3,187	2,659
Deferred income taxes	2,079	2,118
Other current assets	637	818
Total current assets	29,738	26,514
Property, plant and equipment—net	19,397	19,358
Investments	1,503	864
Finance receivables	3,815	3,643
Prepaid pension costs	3,576	3,480
Other assets	2,737	3,329
Total assets	$60,766	$57,188
Liabilities and Deferred Credits		
Accounts payable	$ 4,694	$ 5,045
Payroll and benefit-related liabilities	3,746	3,336
Postretirement and postemployment benefit liabilities	1,301	—
Debt maturing within one year	10,904	7,600
Dividends payable	448	443
Other current liabilities	4,241	4,962
Total current liabilities	25,334	21,386
Long-term debt including capital leases	6,812	8,604
Postretirement and postemployment benefit liabilities	9,082	—
Other liabilities	4,298	2,634
Deferred income taxes	275	4,660
Unamortized investment tax credits	270	350
Other deferred credits	263	181
Total liabilities and deferred credits	46,334	37,815
Minority interests	582	452
Shareowners' Equity		
Common shares par value $1 per share	1,352	1,340
Authorized shares: 2,000,000,000		
Outstanding shares: 1,352,398,000 at December 31, 1993; 1,339,831,000 at December 31, 1992		
Additional paid-in capital	12,028	11,425
Guaranteed ESOP obligation	(355)	(407)
Foreign currency translation adjustments	(32)	65
Retained earnings	857	6,498
Total shareowners' equity	13,850	18,921
Total liabilities and shareowners' equity	$60,766	$57,188

Source: AT&T, 1993 Annual Report, p. 32

Exhibit 11–6   ICI Balance Sheets

At 31 December	Group 1993 £m	Group 1992 £m	Company 1993 £m	Company 1992 £m
ASSETS EMPLOYED				
Fixed assets				
Tangible assets	4,024	5,634	311	353
Investments				
Subsidiary undertakings			6,179	5,800
Participating interests	458	455	268	255
	4,482	6,089	6,758	6,408
Current assets				
Stocks	1,199	2,273	70	417
Debtors	1,887	3,033	1,033	4,641
Investments and short-term deposits	1,467	507	629	–
Cash	194	220	31	12
	4,747	6,033	1,763	5,070
Total assets	9,229	12,122	8,521	11,478
Creditors due within one year				
Short-term borrowings	(145)	(671)	(1)	(17)
Current installments of loans	(220)	(282)	(62)	(75)
Other creditors	(2,087)	(3,424)	(3,774)	(6,031)
	(2,452)	(4,377)	(3,837)	(6,123)
Net current assets (liabilities)	2,295	1,656	(2,074)	(1,053)
Total assets less current liabilities	6,777	7,745	4,684	5,355
FINANCED BY				
Creditors due after more than one year				
Loans	1,717	1,984	263	325
Other creditors	123	168	1,190	1,207
	1,840	2,152	1,453	1,532
Provision for liabilities and charges	585	956	48	35
Deferred Income: Grants not yet credited to profit	39	49	1	4
Minority interests	330	302		
Capital and reserves attributable to parent company				
Called-up share capital	722	714	722	714
Reserves				
Share premium account	561	502	561	502
Revaluation reserve	46	63	–	–
Other reserves		546		541
Profit and loss account	2,588	2,428	1,899	2,027
Associated undertakings' reserves	66	33		
Total reserves	3,261	3,572	2,460	3,070
Total capital and reserves attributable to parent company	3,983	4,286	3,182	3,784
	6,777	7,745	4,684	5,355

Source: ICI, *Annual Report and Accounts 1993*, p. 11.

a major and notable impact because of capital markets globalization and its support of harmonization efforts of the IASC and the IFAC. EU directives have a force of law for the member countries. All member countries, within the range of flexibility allowed, must adhere to the EU directives. The standards issued by the IASC and the IFAC are having increasingly more influence. Many countries and individual companies are voluntarily adopting the standards issued by these two organizations. For example, as of January 1, 1993, Renault adopted the IASC standards for its consolidated financial statements. The *audited* consolidated financial statements of Renault Group for the year ended December 31, 1993 were prepared in accordance with the IASC standards.

In the final analysis, perhaps the most important factor providing momentum toward greater disclosure is the self-interest motive. The players in international markets will be motivated to provide voluntary disclosures if this would help achieve their investment and trade goals. They would do so regardless of the domestic disclosure requirements. *The globalization of markets may thus turn out to be the motivating factor for greater disclosure and harmonization of accounting and auditing principles worldwide.*

Diversity of Accounting Principles and Business Practices

Notwithstanding the trend toward greater disclosure, the lack of harmonization of accounting principles remains a major obstacle for financial statements users outside the country where the issuing company is based. Financial measurement of attributes is heavily influenced by accounting principles. *This leads to an important observation: Different accounting practices may result in reported differences while in fact there may not be any real differences.* According to a study conducted by Schieneman, differences in accounting principles had a significant impact on the financial statements of most of the companies included in the study. When adjusted to U.S. GAAP, net income of one U.K.-based company *dropped* by 27.1 percent, while the net income of a German-based company *went up* by 40.1 percent. The restatement had even more effect on shareholders' equity. The shareholders' equity change was in the range of -32.5 to +60.1 percent. Interestingly, both of these companies were U.K.-based.[3]

Practices in some countries include income smoothing through the use of reserves, or entering irregular items (such as income or loss from discontinued operations) directly into retained earning. As mentioned in Chapter 3, a restatement from one accounting framework to another can be helpful in overcoming such problems. With the information available about the items that are treated differently, the restatement adjustments can easily be made.

An alternative to restatement of financial statements would be to develop the capability to understand and interpret the local generally accepted accounting principles. While it may not be a viable alternative for individuals making their investment decisions, it may be feasible for institutional and corporate investors. The latter may find developing the expertise cost-effective.

---

[3] Gary S. Schieneman, "The Effect of Accounting Differences on Cross Border Comparisons," *International Accounting and Investment Review,* 29 April 1988, pp. 1-14.

Some investment managers prefer not to invest their resources in restatement of financial statements or on developing facility for using local GAAP. They instead feel that they can achieve satisfactory results by diversifying their portfolios to earn desired returns at acceptable risk levels. This approach, admittedly, may not provide the optimal returns per se but may be acceptable if neither of the two analytical approaches discussed above are considered cost-effective in the given situation.

Different business practices. The major problem is not attributable to different accounting practices. Those can be managed to varying levels of satisfaction, as discussed above. *The major problem in financial statement analysis is the influence of different business operating environments.* The interpretation of financial statement analysis is made difficult by differing business practices among countries. An example is the debt ratio of Japanese companies. Japanese companies are typically heavily leveraged. Japanese banks willingly loan funds to the companies considered to have good earning potential. Since the bankers work closely with company management, they are in a position to be aware of the financing needs of the company and also its ability to pay back borrowings. Consequently, the companies tend to rely significantly on debt, rather than equity, as a source of capital.

It is of utmost importance to understand cultural and economic differences to correctly analyze financial statements. The presence of significant environmental differences in which businesses operate makes this understanding critical.

Financial Statement Analysis

The objective of financial statement analysis is to extract useful information for decision making. To accomplish this, a variety of approaches can be used. One approach is to rely on the annual report that includes financial statements, schedules, the notes accompanying the statements, and other important information. The other information contained in the annual report usually discusses management policies, product development and product innovation, market conditions, and the company's plans. A careful review of the annual report may provide an understanding of the company's operating performance, financial position, and possibly its future potential within the context of its operating environment. In this approach no comparison is made with another firm. The complexities associated with international comparisons are thus avoided.

If a comparison between, or among, firms is desired, then two financial analysis alternatives are available. **Financial ratio analysis** enables comparability across firms, i.e., interfirm comparisons. **Trend analysis**, the second alternative, provides intrafirm as well as interfirm comparisons for two or more periods or dates. In the subsequent sections we will discuss these two techniques of financial analysis and related issues.

Financial Ratio Analysis

Financial ratio analysis is done for the evaluation of financial performance and financial position. This helps assess factors such as credit risk and earnings potential. It is also helpful in decision making. If the financial statements of a foreign-based company are not restated, this fact should be taken into account while performing financial statement analysis. The analyst should understand the accounting framework on which the accounting statements have been prepared, and also should understand the foreign business practices and the operating environment. *This is to emphasize that simply restating the statements is not enough to avoid misleading conclusions based on financial statement analysis.*

Ratio analysis is the starting point in developing information desired by the analyst. Ratio analysis is generally classified as described below.[4]

Liquidity ratios. Measures of the enterprise's short-run ability to pay its maturing obligations. Also called *solvency ratios.*

Activity ratios. Measures of how effectively the enterprise is using the assets employed. Also called *turnover ratios* or *efficiency ratios.*

Profitability ratios. Measures of the degree of success or failure of a given enterprise or division for a given period of time.

Coverage ratios. Measures of the degree of protection for long-term creditors and investors. Also called *leverage ratios* or *capital structure ratios.*

Some of the common financial statement ratios are shown for each classification in Exhibit 11–7 on the following page.

Ratios based on the same amounts will be the same regardless of the currency. Therefore, it is unnecessary to convert amounts expressed in different currencies to a single currency. Doing so would not change the ratios.

Example A French company's current assets are F 2.5 million and current liabilities amount to F 2.0 million. The convenience translation (year-end exchange) rate is $1.00 = F 5.2

Current ratio using amounts in F $\quad \dfrac{2,500,000}{2,000,000} \quad = \quad 1.25 \text{ to } 1$

Current ratio using amounts in $ $\quad \dfrac{2,500,000 \div 5.2}{2,000,000 \div 5.2} \quad = \quad 1.25 \text{ to } 1$

This example illustrates that financial ratio analysis can be performed without converting amounts expressed in different currencies to a single currency.

---

[4] Donald E. Kieso and Jerry J. Weygandt, *Intermediate Accounting,* 8th ed (New York: John Wiley & Sons, Inc., 1995), pp. 1301-1303.

Exhibit 11–7	**Common Financial Ratios**	
Classification	**Ratio**	**Computation**
Liquidity	Current ratio	$\dfrac{\text{Current assets}}{\text{Current liabilities}}$
	To determine ability to meet short-term debt.	
Activity	Inventory turnover	$\dfrac{\text{Cost of goods sold}}{\text{Average inventory}}$
	To measure how quickly inventory is sold.	
Profitability	Profit margin	$\dfrac{\text{Net income}}{\text{Sales}}$
	To compare margin to competitors' margins.	
	Rate of return on assets	$\dfrac{\text{Net income}}{\text{Average total assets}}$
	To measure competitive profit efficiency of assets.	
	Rate of return on net worth	$\dfrac{\text{Net income}}{\text{Average net worth}}$
	To measure profit efficiency of stockholders' assets.	
Coverage	Debt ratio	$\dfrac{\text{Debt}}{\text{Total assets}}$
	To analyze the ability to meet long-term debt.	

General Limitations of Financial Ratio Analysis

Ratio analysis has several *general limitations* besides the complexity introduced by different accounting frameworks and business practices worldwide.

- Financial ratios are based on historical cost in most countries. The users may, however, make the erroneous assumption that the costs reflect current prices. The result may be poor decisions.
- In the presence of substantial amounts involving estimates—such as depreciation and amortization—the ratios lose their effectiveness for intercompany comparisons.
- Different companies use different alternatives allowed by accounting standards. Examples include:
  - ✓ Inventory valuation: LIFO, FIFO
  - ✓ Depreciation methods: straight-line, double-declining balance.
  - ✓ Treatment of irregular items: discontinued operations, extraordinary items.

Use of different methods within the same accounting framework makes intercompany comparisons difficult.

- Many important informational items are not included in financial statements. Examples include labor relations, technological developments, investment in new technology, and competitors' actions. Though important to a company's future, these do not enter the accounting system. Omission of such information in the ratios limits their usefulness.

International Financial Ratio Analysis

The above general limitations of financial ratio analysis are intensified in the international context.

- Though many countries have ratios based on historical cost, other countries' financial statements are prepared using current cost basis, hybrid historical-current cost basis, or historical costs basis adjusted for general price-level changes. Argentina, for example, uses current cost, while the U.K. has a hybrid of historical-current costs. In Mexico, historical-cost-based statements are adjusted for general price level changes.

- The varying levels of flexibility for estimating specific items allowed in different countries makes the ratio comparisons more difficult. For example, a maximum of 40 years is allowed for amortization of goodwill in the U.S. Under German accounting regulation, the amortization period for goodwill ranges between 5 to 15 years.

  The acceptable alternatives in the application of accounting principles vary among countries. For example, there is little comparability internationally in accounting treatment of unusual and extraordinary items. In the U.S., the events and transactions considered to be both unusual and infrequent in occurrence are considered extraordinary items. They are required to be segregated from the results of continuing operations, and reported separately on the income statement. In Germany, the Commercial Code requires that extraordinary amounts be disclosed in notes. There is no disclosure requirement in Italy.

  Another example involves discontinued operations. There are no disclosure requirements involving discontinued operations in Germany and Japan. In the Netherlands, the assets of an operation to be discontinued in the near future are valued at net realizable value, and this fact is required to be discussed in the notes. In the U.S., there are detailed reporting and disclosure requirements for discontinued operations. These include their separate reporting from continuing operations and immediate recognition of estimated future operating and disposal losses.

- As discussed earlier, ratio analysis suffers in general from omission of some important information, such as the company's emphasis on product innovation. The problem is exacerbated by the fact that some information that is required to be disclosed in the financial reports in some countries is altogether omitted in other countries. For example, in South Korea no contingent losses are accrued. In Spain, accounting law gives little guidance on loss contingencies and does not address treatment of gain contingencies at all. In Argentina, gain contingencies are accrued if highly probable. In China, there are no accounting treatments or disclosure requirements for contingencies. The current practice in China is that contingent gains or losses are neither accrued nor disclosed. In the U.S., contingent gains are not recorded, and contingent losses may or may not be accrued or disclosed depending on specific circumstances.

- The above discussion focused on the *intensifying effect* of internationalization on the limitations of financial ratio analysis. We will next discuss financial statement analysis in an international context.

Different accounting frameworks. Accounting frameworks differ from country to country. In the absence of restated financial statements, comparison of financial ratios of different companies' financial statements prepared using different accounting framework is a futile exercise.

Different operating environments. Business practices are not uniform throughout the world. If the user of financial analysis is not knowledgeable about the differences, it is quite likely that wrong conclusions will be drawn. The restatement of financial statements alone is not enough to overcome this problem. As mentioned earlier, Japanese companies typically have relatively higher debt to equity ratios than comparable U.S. companies. Knowledgeable analysts would correctly interpret this as a direct result of Japanese business customs. They would know that banks in Japan work closely with their clients' firms and are willing to lend heavily to those considered sound. A Japanese firm's high debt to equity ratio, therefore, indicates bankers' confidence in its management and its earning potential—a positive interpretation rather than a negative reflection on the company's leverage position.

Business practices may also affect profit margins. In some countries it is acceptable to arbitrarily make charges against income to achieve income smoothing. This practice is not allowed in other countries. *This directly affects reported profitability and other ratios, not because of the real income differences, but because of the diversity in income smoothing practices.* This again highlights the importance of understanding business practices in the countries whose financial statements are being analyzed.

The orientation of financial statements poses another challenge. In many countries financial statements are oriented toward investors; in other countries, the orientation is toward creditors. This influences the information content of financial statements, and also the extent to which detailed disclosures are made on individual items.

Influence of tax laws. In order to reduce taxes, it is common practice in some countries to prepare financial statements that purposely minimize reported income. In Italy, the tax law generally applies to any profit presented in financial statements, even if such profit is not required to be recognized according to tax regulations. In Germany, there are many areas where an accounting method selected for income tax purposes is required for financial reporting. Consequently, there are few differences in Germany between income for taxation and income for financial reporting.

Data accuracy. It was mentioned in an earlier section of this chapter that many developing countries do not have the systems capability to collect reliable data. Also, in some cases the data may be deliberately changed to show better than actual performance. The ratios are only as good as the data upon which they are based and the information with which they are compared.[5] Ratios based on inaccurate data would obviously be inaccurate and unreliable for comparison.

Case Study 1: Daimler-Benz

Daimler-Benz was the first German company to list its stock on the New York Stock Exchange. The company reconciled its net income and stockholders' equity to U.S. GAAP—as required by the U.S. Securities and Exchange Commission. Exhibit 11–8 contains a reconciliation of net income, and Exhibit 11–9 shows a reconciliation of stockholders' equity. These two exhibits reconcile the amounts determined in accordance with

Exhibit 11–8   Daimler-Benz Reconciliation of Net Income to U.S. GAAP

	1993	1992
	– in Millions of DM –	
Consolidated net income in accordance with German HGB (Commercial Code)	615	1,451
·/. Minority interest	(13)	(33)
Adjusted net income under German regulations	602	1,418
+/– Changes in appropriated retained earnings:		
provisions, reserves and valuation differences	(4,262)	774
	(3,660)	2,192
Additional adjustments		
+/– Long-term contracts	78	(57)
Goodwill and business acquisitions	(287)	(76)
Business dispositions	–	337
Pensions and other postretirement benefits	(624)	96
Foreign currency translation	(40)	(94)
Financial instruments	(225)	(438)
Other valuation differences	292	88
Deferred taxes	2,627	(646)
Consolidated net income (loss) in accordance with U.S. GAAP		
before cumulative effect of changes in accounting principles		
in accordance with U.S. GAAP	(1,839)	1,402
Cumulative effect of changes in accounting in accordance with U.S. GAAP		
for postretirement benefits other than pensions		
(net of tax of 33 million DM)	–	(52)
Consolidated net profit in accordance with U.S. GAAP	(1,839)	1,350

Source: Daimler-Benz, *Annual Report 1993*, p. 73.

[5] Kieso and Weygandt, p. 1316.

the principles of the German Commercial Code (Handelsgesetzbuch) to those under U.S. GAAP. A review of Exhibit 11–8 demonstrates the drastic impact of the restatement on Daimler's 1993 consolidated net income. Under the German Commercial Code, there was net income in the amount of DM 615 million. A net loss of DM 1.839 billion is reported according to U.S. GAAP for the same period. Based on the information contained in Exhibits 11–8 and 11–9, two profitability ratios are computed in Exhibit 11–10. Consolidated revenue of Daimler-Benz was DM 97.737 billion for 1993. Exhibit 11–10 shows how different accounting frameworks can affect financial ratios.

Exhibit 11–9   Daimler-Benz Reconciliation of Stockholders' Equity to U.S. GAAP

	December 31, 1993 DM in Millions	December 31, 1992 DM in Millions
Stockholders' equity in accordance with German HGB	**18,145**	19,719
'/. Minority interest	(561)	(1,228)
Adjusted stockholders' equity under German regulations	17,584	18,491
+/– Appropriated retained earnings/ (provisions, reserves and valuation differences)	5,770	9,931
	23,354	28,422
Additional adjustments		
+/– Long-term contracts	207	131
Goodwill and business acquisitions	2,284	1,871
Pensions and other postretirement benefits	(1,821)	(1,312)
Foreign currency translation	85	(342)
Financial instruments	381	580
Other valuation differences	(698)	(1,708)
Deferred taxes	2,489	(138)
Stockholders' equity in accordance with U.S. GAAP	**26,281**	27,504

Source: Daimler-Benz, *Annual Report 1993*, p. 73.

Exhibit 11–10 Daimler-Benz Profitability Ratios

Ratio	U.S. GAAP	German GAAP
Profit margin	$\dfrac{(1,839)}{97,737} = (1.88\%)$	$\dfrac{615}{97,737} = 0.63\%$
Rate of return on net worth	$\dfrac{(1,839)}{26,281} = (7.00\%)$	$\dfrac{615}{18,145} = 3.39\%$

Case Study 2: Canadian Pacific Limited

Consolidated financial statements of Canadian Pacific Limited are prepared in accordance with generally accepted accounting principles in Canada, as promulgated by the Canadian Institute of Chartered Accountants. Exhibit 11–11 shows the effect of GAAP differences between the U.S. and Canada on the company's 1993 reported loss. The exhibit also includes a reconciliation between the loss amounts determined under GAAP of the two countries. According to the annual report, the effect on the consolidated balance sheet due to the GAAP differences was not significant (p. 68). Canadian Pacific had total revenues of $6,579.4 million and total assets of $17,134.3 million in 1993. Based on this information, two profitability ratios are shown in Exhibit 11–12 using U.S. GAAP and Canadian GAAP.

Exhibit 11–11 Canadian Pacific Limited U.S. and Canadian GAAP Impact on Income

For the year ended December 31 (in millions, except amounts per share)	1993	1992
Operating income		
Canadian GAAP	$ 915.1	$ 163.2
United States GAAP	856.0	47.4
Income(loss) from continuing operations		
Canadian GAAP	(27.6)	(301.2)
United States GAAP	(18.8)	(454.8)
Net income (loss)		
Canadian GAAP	(190.6)	(478.3)
United States GAAP	(117.8)	(693.9)
Earnings (loss) per ordinary share		
Income (loss) from continuing operations		
Canadian GAAP	(0.09)	(0.95)
United States GAAP	(0.06)	(1.43)
Net income (loss)		
Canadian GAAP	(0.60)	(1.50)
United States GAAP	(0.37)	(2.18)
The following is a reconciliation of net income (loss) under Canadian GAAP to net income (loss) under United States GAAP:		
Net income (loss) — Canadian GAAP	$ (190.6)	$ (478.3)
Increased or (decreased) by:		
Oil and gas	10.7	10.2
Real estate and hotels	(22.8)	(16.3)
Deferred income taxes	65.5	–
Foreign exchange	(22.8)	(81.8)
Pension costs	(22.8)	(21.3)
Post retirement benefits	(4.8)	(45.6)
Other	5.8	1.2
Discontinued operations	64.0	(62.0)
Net income (loss)—United States GAAP	$ (117.8)	$ (693.9)

Source: Canadian Pacific Limited, *Annual Report 1993*, p. 69.

Exhibit 11–12 Canadian Pacific Limited Profitability Ratios

Ratio	U.S. GAAP	Canadian GAAP
Profit margin	$\frac{(117.8)}{6,579.4} = (1.79\%)$	$\frac{(190.6)}{6,579.4} = (2.90\%)$
Rate of return on net worth	$\frac{(117.8)}{17,134.3} = (0.69\%)$	$\frac{(190.6)}{17,134.3} = (1.11\%)$

Case Study 3: Pirelli SpA

Pirelli is one of the largest Italy-based international firms. Exhibit 11–13 shows the adjustments to Pirelli's 1990 net income and stockholders' equity to conform to GAAP of four other European countries.

As shown in the exhibit, when the amounts are adjusted to GAAP of the selected countries, the two ratios are lowest in case of U.K. GAAP and highest for French GAAP.

Exhibit 11–13 Pirelli SpA Adjustments and Selected Ratios

| | Lire billions (except percentages) | | | | |
	Italy	U.K.	Germany	Spain	France
Net income	100	58	60	95	118
Stockholders' equity	3,039	3,286	3,018	2,961	2,996
Profit margin (%)	0.94%	0.54%	0.57%	0.90%	1.11%
Rate of return on net worth (%)	3.29%	1.76%	1.99%	3.21%	3.94%

Sales of Pirelli were 10,603 billion lire in 1990.

Source: J.M. Samuels, R.E. Brayshaw, and J.M. Craner, *Financial Statement Analysis in Europe* (London: Chapman & Hall, 1995).

Case Study 4: Rhône-Poulenc SA

Rhône-Poulenc SA is the largest chemical company in France. Exhibit 11–14 displays adjustments and selected ratios of the company in accordance with GAAP of four other European countries for the year 1990.

The impact of restatements is quite dramatic, as indicated by the exhibit, especially on the rate of return on net worth.

Exhibit 11–14 Rhône-Poulenc SA Adjustments and Selected Ratios

	French franc millions (except percentages)				
	France	Germany	Italy	Spain	U.K.
Net income	1,097	1,604	(702)	(5)	2,951
Stockholders' equity	21,047	2,268	21,796	20,328	1,092
Profit margin (%)	1.39%	2.04%	(0.39)%	0%	3.76%
Stockholders' equity	21,047	2,268	21,796	20,328	1,092
Rate of return on net worth (%)	5.21%	70.72%	(3.45)%	(0.02)%	270.00%

Sales of Rhône-Poulenc were 78,411 million French francs.

Source: J.M. Samuels, R.E. Brayshaw, and J.M. Craner, *Financial Statement Analysis in Europe* (London: Chapman & Hall, 1995).

Trend Analysis

Ratio analysis is for one period or one date. *Trend analysis presents the information for an item for two or more different dates or periods for comparison.* Trend analysis thus provides information about the change taking place in an item and the rate of the change. It is common for companies to present 5- or 10-year summaries of selected data items, and ratios in their annual reports. Examples are shown in Exhibit 11–15 for Toyota and Exhibit 11–16 for Orkla (a Norway-based company). Companies also normally present financial statements for the past one or two years alongside the current year's financial statements (see Exhibits 11–4 through 11–6).

While performing trend analysis for comparison with the data of other companies, it is desirable to convert the amounts to a common base. This enables the analyst to evaluate the rate of growth or decline across time more readily. A common approach is to select the earliest year as the base year. The amount of each succeeding year is then divided by the amount of the base year. When two or more firms are being compared, the same base year should be used for all of the firms.

The trends can be significantly influenced by the base year selected. For this reason, the base year chosen for each firm should be a representative year. This precludes selecting any year with a negative amount as the base year. An illustration of this approach is shown in Exhibit 11–17 for Volkswagen AG and General Motors for the period 1986–1993.

When this analytical technique is used for comparison, no complexity is added by the different currencies—German mark and U.S. dollar in our example. The growth trend is expressed in percentages and not in the currency amounts.

Exhibit 11–15   Toyota Consolidated Financial Summary

Toyota Motor Corporation and Consolidated Subsidiaries
Years ended June 30

	1994	1993	1992	1991	1990
	Vehicle units				
Vehicle factory sales:					
Domestic	2,010,130	2,159,474	2,331,091	2,443,274	2,425,809
Overseas	2,120,716	2,306,742	2,180,742	2,095,233	2,003,336
Total	4,130,846	4,466,216	4,511,833	4,538,507	4,429,145

	Millions of yen	Thousands of U.S. dollars		Millions of yen		
Net sales	¥9,362,732	$94,573,051	¥10,210,749	¥10,163,376	¥9,855,132	¥9,192,838
Net income	125,807	1,270,781	176,465	237,841	431,450	441,302
Total assets	9,657,638	97,551,904	9,414,417	9,582,708	8,988,148	8,431,095
Shareholders' equity	4,829,755	48,785,402	4,762,546	4,718,885	4,577,945	4,235,869
Common stock	261,800	2,644,443	260,513	260,161	255,971	246,783
Capital investment*	330,000	3,333,333	555,900	768,300	804,200	526,200
Depreciation*	400,366	4,044,102	444,810	439,931	379,906	339,413

	Yen	U.S. dollars		Yen		
Amounts per share:						
Net income	¥ 32.95	$ 0.333	¥ 46.04	¥ 61.90	¥ 111.76	¥ 114.21
Dividends	19.00	0.192	19.00	19.00	17.27	15.70
Shareholders' equity	1,297.13	13.102	1,279.69	1,268.12	1,232.05	1,143.54

Equity to assets ratio	50.0%		50.6%	49.2%	50.9%	50.2%

Shares outstanding at year-end (thousands)	3,723,406		3,721,631	3,721,165	3,377,933	3,061,295
Employees at year-end	110,534		109,279	108,167	102,423	96,849

*Not including vehicles for leasing

Notes: 1.   The number of shares used in computing per share amounts has been adjusted to take into account the retroactive effect of stock splits.
2.   Dividends include interim cash dividends.
3.   U.S. dollar amounts have been translated from yen, solely for the convenience of the reader, at the rate of ¥99=US$1, the approximate exchange rate on the Tokyo Foreign Exchange Market on June 30, 1994, the last trading day of the fiscal year.

Source: Toyota, Annual Report 1994, p. 44.

Exhibit 11–16 Orkla Group —Key Figures

		1993	1992	1991	1990	1989
Turnover						
1. Operating revenue	(NOK mill.)	17,858	16,807	16,133	15,465	13,353
2. International sales	(%)	30	28	26	23	20
Profit and Cashflow						
3. Operating profit	(NOK mill.)	1,270	1,190	870	911	894
4. Ordinary net profit	(NOK mill.)	984	203	767	641	651
5. Net cashflow from operations	(NOK mill.)	162	2,236	1,976	83	N/A
6. Maintenance/Environmental investments, net	(NOK mill.)	1,102	794	856	621	N/A
7. Expansion investments	(NOK mill.)	924	802	380	1,261	N/A
Profitability						
8. Operating margin	(%)	7.1	7.1	5.4	5.9	6.7
9. Gross profit margin	(%)	7.4	1.9	5.2	6.5	7.4
10. Return on total capital (Industry area incl. H.O.)	(%)	11.0	11.4	10.5	N/A	N/A
11. Return on capital employed (Industry area incl. H.O.)	(%)	18.0	18.0	12.4	N/A	N/A
12. Return on equity	(%)	15.9	3.5	14.0	15.0	19.3
Capital at 31.12						
13. Market capitalisation	(NOK mill.)	13,358	7,912	7,262	9,458	8,858
14. Book value of total assets	(NOK mill.)	19,492	16.743	17,093	17,044	13,666
15. Book value of equity (incl. minority interests)	(NOK mill.)	6,770	6,043	5,892	5,249	3,830
16. Equity ratio	(%)	34.7	36.1	34.5	30.8	28.0
17. Net interest-bearing debt at 31.12.	(NOK mill.)	7,082	5,119	5,485	5,430	3,882
Shares						
18. No. of shares outstanding (fully diluted) at 31.12.	(x 1,000)	47,420	47,420	47,450	50,994	47,144
19. Average no. of shares outstanding (fully diluted)	(x 1,000)	47,420	47,435	47,610	49,708	47,144
Share-related key figures						
20. Share price at 31.12. Ordinary A-shares	(NOK)	280	167	155	191	196
21. Earnings per share	(NOK)	20.80	4.30	16.10	12.90	13.80
22. Cashflow per share	(NOK)	39.80	31.50	34.50	29.40	27.50
23. Dividend per share	(NOK)	4.10	3.75	3.41	3.18	2.91
24. Payout ratio	(%)	19.6	87.7	21.0	24.8	18.6
25. Price/earnings ratio		13.5	39.0	9.6	14.8	14.2
26. Price/cashflow ratio		7.0	5.3	4.5	6.5	7.1
Personnel						
27. Total employees		15,081	14,679	14,505	14,044	12,676
28. Total man-years		14,532	13,606	13,473	12,871	11,734

Source: Orkla, *Annual Report 1993*, p. 32.

Exhibit 11–17 Annual Sales Trends, Volkswagen AG and General Motors								
	1986	**1987**	**1988**	**1989**	**1990**	**1991**	**1992**	**1993**
Volkswagen AG								
Sales								
(DM Millions)	52,794	54,635	59,221	65,352	68,061	76,315	85,403	76,586
Base year trend (%)	100	103	112	124	129	145	162	145
General Motors								
Sales								
($ millions)	115,610	114,870	123,642	126,932	124,705	123,109	132,242	138,220
Base year trend (%)	100	99	107	110	108	106	114	120

Another variation of this approach is to compute the changes from year to year. Using the information from Exhibit 11–17 for Volkswagen AG, the sales revenue (in DM millions) is 52,794 for 1986 and 54,635 for 1987. Percent change in sales revenue for these two years is computed as follows:

$$\frac{(54{,}635 - 52{,}794)}{52{,}794} \times 100 = 3.5\% \text{ (approximately)}$$

Annual sale change trends for Volkswagen AG and General Motors from 1987 to 1993 are shown in Exhibit 11–18.

Exhibit 11–18 Annual Sales Change Trends (Percentages), Volkswagen AG and General Motors								
	1986	**1987**	**1988**	**1989**	**1990**	**1991**	**1992**	**1993**
Volkswagen AG	–	3.5	8.4	10.4	4.1	12.1	11.9	–10.3
General Motors	–	–0.6	7.6	2.7	–1.8	–1.3	7.4	4.5

A review of Exhibit 11–18 indicates far more volatility in sales from year to year for both companies than was apparent from the sale trends shown in Exhibit 11–17.

Limitations of Trend Analysis

Though trend analysis is informative, it should be used with caution for forecasting. It compares only growth (or decline) and the related volatility from period to period.

There are two major limitations of trend analysis. First, the base year has a significant impact on the long-term trend. For this reason, *the representativeness of the base year selected cannot be overemphasized.* Presence of irregular items, e.g., extraordinary items, in the base year would distort the long-term trend figures.

Second, *the base year cannot be a negative number,* because the trends cannot be developed from using a negative number. For this reason, there may be gaps in the series when year-to-year change trends are being developed. This is illustrated in Exhibit 11–19 for Imperial Chemical Industries PLC.

**Exhibit 11–19 Annual Net Income Change Trends (in millions of £)
Imperial Chemical Industries PLC**

	1989	1990	1991	1992	1993
Net profit (loss) attributable to parent company	1,057	483	542	−570	138
Annual net income changes (%)	–	−54.3	12.2	−205.2	–

The gap in the series for 1993 is because the base year 1992 has a negative number (loss in the amount of £570 million). When such gaps develop, no comparisons with other companies can be made for the affected years in the series.

Foreign currency considerations. In an earlier section of this chapter, it was stated that financial ratios are identical regardless of the currency denomination of the account balances. Therefore, it is unnecessary to convert the balances from a foreign, i.e., local, currency to the domestic currency for ratio analysis.

For the purpose of performing comparative trend analysis, it is not only necessary but desirable to use amounts expressed in the local currency. The reason for this is that the trend data based on amounts translated from a local (foreign) currency to the domestic currency distort the underlying financial relationships. This is true whether the year-end exchange rates are used for translation, or one of the currency translation methods discussed in Chapter 6 is employed.

If the year-end exchange rates are used, a base year must be chosen for the years that are included in the trend analysis. This decision as to which one of the years should be selected as the base year would primarily depend on personal preference. Perhaps the only situation in which a base year guideline exists is when foreign currency balances have been adjusted for changes in the general purchasing power of the currency. In such a case, the year-end exchange rates of the year used as the base year for inflation adjustments should be used.

Example Sales revenue data of a British company for four years are given below.

Year	Sales (£ millions)	Year-End Exchange Rates, £ to $
19x1	600	0.50
19x2	680	0.45
19x3	800	0.60
19x4	980	0.70

(a) Trend analysis using the local currency: $\dfrac{980 - 600}{600} = 63\%$

(b) Trend analysis using 19x1 as the base year: $\dfrac{(980 \div 0.5) - (600 \div 0.5)}{(600 \div 0.5)} = 63\%$

(c) Trend analysis using 19x4 as the base year: $\dfrac{(980 \div 0.7) - (600 \div 0.7)}{(600 \div 0.7)} = 63\%$

(d) Trend analysis using the applicable convenience translation rates at the year-ends 19x1 and 19x4:

$$\dfrac{(980 \div 0.7) - (600 \div 0.5)}{(600 \div 0.5)} = \dfrac{1{,}400 - 1{,}200}{1{,}200} = 17\%$$

As can be seen from (a), (b), and (c), when a base-year's rate is used the trend analysis results are unaffected by translating the local currency using convenience rates. It does not matter whether the 19x1 year-end convenience rate is used, the 19x4 year-end convenience rate is used, or the amounts are not translated at all using any of the convenience rates. However, when we use the year-end convenience rates applicable to the sales amounts of specific years, we get a distortion. This is demonstrated in (d) above.

For translation purposes if, instead of using the year-end rates of the base year, one of the currency translation methods is employed, distortion can result due to the nature of the translation process itself. Using the same data each one of the specific translation methods results in translated amounts that are different in many instances. *These translated amounts, regardless of the translation method used, may be the result of a management decision or merely the result of a translation effect.* Unless an effort is made to isolate exchange rate influences, the trend analysis may be distorted and may lead to misleading conclusions. For these reasons, it is desirable to perform comparative trend analysis in the local currency.

Note to Students

Many financial services, financial journals, and other sources of information provide information about companies and countries. Some of the periodicals include *Economic Times* (India); *Asian Finance* (Hong Kong); *Financial World, Financial Executive, and Financial Times* (U.K.); and *Business Week, Fortune,* and *The Wall Street Journal* (U.S.). Most of the large public accounting firms publish country guides that include helpful information about different countries. The Information Guide series of Price Waterhouse, and the International Tax and Business Guide series of Deloitte Touche Tohmatsu International are especially noteworthy.

Many services provide company information. For example, Global Research Company provides microfiche packages on over 300 companies. Comprehensive databases are also available to compare companies in an industry or across industries. Global Vantage contains data on hundreds of companies in major economic centers of the world. Worldscope/Disclosure has two databases: Global and Emerging Markets. As of September 1995, Worldscope's Global database includes approximately 11,000 companies in 40 countries and in 24 major industry groups. Worldscope's other database, released in 1994, contains financial information and news on emerging markets. The Emerging Markets database includes approximately 1,800 companies in 25 countries and 24 major industries. The Worldscope databases provide fundamental financial data and news headlines for the countries. Data items include:

- **Company profiles**
  Corporate profile
  Business description
  Sales by product segment
  Sales by geographic segment
  Five-year sales, income, and EPS summary
  Listing of officers
- **Financial statements**
  Balance sheet
  Income statement
  Key financial items in U.S. dollars
  Flow of funds statement
  Supplementary data
  Footnotes
- **Ratios (annual & five-year averages)**
  Growth rates
  Profitability ratios

Asset utilization ratios
Leverage ratios
Liquidity
Foreign business statistics

- **Market data (current & historical)**
  Stock price & trading data
  Share data (interim & annual)
  Month-end pricing
  Stock performance ratios
  Stock report footnotes
  Exchange rates
- **Other information**
  Annotated news headlines
  Company-specific accounting practices
    identified
  Free access to multilingual analysts
  Company/country listing

An annotated bibliography of international business resources is available from the California Society of Certified Public Accountants (CSCPA). The CSCPA's *Global Opportunities Resource* features quick references on a variety of international trade, tax, accounting, auditing, and legal subjects. The Global Opportunities State Committee of the CSCPA, of which the lead author of this book is a member, developed this resource.

Chapter Summary

- Several current trends are making financial statement analysis increasingly important.
- Information is vital for global markets' efficiency.
- Reasons for international financial statement analysis include high returns availability, risk diversification, competition, relaxation or removal of ownership restrictions, effect of foreign currency appreciation on investment, and transaction of business.
- Perceived problems in the availability of financial information include reliability of data, adequacy of disclosures, timeliness of information, language and terminology differences, different currencies, and financial statements format differences.
- The current trend is toward greater disclosure. Several organizations have contributed to this trend.
- Globalization of markets appears to be the motivating factor contributing to voluntary disclosures and greater harmonization of accounting and auditing principles.
- Different accounting practices may produce differences in reported amounts while in fact there may be no real differences.

- For a financial analyst, the diversity of business practices worldwide is a greater challenge than the diversity of accounting principles worldwide.

- Two techniques of financial analysis are financial ratio analysis and trend analysis.

- There are several general limitations of financial ratio analysis. The effect of these limitations is compounded when financial ratio analysis is done in the international context.

- It is important to select a representative year as the base year for doing trend analysis since the trends can be significantly influenced by the base year selected.

- The presence of different currencies does not add complexity to trend analysis since trends are expressed in percentages.

- It is desirable to use amounts expressed in local (foreign) currency for trend analysis for several reasons. Translation is not advisable since the translated amounts can distort the results.

Questions for Discussion

1. Define financial statement analysis.

2. Discuss at least four reasons for the increasing importance of financial statement analysis.

3. Is there any effect of an appreciation in a country's currency on the value of an investment already made in that country?

4. Discuss at least three perceived problems related to the availability of financial information in different countries.

5. Name the organizations that are significantly affecting financial reporting of the companies engaged in international business and investment.

6. Identify the most important factor contributing toward voluntary disclosure and toward the harmonization of accounting and auditing principles. Name two companies that are providing voluntary disclosures.

7. Discuss the two alternatives to cope with the diversity of accounting principles worldwide.

8. What is the objective of financial statement analysis?

9. Describe and contrast financial ratio analysis and trend analysis.

10. Describe what these ratios measure: Liquidity, activity, profitability, and coverage.

11. Give one example for each of the four types of ratios listed in Question 10.

12. Discuss at least two general limitations of financial ratio analysis.

13. "The general limitations of financial ratio analysis pose relatively more serious problems when financial ratio analysis is done in the international context." Explain.

14. Why is it important to choose a representative year as the base year in trend analysis?

15. Discuss the two limitations of trend analysis.

16. Why is it desirable to use the amounts expressed in local (foreign) currency for trend analysis?

17. State the base year guideline for trend analysis when foreign currency balances have been adjusted for general price level changes.

18. "Foreign currency balances translated using one of the translation methods may cause distortion due to the translation process." Explain.

19. When *Fortune* released its annual list of the world's top 500 industrial companies on 6 July 1994, the Associated Press stated, "Rankings were skewed by accounting rule changes that made profits appear to climb 133 percent and a strong yen that artificially bolstered Japanese companies." Comment on the Associated Press statement.

Exercises/Problems

11-1 You have completed a financial statement analysis of a successful Japanese company. While comparing results of the analysis to a comparable U.S. company, you made the observation that the Japanese company had a relatively high debt to equity ratio compared with the U.S. company, as summarized below.

	(In millions)		
	Debt	**Equity**	**Debt to Equity Ratio**
Japanese	¥ 40,000	¥ 20,000	2.0
U.S.	$ 200	$ 400	0.5

You are curious to know why there is such a difference in the leverage position of the two supposedly comparable companies.

Required: Explain the factor(s) causing the differences between the two companies. What can you do to overcome the difficulties in such a comparison?

11-2 Imperial Chemical Industries (ICI) is the U.K.'s largest manufacturing company. ICI is listed in the U.S. and therefore is required by the U.S. Securities and Exchange Commission to provide data reconciling U.K. GAAP with U.S. GAAP.

Given below are selected data for the year 1993.

	£ (in millions)	
	U.K. GAAP	**U.S. GAAP**
Sales—continuing operations	8,430	8,430
Net income (loss)—continuing operations	31	(102)
Shareholders' equity (December 31)	3,983	4,320

Required:
(1) Compute the following ratios using U.K. GAAP:
   a. Profit margin
   b. Rate of return on net worth

(2) Do requirement (1) using U.S. GAAP.

(3) Comment on the differences between your solutions in the two requirements.

11-3 Refer to Exhibits 11–5 and 11–6, which contain AT&T and ICI balance sheets respectively.

Required:

(1) Identify the differences in the two balance sheets in terminology and format.

(2) Prepare a balance sheet for ICI Group for the year ended December 31, 1993 using U.S. terminology and format.

(3) Prepare a balance sheet for AT&T for the year ended December 31, 1993 using the U.K. terminology and format.

11-4 Review and analyze the annual report of a foreign company. Also research the operating environment of the country that affects its business practices.

Required: Prepare a 400-500 word report, discussing the following:

(1) Operating environment effects on business practices and financial reporting.

(2) Selected ratio and trend analysis (you choose the ratios and trends).

(3) Your opinion regarding the company's operating performance and financial position.

11-5 Write a 200-250 word report on:

(1) General limitations of financial ratio analysis.

(2) Limitations of financial ratio analysis in the international context.

11-6 In a report of 150-200 words, describe limitations of financial trend analysis, including the foreign currency aspect.

11-7 Refer to Exhibits 11–5 and 11–6 in the chapter.

Required:

(1) Prepare these ratios for ICI and AT&T.

a. Current ratio

b. Debt ratio

(2) Explain what the above ratios measure.

(3) Refer to Exhibit 11–4. Is it possible to compute the current ratio for Volkswagen? Explain.

11-8 Refer to Exhibit 11–15 in the chapter.

Required: Prepare the annual sales trends for Toyota for the period 1990–1994. Use the net sales amounts in yen for your analysis.

11-9 Refer to Exhibit 11–15 in this chapter.

Required: Prepare the annual sales change trends for Toyota for the period 1990–1994. Use the net sales amounts in yen for your analysis.

11-10 Given below is the annual net income (loss) of Renault for the years 1989–1993 in millions of French francs:

	1989	**1990**	**1991**	**1992**	**1993**
Net income (loss)	6,932	1,123	2,467	3,251	(5,225)

Required:

(1) Prepare annual income (loss) trends using 1989 as the base year for the years.

(2) Prepare annual income (loss) change trends for the years.

11-11 Given below are the net income (loss) data for AT&T and General Motors from 1988 through 1993 in millions of U.S. dollars.

	1988	1989	1990	1991	1992	1993
GM	4,856	4,224	(1,986)	(4,453)	(23,498)	2,466
AT&T	(1,230)	3,109	3,104	522	3,807	(3,794)

Required: Compute the annual net income (loss) change trends for the two companies for the year indicated.

11-12 A Japanese company's current assets are ¥100 million and current liabilities amount to ¥300 million. The convenience translation (year-end exchange) rate is $1.00 = ¥99.

Required:

(1) Compute the current ratio using amounts in yen.

(2) Compute the current ratio using amounts in dollars.

(3) Compare your answers in requirements (1) and (2) and comment.

11-13 Sales revenue data of a Norwegian company for four years are given below.

Year	Sales (K millions)	Year-End Exchange Rates K to $
19x1	750	0.17
19x2	800	0.18
19x3	630	0.15
19x4	890	0.14

Required:

(1) Perform trend analysis using the Norwegian krone.

(2) Perform trend analysis using 19x1 as the base year for the exchange rate at year-end.

(3) Perform trend analysis using 19x4 as the base year for the exchange rate at year-end.

(4) Perform trend analysis using the applicable exchange rates at the year-ends 19x1 and 19x4.

(5) Comment on your results in the above four requirements.

11-14 The 1994 Annual Report and Accounts of ICI is contained in the special supplement to this chapter.

Required:

(1) If you are a student in any country other than the U.K., write a two- to three- page report on how ICI's annual report differs from a typical annual report in your country. Some of the following items may be relevant:

a. Convenience translation.

b. Full disclosure principles and significant accounting policies.

c. Valuation principle.

d. Required financial statements.

      e. Format of financial statements.

      f. Depreciation policy (e.g., in Japan and Germany, financial reporting is consistent with tax treatment).

      g. Culture.

      h. Auditor's report.

     Students in the U.K. are not responsible for this requirement.

(2) Perform the ratio analysis using, at the minimum, the ratios described in Exhibit 11–7. You may wish to supplement analysis by using other ratios of your choice.

(3) Perform trend analysis for ICI to determine its annual sales trends, annual sales change trends, and annual net income change trends from 1989 to 1994.

11-15 Reformat ICI's 1994 financial statements, contained in the special supplement to this chapter, to your country's format. Note the important differences, such as valuation, measurement basis, etc. (U.K. students: Instead of the above, review the materials in the special supplement and write a five page report describing the strategies, plans, product leadership, financial results, financial position, and environmental performance of ICI.)

11-16 Review the materials in the special supplement to this chapter. Write answers to the following questions, and also be prepared to discuss your responses in class.

   (1) Company name.

   (2) Base country.

   (3) Statements prepared in:

     a. language

     b. currency

   (4) Auditor's report: How is it similar to or different from your country's auditor's report? What are its contents? What is your understanding of the extent of responsibility assumed by the auditors for discovery of any inaccuracies, lack of transparency, detection of fraud, etc.?

   (5) Is there any reference to the GAAP used in the auditor's report or the notes accompanying financial statements? If yes, what GAAP is used?

   (6) Is a reconciliation to another country's GAAP provided? If so, what country? What are the most significant reconciliation items?

   (7) How are the formats of the financial statements similar to or different from your country's formats? (U.K. students: disregard this question.)

   (8) Are segment disclosures presented? If yes, what type of segments?

   (9) Are reserves used? If yes, what type?

   (10) Is foreign currency translated? If yes, what translation method is used?

   (11) Are any inflation restatements or adjustments made? If yes, what approach is used?

   (12) Are there any unusual or unique disclosures?

   (13) Did any of the disclosures provide insights into culture of the base country (e.g., legal system, religion, etc.).

   (14) Are there any significant terminology differences? (U.K. students: may disregard this question).

Case 1: International Monetary Fund Agrees to Set Up Crisis Warning System

The International Monetary Fund (IMF) has agreed to establish an early warning system to detect Mexican-style currency crises. The 1995 spring meetings of the 179-nation IMF and its sister lending organization, the World Bank, were concluded on April 27.[6] The delegates approved an overhaul of how the IMF conducts its surveillance activities.

The proposals will require increased monitoring of countries deemed to represent the greatest threat to the global economic system as well as expanded requirements on the types of financial information nations will be asked to provide the IMF and financial markets.

Required:
(1) In your opinion, what are the important features in the design of a system such as the one proposed by the IMF?
(2) What would be some of the potential problems in the implementation and operation of such a system?
(3) Provide your recommendation for alleviation or solution of the potential problems you identified in your response to requirement (2).

Case 2: Lustra S.p.A. (B) (Copyright © by the President and Fellows of Harvard College.)[7]

In February 1990, Peter Scala decided not to issue and list Lustra S.p.A.'s common stock in the United States of America. The principal reason was a reluctance to go into the U.S. market with a declining earning per share trend that, in Peter Scala's mind, was simply the result of *Opinion No. 15*'s "arbitrary and unrealistic" rules for computing earnings per share. Instead he decided to explore the possibility of listing the company's stock on the London Exchange as a preliminary step to raising equity capital in the United Kingdom at some future date.

Based on his experience with *Opinion No. 15,* Peter Scala decided to check quickly on the United Kingdom's earnings per share calculation and disclosure rules. Based on his research, he concluded:

- Statements of Standard Accounting Practice (SSAP) 3 required listed companies to show earnings per share on the face of the income statement.
- Earnings per share was defined as the period's after-tax consolidated profit, deducting minority interest and preferred dividends but before taking into account extraordinary items based on the weighted-average share capital eligible for dividends. This figure was known as *basic earnings per share.*
- A second fully diluted earnings per share figure reflecting potential earnings per share dilution from warrants, opinions, or conversion rights should be disclosed, if applicable.

---

[6] The International Monetary Fund approved a voluntary early warning system on April 16, 1996.

[7] Professor David F. Hawkins prepared this case as the basis for class discussion rather than to illustrate either effective or ineffective handling of an administrative situation.

Peter Scala believed this last requirement would not be a problem, since he believed he could limit the potential dilution to an immaterial amount by the calculation methodology he elected to employ. Also Peter Scala believed that U.K. investors did not use fully diluted earnings per share figures in their investment decisions.

During 1991 and 1992 the demand for fashion eyewear was hurt by the global recession. And despite a significant increase in new store openings, Lustra's sales and profits reflected this adverse development. The company's poor financial results and the significant operating demands on Peter Scala's time led him to conclude that any listing decision should be postponed.

Early in the fourth quarter of 1992, Peter Scala decided to restructure the company by closing a number of unprofitable stores, discontinuing a recently-started small chain of specialty stores, and disposing of some excess and slow-moving inventories. The after-tax losses associated with these three actions were:

(Millions of British pounds equivalent at year-end pound-lira exchange rate)

Unprofitable store closings	£0.50
Discontinuance of speciality store business	.35
Inventory disposal	.60
Total loss	£1.45

Lustra's chief financial officer told Peter Scala that the £1.45 million after-tax loss associated with these actions could be treated as an extraordinary item and as such excluded from the company's 1992 earnings per share calculation, as shown in Exhibit 11-20.[8]

Exhibit 11–20 Lustra S.p.A.—Financial Information (millions, except earnings per share)[a]

	1990	1991	1992
Net sales	£86.0	£92.0	£ 81.00
Profit on ordinary activities and attributable to ordinary shareholders	1.05	.7	.85
Extraordinary items	-	-	(1.45)
Profit for the financial year	£1.05	£ 0.7	£(0.60)
Earnings per share[b]	£1.05	£0.70	£ 0.85

[a]Converted to British pounds at the year-end pound-lira exchange rate.
[b]Computation for Italian reporting purposes. Profit on ordinary activities and attributable to ordinary shareholders divided by average number of common shares outstanding.

---

[8] There are no requirements covering extraordinary items or earnings-per-share computation and disclosure in the Italian civil code or in the accounting standards issued by the representative body of the Italian accounting profession.

In early January 1993, encouraged by the 1992 improvement in earnings per share, Peter Scala decided the time had come to get a London listing for the company's stock. The first step was to communicate his decision to Harold Denning, the senior partner of the London office of Peat, Waterhouse & Company, the company's auditors. At this time, the 1992 audit was still in progress. Lustra's 1992 financial statements were due to be released in mid-March.

Peter Scala was surprised to learn from Harold Denning that under a new U.K. accounting standard (*FRS3*) Lustra would not show an improving earnings per share trend in 1992. Instead, 1992 earnings per share would not only be lower than the 1991 figure, they would be negative.

The day after his conversation with Harold Denning, Peter Scala received a letter from Denning explaining the new standard (Exhibit 11–21). Immediately after reading the letter, Scala met with his chief financial officer to reassess his London listing decision.

Required:
(1) Determine Lustra's 1992 basic earnings per share presentation using *FRS3*.
(2) If Lustra proceeds with a London listing application, what adjusted earnings per share figure, if any, should the company include in its 1992 financial report? Why should the company present an adjusted 1992 earnings per share figure? Explain the justification for your adjustment.
(3) Does *FRS3* represent a significant improvement over SSAP3? Discuss.
(4) How might *FRS3* influence Lustra's decision to list on the London Exchange?

Exhibit 11–21   Letter to Peter Scala from Harold Denning

10 January 1993

Mr. Peter Scala
President
Lustra S.p.A.
Lustra Building, Via Saicar 551
Naples, Italy

Dear Peter:

This letter is written to clarify my comments made to you yesterday regarding the format of your 1992 financial statements and earnings per share calculation should you decide to seek a London listing.

Since its formation in 1991, the Accounting Standards Board has undertaken a far-reaching review of U.K. generally accepted accounting principles. This has resulted in major changes to the way companies present their accounts. In line with the recommendations of the Accounting Standards Board, we urge you to adopt *Financial Reporting Standard No. 3 (FRS3)* at the earliest opportunity. This standard replaces *SSAP3*.

The objective of *FRS3* is to highlight a range of important components of financial performance to aid users in their understanding of accounts and to assist them in forming a basis for their assessment of future results and cash flows. The format laid down in *FRS3* for the profit and loss account will be demanded by investors to analyze your financial statements.

The basic *FRS3* format we recommend for Lustra's 1992 profit and loss account in any listing submission is:

	Continuing Operations	Discontinued Operations	Total
Turnover	£XXX	£XXX	£XXX
Cost of sales	XXX	XXX	XXX
Trading profit (loss)	£XXX	£XXX	£XXX
Exceptional items	XXX	XXX	XXX
Operating profit (loss) on ordinary activities	£XXX	£XXX	£XXX
Minority interest	XXX	XXX	XXX
Profit (loss) for the financial year	£XXX	£XXX	£XXX
Profit (loss) per ordinary share	£XXX	£XXX	£XXX

As I explained to you during our phone conversation, *FRS3* limits extraordinary items to very rare occurrences. As the illustrations in *FRS3* clearly indicate, the extraordinary items shown in your Italian-GAAP-based reports no longer qualify as extraordinary items in U.K. GAAP presentations.

Exhibit 11–21 Letter to Peter Scala from Harold Denning (continued)

Under *FRS3*, a business is classified as a discontinued operation if it is clearly distinguishable; has a material effect on the nature and focus of the Group's activities; represents a material reduction in the Group's operating facilities; and either its sale is completed, or if a termination, its former activities have ceased before the earlier of three months after the commencement of the subsequent period and the date on which the financial statements are approved. In line with these new requirements, we believe the charge associated with the discontinuance of your small specialty store business should be reported as a discontinued operation. To conform to *FRS3*, any prior periods presented will have to be restated to show the specialty stores as a discontinued business.

The store closing and inventory disposal losses are business activities that relate to your continuing business. As such, *FRS3* requires that these losses be included in the calculation of continuing-operations-related operating profit on ordinary activities.

FRS3 also deals with the calculation and disclosure of earnings per share data. It requires basic earnings per share to be calculated on the basis of profit for the financial year less preferred dividends, if any. Therefore, the basic earnings per share you would show under U.K. GAAP would be a negative amount rather than a positive amount as reported on your Italian GAAP statements.

When the *FRS3* earnings per share calculation was proposed, it was bitterly opposed by the business and financial analysts communities. They believed it would lead to more volatile earnings and did not reflect the way investors view and use earnings per share data. As a compromise, the Accounting Standards Board agreed to permit companies to disclose an alternative earnings per share figure that the reporting company believed was a more useful one for investors. The requirements are that this alternative fiture be presented with the official one, not be displayed in a more prominent way, and the method used to calculate it be fully disclosed.

We believe that you should consider reporting an alternative earnings per share figure on the face of your 1992 profit and loss account and in the accompanying notes. The presentation of the adjusted earnings per share figure would be accompanied by the following statement: "In the opinion of the directors, the adjustments give a better underlying picture of the Group's performance than the basic earnings per share figure."

Should you decide to proceed with a London listing, we will be delighted to assist you in the preparation of your listing materials. Please let me know your plans as soon as possible so that we can incorporate this matter into our current year-end audit programme.

Sincerely,

Harold Denning
Managing Partner
Peat, Waterhouse & Company

References

Blasch, Doris M., Jerome Kelliher, and William J. Read. "The FASB and the IASC Redeliberate EPS." *The Journal of Accountancy,* February 1996, pp. 43-47.

Choi, Frederick D. S., and Richard M. Levich. "Behavioral Effects of International Accounting Diversity." *Accounting Horizons,* June 1991, pp. 1-13.

————. *The Capital Market Effects of Internal Accounting Diversity.* Homewood, Ill.: Dow Jones–Irwin, 1990.

Coopers & Lybrand. *International Accounting Summaries: A Guide to Interpretation and Comparison.* 2d ed. New York: John Wiley & Sons, Inc., 1993.

Doost, Roger K., and Karen M. Ligon. "How U.S. and European Accounting Practices Differ." *Management Accounting,* October 1986, pp. 38-41.

Fédération des Experts Comptables Européens. *1992 FEE Analysis of European Accounting and Disclosure Practices.* London: Routledge, 1992.

Gray, Sidney J., and Clare B. Roberts. "East-West Accounting Issues: A New Agenda." *Accounting Horizons,* March 1991, pp. 42.-50.

Hofsteder, G. H. *Culture's Consequences. International Differences in Work-Related Values.* Sage, 1980.

Kelly, John F. "The New Dilemma of Cash Versus Earnings." *Financial Executive,* July/August 1989, pp. 29-32.

Lowe, Howard D. "Shortcomings of Japanese Consolidated Financial Statements." *Accounting Horizons,* September 1990, pp. 1-9.

Meek, Gary K., and Sidney J. Gray. "Globalization of Stock Markets and Foreign Listing Requirements: Voluntary Disclosures by Continental European Companies Listed on the London Stock Exchange," *Journal of International Business Studies,* summer 1989, pp. 315-336.

Perera, M. H. B. "Towards a Framework to Analyze the Impact of Culture on Accounting." *The International Journal of Accounting,* vol. 24, no. 1 (1989), pp. 42-56.

Progress on the Environmental Challenge: A Survey of Corporate America's Environmental Accounting and Management. New York: Price Waterhouse, 1994.

Samuels, J. M., R. E. Brayshaw, and J. M. Craner. *Financial Statement Analysis in Europe.* London: Chapman & Hall, 1995.

Schieneman, Gary S. "The Effect of Accounting Differences on Cross Border Comparisons." *International Accounting and Investment Review,* 29 April 1988, pp. 1-14.

Special Committee on Financial Reporting. *Improving Business Reporting—A Customer Focus.* New York: American Institute of Certified Public Accountants, 1994.

Standards for the Dissemination by Countries of Economic and Financial Statistics: A Discussion Draft. Washington, D.C.: International Monetary Fund, 1996.

Sundby, Larry, and Bradley Schwieger. "EC, EZ?" *Journal of Accountancy,* March 1992, pp. 71-76.

Wallace, R. S. Olusegun, and Paul A. Collier. "The 'Cash' in Cash Flow Statements: A Multi-Country Comparison." *Accounting Horizons,* December 1991, pp. 44-52.

Tondkar, Rasoul H., Ajay Adhikari, and Edward N. Coffman. "Adding an International Dimension to Upper-Level Financial Accounting Courses by Utilizing Foreign Annual Reports." *Issues in Accounting Education,* fall 1994, p. 271-281.

Weetman P., and S. J. Gray. "A Comparative International Analysis of the Impact of Accounting Principles on Profits: The U.S.A Versus the U.K., Sweden, and the Netherlands." *Accounting and Business Research,* autumn 1991, pp. 363-379.

―――. "International Financial Analysis and Comparative Corporate Performance: The Impact of U.K. versus U.S. Accounting Principles on Earnings." *Journal of International Financial Management and Accounting,* summer/autumn 1990, pp. 111-130.

Working Group on External Financial Reporting of the Schmalenbach-Gesellschaft-Deutsche Gesellschaft für Betriebswirtschaft. "German Accounting Principles: An Institutionalized Framework." *Accounting Horizons,* September 1995, pp. 92-99.

Wyatt, Arthur. "International Accounting Standards: A New Perspective." *Accounting Horizons,* September 1989, pp. 105-108.

Wygal, Donald E., David E. Stout, and James Volpi. "Reporting Practices in Four Countries." *Management Accounting,* December 1987, pp. 37-46.

Special Supplement: Imperial Chemical Industries Annual Reports

The following pages contain the annual report and accounts, annual review and summary financial statement, and environmental performance report of Imperial Chemical Industries PLC (ICI) for 1994. ICI is one of the largest U.K. based multinationals. ICI is a manufacturer of paint, synthetic materials, explosives, and industrial chemicals. Because of its size and its worldwide operations, ICI's accounting and reporting practices are affected by most of the topics covered in this book.

Our objective is to maximise value for our shareholders by focusing on businesses where we have market leadership, a technological edge and a world competitive cost base. We will promote a culture of continuous improvement in everything we do.

financial highlights

	1994 £m	1993† £m	1992 £m
Financial results – continuing operations*			
Turnover	**9,189**	8,430	7,557
Trading profit before exceptional items°	**588**	325	173
Profit before exceptional items and taxation	**514**	280	163
Exceptional items before taxation	**(106)**	(94)	(595)
Net profit (loss) attributable to parent company	**188**	25	(621)
Earnings and dividends			
Earnings (loss) per £1 Ordinary Share			
Continuing operations – before exceptional items	**37.3p**	19.6p	3.2p
Total earnings (loss)	**26.0p**	17.9p	(79.9)p
Dividend per £1 Ordinary Share (note 2, page 23)	**27.5p**	27.5p	55.0p

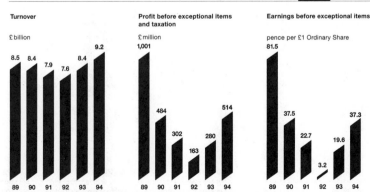

Turnover

£ billion

89	90	91	92	93	94
8.5	8.4	7.9	7.6	8.4	9.2

Profit before exceptional items and taxation

£ million

89	90	91	92	93	94
1,001	484	302	163	280	514

Earnings before exceptional items

pence per £1 Ordinary Share

89	90	91	92	93	94
81.5	37.5	22.7	3.2	19.6	37.3

* Continuing operations – unless otherwise stated, all comparative figures refer to ICI's continuing operations which exclude the results of Zeneca and the Group's European fibres business.

†Restated, see note 5, page 24.
° Unless otherwise stated, all references to trading profit are in respect of trading profit before exceptional items.

ICI today

paints · **materials** · **explosives** · **industrial chemicals** Chemicals & Polymers (C&P) and Tioxide · **regional businesses**

ICI Paints is a world leader in decorative paint, coatings for food and drinks cans, and refinish paints for vehicles. It owes its success to excellent customer service, innovative technology and strong brands such as 'Dulux', 'Glidden' and ICI Autocolor.

ICI Materials produces chemicals and related materials from which products can be fabricated. It focuses on acrylics (used for coatings, baths, lighting products and vehicle components); on high-performance plastic films (uses range from packaging to data storage); and on polyurethanes for applications such as insulation, seat cushioning, shoe soles and adhesives.

ICI Explosives is the world's leading supplier of blasting services including industrial explosives and initiating systems for the mining, quarrying and construction industries. Other activities include making components for vehicle airbags.

C&P is one of the world's largest manufacturers of industrial chemicals. It includes the high-growth, global businesses of pure terephthalic acid (PTA), 'Melinar' PET resins, surfactants, catalysts and 'Klea' CFC-replacements.

  Tioxide is the world's second largest producer of titanium dioxide pigments, used to give whiteness and opacity to products such as paints, plastics, textiles, inks and coatings.

Where market conditions offer clear competitive advantages, the Group invests in opportunities outside its global businesses. Within their markets, ICI's regional businesses aim to excel against both local and international competition.

Herman Scopes
Chief Executive Officer

Bill Madden
Chief Executive Officer

Peter Clinch
Chief Executive Officer

Mike Brogden
Chief Executive Officer, C&P
Alan Pedder
Chief Executive Officer,
Tioxide

Each regional business is managed locally.

19%
21%
Trading profit
Turnover

Trading profit
Turnover

8%
8%
Trading profit
Turnover

39%
45%
Trading profit
Turnover

15%
13%
Trading profit
Turnover

£600m
net operating assets and capital under construction

15,400 employees

£1,250m
net operating assets and capital under construction

8,400 employees

£350m
net operating assets and capital under construction

13,700 employees

£2,200m
net operating assets and capital under construction

17,800 employees

£810m
net operating assets and capital under construction

10,900 employees

ICI has emerged from recession with a strong balance sheet, sound strategies, a competitive cost base, innovative technology and well established positions for its main products in many markets. We are hungry for growth.

chairman's statement

1994 was a better year for the Group. As I had predicted, ICI benefited from the recovery in the world economic cycle.

Sales rose by 9 per cent to £9.2 billion. Profit before exceptional items and tax was 84 per cent higher at £514 million and cash flow was extremely strong with net gearing falling to 3 per cent. The Board has declared a second interim dividend of 17.0p to bring the total for the year to 27.5p.

Corporate governance properly continues to attract a great deal of public attention. ICI's long established record in this area was recognised in January this year when the Company became the first winner of the British Quality of Governance award. This accolade is also a tribute to our Non-Executive Directors whose wisdom, integrity and international experience contribute significantly to our corporate decision making.

As part of good governance, we have always communicated frankly and openly with our shareholders on issues such as directors' contracts and remuneration. This year, you will find an even fuller statement of each director's emoluments in the Notes to the Summary Financial Statement on page 24 of this document. I hope shareholders will find this helpful.

Congratulations are due to our Chief Executive, Ronnie Hampel, who received a knighthood in the 1995 New Year's Honours. As we announced last June, he will succeed me as Chairman on 27 April and Charles Miller Smith, who recently joined us from Unilever, will take his place as Chief Executive on the same date.

Sir Ronald and Mr Miller Smith will make a powerful team. Their particular blend of ICI continuity and external experience will bring precisely the qualities we need to maintain the Group's momentum, and I will hand over my responsibilities with great confidence.

On 1 January 1995 we welcomed George Simpson as a Non-Executive Director. He is Chief Executive of Lucas Industries and his wide business experience will be of great benefit.

Colin Short will retire at the end of April. During his five years on the Board, Colin has made a valuable contribution to the Group and I particularly welcomed his support during the demerger process when he and I worked closely together. We will all miss his calm, expert guidance and wish him well for the future.

At the conclusion of this year's AGM, I shall myself retire after eight exciting and fulfilling years as Chairman. Those years have not been short of challenges with the Stock Market collapse of October 1987, the longest recession for 60 years, the chaos in Eastern Europe which affected the defence and aerospace industries, and the emergence of a rapidly growing chemical industry in Asia Pacific, bringing with it both threats and opportunities. There were also momentous changes in ICI itself – not least the demerger of Zeneca.

The decisions associated with these changes have been difficult and often painful. Nevertheless, the ICI team has responded vigorously to secure the long term prosperity of the Group in today's fiercely competitive world climate.

Throughout this turbulent period, I have greatly appreciated the support of ICI's shareholders as we have sought, year on year in good times and bad, to enhance the value of the Group. I am also extremely grateful for the loyalty and dedication of our employees generally and my close colleagues in particular. I am proud to have served as Chairman of this great Company with its strong tradition of style, quality and good fellowship which I have striven to maintain.

We shall continue to move forward under an excellent management team who are hungry for growth. I wish them every success – plus that little bit of good fortune we all need!

Denys Henderson

Sir Denys Henderson
Chairman

chief executive's review

We now have a family of businesses able to form the core of a growing ICI Group... The task now is to build on the considerable opportunities for growth contained in our chosen portfolio... As we pursue the growth opportunities, we will in no way slacken our resolve to control costs and improve our productivity continuously.

This has been a year of considerable achievement in increasing value for our shareholders. By the end of 1994, our performance in profit and cash was ahead of the market's expectations, and our own, at the time of demerger. With no real help from the global economic upturn until the last quarter, our progress was largely the result of our own efforts in the form of cost-cutting and higher productivity. For this achievement, our employees throughout the world deserve much credit.

Reviews of our individual businesses appear on the following pages, so I need not go into detail here. However, I would like to draw attention to the main themes underlying the year's performance.

Productivity and reshaping

Firstly, greater productivity across all our businesses has contributed to an increase in return on assets. We have stretched the capacity of many of our plants and benefited from business re-engineering as well as the more traditional control of costs. Staff numbers in the Group are down by 6 per cent, after adjusting for acquisitions and divestments, while sales have increased by 9 per cent.

Secondly, we have continued to reshape the portfolio in order to focus still more closely on ICI's global strengths. We have floated EVC International, our joint venture in polyvinyl chloride (PVC), and successfully sold our remaining stake in AECI, following last year's reorganisation in South Africa under which we acquired a majority share

of AECI's explosives division. We have also disposed of our holding in Chemical Company of Malaysia while retaining our stake in ICI Paints (Malaysia). Shortly after the year end, we completed an agreement to divest C&P's ethylene oxide and derivatives business.

Expansion

Thirdly, we have pursued opportunities for profitable growth. The opening by the Chairman of a new paint factory in China marks our first manufacturing presence in this vast potential market. I had the pleasure of opening the new 'Klea' 134a plant in Japan – our third in five years. Other expansions, either sanctioned or announced, include new capacity for 'Klea' 134a in the USA, a new US 'Melinar' plant, an MDI plant in Holland for Polyurethanes, a paint factory in Indonesia, new capacity for pure terephthalic acid (PTA) in Taiwan and, in Pakistan, an expansion of capacity in polyester fibre.

In addition, Paints acquired two new businesses in the USA and Australia, and Explosives has signed an agreement to explore the possibility of joint manufacturing ventures with the Government of China. We are also building a pipeline in Australia to supply competitively-priced ethane to our petrochemical complex at Botany Bay.

Corporate culture

Fourthly, we have kept up the momentum in creating a new corporate culture. Structures have been streamlined with greater emphasis on autonomy, accountability and achievement. New training programmes are helping employees to understand the principles of shareholder value and how they themselves can enhance it. The results are coming through in that staff at all levels are becoming more financially aware. Managers are noticeably more prudent in their use of cash and this has contributed to ICI's strong cash position.

After intensive restructuring, we now have a family of businesses able to form the core of a growing ICI Group. Of course some restructuring will always be necessary and this year's further rationalisation in Explosives is an example. That said, the task now is to build on the considerable opportunities for growth contained in our chosen portfolio. We are well placed to do so.

Towards our targets

As I mentioned in my statement last year, we will measure our progress principally by return on net assets. Last year's figure was over 10 per cent and is a considerable improvement on a year ago. However, all in ICI recognise that it still falls short of our target of 20 per cent per annum averaged over five years. As we pursue the growth opportunities, we will in no way slacken our resolve to control costs and improve our productivity continuously.

Progress will also be measured by our record on safety, health and the environment. This year had its setbacks in the tragic deaths of 12 employees and three contractors – 11 of them in

our explosives operations in South Africa. The sympathies of the Board go to all those affected. No death is acceptable and we will not be satisfied until accidents at work are a thing of the past.

Sadly, these losses came in a year when ICI's overall record was improving. Our new unified policy on safety, health and the environment underlines the importance of an integrated approach and has helped to reduce the number of lost-time injuries to a new low. For the first time this year, one of our businesses – ICI Acrylics – achieved a full 12 months with no lost-time injuries at all. That is our ambition for the Group as a whole.

The environment

ICI's environmental record continues to improve. Our programme of defining the problems inherited from the past is now largely complete and the task of resolving them is well in hand. Our strategy is to ensure that new products and processes do not create problems for the future. Some of our 1995 environmental targets – set in 1990 – have already been met and new goals are now being agreed as we look towards the end of the decade. Details of our environmental performance are in the separate report that accompanies this document.

Improving performance

A year ago I looked forward to an improving performance in 1994. My confidence has been more than justified. Everyone in ICI can be proud of the achievements of the last

Sir Denys Henderson

Denys Henderson retires from ICI at the 1995 Annual General Meeting after 38 years of service – the last 15 on the Board and as Chairman since 1987. His contribution to the Group is immense. We on the Board will miss his leadership, his judgement, his balance and his steadfastness in times of pressure. He will be remembered above all – and deserves so to be – as the Chairman who had the courage to question the fundamental structure of the Group and then to preside over the successful demerger of Zeneca.

All in ICI wish him a long, healthy and happy retirement.

12 months and my thanks go to all our staff for their contribution.

The key now is to grow selectively in our core businesses while continuing the drive for productivity. The winners in our industry will be those that can do both. ICI intends to be among them.

Ronald Hampel

Sir Ronald Hampel
Chief Executive

Sir Denys Henderson

A Director since 1980 and Chairman since 1987. He will retire on 27 April 1995. He is also Chairman of Zeneca Group PLC and The Rank Organisation Plc, and a Non-Executive Director of Barclays PLC and The RTZ Corporation PLC. Aged 62.

Sir Ronald Hampel

A Director since 1985 and Deputy Chairman and Chief Executive since 1993. He will succeed Sir Denys Henderson as Chairman with effect from 27 April 1995. He is also a Non-Executive Director of British Aerospace PLC, the Commercial Union Assurance Company plc and the Aluminium Company of America. Aged 62.

C Miller Smith

Appointed a Non-Executive Director in 1993 and an Executive Director in October 1994, he will succeed Sir Ronald Hampel as Chief Executive with effect from 27 April 1995. He is also a Non-Executive Director of Midland Bank PLC. Aged 55.

Sir Antony Pilkington

Appointed a Non-Executive Director in 1991. He is also Chairman of Pilkington plc. Aged 59.

Miss Ellen R Schneider-Lenné

Appointed a Non-Executive Director in 1991. She is a member of the Board of Managing Directors of Deutsche Bank AG and a Director of Morgan Grenfell Group plc. Aged 52.

C M Short

A Director since 1990, he has territorial responsibility for the Eastern Hemisphere. He is also a Non-Executive Director of United Biscuits (Holdings) plc. He will retire on 30 April 1995. Aged 60.

R J Margetts

A Director since 1992, he is Group Personnel and Group Research and Technology Director, and has territorial responsibility for the Western Hemisphere. He is also a Non-Executive Director of English China Clays plc. Aged 48.

F R Hurn

Appointed a Non-Executive Director in 1993. He is also Chairman and Chief Executive of Smiths Industries plc, and a Director of S G Warburg Group plc. Aged 56.

A G Spall

Appointed a Director in January 1994, he is Group Finance Director and has overview responsibility for insurance, investments and property. Aged 50.

M E Brogden

Appointed a Director in May 1994, he is Group Planning and Group Safety, Health and Environment Director, and is Chief Executive Officer of ICI Chemicals & Polymers. Aged 56.

G Simpson

Appointed a Non-Executive Director in January 1995. He is also Chief Executive of Lucas Industries plc and a Director of Pilkington plc. Aged 52.

Under Article 74 of the Company's Articles of Association, Mr M E Brogden and Mr G Simpson retire together with Mr R J Margetts, Sir Antony Pilkington and Miss Ellen R Schneider-Lenné who retire under Article 92. All are recommended for re-election.

Mr M E Brogden and Mr R J Margetts each has a service contract with the Company, which is subject to termination by either party giving not less than two years' notice to expire on, or at any time after, the third anniversary of the date of appointment.

The Audit Committee and the Remuneration and Nomination Committee comprise all the Non-Executive Directors, except that the Chairman is a member of the Remuneration and Nomination Committee when acting as a Nomination Committee.

Advanced new plastic

In July, ICI announced its decision to build the world's largest single stream plant for PET resin, the raw material for plastic bottles. The new plant in the USA will produce 'Laser +', an advanced version of ICI's 'Melinar' PET which has proved immensely popular with bottle makers in recent years.

Australian pipeline

ICI Australia secured a ten-year supply of ethane – an economic, environmentally-friendly alternative to its present feed-stocks. A new 1,380 km, underground pipeline will carry the ethane from South Australia's Moomba gas field to ICI's ethy-lene plant at Botany. The switch to ethane will make ICI Australia one of the world's most cost-effective ethylene producers.

Tioxide success

In the first year of its joint-venture manufacturing operation in the USA, Tioxide sold the entire production from its half-share in the new titanium dioxide plant in Louisiana. It is now looking at ways to extend the plant's capacity in order to sustain its growing share of the global market.

a year of achievement

Unique cushioning

First launched at the Milan Furniture Fair in 1993, ICI's 'Waterlily' comfort cushioning has completed its first year of sales and has been welcomed by designers and furniture makers for its unique technical properties. The environmental benefits were recognised by an award from the US Environmental Protection Agency.

Paints in China

In March, the Chairman, Sir Denys Henderson, opened a new £15 million paint factory in China. This is ICI's first manufacturing venture in China and an important advance in this huge potential market.

Components for cars

In North America, half the airbags in new cars now include components from ICI Explosives. A third of new air-conditioning systems in North American vehicles use ICI's CFC-alternative, 'Klea' 134a.

it all starts with the customer

ICI succeeds by understanding what customers want and being fast on its feet to meet their needs. World leading technology, skilled people, a responsive organisation and a commitment to working in partnership all contribute to its customers' prosperity and success.

Bath appeal

"We chose 'Asterite' because it offered design flexibility and an excellent range of colours and textures. These features helped us to develop our own unique products."

Kyoichi Inoue, President, Cleanup Corporation, Japan

In Japan, household baths have traditionally been made of stainless steel. Realising that consumers wanted something new and different, Japanese bath manufacturers such as Matsushita Denko and Cleanup Corporation saw a market opportunity based on new materials that ICI was to introduce to Japan.

Working closely with its customers – and with their customers, the general public – ICI developed a new formulation of 'Asterite' artificial marble. (Among other benefits, the high thermal resistance of 'Asterite' eminently suits the Japanese trend towards keeping baths filled and hot 24 hours a day.) ICI also provided technical assistance to help its customers switch their manufacturing to the new material. Sales have soared and 'Asterite' now accounts for a growing proportion of new baths in Japanese homes.

Cutting the cost of blasting

"It is Disputada's policy to implement continuous improvement programmes with all its major suppliers. ICI Explosives played a pioneering role in the implementation of such initiatives."

Ivan Violic, General Manager, Los Bronces Mine, Chile

Disputada, an Exxon mining operation in Chile, needed to reduce costs at one of its copper mines. It found the solution in ICI Explosives' highly developed skills in initiating systems and the planning and computer-modelling of blasts.

The key on ICI's part was not to supply a product but an effect. It guaranteed a given amount of rock, reduced to fragments of specified size, at or below an agreed cost. Under the contract, ICI would carry out the blasting and repay the difference if it failed to reduce Disputada's drilling and blasting costs by a guaranteed percentage.

A small ICI team living and working at Los Bronces open-pit copper mine high in the Andes was able to draw on the full range of ICI Explosives' worldwide expertise to save money for the customer. The target was exceeded and the contract continues.

New material, faster production

"In 1994 we became the first company in Europe to make two litre Coca-Cola contour bottles. We owe part of this success to 'Melinar' which guaranteed good bottle strength and excellent shape retention.

"Now, with the unmatched re-heat properties of 'Laser +', we can blow bottles even faster and have raised our productivity by over ten per cent."

Dr Pietro Bruseschi, Director, IFAP spa, Italy

PET resin is used mainly to make plastic bottles for carbonated soft drinks and mineral water. In some cases, the rate at which bottles could be produced was determined not by the manufacturer's equipment but by the time needed to heat the material before blowing it into shape. More bottles could be made if the resin could absorb heat more quickly.

Aware of the problem, ICI developed 'Laser +', a new version of its highly successful 'Melinar' PET. The product's heat-absorbing qualities mean that bottle lines can now be run much faster. The process also uses less energy per bottle.

paints

£m	92	93	94
Turnover	1,580	1,691	**1,712**
Trading profit	115	101	**122**

"After several years of intensive change, ICI Paints is the most sharply-focused coatings enterprise in the world. Our dedication to three core activities, backed by unrivalled coverage of North America, Europe and Asia Pacific, puts us in a powerful position as the paints industry becomes more international.

"We're now structured in a way that allows our people to concentrate on the essentials – serving the customer, developing exciting new products, improving our manufacturing processes and adding to the value of the business. The prospects in all our main markets are encouraging. The challenge now is to build on the strengths we have developed over recent years."

Herman Scopes – Chief Executive Officer

In a difficult market, a combination of outstanding service and high-quality, innovative products produced a 21 per cent rise in ICI Paints' trading profit.

The business faced stiff competition, generally sluggish markets and sharp increases in the price of raw materials and packaging. Consumers, particularly in North America and Europe, remained extremely price-conscious, so higher costs had to be absorbed by improvements in efficiency and productivity.

Sales continued to grow strongly in Asia Pacific, supported by extensions to existing factories in Thailand, Taiwan and Australia and by new plants in Malaysia and China. The Chinese plant, opened in March, is the Group's first in the country. China offers great potential for sales and ICI Paints is rapidly expanding its distribution network. This year, 100 more Colour Centre display shops were opened in Chinese towns and cities.

In Europe, there was good progress in France, Germany, Ireland and the Benelux countries. Results in North America were an improvement on 1993.

Users of coatings are constantly looking for better performance, easier application and greater value for money. ICI Paints has responded during the year in a number of ways. 'Aquabase', the revolutionary, water-based car refinish paint, has been made available in more markets. The range of can coatings has been broadened, particularly in the Americas. The decorative range in the UK and Continental Western Europe has been supplemented with new products such as 'Roller Coaster', 'Ultra', 'Brushwood', 'Onctua', 'Creatone', 'Silk Reflex' and 'Quantum', each offering fresh benefits to the customer. And the introduction of 'Dulux' in the USA has taken ICI Paints' flagship brand into the world's biggest market.

The business completed two acquisitions – Decratrend, a California-based chain of stores for the professional painter; and Cabots, a supplier of woodcare products in Australia.

"We're now clearly concentrating on the three strong businesses where ICI Materials enjoys competitive advantages and good prospects for growth. We're seeing the benefits of all the streamlining of the last few years and we're pressing on towards even greater productivity. The imperatives now are to grow globally and increase our profitability by offering our customers quality, differentiated products based on strong research and development." Bill Madden – Chief Executive Officer

materials

ICI Materials continues to focus on its three global businesses – acrylics, films and polyurethanes. These now account for over 90 per cent of turnover and all three have seen markets improving during the year. North America has been particularly strong, Europe has improved significantly and Japan has shown signs of recovery.

The second half of the year brought a sharp rise in the price of key raw materials, particularly in acrylics. Although its own product prices have improved, ICI Materials has suffered a squeeze between buying and selling prices.

ICI Acrylics has now integrated the US business acquired in 1993 and its success owes much to the willingness of all employees to learn from each other. The acquisition, along with recent investments, has made ICI Acrylics a global business and the

world's largest producer of methyl methacrylate. The financial benefits of the acquisition have been partly offset this year by the rise in raw material prices and production difficulties in Europe. However, the benefits should become more apparent in 1995.

ICI Films has concentrated on making its plants more productive and now produces far more from the same assets than it did a year ago. It has extended its product range, particularly in packaging, and today is better able to supply exactly what its customers want. In a clear change of culture, staff at every level are more willing to take the initiative in suggesting improvements, satisfying the customer and sharing ideas with colleagues around the world.

ICI Polyurethanes faces rising demand, particularly as many of its products have attractive environmental advantages. Plants are fully loaded and in many cases capacity has been increased. In October, the business announced its intention to build a large MDI plant in Holland – MDI being the basis of most of its products. The innovative, cushioning material, 'Waterlily', has had a successful first year in the market. Designed to offer better environmental performance throughout its lifecycle, it recently won an international award from the US Environmental Protection Agency.

ICI Annual Review and Summary Financial Statement 1994

11

explosives

£m	92	93	94
Turnover	573	643	786
Trading profit	59	51	45

"We're determined to remain the world's number one explosives company. As opportunities increase, we're expanding capacity across the whole spectrum of our business from ammonium nitrate production, to small-scale plants on site at our customers' mines and quarries, to new detonator assembly lines.

"Our aim is to use technology to help our customers succeed. That means going where the mining industry goes and solving problems on the spot. Our growth depends on small, scattered teams of ICI people giving terrific service to their customers."

Peter Clinch – Chief Executive Officer

Despite strong growth in sales and profits in Australia, Asia and South America, overall financial performance in 1994 was disappointing.

In South Africa, demand was seriously affected by the election and subsequent labour unrest. In addition, two separate explosions, with the tragic loss of eleven lives, have accelerated the closure of some plants and the decision to restructure the business using more modern products and processes.

The North American explosives business reported lower profits due to intense competition and substantial increases in the cost of major raw materials. In the UK, losses increased as demand continued to decline with the closure of more coal mines.

The widening geographic spread of the mining industry, together with the introduction of new products, has resulted in decisions to scale down or close old sites. An exceptional charge of £80 million to cover restructuring and closure costs has been provided in the 1994 accounts.

The mining industry continues to seek new, lower cost operations across the globe and ICI is responding by building dedicated explosives plants to support new mines. New facilities include plants in Ghana, Chile, Vietnam and Indonesia with further plants and joint ventures under investigation in several countries.

The new ammonium nitrate plant in Australia is to be doubled in size to keep pace with demand. ICI Explosives is also doubling its capacity for making initiating systems with new facilities in Australia, India, Brazil and South Africa. Further growth and investments are planned for the automotive airbag sector, and the environmental services business in the USA is commissioning its high technology incinerator for civil and military waste explosives.

industrial chemicals
Chemicals & Polymers

"After three difficult years of recession, the self-help measures that raised C&P's profits last year have now been augmented by recovery in our markets. We're determined that these measures should continue during the upswing to make us still more competitive and to protect the business against future downturns.

"Success depends on empowered people. During the year, our staff have responded magnificently by getting the best from our plants and working hard at pleasing our customers. Thanks to their efforts, we've achieved a first-class performance."

Mike Brogden – Chief Executive Officer, ICI Chemicals & Polymers

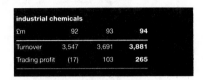

industrial chemicals			
£m	92	93	**94**
Turnover	3,547	3,691	**3,881**
Trading profit	(17)	103	**265**

As world economies improved, so did the markets for most of C&P's products. Selling prices have risen, though many have some way to go to reach those of the late 1980s and justify reinvestment.

The benefit from stronger markets has reinforced the improvement in performance resulting from the radical internal changes of the last few years. Restructuring, cutting costs, raising quality and boosting productivity were having a major impact before the recovery began. As markets improve, the continued emphasis on self-help measures is adding impetus to C&P's progress.

When recovery began, it was crucial that C&P's plants were able to respond – as indeed they did. With many at full stretch, C&P has been working hard to increase capacity.

It was a good year for the growth businesses of PTA, 'Melinar' PET resins, surfactants, catalysts and the CFC-replacement, 'Klea'. Common to all these businesses is technological leadership based on world-class research and processes. In each case there are plans to build on success by expanding capacity still further.

In July, ICI announced a $100 million investment in 'Melinar' PET capacity in the USA to meet rapidly growing demand. The Group is also planning a second PTA plant in Taiwan alongside the first, which is now at full capacity just a little over two years from its opening. Along with another projected PTA plant in Pakistan, the Taiwanese plant will use advanced technology to achieve low-cost production.

Petrochemicals and fertilizers showed an encouraging recovery, but chlor-alkali products remained under competitive pressure for much of the year.

In order to focus on its growth businesses, C&P has divested its West European polypropylene business, its polyols business in the USA and The Monckton Coke & Chemical Company Limited in the UK. EVC, the Group's joint venture in PVC, was successfully floated on the Amsterdam Stock Exchange. In February 1995, C&P completed the disposal of the ethylene oxide and derivatives business.

industrial chemicals
Tioxide

"In the last few years, Tioxide has built up the assets, technologies and market positions it needs for future profitable growth. We intend to use these strengths to expand in our chosen markets, particularly North America and Asia Pacific, while maintaining our leadership in Europe.

"By focusing on sectors where Tioxide has a competitive advantage, and by developing products specifically for these sectors, we hope to enjoy the benefits not only of world economic recovery but of greater added value."

Alan Pedder – Chief Executive Officer, Tioxide Group Limited

1994 brought a sharp recovery in demand as continental Europe followed the USA and the UK out of recession and Japan's economy began to improve. A balance of supply and demand has allowed prices to rise, though they still lag well behind their pre-recession levels. The expected growth in demand in 1995 should lift prices further in all Tioxide's markets.

Despite the recession, Tioxide has invested heavily to bring all its plants into line with environmental standards around the world. This year saw the commissioning of new environmental projects in the UK, France, Spain, Italy, Australia and South Africa. In addition, the recently acquired chloride-process plant in Louisiana, USA, and a new sulphate-process plant in Malaysia both came fully on stream.

The task of starting up so much new production so quickly presented problems at some of the plants. These, however, were resolved during the year and Tioxide was able to increase both its sales and its market share.

The new investments provide environmentally sound capacity just at a time when world demand is recovering. They give Tioxide a strong manufacturing presence in the three main regions of Europe, North America and Asia Pacific as well as in South Africa. They also provide a good balance between the chloride and sulphate production routes.

Tioxide has completed the process of focusing its business on three market sectors – coatings, plastics and specialities. Having thoroughly overhauled its manufacturing, research and marketing functions, it is now concentrating on developing its product line and introducing specialised products within these sectors. It has also set up a new business, Tioxide Materials, to find markets for co-products from the manufacturing process.

Strength in research has made possible a further group of businesses that are helping to extend the range and make Tioxide less susceptible to the economic cycle. These include innovative products such as advanced engineering ceramics, 'Spectraveil' inorganic dispersants increasingly used in cosmetics and suncreams, and a widening range of organometallic compounds for end uses such as catalysts and adhesion promoters.

£m	92	93	**94**
Turnover	1,322	1,416	**1,477**
Trading profit	8	45	**80**

regional businesses

ICI invests in businesses that create value for shareholders. These include not just the global businesses of Paints, Materials, Explosives, Chemicals & Polymers and Tioxide, but also a number of regional businesses where ICI is strong in the local market.

As with the global businesses, ICI continues to streamline its regional portfolio in order to focus on its strengths. During 1994 it completed the disposal of some of its businesses in India and Argentina. It also sold its stake in Chemical Company of Malaysia Berhad to a management buy-out while retaining its 60 per cent holding in ICI Paints (Malaysia) Sdn. Bhd.

Elsewhere ICI invested heavily, sanctioning £250 million in capital projects for regional businesses.

Well over half of ICI's regional sales are in **Australia**. Although drought affected the fertilizers and crop-care businesses, the improving Australian economy produced better results in the chemicals businesses. Plastics, in particular, benefited from rising demand, lower feedstock costs and better international prices, all helped by further rationalisation and strenuous efforts to reduce costs. Two big investments – the ethane pipeline mentioned on page 7 and further capacity in PVC – are important steps

in making ICI Australia a world-competitive business.

In **Pakistan**, polyester fibres had an excellent year and the Group has sanctioned a further expansion of capacity. The strong growth of the country's fibres industry is one of the factors that has led C&P to consider building a PTA plant in Pakistan. The soda ash business also performed well and an extension to the plant was commissioned ahead of schedule in December.

In **India**, sales and trading profit both rose. In rubber chemicals, the price-weakening effect of cheap imports was more than countered by greater efficiencies and lower fixed costs.

In **Canada**, the Forest Products business improved its performance as a result of vigorous cost reductions and more favourable market conditions.

The Duperial Group in **Argentina** had a better year after recent restructuring and now looks set to benefit from the country's economic growth.

research, technology and engineering

The products and processes generated by ICI's research, technology and engineering (RT&E) are central to the Group's ambition of enhancing shareholder value. RT&E helps the Group to outflank its competitors and satisfy its customers more fully. It strengthens the ICI of today and renews it for the future.

1994 has brought further innovation across the Group.

In France and Germany, Paints has launched new gloss and semi-gloss paints with better coverage and half the solvent levels of existing products. It has also introduced a waterborne exterior woodstain system in the UK; waterborne spray-applied linings for the insides of food cans in the USA; and 'Mouldshield' paints from Paints in Australia for use in tropical climates.

Films has the broadest portfolio of polyester films in the industry. The 'Melinex' range has been extended with an easily-peelable seal for yogurt pots and ready-meal containers along with new environmentally-friendly films for labels and food packaging.

Polyurethanes has replaced CFC blowing agents with water in most of its foams.

Explosives uses a suite of computer models to supply sophisticated blasting services to the world's mines and quarries. Its advanced product and process technology provides strong competitive edge as it seeks out new opportunities in countries such as China.

Chemicals & Polymers has further developed its process technology for PTA, 'Melinar' PET and 'Klea' and added new products to its range of PET resins, lubricants, surfactants and environmental catalysts.

Tioxide is developing innovative products such as advanced engineering ceramics, UV-absorbing inorganic dispersants and organo-metallic compounds.

To achieve this spectrum of results, ICI spends around £250 million a year on R&T, including technical service, and has over 4,000 people working full-time in RT&E.

These staff apply their expertise directly to ICI's products and processes. The Group has a core of science and technology skills ranging

from colloids and catalysts to process technology, engineering and manufacturing. These capabilities are networked across ICI so that any business can draw at any time on the Group's total resource.

ICI's core skills are kept up to date through joint research projects in universities around the world. Money spent on academic collaboration rose sharply in 1994 and now totals around £5 million a year.

An important development in 1994 was the emergence of ICI Engineering Technology and its relocation to the technical centres at Runcorn and Wilton in the UK. ICI's corporate engineering staff provide skills and processes vital for business advantage but not sustainable in any one business. The move integrates ICI's engineering capability with the technological and business concerns of the wider Group, so making RT&E projects faster and more effective.

The new subsidiary, Eutech Engineering Solutions Limited, offers engineering services to customers both inside and outside the Group and has just completed a successful first year of trading.

safety, health and the environment

The Group remains committed to a constantly improving record on safety, health and environmental performance.

ICI deeply regrets that twelve employees and three contract workers died on Group business in 1994. Eleven employees died in two separate incidents at ICI's explosives operations in South Africa. After a review by the ICI Executive Directors, the local management has been reinforced and better safety programmes have been implemented.

Despite these sad events, the overall number of reportable injuries fell to a new low during the year. New initiatives have heightened safety awareness among employees and contractors across the Group.

The inaugural winner of the Chief Executive's Safety Award was a team from Paints in Malaysia which achieved remarkable safety standards during the building of a new factory. The 300-strong construction force – mainly contract workers – passed 500,000 man hours without a reportable injury.

ICI makes comprehensive provision for occupational healthcare for its employees and others on site. It also provides all necessary information to its customers to enable its products to be used safely.

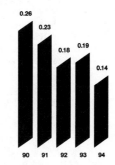

Group reportable injuries
per 100,000 working hours

The Group has also made further progress towards the environmental objectives it set itself in 1990. Details are in the environmental report issued with this Review.

ICI's people

The Group's overall aim is to maximise value for its shareholders. This means releasing the energy of ICI's people and stripping away anything that stifles their creativity.

In 1994, the average number of people employed by the worldwide Group was 67,500. Of this total, 31 per cent are in the UK, 9 per cent in Continental Europe, 22 per cent in the Americas, 20 per cent in Asia Pacific and 18 per cent in other countries.

The reshaping and cost-cutting of the last few years have created a flatter, leaner organisation with devolved responsibilities and fewer obstacles to quick decision-making. These changes are helping to foster the responsive, entrepreneurial spirit of a small organisation within the framework of a large one. The aim is a Group in which everybody knows what is expected of them, has the freedom to take initiatives, is accountable for the result and is properly rewarded for their contribution. Only by becoming this kind of organisation will ICI continue to deliver excellent products and service to its customers.

The Group's training and education are aimed at creating just such a culture. The worldwide Shareholder Value programme encourages staff to identify with their businesses and understand how their actions can help or hinder the growth of shareholder value.

The Group's worldwide expenditure on charitable donations in 1994 amounted to £2.0 million. Of this total, £0.9 million was spent in the UK. In addition, £1.0 million was spent by local units in the UK on communtiy projects. These units also gave some 45 years of staff time to their communities. Within the UK, ICI also spent £1.0 million on academic liaison and related activities. As in previous years, the Company made no donations for political purposes.

ICI Annual Review and Summary Financial Statement 1994

summary financial statement

financial review

Summary Directors' Report :
A review of the business during
1994 and an indication of the future
developments in the Group are
given in the Chairman's Statement,
the Chief Executive's Review and
the Business Review on pages 3 to
15 which are adopted as part of
this Report.

Economic background and turnover

Growth in the OECD at nearly 3% was more than double the rate in 1993 with industrial production recovering even more strongly. The US and UK economies expanded rapidly and Continental Europe recovered from the sharp fall of 1993. Japan also started to recover in the second half of the year.

Total chemical demand in ICI's markets rose by about 5% compared to 1% in 1993 whilst ICI's own sales volumes grew by 7%. Exchange rate movements had little effect on the year's results. Despite much greater demand for chemical products, 1994 was another year of fierce competition making it difficult to raise selling prices, except in Industrial Chemicals' markets in the second half of the year.

Turnover by business sector

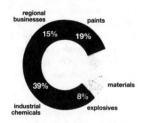

Group turnover of £9,189m was 9% above 1993 reflecting improved

volumes in all geographic markets and selling prices which, on average, were 2% higher.

Encouraging improvements in sales volumes occurred in all businesses except Explosives. Increased turnover in Explosives was primarily due to the inclusion of AECI Explosives Ltd (AEL). Price increases in Industrial Chemicals also made a significant contribution but turnover was affected by the sale of the US polyols and European polypropylene businesses.

Profits before exceptional items

At £588m trading profit was over 80% higher than in 1993, due mainly to the effects of price and volume partly offset by higher raw material costs, primarily in Materials.

Trading profit before exceptional items by business sector

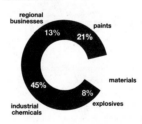

Significant improvements arose in Industrial Chemicals with profits of £265m up by 157% and Materials, where profits have grown fivefold to £76m strengthened by the US Acrylics business acquired in 1993. Regional businesses increased profits by 78%, due mainly to an improved performance in ICI Australia's chemicals business and in Argentina following withdrawal from the PVC business.

Turnover by market

Income from associated undertakings fell sharply by £31m to £14m, due mainly to the Group's disposal of its holding in AECI Limited.

Net interest payable of £88m was slightly less than in 1993, reflecting the lower average level of net indebtedness and the repayment of some high coupon borrowings.

Profit before tax for the year at £514m was 84% higher than in 1993.

The taxation charge was £182m giving an effective rate of 35%. This reflected the utilisation of tax losses in certain overseas subsidiaries as these returned to profit. No ACT was written off in the year.

Productivity

Productivity continued to improve in terms of both turnover per employee (up from £120,000 in 1993 to £136,000) and added value per employee (up from £35,000 to £40,000 in 1994).

During 1994 the major cost reduction and restructuring programmes initiated in 1990 and 1992 contributed an additional £100m to Group pre-tax profit. The annualised rate of savings at the end of the year was £475m compared with 1990. Staff numbers adjusted for divestments and acquisitions fell by 6% in the year.

Exceptional items

The charge against trading profit of £67m was in respect of the restructuring of the Explosives operations, principally in the USA, the UK and South Africa.

The charge against associated undertakings was in respect of exceptional asset write-downs by EVC prior to its flotation. The flotation of EVC, together with the reduction of ICI's holding and the transfer of its related operations to EVC, resulted in a total charge to profit and loss account of £112m.

Net losses on sale or closure of operations included the costs of withdrawing from the nitroglycerine explosives business, the sale of related operations to EVC, the sales of the US polyols and European polypropylene businesses and of ICI's shareholding in Chemical Company of Malaysia Berhad.

Profits on the disposal of fixed assets related to the sale of part of the Group's holding in EVC, the disposal of the remaining holding in AECI and ICI's interest in Westralian Sands Limited.

Earnings and dividends

The Group continues the drive to improve its return on net assets.

Return on net assets*

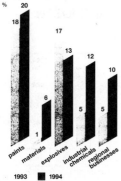

■ 1993   ■ 1994

* trading profit as a % of net operating assets and capital under construction

Earnings from continuing operations before exceptional items increased by over 90% to £270m (1993 £141m). This represented earnings per £1 Ordinary Share of 37.3p compared with 19.6p in the previous year. After exceptional items, total earnings for the year were £188m equivalent to 26.0p per share.

The Annual General Meeting will be asked to confirm a second interim Ordinary dividend to shareholders of 17.0p per £1 Ordinary Share as the final dividend for 1994, payable on 26 April 1995. Together with the interim dividend of 10.5p per £1 Ordinary Share paid on 3 October 1994, this makes a total cash dividend of 27.5p for the year. The gross equivalent including the related tax credit is 34.4p, and the payment of these dividends requires appropriations totalling £199m of which £11m will be met from reserves.

The dividend remains unchanged from 1993 but dividend cover, before exceptional items, has improved to 1.4. The Board's objective is to build dividend cover and to ensure that the future level of dividends will reflect the strength and sustainability of underlying earnings through the trade cycle.

Investments and disposals

Capital expenditure authorised in 1994 amounted to £613m. Major sanctions included the world's largest single stream plant to manufacture 'Melinar' PET in the USA, a 1,380 km ethane pipeline in Australia, a major polyester fibre expansion in Pakistan, additional airbag initiator capacity in North America, increased 'Klea' 134a capacity in the USA and a new decorative paint plant in Indonesia.

Acquisitions in the year included decorative paint outlets in the west of the USA, and a small strategic stake in China's largest polyester fibre producer.

The major disposals in 1994 have already been referred to above.

Capital gearing
£ million

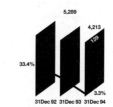

■ Minority interests and shareholders' funds – £m

Net borrowings (total borrowings less cash, investments and short-term deposits) – £m

— Capital gearing – net borrowings as a percentage of net borrowings, minority interests and shareholders' funds – %

Cash flow and finance

The Group's cash flow was strong during the year and capital gearing fell to 3.3%.

The net cash inflow from operating activities was £888m compared to £1,026m in 1993 (which included £200m from the pre-demerger Zeneca operations). Working capital increased only marginally despite a significant increase in sales.

Income from investments was down by £54m reflecting the disposal of the shareholding in AECI, and net interest payable was reduced due to lower net indebtedness.

Tax payments were down due mainly to tax repayments associated with loss relief claims.

Expenditure on fixed assets amounted to £373m and was similar to the 1993 level for continuing operations. Acquisitions of £37m included AEL, and disposals of £310m included £83m in respect of EVC and £80m in respect of AECI.

Net cash inflow, before financing, totalled £775m, of which £223m was used to reduce borrowings and, after taking into account share issues in respect of options, the Group's cash and cash equivalents increased by £562m.

The management of the Group's cash flows continues to be given the highest priority.

ICI Annual Review and Summary Financial Statement 1994

summary group profit and loss account

for the year ended 31 December 1994

	Notes	1994 Continuing operations Before exceptional items £m	1994 Continuing operations Exceptional items £m	1994 Discontinued operations £m	1994 Total £m	1993† Continuing operations Before exceptional items £m	1993† Continuing operations Exceptional items £m	1993† Discontinued operations £m	1993† Total £m
Turnover	1	9,189	–	–	9,189	8,430	–	2,202	10,632
Trading profit (loss)	1	588	(67)	–	521	325	–	294	619
Share of losses less profits of associated undertakings		14	(70)	–	(56)	45	–	2	47
Losses less profits on sale or closure of operations		–	(39)	–	(39)	–	(94)	(59)	(153)
Profits on disposal of fixed assets		–	70	–	70	–	–	–	–
Profit (loss) on ordinary activities before interest	1	602	(106)	–	496	370	(94)	237	513
Net interest payable		(88)	–	–	(88)	(90)	–	(63)	(153)
Profit (loss) on ordinary activities before taxation		514	(106)	–	408	280	(94)	174	360
Tax on profit (loss) on ordinary activities		(182)	18	–	(164)	(101)	(18)	(70)	(189)
Profit (loss) on ordinary activities after taxation		332	(88)	–	244	179	(112)	104	171
Attributable to minorities		(62)	6	–	(56)	(38)	(4)	–	(42)
Net profit (loss) for the financial year		270	(82)	–	188	141	(116)	104	129
Dividends	2								
Cash					(199)				(199)
Demerger									(363)
					(199)				(562)
Loss retained for year					(11)				(433)
Earnings (loss) per £1 Ordinary Share	3	37.3p	(11.3)p	–	26.0p	19.6p	(16.1)p	14.4p	17.9p

Note: Directors' emoluments are set out in note 4, page 23.

statement of group total recognised gains and losses

for the year ended 31 December 1994

	Notes	1994 £m	1993† £m
Net profit for the financial year		188	129
Currency translation differences on foreign currency net investments and related loans		(96)	(23)
Share of other reserve movements of associated undertakings and other items		(7)	–
Total recognised gains and losses relating to the year		85	106
Prior year adjustment	5	(95)	
Total gains and losses recognised since last annual report		(10)	

† Restated (note 5)

summary group balance sheet

at 31 December 1994

	1994 £m	1993† £m
ASSETS EMPLOYED		
Fixed assets		
Tangible assets	**3,861**	4,024
Investments	**171**	458
	4,032	4,482
Current assets	**4,972**	4,747
Total assets	**9,004**	9,229
Creditors due within one year	**(2,608)**	(2,452)
Net current assets	**2,364**	2,295
Total assets less current liabilities	**6,396**	6,777
FINANCED BY		
Creditors due after more than one year		
Loans	**1,522**	1,717
Other creditors	**95**	123
	1,617	1,840
Provisions for liabilities and charges	**675**	680
Deferred income: Grants not yet credited to profit	**30**	39
Minority interests – equity	**338**	330
Shareholders' funds – equity		
Called-up share capital	**724**	722
Reserves	**3,012**	3,166
Total capital and reserves attributable to parent company	**3,736**	3,888
	6,396	6,777
Capital gearing		
Net borrowings (total borrowings less cash, current asset investments and short-term deposits)		
as a percentage of net borrowings, minority interests and shareholders' funds.	**3.3%**	20.2%

reconciliation of movements in shareholders' funds

for the year ended 31 December 1994

	1994 £m	1993† £m
Net profit for the financial year	**188**	129
Dividends		
Cash	**(199)**	(199)
Demerger		(363)
Loss retained for year	**(11)**	(433)
Issues of ICI Ordinary Shares	**10**	67
Goodwill movement	**(48)**	80
Other recognised losses related to the year	**(103)**	(23)
Net reduction in shareholders' funds	**(152)**	(309)
Shareholders' funds at beginning of year	**3,888**	4,197
(1994 originally was £3,983m (1993 £4,286m) before deduction of prior year adjustment of £95m (£89m))		
Shareholders' funds at end of year	**3,736**	3,888

† *Restated (note 5)*

statement of group cash flow

for the year ended 31 December 1994

	1994 £m	1993 £m
Cash inflow from operating activities		
Net cash inflow from trading operations	**1,032**	1,305
Outflow related to exceptional items	**(144)**	(279)
Net cash inflow from operating activities	**888**	1,026
Returns on investments and servicing of finance		
Interest and dividends received	**105**	159
Interest paid	**(182)**	(254)
Dividends paid by parent company	**(199)**	(318)
Dividends paid by subsidiary undertakings to minority interests	**(32)**	(20)
Net cash outflow from returns on investments and servicing of finance	**(308)**	(433)
Tax paid	**(98)**	(144)
Investing activities		
Cash expenditure on tangible fixed assets	**(373)**	(485)
Acquisitions and new fixed asset investments	**(37)**	(286)
Disposals	**310**	443
Repayment of debt by Zeneca	**568**	1,364
Purchase of short-term investments and deposits	**(175)**	(436)
Cash and cash equivalents of Zeneca at date of demerger		(153)
Net cash inflow from investing activities	**293**	447
Net cash inflow before financing	**775**	896
Financing		
Issues of ICI Ordinary Shares	**10**	67
Net decrease in loans	**(199)**	(379)
Net decrease in lease finance	**(30)**	(15)
Net increase (decrease) in short-term borrowings	**6**	(3)
Issue of shares to minorities by subsidiary undertakings	**–**	6
Net cash outflow from financing	**(213)**	(324)
Increase in cash and cash equivalents	**562**	572

auditors' statement

To the Members of Imperial Chemical Industries PLC.

We have examined the Summary Financial Statement on pages 18 to 24.

Respective responsibilities of directors and auditors

The Summary Financial Statement is the responsibility of the Directors. Our responsibility is to issue an independent opinion on the Summary Financial Statement.

Basis of opinion

We conducted our examination in accordance with guidelines issued by the Auditing Practices Board and carried out such procedures as we considered necessary to support our opinion. Our report on the Group's full annual accounts describes the basis of our audit opinion on those accounts.

Opinion

In our opinion the Summary Financial Statement is consistent with the Annual Accounts and Directors' Report of Imperial Chemical Industries PLC for the year ended 31 December 1994 and complies with the requirements of section 251 of the Companies Act 1985 and the regulations made thereunder.

London
6 March 1995

KPMG
Chartered Accountants
Registered Auditors

The Auditors' Report on the full accounts for the year ended 31 December 1994 was unqualified and did not include a statement under sections 237(2) (accounting records or returns inadequate or accounts not agreeing with records and returns) or 237(3) (failure to obtain necessary information and explanations) of the Companies Act 1985.

notes relating to the summary financial statement

1 Segment information

CLASSES OF BUSINESS	Turnover		Trading profit before exceptional items		Profit before interest and taxation after exceptional items	
	1994 **£m**	1993 £m	**1994** **£m**	1993 £m	**1994** **£m**	1993 £m
Continuing operations						
Paints	**1,712**	1,691	**122**	101	**117**	127
Materials	**1,748**	1,494	**76**	14	**83**	(81)
Explosives	**786**	643	**45**	51	**(35)**	51
Industrial Chemicals	**3,881**	3,691	**265**	103	**253**	102
Regional Businesses	**1,477**	1,416	**80**	45	**134**	21
Inter-class eliminations	**(415)**	(373)	**–**	11	**–**	11
Share of losses less profits of associated undertakings					**(56)**	45
	9,189	8,562				
Sales to discontinued operations	**–**	(132)				
	9,189	8,430	**588**	325	**496**	276
Discontinued operations	**–**	2,256	**–**	294	**–**	237
Sales to continuing operations	**–**	(54)				
	–	2,202	**–**	294	**–**	237
	9,189	10,632	**588**	619	**496**	513

2 Dividends

	1994 **pence per** **£1 Share**	1993 pence per £1 Share	**1994** **£m**	1993 £m
Interim, paid 3 October 1994	**10.5p**	10.5p	**76**	76
Second interim, to be confirmed as final, payable 26 April 1995	**17.0p**	17.0p	**123**	123
	27.5p	27.5p	**199**	199
Demerger dividend – This comprised the net assets of Zeneca at date of demerger.				363
			199	562

3 Earnings (loss) per £1 Ordinary Share

	million	million
Earnings (loss) per £1 Ordinary Share has been calculated based on the average Ordinary Shares in issue during the year, weighted on a time basis	**723**	719

4 Remuneration policy and directors' contracts, emoluments and interests in share options

The Company pays competitive wages and salaries to its employees around the world. These include incentive payments which reward enhanced shareholder value. Levels of pay and the structure of arrangements in each country reflect the competitive environment in that country. Whilst ICI does not have global pay scales, it has to have regard to its need to be able to move staff around the world.

The contracts and emoluments of executive directors and senior executives are determined by the Remuneration and Nomination Committee ("the Remuneration Committee"), which for this purpose is composed wholly of non-executive directors of the Company. The remuneration package comprises short, medium and longer term benefits, with the incentive element geared to shareholder value enhancement.

Service contracts – Normally executive directors are employed on rolling contracts subject to two years' notice at any time, save on first appointment, when the contract is for an initial period of three years. Contracts expire at normal retirement age of 62. Sir Denys Henderson's contract as Chairman, and Sir Ronald Hampel's contract as Chief Executive, expire at the conclusion of the AGM in 1995.

The short-term benefits – are an annual salary, health plan and car benefits and participation in the Annual Performance Related Bonus Scheme. No annual cost of living or inflation adjustment is made, but each year the salary scale is measured against external benchmarks to ensure it remains competitive. Annual assessment of each individual executive director's performance is carried out by the Remuneration Committee.

In 1994 there was no adjustment to the executive directors' salary scale and no salary increase was awarded to any executive director, including the Chairman and Chief Executive.

notes relating to the summary financial statement

4   Remuneration policy and directors' contracts, emoluments and interests in share options (continued)

The level of bonus (if any) under the Annual Performance Related Bonus Scheme is determined by the Remuneration Committee on the basis of criteria established at the beginning of the year.

For 1994 the bonus for executive directors was linked entirely to increased earnings per share ("EPS"). The trigger point was established at a covered dividend of 27.5p. This figure was above the budget accepted by the Board as the 1994 plan and significantly above the 19.6p EPS achieved in 1993. The 37.3p achieved EPS in 1994 has resulted in the payment of a bonus at the maximum level of 40%. The level of bonus paid in 1993 was 10%; no bonuses were paid in the previous four years.

The medium-term benefit – is the Bonus Conversion Plan, designed to encourage the conversion of any annual bonus into shares in the Company and the holding of those shares for a minimum of three years. Shares purchased in the Plan are released at the end of a three year retention period and are then matched by an equal number of shares by the Company on which the individual is required to pay income tax.

The long-term benefit – is the Share Option Scheme under which options over the Company's Ordinary Shares may be granted each year to executive directors and senior executives at a multiple of 0.8 times salary for directors (except on first appointment) subject to an overall maximum holding of four times salary.

Post-retirement benefits – All executive directors, other than Mr C M Short and Mr C Miller Smith, are members of the ICI Pension Fund, which is open to all UK employees. The Company made a contribution for all employees, including executive directors in the ICI Pension Fund, at a rate of 13.68% of salary in 1994 except for the Chairman and Sir Ronald Hampel, who are the last two long serving members of the Pension Fund whose contributions were capped at significantly lower levels.

Mr C Miller Smith has a Funded Unapproved Pension Scheme to which the Company makes a contribution equivalent to 25% of his salary. Mr C M Short is entitled by contract to an unfunded pension from the Company on retirement.

	1994 Salary £000	1994 Benefits £000	1994 Bonus £000	Total £000	1993 Total £000
Emoluments of directors					
Remuneration of executive directors					
Sir Denys Henderson – Chairman	313	6	125	**444**	493
Sir Ronald Hampel – Chief Executive	425	12	170	**607**	479
C. Miller Smith (appointed executive director 1 October 1994)	87	3	35	**125**	
M. E. Brogden (appointed 1 May 1994)	167	7	67	**241**	
C. Hampson (retired 29 April 1994)	100	4	40	**144**	342
R. J. Margetts	250	8	100	**358**	255
C. M. Short	300	17	120	**437**	353
A. G. Spall (appointed 1 January 1994)	250	8	100	**358**	
Directors who ceased to be directors of ICI on demerger of Zeneca					367
	1,892	65	757†	**2,714**	2,289
Fees to non-executive directors				**97**	194
Pension fund contributions				**111**	70
Total emoluments				**2,922**	2,553
Remuneration of executive directors 1993	1,815	60	414		

† Excludes the benefit of shares under the Bonus Conversion Plan (see The medium-term benefit, above) which will be included in emoluments in the year in which the benefit of the extra shares provided by the Company is received by the director.

Interests in share options

Directors at 31 December 1994	1 January 1994 Number	Options granted Number	Options granted Weighted average price £	Options exercised Number	Options exercised Exercise price £	Options exercised Market price £	31 December 1994 Number	31 December 1994 Weighted average exercise price £	31 December 1994 Date from which exercisable	31 December 1994 Expiry date
Sir Denys Henderson	177,765						177,765	5.79	2.4.89	28.5.02
Sir Ronald Hampel	281,926						281,926	6.03	2.4.89	24.6.03
C. Miller Smith		178,300	7.85				178,300	7.85	7.11.97	7.11.04
M. E. Brogden	34,560*			1,000	5.26	7.76½	33,560	6.47	3.4.94	22.3.04
R. J. Margetts	154,092	1,371	6.34				155,463	6.00	2.4.89	25.11.03
C. M. Short	52,199						52,199	6.90	3.4.94	25.11.03
A. G. Spall	15,500	58,664	7.53				74,164	7.35	24.6.96	22.3.04

*Interest at date of appointment.

No options lapsed during the year. The options outstanding are exercisable at prices between £4.97 and £7.85. The market price of the shares at 31 December 1994 was £7.48½ and the range during 1994 was £7.28½ to £8.67½.

5   Restatement

All comparative figures for 1993 have been restated to reflect the adoption of the accounting requirements in respect of accounting for post-retirement benefits other than pensions.

6   Approval of Summary Financial Statement

This Summary Financial Statement was approved by the directors on 6 March 1995 and signed on their behalf by Sir Denys Henderson and Mr A G Spall.

shareholder information

Quarterly results

Unaudited trading results of the ICI Group for 1995 are expected to be announced as follows:

First quarter	27 April 1995
Half year	27 July 1995
Nine months	26 October 1995
Full year	22 February 1996

Dividend payments

A second interim dividend for the year 1994, which the Annual General Meeting will be asked to confirm as the final dividend for that year, is payable on 26 April 1995 to Ordinary shareholders registered in the books of the Company on 23 March 1995. Dividends are normally paid as follows:

First interim: Announced with the Half year results and paid in early October.

Second interim: Announced with the Full year results and paid in late April.

Taxation

In certain circumstances, when a shareholder in the UK sells shares, his liability to tax in respect of capital gains is computed by reference to the market value of the shares on 31 March 1982 adjusted for inflation between that date and the date of disposal. The market value of ICI Ordinary Shares at 31 March 1982, for the purposes of capital gains tax, was 309p.

Shares in Zeneca acquired on demerger from ICI will be treated as having a base cost for capital gains tax purposes ascertained by reference to the values of ICI and Zeneca shares on 1 June 1993 calculated in accordance with the provisions of Section 272 of the Taxation of Chargeable Gains Act 1992. The base cost of any holding of ICI shares on that date will be adjusted on the same basis.

The relevant prices on The London Stock Exchange on 1 June 1993 were:

ICI – 631.75p and Zeneca – 625.75p.

Base costs in the pre-demerger ICI shares will, therefore, be split between the post-demerger ICI and Zeneca shares in the proportion:

ICI – 0.50239 and Zeneca – 0.49761.

The Company is not, and has not been, a close company within the provisions of the Income and Corporation Taxes Act 1988.

Auditors

The remuneration and expenses of the Auditors in respect of the statutory report to the members of the Company for the year 1994 amounted to £280,000 (1993: £282,000). The total figure for the Group was £3.5m (1993: £3.4m) which includes charges for audits of subsidiary companies in the UK and overseas, both for the purposes of consolidation into the Group accounts and to meet statutory requirements of the countries in which subsidiaries operate.

Shareholders

The following table analyses the holdings of £1 Ordinary Shares at the end of 1994:

Size of holding	Number of Ordinary shareholders' accounts	Number of shares	%
1-250	120,899	14,432,715	2.0
251-500	65,419	24,400,466	3.4
501-1,000	46,844	33,901,775	4.7
1,001-5,000	25,204	44,149,636	6.1
5,001-10,000	809	5,753,751	0.8
10,001-50,000	762	18,219,501	2.5
50,001-1,000,000	775	171,565,418	23.7
Over 1,000,000	91	411,474,652	56.8
All holdings	260,803	723,897,914	100.0

In addition to the number of registered shareholders shown, there are approximately 43,000 holders of American Depositary Receipts (ADRs). The ADRs, each of which is equivalent to four £1 Ordinary Shares, are issued by Morgan Guaranty Trust Company of New York.

As at 21 February 1995 (one month prior to the date of Notice of Meeting) Morgan Guaranty Trust Company of New York had a non-beneficial interest in 97,811,423 Ordinary Shares of the Company (13.51% of the issued Ordinary Share Capital), all of which were registered in the name of their nominee company, Guaranty Nominees Limited, in respect of ADRs. No other person held an interest in shares, comprising 3% or more of the issued Ordinary Share Capital of the Company, appearing in the register of interests in shares maintained under the provisions of Section 211 of the Companies Act 1985.

ICI Ordinary Shares are listed on The London Stock Exchange and other major European stock exchanges. In the form of ADRs, they are also listed on the New York Stock Exchange.

The Company from time to time files reports with the United States Securities and Exchange Commission. As a standing arrangement, a copy of each such report filed within the preceding 12 months can be inspected by any shareholder or ADR holder during normal business hours at the offices of ICI at 9 Millbank, London, SW1P 3JF and at Olympic Tower, 645 Fifth Avenue, New York.

Personal Equity Plans (PEPs)

Details of the ICI General PEP and the ICI Single Company PEP may be obtained from:
The Plan Manager
Bradford & Bingley (PEPs) Limited
Telephone helpline:
(01274) 555677

Registered Office

Imperial Chemical House
Millbank
London SW1P 3JF
Telephone: (0171) 834 4444

Registrar and Transfer Office

I C Parkinson
PO Box 251
Wexham Road
Slough SL2 5DP
Telephone: (01753) 877008

Auditors

KPMG
8 Salisbury Square
Blackfriars
London EC4Y 8BB

Design
Bamber Forsyth Limited

Text
The Company Writers Limited

Printed in England
by Watmoughs

> Our objective is to maximise value for our shareholders by focusing on businesses where we have market leadership, a technological edge and a world competitive cost base. We will promote a culture of continuous improvement in everything we do.

operating and financial review

CREATING VALUE

ICI's objective is to maximise value for its shareholders. This will be achieved by:

- Providing unrivalled, international service to its customers.
- Focusing on businesses which are, or can become, world leaders and which offer potential for profitable growth.
- Completing the restructuring which will make ICI competitive in all its markets.
- Investing selectively in growth opportunities where ICI enjoys technological or other advantages.
- Increasing the Group's presence in the fast-growing markets of Asia Pacific.
- Investing in research and technology to strengthen existing businesses, develop innovative products and processes and create new businesses to regenerate the Group.
- Maintaining high standards of safety, health and environmental performance.

Share price and FTSE 100 share price index

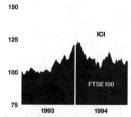

Index

175

150

125

ICI

100

FTSE 100

75

1993   1994

Source: Datastream
The ICI share price prior to 1 June 1993 has been adjusted to reflect the demerger of Zeneca.

ECONOMIC BACKGROUND

The market

As the economic recovery gathered pace in 1994, demand and activity in the leading industrialised economies strengthened considerably. The economies in the Organisation of Economic Co-operation and Development (OECD) grew by nearly 3%, more than double the rate in 1993.

OECD industrial production, which fell slightly in 1993, recovered strongly to grow by over 3%.

This overall improvement reflected developments in all ICI's main markets. The US and UK economies expanded rapidly through the year, although interest rates were raised on several occasions to dampen demand. GDP and industrial production in Continental Europe recovered well from the sharp falls of 1993. Growth in Asia Pacific was at much the same high rate as in 1993, helped by strong expansion in Australia. The Japanese economy started to recover in the second half of the year.

Faster economic growth was accompanied by much greater demand for chemicals and by higher chemical production in most of ICI's markets.

Unless otherwise stated, the Operating and Financial Review refers to ICI's continuing operations. Figures for 1993 have been restated to account for post-retirement benefits other than pensions. See note 2, page 15.

operating and financial review

OECD chemical production volume

percentage changes

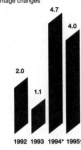

1992 1993 1994* 1995†

* Estimate   † Forecast

While the price of some intermediate chemical products rose sharply, final output prices increased more slowly, particularly in the first half of the year.

Demand and volumes

Total chemical demand in ICI's markets rose by about 5% compared with only 1% in 1993. Within these markets, ICI's own sales volumes grew by 7%. Every market showed an increase with the greatest rises in Asia Pacific, USA, the UK and Germany. Sales volumes increased in all businesses, apart from Explosives where volumes were flat.

Turnover

£ billion

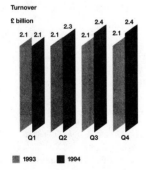

Q1   Q2   Q3   Q4

■ 1993   ■ 1994

ICI's total turnover increased by 9% mainly from higher volumes. Average selling prices increased by 2% and

exchange rate movements had only a minor effect on the year's results.

Competition and prices

Despite buoyant demand and a growing take-up of capacity, 1994 was another year of fierce competition and cost-conscious customers. This made it difficult in most markets to raise selling prices. With some raw material prices increasing sharply, all businesses found their margins under pressure.

After falling in most western European countries in 1993, Industrial Chemicals' selling prices improved strongly in the latter part of 1994 in all the major OECD countries. This reflected strong demand and shortages of many commodity products, especially in North America and Asia Pacific.

BUSINESS DEVELOPMENTS IN 1994

Rising productivity

Productivity continues to improve in terms of both turnover per employee and added value per employee. A major contribution has been ICI's restructuring which has significantly reduced the break-even point for the Group. Improving productivity, both labour and capital, remains a priority for all ICI's businesses.

Group reshaping

Since 1990, the total benefits of ICI's two major restructuring programmes have amounted to £1,130m. Annualised cost savings are now running at £475m.

Since the publication of ICI's last Annual Report, further action has been taken.

Turnover and added value per employee

£000

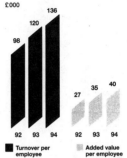

92   93   94   92   93   94

■ Turnover per   Added value
employee   per employee

In November 1994, EVC International NV, a joint venture in PVC between ICI and EniChem S.p.A. of Italy, undertook a global offering involving the issue of new shares and the disposal of shares held by both its parents. EVC is now publicly quoted on the Amsterdam Stock Exchange with ICI's interest reduced from 50% to 15.8%.

In December, ICI sold its remaining 13.3% share in AECI Ltd. The move follows the reorganisation of ICI's interests in South Africa earlier in the year under which ICI acquired a direct 51% stake in AECI's explosives business.

The Group has also restructured its interests in Malaysia, selling its 50.1% holding in Chemical Company of Malaysia Berhad but retaining its 60% stake in ICI Paints (Malaysia) Sdn. Bhd.

Other 1994 disposals were The Monckton Coke & Chemical Company Limited in the UK; the starch-based polyols business in the USA; and the acrylics operation at Compton, California – a disposal required by the US Federal Trade Commission as part of the 1993 nylon-acrylics transactions.

These divestments reflect the Group's strategy of developing its core global businesses and concentrating resources in businesses which can grow and prosper.

operating and financial review

Electricity prices

In February 1994, action by the industry regulator, OFFER, halted the rising trend in electricity prices. However, power costs for large, intensive users are still much higher in the UK than in most European countries and are harming ICI's chlor-alkali business. In addition, the large fluctuations of price within short periods hinder efficient management of the business.

ICI is exploring every avenue for securing better terms, including considering a project for a gas-fired power station at Runcorn.

INVESTMENT FOR THE FUTURE

Creating shareholder value requires market leadership, technological edge and world-competitive costs. ICI has continued to pursue these objectives by investing in its people, its plant and its research and technology.

Training

The Group's Shareholder Value training courses help ICI's people to understand the return that shareholders expect from their investment and how the external financial markets affect the internal financial targets of each business. It also helps them see how their actions can contribute to shareholder value.

Most senior managers around the world have now attended, and the programme is cascading through the organisation, in appropriate form, to all ICI staff.

The Company's Market Focus Bureau is adding corporate management education and training to its portfolio.

Group authorisations and expenditure on fixed assets

	Authorised			Expenditure		
	1992 £m	1993 £m	**1994 £m**	1992 £m	1993 £m	**1994 £m**
Tangible fixed assets						
United Kingdom	91	94	**64**	160	92	**94**
Continental Europe	50	36	**45**	82	68	**38**
The Americas	167	(12)*	**187**	111	78	**117**
Asia Pacific	109	82	**230**	155	93	**108**
Other countries	39	6	**87**	15	17	**28**
	456	206	**613**	523	348	**385**
Total authorised but unspent at end of year				463	321	**549**
Acquisitions and new investments				59	294	**125**
Disposals				(102)	(490)	**(388)**

* Adjusted for Tioxide capacity in North America previously sanctioned but subsequently substituted by investment in joint venture.

Capital expenditure

Fixed capital expenditure in 1994 stood at £385m. The figure is expected to rise in 1995 as opportunities for profitable growth in ICI's core businesses are pursued.

During the year the Group sanctioned capital expenditure of £613m. This is being spent on a large number of projects worldwide.

In the USA, C&P will expand its 'Klea' 134a plant and build a new 'Melinar' PET plant to manufacture the innovative 'Laser +' co-polymer. ICI Explosives will strengthen its position in automotive airbags with a new igniter line in the USA. ICI Paints is to build a new factory in Indonesia to help meet rising demand in Asia Pacific.

Among the regional businesses, ICI Australia will benefit from a 1,380 km pipeline carrying ethane to its plant at Botany Bay. The use of ethane, along with modifications to the plant itself, will make ICI Australia a world-competitive producer of ethylene. Following the closure of outdated assets in New South Wales, ICI Australia will also double capacity at its PVC plant in Victoria. In Pakistan, an expansion of capacity in polyester fibre

will enhance competitiveness and take advantage of a rapidly growing market.

As well as projects already sanctioned, the Group announced plans for a £100 million MDI plant in Holland for ICI Polyurethanes. It is also considering expanding its production of PTA by enlarging its plant in Taiwan and building a new plant in Pakistan.

The decision in March 1994 to take a 2.5% share in the flotation of Yizheng Chemical Fibre Company reflects the growing strategic importance of China and the value to ICI of its major PTA trading relationships in Asia Pacific. Yizheng is China's largest producer of polyester fibre.

Research and technology (R&T)

ICI is committed to developing innovative and competitive products and processes. It currently employs over 4,000 people in research, technology and engineering. Research expenditure in 1994 totalled £241m, including £57m spent on technical service.

ICI continues to make its R&T more effective by integrating it closely with the strategy and objectives of the businesses. This is leading to a much improved contribution by ICI's

operating and financial review

scientists and engineers to business success through direct exposure to the marketplace.

OUTLOOK

Market growth

The stronger economic growth of 1994 is expected to continue in 1995 with GDP in the OECD area expanding by about 3%. In the USA and the UK, the growth of GDP is forecast to slow to more sustainable rates as policies to constrain inflationary pressures take effect. On the other hand, the upswing in Continental Western Europe is expected to strengthen, as is the Japanese economy.

With the authorities in many countries tightening monetary conditions and reducing public sector deficits, inflationary pressures in the OECD are expected to moderate for this stage of the economic cycle. OECD inflation is forecast to accelerate to nearly 3% compared with about 2.5% in 1994.

Having expanded much faster than GDP or industrial production during 1994, chemical demand is likely to grow less rapidly in 1995. The rate, however, is expected to be above that of GDP.

Sales and prices

In 1995, ICI's sales volumes should continue to increase broadly in line with the growth of chemical demand in the Group's main markets. As in 1994, the fastest growth in sales is expected to be in Asia Pacific. The outlook in other major markets is for continued growth at slightly slower rates than in 1994.

With supply pressures in many products and in all the main regions,

chemical selling prices are likely to increase at faster rates than in 1994. However, some raw material prices are also expected to increase more quickly.

Real GDP growth

percentage changes (%)

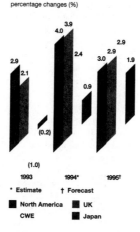

* Estimate   † Forecast

■ North America   ■ UK
  CWE   ■ Japan

Investment

Initiatives by the Group to grasp market opportunities are well advanced. They include further expansion for Paints in Thailand and Indonesia, building on new production in China and Australia. In 1996, Explosives will expand ammonium nitrate facilities at Yarwun, Australia, and open a new driver-side airbag igniter line in the USA.

The CFC replacement, 'Klea', continues to grow with a plant expansion due to be commissioned in the UK in 1995 and further capacity becoming available in the USA in 1996. With plans for new plants, the PTA business continues to reinforce its position as a global player. In Materials, Acrylics and Polyurethanes plan extensions of capacity in Europe, the USA, China and Taiwan.

FINANCIAL REVIEW

Profits before exceptional items

Trading profit amounted to £588m, more than 80% higher than the previous year which in turn was double that in 1992. The increase was due primarily to sales volume and improved productivity together with higher selling prices achieved in Industrial Chemicals, particularly in the second half of the year. Selling prices in other international businesses remained under pressure and, with raw material price increases, margins in these businesses were squeezed.

Significantly improved performances came from Industrial Chemicals (profits of £265m up by 157%), Materials (where profits have increased fivefold to £76m) and from Regional Businesses (up 78% at £80m).

Income from associated undertakings at £14m was lower by £31m, mainly reflecting the reduced investment in AECI which ceased to be equity accounted from the beginning of 1994. (This remaining holding of 13% was sold in December 1994).

Net interest payable at £88m was slightly lower than the previous year due to the lower average level of net indebtedness and the repayment of some high coupon borrowings.

Exceptional items

The exceptional charge of £67m against trading profit relates to the Explosives business and comprises the costs of exiting from the US aerospace business, the closure of the initiating systems facility in Scotland and restructuring operations principally in the US, the UK and South Africa. The charge against associated undertakings of £70m was the Group's share of the write-down of assets by EVC, as part of

operating and financial review

its flotation referred to on page 2. Losses on sale or closure of operations consisted of losses arising on the sale of related operations to EVC, the exit from the Group's worldwide nitro-glycerine explosives business and the closure of operations in Canada and Argentina. These were partly offset by profits on the sale of the US polyols business, the European polypropylene business, and the 50% holding in Chemical Company of Malaysia Berhad. Profits on the sale of fixed assets consisted of gains on the disposal of the remaining 13% holding in AECI, the disposal of 2.8m shares in EVC, and the 45% holding in Westralian Sands Limited.

Profit before exceptional items and taxation

£ million

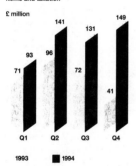

| Q1 | Q2 | Q3 | Q4 |
1993 ■ 1994

Taxation

The taxation charge on profit before exceptional items was £182m representing a rate of 35% (1993 36%). This reflected the utilisation of past losses in certain overseas countries as profitability returned. No ACT was written off in the year. The exceptional taxation credit of £18m related to relief on the Explosives rationalisation costs, partly offset by tax on gains arising on the disposal of fixed assets referred to above.

Earnings and dividends

The profit after taxation, but before exceptional items, amounted to £332m, an improvement of over £150m compared to the previous year. Earnings before exceptional items attributable to minority interests were £62m, significantly higher than 1993's figure of £38m and due mainly to the improved performance of ICI Australia and the acquisition of AECI Explosives Ltd (AEL) at the beginning of the year. The net profit before exceptional items attributable to shareholders of £270m was over 90% higher than in 1993 producing earnings per share of 37.3p compared to 19.6p in the previous year. Exceptional items reduced earnings per share by 11.3p to 26.0p.

As previously stated, the Board's objective is to build dividend cover and to ensure that the future level of dividends will reflect the strength and sustainability of underlying earnings through the trade cycle. The interim dividend of 10.5p per £1 Ordinary Share paid in October, together with the recommended second interim dividend of 17.0p, makes a total dividend for 1994 of 27.5p per share.This is the same level as last year and results in dividend cover, before exceptional items, of 1.4.

Shareholders' funds

In arriving at the total recognised gains for the year, the net profit of £188m has been reduced by translation losses of £96m, due primarily to the effects of the depreciation of the US dollar.

On 1 January 1994, shareholders' funds stood at £3,888m which were increased by total recognised gains of £85m and the issue of shares under employee share schemes of £10m. Goodwill of £48m, primarily in respect of the acquisition of AEL, and dividends of £199m have reduced

shareholders' funds to give a year end balance of £3,736m.

Capital structure

At 31 December 1994, the ICI Group's net indebtedness (net of cash and short-term investments) was £139m (1993 £1,071m) and net gearing stood at 3.3% (1993 20.2%).

The Group's loans are denominated mainly in US dollars and European currencies, including sterling, and have an average maturity of five years. The currency and interest rate exposure arising on borrowings, and cash not immediately required by the business, is managed on a net basis, through the use of interest rate and currency swaps to reduce, where possible, the currency and interest rate risk of the Group. Further information on financial instruments is given in Notes 5, 8 and 20 relating to the Accounts.

The most significant impact of this approach is that the exposure created by the US dollar and US dollar related long-term loans (£1,078m, of which £923m is fixed rate) has been reduced, by holding cash in US dollars and by transacting interest rate and cross-currency swaps, into a net exposure of approximately £280m equivalent, of which £140m is at fixed rates.

The currency disposition of the Group's net debt takes into account the availability and cost of funding in varying currencies, the effectiveness of currency debt as a hedge against future cashflows, and the sensitivity of Group gearing and earnings ratios to exchange rate movements.

Treasury policies

Group Treasury operates as a cost centre, its purpose being to reduce or eliminate financial risk and to invest cash assets safely and profitably within policies, financing plans and

operating and financial review

monitoring procedures approved by the Board. These policies and procedures include controls surrounding the usage of financial instruments in managing the Group's risk. Group Treasury does not undertake any trading activity in financial derivatives.

The Group's exposure to credit risk is controlled by continuously reviewing the credit ratings of counterparties and limiting the aggregate credit exposure to any one of them.

Currency hedging

The Group uses the forward foreign exchange markets to hedge its net transactional currency exposures 100%.

The Group selectively hedges its anticipated cash flow exposures for up to 12 months ahead using forward contracts and purchased currency options. At the year end, cover for this purpose of a net £330m was in place, representing approximately 55% of the Group's anticipated currency exposures.

Liquidity and investments

The Group has at its disposal over £800m equivalent in unutilised committed credit facilities with varying maturities up to 1997 and substantial uncommitted facilities.

Surplus funds are invested in high quality liquid marketable instruments including money market instruments, government securities, repurchase agreements and mortgage backed securities. The interest rate risk on these investments is managed on a net basis with the Group's borrowings. £210m equivalent of the Group's cash assets are managed by external fund managers under guidelines consistent with the Group's overall currency and interest rate policies.

The Group considers the possibility of material loss in the event of non-performance by a financial counter-party to be unlikely.

Cash flows

The Group continues to exercise tight management disciplines over its cash flows. The Group's cash flow was strong during the year and the capital gearing of the Group fell from 10.5% (after taking account of the repayment by Zeneca of its £575m loan) to 3.3%.

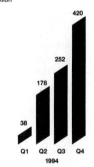

Net cash inflow from operating activities
£ million

- Q1: 38
- Q2: 178
- Q3: 252
- Q4: 420

1994

Operating cash inflow of £888m was down by £138m compared to 1993. Cash flows for 1993 included the cash flows of Zeneca prior to its demerger on 1 June 1993 and included £200m of operating cash flow. Outflow due to working capital increased only marginally despite a significant increase in sales. Expenditure on rationalisation programmes begun in previous years is now nearing completion, which principally accounts for the reduction in exceptional cash outflows.

The cash outflow from returns on investments and servicing of finance reflected a lower level of dividend receipts (due to disposals of investments) as well as lower interest

received on cash investments. Interest payments were significantly lower due to the lower level of net debt. Dividend payments in 1993 included the higher final dividend for 1992 prior to the demerger.

Tax paid was £98m, £46m lower than in 1993 due primarily to tax repayments associated with loss relief claims.

The net cash inflow from investing activities was £154m lower than in 1993. Reduced cash inflows arising from a reduction in debt repayments by Zeneca together with lower disposal proceeds (including EVC and AECI in 1994 and Fibres in 1993) partly offset by lower outflows for acquisitions (including Acrylics in 1993) were the principal factors.

Net cash inflow, before financing, totalled £775m of which £223m was used to reduce the Group's net debt. With the issue of shares to satisfy the exercise of options, cash and cash equivalents increased by £562m during the year.

A valuation of the ICI Pension Fund was carried out by the Company's actuaries which revealed a deterioration in its solvency position as at 31 March 1994. Payments into the Fund are being accelerated and further details are given in Note 33 to the Accounts on page 32.

board of directors

Sir Denys Henderson

A Director since 1980 and Chairman since 1987. He will retire on 27 April 1995. He is also Chairman of Zeneca Group PLC and The Rank Organisation Plc, and a Non-Executive Director of Barclays PLC and The RTZ Corporation PLC. Aged 62.

Sir Ronald Hampel

A Director since 1985 and Deputy Chairman and Chief Executive since 1993. He will succeed Sir Denys Henderson as Chairman with effect from 27 April 1995. He is also a Non-Executive Director of British Aerospace PLC, the Commercial Union Assurance Company plc and the Aluminium Company of America. Aged 62.

C Miller Smith

Appointed a Non-Executive Director in 1993 and an Executive Director in October 1994, he will succeed Sir Ronald Hampel as Chief Executive with effect from 27 April 1995. He is also a Non-Executive Director of Midland Bank PLC. Aged 55.

Sir Antony Pilkington

Appointed a Non-Executive Director in 1991. He is also Chairman of Pilkington plc. Aged 59.

Miss Ellen R Schneider-Lenné

Appointed a Non-Executive Director in 1991. She is a member of the Board of Managing Directors of Deutsche Bank AG and a Director of Morgan Grenfell Group plc. Aged 52.

C M Short

A Director since 1990, he has territorial responsibility for the Eastern Hemisphere. He is also a Non-Executive Director of United Biscuits (Holdings) plc. He will retire on 30 April 1995. Aged 60.

R J Margetts

A Director since 1992, he is Group Personnel and Group Research and Technology Director, and has territorial responsibility for the Western Hemisphere. He is also a Non-Executive Director of English China Clays plc. Aged 48.

F R Hurn

Appointed a Non-Executive Director in 1993. He is also Chairman and Chief Executive of Smiths Industries plc and a Director of S G Warburg Group plc. Aged 56.

A G Spall

Appointed a Director in January 1994, he is currently Group Finance Director and has overview responsibility for insurance, investments and property. Aged 50.

M E Brogden

Appointed a Director in May 1994, he is Group Planning and Group Safety, Health and Environment Director, and is Chief Executive Officer of ICI Chemicals & Polymers. Aged 56.

G Simpson

Appointed a Non-Executive Director in January 1995. He is also Chief Executive of Lucas Industries plc and a Director of Pilkington plc. Aged 52.

Under Article 74 of the Company's Articles of Association, Mr M E Brogden and Mr G Simpson retire together with Mr R J Margetts, Sir Antony Pilkington and Miss Ellen R Schneider-Lenné who retire under Article 92. All are recommended for re-election.

Mr M E Brogden and Mr R J Margetts each has a service contract with the Company, which is subject to termination by either party giving not less than two years' notice to expire on, or at any time after, the third anniversary of the date of appointment.

The Audit Committee and the Remuneration and Nomination Committee comprise all the Non-Executive Directors, except that the Chairman is a member of the Remuneration and Nomination Committee when acting as a Nomination Committee.

directors' report

The Directors of Imperial Chemical Industries PLC present their Annual Report for the year ended 31 December 1994 together with the Accounts of the Company for the year. These will be laid before the shareholders at the Annual General Meeting to be held on Thursday, 27 April 1995.

Principal activities

The principal activities of the Company are research, manufacture and sale of paints, materials, explosives and industrial chemicals. A review of the Company and its subsidiaries' businesses, including research and development, is given on pages 3 to 5 and 10 to 16 of the Annual Review and Summary Financial Statement and in the Operating and Financial Review on pages 1 to 6 of this Report.

Dividends

The Directors have declared the payment of a second interim dividend of 17.0 pence per Ordinary Share to be paid on 26 April 1995 to Ordinary shareholders registered in the books of the Company on 23 March 1995. An interim dividend of 10.5 pence per Ordinary Share was paid on 3 October 1994 making a total of 27.5 pence (1993 – 27.5 pence).

Share capital

Changes in the Company's Ordinary share capital during the year are given in Note 22 on page 27.

Purchase of own shares

The Directors are authorised by the shareholders to purchase, in the market, the Company's own shares, as is permitted under the Company's Articles of Association. Although no such purchases have been made, the Directors will seek to renew the authority from its

shareholders at the Annual General Meeting.

Directors

The names of the Directors of the Company at the date of this Report and brief biographical details are given on page 7.

Mr C Hampson and Mr P A Volcker retired from the Board on 29 April 1994.

At no time during the year has any Director had any material interest in a contract with the Company, being a contract of significance in relation to the Company's business. A statement of Directors' interests in the shares and debentures of the Company and its subsidiaries is set out in Note 39 on page 36.

Directors' and officers' liability insurance

The Company maintains directors' and officers' liability insurance which provides insurance cover for Directors and Officers of Group companies, including those of the Company.

Employment policies

To encourage all employees to make a full contribution to business success, ICI has extensive arrangements for team and individual employee involvement in continuous improvement activities. This is backed-up by a streamlined system of consultation which makes sure that management opinion and employee views are brought together at every relevant management level.

It is ICI's policy that there should be no discrimination against any person for any reason that is not relevant to the effective performance of their job. The Group aims to attract, retain and motivate people by recognising and rewarding superior performance; to ensure that people are equipped and trained to perform well; to communicate

effectively within the organisation and to encourage initiative and innovation.

In accord with the Company's equal opportunity policy, disabled people are given the same consideration as others when they apply for jobs. Depending on their skills and abilities, they enjoy the same career prospects and scope for realising their potential as other employees.

After one year of operation, most of ICI's businesses are continuing with Profit Related Pay schemes. These reward employees' contribution by paying a bonus to each employee which is dependent on the performance of the business in which the employee is engaged. A new Sharesave scheme for UK employees was introduced in 1994.

Political and charitable donations

The Group's worldwide expenditure on charitable donations in 1994 amounted to £2.0m. Of this total, £0.9m was spent in the UK. The Company made no donations for political purposes.

Taxation status

The Company is not, and has not been, a close Company within the provisions of the Income and Corporation Taxes Act 1988.

Auditors

On 6 February 1995, the Auditors changed the name under which they practise to KPMG and, accordingly, they have signed their report in their new name. KPMG have expressed their willingness to continue in office as auditors of the Company, and a resolution to propose their re-appointment and to authorise the Directors to agree their remuneration will be put to the Annual General Meeting.

directors' report

Annual general meeting

The Notice of Annual General Meeting to be held on Thursday, 27 April 1995 is contained in a separate letter from the Chairman accompanying this Annual Report and Accounts.

Corporate governance

The Company remains in full compliance with the Code of Best Practice published in December 1992 by the Committee on the Financial Aspects of Corporate Governance, in respect of the provisions of the Code currently in force. The Auditors have confirmed to the Directors that they are satisfied that this statement appropriately reflects the Company's compliance with the Code, insofar as it relates to the paragraphs of the Code which The London Stock Exchange has specified for their review. They have also confirmed that, with respect to the Directors' comments on going concern set out below, the Directors have provided the disclosures required by paragraph 4.6 of the Code (as supplemented by the related guidance for directors) and such statement is not inconsistent with the information of which they are aware based on their audit work on the financial statements. They have carried out their review in accordance with Bulletin 1994/1 issued by the Auditing Practices Board, which does not require them to extend their normal audit work in order to express a separate opinion on the ability of a company to continue in operational existence.

Internal control

The Directors are responsible for the Group's system of internal control. The Audit Committee has reviewed the effectiveness of the system from information provided by the management and the internal auditors.

This can provide only reasonable and not absolute assurance of meeting control objectives.

The key elements of the control system which have been established are as follows:-

Within the financial and overall objectives for the Group, agreed by the Board, the management of the Group as a whole is delegated to the Chief Executive and the Executive Directors. The conduct of ICI's individual businesses is delegated to the Chief Executive Officers of the International Businesses, the Chief Executives of major subsidiaries and the Regional Executive. They are accountable for the conduct and performance of their businesses within the agreed business strategy. They have full authority to act subject to the reserved powers and sanctioning limits laid down by the Board and to Group policies and guidelines.

Units are responsible for meeting the defined reporting timetables and compliance with Group accounting manuals which set out accounting policies, controls and definitions.

The Audit Committee receives reports from the internal and external auditors on a regular basis.

The Group's strategic direction is regularly reviewed by the Board, and the Executive Directors consider the strategy for the individual businesses on approximately an annual basis. Annual plans and performance targets for each business are set by the Executive Directors and reviewed at Group level by the Board in the light of the overall objectives.

Directors receive a summary of financial results monthly from each business, and the Group's published quarterly financial statements are based on a standardised reporting process.

Controls are designed to ensure that all activities operate efficiently,

effectively and to high ethical standards.

On completion of all major investments, post event reviews are carried out by the relevant Businesses and reviewed by the Executive Directors. This process helps improve the quality of business judgements through the understanding and experience gained.

The Audit Committee, on behalf of the Board, receives a written annual assurance from senior managers of the adequacy of the controls in the operations for which senior managers are responsible. The Audit Committee reviews these assurances and the reports from the internal audit function and the external auditors. Corrections to any weaknesses found are monitored and controls are developed to match changing circumstances.

Going concern

The operation of the Group's control procedures gives the Directors a reasonable expectation that the Group has adequate resources to continue in operation for the foreseeable future. Accordingly they continue to adopt the going concern basis in preparing the Group accounts.

On behalf of the Board

V O White
Secretary

6 March 1995

Registered office
Imperial Chemical House
Millbank
London SW1P 3JF

Registered number: 218019

financial statements

Company law requires the Directors to prepare financial statements for each financial year which give a true and fair view of the state of affairs of the Company and Group and of the profit or loss for that period. In preparing those financial statements, the Directors are required to:

- select suitable accounting policies and then apply them consistently;
- make judgements and estimates that are reasonable and prudent:

- state whether applicable accounting standards have been followed, subject to any material departures disclosed and explained in the financial statements;
- prepare the financial statements on the going concern basis unless it is inappropriate to presume that the Group will continue in business.

The Directors are responsible for keeping proper accounting records which disclose with reasonable accuracy

at any time the financial position of the Company and to enable them to ensure that the financial statements comply with the Companies Act 1985. They have a general responsibility for taking such steps as are reasonably open to them for safeguarding the assets of the Group and to prevent and detect fraud and other irregularities.

auditors' report

To the Members of Imperial Chemical Industries PLC.
We have audited the financial statements on pages 11 to 37.

Respective responsibilities of directors and auditors

As described above, the Company's Directors are responsible for the preparation of the financial statements. It is our responsibility to form an independent opinion, based on our audit, on those statements and to report our opinion to you.

Basis of opinion

We conducted our audit in accordance with Auditing Standards issued by the Auditing Practices Board. An audit includes examination, on a test basis, of evidence relevant to the amounts and disclosures in the financial statements. It also includes an

assessment of the significant estimates and judgements made by the Directors in the preparation of the financial statements and of whether the accounting policies are appropriate to the Group's circumstances, consistently applied and adequately disclosed.

We planned and performed our audit so as to obtain all the information and explanations which we considered necessary in order to provide us with sufficient evidence to give reasonable assurance that the financial statements are free from material misstatement, whether caused by fraud or other irregularity or error. In forming our opinion we also evaluated the overall adequacy of the presentation of information in the financial statements.

Opinion

In our opinion the financial statements give a true and fair view of the state of affairs of the Company and the Group as at 31 December 1994 and of the profit of the Group for the year then ended and have been properly prepared in accordance with the Companies Act 1985.

KPMG
Chartered Accountants
Registered Auditors
London
6 March 1995

accounting policies

The accounts are prepared under the historical cost convention and in accordance with the Companies Act 1985 and applicable accounting standards. The following paragraphs describe the main policies. The accounting policies of some overseas subsidiaries do not conform with UK Accounting Standards and, where appropriate, adjustments are made on consolidation in order to present the Group accounts on a consistent basis.

Depreciation

The Group's policy is to write-off the book value of each tangible fixed asset to its residual value evenly over its estimated remaining life. Reviews are made periodically of the estimated remaining lives of individual productive assets, taking account of commercial and technological obsolescence as well as normal wear and tear. Under this policy it becomes impracticable to calculate average asset lives exactly; however, the total lives approximate to 22 years for buildings and 17 years for plant and equipment. Depreciation of assets qualifying for grants is calculated on their full cost.

Foreign currencies

Profit and loss accounts in foreign currencies are translated into sterling at average rates for the relevant accounting periods. Assets and liabilities are translated at exchange rates ruling at the date of the Group balance sheet. Exchange differences on short-term currency borrowings and deposits are included with net interest payable. Exchange differences on all other transactions, except relevant foreign currency loans, are taken to trading profit. In the Group accounts, exchange differences arising on consolidation of the net investments in overseas subsidiary undertakings and associated undertakings are taken to reserves, as are differences arising on equity investments denominated in foreign currencies in the Company accounts. Differences on relevant foreign currency loans are taken to reserves and offset against the differences on net investments.

Goodwill

On the acquisition of a business, fair values are attributed to the net assets acquired. Goodwill arises where the fair value of the consideration given for a business exceeds such net assets. UK Accounting Standards require that purchased goodwill be eliminated from the balance sheet either upon acquisition against reserves or by amortisation over a period. Elimination against reserves has been selected as appropriate to the goodwill purchases made during recent years. On the subsequent disposal or termination of a previously acquired business, the profit or loss on disposal or termination is calculated after charging the amount of any related goodwill previously taken to reserves.

Leases

Assets held under finance leases are capitalised and included in tangible fixed assets at fair value. Each asset is depreciated over the shorter of the lease term or its useful life. The obligations related to finance leases, net of finance charges in respect of future periods, are included as appropriate under creditors due within, or creditors due after, one year. The interest element of the rental obligation is allocated to accounting periods during the lease term to reflect a constant rate of interest on the remaining balance of the obligation for each accounting period. Rentals under operating leases are charged to profit and loss account as incurred.

Pension costs

The pension costs relating to UK retirement plans are assessed in accordance with the advice of independent qualified actuaries. The amounts so determined include the regular cost of providing the benefits under the plans which should be a level percentage of current and expected future earnings of the employees covered under the plans. Variations from the regular pension cost are spread on a systematic basis over the estimated average remaining service lives of current employees in the plans.

With minor exceptions, non-UK subsidiaries recognise the expected cost of providing pensions on a systematic basis over the average remaining service lives of employees in accordance with the advice of independent qualified actuaries.

Associated undertakings

The Group's share of the profits less losses of significant associated undertakings is normally included in the Group profit and loss account on the equity accounting basis. The holding value of significant associated undertakings in the Group balance sheet is calculated by reference to the Group's equity in the net tangible assets of such undertakings, as shown by the most recent accounts available, adjusted where appropriate. Proportional consolidation is adopted where this more accurately reflects the Group's interest in an associated undertaking.

Research and development

Research and development expenditure is charged to profit in the year in which it is incurred.

Stock valuation

Finished goods are stated at the lower of cost and net realisable value, raw materials and other stocks at the lower of cost and replacement price; the first in, first out or an average method of valuation is used. In determining cost for stock valuation purposes, depreciation is included but selling expenses and certain overhead expenses are excluded.

Taxation

The charge for taxation is based on the profit for the year and takes into account taxation deferred because of timing differences between the treatment of certain items, including post-retirement benefits, for taxation and for accounting purposes. However, no provision is made for taxation deferred by reliefs unless there is reasonable evidence that such deferred taxation will be payable in the future.

Environmental liabilities

The Group is exposed to environmental liabilities relating to its past operations, principally in respect of soil and ground-water remediation costs. Provisions for these costs are made when expenditure on remedial work is probable and the cost can be estimated within a reasonable range of possible outcomes.

group profit and loss account

for the year ended 31 December 1994

	Notes	1994 Continuing operations Before exceptional items £m	1994 Continuing operations Exceptional items £m	1994 Discontinued operations £m	1994 Total £m	1993† Continuing operations Before exceptional items £m	1993† Continuing operations Exceptional items £m	1993† Discontinued operations £m	1993† Total £m
Turnover	4	9,189	–	–	9,189	8,430	–	2,202	10,632
Operating costs	3,5	(8,691)	(67)	–	(8,758)	(8,228)	–	(1,941)	(10,169)
Other operating income	5	90	–	–	90	123	–	33	156
Trading profit (loss)	3,4,5	588	(67)	–	521	325	–	294	619
Share of losses less profits of associated undertakings	3,7	14	(70)	–	(56)	45	–	2	47
Losses less profits on sale or closure of operations	3	–	(39)	–	(39)	–	(94)	(59)	(153)
Profits on disposal of fixed assets	3	–	70	–	70	–	–	–	–
Profit (loss) on ordinary activities before interest	4	602	(106)	–	496	370	(94)	237	513
Net interest payable	8	(88)	–	–	(88)	(90)	–	(63)	(153)
Profit (loss) on ordinary activities before taxation		514	(106)	–	408	280	(94)	174	360
Tax on profit (loss) on ordinary activities	9	(182)	18	–	(164)	(101)	(18)	(70)	(189)
Profit (loss) on ordinary activities after taxation		332	(88)	–	244	179	(112)	104	171
Attributable to minorities		(62)	6	–	(56)	(38)	(4)	–	(42)
Net profit (loss) for the financial year		270	(82)	–	188	141	(116)	104	129
Dividends	10								
Cash					(199)				(199)
Demerger									(363)
					(199)				(562)
Loss retained for year	23				(11)				(433)
Earnings (loss) per £1 Ordinary Share	11	37.3p	(11.3)p	–	26.0p	19.6p	(16.1)p	14.4p	17.9p

statement of group total recognised gains and losses

for the year ended 31 December 1994

	Notes	1994 £m	1993† £m
Net profit for the financial year		188	129
Currency translation differences on foreign currency net investments and related loans		(96)	(23)
Share of other reserve movements of associated undertakings and other items		(7)	–
Total recognised gains and losses relating to the year		85	106
Prior year adjustment	2	(95)	
Total gains and losses recognised since last annual report		(10)	

† Restated (note 2)

balance sheets

at 31 December 1994

	Notes	Group 1994 £m	Group 1993† £m	Company 1994 £m	Company 1993† £m
ASSETS EMPLOYED					
Fixed assets					
Tangible assets	12	**3,861**	4,024	**424**	311
Investments					
Subsidiary undertakings	13			**6,883**	6,179
Participating and other interests	14	**171**	458	**56**	268
		4,032	4,482	**7,363**	6,758
Current assets					
Stocks	15	**1,233**	1,199	**88**	70
Debtors	16	**1,980**	1,887	**1,197**	1,033
Investments and short-term deposits	17	**1,524**	1,467	**232**	629
Cash	17	**235**	194	**37**	31
		4,972	4,747	**1,554**	1,763
Total assets		**9,004**	9,229	**8,917**	8,521
Creditors due within one year					
Short-term borrowings	18	**(142)**	(145)	**(50)**	(1)
Current instalments of loans	20	**(181)**	(220)	**(63)**	(62)
Other creditors	19	**(2,285)**	(2,087)	**(4,840)**	(3,774)
		(2,608)	(2,452)	**(4,953)**	(3,837)
Net current assets (liabilities)		**2,364**	2,295	**(3,399)**	(2,074)
Total assets less current liabilities		**6,396**	6,777	**3,964**	4,684
FINANCED BY					
Creditors due after more than one year					
Loans	20	**1,522**	1,717	**200**	263
Other creditors	19	**95**	123	**1,141**	1,190
		1,617	1,840	**1,341**	1,453
Provisions for liabilities and charges	21	**675**	680	**40**	51
Deferred income: Grants not yet credited to profit		**30**	39	**1**	1
Minority interests – equity		**338**	330		
Shareholders' funds – equity					
Called-up share capital	22	**724**	722	**724**	722
Reserves					
Share premium account		**569**	561	**569**	561
Revaluation reserve		**37**	46	**–**	–
Associated undertakings' reserves		**60**	66		
Profit and loss account		**2,346**	2,493	**1,289**	1,896
Total reserves	23	**3,012**	3,166	**1,858**	2,457
Total capital and reserves attributable to parent company (page 14)		**3,736**	3,888	**2,582**	3,179
		6,396	6,777	**3,964**	4,684

† Restated (note 2)

The accounts on pages 11 to 37 were approved by the Board of Directors on 6 March 1995 and were signed on its behalf by:

Sir Denys Henderson Director
A G Spall Director

statement of group cash flow

for the year ended 31 December 1994

	Notes	1994 £m	1993 £m
Cash inflow from operating activities			
Net cash inflow from trading operations	24	**1,032**	1,305
Outflow related to exceptional items	25	**(144)**	(279)
Net cash inflow from operating activities		**888**	1,026
Returns on investments and servicing of finance			
Interest and dividends received	26	**105**	159
Interest paid		**(182)**	(254)
Dividends paid by parent company		**(199)**	(318)
Dividends paid by subsidiary undertakings to minority interests		**(32)**	(20)
Net cash outflow from returns on investments and servicing of finance		**(308)**	(433)
Tax paid		**(98)**	(144)
Investing activities			
Cash expenditure on tangible fixed assets	12	**(373)**	(485)
Acquisitions and new fixed asset investments	27	**(37)**	(286)
Disposals	28	**310**	443
Repayment of debt by Zeneca		**568**	1,364
Purchase of short-term investments and deposits		**(175)**	(436)
Cash and cash equivalents of Zeneca at date of demerger			(153)
Net cash inflow from investing activities		**293**	447
Net cash inflow before financing		**775**	896
Financing			
Issues of ICI Ordinary Shares		**10**	67
Net decrease in loans		**(199)**	(379)
Net decrease in lease finance		**(30)**	(15)
Net increase (decrease) in short-term borrowings		**6**	(3)
Issue of shares to minorities by subsidiary undertakings		**–**	6
Net cash outflow from financing	29	**(213)**	(324)
Increase in cash and cash equivalents	30	**562**	572

reconciliation of movements in shareholders' funds

for the year ended 31 December 1994

	1994 £m	1993† £m
Net profit for the financial year	**188**	129
Dividends		
Cash	**(199)**	(199)
Demerger		(363)
Loss retained for year	**(11)**	(433)
Issues of ICI Ordinary Shares	**10**	67
Goodwill movement	**(48)**	80
Other recognised losses related to the year	**(103)**	(23)
Net reduction in shareholders' funds	**(152)**	(309)
Shareholders' funds at beginning of year	**3,888**	4,197
(1994 originally was £3,983m (1993 £4,286m) before deduction of prior year adjustment of £95m (£89m))		
Shareholders' funds at end of year	**3,736**	3,888

† *Restated (note 2)*

notes relating to the accounts

1 Composition of the Group

The Group accounts consolidate the accounts of Imperial Chemical Industries PLC (the Company) and its subsidiary undertakings, of which there were 363 at 31 December 1994. Owing to local conditions and to avoid undue delay in the presentation of the Group accounts, 62 subsidiaries made up their accounts to dates earlier than 31 December, but not earlier than 30 September; one subsidiary makes up its accounts to 31 March but interim accounts to 31 December are drawn up for consolidation purposes.

2 Basis of presentation of financial information

At an Extraordinary General Meeting on 28 May 1993 the shareholders of ICI approved a resolution to demerge its bioscience operations ("Zeneca"). The demerger was effective 1 June 1993 and Zeneca has operated as a separate, publicly listed company since that date.

The results of Zeneca to the date of demerger and of the European nylon fibres business were reported as discontinued operations in the 1993 Group Profit and Loss Account together with the loss on disposal of the fibres business. The 1993 Group Cash Flow Statement includes the cash flows of Zeneca to the date of demerger.

The results reflect the initial adoption of the accounting requirements of pronouncement UITF6 "Accounting for Post-retirement Benefits other than Pensions". The cumulative cost of the benefits relating to previous years has been recognised in the accounts as a prior year adjustment and comparative figures for 1993 have been restated. The effect on continuing operations of implementing this new accounting policy was to reduce trading profit for the year by £12m (1993 £10m), to reduce the tax charge by £4m (1993 £4m) and to reduce the value of Group reserves at 1 January 1994 by £95m (1993 £89m) (Company £3m, 1993 £3m).

The Accounting Standards Board published Financial Reporting Standard No.4 – "Capital Instruments" in December 1993, No.5 – "Reporting the Substance of Transactions" in April 1994, No.6 – "Acquisitions and Mergers" in September 1994 and No.7 – "Fair Values in Acquisition Accounting" in September 1994 all of which have been applied to the 1994 Accounts.

3 Exceptional items before tax

	1994 Continuing operations £m	1994 Discontinued operations £m	Total £m	1993 Continuing operations £m	1993 Discontinued operations £m	Total £m
Charged in arriving at trading profit (loss)						
Provisions for restructuring in the Explosives business, principally severance costs of £44m and asset write-downs and demolition of £13m	(67)	–	(67)	–	–	–
Charged after trading profit (loss)						
Share of losses of associated undertakings*	(70)	–	(70)	–	–	–
Losses less profits on sale or closure of operations and related provisions						
Losses/provisions*	(78)	–	(78)	(148)	(72)	(220)
Profits	39	–	39	54	13	67
	(39)	–	(39)	(94)	(59)	(153)
Profits on disposal of fixed assets*	70	–	70	–	–	–
Exceptional items within profit (loss) on ordinary activities before taxation	(106)	–	(106)	(94)	(59)	(153)

* Exceptional items include the following relating to the flotation and partial disposal of EVC International NV:

   (i) £70m being a write-down of assets by EVC as part of the flotation (included in share of losses less profits of associated undertakings),

   (ii) £55m being losses on sale of residual operations to EVC (included in losses on sale or closure of operations) and

   (iii) £13m being profit on disposal of shares in EVC (included in profits on disposal of fixed assets).

notes relating to the accounts

4 Segment information

CLASSES OF BUSINESS

	Turnover		Trading profit before exceptional items		Profit before interest and taxation after exceptional items	
	1994 £m	1993 £m	**1994 £m**	1993 £m	**1994 £m**	1993 £m
Continuing operations						
Paints	**1,712**	1,691	**122**	101	**117**	127
Materials	**1,748**	1,494	**76**	14	**83**	(81)
Explosives	**786**	643	**45**	51	**(35)**	51
Industrial Chemicals	**3,881**	3,691	**265**	103	**253**	102
Regional Businesses	**1,477**	1,416	**80**	45	**134**	21
Inter-class eliminations	**(415)**	(373)	**–**	11	**–**	11
Share of losses less profits of associated undertakings					**(56)**	45
	9,189	8,562				
Sales to discontinued operations	**–**	(132)				
	9,189	8,430	**588**	325	**496**	276
Discontinued operations	**–**	2,256	**–**	294	**–**	237
Sales to continuing operations	**–**	(54)				
	–	2,202	**–**	294	**–**	237
	9,189	10,632	**588**	619	**496**	513

The Group's policy is to transfer products internally at external market prices. Inter-class turnover affected several businesses the largest being sales from Industrial Chemicals to Materials of £178m (1993 £163m).

	Total assets less current liabilities		Capital expenditure (note 12)		Depreciation (note 12)	
	1994 £m	1993 £m	**1994 £m**	1993 £m	**1994 £m**	1993 £m
Continuing operations						
Paints	**578**	533	**61**	65	**36**	38
Materials	**1,162**	1,221	**53**	58	**108**	109
Explosives	**333**	302	**50**	46	**43**	24
Industrial Chemicals	**1,995**	2,160	**146**	122	**158**	159
Regional Businesses	**756**	790	**75**	57	**68**	87
Net operating assets	**4,824**	5,006				
Net non-operating assets	**1,572**	1,771				
	6,396	6,777	**385**	348	**413**	417
Discontinued operations	**–**	–	**–**	117	**–**	88
	6,396	6,777	**385**	465	**413**	505

Net non-operating assets include assets in course of construction, investments in participating and other interests, current asset investments, short-term deposits and cash less short-term borrowings and current instalments of loans, and debtors and creditors relating to taxes and dividends.

notes relating to the accounts

4 Segment information (continued)

GEOGRAPHIC AREAS

The information opposite is re-analysed in the table below by geographic area. The figures for each geographic area show the turnover and profit made by, and the net operating assets owned by, companies located in that area; export sales and related profits are included in the areas from which those sales were made.

	Turnover		Trading profit before exceptional items		Profit before interest and taxation after exceptional items	
	1994 £m	1993 £m	**1994 £m**	1993 £m	**1994 £m**	1993 £m
Continuing operations						
United Kingdom						
Sales in the UK	**1,978**	1,927				
Sales overseas	**1,644**	1,566				
	3,622	3,493	**130**	38	**98**	46
Continental Europe	**1,392**	1,486	**56**	21	**66**	32
The Americas	**2,567**	2,409	**169**	118	**141**	(11)
Asia Pacific	**2,182**	1,871	**178**	107	**202**	108
Other countries	**414**	374	**53**	40	**43**	55
	10,177	9,633	**586**	324	**550**	230
Sales to discontinued operations	**–**	(132)				
Inter-area eliminations	**(988)**	(1,071)	**2**	1	**2**	1
Share of losses less profits of associated undertakings					**(56)**	45
	9,189	8,430	**588**	325	**496**	276
Discontinued operations	**–**	2,256	**–**	294	**–**	237
Sales to continuing operations	**–**	(54)				
	–	2,202	**–**	294	**–**	237
	9,189	10,632	**588**	619	**496**	513

Inter-area turnover shown above includes sales of £359m (1993 £682m) from the United Kingdom to overseas subsidiaries.

	Net operating assets		Turnover by customer location	
	1994 £m	1993 £m	**1994 £m**	1993 £m
Continuing operations				
United Kingdom	**1,514**	1,531	**2,001**	1,876
Continental Europe	**531**	575	**1,834**	1,678
The Americas	**1,211**	1,362	**2,515**	2,383
Asia Pacific	**1,411**	1,424	**2,256**	1,957
Other countries	**157**	114	**583**	536
	4,824	5,006	**9,189**	8,430
Discontinued operations	**–**	–	**–**	2,202
	4,824	5,006	**9,189**	10,632

EMPLOYEES	1994		1993	
	Continuing operations	**Total**	Continuing operations	Total
Average number of people employed by the Group in				
United Kingdom	**21,200**	**21,200**	24,400	31,600
Continental Europe	**6,300**	**6,300**	7,200	11,500
The Americas	**15,000**	**15,000**	16,400	20,700
Asia Pacific	**13,200**	**13,200**	13,300	14,000
Other countries	**11,800**	**11,800**	9,100	9,300
Total employees	**67,500**	**67,500**	70,400	87,100

The number of people employed by the Group at the end of 1994 was 64,800 (1993 67,000).

notes relating to the accounts

5 Trading profit (loss)

	1994				1993			
	Continuing operations		Discontinued operations	Total	Continuing operations		Discontinued operations	Total
	Before exceptional items	Exceptional items			Before exceptional items	Exceptional items		
	£m	£m	£m	£m	£m	£m	£m	£m
Turnover	**9,189**	**–**	**–**	**9,189**	8,430	–	2,202	10,632
Operating costs								
Cost of sales	**(6,502)**	**(27)**	**–**	**(6,529)**	(6,095)	–	(1,124)	(7,219)
Distribution costs	**(608)**	**(5)**	**–**	**(613)**	(594)	–	(90)	(684)
Research and development	**(184)**	**–**	**–**	**(184)**	(177)	–	(189)	(366)
Administrative and other expenses	**(1,397)**	**(35)**	**–**	**(1,432)**	(1,362)	–	(538)	(1,900)
	(8,691)	**(67)**	**–**	**(8,758)**	(8,228)	–	(1,941)	(10,169)
Other operating income								
Government grants	**8**	**–**	**–**	**8**	10	–	1	11
Royalties	**25**	**–**	**–**	**25**	25	–	18	43
Other income	**57**	**–**	**–**	**57**	88	–	14	102
	90	**–**	**–**	**90**	123	–	33	156
Trading profit (loss)	**588**	**(67)**	**–**	**521**	325	–	294	619
Total charge for depreciation included above	**404**	**7**	**–**	**411**	398	–	88	486
Gross profit, as defined by the Companies Act 1985	**2,687**	**(27)**	**–**	**2,660**	2,335	–	1,078	3,413

Forward contracts hedging foreign currency working capital are revalued at year end and gains and losses are included in trading profit. Forward contracts and currency options hedging other anticipated cash flows are not revalued but, on realisation, gains and losses net of option premia are included in trading profit in the period that the hedged cash flow occurs. Net gains/losses deferred at year end were not material. Option premia are included in debtors until realised.

6 Note of historical cost profits and losses

There were no material differences between reported profits and losses and historical cost profits and losses on ordinary activities before tax in either 1994 or 1993.

7 Share of losses less profits of associated undertakings

| | 1994 | | | 1993 | | |
| | Continuing operations | Discontinued operations | Total | Continuing operations | Discontinued operations | Total |
	£m	£m	£m	£m	£m	£m
Share of losses less profits						
Share of undistributed losses less profits	**(59)**	**–**	**(59)**	11	2	13
Dividend income						
Listed companies	**2**	**–**	**2**	8	–	8
Unlisted companies	**5**	**–**	**5**	22	–	22
	7	**–**	**7**	30	–	30
Share of losses less profits before taxation	**(52)**	**–**	**(52)**	41	2	43
Amounts written off investments (including provisions raised £8m (1993 £1m) and released £4m (1993 £5m))	**(4)**	**–**	**(4)**	4	–	4
	(56)	**–**	**(56)**	45	2	47
Of which accounted for as exceptional	**(70)**	**–**	**(70)**	–	–	–

The reduction in ICI's interest in AECI Ltd, effective from the beginning of the year, and in EVC International NV, in November, has resulted in these investments ceasing to be equity accounted from those dates.

notes relating to the accounts

8 Net interest payable

	1994 Continuing operations £m	1994 Discontinued operations £m	Total £m	1993 Continuing operations £m	1993 Discontinued operations £m	Total £m
Interest payable and similar charges						
Bank loans, overdrafts and other loans wholly repayable within five years	100	–	100	151	1	152
Other loans not wholly repayable within five years	86	–	86	101	–	101
Interest between continuing and discontinued operations				–	62	62
	186	–	186	252	63	315
Interest receivable and similar income						
Listed investments	(10)	–	(10)	(4)	–	(4)
Unlisted investments and short-term deposits	(88)	–	(88)	(96)	–	(96)
Interest between continuing and discontinued operations				(62)	–	(62)
	(98)	–	(98)	(162)	–	(162)
Net interest payable	88	–	88	90	63	153

Interest on cross-currency and interest rate swaps is accrued and included with the interest flows of the underlying borrowing. Forward rate agreements are not revalued but, on realisation, gains or losses are spread over the period of the hedged borrowing or deposit. Net gains/losses deferred at year end were not material.

Interest allocated to discontinued operations in 1993 consisted of the interest applicable to Zeneca based on the debt assumed by Zeneca prior to demerger. No interest was allocated in that year in respect of the discontinued fibres business.

9 Tax on profit (loss) on ordinary activities

	1994 Continuing operations Before exceptional items £m	1994 Continuing operations Exceptional items £m	1994 Discontinued operations £m	Total £m	1993 Continuing operations Before exceptional items £m	1993 Continuing operations Exceptional items £m	1993 Discontinued operations £m	Total £m
ICI and subsidiary undertakings								
United Kingdom taxation								
Corporation tax	72	(1)	–	71	2	4	60	66
Double taxation relief	(11)	–	–	(11)	(2)	–	–	(2)
Deferred taxation	5	(13)	–	(8)	7	2	(13)	(4)
	66	(14)	–	52	7	6	47	60
Overseas taxation								
Overseas taxes	110	5	–	115	87	8	34	129
Deferred taxation	2	(9)	–	(7)	(6)	4	(11)	(13)
	112	(4)	–	108	81	12	23	116
	178	(18)	–	160	88	18	70	176
Associated undertakings	4	–	–	4	13	–	–	13
Tax on profit (loss) on ordinary activities	182	(18)	–	164	101	18	70	189

UK and overseas taxation has been provided on the profits (losses) earned for the periods covered by the Group accounts. UK corporation tax has been provided at the rate of 33 per cent (1993 33 per cent).

The exceptional tax credit in 1994 is in respect of the Explosives restructuring costs and the transfer of operations to EVC partially offset by tax on disposals of other operations in the US and Australia. Taxation attributable to discontinued operations in 1993 comprised the taxation on the operating results of the discontinued businesses to the date of demerger/disposal together with tax relief on the losses on sale of the fibres business. The exceptional tax charge in 1993 reflected taxation on profits on disposals; losses on disposals, principally goodwill, did not attract significant tax relief.

notes relating to the accounts

9 Tax on profit (loss) on ordinary activities (continued)

Deferred taxation

The amounts of deferred taxation accounted for at the balance sheet date and the potential amounts of deferred taxation are disclosed below.

	Group		Company	
	1994 **£m**	1993 £m	**1994** **£m**	1993 £m
Accounted for at balance sheet date (note 21)				
Timing differences on UK capital allowances and depreciation	**182**	178	**69**	36
Miscellaneous timing differences	**(92)**	(90)	**(38)**	(17)
	90	88	**31**	19
Not accounted for at balance sheet date				
Timing differences on UK capital allowances and depreciation	**–**	–	**–**	–
Miscellaneous timing differences	**22**	(18)	**–**	(11)
	22	(18)	**–**	(11)
Full potential deferred taxation	**112**	70	**31**	8

10 Dividends

	1994 **pence per** **£1 Share**	1993 pence per £1 Share	**1994** **£m**	1993 £m
Interim, paid 3 October 1994	**10.5p**	10.5p	**76**	76
Second interim, to be confirmed as final, payable 26 April 1995	**17.0p**	17.0p	**123**	123
	27.5p	27.5p	**199**	199
Demerger dividend – This comprised the net assets of Zeneca at date of demerger.				363
			199	562

11 Earnings (loss) per £1 Ordinary Share

	1994 **£m**	1993 £m
Net profit for the financial year before exceptional items – continuing operations	**270**	141
Exceptional items after tax and minorities – continuing operations	**(82)**	(116)
Net profit on discontinued operations		104
Net profit for the financial year	**188**	129
	million	million
Average Ordinary Shares in issue during year, weighted on a time basis	**723**	719
	pence	pence
Earnings per £1 Ordinary Share before exceptional items – continuing operations	**37.3**	19.6
Earnings per £1 Ordinary Share – total operations	**26.0**	17.9

The effect on earnings per £1 Ordinary Share of the issue of shares under option (note 22) would not be material.

Earnings per £1 Ordinary Share before exceptional items for continuing operations has also been calculated to exclude the impact of exceptional items and, in respect of 1993, of discontinued operations as these can have a distorting effect on earnings and therefore warrant separate consideration.

notes relating to the accounts

12 Tangible fixed assets

	Land and buildings	Plant and equipment	Payments on account and assets in course of construction	Total
	£m	£m	£m	£m
GROUP				
Cost or as revalued				
At beginning of year	1,285	6,609	267	**8,161**
Exchange adjustments	(1)	(14)	3	**(12)**
New subsidiary undertakings	23	23	4	**50**
Capital expenditure			385	**385**
Transfers of assets into use	33	292	(325)	
Disposals and other movements	(93)	(511)	(1)	**(605)**
At end of year	1,247	6,399	333	**7,979**
Depreciation				
At beginning of year	458	3,679		**4,137**
Exchange adjustments	2	4		**6**
Disposals and other movements	(45)	(393)		**(438)**
Charge for year	40	373		**413**
At end of year	455	3,663		**4,118**
Net book value at end 1994	792	2,736	333	**3,861**
Net book value at end 1993	827	2,930	267	4,024

The Group depreciation charge of £413m, shown above, comprises £411m charged in arriving at trading profit and £2m charged within losses on sale or closure of operations.

Capital expenditure in the year of £385m includes capitalised finance leases of £7m; creditors for capital work done but not paid for increased by £5m; the resulting cash expenditure on tangible fixed assets was £373m.

The net book value of the tangible fixed assets of the Group includes capitalised finance leases of £24m (1993 £39m) comprising cost of £104m (£114m) less depreciation of £80m (£75m). In respect of capitalised leases the depreciation charge for the year was £5m (1993 £4m) and finance charges were £4m (£7m).

Included in land and buildings is £228m in respect of the cost of land which is not subject to depreciation.

	Land and buildings	Plant and equipment	Payments on account and assets in course of construction	Total
COMPANY				
Cost				
At beginning of year	165	508	11	**684**
Capital expenditure			23	**23**
Transfers of assets into use	3	16	(19)	
Transfers from (to) subsidiary undertakings	2	191	(4)	**189**
Disposals and other movements	(3)	(23)	–	**(26)**
At end of year	167	692	11	**870**
Depreciation				
At beginning of year	44	329		**373**
Transfers from subsidiary undertakings		43		**43**
Disposals and other movements	6	(30)		**(24)**
Charge for year	5	49		**54**
At end of year	55	391		**446**
Net book value at end 1994	112	301	11	**424**
Net book value at end 1993	121	179	11	311

notes relating to the accounts

12 Tangible fixed assets (continued)

	Group		Company	
	1994 **£m**	1993 £m	**1994** **£m**	1993 £m
The net book value of land and buildings comprised				
Freeholds	**729**	750	**111**	120
Long leases (over 50 years unexpired)	**54**	71	**1**	1
Short leases	**9**	6	**–**	–
	792	827	**112**	121

	Group			
	Land and buildings		Plant and equipment	
	1994 **£m**	1993 £m	**1994** **£m**	1993 £m
Revalued assets included in tangible fixed assets				
At revalued amount	**104**	102	**127**	129
Depreciation	**41**	37	**112**	112
Net book value	**63**	65	**15**	17
At historical cost	**57**	57	**129**	130
Depreciation	**31**	31	**120**	119
Net book value	**26**	26	**9**	11

13 Investments in subsidiary undertakings

	Shares £m	Loans £m	Total **£m**
Cost			
At beginning of year	4,606	1,721	**6,327**
Exchange adjustments	(10)	(67)	**(77)**
Transfers to subsidiary undertakings	(2,853)	(511)	**(3,364)**
Transfers from subsidiary undertakings	207	29	**236**
New investments/new loans	3,624	582	**4,206**
Disposals/loans repaid/transfers	(12)	(278)	**(290)**
At end of year	5,562	1,476	**7,038**
Provisions			
At beginning of year	(147)	(1)	**(148)**
Exchange adjustments	3	–	**3**
Additions	(21)	–	**(21)**
Disposals	11	–	**11**
At end of year	(154)	(1)	**(155)**
Balance sheet value at end 1994	5,408	1,475	**6,883**
Balance sheet value at end 1993	4,459	1,720	6,179

Cost includes scrip issues capitalised £6m (1993 £6m).

	1994 **£m**	1993 £m
Shares in subsidiary undertakings which are listed investments		
Balance sheet value	**5**	5
Market value	**63**	81

None of the listed investments were listed on The London Stock Exchange.

The Company's investment in its subsidiary undertakings consists of either equity or long term loans, or both. Normal trading balances are included in either debtors or creditors. Information on principal subsidiary undertakings is given on page 37.

notes relating to the accounts

14 Investments in participating and other interests

	Associated undertakings		Other investments	Total
	Shares	Loans	Shares	
	£m	£m	£m	£m
GROUP				
Cost				
At beginning of year	398	7	–	**405**
Exchange adjustments	(18)	–	–	**(18)**
Additions	22	6	7	**35**
Reclassification	(137)	–	137	
Disposals and repayments	(213)	(5)	–	**(218)**
Other movements	(8)	(5)	–	**(13)**
At end of year	44	3	144	**191**
Share of post-acquisition reserves less losses				
At beginning of year	66			**66**
Exchange adjustments	(11)			**(11)**
Retained losses less profits	(63)			**(63)**
Reclassification	74			**74**
Disposals	3			**3**
Other movements	(9)			**(9)**
At end of year	60			**60**
Provisions				
At beginning of year	(13)	–	–	**(13)**
Exchange	(1)	–	–	**(1)**
Net additions in year	(4)	–	–	**(4)**
Reclassification	–	–	(74)	**(74)**
Disposals	7	–	(2)	**5**
Other movements	7	–	–	**7**
At end of year	(4)	–	(76)	**(80)**
Balance sheet value at end 1994	100	3	68	**171**
Balance sheet value at end 1993	451	7	–	458
The above investments included				
1994				
Listed investments – balance sheet value	–	–	57	**57**
– market value	–	–	72	**72**
1993				
Listed investments – balance sheet value	145	–	–	145
– market value	234	–	–	234

None of the listed investments were listed on The London Stock Exchange.

Information on principal associated undertakings is given on page 36.

notes relating to the accounts

14 Investments in participating and other interests (continued)

	Associated undertakings		Other investments	Total
	Shares	Loans	Shares	
	£m	£m	£m	£m
COMPANY				
Cost				
At beginning of year	271	6	–	**277**
Exchange adjustments	15	–	–	**15**
Additions	14	–	–	**14**
Transfers from subsidiary undertakings	40	–	–	**40**
Reclassification	(151)	–	151	
Disposals	(184)	(6)	–	**(190)**
At end of year	5	–	151	**156**
Provisions				
At beginning of year	(3)	(6)	–	**(9)**
Additions	–	–	(99)	**(99)**
Disposals	2	6	–	**8**
At end of year	(1)	–	(99)	**(100)**
Balance sheet value at end 1994	4	–	52	**56**
Balance sheet value at end 1993	268	–	–	268
The above investments included				
1994				
Listed investments - balance sheet value	–	–	52	**52**
- market value	–	–	66	**66**
1993				
Listed investments - balance sheet value	–	–	–	–

None of the listed investments were listed on The London Stock Exchange.

15 Stocks

	Group		Company	
	1994	1993	**1994**	1993
	£m	£m	**£m**	£m
Raw materials and consumables	**418**	396	**23**	18
Stocks in process	**75**	84	**8**	4
Finished goods and goods for resale	**740**	719	**57**	48
	1,233	1,199	**88**	70

16 Debtors

	Group		Company	
	1994	1993	**1994**	1993
Amounts due within one year				
Trade debtors	**1,360**	1,214	**42**	1
Amounts owed by subsidiary undertakings			**993**	912
Amounts owed by associated undertakings	**9**	18	**–**	–
Other debtors	**260**	341	**26**	25
Prepayments and accrued income*	**112**	104	**31**	24
	1,741	1,677	**1,092**	962
Amounts due after more than one year				
Advance corporation tax recoverable	**–**	–	**56**	29
Prepayments and other debtors*	**239**	210	**49**	42
	239	210	**105**	71
	1,980	1,887	**1,197**	1,033

* Includes prepaid pension costs (note 33).

notes relating to the accounts

17 Current asset investments and short-term deposits

	Group		Company	
	1994 **£m**	1993 £m	**1994** **£m**	1993 £m
Securities listed on The London Stock Exchange	**75**	–	**58**	–
Other listed investments	**187**	–	**59**	–
Total listed investments	**262**	–	**117**	–
Unlisted investments and short-term deposits	**1,262**	892	**115**	54
	1,524	892	**232**	54
Amounts owed by Zeneca	**–**	575	**–**	575
	1,524	1,467	**232**	629
Included in cash and cash equivalents (note 30)	**941**	464		
Market value of listed investments	262	–	117	–

Included in unlisted investments and short-term deposits and cash are amounts totalling £61m (1993 £nil) held by the Group's insurance subsidiaries, of which some £49m (1993 £nil) is not readily available for the general purposes of the Group.

18 Short-term borrowings

Bank borrowings				
Secured by fixed charge	**3**	3	**–**	–
Secured by floating charge	**4**	3	**–**	–
Unsecured	**82**	56	**50**	1
	89	62	**50**	1
Other borrowings (unsecured)	**53**	83	**–**	–
	142	145	**50**	1
Included in cash and cash equivalents (note 30)	**136**	144		

19 Other creditors

Amounts due within one year				
Trade creditors	**993**	888	**128**	130
Amounts owed to subsidiary undertakings			**4,386**	3,341
Amounts owed to associated undertakings	**8**	6	**5**	5
Corporate taxation	**233**	164	**97**	78
Value added and payroll taxes and social security	**76**	81	**6**	8
Other creditors*	**539**	531	**57**	62
Accruals	**313**	294	**38**	27
Dividends to Ordinary Shareholders	**123**	123	**123**	123
	2,285	2,087	**4,840**	3,774
Amounts due after more than one year				
Amounts owed to subsidiary undertakings			**1,136**	1,186
Other creditors*	**95**	123	**5**	4
	95	123	**1,141**	1,190

* Includes obligations under finance leases (note 31) and accrued pension costs (note 33).

notes relating to the accounts

20 Loans

	Repayment dates	Group 1994 £m	1993 £m	Company 1994 £m	1993 £m
Secured loans					
US dollars	1995/1998	**55**	71		
Australian dollars		**–**	18		
Other currencies	1995/2004	**113**	135		
Total secured		**168**	224		
Secured by fixed charge – bank loans		**163**	205		
– other		**–**	14		
Secured by floating charge – bank loans		**5**	5		
Unsecured loans					
Sterling					
9¾% to 11¼% Bonds	1995/2005	**263**	325	**263**	325
Others	1995/2002	**98**	74		
		361	399	**263**	325
US dollars					
8% eurodollar Bonds	1996	**64**	68		
8⅞% Debentures	2006	**160**	169		
7.83% to 8.9% medium-term Notes	1995/2002	**61**	68		
8¾% Notes	2001	**160**	169		
7⅝% Notes	1997	**144**	152		
9½% Notes	2000	**192**	203		
7½% Notes	2002	**128**	135		
Others	1995/2005	**15**	18		
		924	982		
Australian dollars (13.5%)	1995	**37**	62		
Swiss francs (4½% to 6¾%)	1997/1999	**195**	220		
Other currencies	1995/2005	**18**	50		
Total unsecured		**1,535**	1,713	**263**	325
Total loans		**1,703**	1,937	**263**	325

The Group has entered into currency swap, interest rate swap and forward rate agreements to manage the interest rate and currency exposures arising on borrowings and cash not immediately required by the business. At 31 December 1994, the Group had agreements outstanding with commercial banks which had principal amounts of £1,450m (1993 £1,763m) equivalent at the exchange rate on that date. Principal amounts under cross-currency agreements are revalued to balance sheet rates and any exchange gains or losses arising are included in the total sterling value of Group loans. The amount attributed to cross-currency swaps included in the above total is £9m (1993 (£5m)).

notes relating to the accounts

20 Loans (continued)

	Group		Company	
Loan maturities	**1994** **£m**	1993 £m	**1994** **£m**	1993 £m
Bank loans				
Loans or instalments thereof are repayable				
After 5 years from balance sheet date				
Lump sums	**8**	–		
Instalments	**53**	82		
	61	82		
From 2 to 5 years	**138**	129		
From 1 to 2 years	**45**	43		
Total due after more than one year	**244**	254		
Total due within one year	**46**	42		
	290	296	–	–
Other loans				
Loans or instalments thereof are repayable				
After 5 years from balance sheet date				
Lump sums	**851**	1,018	**200**	200
Instalments	**–**	6	**–**	–
	851	1,024	**200**	200
From 2 to 5 years	**361**	304	**–**	–
From 1 to 2 years	**66**	135	**–**	63
Total due after more than one year	**1,278**	1,463	**200**	263
Total due within one year	**135**	178	**63**	62
	1,413	1,641	**263**	325
Total loans				
Due after more than one year	**1,522**	1,717	**200**	263
Due within one year	**181**	220	**63**	62
Total loans	**1,703**	1,937	**263**	325
Aggregate amount of loans repayable by instalments any of which fall due after 5 years	**180**	200	**–**	–

21 Provisions for liabilities and charges

	At beginning of year	Profit and loss account	Net amounts paid or becoming current	Exchange and other movements	**At end** **of year**
	£m	£m	£m	£m	**£m**
GROUP					
Deferred taxation (note 9)†	88	(15)	–	17	**90**
Advance corporation tax recoverable	(29)	–	–	(40)	**(69)**
Employee benefits * †	292	51	(27)	5	**321**
Reorganisation, environmental and other provisions	329	99	(78)	(17)	**333**
	680	135	(105)	(35)	**675**
COMPANY					
Deferred taxation (note 9)†	19	12	–	–	**31**
Advance corporation tax recoverable	–	–	–	(19)	**(19)**
Other provisions†	32	17	(22)	1	**28**
	51	29	(22)	(18)	**40**

* Includes provisions for unfunded pension costs (note 33).
† Restated at 1 January 1994 to include prior year adjustment in respect of post-retirement healthcare obligations (notes 2 and 34).
No provision has been released or applied for any purpose other than that for which it was established.

22 Called-up share capital of parent company

	Authorised	Allotted, called-up and fully paid	
		1994	1993
	£m	**£m**	£m
Ordinary Shares (£1 each)	**724**	**724**	722
Unclassified shares (£1 each)	**126**		
	850	**724**	722

The number of Ordinary Shares issued during the year, wholly in respect of the exercise of options totalled 1.8m.

At 31 December 1994 there were options outstanding in respect of 8.3m Ordinary Shares of £1 under the Company's share option schemes for staff (1993 6.0m) normally exercisable in the period 1995 to 2004 (1994 to 2003) at subscription prices of £4.32 to £13.81 (£3.04 to £13.81). The weighted average subscription price of options outstanding at 31 December 1994 was £6.43.

Options granted to directors are shown in note 39.

During 1994 movements in the number of shares under option comprised new options issued £4.5m, options exercised £1.8m, and options lapsed or waived £0.4m. At the end of 1994 there were 15.3m shares available for the granting of options (1993 19.3m).

notes relating to the accounts

23 Reserves

	Share premium account £m	Revaluation £m	Associated under-takings £m	Profit and loss account £m	**1994 Total £m**	1993 Total £m
GROUP						
Reserves attributable to parent company						
At beginning of year as previously stated						3,572
Prior year adjustment (note 2)						(89)
At beginning of year as restated	561	46	66	2,493	**3,166**	3,483
Profit (loss) retained for year			(63)	52	**(11)**	(433)
Amounts taken direct to reserves						
Share premiums	8				**8**	59
Goodwill				(48)	**(48)**	80
Exchange adjustments		(6)	(11)	(79)	**(96)**	(23)
Share of other reserve movements						
of associated undertakings and other items			(9)	2	**(7)**	–
	8	(6)	(20)	(125)	**(143)**	116
Other movements between reserves		(3)	77	(74)		
At end of year	569	37	60	2,346	**3,012**	3,166

In the Group accounts, £33m of net exchange gains (1993 losses £26m) on foreign currency loans have been offset in reserves against exchange losses (1993 gains) on the net investment in overseas subsidiaries and associated undertakings.

The movement in goodwill includes £54m of goodwill written off on the acquisition of new subsidiaries and £6m relating to goodwill transferred to the profit and loss account on the disposal of subsidiaries.

The cumulative amount of goodwill resulting from acquisitions during 1994 and prior years, net of goodwill attributable to subsidiary undertakings or businesses demerged or disposed of prior to 31 December 1994, amounted to £657m (1993 £609m).

There are no significant statutory or contractual restrictions on the distribution of current profits of subsidiary or associated

undertakings; undistributed profits of prior years are, in the main, permanently employed in the businesses of these companies. The undistributed profits of Group companies overseas may be liable to overseas taxes and/or UK taxation (after allowing for double taxation relief) if they were to be distributed as dividends. No provision has been made in respect of potential taxation liabilities on realisation of assets at restated or revalued amounts or on realisation of associated undertakings at equity accounted value.

For the purpose of calculating the basis of the borrowing limits in accordance with the Articles of Association, the total of the sums standing to the credit of capital and revenue reserves of the Company and its subsidiary undertakings, to be added to the nominal amount of the share capital of the Company, was £3,636m at 31 December 1994.

	Share premium account £m	Profit and loss account £m	**1994 Total £m**	1993 Total £m
COMPANY				
Reserves				
At beginning of year as previously stated				3,070
Prior year adjustment (note 2)				(3)
At beginning of year as restated	561	1,896	**2,457**	3,067
Loss retained for year		(579)	**(579)**	(646)
Amounts taken direct to reserves				
Share premiums	8		**8**	59
Exchange adjustments		(28)	**(28)**	(23)
	8	(28)	**(20)**	36
At end of year	569	1,289	**1,858**	2,457

By virtue of S230 of the Companies Act 1985, the Company is exempt from presenting a profit and loss account.

notes relating to the accounts

24 Net cash inflow from trading operations

	1994 £m	1993 £m
Trading profit	521	619
Exceptional charges within trading profit	67	–
Trading profit before exceptional items	588	619
Depreciation	404	486
Stocks (increase) decrease	(65)	130
Debtors increase	(161)	(87)
Creditors increase	210	189
Other non-cash movements, including exchange	56	(32)
	1,032	1,305

Net cash inflow from trading operations in 1993 included £251m relating to discontinued Zeneca operations.

25 Outflow related to exceptional items

This includes expenditure charged to exceptional provisions relating to business rationalisation and restructuring and for sale or closure of operations, including severance and other employee costs, plant demolition and site clearance. The major part of the 1994 expenditure relates to provisions raised in 1992.

Exceptional items outflow in 1993 included £51m relating to discontinued Zeneca operations.

26 Interest and dividends received

	1994 £m	1993 £m
Dividends received from equity accounted associated undertakings	6	31
Other dividends received	2	4
Interest received	97	124
	105	159

27 Acquisitions and new fixed asset investments

	1994 £m	1993 £m
Acquisitions and new fixed asset investments		
Acquisitions of subsidiary undertakings involving		
Fixed assets	50	299
Current assets	56	60
Total liabilities	(36)	(107)
Minority interests	(15)	–
Net assets of subsidiary undertakings acquired	55	252
Goodwill	54	31
Fair value of consideration for subsidiary undertakings	109	283
Investment in equity accounted undertakings	9	11
Other investments	7	1
	125	295
Consideration for acquisitions and new fixed asset investments		
Cash and cash equivalents acquired	1	7
Non-cash consideration	78	–
Deferred consideration	9	2
Net cash investment	37	286
	125	295

Fixed and current assets are adjusted to fair value based on external valuations and internal reviews.

The principal acquisition in the year was a 51% interest in AECI Explosives Limited.

notes relating to the accounts

28 Disposals

	1994 £m	1993 £m
Disposals in the year resulted in the following net asset movements		
Tangible fixed assets	**166**	263
Investments in participating interests	**205**	4
Other net current assets	**54**	205
Creditors due after more than one year	**(6)**	(2)
Provisions for liabilities and charges	**(29)**	89
Minority interests	**(31)**	7
	359	566
Goodwill	**(6)**	111
Profit and loss account		
Ordinary activities	**(9)**	–
Exceptional items	**44**	(140)
	388	537
Satisfied by		
Cash consideration	**310**	443
Non-cash consideration	**78**	–
Deferred consideration	**–**	94
	388	537

The cash consideration for disposals comprises £77m (1993 £408m) in respect of disposals of operations, £120m (£4m) in respect of equity accounted participating interests, £80m (nil) in respect of other investments and £33m (£31m) in respect of tangible fixed assets. £272m (1993 £439m) of the cash consideration was accounted for as exceptional.

Apart from the disposal proceeds, the contribution of the businesses and subsidiary undertakings divested in 1994 to the cash flows for the year was not material.

29 Changes in financing during the year

	Share capital £m	Share premium account £m	Loans £m	Finance leases £m	Short-term borrowings* £m	Total £m
At beginning of 1993	714	502	2,266	94	4	3,580
Exchange adjustments			21	(1)	–	20
New finance	8	59	31	6	–	104
Finance repaid			(410)	(15)	(3)	(428)
Introduced by acquisitions			72†	–	–	72
Zeneca demerger			(62)	(9)	–	(71)
Other movements			19	–	–	19
At beginning of 1994	722	561	1,937	75	1	**3,296**
Exchange adjustments			(33)	2	–	**(31)**
New finance	2	8	93	7	6	**116**
Finance repaid			(292)	(30)	–	**(322)**
Other movements			(2)	(1)	(1)	**(4)**
At end of 1994	724	569	1,703	53	6	**3,055**

* Amount of short-term borrowings repayable more than 3 months from date of advance.

† The increase in loans due to acquisitions includes £69m in respect of the Group's investment in Louisiana Pigment Company, L.P.

No new finance was raised from the issue of shares to minorities in 1994 (1993 £6m).

notes relating to the accounts

30 Cash and cash equivalents

	1994 £m	1993 £m
Balance of cash and cash equivalents		
Cash	235	194
Investments and short-term deposits which were within 3 months of maturity when acquired (note 17)	941	464
Short-term borrowings repayable within 3 months from date of advance (note 18)	(136)	(144)
	1,040	514
Change in the balance of cash and cash equivalents		
At beginning of year	514	(56)
Exchange adjustments	(36)	(2)
Increase for year	562	572
At end of year	1,040	514

31 Leases

	1994			1993		
Total rentals under operating leases, charged as an expense in the profit and loss account	Continuing operations £m	Discontinued operations £m	Total £m	Continuing operations £m	Discontinued operations £m	Total £m
Hire of plant and machinery	67	–	67	69	2	71
Other	41	–	41	43	12	55
	108	–	108	112	14	126

	Group		Company	
Commitments under operating leases to pay rentals during the year following the year of these accounts, analysed according to the period in which each lease expires	1994 £m	1993 £m	1994 £m	1993 £m
Land and buildings				
Expiring within 1 year	7	4	–	–
Expiring in years 2 to 5	14	18	1	1
Expiring thereafter	13	30	1	1
	34	52	2	2
Other assets				
Expiring within 1 year	9	10	1	5
Expiring in years 2 to 5	27	35	1	1
Expiring thereafter	17	7	1	2
	53	52	3	8
Obligations under finance leases comprise				
Rentals due within 1 year	46	31	1	–
Rentals due in years 2 to 5	10	39	2	–
Rentals due thereafter	–	31	1	–
Less interest element	(3)	(26)	(1)	–
	53	75	3	–

Obligations under finance leases are included in other creditors (note 19).

The Group had no commitments under finance leases at the balance sheet date which were due to commence thereafter.

notes relating to the accounts

32 Employee costs

| | 1994 | | | 1993 | | |
	Continuing operations	Discontinued operations	Total	Continuing operations	Discontinued operations	Total
	£m	£m	£m	£m	£m	£m
Salaries	**1,340**	**–**	**1,340**	1,421	405	1,826
Social security costs	**132**	**–**	**132**	138	52	190
Pension costs	**154**	**–**	**154**	137	38	175
Other employment costs	**76**	**–**	**76**	45	23	68
	1,702	**–**	**1,702**	1,741	518	2,259
Less amounts allocated to capital and to provisions set up in previous years	**(26)**	**–**	**(26)**	(59)	(21)	(80)
Severance costs charged in arriving at profit before tax	**115**	**–**	**115**	60	17	77
Employee costs charged in arriving at profit before tax	**1,791**	**–**	**1,791**	1,742	514	2,256

The average number of people employed by the Group in 1994 was 67,500 (1993 87,100) all of whom were engaged in continuing operations (1993 70,400).

33 Pension costs

Group

The Company and most of its subsidiaries operate retirement plans which cover the majority of employees (including directors) in the Group. These plans are generally of the defined benefit type under which benefits are based on employees' years of service and average final remuneration and are funded through separate trustee-administered funds. Formal independent actuarial valuations of the Group's main plans are undertaken regularly, normally at least triennially and adopting the projected unit method.

The actuarial assumptions used to calculate the projected benefit obligation of the Group's pension plans vary according to the economic conditions of the country in which they are situated. The weighted average discount rate used in determining the actuarial present values of the benefit obligations was 8.7%. The weighted average expected long-term rate of return on investments was 8.8%. The weighted average rate of increase of future earnings was 5.9%.

The actuarial value of the fund assets of these plans at the date of the latest actuarial valuations was sufficient to cover 92% of the benefits that had accrued to members after allowing for expected future increases in earnings; their market value was £5,747m.

The total pension cost for the Group for 1994 was £154m (1993 continuing operations – £137m). Accrued pension

costs amounted to £29m (1993 £29m) and are included in other creditors (note 19); provisions for the benefit obligation of a small number of unfunded plans amounted to £130m (£119m) and are included in provisions for employee benefits (note 21). Prepaid pension costs amounting to £69m (£48m) are included in debtors (note 16).

ICI Pension Fund

The ICI Pension Fund accounts for approximately 80% of the Group's plans in asset valuation and projected benefit terms.

An actuarial valuation of the ICI Pension Fund was carried out as at 31 March 1994. From that date the Company will make payments into the Fund to reflect the extra liabilities arising from early retirement as retirements occur. In addition, the Company has agreed to make accelerated contributions to the Fund over the next six years commencing with £75m in 1995. The solvency ratio on a current funding level basis which assumes a cessation of operations is 96% and the deficit of £189m in market value terms will be eliminated over a three year period. The deficit in the Fund has been taken into account in arriving at the employers' pension cost charged in the accounts from 1 April 1994 by being amortised as a percentage of pensionable emoluments over the expected working lifetime of existing members.

34 Healthcare costs

The Group provides in North America, and to a lesser extent in some other countries, certain unfunded healthcare and life assurance benefits for retired employees. At 31 December 1994 approximately 28,000 current and retired employees were eligible to benefit from these schemes.

As stated in note 2, the results reflect the initial adoption of the accounting requirements of pronouncement UITF 6 "Accounting for Post-retirement Benefits other than Pensions" and the liabilities in respect of these benefits are now fully

accrued. The total post-retirement healthcare cost for the Group for 1994 was £16m and the provision at the year end was £153m.

In respect of the Group's major US plans the costs and provisions were determined on an actuarial basis using a discount rate of 7.25%. Healthcare cost rate increases range from 9.0% to 11.0% for 1994 and are assumed to gradually decrease to 5.0%.

notes relating to the accounts

35 Commitments and contingent liabilities

	Group		Company	
	1994 **£m**	1993 £m	**1994** **£m**	1993 £m
Commitments for capital expenditure not provided for in these accounts (including acquisitions)				
Contracts placed for future expenditure	**274**	80	**4**	2
Expenditure authorised but not yet contracted	**275**	243	**14**	23
	549	323	**18**	25

Contingent liabilities existed at 31 December 1994 in connection with guarantees and uncalled capital relating to subsidiary and other undertakings and guarantees relating to pension funds, including the solvency of pension funds. The maximum contingent liability in respect of guarantees of borrowings and uncalled capital at 31 December 1994 was £25m (1993 £18m) for the Group; the maximum contingent liability for the Company, mainly on guarantees of borrowings by subsidiaries, was £1,247m (1993 £1,337m).

The Group is also subject to contingencies pursuant to environmental laws and regulations that in the future may require it to take action to correct the effects on the environment of prior disposal or release of chemical substances by the Group or other parties. The ultimate requirement for such actions, and their cost, is inherently difficult to estimate, however provisions have been established at 31 December 1994 in accordance with the accounting policy noted on page 11. It is believed that, taking account of these provisions, the cost of addressing currently identified environmental obligations is unlikely to impair materially the Group's financial position.

The Glidden Company is a defendant, along with numerous other paint and former lead pigment manufacturers, in a number of suits in the US, several of which purport to be class actions, seeking damages for alleged personal injury caused by lead-based paint or for the costs of removing lead-based paint. Glidden stopped manufacturing lead pigments in the 1950s and lead-based consumer paints in the 1960s. The suits involve substantial claims for damages and an adverse ruling against Glidden could lead to additional claims. Several US State legislatures and the US Congress are considering proposed bills that could adversely affect Glidden's position in

pending or possible future cases, including proposals that could add additional grounds for legal liability or that would permit suits otherwise time-barred. Glidden believes that it has strong defences and intends to continue to deny all liability and to defend all actions vigorously.

In December 1992, ICI Explosives USA Inc. received a subpoena from a grand jury sitting in Fort Worth, Texas, with respect to what appears to be an industry-wide antitrust investigation of the US explosives business. The company is co-operating with the investigation, the results of which are unlikely to be known for some time. However, violation of US antitrust laws, if established, can result in the payment of substantial penalties and damages.

The Group is also involved in various other legal proceedings, principally in the UK and US, arising out of the normal course of business. The Group does not believe that the outcome of these proceedings will have a material effect on the Group's financial position.

The Company has given certain indemnities in the course of disposing of companies and businesses and also in connection with the demerger of Zeneca. These and other guarantees and contingencies arising in the ordinary course of business, for which no security has been given, are not expected to result in any material financial loss.

Significant take-or-pay contracts entered into by subsidiaries are as follows:

(i) the purchase of electric power which commenced April 1993 for 15 years. The present value of the remaining commitment is estimated at £679m.

(ii) the supply of ethane which will commence May 1996 for 10 years. The present value of this commitment is £105m.

36 Statutory and other information

Included in debtors is an interest-free loan of £45,000 (1993 £45,000) to one (one) officer of the Company. This loan was provided in accordance with the Company's policy of providing housing assistance to staff who have been transferred.

Remuneration of auditors charged in the Group accounts for 1994 was £3.5m (1993 £3.4m); fees paid to the auditors of the parent Company for services other than statutory audit supplied to the Company and its UK subsidiaries during 1994 totalled £0.9m (1993 £2.3m).

In November 1994, as part of the Group's restructuring in Malaysia, ICI disposed of its 50.1% interest in Chemical Company of Malaysia Berhad (CCM), to companies owned by three directors of CCM, Mr Chen Yeng Khan, Mr Oh Kim Sun and Mr Lim Say Chong. The consideration comprised cash of £25m together with 25% of the share capital of ICI Paints (Malaysia) Sdn. Bhd. (value approximately £20m) owned by CCM.

notes relating to the accounts

37 Remuneration policy

The Company pays competitive wages and salaries to its employees around the world. These include incentive payments which reward enhanced shareholder value. Levels of pay and the structure of arrangements in each country reflect the competitive environment in that country. Whilst ICI does not have global pay scales, it has to have regard to its need to be able to move staff around the world.

38 Contracts and emoluments of directors

Framework and objectives – The contracts and emoluments of executive directors and senior executives are determined by the Remuneration and Nomination Committee ("the Remuneration Committee"), which for this purpose is composed wholly of non-executive directors of the Company.

The objective of the Company's remuneration policy is to provide remuneration in form and amount which will attract, retain, motivate and reward high calibre executive directors and senior executives. It must, therefore, be competitive with other companies. To this end, the remuneration package comprises short, medium and longer term benefits, with the incentive element geared to shareholder value enhancement as outlined in the circular to shareholders for the 1994 AGM.

Service contracts – Normally executive directors are employed on rolling contracts subject to two years' notice at any time, save on first appointment, when the contract is for an initial period of three years. Contracts expire at normal retirement age of 62. Sir Denys Henderson's contract as Chairman, and Sir Ronald Hampel's contract as Chief Executive, expire at the conclusion of the AGM in 1995.

The short-term benefits – are an annual salary, health plan and car benefits and participation in the Annual Performance Related Bonus Scheme. The salaries are set at competitive base levels established from surveys of similar companies; they are within a range of up to 130% of base level (the salary at appointment) to allow the Remuneration Committee to reward the performance and experience of executive directors. No annual cost of living or inflation adjustment is made to this scale, but each year it is measured against external benchmarks to ensure it remains competitive. Annual assessment of each individual executive director's performance is carried out by the Remuneration Committee.

In 1994 there was no adjustment to the executive directors' salary scale and no salary increase was awarded to any executive director, including the Chairman and Chief Executive.

The level of bonus (if any) under the Annual Performance Related Bonus Scheme is determined by the Remuneration Committee on the basis of criteria established at the beginning of the year to encourage performance in a manner which the Remuneration Committee considers will contribute most to increasing shareholder value for that year. The maximum bonus available to executive directors, including the Chairman and Chief Executive, is 40%.

For 1994 the bonus for executive directors was linked entirely to increased earnings per share ("EPS"). The trigger point was established at a covered dividend of 27.5p. This figure was above the budget accepted by the Board as the 1994 plan and significantly above the 19.6p EPS achieved in 1993. The 37.3p achieved EPS in 1994 has resulted in the payment of a bonus at the maximum level of 40%. The level of bonus paid in 1993 was 10%; no bonuses were paid in the previous four years.

The medium-term benefit – is the Bonus Conversion Plan, introduced at the beginning of 1994, designed to encourage the conversion of any annual bonus (as described above) into shares in the Company and the holding of those shares for a minimum of three years. Under the Plan, the recipient of a bonus may elect to have shares purchased at market value in the Plan with his net bonus after tax. Shares purchased in the Plan are released at the end of a three year retention period and are then matched by an equal number of shares by the Company on which the individual is required to pay income tax.

The long-term benefit – is the Share Option Scheme (renewed in May 1994) under which options over the Company's Ordinary Shares may be granted each year to executive directors and senior executives at a multiple of 0.8 times salary for directors (except on first appointment) subject to an overall maximum holding of four times salary. All options under the 1994 Scheme are subject to performance conditions on exercise as determined by the Remuneration Committee. Exercise of options granted during the year under the 1994 Scheme are subject to satisfaction of one of two conditions – one related to total shareholder return exceeding the return on the FTSE All Share Index over three years, and the other to improved earnings per share being 2% greater than the change in the RPI over a three year period. Options must be held for three years before they are exercised and lapse if not exercised within ten years from grant.

The shares within both the Share Option Scheme and the Bonus Conversion Plan do not dilute shareholders' equity as they are bought in the market and held by a trust.

Post-retirement benefits – All executive directors, other than Mr C M Short and Mr C Miller Smith, are members of the ICI Pension Fund, which is open to all UK employees and which provides pensions and other benefits to members within Inland Revenue limits. The Company made a contribution for all employees, including executive directors in the ICI Pension Fund, at a rate of 13.68% of salary in 1994 except for the Chairman and Sir Ronald Hampel, who are the last two long serving members of the Pension Fund whose contributions were capped at significantly lower levels.

Mr C Miller Smith has a Funded Unapproved Pension Scheme to which the Company makes a contribution equivalent to 25% of his salary. Mr C M Short is entitled by contract to an unfunded pension from the Company on retirement.

notes relating to the accounts

38 Contracts and emoluments of directors (continued)

Emoluments of directors

	1994				1993
	Salary £000	Benefits £000	Bonus £000	**Total £000**	Total £000
Remuneration of executive directors					
Sir Denys Henderson – Chairman	313	6	125	**444**	493
Sir Ronald Hampel – Chief Executive	425	12	170	**607**	479
C. Miller Smith – Chief Executive designate	87	3	35	**125**	
(appointed executive director 1 October 1994)					
M. E. Brogden (appointed 1 May 1994)	167	7	67	**241**	
C. Hampson (retired 29 April 1994)	100	4	40	**144**	342
R. J. Margetts	250	8	100	**358**	255
C. M. Short	300	17	120	**437**	353
A. G. Spall (appointed 1 January 1994)	250	8	100	**358**	
Directors who ceased to be directors of ICI on demerger of Zeneca					367
	1,892	65	757†	**2,714**	2,289
Fees to non-executive directors				**97**	194
Pension fund contributions				**111**	70
Total emoluments				**2,922**	2,553
Remuneration of executive directors 1993	1,815	60	414		

† Excludes the benefit of shares under the Bonus Conversion Plan (see The medium-term benefit, page 34) which will be included
in emoluments in the year in which the benefit of the extra shares provided by the Company is received by the director.

The emoluments of the Chairman, inclusive of pension fund contributions (£362; 1993 £616) and bonuses (£125,000; 1993 £106,000),
were £444,000 (1993 £494,000). The emoluments of the highest paid director, inclusive of pension fund contributions
(£370; 1993 £1,026) and bonuses (£170,000; 1993 £78,000), were £608,000 (1993 £480,000).

The emoluments of non-executive directors, inclusive of Mr C Miller Smith until he became an executive director on 1 October 1994
(£16,000; 1993 £11,000), and of executive directors who ceased to be directors of ICI on demerger of Zeneca were within the
following bands:

Emoluments £	Number		Emoluments £		Number	
	1994	1993			**1994**	1993
Non-executive directors						
5,001 – 10,000		4	20,001 – 25,000		**3**	2
10,001 – 15,000	**1**	1	85,001 – 90,000			1
15,001 – 20,000	**1**	1				
Executive directors who ceased to be						
directors of ICI on demerger of Zeneca						
95,001 – 100,000		1	155,001 – 160,000			1
105,001 – 110,000		1				

Two executive directors and one non-executive director were directors for part of 1994. Three executive directors and six
non-executive directors were directors for part of 1993.

	1994 £000	1993 £000
Pensions in respect of service of former directors paid by the Company	124	52

notes relating to the accounts

39 Directors' interests in shares and debentures

The interests at 31 December 1994 of the persons who on that date were directors (including the interests of their families) in shares and debentures of the Company and its subsidiaries, are shown below. Their interests at 1 January 1994 (or, if appointed during 1994, at their date of appointment) are shown in parentheses where these differ from the holdings at the year end.

	ICI Ordinary Shares	
Sir Denys Henderson	21,274	
Sir Ronald Hampel	6,377	
C. Miller Smith	500	
M. E. Brogden	1,273	(273)
F. R. Hurn	500	
R. J. Margetts	4,798	
Sir Antony Pilkington	500	
Miss Ellen R. Schneider-Lenné	500	
C. M. Short	55,266	
A. G. Spall	3,565	(3,561)

On 23 February 1995 Mr C Miller Smith purchased an additional 4,000 Ordinary Shares. During the period 1 January 1995 to 23 February 1995, there was no other change in the interests of directors shown in this note.

Options to subscribe for Ordinary Shares granted to and exercised by directors during 1994 are included in the table below:

	1 January 1994	Options granted		Options exercised			31 December 1994			
Directors at 31 December 1994	Number	Number	Price £	Number	Exercise price £	Market price £	Number	Weighted average exercise price £	Date from which exercisable	Expiry date
Sir Denys Henderson	160,900						160,900	5.59	2.4.89	28.5.02
	16,865						16,865	7.71†	2.9.90	2.9.97
Sir Ronald Hampel	281,926						281,926	6.03	2.4.89	24.6.03
C. Miller Smith		178,300	7.85				178,300	7.85†	7.11.97	7.11.04
M. E. Brogden	24,760*			1,000	5.26	7.76½	23,760	6.03	3.4.94	24.6.03
	9,800*						9,800	7.55†	22.3.97	22.3.04
R. J. Margetts	154,092	1,371	6.34				155,463	6.00	2.4.89	25.11.03
C. M. Short	52,199						52,199	6.90	3.4.94	25.11.03
A. G. Spall	15,500	1,164	6.34				16,664	6.64	24.6.96	24.6.03
		57,500	7.55				57,500	7.55†	22.3.97	22.3.04

* Interest at date of appointment.
† Exercise price exceeds market price at 31 December 1994.

No options lapsed during the year. The options outstanding are exercisable at prices between £4.97 and £7.85. The market price of the shares at 31 December 1994 was £7.48½ and the range during 1994 was £7.28½ to £8.67½. The Register of Directors' Interests (which is open to shareholders' inspection) contains full details of directors' shareholdings and options to subscribe for shares.

principal associated undertakings

at 31 December 1994

	Issued share and loan capital at date of latest available audited accounts			
	Class of capital	£m	Held by ICI %	Principal activities
IC Insurance Ltd England	Ordinary	–	49†	Insurance and reinsurance underwriting
Louisiana Pigment Company, L.P. USA	Partnership		50†	Manufacture of titanium dioxide pigments

† Held by subsidiaries

The accounting and reporting date of principal associated undertakings is 31 December.

The country of registration or incorporation is stated below each company. The principal operations of IC Insurance Ltd are carried out in the UK and those of Louisiana Pigment Company, L.P. in the USA.

The principal place of business of Louisiana Pigment Company, L.P. (LPC) is 3300 Bayou d'Inde Road, Westlake, Louisiana 70669-0070, USA. The Group's share of the results of LPC is proportionately consolidated in the Group profit and loss account and balance sheet. LPC is managed through a management board on which the Group and the Group's joint venture partner, NL Kronos, are represented.

principal subsidiary undertakings

at 31 December 1994

	Class of capital	Held by ICI %	Principal activities
EUROPE			
Deutsche ICI GmbH Germany	Ordinary	100†	Manufacture of chlorine, caustic soda, specialty plastics, paints and polyurethanes; merchanting of other ICI products
ICI Chemicals & Polymers Ltd England	Ordinary	100†	Manufacture of chemicals, plastics and fertilisers; merchanting of ICI and other products
ICI Finance PLC England	Ordinary	100†	Financial services
ICI France SA France	Ordinary	100†	Merchanting of ICI products
ICI Holland BV The Netherlands	Ordinary	100†	Manufacture of bulk and specialty plastics, films, and polyester polymers and polyurethane chemicals; merchanting of other ICI products
Tioxide Group Ltd England	Ordinary	100†	Manufacture of titanium dioxide pigments
THE AMERICAS			
ICI American Holdings Inc USA	Common	100†	Manufacture of acrylics, films, paints, composites, polyurethanes and chemicals; merchanting of other ICI products
ICI Canada Inc Canada	Common Preference	100† 100†	Manufacture of industrial explosives and initiating systems, paints, chlor-alkali and other chemicals; merchanting of ICI and other products
ICI Explosives USA Inc USA	Common	100†	Manufacture of industrial explosives and initiating systems
OTHER COUNTRIES			
AECI Explosives Ltd Republic of South Africa	Ordinary	51†	Manufacture of industrial explosives and initiating systems
ICI Australia Ltd Australia (Accounting and reporting date 30 September)	Ordinary*	62†	Manufacture and distribution of chemicals and other products including fertilisers and crop care, industrial and specialty chemicals, consumer and effect products, plastics and performance of related services
ICI China Ltd Hong Kong and China	Ordinary	100†	Merchanting of ICI and other products
ICI India Ltd India (Accounting date 31 March; reporting date 31 December)	Equity*	51	Manufacture of industrial explosives, paints, agrochemicals, pharmaceuticals, polyurethanes, catalysts, rubber chemicals and surfactants
ICI Japan Ltd Japan	Ordinary	100†	Manufacture of polyester films and acrylics compounds; merchanting of ICI and other products
ICI Pakistan Ltd Pakistan	Ordinary*	61†	Manufacture of polyester staple fibre, soda ash, paints, specialty chemicals, calcium carbonate, formulation of agrochemicals; toll manufacture and import of pharmaceutical and animal health products; merchanting of general chemicals
ICI Taiwan Ltd Republic of China	Ordinary	56 44†	Manufacture of fibre intermediates, paints and polyurethanes; merchanting of ICI and other products

* Listed
† Held by subsidiaries

The country of principal operations and registration or incorporation is stated below each company. The accounting dates of principal subsidiary undertakings are 31 December unless otherwise stated.

sources and disposal of value added

for the year ended 31 December 1994

	Continuing operations £m	1994 Discontinued operations £m	Total £m	Continuing operations £m	1993† Discontinued operations £m	Total £m
SOURCES OF INCOME						
Sales turnover	9,189	–	9,189	8,430	2,202	10,632
Royalties and other trading income	82	–	82	113	32	145
Less materials and services	(6,556)	–	(6,556)	(6,111)	(1,351)	(7,462)
Value added by manufacturing and trading activities	**2,715**	–	**2,715**	2,432	883	3,315
Share of profit less losses of associated undertakings	14	–	14	45	2	47
Value added related to exceptional items taken below trading profit	(37)	–	(37)	(52)	(47)	(99)
Total value added	**2,692**	–	**2,692**	2,425	838	3,263
DISPOSAL OF TOTAL VALUE ADDED						
Employees						
Employee costs charged in arriving at profit before tax	1,791	–	1,791	1,742	514	2,256
Governments						
Corporate taxes	164	–	164	119	70	189
Less grants	(8)	–	(8)	(10)	(1)	(11)
	156	–	156	109	69	178
Providers of capital						
Interest cost of net borrowings	88	–	88	90	63	153
Dividends to shareholders						
Cash	199	–	199	199	–	199
Demerger				363	–	363
Minority shareholders in subsidiary undertakings	56	–	56	42	–	42
	343	–	343	694	63	757
Re-investment in the business						
Depreciation	413	–	413	417	88	505
(Loss) profit retained	(11)	–	(11)	(537)	104	(433)
	402	–	402	(120)	192	72
Total disposal	**2,692**	–	**2,692**	2,425	838	3,263

† Restated (Note 2 to the Annual Accounts)

This table is based on the audited accounts; it shows the total value added to the cost of materials and services purchased from outside the Group and indicates the ways in which this increase in value has been disposed.

group financial record

for the years ended 31 December

	1994 £m	1993 £m	1992 £m	1991 £m	1990 £m	1989 £m
Profit and loss account						
CONTINUING OPERATIONS						
Turnover	**9,189**	8,430	7,557	7,942	8,444	8,549
Trading profit before exceptional items	**588**	325	173	343	380	767
Exceptional items charged to trading profit	**(67)**	–	(346)	–	–	–
Trading profit after exceptional items	**521**	325	(173)	343	380	767
Associated undertakings – before exceptional items	**14**	45	41	(4)	130	231
Associated undertakings – exceptional profits (losses)	**(70)**	–	(19)	27	376	46
Profits (losses) on sale or closure of operations	**(39)**	(94)	(207)	16	(44)	8
Provisions for costs of fundamental reorganisation and restructuring	**–**	–	(23)	–	(357)	–
Profits less losses on disposal of fixed assets	**70**	–	–	7	32	26
Net interest payable	**(88)**	(90)	(51)	(37)	(26)	3
Profit (loss) before taxation	**408**	186	(432)	352	491	1,081
Taxation	**(164)**	(119)	(187)	(122)	(180)	(391)
Attributable to minorities	**(56)**	(42)	(2)	(22)	(20)	(67)
Net profit (loss) – continuing operations	**188**	25	(621)	208	291	623
DISCONTINUED OPERATIONS – Net profit	**–**	104	51	334	192	434
Net profit (loss) attributable to parent company	**188**	129	(570)	542	483	1,057
Balance sheet						
Tangible fixed assets	**3,861**	4,024	5,634	5,128	4,947	4,856
Investments	**171**	458	455	396	461	753
Current assets	**4,972**	4,747	6,033	5,546	5,449	5,727
Total assets	**9,004**	9,229	12,122	11,070	10,857	11,336
Creditors due within one year	**(2,608)**	(2,452)	(4,377)	(3,410)	(3,406)	(3,618)
Total assets less current liabilities	**6,396**	6,777	7,745	7,660	7,451	7,718
Creditors due after more than one year	**1,617**	1,840	2,152	1,922	1,802	1,699
Provisions and deferred income	**705**	719	1,005	658	692	670
Minority interests	**338**	330	302	288	286	335
Shareholders' funds	**3,736**	3,888	4,286	4,792	4,671	5,014
	6,396	6,777	7,745	7,660	7,451	7,718
Capital gearing						
Net borrowings (total borrowings less cash, current asset investments and short-term deposits) as a percentage of net borrowings, minority interests and shareholders' funds	**3.3**	20.2	33.4	23.6	25.6	28.6
Cash flow						
Net cash inflow from operating activities	**888**	1,026	926	1,458	1,728	1,518
Net cash outflow from returns on investments and servicing of finance	**(308)**	(433)	(610)	(594)	(564)	(492)
Tax paid	**(98)**	(144)	(98)	(286)	(412)	(593)
Net cash inflow (outflow) from investing activities	**293**	447	(672)	(434)	(345)	(1,002)
Net cash inflow (outflow) before financing	**775**	896	(454)	144	407	(569)
Net cash inflow (outflow) from financing	**(213)**	(324)	(24)	189	157	69
Increase (decrease) in cash and cash equivalents	**562**	572	(478)	333	564	(500)
Return on assets						
Profit (loss) before loan interest and exceptional items as a percentage of assets employed (average total assets less current liabilities)						
Continuing operations	**10.2**	6.7				
Total	**10.2**	9.5	9.8	13.0	14.2	22.8

Note: Data for 1989 to 1992 have not been restated for post-retirement healthcare costs; the cumulative adjustment at 1 January 1993 was an increase in provisions and deferred income and a decrease in shareholders' funds of £89m.

shareholder information

Quarterly results

Unaudited trading results of the ICI Group for 1995 are expected to be announced as follows:

First quarter	27 April 1995
Half year	27 July 1995
Nine months	26 October 1995
Full year	22 February 1996

Dividend payments

A second interim dividend for the year 1994, which the Annual General Meeting will be asked to confirm as the final dividend for that year, is payable on 26 April 1995 to Ordinary shareholders registered in the books of the Company on 23 March 1995. Dividends are normally paid as follows: First interim: Announced with the Half year results and paid in early October. Second interim: Announced with the Full year results and paid in late April.

Taxation

In certain circumstances, when a shareholder in the UK sells shares, his liability to tax in respect of capital gains is computed by reference to the market value of the shares on 31 March 1982 adjusted for inflation between that date and the date of disposal. The market value of ICI Ordinary Shares at 31 March 1982, for the purposes of capital gains tax, was 309p.

Shares in Zeneca acquired on demerger from ICI will be treated as having a base cost for capital gains tax purposes ascertained by reference to the values of ICI and Zeneca shares on 1 June 1993 calculated in accordance with the provisions of Section 272 of the Taxation of Chargeable Gains Act 1992. The base cost of any holding of ICI shares on that date will be adjusted on the same basis.

The relevant prices on The London Stock Exchange on 1 June 1993 were: ICI – 631.75p and Zeneca – 625.75p.

Base costs in the pre-demerger ICI

shares will, therefore, be split between the post-demerger ICI and Zeneca shares in the proportion: ICI – 0.50239 and Zeneca – 0.49761.

Auditors

The remuneration and expenses of the Auditors in respect of the statutory report to the members of the Company for the year 1994 amounted to £280,000 (1993: £282,000). The total figure for the Group was £3.5m (1993: £3.4m) which includes charges for audits of subsidiary companies in the UK and overseas, both for the purposes of consolidation into the Group accounts and to meet statutory requirements of the countries in which subsidiaries operate.

Shareholders

The following table analyses the holdings of £1 Ordinary Shares at the end of 1994:

Size of holding	Number of Ordinary shareholders' accounts	Number of shares	%
1-250	120,899	14,432,715	2.0
251-500	65,419	24,400,466	3.4
501-1,000	46,844	33,901,775	4.7
1,001-5,000	25,204	44,149,636	6.1
5,001-10,000	809	5,753,751	0.8
10,001-50,000	762	18,219,501	2.5
50,001-1,000,000	775	171,565,418	23.7
Over 1,000,000	91	411,474,652	56.8
All holdings	260,803	723,897,914	100.0

In addition to the number of registered shareholders shown, there are approximately 43,000 holders of American Depositary Receipts (ADRs). The ADRs, each of which is equivalent to four £1 Ordinary Shares, are issued by Morgan Guaranty Trust Company of New York.

As at 21 February 1995 (one month prior to the date of Notice of Meeting) Morgan Guaranty Trust Company of New York had a non-beneficial interest in 97,811,423 Ordinary Shares of the Company (13.51% of the issued Ordinary Share Capital), all of which were registered in the name of their

nominee company, Guaranty Nominees Limited, in respect of ADRs. No other person held an interest in shares, comprising 3% or more of the issued Ordinary Share Capital of the Company, appearing in the register of interests in shares maintained under the provisions of Section 211 of the Companies Act 1985.

ICI Ordinary Shares are listed on The London Stock Exchange and other major European stock exchanges. In the form of ADRs, they are also listed on the New York Stock Exchange.

The Company from time to time files reports with the United States Securities and Exchange Commission. As a standing arrangement, a copy of each such report filed within the preceeding 12 months can be inspected by any shareholder or ADR holder during normal business hours at the offices of ICI at 9 Millbank, London, SW1P 3JF and at Olympic Tower, 645 Fifth Avenue, New York.

Personal Equity Plans (PEPs)

Details of the ICI General PEP and the ICI Single Company PEP may be obtained from:
The Plan Manager
Bradford & Bingley (PEPs) Limited
Telephone helpline: (01274) 555677

Registered Office

Imperial Chemical House
Millbank
London SW1P 3JF
Telephone: (0171) 834 4444

Registrar and Transfer Office

I C Parkinson
PO Box 251
Wexham Road
Slough SL2 5DP
Telephone: (01753) 877008

Auditors

KPMG
8 Salisbury Square
Blackfriars
London EC4Y 8BB

3   **EXECUTIVE SUMMARY**

a summary of
performance
1994

This, our fourth annual environmental performance report, describes progress towards meeting the objectives we set ourselves in 1990. For the first time we detail actions being taken by individual businesses within the ICI Group.

The good progress made in reducing wastes in previous years has been maintained in 1994, especially the continued reduction of wastes to air and to water.

Although the total amount of waste we produced in 1994 is at a similar level to 1993, this is due mainly to increased production of gypsum, an environmentally benign material, produced by Tioxide in neutralising its waste acid in its new treatment facilities. Tioxide is now selling gypsum as a product and sales are growing rapidly. In the future, the Group's total volume of waste will reduce as new markets are found.

There has been a continued improvement in energy efficiency across the Group.

Our achievements have been brought about through a combination of good management, training, attention to detail and safety, the introduction of new technologies and improved processes that reduce the impact of our operations on the environment. The closure of some outdated plants and our withdrawal from certain markets has also helped.

We have continued to improve our compliance performance with the increasingly stringent regulations being applied around the world, but we are still not perfect. I was disappointed by the number of times we were prosecuted and fined for breaking environmental laws and regulations. Our goal remains total compliance.

Environmental pressures are providing us with business opportunities to develop and market a wide range of new technologies and products that satisfy an ever-growing demand for goods with sound environmental performance.

We have proved, not least to ourselves, that target-setting is an effective way to motivate our staff to improve the management of our operations. We are now devising a new set of challenging goals covering safety and health, as well as the environment, to support continuous improvement by the Group into the next century. These will be finalised this year.

Finally, congratulations to Chris Hampson, our former director in charge of safety, health and the environment, now retired from ICI, on receiving the CBE for services to environmental protection. He was instrumental in initiating these detailed reports against defined objectives.

4 **PROGRESS IN 1994**

to focus our efforts on environmental improvement we set ourselves **four main objectives** in 1990

these two pages summarise our progress.

OBJECTIVE

1

ICI requires all its new plants to be built to standards that will meet the regulations it can reasonably anticipate in the most environmentally demanding country in which it operates that process. This will normally require the use of the best environmental practice within the industry.

All plants designed and built during 1994 have met the objective.

This includes the world's largest single stream manufacturing plant for ICI's 'Melinar' PET (polyethylene terephthalate) at Fayetteville, US. It is scheduled to begin production in 1996.

We are building a new £16 million manufacturing plant for waterborne paints in Cikarang, Indonesia. It will incorporate the latest computerised process technology. We intend this to be a zero-liquid effluent plant, the same as the recently opened paint production facility in Nilai, Malaysia.

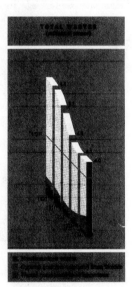

OBJECTIVE

2

ICI will reduce wastes by 50% by 1995, using 1990 as the baseline year. The company will pay special attention to wastes which are hazardous. In addition, ICI will try to eliminate all off-site disposal of environmentally harmful wastes.

• Total waste emissions to air, water and land are 27% lower than 1990, the baseline year. This is the same as 1993 although production has increased.

• Hazardous wastes are reduced by 65%, a small improvement on 1993. Hazardous waste to water is 82% lower than in 1990.

• Hazardous wastes represent only 4% of our total wastes.

• Non-hazardous wastes to air and water have been reduced each year and are now 48% and 44% lower respectively than in 1990.

• Although non-hazardous waste to land has increased by 31% since 1990, this is because of a major change in the way certain acid wastes are dealt with.

These are now neutralised in a process that creates gypsum - an environmentally benign material - for which we are developing new markets. Sales are growing and this will reduce the amount of gypsum going to landfill.

For more information on our wastes, where they go, and our progress in their reduction, see pages 15,16 & 17.

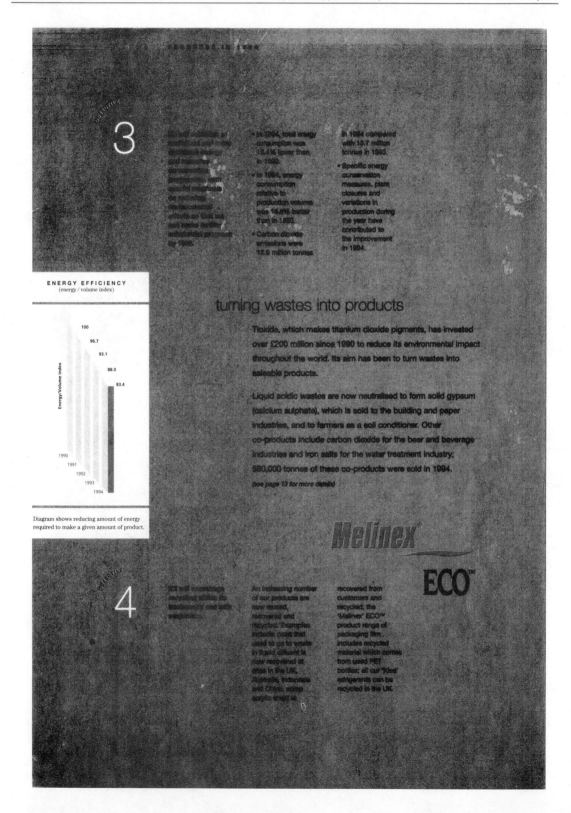

ENERGY EFFICIENCY
(energy / volume index)

100

96.7

93.1

88.0

83.4

Energy/Volume index

1990
1991
1992
1993
1994

Diagram shows reducing amount of energy
required to make a given amount of product.

- In 1994, total energy consumption was 15.4% lower than in 1990.
- In 1994, energy consumption relative to production volume was 16.6% better than in 1990.
- Carbon dioxide emissions were 12.9 million tonnes

in 1994 compared with 13.7 million tonnes in 1993.

- Specific energy conservation measures, plant closures and variations in production during the year have contributed to the improvement in 1994.

turning wastes into products

Tioxide, which makes titanium dioxide pigments, has invested over £200 million since 1990 to reduce its environmental impact throughout the world. Its aim has been to turn wastes into saleable products.

Liquid acidic wastes are now neutralised to form solid gypsum (calcium sulphate), which is sold to the building and paper industries, and to farmers as a soil conditioner. Other co-products include carbon dioxide for the beer and beverage industries and iron salts for the water treatment industry; 580,000 tonnes of these co-products were sold in 1994.

(see page 13 for more details)

An increasing number of our products are now reused, recovered and recycled. Examples include paint that used to go to waste in liquid effluent is now recovered at sites in the UK, Australia, Indonesia and China; some acrylic sheet is

recovered from customers and recycled; the 'Melinex' ECO™ product range of packaging film includes recycled material which comes from used PET bottles; all our 'Klea' refrigerants can be recycled in the UK.

we estimate about £430 million of our **expenditure** was on safety, health and the environment in 1994

of which about £210 million was spent on the environment.

There are four main areas where we spend money on the environment.

1 **Developing environmentally sound products and processes** We put considerable effort into developing products and processes which meet the fast growing demand for goods with a sound environmental performance. We spend money on research, technology and engineering, building plants and providing technical services to customers. These costs are not directly labelled as environmental expenditure.

2 **New plants** Whenever new plants are built anywhere in the world they are designed to keep their impact on the environment to a minimum - up to one quarter of the building costs can be attributed to safety, health and the environment. This makes good business and environmental sense because a clean plant will be more efficient, produce less waste and therefore cost less to run. This will eventually reduce our annual running costs for environmental protection.

3 **Wastes** The cost of dealing with our wastes is charged against the profits for the year. This charge will include, where appropriate, the depreciation on assets (eg clean-up technologies) which have been built to improve standards at existing plants.

4 **Cleaning up contaminated land and groundwater** Such contamination is inherited from the industrial practices of the past, before the effects on the environment were known.

Our policy is to include in the accounts the full cost of cleaning up as soon as a decision has been taken to remediate and when the costs can be estimated, although there may be a period of time before work is undertaken.

We recognise the amount of money spent on the environment does not necessarily reflect a company's environmental performance. It is also difficult to compare environmental expenditures published by companies in the same industry because of different accounting conventions.

The most successful chemical companies will be those that reduce their environmental costs through resolving historical problems, running clean plants and developing environmentally sound products.

our **mistakes** and compliance with the law

ICI was prosecuted and fined for breaking environmental laws on 13 occasions in 1994. The infringements were unintentional but clearly unacceptable. Despite this, we have improved our compliance with worldwide environmental regulations. Our goal remains total compliance with the law wherever we operate. *(see page 18 for further details).*

ICI operates throughout the world. Our Safety, Health and Environment (SHE) Policy commits us, as a minimum, to operate to the same high standards worldwide. This can be challenging in countries which have cultures, standards, attitudes and laws that are different from - but not necessarily less rigorous - than those in, say, Europe or North America.

conforming to **world standards**

Take Taiwan, where ICI has six different business operations. These include a PTA (pure terephthalic acid) plant - our single largest overseas investment - and the Kaoshiung Monomer Company (KMC), a joint venture between ICI and a Taiwanese company producing methyl methacrylate monomer for acrylics production.

Taiwan is about 100 miles wide and 200 miles long. Eighty per cent of the island is mountainous and uninhabitable and the population of 21 million is confined to living and working in the narrow west coastal strip. This creates major problems including dense housing, a lot of traffic and air pollution.

Taiwan's remarkable economic success in recent years is largely due to the nation's adaptability and the people's strong entrepreneurial spirit. As in many parts of the world, awareness about the environment and safety has grown. The Environmental Protection Administration has introduced very tough environmental laws. Our PTA plant which was constructed in 1990 to contemporary high standards has recently been required to upgrade its waste water treatment works to meet even tighter Taiwanese regulations.

Our KMC plant is located in one of the busiest petrochemicals complexes on the island where no fewer than 11 different companies operate. Government and industry have co-operated in establishing a pollution monitoring centre for the entire complex. KMC has 91 emissions detectors linked to the centre which operates 24 hours a day.

Increasing concern for the environment and safety in Taiwan is good news for ICI. It supports our commitment to conform to the highest international standards, and to promote good environmental performance and good safety practice among our workforce. As a leading exponent of "Responsible Care" in Taiwan, we share our SHE knowledge with government agencies and other chemical companies.

working towards **sustainable development**

The United Nations has started a worldwide debate, led by Norway, to develop patterns of production and consumption that can be sustained. ICI supports these efforts and is contributing to the debate through its membership of the World Business Council for Sustainable Development.

Our commitment to the worldwide chemical industries' "Responsible Care" initiative and the International Chamber of Commerce's "Business Charter for Sustainable Development" is written into the ICI Group SHE Policy.

8   ICI PAINTS

Main impacts on the environment

Paints manufacture consumes mainly water, raw materials and energy. Paints also affect the environment when used, for example by the emission of volatile organic compounds (VOCs) to the air. As with any well-established manufacturer we also have to deal with environmental issues from the past such as land contamination at some of our older sites.

ICI paints is one of the world's largest suppliers of **paint**

for decoration, refinishing vehicles and coating food cans. Paints protect, preserve and prolong the life of the items they cover and add colour to our lives.

Actions taken

Cutting waste Minimising waste and reducing the use of water in manufacturing are integral parts of our operations. Recent examples are: all water discharges have been eradicated from our new plant at Nilai, Malaysia; a company-wide programme encourages the recycling and reuse of water; sites in the UK, Australia, Indonesia and China recover paint that previously went to waste in liquid effluent.

Reducing VOC emissions All VOCs used in paint eventually end up in the atmosphere. The overall level of these emissions is decreasing as we produce more waterborne paints, improve our practices and processes to reduce the use of organic solvents and improve environmental controls in our plants.

Protecting our sites We commissioned tests and reports on all our property in 1994 as part of our ongoing programme to prevent spillage, improve our working practices and prevent contamination.

Product stewardship We want our customers to make the best use of our products and handle them safely - we provide all the necessary information to achieve this. We also seek to encourage the use of waterborne products by informing customers and the market place, and by working with governments and other organisations. We have taken major initiatives in the post-consumer waste area to promote recycling, reuse and reduction.

BUSINESS HIGHLIGHT

Cuts in hazardous wastes have already exceeded the Group's reduction target. Our ultimate aim is to eradicate these wastes altogether.

9   **ICI EXPLOSIVES**

we are the world's leading supplier of **explosives** and blasting services for mining, quarrying and construction

Main impacts on the environment
Our products and processes affect the environment during manufacture, use and disposal. The manufacturing process creates emissions, particularly solid waste, including the release locally of ammonium nitrate, and the generation of solid waste and aqueous effluent. On older sites, contaminated land is an issue which has to be managed responsibly.

Actions taken

Cutting waste Modern manufacturing methods ensure that our operations have minimal impact on the environment. For example, we have reduced the amount of particulate ammonium nitrate which escapes from our plants by using a new in-house technology. The new process has the added benefit of reducing our energy consumption too.

Disposing of explosives We have installed a high-temperature rotary kiln incinerator at our Joplin Site in the US, which will be used to destroy sub-standard explosives and surplus munitions from North America.

Clean-up Our special Land Reclamation Group is looking at the extent of the problem and finding the best solutions. We plan to spend nearly £7 million in 1995 on site demolition and clean-up in the UK, Asia Pacific and the Americas.

Cleaner products ICI Explosives in Australia has developed a new and popular product called 'PowerGel Clear' which dramatically reduces the amount of nitrogen dioxide formed in a blast.

BUSINESS HIGHLIGHT

Our Environmental Services business in the US disposes of unwanted explosives and munitions in an environmentally acceptable way.

ICI's **materials** is made up of ICI acrylics, ICI films and ICI polyurethanes

ICI ACRYLICS

We are the world's largest producer of methyl methacrylate (MMA), used in the manufacture of a wide range of products such as baths, signs, lighting products and vehicle parts.

Main impacts on the environment
MMA manufacture consumes energy and water and demands the careful handling of toxic intermediates. The process creates solid and liquid wastes and air emissions. When they are used, acrylic resins affect the environment by the emission of volatile organic compounds (VOCs).

Actions taken

Cutting wastes The further reduction of acidic ammonium sulphate waste in water is a priority worldwide. For example, we plan to further reduce acid discharges by 85% at our Teesside, UK, plant, in accord with the National Rivers Authority programme to re-stock the River Tees with salmon in 1995.

BUSINESS HIGHLIGHT

The technology used in "Recovery" allows scrap acrylic sheet to be recycled back to the monomer to make new high quality 'Perspex' sheet.

Recycling We recycle acrylic waste material in our manufacturing process. We have launched a scheme called "Recovery" to recycle scrap acrylic sheet from customers.

Reformulating products We are involved in reformulating acrylic resins to replace organic solvents with water-based alternatives. We are also using Life Cycle Assessments to understand the environmental performance of our products from their manufacture, through their use and finally to their eventual disposal.

ıı   **ICI MATERIALS**

BUSINESS HIGHLIGHT

We are a leader in
CFC-free foam-
blowing technology
for all applications.
We promote the
technology
throughout the world
including developing
countries.

ICI FILMS

ICI Films makes specialist high-performance
plastic film, used for a wide variety of
applications, such as data storage
and packaging.

Main impacts on the environment

Our main raw materials are polymers and their
precursors, and our manufacturing processes
use energy, water and organic solvents.
Wastes include unusable polymers and
discarded packaging materials. Our main
environmental issues are solid wastes (mainly
polymers) which are landfilled and ground
water contamination at some of our sites.

Actions taken

Cutting waste Waste reduction has been
achieved by improving the efficiency of our
processes, removing water from waste, and by
recycling more polymers, cardboard, solvents,
lubricants, paper and wood. We have also just
installed a thermal oxidiser at our US plant in
Fayetteville, North Carolina.

Ground and groundwater contamination We
have further investigated and assessed the
degree of contamination at our sites. Two of
our UK sites have removed contamination
already and other sites are preparing to do so.
Novel bio-remediation techniques have been
pioneered at Dumfries, UK.

Recycling New recyclable packaging systems
have been developed. The 'Melinex' ECO™
product range has been developed in the US
to include recycled material. Several of these
films now contain a minimum of 25% post-
consumer recycled waste, which comes from
recycled PET bottles.

BUSINESS HIGHLIGHT

The new 'Melinex' ECO™
packaging product range
in the US each year uses
over 44 million discarded
soft drink PET bottles,
which would have gone
to landfill.

ICI POLYURETHANES

We are the world's second biggest maker of
polyurethane chemicals and systems. Our
products range from soft, comfortable foam
used in furniture to hard, energy-saving
construction boards in buildings and
refrigeration systems.

Main impacts on the environment

Making polyurethane chemicals produces air
emissions, liquid effluent and solid waste
(almost all as common salt - sodium chloride).
The hazardous nature of some of the
chemicals used in the process demands that
we design, build and operate our plants to the
highest standards.

Actions taken

Waste reduction We operate a special
environmental scheme which targets
hazardous waste, substance by substance.
Achievements in 1994 include: the
commissioning of a gas-separation unit, called
PRISM, in our aniline plant at Wilton, UK,
which uses membrane technology to reduce
methane and other hydrocarbon emissions by
over 3,700 tonnes a year; and the reduction by
more than one third of the chemicals oxygen
demand in the liquid effluent of our polyols
plant at Rozenburg, The Netherlands.

Product Improvements 'Waterlily' comfort
cushioning minimises environmental impact
throughout its life cycle. It uses water as the
blowing agent instead of CFCs. MDI binders
are used to convert waste from straw and
cotton into low-cost packaging, furniture and
building materials.

ICI is one of the largest manufacturers of industrial **chemicals & polymers**

ICI Chemicals & Polymers (C&P) has five major business units. They are: Petrochemicals & Fertilizers; Polyester Intermediates & Polymers which manufactures pure terephthalic acid (PTA) and 'Melinar' PET resins; Chlor-Chemicals; Surfactants & Chemicals; and Fluorochemicals which manufactures the 'Klea' range of CFC replacements.

Main impacts on the environment

C&P is a major chemicals manufacturer using oil, natural gas and salt. Oil and gas are transformed into the building blocks used in a wide range of products, such as plastics for soft drinks bottles. Salt is converted in an energy-intensive process into chlorine, an essential chemical for industry and society. Our activities can, and do, have an impact on the environment. For example, we handle materials that are flammable and toxic, making it vitally important for us to ensure that the substances are adequately and properly contained. We consume energy and create wastes that are emitted to the environment under strict legal control.

Actions taken

Waste reduction A major waste treatment plant, under construction at our Runcorn, UK, site, will enable us to reduce by 90% hazardous waste emissions to the air and water from our Merseyside operations. Other examples include: the development of a new wetting agent at our Thorndale plant in the US which replaces alcohol and reduces air emissions by 94%; a new £370,000 water treatment plant at our Mevisa site in Spain which reduces organic waste by 80%, solid waste by 50% and energy use by 30%; and the use as fertilizers of nitrogen and phosphorus-rich sludges from our Chocques, France, wastewater treatment plant.

Product stewardship Large containers (from 30 to 300 gallon capacity) in which our 'Fluon' powders and resins are packaged can now be reused or recycled (according to the type) after changes in design and collection systems. Recycling and/or reuse is now cheaper and easier for customers and the containers no longer go to waste. All 'Klea' refrigerants (our ozone benign replacements for CFCs) can now be recycled in the UK.

Improved products A new textile scouring product called 'Lanaryl' RK, which is almost completely biodegradable, has been developed to replace aromatic and chlorinated hydrocarbon solvents. Formaldehyde-free dye fixing agents, called 'Matexil' FC-ER and 'Fixogene' E, have been developed for the textile industry. The worldwide production of 'Klea' 134a at our plants in the UK, the US and Japan continues to grow as CFCs are phased out under international agreement.

BUSINESS HIGHLIGHT

By 1994 our hazardous waste production was less than one third of that in 1990.

Titanium dioxide is used in a wide range of products such as paints, paper, plastics, printing inks, ceramics and in a high-purity form in food and cosmetics.

at **tioxide** we produce titanium dioxide pigments that are used to give whiteness and opacity

Main impacts on the environment
Titanium dioxide is produced from titanium ores such as ilmenite by two possible processes, one called sulphate and the other chloride. We use both. Their respective impacts on the environment depend more on the choice of ore, the waste treatment techniques used and whether a use can be found for the co-products, rather than on the choice of manufacturing route alone. Acid waste from the sulphate process can be recycled or neutralised. Neutralisation produces gypsum, a naturally occurring, benign substance, which can be developed into co-products for the construction and agricultural industry or safely disposed to landfill.

Actions taken

Improving performance We have chosen different solutions to reduce the impact on the environment made by our factories around the world, depending on the economics and the environmental requirements at each location. During 1994, we commissioned major new environmental projects at our plants at Calais, France; Grimsby, UK; Burnie, Australia; Huelva, Spain and Umbogintwini, South Africa.

From waste to product We are developing markets for co-products that were previously treated as waste. These include chemicals that can be used to treat water, soil conditioners and fertilizers, and materials for the building trade. In 1994, sales of co-products by volume

exceeded that of titanium dioxide itself. We also opened a joint venture soil nutrient business called Oligo, in Huelva, Spain.

Life Cycle Assessment LCA is revealing that the overall impact of titanium dioxide manufacture depends on raw material selection and the degree of co-product sales and effluent treatment, rather than a simple choice between the manufacturing routes. Further stages of the LCA study will be carried out in 1995.

Standards All our pigment plants are registered to the quality management standard ISO 9002 and during 1994 our sites started a programme of work leading towards registration to the environmental management standard BS7750.

BUSINESS HIGHLIGHT

Sales of co-products - once waste - were 580,000 tonnes in 1994. We intend to increase these to over 800,000 tonnes in 1995.

Tioxide produces its own environmental report. Copies can be obtained from Anita Hunt, Tioxide Group Headquarters, Lincoln House, 137-143 Hammersmith Road, London W14 0QL, UK

14   ICI REGIONAL BUSINESSES

regional
businesses operate in Argentina, Australia, Canada, India and Pakistan

ICI's main businesses operate internationally, but in addition, there are several businesses which are more local in their scope.

In Argentina, we make industrial chemicals, plastics and chemicals from the wine making process; in Australia, we make industrial chemicals, plastics, paints, commercial explosives and fertilizers; in Canada we are in chlor-alkali manufacture; in India our manufacturing includes industrial explosives, paints, agrochemicals and polyurethanes; and in Pakistan we make polyester fibre, soda ash and specialty chemicals.

Main impacts on the environment
Because of our wide range of activities we create a number of equally broad pressures on the environment including the use of energy, water and natural resources and generate solid and liquid wastes and air emissions.

Actions taken

Cleaner production In Australia, a new 1,380 km cross-country pipeline will bring ethane from Cooper Basin in South Australia to our Botany site, near Sydney, as a replacement for the existing naphtha feedstock. This will provide a use for the previously wasted ethane and reduce energy consumption and air emissions from the Botany operations.

Cleaning up ground and groundwater contamination is important in Canada and Australia. For example, in Australia, past activities at the Botany site from a time when environmental standards were not as high have contributed to some contamination. Investigations are being undertaken to decide on the most appropriate remedial action. More than A$3 million will be spent on this project in the next two years.

Emergency procedures ICI's Ennore Works in India played a successful and key role in introducing a United Nations programme called "Awareness and Preparedness for Emergency at Local Levels" (APELL).

Site improvement At Khewra, Pakistan, we have planted over 55,000 trees and shrubs in a programme called "Project Green" on abandoned lime beds adjacent to the soda ash works. This is being carried out to demonstrate to the community that the lime beds do not contain hazardous chemicals as well as generally improving the aspect of the site.

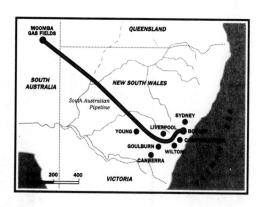

Every year the leading industrial countries produce over nine billion tonnes of waste. Households are responsible for about six per cent of this and manufacturing industry accounts for 17 per cent. The remainder comes from agriculture, mining, power generation, demolition and sewage.

Everyone has a responsibility to reduce waste to a minimum. These pages describe ICI's main wastes, explain where they go and show our progress in their reduction. The data presented in this section represent actual annual totals and have not been corrected for production volume.

environmental **data**

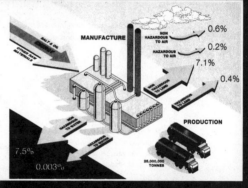

Wastes compared with output

Our hazardous waste constitutes only 0.7 per cent by volume of our output - everything we make and sell - which we estimate was 25 million tonnes in 1994.

The diagram shows the routes of disposal of waste expressed as a percentage of our total output.

how we performed

We divide our wastes into hazardous (defined by national legislation) and non-hazardous. Some of these wastes are emitted to the air, some to water (rivers and seas) and some are disposed of on land. These graphs show our wastes by weight, their classification, where they went and progress since 1990.

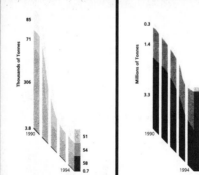

16   **ICI DATA**

hazardous wastes
what they are and reductions achieved

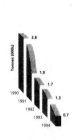
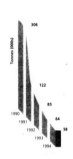
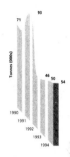

To air Mainly volatile organic compounds (VOCs) which evaporate in air at normal temperatures.

Progress down 40 per cent on 1990 levels.

* Licensed waste treatment contractors are audited by and on behalf of ICI to ensure operating standards are maintained to legal requirements and ICI's own standards.

To water Mostly metals and compounds and mainly chromium and zinc compounds.

Progress down 82 per cent on 1990 levels.

To land on site Includes disposal of wastes, such as chlorinated hydrocarbons, to licensed land disposal on ICI property.

Progress down 81 per cent on 1990 levels.

To land off site Generally contain small amounts of hazardous components. Sent for treatment (mainly incineration and landfill) by outside licensed contractors.*

Progress down 24 per cent on 1990 levels.

non-hazardous wastes
what they are and reductions achieved

■ Particulates to air

Inorganic gases to air

■ To water

■ To land on site

■ To land off site

■ Non-process waste

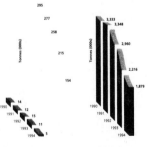
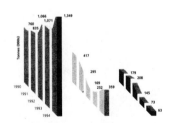

To air Products of burning coal and oil include nitrogen oxides, sulphur oxides, particulates and dust. We are using more natural gas and power generators that produce both heat and power. They reduce emissions and use fuel more efficiently.

Progress down 48 per cent on 1990 levels.

To water Nearly one quarter of non-hazardous waste is salty water (brine). These wastes have little effect on the environment and are considered too expensive to reduce. A large amount of acidic effluent has been neutralised to gypsum.

Progress down 44 per cent on 1990 levels.

To land on site and off site
Large volumes of wastes, such as gypsum and fly-ash from power stations, are sent to landfill. Non-process waste is mainly demolished building materials.

Wastes up 31 per cent on 1990 levels.

This increase is because acidic wastes are now neutralised in a process that creates gypsum - an environmentally benign material for which we are developing new sales opportunities. This will reduce the amount of gypsum going to landfill.

ICI DATA

ICI **substance emissions**
data* (tonnes) 1994

The chemicals listed are substances with recognised potential environmental impact and are drawn from UK, US and European environmental regulations.

Inorganic Compounds	Air	Water	Land	Metals & Compounds	Air	Water	Land
Sulphuric Acid	54	275510	23	Manganese	13	2381	15
Sulphur Dioxide	54077	-	-	Vanadium	-	582	<1
Carbon Monoxide	41906	-	-	Chromium	<1	219	17
Ammonium Sulphate	8	22085	-	Zinc	1	203	6
Nitrogen Dioxide	18069	-	-	Cobalt	6	50	7
Ammonium Nitrate	400	8140	2617	Copper	2	10	22
Nitric Acid	-	8072	-	Antimony	<1	1	30
Nitrous Oxide	4403	-	-	Mercury	4	1	16
Ammonia	926	384	-	Nickel	2	19	4
Asbestos	-	-	637	Lead	7	13	1
Chlorine	6	480	32	Arsenic	-	2	1
Hydrochloric Acid	246	<1	4	Barium	<1	1	-
Hydrogen Cyanide	161	-	-	Cadmium	-	<1	<1
Phosphoric Acid	-	17	-				
Cyanide Compounds	-	10	-				
Hydrogen Fluoride	2	-	3				
Hydrogen Sulphide	2	-	-				
Hydrazine	-	<1	-				

Organic Compounds	Air	Water	Land		Air	Water	Land
				Propylene	186	-	-
1,2-Dichloroethane	2817	3	8496	Chloroprene	-	-	184
Ethylene	5182	-	-	Chloropentafluoroethane	182	1	-
Acetic Acid	1048	3274	402	Dichlorodifluoromethane	54	<1	122
Methanol	2424	1164	456	Vinylidene Chloride	114	<1	23
Ethylene Glycol	1847	1353	20	Phenol	10	71	49
1,2-Dichloroethylene	2041	<1	275	Chlorobenzene	93	<1	10
P-Xylene	2009	2	-	Methyl Ethyl Ketone	97	-	-
1,1,2-Trichloroethane	97	<1	1769	Chloroethane	93	-	2
Carbon Tetrachloride	69	1	1752	Trichlorobenzene	-	-	75
Vinyl Chloride	1340	13	4	Formaldehyde	9	60	-
1,1,2,2-Tetrachloroethane	2	<1	1249	Ethyl Benzene	67	-	-
Xylene	1063	27	-	Glycol Ethers	<1	64	-
Chloromethane	1006	4	10	Cumene	55	-	-
2-Nitrophenol	-	97	891	1,3-Butadiene	55	-	-
Tetrachloroethylene	215	1	748	Ethane 1,1,2-Trichloro			
Acetone	897	53	<1	1,2,2-Trifluoro	-	<1	40
Benzene	801	79	6	Dichlorotetrafluoroethane	22	<1	5
Trichloroethylene	536	1	280	Methyl Isobutyl Ketone	18	1	-
Aniline	14	304	467	4,4-Methylenedianiline	1	2	15
Hexachloro-1,3-Butadiene	-	-	759	Dinitrotoluene	5	-	10
1,1,1,2-Tetrachloroethane	2	<1	728	Propylene Oxide	12	-	-
Methyl Methacrylate	543	46	-	1,4-Dioxane	-	10	-
Carbonyl Sulphide	572	-	-	Ethyl Acrylate	4	<1	-
Chloroform	229	11	297	Isopropyl Alcohol	3	<1	-
Dichloroethane	422	1	105	Butyl Acrylate	2	-	-
Nitrobenzene	1	242	199	1,2-Dichlorobenzene	1	-	1
Toluene	263	89	12	Carbon Disulphide	2	-	-
Bromomethane	360	-	-	Hexachloroethane	-	-	1
Dichloromethane	342	4	-	Dibutyl Phthalate	-	1	-
Acetaldehyde	172	162	-	Hydroquinone	<1	-	<1
1,1,1-Trichloroethane	204	1	45	Hexachlorobenzene	-	<1	<1
Cyclohexane	231	-	-	N-Butyl Alcohol	<1	-	-
Ethylene Oxide	195	-	-	Trichlorofluoromethane	-	<1	-

* These data are aggregated from 55 ICI manufacturing sites around the world to illustrate the substances being released and the receiving media. These categories do not correspond to groupings already used in this report. Contact your site manager for detailed local information.

18   I C I   D A T A

complying with the **law**

We carry out hundreds of thousands of tests on our emissions throughout ICI every year to determine that our operations are in compliance with local regulations. Environmental laws around the world are strict and becoming stricter, as a reflection of the increased concern for the environment. Our aim is to comply with the law as a minimum standard, but we sometimes fail. Nevertheless our compliance continues to improve.

compliance with
regulatory standards

Year		%
1990		**90%**
1991		**90%**
1992	Air	**96%**
	Water	**94%**
1993	Air	**98%**
	Water	**95%**
1994	Air	**99%**
	Water	**98%**

prosecutions,
penalties 1994

In the UK

• Fined £2,000 for release of ammonia from fertilizer manufacture.

• Fined £15,000 for over-filling a storage tank of potassium hydroxide.

In North America

• Fined US$25,000 for an administration violation for failing to register three vents.

• Fined US$1,000 on six occasions for out-of-consent discharges following heavy rain.

In South America

• Notice of fine issued for exceeding permissable emission of sulphur dioxide. The size of the fine is pending.

In Australia

• Fined A$500 for release of PVC/VCM after the rupture of a bursting disc.

• Fined A$500 for over-filling an ethylene oxide storage tank.

• Fined A$2,500 for release of liquid to a surface-water pond.

complaints by the public

In 1994, 986 people made a complaint to the company. The figure includes some complaints about incidents in which we were not involved. Some incidents received multiple complaints. We responded to all complainants and provided the requested information. Over half the complaints were in the UK, which reflects ICI's large manufacturing presence in the country.

awards

• US EPA Stratospheric Ozone Protection Award to ICI Polyurethanes, for the development of 'Waterlily' comfort cushioning.

• Commendation for ICI Explosives in the Scottish Environmental Awards for Business 1994.

• ICI's Glidden paints plant at Huron, Ohio, won the Pollution Prevention Award of the National Paint and Coatings Association in the US.

• Business/Industry Award in the Great Grimsby Environment Awards won by Tioxide, Grimsby, UK.

Chapter 12

Auditing Issues for Global Operations

Internal auditing and external auditing are two separate but related functions. The two audit functions share a common objective—to determine reliability of accounting information. In this chapter we will discuss issues related to internal as well as external auditing.

Internal Auditing

Internal auditing is defined as an objective evaluation of operations and control systems of an organization to determine whether its policies and procedures are being followed and also whether its resources are safeguarded and used efficiently to achieve organizational objectives. The objectives of internal auditing, based on the above definition, are to determine whether:

- Management and accounting controls are in place and are effective.
- Assets are safeguarded and used efficiently.

The importance of an internal audit function increases as operations of an organization become geographically dispersed. It is easy to understand the underlying reasons—internal audit deals with two areas that are dear to the heart of management of a company: Management is interested in compliance with its policies, and management is interested in safeguarding of assets and their proper use.

Global Trends in Internal Auditing

The importance and practice of internal auditing is increasing worldwide. This is especially the case in North America, Japan, Western Europe, Israel, and India. In many countries internal auditing is required by law. Several factors have contributed to the enhanced status of internal auditing.

Audit committees. The role of boards of directors has been redefined during the last 10 to 15 years. The boards are being held by stockholders to much higher levels of accountability than in the past. Also, the trend toward having directors on the board who are from outside the organization has been gaining popularity. A recent survey of the 100 largest publicly held U.S.-based multinationals has revealed that they have been recruiting a large number of outsiders to their boards of directors, while getting rid of insiders. According to this survey, conducted by the Spencer Stuart consulting firm, the typical board of directors in 1994 contained four times as many outside directors as inside directors. Incidentally, the ratio was three outsiders to one insider in 1993 and two outsiders to one insider in 1989.[1]

---

[1] Arthur M. Louis, "Firms Seek Outsiders as Directors," *San Francisco Chronicle,* 17 June 1994, sec. E, p. 1.

These developments have shifted the balance of power from top operating executives to the board of directors. One outcome of the shift in power has been widespread creation and use of audit committees. Typically, the audit committee consists of members of the board of directors, the majority of whom are usually from outside the organization. The internal auditors of the organization often report directly to the audit committee. An important factor contributing to the establishment of audit committees has been the Foreign Corrupt Practices Act (FCPA). The impact of FCPA has been felt worldwide due to its broad scope and its penalty provisions. A later section of this chapter discusses FCPA in detail. In the U.K., the recommendations of the Committee on the Financial Aspects of Corporate Governance (commonly known as the Cadbury Committee, after its chairman) are expected to result in an expanded role for audit committees of companies listed on the London Stock Exchange. In the U.S., the New York Stock Exchange, the American Stock Exchange, and the automated quotation system of the National Association of Security Dealers (DASDAQ) require that all companies listed on those security markets have audit committees. The New York Stock Exchange mandates that the audit committees consist of non-management directors only, while the American Stock Exchange and NASDAQ require that the majority be non-management directors. The Committee of Sponsoring Organizations (COSO) of the Treadway Commission considers an effective internal audit function to be important for reliability and integrity of financial and operational information. COSO has also stated that an enlightened and proactive audit committee is a powerful agent for corporate self-regulation.

Technological advances. Major advances in communication and information technologies have made internal auditing more necessary as well as more feasible. Speed of electronic transfers and computerization of information systems have raised new concerns about both asset security and data security. This makes the role of internal auditing more important. The new technologies enable the internal auditor to perform audit tests and analyses faster and more economically.

Reliance of external auditors on internal audit reports. For cost savings and to avoid unnecessary duplication, it is common for external auditors to rely on internal audit reports, as discussed in a later section. This further enhances the importance of the internal audit function.

Complexity of international operations. Conceptually there is no difference between internal audit of domestic operations and internal audit of international operations. However, international operations add certain complexities that necessitate adaptations and adjustments.

- Geographic distance makes it impossible to oversee distant operations through physical observation and visual inspection.
- Knowledge of local laws is essential to ensure their compliance. Local laws apply to a multitude of operational areas, e.g., environmental pollution, product safety, and employment, to name a few. In France, for example, a new penal code took effect on March 1, 1994 that, for the first time, makes corporations, small companies, and nonprofit groups accountable for endangering others. The code contains penalty provisions for environmental terrorism, including willful pollution.

- Business practices are different throughout the world. In some countries (for example, Japan) banks typically do not return cancelled checks. In other countries, confirmation of receivables and payables is not a customary practice.
- Each country has its own monetary unit.
- Local records are kept in the local language and create translation problems. Translation problems may be compounded by differences in accounting terminology. Even when the language is the same, accounting terms may have different meanings. For example, the term "stock" has a different meaning in the U.K. (inventory) than it does in the U.S. (ownership shares).
- Different cultural practices often require that the top management make decisions by balancing many conflicting factors. The trade-offs thus required make such decisions more complex than they would have been in purely domestic operations.
- The degree to which the infrastructure of a country is developed has a direct impact on the design of internal control system and internal audit function.
- Lack of availability of skilled internal auditors may be a problem in some countries.

These are just some examples of the complexities in international operations. Internal auditors can provide in-house consulting expertise for problem solving in a complex environment.

Policy Formulation in Different Cultures

Cultural realities must be confronted and issues resolved to ensure that corporate policies are well thought out and well articulated. This requires taking into account cultural differences, company goals, and business ethics. Some issues are easy to resolve, e.g., pork in company functions should not be served in Israel or in Muslim countries. Other issues are more complex and can be addressed only after analyzing them and then articulating a clear corporate policy. An important consideration to keep in mind is that MNC operations are not confined to one part of the world. *MNCs are corporate citizens of a country as well as of the world.* Some claim that cultural differences preclude applying one set of ethical standards worldwide. Research findings, however, indicate that despite cultural differences, standards of moral judgment do not vary significantly among countries.[2] Therefore, ethical considerations become critically important variables in the decision process to ensure long-run approach, rather than short-run gains. According to a recent poll, instituting formal ethical policies in a company leads to lower internal control costs for the company.[3]

This is not to imply that these are easily resolved dilemmas. However, proper focus does help. *Formulation of corporate policy should focus on long-run results rather than short-term expediency.* The leadership and attitude of top management coupled with a proactive management style can go a long way toward cultivation of a corporate culture in which constructive ideas are accepted, nourished, and given a chance to flourish. A performance evaluation system that takes into account performance in the areas of cultural sensitivity,

---

[2] Robert B. Sweeney, "Ethics in an International Environment," *Management Accounting,* February 1991, p. 27.

[3] "Ethics Policies Help Reduce Internal Control Costs," *Journal of Accountancy,* April 1994, p. 14.

innovation, and long-run approach can provide the incentives to motivate managers and employees in behaving in a manner consistent with corporate policies.

Internal Auditing in the International Environment

As mentioned in an earlier section, international operations add certain complexities to internal auditing. Fortunately, some of those complexities are decreasing, for two reasons.

First, the ever-increasing magnitude and importance of international business has resulted in greater uniformity in business practices worldwide. Differences in business practices in different parts of the world are not as pronounced as they used to be. For example, written agreements are commonly accepted now in most countries where local customs previously dictated otherwise.

Second, advancements in technology such as computers, faxes, bar-coding, and scanners have alleviated many problems posed by geographic distance or lack of well-developed infrastructure within a country. Communication systems are now more efficient and less costly than they were a few years ago. A country's poor postal system, for example, would probably not pose as much of a problem now as it did a few years ago.

Structure of the Internal Audit Organization

The internal audit function is a management function. The management sets organizational policies and establishes a system of internal control that includes internal audit function. One of the decisions involving the internal audit function is the structure of the internal auditing organization itself. *While selecting an organizational structure for internal audit function, independence of the internal audit staff should be of paramount concern.* This is why in many organizations internal auditors report directly to the board of directors, or a committee of the top corporate executives, or both.

Benefits of any system should outweigh its costs. Even when costs of training a cadre of local professional staff appear to be exorbitant at first glance, the manager should take into account the resultant benefits from such training as well as the costs of an ill-trained internal audit staff that does not possess the necessary skills.

Standardization of the internal control reporting system to the extent possible, and ensuring that the staff has the necessary training to understand and interpret report content can go a long way toward overcoming many potential problems posed by different languages, and by different accounting principles and procedures. Even when detailed records are kept in local language (using local accounting procedures), standardized reports can be quite satisfactory. This can be accomplished only with a skilled internal audit staff.

Forms of internal audit organizations. An internal audit organization structure reflects management philosophy, availability of qualified staff, and extent of international operations. We will briefly describe six models including centralized, decentralized, and four hybrid structures.

1. *Centralized.* In this type of organization, there is only one central internal audit organization that is located at the headquarters of the parent company. The internal auditors travel to various parts of the world where operations are located to perform internal audit, and to perform other functions such as quality control, audit research, liaison with external auditors, training, and technical support.

2. *Decentralized.* Internal auditors are on locations throughout the world, wherever international operations are located. Each international operation has its own internal audit organization.

3. *Resident staff and regional reviewers.* Work of the resident internal auditors is reviewed by the regional reviewers to ensure uniformity. Independent review from regional staff also enhances the degree of reliability of the reports.

4. *Regional audit staff.* The regional staff is responsible for performing audits in all of the operations in the region. This model has recently been gaining popularity among many multinationals.

5. *Resident staff and central reviewers.* The resident internal auditors located on site perform the audit work. Their work is periodically reviewed by the traveling members of the parent company's central internal audit staff.

6. *Resident staff and regional and central reviewers.* Resident staff conducts the internal audits. Regional reviewers, responsible for certain geographical areas, oversee their work to ensure compliance with the parent company policies. The central staff from headquarters makes periodic reviews to ensure reporting uniformity throughout all the regions.

Each of these six models has its strengths and weaknesses. Unless there are only a few small international operations, the centralized organization model would not be feasible. The decentralized model may not be economical, and generally it would not provide adequate reliability and assurance of uniformity. The four hybrid models require the parent company management to choose from combinations that involve making trade-offs. There is no one model that is most appropriate for all situations. However, certain guidelines may be helpful in making the choice:

- Because of familiarity with local language, culture, business customs, and contacts, resident staff can usually get the job done more easily when cooperation from outsiders is needed. Confirmation of accounts receivable, for example, would be impossible without the cooperation from outsiders (customers).

- Costs of travel to various international locations where operations are located would be substantial for regional and central staff.

- Travel for performing an internal audit or conducting a review usually causes discomfort and fatigue. This may have an adverse effect on the performance of the traveling internal audit staff.

- Operating people at an international location may not be as trusting of someone who is not permanently at their location.

- The recommendation of a visiting auditor from central headquarters or from a regional office may not be as readily accepted by the local operating managers, again because of lack of trust.

- The local auditor can make recommendations to the local operating managers in a timely manner, thus making it possible for them to take corrective action without unnecessary delay.

All of the above points are interrelated. *Monetary costs* should not be considered in isolation but rather with all other factors affecting *quality* of internal audit reports. Quality is directly related to the knowledge, skill, and expertise of people performing the internal audit. *Quality is necessary to achieve reliability and comparability.* This leads us to suggest that a combination of local staff with regional and/or central staff would be appropriate in most situations. Regional or central staff can be beneficial because a high level of expertise can be assumed due to the size of the talent pool available to the parent company. The regional or central staffs are likely to have some or all of these advantages:

- Greater familiarity with parent company policies and more knowledge about top management's expectations of subsidiary operations because of frequent contacts with headquarters.
- Broad-based experience on different locations and settings, which provides valuable service to local operating managers. These staffs may be able to quickly identify problems and provide solutions because of their encounters with similar problems on other locations. In addition, they can share information with local managers about innovations introduced in operations elsewhere.
- Involvement in internal audit reports of many operations can ensure a higher degree of reporting comparability.
- Freedom from undue influence of local operating managers and local controllers. Detachment from local operations tends to make them more objective—thus enhancing the reliability of their reports. Culture plays an important role in the influence that local controllers and managers can have on internal auditors.[4]

. . . Boeing statistics offer one insight into how flying procedures work in the air. Its safety team has plotted accident rates for countries against various measurements of culture devised by social anthropologists. Two regions where accidents are more frequent than in America or Europe, and where pilot deviation from procedure scores highest as a cause of accidents, are Latin America and Asia. These regions also score high on an anthropological scale, known as the Hoffstede power-distance index, which measures the power relationship between two people as perceived by the weaker. Translated to the flight deck, that means that an Asian or a Latin American co-pilot is wonderfully obedient but less likely than his American or European counterpart to tell his boss that he is about to fly into a mountain—until it is too late. It is a high price to pay for deference.

Internal audit is an integral part of an internal control system. It provides feedback and may result in changing the goals of the parent company, or the expected level of performance from the international operation. It would be erroneous to assume, therefore, that the

---

[4] "Air Crashes—But Surely . . . ," *Economist,* 4 June 1994, pp. 86-87.

corrective action always takes place at the local level. It should also be noted that when central or regional staff is involved in the internal audit, it is a common practice for them to report *both* to the central headquarters and the managers of local operations. By reporting to the local managers, they make it possible for the local managers to take corrective action without any unnecessary delay. It also fosters a more cooperative attitude on the part of the local managers towards central or regional internal audit staff. The central or regional staff needs to have excellent interpersonal skills, and should display sensitivity toward local managers to avoid conflicts.

Foreign Corrupt Practices Act

The **Foreign Corrupt Practices Act** (FCPA) was passed by the U.S. Congress in 1977 and revised in 1988. Although it is a U.S. law, its impact has been felt worldwide due to its scope. The FCPA has implications both for internal audit and external audit. The act was passed as a result of discovery by the U.S. Securities and Exchange Commission that hundreds of U.S. based multinational companies had made illegal or questionable payments to foreign government officials and politicians amounting to hundreds of millions of dollars. These payments were either not recorded or were recorded improperly to conceal their nature.

The intent of the FCPA is to curb influence peddling. **Influence peddling** involves providing monetary or nonmonetary benefits to a person in a position of authority in exchange for an action by the person that benefits the company—an action that normally would not have been taken without the monetary or nonmonetary benefit. An example of influence peddling is to bribe a government official who has authority to award contracts in exchange for receiving a contract. For example, in June 1994, a federal grand jury indicted Lockheed Corporation and two of its executives for fraud and corruption involving a sale of three C-130 transport planes in 1989. The indictment alleged that the company, through its high level officials, violated the Foreign Corrupt Practices Act. U.S. federal authorities claimed that Lockheed illegally paid more than $1 million for help in securing a $79 million government contract for the company.

The scope of the FCPA is quite broad. It makes it illegal for all U.S. firms, their affiliates, and agents to bribe government officials both within the U.S. as well as outside the U.S. Firms and executives can face criminal and civil prosecution if convicted of violation. The criminal penalties include fines of up to $2 million for the company, and up to $100,000 for the executive with a prison term of up to five years. The 1988 revision added a civil penalty of up to $10,000 for executives, which cannot be paid by the company.

Accounting implications. The accounting implications of the FCPA include the provisions listed below.

- *Recordkeeping provisions.* Books, records, and accounting should be accurate reflections of business transactions.
- *Internal control provisions.* All firms must develop and maintain a system of internal control to ensure that:
  - ✓ Transactions are executed with management authorization.

> ✓ Transactions are recorded in a manner that permits preparation of financial statements in conformity with generally accepted accounting principles or other applicable standards.
> ✓ Accountability of assets is maintained. Only authorized personnel have access to assets.
> ✓ Recorded accountability of assets is regularly compared with existing assets. In case of discrepancies, appropriate action is taken.

In essence, the FCPA requires that all payments, including improper payments, must be recorded and disclosed. Firms and their executives can face criminal and civil prosecution for either of these violations:

- Company books are not kept properly.
- An adequate system of internal control is not developed and implemented.

Note that although the FCPA prohibits payments for influence peddling, it does not prohibit facilitating payments. **Facilitating payments** are payments made to influence an official to take an action that the official must take anyway. The objective is to speed up the process.

The FCPA applies to both domestic and foreign corporations that are registered under Section 12 of the Securities Act of 1934 or that are required to file reports under Section D of that act. The FCPA has been a major contributor to many recent actions that have upgraded the status of internal auditing. These include:

- Adoption of codes of ethical conduct by many companies and strengthening of codes by others.
- Strengthening of internal control systems.
- Increasing the number of outside directors on the board.
- Formation of audit committees.

It is clear that the FCPA has had, and will continue to have, worldwide impact.

Institute of Internal Auditors

The **Institute of Internal Auditors** (IIA), established in 1941, is the most influential international organization in the development of internal auditing standards. Based in the U.S., the organization has over 50,000 members in more than 100 countries. The IIA has taken a leadership role in the development of the internal auditing profession and has published *Codification of Standards for the Professional Practice of Internal Auditing.* It includes the IIA pronouncements listed below.

- General Standards (Appendix 12A)
- Specific Standards
- Guidelines
- Statement of Responsibilities
- Code of Ethics (Appendix 12B)

As of early 1995, the *Codification of Standards* was available in 12 different languages, including French, Chinese, Arabic, German, Japanese, Hebrew, and Spanish. In addition, the IIA regularly publishes the *Internal Auditor, IIA Today, Pistas de Auditoria,* and the *IIA Educator.* The IIA is the sponsoring organization for the certification program called Certified Internal Auditor (CIA). Currently about 6,000 candidates take the examination annually at over 200 sites around the world. The language options for the examination are English, Spanish, and French. Besides passing the examination, the candidates must have two years of practical experience in internal auditing before certification. The IIA also organizes an annual international conference of internal auditors. The 1995 conference was held in France.

The IIA influences international auditing through participation in the United Nations' internal audit group, called the International Organization of Supreme Audit Institutions, as well as the International Federation of Accountants. The IIA is also involved in cooperative projects with several national and regional audit organizations. One of the regional organizations with which the IIA has a strong alliance is the **European Confederation of Institutes of Internal Auditing** (ECIIA). The ECIIA is comprised of 17 internal audit organizations representing 18 European nations plus Israel.

Currently the IIA's Global Union Steering Committee is actively working toward forming a Global Union of Institutes of Internal Auditing. One of the foremost objectives of the proposed Global Union is to foster a strong and cohesive profession on a worldwide basis.

Coordination of Internal Audits with External Audits

Coordination of the internal and external audit functions is desirable to ensure that the audit scope is adequate and there is minimal duplication of efforts. The IIA's *Statement on Internal Audit Standard 5,* "The Internal Auditors' Relationship with Independent Outside Auditors," specifies that there should be maximum coordination between internal and external auditors. The International Federation of Accountants also addressed the issue in the *International Standard on Auditing 10,* "Using the Work of an Internal Auditor." This pronouncement requires the external auditor to evaluate the internal audit function. The standard also contains guidance regarding the procedures that should be considered by the external auditor in assessing the work of an internal auditor for the purpose of using that work.

Even though external auditors cannot substitute the work of internal auditors for their own work, the scope of work for an external audit may be affected by internal auditors' work. The extent to which this happens depends primarily on the assessment of competence and objectivity of internal auditors by external auditors. All large international public accounting firms have policies on relations with a client's internal auditors. Internal auditors may perform some procedures that would otherwise be performed by external auditors, provided the external auditors supervise and test internal auditors' work.

Since the internal audit function is an important aspect of an internal control system, an understanding of internal audit function by external auditors also contributes to their evaluation of overall internal control system of the client company.

External Auditing

External audits are performed by public accountants. During the audit, external auditors perform the necessary audit procedures to the financial statements and supporting evidence to determine whether the financial statements are in conformity with applicable standards. If the auditor's opinion states that the statements conform to the standards, it lends credibility to the representations contained in the financial statements. The opinion of the external auditor is especially important for the parent company, investors, and creditors. The parent company can rely on the financial statements of international operations for preparation of consolidated financial statements and for decision making. The investors and creditors use financial statements audited by external auditors to make their decisions. It is critical for a multinational company to make its audited financial statements available to regulatory agencies, investors, creditors, and security analysts for the purposes of listing its securities on international security exchanges, and for actively participating in international capital markets.

External Audit Objective

The basic objective of the external audit is the same in all countries—to determine if the financial statements are properly prepared. The external auditors audit financial statements and supporting evidence by applying the auditing standards. Though the objective is the same, external audits are performed differently in different countries since *accounting standards as well as auditing standards differ from country to country.*

Accounting standards. A prerequisite for conducting an external audit is that the external auditor must be knowledgeable of the country's accounting standards and have the expertise in their application. As we discussed in Chapter 1, accounting standards differ worldwide. Therefore, financial statements prepared in conformity with accounting standards of one country are not comparable to financial statements prepared in conformity with accounting standards of another country. For example, in some countries plant assets can be written-up subsequent to their acquisition, a practice that is not acceptable in other countries. The representations made by the financial statements in conformity with different standards require different audit emphases and procedures.

Auditing standards. The auditing standard-setting process differs from country to country. In some countries, auditing standards are set by the public accounting profession. In other countries, auditing standards are based on government requirements as mandated in the countries' laws and regulations. Then there are countries where both public accounting profession and government participate in audit standard-setting process.

In countries where statutory audit requirements exist, e.g., Germany, the purpose of the external audit is primarily to ensure that the financial records are kept and the financial statements are prepared according to legal requirements. In countries where the public accounting profession has assumed the primary responsibility to set auditing standards, an external audit is conducted using generally accepted auditing standards. These auditing standards are set by the profession to determine whether the financial statements are in conformity with generally accepted accounting principles.

Regardless of who sets auditing standards, the standards and audit procedure requirements themselves vary from country to country. For example, independent confirmation of accounts receivable and physical observation of inventory are required in some countries, while no such requirement exists in other countries.

External Auditing in the International Environment

As we discussed in the last section, the objective of an external audit is the same throughout the world—to determine the conformity of financial statements to applicable accounting standards. As we noted earlier, accounting standards as well as auditing standards differ from country to country. These factors add extra dimensions to audits conducted in an international setting.

For a multinational company with operations in many different parts of the world, it is not usually feasible to send external auditors from the base country to each of the locations of international operations, for several reasons:

- Geographic distance makes travel costly, and usually has an adverse effect on the performance of the auditor due to unfamiliar surroundings and fatigue.
- Thorough knowledge of applicable accounting standards and the expertise in auditing standards of a country can only be acquired through training and practical experience in that country.
- In many countries, legal requirements have a direct and significant impact on the external audit. This requires an orientation that is different from the orientation in countries with few legal implications for an external audit.
- Business customs differ among countries. Familiarity with business customs of a country may be necessary to collect and test the supporting evidence for successful completion of the audit.

The above points favor using an external auditor who practices in the country where an international operation is located. However, there is a need to have a coordination mechanism with the parent company. The quality of an external audit in an international setting depends heavily on the qualifications of an external auditor.

Qualifications. Education, experience, and certification requirements for external auditors vary in different parts of the world. For example, in some countries, an external auditor is not required to have any formal education and training in the audit function. This is especially the case in several countries with statutory audit requirements. Coordination is necessary to ensure that qualifications of the external auditor are satisfactory to meet the parent company's needs for reliable information.

Fortunately, the problem is not as serious as it may seem. In this age of global financial markets, advanced communication systems, and sophisticated data processing technology, large as well as small multinational firms can rely on the expertise of public accounting firms that have the capability to perform external audits in different parts of the world. An obvious example is the "Big Six" accounting firms. The **Big Six** includes Arthur Andersen, KPMG Peat Marwick, Deloitte Touche Tohmatsu, Ernst & Young, Coopers & Lybrand, and Price

Waterhouse. Each of these firms has offices throughout the world. In the countries where these firms do not have offices, they have a "representative," a "correspondent," or "associated" firms. For example, Coopers & Lybrand had member and associated firms in 126 countries in 1994.[5] The **representative, correspondent,** or **associated firms** are locally owned accounting firms. They have a common code of ethics and audit practice guidelines with the Big Six firm. This ensures a high degree of uniformity and mutual reliance. It would be erroneous, however, to assume that the Big Six are the only players in the international audit arena. Many small to medium-sized firms also have become involved in international auditing by having a correspondent relationship with local firms in other countries.

Auditor's report. The auditor's report communicates the results of the external audit, and the format of the report is necessarily mandated by the nature of the audit. Since there are no worldwide uniform accounting and auditing standards, there is no worldwide uniform format of an auditor's report. In this section we will briefly discuss salient features of the standard format of an auditor's report in France, Germany, Australia, the Netherlands, and the U.S. Examples of these reports are presented in Exhibits 12–1 through 12–5.

The auditor's report for Renault, a French conglomerate, is presented in Exhibit 12–1. Examples of the auditor's report for two well-known multinationals, Daimler-Benz and Foster's Brewing Group Limited, are contained in Exhibits 12–2 and 12–3. All three of these reports make specific reference to legal provisions and to professional standards. The auditor's reports in the latter two cases use the term *true and fair view.*

The auditor's report for Philips Electronics N.V. in Exhibit 12–4 is noteworthy for its brevity. The opinion states that financial statements comply with Dutch legal requirements. This is an interesting example in which accounting standards promulgated by both the accounting profession and the government are applicable.

Finally, Exhibit 12–5 displays the standard auditor's report in the U.S. The report states whether the financial statements are in accordance with generally accepted accounting principles. It is required that title of the report include the word *independent.* The standard report consists of three paragraphs covering introduction, scope, and opinion.[6]

- The *introduction* paragraph delineates the responsibilities for the financial statements between management and the external auditor. The auditor audits the financial statements, but they remain management's responsibility.
- The *scope* paragraph summarizes the essential aspects of an audit. It states that the audit was conducted in accordance with generally accepted auditing standards, and explicitly spells out an auditor's objective: to be reasonably satisfied that the financial statements have been prepared without material error.
- The *opinion* paragraph indicates whether financial statements "present fairly in all material respects [the financial position, results of operations, and cash flows] in conformity with generally accepted accounting principles."

---

[5] *Foreign Currency Translation and Hedging* (New York: Coopers & Lybrand, 1994), pp. 271-273.

[6] *An Analysis of the New Auditor's Report* (New York: Touche Ross, 1988), pp. 2-3.

In contrast to the auditor's report in Germany, the U.S. auditor's report does not refer to a management (business review) report.

Exhibit 12–1   Auditor's Report: France

Statutory Auditors' General Report
Year ended December 31, 1993

In our capacity as statutory auditors, we present our report on:
- the audit of the financial statements of Régie Nationale des Usines Renault S.A.,
- the specific procedures as required by law, for the year ended December 31, 1993.

I. OPINION ON THE FINANCIAL STATEMENTS
We have audited the financial statements, applying the procedures which we considered necessary, in accordance with the standards of our profession.

In our opinion, the financial statements present fairly the results of operations and the financial position of the Régie Nationale des Usines Renault S.A. at December 31, 1993 and for the year then ended, in accordance with French accounting regulations.

II. PROCEDURES
We have also performed the specific procedures prescribed by law, in accordance with the standards of our profession.

We have no observation regarding the fairness of the information in the report of the Board of Directors and the other information addressed to shareholders concerning the financial position of the company or its consistency with the financial statements.

Paris, April 13, 1994

The Statutory Auditors

DELOITTE TOUCHE TOHMATSU	Michel POISSON	ERNST & YOUNG Audit
BDA		Department of HSD-CJ
Jacques MANARDO		Patrice COSLIN Marc STOESSEL

Source: Renault Group, *Annual Report 1993*, Paris, 1994, p.46

True and fair view. The true and fair view (TFV) concept was briefly discussed in Chapter 2. The concept has been adopted in the *Fourth Directive* of the EU, and in the corresponding commercial laws of the U.K., France, and Germany. In spite of the common terminology, differences in meaning exist from country to country. According to David Alexander, "countries are tending to interpret TFV in the context of national culture, national accounting tradition, and national GAAP."[7] It is interesting to note that there is no consensus on the

---

[7]   David Alexander, "A European True and Fair View?" *The European Accounting Review,* 1 (1993), p. 59.

Exhibit 12–2   Auditor's Report: Germany

We rendered an unqualified opinion on the consolidated financial statements and the business review report in accordance with §322 HGB (German Commercial Code). The translation of our opinion reads as follows:

"The consolidated financial statements, which we have audited in accordance with professional standards, comply with the legal provisions. With due regard to the generally accepted accounting principles, the consolidated financial statements give a true and fair view of the assets, liabilities, financial position and results of operations of the Daimler-Benz group. The business review report, which summarizes the state of affairs of Daimler-Benz Aktiengesellschaft and that of the group, is consistent with the financial statements of Daimler-Benz Aktiengesellschaft and the consolidated financial Statements."

Frankfurt/Main, March 22, 1995

KPMG Deutsche Treuhand-Gesellschaft
Aktiengesellschaft
Wirtschaftsprüfungsgesellschaft

Zielke   Dr. Koschinsky
Wirtschaftsprüfer   Wirtschaftsprüfer
"Certified Public Accountant"   "Certified Public Accountant"

Source: Daimler-Benz Group, *Annual Report 1994* (Frankfurt/Main, 1995), p. 85.

---

operational definition of TFV. Alexander suggests, "In most situations TFV will work indirectly through influence on accounting and reporting regulation. This requires proper and sensible regulation prepared with rigour and intellectual honesty." He concludes, "The way forward, with TFV as with financial reporting as a whole, is through increasing conceptually based understanding of what financial statements are trying to do and how they can best do it, coupled with exploration and education of actions and attitudes across Europe and beyond."[8]

Present fairly. The American Institute of Certified Public Accountants' Statement on Auditing Standards No. 69 explains the meaning of the phrase "present fairly" as used in the independent auditor's report. According to the standard, the independent auditor's judgment concerning the "fairness" of the overall presentation of financial statements should be applied *within the framework of generally accepted accounting principles.* The auditor's opinion that financial statements present fairly an entity's financial position, results of operations, and cash flows in conformity with generally accepted accounting principles should be based on the auditor's judgment on the following issues:[9]

---

[8] *Ibid.,* p. 75.

[9] American Institute of Certified Public Accountants, *Codification of Statements on Auditing Standards* (Chicago, Ill: Commerce Clearing House, Inc., 1995), pp. 313-314.

Exhibit 12–3   Auditor's Report: Australia

Independent Audit Report to the Members of Foster's Brewing Group Limited

Scope

We have audited the financial statements of the Company for the year ended 30 June 1994 as set out on pages 28 to 68. The financial statements consist of the accounts of the Company and the consolidated accounts of the economic entity comprising the Company and the entities it controlled at the end of, or during, the financial year. The Company's directors are responsible for the preparation and presentation of the financial statements and the information they contain. We have conducted an independent audit of these financial statements in order to express an opinion on them to the members of the Company.

Our audit has been conducted in accordance with Australian Auditing Standards to provide reasonable assurance as to whether the financial statements are free of material misstatement. Our procedures included examination, on a test basis, of evidence supporting the amounts and other disclosures in the financial statements, and the evaluation of accounting policies and significant accounting estimates. These procedures have been undertaken to form an opinion as to whether, in all material respects, the financial statements are presented fairly in accordance with Australian Accounting Standards and the Corporations Law so as to present a view which is consistent with our understanding of the Company's and the economic entity's state of affairs, the results of their operations and their cash flows.

We have not acted as auditors of the controlled entities identified in note 30 to the financial statements. We have, however, received sufficient information and explanations concerning these controlled entities to enable us to form an opinion on the consolidated accounts.

The audit opinion expressed in this report has been formed on the above basis.

Audit Opinion

In our opinion the financial statements of the Company are properly drawn up:
- (a) so as to give a true and fair view of:
    - (i)   the state of affairs at 30 June 1994 and the results and cash flows for the financial year ended on that date of the Company and the economic entity; and
    - (ii) the other matters required by Divisions 4, 4A and 4B of Part 3.6 of the Corporations Law to be dealt with in the financial statements;
- (b) in accordance with the provisions of the Corporations Law; and
- (c) in accordance with applicable accounting standards and Australian Accounting Standards.

[signature]   [signature]

Price Waterhouse   Paul V. Brasher

Chartered Accountants   Partner

Source: Foster's Brewing Group Limited, Annual Report 1994 (South Yarra, Victoria, 5 September 1994), p. 68.

Exhibit 12–4   Auditor's Report: Netherlands

Auditors' report

We have audited the financial statements of Philips Electronics N.V. for the year 1994. We conducted our audit in accordance with generally accepted auditing standards.

In our opinion these financial statements present fairly the financial position of the Company at December 31, 1994 and the results for the year then ended, and also comply with other Dutch legal requirements for financial statements.

Eindhoven, February 21, 1995
KPMG Accountants N.V.

Source: Philips Electronics, *Annual Report 1994* (Eindhoven, Netherlands, 1995), p. 73.

- The accounting principles selected and applied have general acceptance.
- The accounting principles are appropriate in the circumstances.
- The financial statements, including the related notes, are informative of matters that may affect their use, understanding, and interpretation.
- The information presented in the financial statements is classified and summarized in a reasonable manner.
- The financial statements reflect the underlying transactions and events in a manner that presents the financial position, results of operations, and cash flows within a range of acceptable limits.

The reporting standard further states that generally accepted accounting principles recognize the importance of reporting transactions and events in accordance with their substance. In other words, substance overrides form.

Independent Auditing Environment in Selected Countries

In this section we will look at auditing practices in the eleven countries and observe some notable trends.

Australia.   The Corporation Law requires audit of the annual financial statements of nearly all public companies by external auditors. External (registered) auditors are initially appointed by the board of directors and are reappointed by shareholders. They continue their engagement indefinitely until the time when the shareholders appoint new auditors *with the approval* of the Australian Securities Commission, a governmental body.

Registered company auditors must be independent of the client and also meet the professional qualification criteria. Professional criteria include the following.

- Membership in the Institute of Chartered Accountants in Australia, or the Australian Society of Certified Practicing Accountants. In rare cases, a degree from a

---

Exhibit 12–5   Auditor's Report: United States

Report of Independent Auditors

To the Shareowners of AT&T Corp.:

We have audited the consolidated balance sheets of AT&T Corp. and subsidiaries (AT&T) at December 31, 1994 and 1993, and the related consolidated statements of income and cash flows for the years ended December 31, 1994, 1993 and 1992. These financial statements are the responsibility of AT&T's management. Our responsibility is to express an opinion on these financial statements based on our audits.

We conducted our audits in accordance with generally accepted auditing standards. Those standards require that we plan and perform the audit to obtain reasonable assurance about whether the financial statements are free of material misstatement. An audit includes examining, on a test basis, evidence supporting the amounts and disclosures in the financial statements. An audit also includes assessing the accounting principles used and significant estimates made by management, as well as evaluating the overall financial statement presentation. We believe that our audits provide a reasonable basis for our opinion.

In our opinion the financial statements referred to above present fairly, in all material respects, the consolidated financial position of AT&T at December 31, 1994 and 1993, and the consolidated results of their operations and their cash flows for the years ended December 31, 1994, 1993 and 1992, in conformity with generally accepted accounting principles.

As discussed in Note 2 to the financial statements, in 1993 AT&T changed its methods of accounting for postretirement benefits, postemployment benefits and income taxes.

[Coopers & Lybrand LLP, signature only]
1301 Avenue of the Americas
New York, New York
January 24, 1995

Source: AT&T, *1994 Annual Report* (New York, 1995), p. 29.

---

recognized educational institution that includes studies of accounting and company law may be substituted for the membership requirement in either of the two professional organizations.

- A minimum of three years of professional experience in accounting and auditing.

The Corporation Law is the major source of auditing standards in Australia and it prescribes the format of the auditor's standard report. The auditor's report addresses whether the company's financial statements provide a *true and fair view*. The auditor's report specifically states whether financial statements conform to the Corporation Law.[10]

---

[10] Coopers and Lybrand, International Accounting Summaries, 2d ed. (New York: John Wiley & Sons, Inc., 1993), p. A-24.

The Institute of Chartered Accountants in Australia and the Australian Society of Certified Practicing Accountants issue auditing pronouncements. Both of these organizations are members of the International Federation of Accountants (IFAC). Their pronouncements, providing guidance on ethical conduct and auditing procedures, are usually identical to the IFAC's guidelines on these matters.

Brazil. Public companies and financial institutions are required to publish financial statements audited by independent auditors registered with the Securities Exchange Commission. The board of directors of a company selects independent auditors. The Corporate Law requires that the financial statements must be published within a specified time range before the general annual meeting of shareholders.

An independent auditor's qualifications in Brazil include membership in a professional organization in Brazil. This means meeting education and practical experience requirements for admission as a member of the professional organization.

Auditing standards in Brazil are set primarily by The Federal Accounting Council. On a smaller scale, the Brazilian Accountants Institute and the Securities Exchange Commission are also involved in the audit standard-setting process. The Brazilian Accountants Institute is a member of the IFAC. Its auditing pronouncements generally conform with the IFAC guidelines.[11]

Canada. An audit is required of all public corporations and large private companies. According to the federal Canada Business Corporations Act, the shareholders of a corporation are required to appoint an auditor annually. The auditor must be independent of the corporation, its affiliates, and officers.

There are no national laws prescribing minimum qualification requirements for auditors. Some of the provinces issue licenses for auditors. In such cases, the licensing requirements usually include education and experience requirements for qualification. Regardless of qualifications, all auditors are required to follow generally accepted auditing standards.[12] The Canadian Institute of Chartered Accountants (CICA) establishes both accounting and auditing standards. They are contained in the CICA Handbook. In general, Canadian auditing standards are similar to the IFAC's standards and guidelines.

France. The Company Law of 1966 requires statutory audits of all business companies except small partnerships and small corporations. In addition, a statutory audit is required of nonprofit organizations engaged in commercial activities that meet specified size criteria, and of governmental bodies not using governmental accounting while conducting commercial activities. The auditor is required to verify the truthfulness of information other than the financial statements, such as the contents of the board of directors report. *Any violations of the Company Law must be reported to the public prosecutor. Failure to report such a violation is considered a criminal offense.*

---

[11] *Brazil—International Tax and Business Guide* (New York: Deloitte Touche Tohmatsu International, 1993), p. 51.

[12] *Coopers and Lybrand, International Accounting Summaries,* 2d ed. (New York: John Wiley & Sons, Inc., 1993), p. C-1.

Shareholders appoint a statutory auditor for a six-year term, subject to reelection an unlimited number of times. Auditors can be dismissed by court only when dismissal is requested by shareholders, the board of directors, or some other appropriate authority. The public prosecutor also has the authority to dismiss statutory auditors for some criminal offenses.[13]

Statutory auditors must be independent of their clients. In performing their audit, statutory auditors may engage experts or colleagues to assist in their audit work. Many audit firms work closely with consultants who have expertise in special areas. *All statutory auditors are registered on an approved list kept by the Appeal Court, and must be members of the National Association of Statutory Auditors.* Statutory auditors prepare two kinds of reports after completion of audit work: reports to management and reports to shareholders. The main source of auditing standards is the National Council of Statutory Auditors. Auditing standards are very similar to the IFAC guidelines and are periodically updated for conformance to the IFAC standards.

The *reports to management* are required under Company Law. Under this requirement, the statutory auditor reports to the board of directors *orally or in writing* on matters such as the audit procedures performed, actions recommended to improve quality of balance sheet and financial records, and discovery of any errors or improprieties. The reports to management also include audit adjustments, if any, and their effect on current and preceding period's income.

The *reports to shareholders* of a corporation express the opinion on the financial statements. The opinion may be unqualified, qualified, adverse, or disclaimer of an opinion. In case of a fraudulent balance sheet, the statutory auditor is required by law to communicate the findings to the public prosecutor.[14]

Germany. The German Commercial Code requires that annual financial statements of all except small corporations (as specified in the code) must be audited. All corporations listed on the stock exchange regardless of size are required to be audited.

Starting January 1, 1995, the financial statements of limited liability companies and limited partnership are subject to the same requirements as corporations. Limited liability companies have their own legal identity similar to corporations. Limited partnerships do not have separate legal identities. They may, however, engage in business transactions, and also may be subject to legal claims by other parties. This new requirement is a direct result of EU accounting regulations, which are now incorporated into German law.

Auditors are appointed by shareholders each year. An auditor must generally be a German certified public accountant or a certified public accounting firm. Auditors must be independent of the client. They must not own shares in the companies they audit, and may not be employees or members of the board of directors.

---

[13] *France: International Tax and Business Guide* (New York: Deloitte Touche Tohmatsu International, 1995), p. 57.

[14] *The Auditing Profession in France,* 2d ed., revised (New York: American Institute of Certified Public Accountants, 1992), pp. 9-17.

There are two professional organizations for auditors: the Chamber of Certified Public Accountants and the Institute of Certified Public Accountants. Auditors are required to be members of the Chamber of Certified Public Accountants. The Institute of Certified Public Accountants has issued statements on audit standards within the legal framework.[15] Compliance with the IFAC audit guidelines depends on whether they are incorporated in German audit standards.

The German Commercial Code requires the independent auditors to report whether the financial statements comply with legal provisions, give a *true and fair view* of financial position and results of operations, and are in conformity with required accounting standards.

Japan. The Commercial Code requires stockholders of all corporations to elect statutory auditors. In addition, large corporations (discussed later) and corporations subject to the Securities and Exchange Law must appoint an independent auditor.

Statutory auditors. There are no established professional qualifications for statutory auditors, and typically they are not professional accountants. The statutory auditor expresses an opinion as to whether the performance of the company's directors is in conformity with requirements of the Commercial Code. A statutory auditor may receive a portion of the corporation's profits as a bonus. Though usually not independent, the statutory auditor cannot be an employee or a director of the corporation.

Large corporations. Large corporations (defined in terms of the size of share capital or total liabilities) must have at least three statutory auditors and a board of statutory auditors. Financial statements of every large corporation are subject to both an independent audit and a statutory audit. Statutory auditors of large corporations must report on the appropriateness of the financial statements and express an opinion on the independent auditor's report.

Independent auditors. Independent auditors are either CPAs or an audit corporation. The Securities and Exchange Law and the Commercial Code have different requirements regarding professional duties of independent auditors.

- The Securities and Exchange Law requires an independent auditor to express an opinion as to whether the financial statements are a fair representation of the financial position and results of operations of the company.
- The Commercial Code requires that the independent auditor express an opinion as to whether financial statements are in compliance with the Commercial Code and the company's articles of incorporation.

The appointment procedures prescribed for independent auditors differ between the Commercial Code and the Securities and Exchange Law.

- For Commercial Code purposes, the appointment is in two steps. First, the candidates for appointment are approved by the statutory auditors. Subsequently, shareholders appoint the independent auditors.

---

[15] *Germany: International and Tax Guide* (New York: Deloitte Touche Tohmatsu International, 1995), pp. 76-77.

- Under the Securities and Exchange Law, the independent auditors are appointed by the board of directors. They are initially appointed for a one-year term but are eligible for automatic reappointment.

The independent auditors of a corporation submit their report on financial statements to the statutory auditors. The statutory auditors present their report to the board of directors. Guidelines for submission of reports from one level to the next include a specified time frame that varies according to the size of corporation.

Auditing profession. The Japanese Institute of Certified Public Accountants (JICPA) is the only professional accounting and auditing organization in Japan. It's Audit Committee is involved in establishing professional standards and ethics. There are relatively few Certified Public Accountants in Japan when compared with other industrialized countries. This is attributable to rigorous examination standards and experience requirements.

Auditing standards are incorporated into Japanese law. Therefore, the degree of consistency of Japanese audit standards with the IFAC standards depends on the extent to which the IFAC standards are incorporated in laws. The financial statements subject to independent audit include the balance sheet and the income statement. For corporations that are subject to the Securities and Exchange Law, both the financial statements of the parent company and the consolidated financial statements receive independent audit.[16]

Mexico. A statutory audit is required for all corporations, and the statutory auditor presents an annual report to shareholders. The statutory auditor is not required to be a public accountant. However, it is common practice to appoint public accountants to this position.

All companies that are registered with the National Securities Commissions and file a tax report are subject to annual audit requirements, as are the companies filing a consolidated tax return. The audited financial statements include a balance sheet, income statement, statement of changes in shareholders' equity, and statement of changes in financial position.

The financial statements are required to be adjusted for inflation in accordance with Mexican Accounting Principles Bulletin *Accounting for the Effects of Inflation in the Financial Information and Amendments.* The Mexican Institute of Public Accountants has issued *Auditing Procedures Applicable to the Examination of Financial Statement Items Modified to Reflect the Effects of Inflation* to provide guidance on audit procedures for inflation accounting.

Auditors are appointed by shareholders. When an audit firm conducts the audit, *the member of the firm signing the report is individually responsible.* The auditor's opinion states whether the financial statements present fairly the financial position of the company, the results of its operations, and changes in its financial position.

Auditing standards in Mexico are established by the Auditing Standards and Procedures Commission of the Mexican Institute of Public Accountants. General auditing standards in Mexico are very similar to the corresponding U.S. standards. The Code of Professional Ethics

---

[16] *Japan: International Tax and Business Guide* (New York: Deloitte Touche Tohmatsu International, 1994), pp. 51-53.

prohibits a public accountant from acting as an auditor of a company under circumstances that may affect his or her actual or apparent independence. The ethics code also requires that independent auditors who sign audit reports must be Certified Public Accountants. The Mexican Institute of Public Accountants is a member of the IFAC. Mexico's auditing standards are similar to the IFAC's auditing guidelines, including the scope of statutory audits.[17]

Netherlands. Financial statements of all companies except qualifying small companies require statutory audit by independent auditors appointed by shareholders at a general meeting.

The independent auditor must be either a member of the Netherlands Institute of Registered Accountants, or a foreign auditor who has been authorized by the Minister of Economic Affairs. An auditor must be independent of the company to be audited. This includes not having any financial interest in the company.

In addition to an opinion on the financial statements, the independent auditor is required to ascertain whether the directors' report meets the legal requirements and is consistent with the financial statements. Independent auditors are also required to determine if all of the required disclosures have been included. Requirements for disclosures vary in the Netherlands depending on the size of the company.

There is no explicit requirement for Dutch auditors to follow IFAC guidelines. However, The Netherlands Institute of Registered Accountants is a member of the IFAC and has issued statements on auditing standards that are largely based on the IFAC guidelines. For all practical purposes, IFAC audit standards are complied with in the Netherlands.[18]

Nigeria. Shareholders of every company incorporated under the provision of the Companies and Allied Matters Decree (CAMD) of 1990 are required to appoint an independent auditor annually. The auditor must be a licensed member of the Institute of Chartered Accountants of Nigeria (Institute). To qualify for membership and the license, the independent auditor must have passed the examination conducted by the Institute and have completed a minimum of 2.5 years of continuous full-time approved practical training under the supervision of a licensed member of the Institute.

The independent auditors have a statutory responsibility and a professional responsibility. To perform their *statutory responsibility,* the auditor's report should include an opinion as to whether:

- The financial statements give a true and fair view of the state of affairs of the company, its profits, and its sources and applications of funds;
- The financial statements have been prepared in accordance with the CAMD and other relevant legislation.

[17] *Mexico: International Tax and Business Guide* (New York: Deloitte Touche Tohmatsu International, 1995), pp. 47-48.

[18] *Netherlands: International Tax and Business Guide* (New York: Deloitte Touche Tohmatsu International, 1994), pp. 53-54.

The *professional responsibility* requires the auditor to report whether the financial statements are in compliance with the Statements of Accounting Standards issued by the Nigerian Accounting Standards Board, and with International Accounting Standards issued by the International Accounting Standards Committee.

The independent auditor is required under CAMD provisions to ascertain whether the information contained in the directors' report is consistent with the financial statements. There is no requirement for the auditor's report to state whether the financial statements conform to generally accepted accounting principles. However, when expressing a *true and fair view* opinion, the auditor should be satisfied that all relevant Statements of Accounting have been complied with except in those situations where such compliance would render the financial statements misleading. The Institute requires the independent auditors to be independent of the company being audited.[19]

The Institute has established an Auditing Standards Committee to issue pronouncements on auditing principles, procedures, and techniques. The Institute has adopted most of the auditing guidelines issued by the IFAC.

United Kingdom. The term *corporation* is not commonly used in the U.K. The Companies Act requires that every active, limited liability company, public or private, must appoint independent and professionally qualified auditors. A limited liability company with share capital is the most common form of business organization in the U.K. Incorporation of *both* public (with many shareholders) or private (with very few shareholders) limited liability companies is under the Companies Act. *Limited liability companies are not separate forms of legal entity.*

The auditor or audit firm reports whether the financial statements:

- Present a true and fair view of the company's financial positions, results of its operations, and its cash flow. Small companies are not required to have their cash flow statement audited.
- Have been prepared in conformance with the Companies Act. The commonly used term for financial statements in the U.K. is "accounts."

Independent auditors in the U.K. are appointed by shareholders of the company at its annual general meeting. If auditors choose to resign, their resignation must be accompanied by a statement, if warranted, of the circumstances of their resignation. A copy of this statement must be submitted to the Companies Registry.

Independent auditors have a statutory requirement to include certain information in their report if the information is not disclosed in financial statements. The information is mostly related to transactions between the company and its directors.

In addition to the Companies Act, other duties of auditors are contained in Auditing Standards and Guidelines issued by the Auditing Practice Board. The Auditing Practices

---

[19] Coopers & Lybrand, *The Accounting Profession in Nigeria* (New York: American Institute of Certified Public Accountants, 1993), pp. 1-13.

Board is a committee of the Consultative Committee of Accounting Bodies. Independent auditors are expected to follow these standards and guidelines during their audit.

The Companies Act was amended in 1989 to conform to provisions of the EU Eighth Directive. The objective is to harmonize qualifications of the auditors who are entitled to carry out audits in the European Union.

It is against the law for an independent auditor to hold any office in the company being audited. An independent auditor must be a member of one of the five specified accounting professional organizations in the U.K. and Ireland. The professional bodies have stricter rules for professional independence than the legal requirement.

The U.K. professional accounting bodies are members of the IFAC. Their authoritative pronouncements on audit standards and guidelines are consistent with the IFAC's audit requirements. Therefore, audits in the U.K. do not differ from the IFAC guidelines. [20]

United States. Corporate laws of various states in the U.S. typically do not require appointment of an independent auditor. The Securities and Exchange Commission and the national securities exchanges, however, generally require that the financial statements filed with them must be audited. Independent auditors are usually appointed by directors of nonpublic companies, and by stockholder approval for public companies.

Generally accepted auditing standards are issued by the Auditing Standards Board of the American Institute of Certified Public Accountants (AICPA) in the form of *Statements on Auditing Standards* (SASs). The U.S. generally accepted auditing standards, presented in Appendix 12C, are contained in *SAS 1*. Independent auditors are required to comply with these standards *and* all the SASs while performing an audit. Though the standards are formulated by the Auditing Standards Board, their requirements are often influenced directly by the Securities and Exchange Commission and court decisions, and indirectly by pressure from the U.S. Congress. In most respects the auditing standards are consistent with the IFAC requirements.

The AICPA's *Code of Professional Conduct,* presented in Appendix 12D, requires that the certified public accountant must be independent (both in fact and in appearance) of the client company. They are required to possess integrity and objectivity.

Each state has its own board of accountancy to regulate the practice of public accounting within the state. All states have licensing requirements for the practice of public accounting. A public accountant can be licensed without being a member of the AICPA. In most states, only licensed Certified Public Accountants (CPAs) can perform independent audits. The annual financial statements filed with the SEC are required to be audited by, and the auditor's report is required to be signed by, licensed certified public accountants. All state boards of accountancy are state governmental agencies. There is no federal agency that grants license to practice public accounting nationwide in the U.S.

---

[20] *United Kingdom: International Tax and Business Guide,* (New York: Deloitte Touche Tohmatsu International, 1995), pp. 71-74.

Generally each state requires that an individual meet three requirements to become a licensed certified public accountant.

- *Pass the CPA examination.*
- *Achieve a minimum level of higher education.* Most states require a baccalaureate degree with the equivalent of a major in accounting. Some states require education equivalent to a master's degree.
- *Obtain professional experience.* States vary in their experience requirements—both the type and its length. Most states require two to three years of experience in public accounting before a license to practice as a certified public accountant is granted.

Reciprocity among states—allowing a licensed CPA from another state to practice in the state without requiring him or her to obtain a license—depends on the laws of each state.

Independent auditors in the U.S. are required to consider "inherent risk" brought about by economic conditions while planning an audit. *The auditors should include global risks among the risk factors.*[21]

> In the past there has been a tendency to think of the U.S. economy when considering general economic conditions. Today, however, auditors must consider many global economic and financial aspects. Some clients will have operations in foreign countries, other clients will export products to foreign countries, and most clients will compete with goods and services from foreign countries. Thus, such factors as fluctuations in foreign exchange rates, restrictive international trade agreements, and political instability will create audit risks for many U.S. clients. Changes in foreign exchange rates may increase the cost of a client's exports, decrease the cost of competitors' imports, or create losses on repatriation of earnings from some foreign countries. Restrictive international trade agreements may restrict or impose tariffs on imports or exports. Political instability may jeopardize foreign markets. All of these factors create risks that should be considered when planning the audit. For example, the imposition of a tariff on a U.S. product may reduce the export sales of that product and increase the risk of excess inventory. The auditor may plan extended tests of the inventory valuation assertion in this case.

In their reports on financial statements, the U.S. auditors express an opinion as to whether the financial statements present fairly the corporation's financial position, results of operations, and cash flows in accordance with generally accepted accounting principles.

Report on financial statements prepared for use in other countries. With internationalization of business, auditors in the U.S. may be appointed to audit and report on financial statements of a U.S. entity that are prepared in conformity with accounting principles of another country, for use outside of the U.S.

---

[21] Donald H. Taylor and G. William Glezen, *Auditing: Integrated Concepts and Procedures,* 6th ed. (New York: John Wiley & Sons, Inc., 1994), pp. 299-300.

If the financial statements (in conformity with generally accepted accounting principles of another country) are prepared for use *only* outside the U.S., the auditor may issue either one of the two forms of report.

1. A U.S.-style report modified to report on the accounting principles of another country.

2. The report form of the other country, whose accounting principles were used for preparation of the financial statements.

Opinions based on another auditor's report. An independent auditor may report on consolidated or combined financial statements, even if the auditor did not audit every entity in the consolidated or combined group. This happens when the principal auditor does not have an office in the country where the client has significant operations. Let us assume that the U.S.-based parent, Schoenen Company, has three subsidiaries: Sohail Company in Singapore, Younas Company in Pakistan, and Sajid Company in Abu Dhabi. Only Schoenen Company and Younas Company were audited by the principal auditor, while Sohail Company and Sajid Company were audited by local auditing firms. This is shown in Exhibit 12–6.

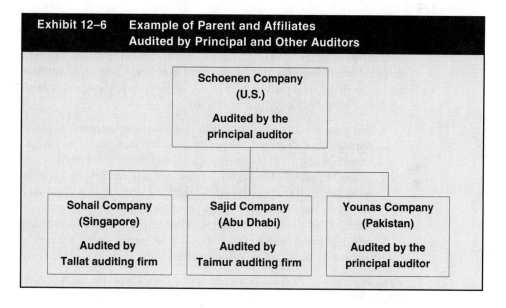

Exhibit 12–6   Example of Parent and Affiliates
Audited by Principal and Other Auditors

The principal auditor must decide whether or not to refer to other auditors' reports. If the principal auditor decides not to refer to other auditors' reports, there is no modification in the report on financial statements of the consolidated or combined entity. *In this case, the principal auditor is assuming responsibility for the other auditors' work.*

If the principal auditor decides, instead, to refer to the report of other auditors, the scope of the work done by the other auditors must be described in the principal auditor's report. *By making reference to other auditors' reports, the principal auditor is indicating the degree of responsibility each auditor is assuming in the report.*

Note: The purpose of reference to other auditors' reports is only to clearly divide the extent of responsibility assumed by each auditor. Such a reference is not considered a qualified opinion.

Audit considerations for the SEC. The SEC generally finds only unqualified opinions acceptable. Thus companies that file their financial statements with the SEC have the *de facto* requirement of resolving any issues regarding the acceptability of their accounting practices. There is one exception: For financial statements of foreign companies that are prepared in accordance with Form 20-F, the SEC will accept an auditor's opinion that is qualified for noncompliance with the industry or geographic segment reporting requirement of U.S. generally accepted accounting principles.[22]

The AICPA requires that its members notify the SEC of changes in auditors for SEC registrants. A CPA firm that has been the auditor for an SEC registrant and has resigned, declined to stand for reelection, or been dismissed is required to report that fact directly in writing to the former SEC client, with a simultaneous copy sent directly by the firm to the chief accountant of the SEC. This letter must be sent by the end of the fifth business day following the CPA firm's determination that the client-auditor relationship has ended.[23]

Worldwide Harmonization of Auditing Standards

Worldwide harmonization of auditing standards is made difficult by the fact that generally accepted accounting principles are different worldwide. Required qualifications for auditors also differ in different parts of the world. Cultural issues related to harmonization have been addressed eloquently by Arthur R. Wyatt.[24]

> We must all come to understand that internationalization is not an effort to remake the professional accounting and auditing world in the image of any one culture. While it is clear that emerging standards in both accounting and auditing reflect the needs of those economies that rely on a diverse source of capital providers, those standards will, it is hoped, emerge as a blending of the best standards found in practice and a rejection of notions tried and found wanting. The fact that the standards that are emerging will require some adjustments to practices found in all societies should be of some comfort to those who fear the process is dominated by a single culture.

Despite all obstacles, there is a clear trend toward worldwide harmonization of auditing standards. *Internationalization of capital markets is the driving force behind this trend, and its impact is quite evident.*

There are many organizations attempting to harmonize auditing standards. Three of the most prominent players in this arena are the International Federation of Accountants (IFAC), the International Organization of Securities Commissions (IOSCO), and the European Union.

---

[22] *United States: International Tax and Business Guide (New York: Deloitte Touche Tohmatsu International, 1994), pp. 55-64.*

[23] American Institute of Certified Public Accountants, The CPA Letter, November 1992, p. 4i.

[24] American Institute of Certified Public Accountants, "Global Perspectives," Journal of Accountancy, January 1993, p. 66.

International Federation of Accountants

The IFAC is a worldwide organization of national professional accounting organizations. Member organizations are recognized by law or by consensus in their countries. The IFAC was established in 1977 to promulgate international standards of auditing, ethics, education, and training. In January 1983, the IFAC and the IASC entered an agreement of "mutual commitments" for close cooperation and consultations with each other. Membership in the IFAC automatically includes membership in the IASC. The IFAC has several standing technical committees, some of which are described next.

International Auditing Practices. This committee has the responsibility for standards on generally accepted auditing practices and on related services.

Education. The committee issues guidelines on, and standards for, education and training of professional accountants.

Forum on Ethics. The forum issues pronouncements on ethics and related issues. The outline of the IFAC's code of ethics is shown in Appendix 12E. The code requires that an auditor have integrity, objectivity, and independence. The independence criterion requires independence both in fact and in appearance. It contains a confidentiality standard and prohibits disclosure of confidential information acquired during the course of performing professional services "unless there is a legal or professional right or duty to disclose."

Financial and Management Accounting. Statements issued by this committee cover application of accounting concepts for managerial decision making. The statements and studies deal with a variety of management accounting issues. For example, a study issued in October 1992 concluded that higher quality management can result from improvements in management accounting techniques such as just-in-time and executive information systems.[25]

Public Sector. The committee issues accounting and auditing guidelines for the public sector.

Information Technology. This committee considers the impact of technology on the accounting profession.

International Organization of Securities Commissions

Membership of this influential organization consists of more than 115 securities regulatory agencies from around the world, including the U.S. Securities and Exchange Commission. The members represent coverage of 85 percent of the world's capital markets.[26] The IOSCO is working with the IFAC and IASC to develop international auditing and accounting standards that will meet the needs of global capital markets and the international business community.

A major part of IOSCO's efforts is to reduce obstacles to the free flow of capital in the global markets. At its October 1992 conference, IOSCO approved a resolution to endorse IFAC's

---

[25] *Impact of Information Technology on the Accountancy Profession* (New York: International Federation of Accountants, October 1992).

[26] *IOSCO Annual Report 1994* (Montreal: IOSCO, 1995).

International Standards on Auditing (ISAs) as an acceptable basis for use in cross-border offerings and continuous reporting for foreign issuers. The IOSCO declared ISAs to be a comprehensive set of auditing standards, and audits conducted in accordance with them can be relied on by securities regulatory authorities for multinational reporting purposes. The IOSCO has recommended to its members that they take all steps necessary and appropriate in their respective jurisdictions to accept audits conducted in accordance with the IFAC's International Standards on Auditing.[27]

European Union

The Eighth Directive of the European Union covers various aspects of the qualifications of statutory auditors. Adopted in 1984, the *Eighth Directive* deals with auditing of financial statements of companies in EU countries, and specifies that they be consistent with EU law. It also deals with statutory audits of consolidated statements. The directive sets qualifications for auditors and the firms conducting audits, including education and experience requirements. In addition, the Directive deals with ethical matters such as independence, and includes sanctions for cases in which audits are not conducted as prescribed by statute.

Other Organizations

There are many other international and regional organizations working toward the goal of greater harmonization of auditing standards. Those include the United Nations and the OECD. The United Nations Intergovernmental Working Group of Experts on International Standards of Accounting and Reporting has submitted several recommendations to the IFAC for consideration.

Appendix 12A Standards for the Professional Practice of Internal Auditing

Independence. Internal auditors should be independent of the activities they audit.

Organizational status. The organizational status of the internal auditing department should be sufficient to permit the accomplishment of its audit responsibilities.

Objectivity. Internal auditors should be objective in performing audits.

Professional proficiency. Internal audits should be performed with proficiency and due professional care.

The internal auditing department

Supervision. The internal auditing department should provide assurance that internal audits are properly supervised.

---

[27] "IOSCO Endorses IFAC Auditing Standards," *Journal of Accountancy,* February 1993, p. 7.

Staffing. The internal auditing department should provide assurance that the technical proficiency and educational background of internal auditors are appropriate for the audits to be performed.

Knowledge, skills, and disciplines. The internal auditing department should possess or should obtain the knowledge, skills, and disciplines needed to carry out its audit responsibilities.

Supervision. The internal auditing department should provide assurance that internal audits are properly supervised.

The internal auditor

Compliance with standards of conduct. Internal auditors should comply with professional standards of conduct.

Knowledge, skills, and disciplines. Internal auditors should possess the knowledge, skills, and disciplines essential to the performance of internal audits.

Human relations and communications. Internal auditors should be skilled in dealing with people and in communicating effectively.

Continuing education. Internal auditors should maintain their technical competence through continuing education.

Scope of work. The scope of internal auditing should encompass the examination and evaluation of the adequacy and effectiveness of the organization's system of internal control and the quality of performance in carrying out assigned responsibilities.

Reliability and integrity of information. Internal auditors should review the reliability and integrity of financial and operating information and the means used to identify, measure, classify, and report such information.

Compliance with policies, plans, procedures, laws, and regulations. Internal auditors should review the systems established to ensure compliance with those policies, plans, procedures, laws, and regulations that could have a significant impact on operations and reports and should determine whether the organization is in compliance.

Safeguarding assets. Internal auditors should review the means of safeguarding assets and, as appropriate, verify the existence of such assets.

Economical and efficient use of resources. Internal auditors should appraise the economy and efficiency with which resources are employed.

Accomplishment of established objectives and goals for operations or programs. Internal auditors should review operations or programs to ascertain whether results are consistent with established objectives and goals and whether the operations or programs are being carried out as planned.

Performance of audit work. Audit work should include planning the audit, examining and evaluating information, communicating results, and following up.

Planning the audit. Internal auditors should plan each audit.

Examining and evaluating information. Internal auditors should collect, analyze, interpret, and document information to support audit results.

Communicating. Internal auditors should report the results of their audit work.

Following up. Internal auditors should follow up to ascertain that appropriate action is taken on reported audit findings.

Management of the internal auditing department. The director of internal auditing should properly manage the internal auditing department.

Purpose, authority, and responsibility. The director of internal auditing should have a statement of purpose, authority, and responsibility for the internal auditing department.

Planning. The director of internal auditing should establish plans to carry out the responsibilities of the internal auditing department.

Policies and procedures. The director of internal auditing should provide written policies and procedures to guide the audit staff.

Personnel management and development. The director of internal auditing should establish a program for selecting and developing the human resources of the internal auditing department.

External auditors. The director of internal auditing should coordinate internal and external audit efforts.

Quality assurance. The director of internal auditing should establish and maintain a quality assurance program to evaluate the operations of the internal auditing department.

Source: *Codification of Standards for the Professional Practice of Internal Auditing* (Altamonte Springs, Fla.: Institute of Internal Auditors, 1993), pp. 5-8.

Appendix 12B   Internal Auditor Code of Ethics

Purpose

A distinguishing mark of a profession is acceptance by its members of responsibility to the interests of those it serves. Members of the Institute of Internal Auditors (Members) and Certified Internal Auditors (CIAs) must maintain high standards of conduct in order to effectively discharge this responsibility. The Institute of Internal Auditors (Institute) adopts this *Code of Ethics* for Members and CIAs.

Applicability

This Code of Ethics is applicable to all Members and CIAs. Membership in The Institute and acceptance of the "Certified Internal Auditor" designation are voluntary actions. By acceptance, Members and CIAs assume an obligation of self-discipline above and beyond the requirements of laws and regulations.

The standards of conduct set forth in this Code of Ethics provide basic principles in the practice of internal auditing. Members and CIAs should realize that their individual judgment is required in the application of these principles.

CIAs shall use the "Certified Internal Auditor" designation with discretion and in a dignified manner, fully aware of what the designation denotes. The designation shall also be used in a manner consistent with all statutory requirements.

Members who are judged by the Board of Directors of The Institute to be in violation of the standards of conduct of the Code of Ethics shall be subject to forfeiture of their membership in The Institute. CIAs who are similarly judged also shall be subject to forfeiture of the "Certified Internal Auditor" designation.

Standards of Conduct

- Members and CIAs shall exercise honesty, objectivity, and diligence in the performance of their duties and responsibilities.

- Members and CIAs shall exhibit loyalty in all matters pertaining to the affairs of their organization or to whomever they may be rendering a service. However, Members and CIAs shall not knowingly be a party to any illegal or improper activity.

- Members and CIAs shall not knowingly engage in acts or activities which are discreditable to the profession of internal auditing or to their organization.

- Members and CIAs shall refrain from entering into any activity which may be in conflict with the interest of their organization or which would prejudice their ability to carry out objectively their duties and responsibilities.

- Members and CIAs shall not accept anything of value from an employee, client, customer, supplier, or business associate of their organization which would impair or be presumed to impair their professional judgment.

- Members and CIAs shall undertake only those services which they can reasonably expect to complete with professional competence.

- Members and CIAs shall adopt suitable means to comply with the *Standards for the Professional Practice of Internal Auditing.*

- Members and CIAs shall be prudent in the use of information acquired in the course of their duties. They shall not use confidential information for any personal gain nor in any manner which would be contrary to law or detrimental to the welfare of their organization.

- Members and CIAs, when reporting on the results of their work, shall reveal all material facts known to them which, if not revealed, could either distort reports of operations under review or conceal unlawful practices.

- Members and CIAs shall continually strive for improvement in their proficiency, and in the effectiveness and quality of their service.

- Members and CIAs, in the practice of their profession, shall be ever mindful of the obligation to maintain the high standards of competence, morality, and dignity promulgated by The Institute. Members shall abide by the Bylaws and uphold the objectives of The Institute.

Source: Codification of Standards for the Professional Practice of Internal Auditing (Altamonte Springs, Fla.: Institute of Internal Auditors, 1993), pp. 93-95.

Appendix 12C   U.S. Generally Accepted Auditing Standards

General Standards

1. The audit is to be performed by the person or persons having adequate technical training and proficiency as an auditor.
2. In all matters relating to the assignment, an independence in mental attitude is to be maintained by the auditor or auditors.
3. Due professional care is to be exercised in the performance of the audit and the preparation of the report.

Standards of Field Work

1. The work is to be adequately planned and assistants, if any, are to be properly supervised.
2. A sufficient understanding of the internal control structure is to be obtained to plan the audit and to determine the nature, timing, and extent of tests to be performed.
3. Sufficient competent evidential matter is to be obtained through inspection, observation, inquiries, and confirmations to afford a reasonable basis for an opinion regarding the financial statements under audit.

Standards of Reporting

1. The report shall state whether the financial statements are presented in accordance with generally accepted accounting principles.
2. The report shall identify those circumstances in which such principles have not been consistently observed in the current period in relation to the preceding period.
3. Informative disclosures in the financial statements are to be regarded as reasonably adequate unless otherwise stated in the report.
4. The report shall either contain an expression of opinion regarding the financial statements, taken as a whole, or an assertion to the effect that an opinion cannot be expressed. When an overall opinion cannot be expressed, the reasons therefor should be stated. In all cases where an auditor's name is associated with financial statements, the report should contain a clear-cut indication of the character of the auditor's work, if any, and the degree of responsibility the auditor is taking.

Source: American Institute of Certified Public Accountants, *Codification of Statements on Auditing Standards* (Chicago: Commerce Clearing House, Inc., 1995), pp. 21-22.

Appendix 12D   The AICPA's Code of Professional Conduct

In the U.S., various state boards of accountancy, state CPA societies, and the American Institute of Certified Public Accountants have codes of professional conduct. The AICPA code is often a model for the codes of state accountancy boards and state CPA societies. The Code has two sections:

Principles of professional conduct are concepts that are the framework of the Code.

Rules of professional conduct are rules that govern the performance of professional services and identify both acceptable and unacceptable behavior.

Principles of Professional Conduct

Principles of Professional Conduct contain guidelines about the proper behavior of CPAs and cover the following areas.

Statement of the purpose of the principles. A key feature of the AICPA Code of Professional Conduct is that many of its provisions hold the members to standards higher than laws and governmental regulations.

Responsibilities. CPAs are reminded that they have responsibilities to their clients, their employers, and the general public.

The public interest. This following statement delineates the CPAs' obligation: "When members observe their responsibility to the public, the interests of clients and employers also are best served."

Integrity. This section emphasizes that members should discharge their professional responsibilities with integrity.

Objectivity and independence. Perhaps this is the most important of all the standards in the code. Independence is often defined as the ability to act with integrity and objectivity. Independence is an integral aspect of auditing and precludes certain relationships that may appear to impair objectivity in providing auditing services. This standard requires both independence in fact (mental attitude) and independence in appearance (the public image). No direct ownership of stock of an audit client, no matter how small, is allowed.

Due care. This section emphasizes that CPAs should be competent and diligent in doing their work. CPAs should know the limitations of their competence. If the CPA lacks a certain qualification, he or she should either consult with someone who has the qualification or refer the client to someone who is knowledgeable in the area.

Scope and nature of services. The rendering of certain nonaudit services to audit clients sometimes raises questions about conflicts of interest. This standard suggests that an auditor use the guidelines listed here to resolve such questions.

- Be member of a firm that has good internal quality control procedures.
- Consider seriously if nonaudit services provided to audit clients might create or appear to create conflicts of interest.

- Consider whether a nonaudit service is consistent with the CPA's professional role, and if it is a reasonable extension of services offered by the profession.

Rules of Professional Conduct

Rules of professional conduct are specific because they identify actions and relationships in which the CPA should not engage.

Independence. (Rule 101)

> A member in public practice shall be independent in the performance of professional services as required by standards promulgated by bodies designated by Council.

This rule holds professionals to an ethical standard higher than requirements of laws or regulations.

Financial relationships. Independent auditors who are members of the AICPA, or their firms, cannot invest in the client's securities during a professional engagement or when expressing an opinion on the financial statements. The SEC has a similar rule disallowing direct financial interest in audit clients.

Business relationships. Independent auditors who are members of the AICPA, or their firms, cannot have any business relationship with a client during a professional engagement or at the time of expressing an opinion. Examples of business relationships include acting as a promoter, underwriter, or voting trustee; serving as a director or officer; and acting as a trustee for any pension or profit-sharing trust of the client.

Integrity and objectivity. (Rule 102)

> In the performance of any professional service, a member shall maintain objectivity and integrity, shall be free of conflicts of interest, and shall not knowingly misrepresent facts or subordinate his or her judgment to others.

General standards. (Rule 201)

> A member shall comply with the following standards and with any interpretations thereof by bodies designated by Council.
>
> a. *Professional competence.* Undertake only those professional services that the member or the member's firm can reasonably expect to be completed with professional competence.
>
> b. *Due professional care.* Exercise due professional care in the performance of professional services.
>
> c. *Planning and supervision.* Adequately plan and supervise the performance of professional services.
>
> d. *Sufficient relevant data.* Obtain sufficient relevant data to afford a reasonable basis for conclusions or recommendations in relation to any professional services performed.

The standards listed above are applicable to all AICPA members, including those not in public accounting.

Compliance with standards. (Rule 202)

> A member who performs auditing, review, compilation, management consulting, tax, or other professional services shall comply with standards promulgated by bodies designated by Council.

Accounting principles. (Rule 203) This rule applies to AICPA members who perform audits and certain other specified services.

> A member shall not (1) express an opinion or state affirmatively that the financial statements or other financial data of any entity are presented in conformity with generally accepted accounting principles or (2) state that he or she is not aware of any material modifications that should be made to such statements or data in order for them to be in conformity with generally accepted accounting principles, if such statements or data contain any departure from an accounting principle promulgated by bodies designated by Council to establish such principles that has a material effect on the statements or data taken as a whole. If, however, the statements or data contain such a departure and the member can demonstrate that due to unusual circumstances the financial statements or data would otherwise have been misleading, the member can comply with the rule by describing the departure, its approximate effects, if practicable, and the reasons why compliance with the principle would result in a misleading statement.

In exceptional circumstances, AICPA members may express unqualified opinions on financial statements that use accounting principles other than those in authoritative pronouncements. This is permitted only if the auditor believes that an application of a pronouncement on accounting principles would render the financial statements misleading. Such exceptions, e.g., a new law, are rare. The auditor may be required to prove that exceptions are justified under the circumstances.

Confidential client information. (Rule 301) This rule requires that information about the client obtained during an audit should be held in confidence. However, this requirement of confidentiality does not extend to incomplete or improper disclosures in the financial statements. For example, if a lawsuit against the audit client is not disclosed in the financial statements, then independent auditors should disclose this finding in their report, provided the possible consequences of the lawsuit are material.

> A member in public practice shall not disclose any confidential client information without the specific consent of the client.

> This rule is not to be construed to (1) relieve a member of his or her professional obligations under Rules 202 and 203, (2) affect in any way the member's obligation to comply with a validly issued and enforceable subpoena or summons, or to prohibit a member's compliance with applicable laws and govern-

ment regulations, (3) prohibit review of a member's professional practice under AICPA or state CPA society or Board of Accountancy authorization, or (4) preclude a member from initiating a complaint with, or responding to any inquiry made by, the professional ethics division or trial board of the AICPA or a duly constituted investigative or disciplinary body of a state CPA society or Board of Accountancy.

Members of any of the bodies identified in (4) and members involved with professional practice reviews identified in (3) should not use to their own advantage or disclose any member's confidential client information that comes to their attention in carrying out those activities. This prohibition is not to restrict members' exchange of information in connection with the investigative or disciplinary proceedings described in (4) or the professional practice reviews described in (3).

The rule on confidentiality allows the auditors to provide simultaneous audit services to competing clients, but prohibits them from disclosing confidential information.

Contingent fees. (Rule 302) CPAs are prohibited from making their fees contingent on their findings or on the result of their audit, review, certain compilation services, examination of prospective financial statements, or preparation of an original or amended tax return or claim for a tax refund. Contingent fee arrangements are permitted when none of these services is performed for a client. The contingent fees rule is presented below.

A member in public practice shall not

(1) Perform for a contingent fee any professional services for, or receive such a fee from, a client for whom the member or the member's firm performs,

(a) an audit or review of a financial statement; or

(b) a compilation of a financial statement when the member expects, or reasonably might expect, that a third party will use the financial statement and the member's compilation report does not disclose a lack of independence; or

(c) an examination of prospective financial information; or

(2) Prepare an original or amended tax return or claim for a tax refund for a contingent fee for any client.

The prohibition in (1) applies during the period in which the member or the member's firm is engaged to perform any of the services listed above and the period covered by any historical financial statements involved in any such listed services. Except as stated in the next sentence, a contingent fee is a fee established for the performance of any service pursuant to an arrangement in which no fee will be charged unless a specified finding or result is attained, or in which the amount of the fee is otherwise dependent upon the finding or result of such service. Solely for purposes of this rule, fees are not regarded as being contingent if fixed by courts or other public authorities, or, in tax matters, if determined based on the results of judicial proceedings or the findings of governmental agencies.

A member's fee may vary depending, for example, on the complexity of services rendered.

Responsibilities to colleagues. This section, presently empty, is reserved for any possible future rules. No such rules are likely.

Acts discreditable. (Rule 501) The rule is to emphasize that good reputation is important for public confidence in CPAs.

A member shall not commit an act discreditable to the Profession.

Advertising and other forms of solicitation. (Rule 502) The rule on advertising and other forms of solicitation has been changed in recent years. Given below is the current rule.

A member in public practice shall not seek to obtain clients by advertising or other forms of solicitation in a manner that is false, misleading, or deceptive. Solicitation by the use of coercion, overreaching, or harassing conduct is prohibited.

Commissions and referral fees. (Rule 503) This rule is to discourage potential conflicts of interest in providing services to clients.

A. *Prohibited commissions.*

A member in public practice shall not for a commission recommend or refer to a client any product or service, or for a commission recommend or refer any product or service to be supplied by a client, or receive a commission, when the member or the member's firm also performs for that client:

(a) an audit or review of a financial statement; or

(b) a compilation of a financial statement when the member expects, or reasonably might expect, that a third party will use the financial statement and the member's compilation report does not disclose a lack of independence; or

(c) an examination of prospective financial information.

This prohibition applies during the period in which the member is engaged to perform any of the services listed above and the period covered by any historical financial statements involved in such listed services.

B. *Disclosure of permitted commissions.*

A member in public practice who is not prohibited by this rule from performing services for or receiving a commission and who is paid or expects to be paid a commission shall disclose that fact to any person or entity to whom the member recommends or refers a product or service to which the commission relates.

C. *Referral fees.*

Any member who accepts a referral fee for recommending or referring any service of a CPA to any person or entity or who pays a referral fee to obtain a client shall disclose such acceptance or payment to the client.

Form of organization and name. (Rule 505)

A member may practice public accounting only in a form of organization permitted by state law or regulation whose characteristics conform to resolutions of Council.

A member shall not practice public accounting under a firm name that is misleading. Names of one or more past owners may be included in the firm name of a successor organization. Also, an owner surviving the death or withdrawal of all other owners may continue to practice under a name which includes the name of past owners for up to two years after becoming a sole practitioner.

A firm may not designate itself as "Members of the American Institute of Certified Public Accountants" unless all of its owners are members of the Institute.

State laws provide the forms of organization available to CPA firms.

Source: American Institute of Certified Public Accountants, *Code of Professional Conduct* (New York: AICPA, 1991).

Appendix 12E   The IFAC's International Code of Ethics

Part A: Applicable to all professional accountants

Section 1	Objectivity
Section 2	Resolution of ethical conflicts
Section 3	Professional competence
Section 4	Confidentiality
Section 5	Tax practice
Section 6	Cross border activities
Section 7	Publicity

Part B: Applicable to professional accountants in public practice

Section 8	Independence
Section 9	Fees and commissions
Section 10	Activities incompatible with the practice of public accountancy
Section 11	Clients' monies
Section 12	Relations with other professional accountants in public practice
Section 13	Advertising and solicitation

Note to Students

This chapter deals with internal and external auditing issues within the global context. As you have learned from studying the chapter, both audit functions have been, and will continue to be, influenced by environmental factors.

The career opportunities in internal auditing are becoming increasingly attractive because of global operations. This career option is overlooked by many students.

The references at the end of this chapter include many listings to enrich your understanding of various topics discussed in the chapter. One of the listed items is especially recommended: *The Philosophy of Auditing* by Mautz and Sharaf. This little book is a classic, and deals primarily with independent auditing. It is concise, enjoyable to read, and intellectually exciting.

Chapter Summary

- Internal auditing and external auditing share a common objective—to determine the reliability of accounting information.

- The internal audit is performed to determine whether an organization's policies and procedures are being followed, and whether its assets are safeguarded and used efficiently.

- Factors contributing to enhancement of internal auditing include audit committees, technological advances, reliance of external auditors on internal audit reports, and international operations.

- Policy formulation in different countries should take into account cultural differences, company goals, and business ethics.

- Top management's attitude and its leadership are critical factors in cultivation of a healthy corporate culture for long-term survival of an organization.

- Internal audit organizations can take various forms. While making a selection, the independence of internal auditors should be the uppermost consideration.

- The Foreign Corrupt Practices Act, though a U.S. law, has had worldwide impact.

- The Institute of Internal Auditors is the most influential organization in the development of internal auditing standards.

- The basic objective of external audit is to determine if the financial statements are properly prepared.

- External audits are performed differently in different countries because accounting and auditing standards differ among countries.

- Many public accounting firms, especially the "Big Six," provide external audit services throughout the world.

- The true and fair view concept has been adopted in the EU Fourth Directive.

- "Present fairly," as used in the U.S., requires an independent auditor to use judgment on several issues.
- Many countries have either successfully adopted the IFAC audit standards, or have changed national auditing standards to make them consistent with the IFAC standards.
- Many countries require statutory audits to determine whether the financial statements are in compliance with applicable laws.
- The IFAC, the IOSCO, and the EU are among the most prominent organizations attempting to harmonize auditing standards.

Questions for Discussion

1. The scope of internal auditing is limited to determining the reliability of the financial statement. Do you agree? Explain.

2. What are the two objectives of internal auditing?

3. Name and discuss at least three global trends in internal auditing.

4. Describe the impact of technological advances on internal auditing.

5. Identify and discuss at least four complexities brought on by international operations in the practice of internal auditing.

6. Discuss the role of ethics in policy formulation.

7. Can company management help set the "right tone" for corporate culture? Explain.

8. What are the two factors that have contributed to alleviating or eliminating some of the complexities associated with internal auditing of international operations?

9. The regional or central staff involved in internal audit of local operations should report to both the central headquarters and the managers of local operations. Do you agree? Explain.

10. Does the FCPA apply to corporations operating only within the U.S.?

11. Identify and describe the two accounting implications of the FCPA.

12. How is the scope of external audit affected by the work of internal auditors?

13. State the main reason why external audits are performed differently in different countries.

14. Why is it important to coordinate external audit of a local operation with the parent company's external auditor?

15. The true and fair view concept has a common meaning in all the countries where it is applied. Do you agree? Explain.

16. What are the three general requirements to be licensed as a Certified Public Accountant in the U.S.?

17. The financial statements of a company are prepared in conformity with generally accepted accounting principles of another country, for use only outside the U.S. Can a U.S. auditor audit such financial statements and report on them? Explain.

18. Name the two most important organizations concerned with harmonization of auditing standards worldwide.

19. The scope of the activities of the IFAC is limited to international auditing standards. Do you agree? Explain.

20. (Appendixes) The independence of an independent auditor differs from that of an internal auditor. How?

Exercises/Problems

12-1 The chapter lists six forms of internal audit organization for a multinational operation.

Required: Describe each of these six forms and provide comments regarding the relative strengths and weaknesses of each.

12-2 In addition to the high level of expertise, four other reasons are provided for involvement of regional or central staff in internal auditing of international operations.

Required: List those reasons in their order of importance (as determined by you), starting with the most important. Give reasons why you chose that listing order.

12-3 The FCPA makes a distinction between two types of payments: influence peddling and facilitating.

Required: Describe each type of payment and give at least two examples of each type.

12-4 Review the auditor's reports shown in Exhibits 12–1 through 12–5.

Required: Prepare an analysis to compare the reports contained in the five exhibits.

12-5 Prepare a matrix analysis of the external auditing in the eleven countries discussed in the chapter. The analysis should include, at the minimum, the following:

    a. Scope: What types of companies are required to be audited?
    b. The type of audit(s) required, e.g., independent, statutory, etc.
    c. Qualifications of different types of auditors.
    d. Procedures for appointment of auditors.
    e. Source(s) of generally accepted auditing standards.
    f. National auditing standards consistency with IFAC standards: identical, similar, etc.

12-6 Refer to the previous problem. Make interpretive and evaluative statements based on your analysis in the previous problem.

12-7 Aliya International is a multinational company based in the U.S. It has five subsidiaries, which are listed below with their location and whether the auditing firm is local.

Subsidiary	Location	Local Independent Auditors?
Sharma Ltd.	London, U.K.	Yes
Diljeet Co.	Jullunder, India	Yes
Rashid Co.	Islamabad, Pakistan	Yes
Epstein Corp.	Los Angeles, U.S.A.	No
Rabin Co.	Toronto, Canada	No

Epstein Corp. and Rabin Co. are audited by the same auditing firm that audits the parent company, Aliya International.

Describe the report options available to the principal auditor of the parent company for expressing an opinion on consolidated financial statements. Specifically include a mention of the responsibility assumed by the principal auditor in each option.

12-8   Reread the quote from Arthur R. Wyatt in the chapter.

Do you agree with Mr. Wyatt's assertions relating to harmonization? Is it possible to reconcile differing needs of different economies with harmonization? Is it possible to harmonize standards without diluting the cultural imprints on auditing standards of a country? Discuss these issues. Feel free to raise and discuss additional issues relevant to harmonization.

12-9   Select a publication from the references listed at the end of the chapter. Critique the publication in 200 to 300 words.

12–10   Write a 200 to 300 word report on the organizations working toward harmonization of auditing standards.

Case 1: The Politics of Mutual Recognition

Daimler-Benz was the first Germany-based multinational to file with the U.S. Securities and Exchange Commission for a listing on the New York Stock Exchange. This occurred in 1993. The reconciliation of Daimler-Benz's income between the U.S. and German GAAP resulted in some interesting numbers. Under German GAAP, Daimler reported income of DM 602 million for the year ended December 31, 1993. That income turned into a loss of DM 1.839 billion under U.S. GAAP. *The principal differences were the items that under U.S. GAAP were charged against current period income, but under German GAAP had been made to reserves (appropriated against retained earnings) in prior periods.*

The annual congress of the Fédération des Experts Comptables Européens, held in September 1993 in Copenhagen, had a panel discussion. The question posed was "What is the future of mutual recognition of financial statements and is comparability really necessary?" The panelists included Walter Schuetze, Chief Accountant of the SEC; Dr. Herbert Biener, from the German Justice Ministry; and David Cairns, Secretary General of the International Accounting Standards Committee.

Their three different viewpoints were reported in the *European Accounting Review.*[28]

Mr. Schuetze argued:[29]

> I believe that it is, in large part, the SEC's commitment to a financial reporting system with the objective of providing full disclosure to investors that has made the U.S. securities markets attractive for global as well as domestic capital formation. Such transparency must, in my personal view, be a primary ingredient in any standards that are to receive worldwide recognition.

Dr. Biener stated:[30]

> Financial reporting is not an end in itself, but is intended to provide information that is useful in making business and economic decisions and for making choices among alternative uses of scarce resources in the conduct of business and economic activities. In the FASB Statement of Concepts, it is clearly stated that investor-owned business enterprises are the most important category in the USA and that investor-owners are usually more interested in returns from dividends and market-price appreciation of their securities than in active participation in directing corporate affairs. It is obvious that this interest has first priority in developing accounting standards in the USA. This may not be so in Continental Europe, where the protection of creditors, shareholders, employees and the enterprise itself seems to have priority. If Continental Europe is now faced with the problem of changing fundamental accounting standards towards Anglo-American objectives, the positive and negative effects on the whole economy and on all interested parties, especially on the decision-making process of managers, shareholders, investors, bankers and other lenders, employees, governments, including tax authorities, and last but not least on the strength of enterprises, should be examined and discussed before any political decisions are made.

Mr. Cairns stated:[31]

> International Accounting Standards are developed through an international due process that involves accountants, financial analysts and other users of financial statements, the business community, stock exchanges, regulatory authorities and other interested organizations from around the world. National standard-setting bodies are increasingly involved in that process. International Accounting

---

[28] "The Politics of Mutual Recognition," *European Accounting Review,* vol. 3, no. 2 (1994), pp. 329-352.

[29] *Ibid.,* p. 334.

[30] *Ibid.,* pp. 339-340.

[31] *Ibid.,* p. 349.

Standards deal with most of the topics that are important internationally in the presentation of general purpose financial statements.

Required: Discuss the three viewpoints. Which one is the most acceptable to you? Provide reasons to support your preference.

Case 2: Lustra S.p.A. (Copyright © by the President and Fellows of Harvard College.)[32]

Peter Scala, president of Lustra S.p.A., Naples, Italy, quietly reflected on the contents of a letter he had sent the day before to his company's U.S. certified public accountant (Exhibit 12–13) in response to an earlier letter from the firm's U.S. certified public accountant (Exhibit 12–12). Scala's letter detailed his reaction to a significant accounting controversy that had arisen during the company's preparation for a planned U.S. issuance of its common stock. Of immediate concern to Peter Scala was what strategy he should adopt in reply to the auditor's anticipated response to his letter.

Background. Lustra was a distributor and retailer of fashion eyewear. The firm had been founded in 1965 by the late John Scala in Naples, Italy. In 1977, the company went public with an offering of common stock on the Milan Exchange. In 1982, Peter replaced his father as president. In 1987, Lustra opened two retail outlets in New York. From 1965 to 1989, sales and profits had grown steadily each year. 1989 proved to be Lustra's best year with profits after tax of over $3.0 million, as shown in Exhibit 12–7.[33]

Exhibit 12–7 Lustra S.p.A.—Financial Information		
	1988	1989
Net sales (millions)	$102.3	$108.6
Gross margin (millions)	52.4	53.4
Profit after tax (millions)	3.00	3.05
Earnings per share*	3.00	3.05

*Computations for Italian reporting purposes. Net income divided by average number of common shares outstanding.

Financing activities. Since 1977, Lustra had twice sought significant external financing in Italy to fund the company's expansion. Exhibit 12–8 details the company's capital structure and common stock prices for 1988 and 1989.

In September 1985, a common stock issue with warrants added 200,000 common shares to Lustra's equity base. The warrants, issued one for each common share acquired, permitted the purchase of one additional share of common stock for $10 cash until September 2000.

---

[32] Professor David F. Hawkins prepared this case as the basis for class discussion rather than to illustrate either effective or ineffective handling of an administrative situation. Adapted from case materials prepared by D. P. Frolin and J. F. Smith.

[33] All financial data have been restated to their U.S. dollar equivalent.

Exhibit 12–8   Partial Capital Structure and Common Stock Prices

	1988	1989
Common shares outstanding	1,000,000	1,000,000
Warrants outstanding	200,000	200,000
Exercise price $10, Expiration date September,		
2000. Common shares reserved for exercise	200,000	200,000
Convertible debentures 9-1/8%. Face value outstanding	0	$7,200,000
Maturity date, 2014, Conversion price $20.		
Common shares reserved for conversion	0	360,000

Common stock price—Milan Exchange*

	1988	1989	Close	Average
First quarter	6-5/8	6-3/4	12-1/4	10
Second quarter	7	7-7/8	17	15-1/4
Third quarter	8-1/8	8-3/4	14-1/2	17-5/8
Fourth quarter	9-7/8	5-5/8	9-3/4	12-1/8
Year	8	13-3/4		

*The stock traded below $10 prior to 1988.

In June 1989, the company issued subordinated convertible debentures with a face value of $7.2 million, a 9-1/8% coupon rate of interest, and a life of 25 years. Each debenture was convertible after June 1991 into Lustra common stock at a conversion price of $20 per share. Thus, each $1,000 debenture was equivalent to 50 shares of common stock.

The relatively small size of the debenture issue resulted in somewhat limited distribution of the initial offering in a very thin and inactive secondary market. The debentures were offered and sold out on June 29 and the first trade in the over-the-counter secondary market occurred on July 5, as per Exhibit 12–9.

Exhibit 12–9   9-1/8% Convertible Debentures

Date	Event	Price	Average Italian Aa Equivalent Corporate Bond Yield
June 29	Issue priced and marketed	98	14.25%
July 5	First trade secondary market	97	14.50%

In order to finance the expansion of Lustra's U.S. business, Peter Scala planned to sell Lustra stock in the United States.

1989 annual report. During preparations for the planned U.S. underwriting, Peter Scala was informed by his independent auditors, Peat, Waterhouse & Co., that the 1989 earnings per share computations that he had prepared for Italian financial statement purposes and shown in Exhibit 12–7 were not acceptable under *Accounting Principles Board (APB) Opinion No. 15*. The senior official in charge of the audit indicated that Lustra S.p.A. had failed to include as common stock equivalents the convertible debentures issued in 1989 and the outstanding common stock warrants issued in 1985. The requirements to treat both as common stock equivalents was explained as follows:

- 9-1/8% Convertible Debentures: The effective yield, based on its market price, was less than two-thirds of the then-average Italian equivalent of the Aa corporate bond yield. Thus, the convertible qualifies as a common stock equivalent and must be counted in primary and fully diluted earnings per share on an "as if" converted basis.
- Common Stock Warrants: The market price of the common stock during the year exceeded the exercise price of the warrant, hence, they are dilutive and must be counted as outstanding during the year in the primary and fully diluted earnings per share figures using the "treasury stock" method of calculation.

The audit senior proposed that the earnings per share figures shown in Exhibit 12–10 be published with the financial statements. Supporting calculations for the treasury stock method appear in Exhibit 12–11.

Exhibit 12–10   U.S. Auditor's Calculation of Earnings per Share

	Primary Earnings per Share	
	1988	**1989**
Profit after tax (000s omitted)	$3,000	$3,050
Add back after-tax interest savings on convertible debentures (tax rate = 46%)	0	177
Profit after-tax (adjusted)	$3,000	$3,227
Common shares outstanding (000 omitted)	1,000	1,000
Adjustments:		
Add conversion of debentures	0	180
Add exercise of warrants	0	47.6
Common shares outstanding (adjusted)	1,000	1,227.6
Primary earnings per share	**$3.00**	**$2.63**

	Fully Diluted Earnings Per Share	
	1988	**1989**
Profit after tax (adjusted; 000s omitted)	$3,000	$3,277
Common shares outstanding (000s omitted)	1,000	1,227.6
Add additional shares outstanding upon exercise of warrants based on closing (not average) prices	0	12.6
Common shares outstanding (adjusted)	1,000	1,240.2
Fully diluted earnings per share	**$3.00**	**$2.60**

Peter Scala's reaction to the audit senior's proposal was initially one of bewilderment, soon replaced by anger. The U.S. rules seem to make no sense.

Exhibit 12–11   Adjustment to Common Shares Outstanding for Warrants, using the Treasury Stock Method

For primary EPS: Using average common stock price.

1988—Antidilutive, no adjustment.

1989—	Quarter	Exercise	(000s omitted) Purchase	Increment
	1	200	200	0
	2	200	131.1	68.9
	3	200	113.5	86.5
	4	200	164.9	35.1
	Total			190.5
	Average			47.6

For fully diluted EPS: Using higher of average or closing quarterly common stock price.

1988—Antidilutive, no adjustment.

1989—	Quarter	Exercise	(000s omitted) Purchase	Increment
	1	200	163.3	36.7
	2	200	117.6	82.4
	3	200	113.5	86.5
	4	200	164.9	35.1
	Total			240.7
	Average			60.2

Additional shares over primary (60.2-47.6) = 12.6

Peter Scala and his controller discussed the matter at length with Donna Christiansen, audit partner responsible for the Lustra audit. The result was a stalemate—Christiansen maintained that her hands were tied by *APB Opinion No. 15,* and Scala insisted that the rules were arbitrary and unfair and that he would have difficulty abiding by them. The meeting ended on strained terms. In the days following, Scala had several telephone conversations with Ms. Christiansen and with Mr. Mark DuMond, the partner-in-charge of the New York office of Peat, Waterhouse & Co. Three days later, Peter Scala received a letter from Mr. DuMond stating the position that Peat, Waterhouse & Co. intended to maintain in this matter. This letter appears as Exhibit 12–12. On the following day, Peter Scala drafted a reply to Mr. DuMond. This reply is shown in Exhibit 12–13.

Required:

(1) If you were Ms. Christiansen, how would you explain the rationale supporting *APB Opinion No. 15?*

(2) Should Lustra adopt *APB Opinion No. 15* for Italian reporting purposes?

(3) Does it really matter what earnings per share figure Lustra reports? For instance, will the security market be influenced by this figure?

Exhibit 12–12 Auditor's Position Letter to Client

6 June 1990

Mr. Peter Scala
President
Lustra S.p.A.
Lustra Building, Via Saicar 551
Naples, Italy

Dear Peter:

This letter is written in follow-up to the telephone conversations that you had with Ms. Donna Christiansen and me earlier today concerning the computation of earnings per common share for the year ended December 31, 1989, for inclusion in your Security and Exchange filing in connection with your forthcoming public offering in the United States.

After giving careful consideration to all factors pertinent to the computation of earnings per common share as outlined in *APB Opinion No. 15,* it is the unanimous opinion of the National Accounting and Auditing Policy Committee of our firm that Lustra's convertible debentures (even though issued in Italy) and the company's warrants must properly be included as common stock equivalents in this computation. The Committee also noted that, even if the convertible debentures were not counted as common stock equivalents, thereby included in the primary earnings per share calculations, they would always be counted as converted in the fully diluted earnings per share calculation. Thus, in any case, the decline in earnings per share from 1988 to 1989 would be published on the face of the income statement.

It is our official position that if the earnings per common share included in the financial statements are not computed in accordance with *APB Opinion No. 15,* we will be unable to issue an unqualified opinion and must indicate that the computation is not within generally accepted accounting principles.

Sincerely,

Mark DuMond
Partner
Peat, Waterhouse & Company

/pbh

Exhibit 12–13   Client's Response to Auditor's Position Letter

June 9, 1990

Mr. Mark DuMond, Partner
Peat, Waterhouse & Co.
One Lander Street
New York, NY 10021

Dear Mark:

I am very disappointed in the position you and your firm seem to have adopted on Lustra's per-share calculation.

In my opinion, the rules in question are arbitrary at best and they are unfair to Lustra because they present a distorted picture of the current year's operations. I have always believed that it was our obligation to present true and fair financial statements to our shareholders. Consequently, when we have found Italian accounting practices unsatisfactory, we have turned to the International Accounting Standards for our accounting guidance. There is no comparable accounting standard in effect in Italy or in the International Accounting Standards to *APB Opinion No. 15*. I now find it distressing to be forced to issue what I consider to be misleading statements in order to comply with your country's listing requirements.

With regard to the convertible debentures, I believe, inherent in the argument that these securities should be deemed converted to common shares for earnings per share computations is the assumption that conversion is imminent (or at least highly probable) in the foreseeable future. In point of fact, the rational investor will not convert to common shares until such time as the market price of the common exceeds the conversion price of $20 per share. Given the current market price of 9-1/4 and the downward price trend, it would appear that the probability of conversion in the foreseeable future is, in fact, nil. Further, if Lustra's earnings per share are computed as prescribed by *APB Opinion No. 15,* the resulting decrease in earnings per share will likely further depress the market price, thereby even further lessening the probability of conversion.

It is interesting to note that, if what you have identified to be the Italian equivalent of the average Aa corporate bond yield at the issue date of the convertible debenture issue had been slightly lower, your position would reverse; or, if Lustra's debenture interest rate had been slightly higher, your position would reverse. Furthermore, if you would have bothered to check the record, you would also see that, against the average Aa corporate bond yield for the full year, the convertible debenture issue would more than meet the corporate bond yield test and be excluded from the common stock equivalent category.

1989 was a year of interest rate turmoil. Interest rates changed numerous times. Under such conditions it hardly seems appropriate for the accounting treatment for a 25-year debenture to depend on the average interest rate in effect on a particular day, or even during a particular week.

Furthermore, when we sold the convertible debenture, we did not anticipate that one day we would seek financing in U.S. markets. If we had, I can assure you that we would have priced the convertible issue to remove it from the primary-earnings-per-share category. Now, after the fact, to impose this U.S. accounting rule on us is unfair.

Exhibit 12–13 Client's Response to Auditor's Position Letter (continued)

Concerning the warrants, again inherent in the argument that the warrants should be deemed exercised for earnings per share computations is the assumption that actual exercise is imminent (or at least highly probable) in the foreseeable future. In point of fact, the rational investor will never exercise a warrant until it expires. Lustra's warrants expire in 2000, nearly ten years hence. The fact that the market price of our common shares exceeded the warrant exercise price at various times during 1989 means absolutely nothing regarding the probability of exercise by the holder of the warrant; its only effect is to change the price of the warrant in the marketplace. We realize that the earnings per share impact of the warrants is relatively insignificant this year. The problem is in the future as our share price rises and the earnings per share impact becomes more significant.

I am also troubled by the fact that the financial statements we issue to our Italian investors will henceforth show different earnings than those reported to our U.S. investors. This discrepancy will cause confusion that, I believe, will not help our stock price in either country.* Also, your lower 1989 earnings per share figures will make it more difficult for us to sell securities in the U.S. After all, who wants to invest in an IPO when the earnings are already sliding down? Maybe we will have to abandon our U.S. financing plan.

I have come to the conclusion that — as you say in America — "the bottom line" is this: in order to go ahead with our U.S. equity issue, we must conform to U.S. GAAP, including *APB Opinion No. 15*. Frankly, I am hesitant to go forward with the U.S. underwriting. Selling shares following a decline in earnings per share is not likely to enhance their value. Before our final decision on whether to proceed with the U.S. underwriting, please check the rules once again to see if it is truly necessary to report the figures you propose.

In the meantime, I hope you will assist me to understand the reasoning behind *APB Opinion No. 15* so that I can in turn help my Board to understand why we must now report different earnings per share to our Italian and U.S. investors. Perhaps, when I understand *APB Opinion No. 15* better, Lustra may even want to use it for our Italian reports; but I am not prepared to do so at this time.

Very truly yours,

Peter Scala
President, Lustra S.p.A.

---

*For U.S. listing purposes, Lustra S.p.A. had to adopt U.S. GAAP for financial statements issued to U.S. investors. Because of the nature of the business, the fact that it had grown without acquisitions, and Peter Scala's insistence on high-quality accounting practices, the net income the company reported for U.S. and Italian listing purposes was essentially the same.

References

Accounting Standards Committee. "Legal Opinion on 'True and Fair.'" *Accountancy,* November 1983.

Alexander, David. "A European True and Fair View?" *The European Accounting Review,* vol. 2, no. 1 (1993), pp. 59-80.

———. *Financial Reporting.* London: Chapman & Hall, 1990.

American Institute of Certified Public Accountants. *Codification of Statements on Auditing Standards.* Chicago: Commerce Clearing House, Inc., 1995.

Barroso, Manuel. "The Globetrotting Auditor." *Internal Auditor,* August 1995, pp. 22-23.

Bisgay, Louis. "International Audit Standards Okayed." *Management Accounting,* January 1993.

Bloom, R., and M. Ahmed Naciri. "An Analysis of the Accounting Standard Setting Framework in Two European Countries: France and the Netherlands." *Advances in International Accounting.* Vol. 2. London: IAI Press, Inc., 1988, pp. 69-85.

Brazil: International Tax and Business Guide. New York: Deloitte Touche Tohmatsu International, 1993.

Burchell, S., C. Clubb, and A.G. Hopwood, "Accounting in Its Social Context: Towards a History of Value Added in the United Kingdom." *Accounting, Organizations and Society,* vol. 10, no. 4, (1985), pp. 5-27.

Busse von Colbe, W. "A True and Fair View: A German Perspective." *EEC Harmonisation: Implementation and Impact of the Fourth Directive,* edited by Gray, S.J., and A.G. Coenenberg. North Holland: Elseview, 1984, pp. 121-128.

Chastney, J.G. *True and Fair View: History, Meaning and the Impact of the Fourth Directive.* London: Institute of Chartered Accountants in England and Wales, 1975.

Commission of the European Communities. *The Accounting Harmonisation in the EC: Problems of Applying the 4th Directive on the Annual Accounts of Limited Companies.* Luxembourg: Office for Official Publications of the EC, 1990.

Coopers & Lybrand. *The Accounting Profession in Nigeria.* New York: American Institute of Certified Public Accountants, 1993.

———. *International Accounting Summaries,* 2d ed. New York: John Wiley & Sons, Inc., 1993.

Current Issues for Audit Committees: 1993. New York: Coopers & Lybrand, 1993.

European Survey of Published Financial Statements in the Context of the Fourth EC Directive. Brussels: Fédération des Experts Comptables Européens, 1989.

Fédération des Experts Comptables Européens. *Analysis of European Accounting and Disclosure Practices.* London: Routledge, 1992.

Foreign Currency Translation and Hedging. New York: Coopers & Lybrand, 1994.

France: International Tax and Business Guide. New York: Deloitte Touche Tohmatsu International, 1995.

Germany: International Tax and Business Guide. New York: Deloitte Touche Tohmatsu International, 1995.

Hill, Robert, and M. Zafar Iqbal. "Auditing Standards: Reflective or Prospective." *The Woman CPA,* January 1983, pp. 14-18.

Hopwood, A. G. "Ambiguity, Knowledge and Territorial Claims: Some Observations on the Doctrine of Substance over Form," *British Accounting Review,* March 1990.

Hussein, Mohamed E.A. "Culture and Financial Reporting: a U.S.: Dutch Comparison." *De Accountant.* Amsterdam: NIVRA, October 1993.

IFAC Auditor's Legal Liability Task Force. *Auditors' Legal Liability in the Global Marketplace: A Case for Limitation.* New York: International Federation of Accountants, 1995.

IFAC Handbook 1995: Technical Pronouncements. New York: International Federation of Accountants, 1995.

IFAC Towards the 21st Century: Strategic Directions for the Accountancy Profession. New York: International Federation of Accountants, 1992.

Impact of Information Technology on the Accountancy Profession. New York. International Federation of Accountants, October 1992.

Internal Audit in Leading Financial Institutions: A Worldwide Study of the Changing Landscape. New York: Deloitte Touche Tohmatsu International, 1995.

International Code of Ethics for Professional Accountants. New York: International Federation of Accountants, July 1992.

International Task Force on Corporate Governance of the International Capital Markets Group, *Who Holds the Reins? An Overview of Corporate Governance Practice in Japan, Germany, France, United States of America, Canada, and the United Kingdom.* London: International Capital Markets Group, 1995.

Japan: International Tax and Business Guide. New York: Deloitte Touche Tohmatsu International, 1994.

Maijoor, S. J. *The Economics of Accounting Regulation: Effects of Dutch Accounting Regulation for Public Accountants and Firms.* Maastricht: Datawyse, 1991.

Mautz, R. K., and Hussein A. Sharaf. *The Philosophy of Auditing.* Sarasota, Fla.: American Accounting Association, 1961.

Mexico: International Tax and Business Guide. New York: Deloitte Touche Tohmatsu International, 1995.

Netherlands: International Tax and Business Guide. New York: Deloitte Touche Tohmatsu International, 1994.

Nobes, Christopher W. *Financial Reporting in the UK and the EEC: Mutual Influences.* London: Certified Accountants Publications, 1986.

Nobes, Christopher W., and R. H. Parker (eds.). *Comparative International Accounting.* Englewood Cliffs, N.J.: Prentice-Hall, 1991.

Raghunandan, K, and D. V. Rama. "Management Reports after COSO." *Internal Auditor,* August 1994, pp. 54-59.

Ratliff, Richard L., and Stephen M. Beckstead. "How World-Class Management Is Changing Internal Auditing." *Internal Auditor,* December 1994, pp. 38-44.

Rutherford, B. A. "The True and Fair View Doctrine: A Search for Explication." *Journal of Business Finance and Accounting,* winter 1985.

Schoonderbeek, J. W., A. van Putten, and J. Bloemarts. "The Tripartite Accounting Standards Committee." *Pilot 10.* Amsterdam: NIVRA, 1980.

Sears, Brian. "Multinational Auditing." *Internal Auditor,* October 1994, pp. 28-31.

Smith, Gerald P. "Horses of Another Color." *Internal Auditor,* August 1995, pp. 18-21.

Standards for the Professional Practice of Internal Auditing. Altamonte Springs, Fla: The Institute of Internal Auditors, 1978.

Statement of Policy of IFAC Council, Assuring the Quality of Audit and Related Services. New York: International Federation of Accountants, July 1992.

United Kingdom: International Tax and Business Guide. New York: Deloitte Touche Tohmatsu International, 1995.

United States: International Tax and Business Guide. New York: Deloitte Touche Tohmatsu International, 1994.

van Hulle, K. "Harmonization of Accounting Standards: A View from the European Community." *The European Accounting Review,* vol. 1, no. 1 (1992), pp. 161-172.

van der Tas, L. *Harmonisation of Financial Reporting: With a Special Focus on the European Community.* Maastricht: Datawyse, 1992.

Verschoor, Curtis C. "U.K. Expands Role of Audit Committees." *Management Accounting,* December 1993, pp. 44-47.

Walton, P.J. "The True and Fair View: A Shifting Concept". *Occasional Research Paper No. 7.* London: Chartered Association of Certified Accountants, 1991.

Zeff, Stephen A. "International Accounting Principles and Auditing Standards." *The European Accounting Review,* 1993, pp. 403-410.

Zeff, Stephen A., F. vander Wel, and K. Camfferman. *Company Financial Reporting: A Historical and Comparative Study of Dutch Regulatory Process.* Amsterdam: North Holland, 1992.

Chapter 13

Developing Countries: The Emerging World Economic Order

Rapid-fire economic development of many Third World countries in Asia and Latin America has resulted in the emergence of a new world economic order that is reshaping the world. Three billion people in the world are participants in the free markets today; ten years ago the number was only one billion. This is an economic development of historic proportions.

Levels of literacy, economic development, technology, and infrastructure development vary widely among the developing countries. Nevertheless, they share many common economic and societal problems. The accounting profession has opportunities to make important contributions to facilitate their economic growth, as discussed later in this chapter.

Economic Progress and Potential

The eighteenth century Scottish political economist Adam Smith stated: "If a foreign country can supply us with a commodity cheaper than we ourselves can make it, better buy it off them with some part of our own industry." Were he alive today, Adam Smith would be very pleased. His advice has received wide acceptance all over the world in recent years—regardless of national or geographic boundaries.

Movement from socialistic to free market economies is nowhere more evident than in Asia. China and India are among the recent converts. These two countries have a combined population of over 2 billion. Other countries in Asia making fast transformation to a free market system include Pakistan, Bangladesh, Sri Lanka, Nepal, Vietnam, Indonesia, and Malaysia. The governments in many Latin American countries also have recently accelerated their movement toward a free market system. Notable among such countries are Chile, Argentina, Peru, Brazil, and Mexico.

The developing countries are inviting foreign investors for both direct and indirect investments. In many countries, there has been a drastic shift in attitude toward foreign investors. Until recent years, the presence of foreign companies was often viewed with suspicion and sometimes with hatred when they were perceived as a symbol of Western dominance. Now most developing countries apparently have concluded that they can achieve economic prosperity only through integration with the global economy—not by economic isolation from the rest of the world. The results have been spectacular, as shown in Exhibit 13–1.[1]

In recent years, industrial production in developing countries has averaged over 4.5 percent yearly while the average rate has been 0.1 percent in industrialized countries. A projection for growth in selected world economies, including Asia, is shown in Exhibit 13–2.

---

[1] Adapted from *Business Week*, 3 October 1994, p. 103.

Exhibit 13–1 Annual Percentage Growth of Gross Domestic Product

	1993	1994*	1995*
Europe	-0.5	2.7	2.7
U.S.	3.0	2.6	3.1
Japan	0.1	0.8	1.1
Asia excluding Japan	NA	10.7	8.8
Latin America	NA	12.8	12.6

*Estimates

Source: Morgan Stanley & Co.

Exhibit 13–2 GDP Growth for Selected Global Regions

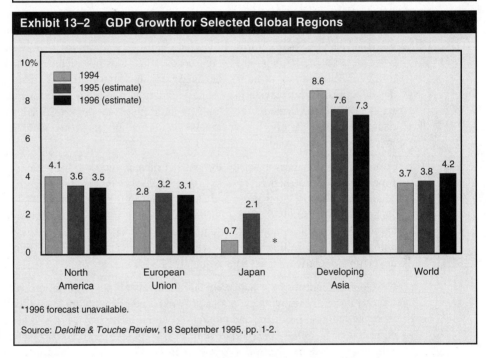

*1996 forecast unavailable.

Source: *Deloitte & Touche Review,* 18 September 1995, pp. 1-2.

Southeast Asia has a large population of low-wage and well-educated workers. *This region remains the most economically vibrant on earth.* In 1994 there was a growth rate of 7 percent or more in Indonesia, Malaysia, Thailand, and Singapore. Economists have forecast the growth for 1995 to be equally impressive. The economic growth has brought economic prosperity, thus creating a sizable middle class. Consequently, many products now manufactured in Southeast Asia are not just for export but also to meet domestic demand from this newly created middle class. This has also motivated many of the richest Southeast Asians to invest in the region.[2] Recently, Japan's investment focus has shifted toward Asia.

[2] "SE Asian Dragons' Economies Still Spark," San Francisco Chronicle, 3 January 1995, p. D6.

Privatization and Economic Reforms

There are two major driving forces behind this new economic momentum in Third World countries: privatization of state-owned enterprises and introduction of economic reforms. Privatization has resulted in private ownership of enterprises that were previously owned by governments. Free market forces are transforming such enterprises into efficient and competitive entities. Economic reforms have resulted in the removal of restrictive policies on trade and investments, such as currency-flow restrictions, high tariffs, import quotas, and limits on equity ownership by foreign investors. *The push for privatization and economic reforms has come from two major sources: The World Bank, and donor countries providing economic assistance to the developing countries.*

Thanks to privatization and economic reforms, the outcome has been a surge in trade between the developing countries and industrialized countries, and also among the developing countries. In addition, investment funds are flowing relatively easily to different parts of the globe in search of high returns. In the later part of 1994, approximately $1.5 trillion was being held in international-equity portfolios. This does not include another $50 to $100 billion in discretionary accounts managed by hedge fund managers.[3] The opportunities in developing countries play an increasingly important role in the investment decisions, since returns that can be earned in developing countries surpass those available in industrialized countries. Consequently, the developing countries are attracting increasing amounts of investments from abroad.

Foreign fund managers make up the bulk of outside investors in Asian security markets. Emerging Asian markets favored by foreign investors include those in Taiwan, Indonesia, Thailand, Malaysia, Singapore, and Hong Kong. In the later part of 1994, investment by Japanese mutual funds (called securities investment trusts) in Asia outside of Japan was approximately $11 billion. U.S. mutual funds dedicated to non-Japanese Asian equities amounted to $12 billion. At 1994 year-end, direct and indirect foreign investments in developing countries totaled approximately $88 billion.

Developing countries have achieved varying levels of industrialization. While some countries are currently enjoying economic growth based primarily on their advantages of cheap labor, agricultural products, and natural resources, others have evolved beyond that developmental stage. *Some East Asian countries are currently at the point where they are soon expected to make the transition to fully industrialized, high technology status.* In fact, one of the Four Tigers of Asia, Singapore, became Southeast Asia's first developed economy on January 1, 1996. The other three of the Four Tigers of Asia—Taiwan, South Korea, and Hong Kong—plus Thailand are considered to be among those next in line to achieve this status. Singapore is an exporter of high technology products and is also exporting its telecommunications expertise. Taiwan manufactures entire personal computers (PCs) as well as key parts for some of the largest computer manufacturers in the world, such as Apple and Compaq.

---

[3] Dean Foust, Karen Lowry Miller, and Bill Javetski, "Financing World Growth," *Business Week*, 3 October 1994, p. 102.

Asian and Latin American markets are becoming vital to many companies in the U.S., Japan, and Western Europe. Corporations such as Coca-Cola, Siemens, Hitachi, ABB Asea Brown Boveri, Mitsubishi, Alcatel-Alsthom, and Procter & Gamble are focusing on high-growth Asian and Latin American countries. This is necessary for their own long-term growth since developing countries have billions of consumers with improving incomes. According to the findings of a recent survey, the importance of global operations intensifies for U.S. companies as corporate size grows. American firms without foreign plants or joint ventures experience a sharp erosion in profitability as sales move above $1 billion. Further, a small firm with annual sales below $500 million may lose opportunities for expansion by remaining domestic. *Not only is size no obstacle to international expansion, but early entry into the global markets may be a clear sign of success.*[4]

A 1994 study by Ernst & Young concluded that approximately 48 percent of U.S.-based multinational enterprises planned to increase their investments in emerging markets during the next five years. The top ten emerging markets *by rank* are:

1. China	6. Brazil
2. India	7. Malaysia
3. Indonesia	8. Argentina
4. Mexico	9. Hong Kong
5. Thailand	10. Taiwan

The results of this study were based on the information from chief executive officers, chief financial officers, corporate planning directors, and international operations directors at 230 of the world's 1,000 largest multinational corporations.[5]

Regulatory Controls on Security Trading

According to many economists and financial analysts, Asian economies will grow at an annual average rate of 8 percent through the year 2010. A strong regulatory framework for security markets is a prerequisite to building investor confidence. Although investors from the West are often frustrated by the lack of adequate controls in the emerging security trading centers, they often cannot resist the high returns. For example, foreign investors take up to 60 percent of market share in Hong Kong. In recent years the governments in several developing countries have taken active steps to regulate security trading. For example, the government of India has empowered the Securities and Exchange Board of India to control the country's 21 security exchanges. Malaysia and Thailand have formed new securities commissions, while Indonesia has privatized its stock exchanges.

Infrastructure as a Competitive Weapon

As mentioned earlier, individual developing countries are at different stages of industrial and technological development. Some are still heavily reliant on their competitive advan-

---

[4] "Weighing Strategic Options," *Deloitte & Touche Review,* 18 April 1994, p. 2.

[5] *Multinational Investments in Emerging Markets* (Ernst & Young: New York, 1994).

tages of cheap labor, agriculture, and natural resources, while others will soon join the league of industrialized, high technology countries.

Many of the developing countries that are dependent on their competitive advantage of low-cost labor, export of agricultural products, or vast natural resources recognize that these advantages will disappear in the future. They are striving to become more industrialized to prepare for the future. A recent example of such a country is the kingdom of Saudi Arabia. The development of infrastructure has become a top priority to achieve this goal for several reasons.

- To produce high-quality goods and services that can withstand competitive pressures in global markets.
- To attract foreign investments that, in the absence of essential infrastructure, would not be made.
- To meet the needs for infrastructure resulting from growth already achieved.

Demand for energy, telecommunications, and transportation networks, therefore, comes from the plans to develop future competitive ability, to attract foreign investments, and to meet already existing needs. According to the Asian Development Bank estimates, the Asian countries excluding Japan will spend $1 trillion by the year 2000 on infrastructure development. Some believe this estimate is too conservative. For example, Hong Kong's Peregrine group estimates that ten developing countries in Asia will spend over $1.9 trillion by the year 2000 on infrastructure.[6] This is shown in Exhibit 13–3. Such vast expenditures are bound to have major social and environmental impacts—perhaps even greater than the economic impact.

Exhibit 13–3	Spending on Infrastructure (Billions of Dollars) by 2000			
	__Total__	__Trans-portation__	__Power__	__Telecommu-nications__	__Other__
ASEAN	$ 222.4	$ 74.0	$64.1	$21.0	$ 63.3
China	1,047.6	968.4	54.0	25.2	NA
Hong Kong	66.8	23.2	12.8	1.2	29.6
South Korea	356.5	132.3	46.2	32.3	145.7
Taiwan	246.5	124.3	28.5	9.6	84.1
	$1,939.8	$1,322.2	$205.6	$89.3	$322.7

The Association of Southeast Asian Nations (ASEAN) is the most important trading bloc in Southeast Asia. The member countries include Brunei, Indonesia, Malaysia, the Philippines, Singapore, Thailand, and Vietnam. The ASEAN member countries plan to establish a free-trade area by 2003. This will be accomplished by reducing tariffs to a maximum of 5 percent by January 2003, by six of the seven member countries. Vietnam has until January

---

[6] Adapted from *Business Week*, 28 November 1994, p. 66. When this report was published, ASEAN had only six members. Vietnam was admitted to ASEAN in 1995.

2006 to make the tariff cuts. The tariff reduction process was started in 1993. Japan has made direct investments of $20 billion in ASEAN member countries since 1990. The flow of investment from Japan is accelerating as Japanese companies search to find cheap labor markets to offset the impact of the strong yen.

Technology transfer and development of human capital. As a result of the active participation by many American, Japanese, and Western European companies in this infrastructure development, it is expected that transfers of advanced technologies to developing countries will occur. The developing countries will also acquire human capital in the form of a cadre of highly skilled technocrats, managers, machinists, and technicians. This human capital will develop as a direct outcome of hands-on involvement in the complex infrastructure projects. Most of the developing countries have sizable pools of highly educated individuals, many with advanced degrees from the U.S. and Europe. The missing ingredient for many, until now, has been practical experience through involvement in complex projects.

Many companies from industrialized countries are competing with one another for infrastructure development contracts. In order to be successful in this pursuit, the companies may benefit from adopting the following strategies to gain a competitive advantage:[7]

- Willingness to transfer advanced technology at low prices.
- Forming long-term alliances through continual transfer of newer technologies, instead of concentrating on one-time sales.
- Willingness to develop human capital by sharing knowledge and expertise.
- Providing financing at a price the Asians consider reasonable.
- Avoiding the perception of making excessive profits.

Japanese companies are generally found to be more reluctant to transfer advanced technology than companies from the U.S., France, and Germany.

Problems and Challenges

Many developing countries have made impressive progress in economic growth and industrial development in recent years. Unfortunately, growth and industrialization also intensify many major problems, such as pollution and natural resource depletion. Without solutions to these problems, hard-earned economic gains may be endangered. In this section we will look at some of the problems and challenges facing developing countries. This is necessary so that we can understand their environments. It will help us later to focus on the role of accounting in finding solutions to many of these problems.

Population Growth

High population growth rates continue to exacerbate the already existing overpopulation problem in developing countries. Developing countries include three of the four most populous nations in the world.

---

[7] William J. Holstein, "Building the New Asia," *Business Week,* 28 November 1994, pp. 65-68.

Country	Population (1994)
China	1,200 million
India	920 million
Indonesia	190 million

The world's population is estimated at over 5.5 billion, and Southeast Asia accounts for 60 percent of this number. India and China together account for approximately 40 percent of the world's total population. The population growth rate has been brought under some control in several countries, notably in Bangladesh, China, India, Indonesia, Hong Kong, South Korea, Singapore, Taiwan, and Thailand. Family planning programs have helped reduce the average number of children born per woman in developing countries from 6.0 in the late 1960s to 3.5 currently. The fertility rate in China is currently below the population replacement level of 2.1 children per woman. The population growth rates, however, remain high in many other developing countries.

Overpopulation is generally acknowledged to be the major cause of environmental pollution, global warming, and depletion of natural resources. Overpopulation also burdens the economy of a developing country and makes it difficult to provide food, education, housing, health care, and employment for a population that is continuously increasing. Child labor—putting young children to work at a very early age—is a sad byproduct of overpopulation in many countries.

Environmental Pollution

Industrial development and population growth have fueled the problem of environmental pollution and natural resource depletion. Deforestation, air and water pollution, toxic waste, and loss of farmland due to urban sprawl are just a few examples. Automobiles are a major source of air pollution in most developing countries. In New Delhi, 64 percent of total air pollutants was estimated to be contributed by automobile emissions.[8] Smog is so thick over Benxi, a city of one million in northeastern China, that, according to a *Business Week* report, the city does not appear on satellite maps.

Environmental negligence has often been fostered by the desire for industrialization—regardless of environmental costs. Chile typifies this dilemma. The Chilean capital city, Santiago, has a serious smog problem blamed mainly on a fleet of 10,000 outmoded diesel buses. The extremely poor air quality has forced the government to declare pre-emergency or emergency air conditions many times, advising children to stay home from school and avoid exercise for part or all of the day. The smog problem is even worse in Mexico City. Chile faces other serious environmental problems including water pollution, destruction of ancient subarctic rain forests, ozone depletion that has resulted in severe ultraviolet contamination in Punta Arenas (reportedly blinding farm and wild animals), toxic waste disposal, and extensive topsoil erosion.[9]

---

[8] "Rising Pollution in Delhi Makes Living Hazardous," *India West,* 2 December 1994, p. 54.

[9] Alexandra Huneeus, "Environmental Mess Prompts Warning by U.S.," San Francisco Chronicle, 7 October 1992, p. A11.

Corruption

Corruption is a serious threat to economic and social health of most, if not all, developing countries. The impact of corruption is far more serious in countries that already are suffering from acute scarcity of economic resources. *Diversion of the precious economic resources from economic development causes misallocation of resources in the countries that can least afford it.* Widespread corruption has compelled many heads of state of developing countries to publicly address this issue. For example, recently the president of an Asian country referred to corruption as a national problem needing a nonpartisan approach.

In most cases, the acceptance of bribes by government officials, including judges, is attributed to their low salaries. This, of course, provides an explanation but not a justification. Even the United Nations has not received immunity from this problem. In some countries where UNICEF (the UN children's fund) has developmental programs, it had to pay "salary supplements" to government officials as an incentive to carry out programs. Auditors for UNICEF warned in 1994 that "while the payment of salary supplements may ensure the achievement of immediate program objectives and lead to more successful policy execution, in the long run it will endanger the sustainability of development effort and erode national capacity building."[10] A subtler form of corruption, nepotism, is also widespread in many developing countries. **Nepotism** means that relatives of those in power tend to easily obtain business licenses, lucrative government contracts, real estate deals, high-level government jobs, and other forms of patronage.

Many countries, such as South Korea and China, have started concerted efforts to crack down on corruption. However, such efforts often face tough resistance. In several cultures, bribe payments have come to be regarded as harmless tips or donations, thus making them quasi-acceptable. According to a South Korean government estimate, this vast underground economy makes up 10 percent of the country's gross national product. A survey published in February 1994 showed that 46.3 percent of businessmen still bribe government officials in South Korea.[11] These examples of South Korean practices are given here to illustrate the problem that exists widely among the developing countries, and are not to imply that the problem in South Korea is more serious than in other countries. Similar examples of rampant corruption can easily be found in many other developing countries.

Political Instability and Civil Unrest

Many developing countries are suffering from political instability and civil unrest to varying degrees. Specific causes of political instability and social disorder vary from country to country. However, the common factors contributing to the problem are ethnic and religious conflicts, regional disputes, political feuds, and governmental corruption and incompetence. *The root causes, according to knowledgeable observers, are economic deprivation and systematic discrimination based on social stratification.*

---

[10] "U.N. Relief Agency Warns Against Bribes, Payments," *San Francisco Chronicle,* 25 December 1994, p. C13.

[11] "Despite Kim's Reforms, South Korea's Culture of Bribery Thrives," *San Francisco Chronicle,* 20 April 1994, p. A12.

Why is political stability and social order important? Today more and more economists believe that it is politics, policies, and institutions that help or hurt growth.[12]

> . . . burgeoning bureaucracies and interest groups in both developing and industrialized nations can throw sand in the economic gears and lead to political paralysis or instability. And political instability is one surefire predictor of poor economic performance, says Harvard University economist Alberto Alesina. . . . In developing countries, the accompanying uncertainty reduces investment and encourages capital flight, while among industrialized nations, instability leads to poor policy choices. "If a government is unlikely to be reelected, it has an incentive to follow particularly shortsighted policies," argues Alesina.

According to Moeen Qureshi a former Vice President of the World Bank, "It is futile to expect a sustained flow of foreign capital if peaceful conditions do not exist."[13] A 1994 survey of the Global 1000 by Ernst & Young reported that the companies feel the highest barrier to their investment in a country is political instability.[14]

Other Problems

Other major problems facing developing countries are:

- High rates of inflation.
- Unstable currency.
- Heavy national debt and deficit spending.
- Politicization of decision making for development projects.

It is difficult to isolate these problems from those discussed above. They are all interrelated. For example, heavy government deficit spending contributes to a high rate of inflation, which in turn often contributes to currency instability. Currency instability often leads to the exodus of foreign capital. When foreign investors withdraw, a government's ability to pay its debts and to finance operations is adversely affected. Inability of a government to pay its debts when due creates a *major* financial crisis.

This phenomenon occurred recently in Mexico after the devaluation of the peso in December 1994. As a result of foreign investors' lack of confidence in Mexican securities, the government of Mexico was able to sell only $64 million of a total $400 million in dollar-indexed bonds in early January 1995. The impact of this crisis of confidence was felt not only in the Mexican stock market but also in other Latin American markets—Argentina, Brazil, and Chile.

Double-digit and sometimes triple-digit inflation rates persist in many countries. It is necessary to curb high inflation to achieve sustained fast economic growth. Many developing

---

[12] Karen Pennar, Geri Smith, Rose Brady, Dave Lindorff, and John Rossant, "Is Democracy Bad for Growth?" *Business Week,* 7 June 1993, pp. 85-86.

[13] Vasantha Arora, "Ex-Pak PM Concerned Over Law and Order," *India West,* 16 December 1994, p. 26.

[14] *Multinational Investments in Emerging Markets* (Ernst & Young: New York, 1994).

countries, such as Turkey and India, also need to curtail their reliance on heavy government deficit spending, which often leads to high inflation rates. For dozens of developing countries, heavy debt is having a crippling effect on economic growth and is keeping away investments from abroad. Major debtor nations include Brazil, Mexico, and India.

The politicization of development projects often results in low quality decisions. A highly politicized decision-making model often results in project delays and suboptimal decisions. Some analysts believe this to be the main reason for problems with infrastructure projects in some countries.

Operating Environment Challenges for Multinationals

Multinational companies operating in developing countries have tremendous opportunities to benefit from their growth economies. With the opportunities come the challenges related to the operating environment existing in developing countries. To succeed, companies operating in developing countries must be aware of the problems, and formulate strategies and plans to cope with them. In this section we will outline some additional problems commonly encountered by multinational companies while doing business in developing countries.

In many countries there are strict business regulations, sometimes directed primarily toward multinational companies. For example, Egypt and India have labor policies covering the employment of local citizens. Many foreign contractors and managers complain that the regulations give virtually permanent protection to the local workers they hire. Some countries, including Taiwan, have stiff rules restricting capital remittances by foreigners. Many countries continue to have protectionist policies such as high import tariffs and prohibition, and importing many products is prohibited. A few countries have strict exit policies that make it difficult for a multinational company to curtail its operations in an orderly and efficient manner. This can cause major problems for a company that is restructuring its operations.

Governmental red tape and bureaucratic obstacles, both in government and in other institutions, often frustrate managers of multinational companies. It may take months, or even years, to get a decision after submission of an application for approval of a project.

Lack of a skilled workforce in adequate supply is a problem in many countries. In some cases, the education system appears to be insensitive to the actual needs of the labor market.

Some countries have inadequate legal and banking systems. A comprehensive legal system provides protection to investors and creditors and a banking system facilitates transactions. Both are critical for transnational companies to conduct business. Lack of infrastructure creates significant obstacles and further compounds the problem. Several countries in Indochina, for example, Cambodia and Laos, suffer from inadequate legal and banking systems and poor infrastructure. Other problems in some countries include inadequate energy supplies, non-convertible currencies, and inefficient judicial systems. In spite of the problems related to operating environments, however, most analysts believe that there is tremendous opportunity at present and immense potential for the future in developing countries.

Role of Accounting

Economic reforms and economic growth in developing countries have brought the role of accounting to the limelight. Accountants have a vital role to play in this new economic world order. Accounting systems record and report the transactions involving transfer of goods, services, and financial resources. This is necessary to meet the information needs of—among others—multinational enterprises, global capital markets, and international investors. In addition, accounting provides useful information to corporate managers and technocrats for policy formulation and decision making.

Accounting Profession

Accounting practices in a country are heavily influenced by its political and economic system. *When there is a drastic change in the political or economic system of the country, it is bound to change the objectives of financial reporting.* In developing countries, such as China, the movement toward a market-oriented economy has necessitated a revision of the financial reporting system. *This revision in accounting and disclosure standards is considered essential for the success of economic reforms.*[15] In the countries that used to have totally planned economies, the traditional focus of accounting was on the stewardship concept. The transition to a market economy makes the information on operating and financial performance of primary importance. This major shift in the financial reporting objectives requires reorientation on the part of accountants. Developing countries have taken active steps to address these issues. For example, Deloitte Touche Tohmatsu International is assisting in the development of continuing professional education for the Chinese Institute of Certified Public Accountants. Also, Western accounting firms have entered into joint ventures for conducting audits with Chinese accounting firms. An important reason cited for such joint ventures is that it will help upgrade accounting standards in China. The upgrading is expected to eventually help attract foreign financial capital.[16] Deloitte Touche Tohmatsu International is also working with the Chinese Ministry of Finance in developing accounting standards that will be consistent with "internationally accepted norms."[17] Other countries—South Africa, for example—are adopting IASC's International Accounting Standards.[18]

The International Organization of Securities Commissions will continue to play a key role in providing the impetus to the development of financial reporting standards because many developing countries are seeking to list their securities in other countries and most of these countries have stock exchanges open to foreign investors.

---

[15] Gary M. Winkle, H. Fenwick Huss, and Chen Xi-Zhu, "Accounting Standards in the People's Republic of China: Responding to Economic Reforms," *Accounting Horizons,* September 1994, p. 48.

[16] "Andersen, Peat Both Open Chinese Joint Ventures," *Accounting Today,* 11 May 1992, p. 44.

[17] N. McGrath, "Sorting Out the Numbers," *Asian Business,* May 1993, p. 9.

[18] "South Africa—Adoption of International Accounting Standards," *IASC Insight,* March 1994, p. 3.

Accounting Education

Accounting educators in the developing countries that have adopted economic reforms and privatization policies face the challenge of restructuring accounting curricula to reflect the impact of these changes. As stated earlier, the revision of accounting and disclosure standards is essential for the success of economic reforms. The accountant's role and the education and training of accountants is also critical to successful implementation of economic reforms.[19] It is vital to revise financial reporting systems and to develop accounting curricula to support economic reforms that enhance integration with the global economy.

Specific Opportunities and Challenges

We now focus on some of the specific opportunities and challenges in the developing countries for the accounting profession.

- The strategic decisions involving infrastructure projects are of critical importance to the developing countries since they have a direct effect on their future competitive ability. The speed and quality of decision making (along with the existence of a competitive private sector) are important factors.[20] *The countries that allow decisions to be made by qualified technocrats or nonpartisan consortiums, rather than by politicians, are making faster progress.* Accountants possess the analytical skills to provide technical support to civilian authorities. Cost-benefit analysis, project cost estimation, and developing post-completion control systems are just a few of the examples.
- The management of infrastructure projects is a challenge for the companies working on the projects. Accountants can make important contributions by developing systems for project management and project control.
- Corruption is acknowledged to be a major problem in many developing countries. As stated earlier, corruption causes misallocation of economic resources and is undesirable anywhere, anytime. However, the effects of corruption are relatively more adverse on the economies of developing countries since these countries can least afford misallocation of scarce resources. Accountants can help alleviate this problem by designing and developing internal control systems to detect fraud and waste. Internal auditing has a natural role in the efforts to curb corrupt practices. The internal audit function includes the examination and evaluation of the adequacy and effectiveness of an organization's internal control system. Internal audits also assess the quality of performance in carrying out assigned responsibilities.[21] Regular internal audits in themselves are a deterrent to corrupt and wasteful practices.

---

[19] Gary M. Winkel, H. Fenwick Huss, and Qiwen Tang, "Accounting Education in the People's Republic of China: An Update," *Issues in Accounting Education,* fall 1992, p. 180.

[20] Holstein, pp. 63-67.

[21] *The Statement of Responsibilities of Internal Auditing* (New York: Institute of Internal Auditors, 1990).

- The lack of data accuracy is common in developing countries. As has been observed, "It takes accurate numbers to institute free-market reforms."[22] Internal auditors, by reviewing the reliability and integrity of financial and operating information, can help achieve the accuracy of data critical to successful implementation of economic reforms.
- A problem in many developing countries is that policy formulation is not necessarily followed by policy implementation. Internal audits can help ensure that economic reforms are implemented as planned.
- All cultures have values implying what is "good" or acceptable. A review of the cross-cultural literature suggests that there are international differences in perceptions of what constitutes ethical behavior. Several researchers have found cross-national differences in ethical reasoning in a business context.[23] Values in different countries could possibly be in apparent conflict with corporate ethical policies. Through their adherence to codes of professional ethics (e.g., the Institute of Management Accountant's *Standards of Ethical Conduct for Management Accountants*), accountants are knowledgeable about professional ethics. They can be helpful in the development of ethical guidelines for use in diverse cultural settings by the operating managers.

Apart from culturally based ethical dilemmas, the management of an organization can benefit from contributions by management accountants in the ethics area in general. Accountants can design incentive systems that reward ethical behavior of employees. The management accountant is in a unique position to encourage ethical conduct within the company by quantifying the potential losses from litigation, loss of reputation, and punitive government action. Management accountants can help prepare or revise policies and mission statements that reflect the management's commitment to responsible and ethical behavior.[24] Internal auditors, through their periodic audits, can determine if the organization's established ethical policies are being followed.

- Cost accounting clearly has a major role. Estimating costs of proposed infrastructure projects has been mentioned earlier. Another example is the cost-benefit analysis to determine whether a state enterprise is achieving its economic and social objectives. Findings of such analyses can help in the decision as to whether a particular public enterprise should be privatized. Besides cost accounting, internal auditing has a role in such a decision-making process. It is commonly acknowledged that the public sector tends to be inefficient. Internal audits can be conducted to see if there is efficient use of resources by public sector entities.

---

[22] Christopher Farrell, Joyce Barnathan, and Elisabeth Malkin, "Statistics Can't Be Damn Lies Any Longer," *Business Week,* 7 November 1994, p. 118.

[23] Jeffrey R. Cohen, Laurie W. Pant, and David J. Sharp, "Culture-Based Ethical Conflicts Confronting Multinational Accounting Firms," *Accounting Horizons,* September 1993, p. 2.

[24] Debra R. Meyer, "More on Whistleblowing," *Management Accounting,* June 1993, p. 26.

- The governmental accounting area in developing countries is full of opportunities. For example, accountants can help develop a regulatory framework for securities trading. Some of the dubious practices in emerging markets have included illegal shares sales, share price manipulation, and insider trading. Placement of a strong regulatory framework helps bolster investor confidence. Lack of regulatory controls has resulted in securities scandals in many developing countries. Another area in governmental accounting in dire need of attention is a system for regular reporting on the economic performance of public enterprises. This is an area where accountants can make significant contributions.

- Development of financial accounting and reporting standards is necessary for the development of financial structure. The need in this area is far from being satisfied. Investors need meaningful and informative financial reports for decision making. The development of reporting and disclosure requirements for security registration and for periodic reporting by listed companies helps meet investors' needs for making informed decisions.

- Tax accounting in developing countries has been identified by many as an area of great opportunity for accountants. Many developing countries need to simplify and improve their taxation and tax-collection systems. In addition, investors and companies doing business in these countries need information about tax laws and regulations for tax planning, for tax law compliance, and for making decisions.

- Environmental accounting is expected to receive increasingly greater attention in developing countries because of rapid growth and also because of plans for infrastructure development. The environmental impact of economic growth is already being felt in all developing countries. Rapid infrastructure development can only intensify the environmental impact. Accounting practitioners as well as accounting researchers have an excellent opportunity to make significant contributions in environmental accounting. For researchers, the developing countries provide a laboratory setting to test hypotheses in the environmental accounting area, and to identify accounting and reporting issues relating to environmental costs and liabilities. There has been increasing interest for environmental information by financial statement users. Some of the important issues requiring attention in the environmental accounting area are:

  - Identification of environmental costs.
  - Environmental liabilities and their recognition and measurement.
  - Disclosure of environmental costs and liabilities.
  - Environmental contingent liabilities.
  - Disclosure of environmental accounting policies.
  - Disclosure of future environmental expenditures.
  - Cost analysis in areas such as energy and waste.
  - Cost-benefit analysis of environmental improvement programs.

- Development of business codes in the legal framework (e.g., investment and banking codes) is another area where accountants have the expertise to provide technical support to those who have the responsibility for developing a legal framework. In many developing countries, lack of a comprehensive legal framework and banking system are major obstacles to trade and investments.

Clearly, accountants are not mere spectators in the global economy. They are active participants. Their skills, expertise, and talents are needed by all players in the arena of global economy—governments, investors, capital market regulators, and corporations. For example, Arthur Andersen has developed a plan for a new management structure for the Bombay Stock Exchange—the oldest exchange in Asia. The new management structure is an attempt to introduce operational reforms. During 1992, Coopers & Lybrand undertook 365 privatization assignments in 64 countries. Accountants have exciting opportunities to make important professional contributions that will help efficient allocation of resources in the new world economic order.

Note to Students

As you study this chapter, you realize that developing countries provide exciting opportunities. Accounting professionals can make significant contributions to facilitate decision making related to economic development of these countries.

To keep abreast of the developments in this dynamic area of emerging economies, the following periodicals are especially valuable: *The Asian Wall Street Journal Weekly*, *Economist*, *Far Eastern Economic Review* (published in Hong Kong), *India West*, *The Economic Times* (India's main financial daily newspaper), *Business India*, *Gulf News* (published in the United Arab Emirates), Beijing's *Economic Daily*, *Business Week*, *Fortune*, and *Financial Times*.

Please grasp the important idea that the developing countries go through an evolutionary process. They usually start out as sources of cheap labor and evolve into industrialized countries. Taiwan appears to have almost completed this evolutionary process and other countries, notably South Korea and Singapore, are not far behind.

Chapter Summary

- The phenomenal economic growth of developing countries is resulting in a new world economic order.
- The most drastic shift from centrally planned economies to free market economies has occurred in Asia.
- Developing countries are inviting both direct and indirect investments from abroad.
- Southeast Asia is considered to be the most economically vibrant region in the world.
- Privatization and economic reforms are the two major driving forces behind the explosive economic growth and development in the Third World countries.
- The World Bank and rich countries providing aid have been instrumental in motivating developing countries to move toward privatization and economic reform.

- Recently there has been an increase in international trade and investment in developing countries.

- Developing countries cover a wide spectrum in terms of the levels of industrialization.

- Markets in developing countries are becoming increasingly important to business enterprises in developed countries.

- Governments in many developing countries have recently introduced security regulations.

- Infrastructure development is being given high priority by many developing countries for a multitude of reasons.

- As a byproduct of infrastructure development, developing countries will acquire high technology and human capital.

- Developing countries share many common problems that threaten erosion of past gains and also future growth.

- Many challenges accompany the opportunities for multinational companies in developing countries.

- The accounting profession and accounting education have an important role in the emerging economies of the world.

- Many opportunities exist for accountants in numerous areas such as internal auditing, cost accounting, financial accounting, governmental accounting, taxation accounting, and ethics.

- Environmental accounting is a fertile area for accounting practitioners and accounting researchers for making significant contributions.

Questions for Discussion

1. How many people live in countries with market-oriented economic systems? What was the number a decade ago?

2. Name the continent that has had the most visible shift to free market economies.

3. Name three countries in Asia making progress to a free market system.

4. Name two countries in Latin America that are moving toward a market-oriented system.

5. Describe the shift in attitude in many developing countries regarding foreign investment.

6. Name the region in the world considered to be most economically dynamic.

7. What was the minimum growth rate in the Southeast Asian countries of Indonesia, Malaysia, Thailand, and Singapore for 1994?

8. Name the two major driving forces for economic momentum in developing countries.

9. Describe the impact of privatization on previously state-owned enterprises.

10. Give three examples of economic reforms.

11. What forces have provided the impetus for privatization and economic reforms?

12. Name three emerging Asian markets favored by foreign investors.

13. Returns on investment that can be earned in developing countries are higher than those available in industrialized countries. Do you agree?

14. Name three of the countries soon expected to achieve fully industrialized status.

15. Why are the markets in developing countries becoming increasingly important to companies in industrialized countries?

16. Is small size an obstacle to international expansion? Explain.

17. Name five countries considered most important by the respondents to the Ernst & Young's 1994 survey.

18. Why is infrastructure development considered to be so important by many developing countries?

19. What is a conservative estimate for infrastructure expenditures by developing countries by the year 2000?

20. How will educated individuals in developing countries benefit from their active involvement in infrastructure development projects?

21. Name two problems that are intensified by growth and industrialization.

22. What is the major cause of environmental pollution, global warming, and depletion of natural resources?

23. Why does corruption have a relatively more drastic impact on a developing country?

24. What is nepotism?

25. What are the root causes of political instability and social disorder?

26. Name three of the factors that contribute to political stability and social unrest.

27. What are the consequences of political instability in developing countries? In industrialized countries?

28. List some of the challenges facing developing countries.

29. What is the role of accounting in emerging economies?

30. How are financial reporting and disclosure affected by a shift from socialistic to market oriented systems?

31. How can accountants be helpful in the strategic decisions made for infrastructure projects?

32. What accounting area is clearly a natural for designing and implementing control systems to curb corruption?

33. What kinds of opportunities exist in developing countries for governmental accounting?

Exercises/Problems

13-1 Many developing countries consider the development of infrastructure critical for continued growth.

Required:
(1) Describe what is meant by infrastructure. Give specific reasons why infrastructure development is considered a necessity by many developing countries.
(2) Discuss the role of decision making in infrastructure development.

13-2 The chapter describes the strategies companies should adopt to gain competitive advantage in obtaining infrastructure development contracts.

Required:
(1) Describe and critique those strategies.
(2) Explain if those strategies will work in countries that have a high degree of political instability and social unrest.

13-3 Select an Asian country that has had political instability in recent years. Research the impact of political instability on the country's economic development. Prepare a two-page report of your research findings.

13-4 Do the requirements in Problem 13-3 for an African country.

13-5 Do the requirements in Problem 13-3 for a Latin American country

13-6 In a report of approximately one to two pages, describe how internal auditing can contribute in many different ways in developing countries. Focus especially on the accounting and other internal controls.

13-7   Describe the role of cost accounting in facilitating economic growth of a developing country in a report of approximately one to two pages.

13-8   If a multinational enterprise is operating in a country, it should respect the country's cultural values and not attempt to impose the values of a foreign culture, i.e., the base country of the multinational. Do you agree? Disagree? Provide reasons to support your answer.

13-9   The following remarks were made by Pehr Gyllenhammar, Chairman of Volvo, as the keynote speaker at the 14th World Congress of Accountants in Washington, D.C., in October 1993:

> The world economy in the 1990s is operating with an entirely different set of systems than those of the 1950s and 1960s. But there was in those days, whether you liked it or not, someone clearly in charge of the systems. There was a responsibility for stability, and the United States assumed that responsibility. In today's multipolar world, there is no clear leadership. No one has the power or the means to assume responsibility for managing the new systems. And we don't seem to be able to do it collectively.
>
> So the global economy of the 1990s is leaderless—and we have plenty of recent and current evidence of this—while at the same time there is a lengthening agenda of issues requiring leadership. The risk is that we will be driven by accident and not by design. So what will we call the 1990s—the no-navigation 1990s? And what lessons can we learn from where we are now and how we got here?
>
> Lesson number one is that international leadership is indispensable but is now in short supply. Vulgar election and cheap-shot referendum campaigns will not help. A leaderless global economy is likely to be highly accident-prone, putting at stake our institutions and our stability.
>
> Lesson number two is to focus on fundamentals, the very simple things that were so often seemingly forgotten in the 1980s. Soul-searching for subtleties is not the task at this point. Productivity is still the source of wealth creation, certainly not inflated asset values and financial engineering. Leverage is not good when it gets out of hand, that is, when it stretches the balance sheets.
>
> Lesson number three is, don't believe the market can solve everything. It was only a couple of years ago when we were told there would never again be a shortage of capital; now banks hardly lend money. And in today's economic climate we should not rely on the market's returning to 'normal.'

Required: Comment on the above statements by Mr. Gyllenhammar.

13-10   Below are excerpts from an article "Is Democracy Bad for Growth?" published in *Business Week* (7 June 1993, p. 84).

> But that freedom of choice is hardly a prerequisite for economic growth. On the contrary, it often seems to hinder it. India has languished under democratic

leadership, while Chile and South Korea, both dictatorships until recently, are success stories. Today, capitalism thrives without democracy, as the rapid growth charted by China's communist leaders amply demonstrates.

Nor does democracy ensure growth for the world's leading industrialized nations. Many are mired in recession or sluggish recovery, and democratic governments from Italy to Japan have been damaged by scandal and aren't delivering growth. Just a few years after the fall of the Berlin Wall and communism's failure in Eastern Europe, democracy's weaknesses seem glaring.

Just what is the relationship between democracy and growth? John F. Helliwell, an economist at the University of British Columbia, compared economic results for nearly 100 nations from 1960 to 1985 and concluded that there was a slight downdraft for democracies compared with nondemocracies or authoritarian regimes. His findings confirm the view that over the near term, authoritarian governments, especially those that offer citizens "economic rights" such as the protection of private property, can achieve strong results.

Required: Comment on the above statement. Provide reasons to support your statements.

13-11 The chapter mentions several challenges (problems) that make it more difficult to take advantage of the opportunities in developing countries. These include legal, work force, banking, and infrastructure problems, among others. Take one or more of these problems and discuss how a multinational might structure and conduct its operations to profit despite the obstacles. Hint: There is no "correct" answer for this problem, but some answers are certainly more thoughtful than others.

13-12 Research the current state of the accounting profession and prepare a report not exceeding 500 words for one or more of the following. Be prepared to discuss your findings in class.
(1) A Latin American country.
(2) An Asian country.
(3) An African country.

13-13 Research the current state of accounting education and prepare a report not exceeding 500 words for one or more of the following. Be prepared to discuss your findings in class.
(1) A Latin American country.
(2) An Asian country.
(3) An African country.

Case: Corruption—An Effective Equalizer of the Free Market System? And Don't Forget Mutual Pleasure!

In its 21 August 1995 issue, *Fortune* published an article on corruption in Asia, accompanied by a chart titled "Asia Corrupt-O-Meter."[25] The article stated that American companies seeking business in Asia face a dilemma: Huge, attractive emerging huge markets (with billions of consumers) are also the most corrupt in Asia. The article was based on a report by the Hong Kong-based firm, Political & Economic Risk Consultancy Ltd. The firm has been analyzing corruption and political stability for more than a decade. According to the consulting firm, paying off government officials to gain business can add 5 percent to operating costs in China.

The article stated that what bothers business executives most is their inability to take legal recourse against "squeeze tactics." The suggested solution by the consultancy firm was to learn how the system works in each place, and cultivate local leaders without giving them questionable payments. The author of the *Fortune* article was less than fully convinced by this approach. "Easier said than done," he stated, "particularly when competitors show up with briefcases full of cash."[26]

Political & Economic Risk Consultancy Ltd. compiled the corruption rating by surveying both its own analysts and 95 corporate managers from North America, Europe, and Australia. For comparison, the 95 managers rated corruption in their home countries at an average of 2.12 on a scale of 1 (least corrupt) to 10 (most corrupt). Singapore was rated at 1.19 and Japan at 1.97. According to Kenneth Sawka, an analyst at the Futures Group (a U.S. firm that advises companies on strategies), Asia is not the most corrupt region for business. He stated that corruption, for example, is far more pervasive and brash in Russia than in China. Following publication of the article, some interesting viewpoints were expressed by readers who wrote letters to the *Fortune* editor. The Managing Director of a firm in Thailand wrote:[27]

> The practice not only reflects the mutual consent of the giver and taker but also implies mutual pleasure, and should be called anything but "corruption." Giving money for favors is embedded in human nature. It spreads the wealth around and acts as an effective equalizer of the free-market system. The strongest and the biggest do not always win over the little guys with this system. And what is wrong with that?

> Perhaps a more appropriate title for the table you labeled "Asia Corrupt-O-Meter" would be "Business Opportunity Cost Index," or "In-Country Wealth Distribution Program Cost Index." You should also rank all the countries in the world. I bet the U.S. would be in the top five.

[25] Louis Kraar, "How Corrupt is Asia," *Fortune*, 21 August 1995, p. 26.

[26] *Ibid.*

[27] *Fortune*, 18 September 1995, p. 14.

A reader in the U.S. wrote:[28]

> Why do we insist on preaching morality? Payoffs are against American law. That law restricts our investing in the rest of the world. To us it may be a perception of corruption; to others it is a business expense. What I call blatant corruption is the boondoggles, lobbies, etc. right on our home ground. They are causing more harm to our economy than foreign payoffs.

A letter from a Ph.D. candidate in economics from China, studying at a U.S. university, appeared in the next issue of *Fortune:*[29]

> Basically, paying bribes is just a redistribution of wealth among different economic agents within the system. It makes more sense to view corruption in China as a way to privatize the state-owned economy.

> For example, a businessman friend from Korea gave a Chinese customs officer two gold necklaces and got a whole container of goods entered without paying one penny of customs tax. Because the two necklaces cost much less than the customs tax he should pay, his operating cost is actually lower.

> The real problem for an American businessman in China could be how to find the right person to bribe. But the cost of this learning process should not add 5 percent to operating costs if you are reasonably smart. And I've been amazed at how smart those foreign business people I met in Beijing are, and how fast they learn.

Required:
(1) Comment on the methodology used by Political & Economic Risk Consultancy Ltd. to analyze and rate countries on a corruption scale.
(2) Can bribes be viewed just as an expense of doing business? Why or why not?
(3) One of the readers stated that domestic lobbying in the U.S. does more harm to the U.S. economy than foreign payoffs. Do you agree? Give reasons for your position.
(4) The readers who wrote letters to the editor of *Fortune* made provocative comments regarding the "benefits" of paying bribes. List those claimed benefits and critique each one.
(5) What is your opinion of the solution proposed by the firm to avoid paying bribes? Do you think this would be an effective approach? Give reasons.
(6) Can you think of an approach that would be more effective?

---

[28] *Ibid.*

[29] *Fortune,* 2 October 1995, p. 29.

References

Accounting Standards Committee. *The Corporate Report.* London: Institute of Chartered Accountants in England and Wales, 1975.

Aguilar, Linda M., and Mike A. Singer. "Big Emerging Markets and U.S. Trade." *Economic Perspectives,* July/August 1995, pp. 2-13.

Arora, Vasantha. "Communist Basu Turns Realist for Dollars." *India-West,* 30 June 1995.

"ASEAN Plans Tariff Cuts on Farm Items." *Gulf News* (United Arab Emirates), 26 August 1995, p. 17.

"Asia's Competing Capitalisms." *The Economist,* 24 June 1995, pp. 16-17.

Barnathan, Joyce, Pete Engardio, Ellen White, Dave Lindorff, and Greg Burns. "Has Singapore Got What It Takes to Be a Finance Powerhouse?" *Business Week,* 20 March 1995, pp. 54-56.

Barrett, Amy. "It's a Small (Business) World." *Business Week,* 17 April 1995, pp. 96-101.

Baydoun, N., and R. Willett. "Cultural Relevance of Western Accounting Systems to Developing Countries." *ABACUS,* March 1995, pp. 67-92.

Bebbington, J. "The European Community Fifth Action Plan: Towards Sustainability." *Social and Environmental Accounting,* vol. 13, no. 1 (1993), pp. 9-11.

Business, Accountancy and the Environment: A Policy and Research Agenda. London: Institute of Chartered Accountants in England and Wales, 1992.

China: A Guide for Businessmen and Investors. Coopers & Lybrand CIEC: Beijing, China, 1993.

Cohen, Jeffrey R., Laurie W. Pant, and David J. Sharp. "Culture-Based Ethical Conflicts Confronting Multinational Accounting Firms." *Accounting Horizons, September 1993, pp. 1-13.*

Coopers & Lybrand. *Mexico: A Business and Investment Guide.* New York: American Institute of Certified Public Accountants, July 1994.

Dawson, Margaret. "Two Tigers Sharpen Up Their Markets." *Business Week,* 24 October 1994, pp. 50-51.

Environmental Accounting and Auditing: Survey of Current Activities and Developments. Bruxelles: Fédération des Experts Comptables Européens, 1993.

Environmental Accounting: The Issues. Pittsburgh, Penn.: Price Waterhouse, 1991.

Environmental Costs: Accounting and Disclosure—A Price Waterhouse Desktop Resource. Pittsburgh, Penn.: Price Waterhouse, 1992.

Environmental Costs and Liabilities: Accounting and Reporting Issues. Canadian Institute of Chartered Accountants: Toronto, Canada, 1993.

"GE's Brave New World." *Business Week,* 8 November 1993, pp. 64-70.

Glasgall, William, Dave Lindorff, Drusilla Menaker, Ian Katz, Elisabeth Malkin, and Bill Javetski. "Global Investing." *Business Week,* 11 September 1995, pp. 68-78.

Gray, R. H. *Accounting for the Environment.* London: Paul Chapman Publishing Ltd., 1993.

Gray, R. H., and Bebbington, K. J. "Accounting Environment and Sustainability." *Business Strategy and the Environment,* summer (Part 2), 1993, pp. 1-11.

Gray, R. H., and Symon, I. W. "An Environmental Audit by any other Name. . . ." *Integrated Environmental Management,* 6 February 1992, pp. 9-11.

Gyllenhammar, Pehr. "The Global Economy: Who Will Lead Next?" *Journal of Accountancy,* January 1993, pp. 61-64.

Hurt, Harry III. "It's Time to Get Real About Mexico." *Fortune,* 4 September 1995, pp. 98-106.

"India Plans End to Protectionism." *Gulf News* (United Arab Emirates), 26 August 1995, p. 21.

KPMG Peat Marwick. *International Survey of Environmental Reporting.* London: KPMG National Environment Unit, 1993.

"The Last Frontier: Phone Frenzy in the Developing World Is Charging up the Telecom Industry." *Business Week,* 18 September 1995, pp. 98-114.

Macve, R., and A. Carey, eds. *Business, Accountancy and the Environment: A Policy and Research Agenda.* London: Institute of Chartered Accountants in England and Wales, 1992.

Madhavmohan, V. K. "Reforms Must Address Disparity in Incomes." *India-West,* 7 April 1995, pp. 4-6.

Maltby, J. "Review of 'Environmental Auditing and the Role of the Accounting Profession.'" *Accounting and Business Research,* winter 1993.

Matthews, M. R. *Socially Responsible Accounting.* London: Chapman and Hall, 1993.

The Measurement of Corporate Social Performance. New York: American Institute of Certified Public Accountants, 1977.

Moshavi, Sharon, Pete Engardio, Shekhar Hattangadi, and Dave Lindorff. "India Shakes Off Its Shackles." *Business Week,* 30 January 1995, pp. 48-49.

Multinational Investments in Emerging Markets. New York: Ernst & Young, 1994.

Nakarmi, Laxmi, Joan Warner, and Margaret Dawson. "Two Tigers Sharpen up Their Markets." *Business Week,* 24 October 1994, pp. 50-51.

Neff, Robert, Michael Shari, Joyce Barnathan, Margaret Dawson, and Edith Updike. "Japan's New Identity." *Business Week,* 10 April 1995, pp. 108-114.

Owen, D., ed. *Green Reporting.* London: Chapman and Hall, 1992.

Perks, R. W. *Accounting and Society.* London: Chapman and Hall, 1993.

Power, Christopher, Rose Brady, Joyce Barnathan, and Karen Lowry Miller. "Second Thoughts on Going Global." *Business Week,* 13 March 1995, pp. 48-49.

Riahi-Belkaoui, Ahmed. *Accounting in the Developing Countries.* London: Quorum Books, 1994.

Salter, S. B., and F. Niswander. "Cultural Influence on the Development of Accounting Systems Internationally: A Test of Gray's [1988] Theory." *Journal of International Business Studies,* vol. 26, no. 2 (1995), pp. 379-397.

Saudagaran, S. M., and G. C. Biddle. "Foreign Listing Location: A Study of MNCs and Stock Exchanges in Eight Countries." *Journal of International Business Studies,* vol. 26, no. 2, pp. 319-341.

Stead, W. E., and J. G. Stead. *Management for a Small Planet.* Newbury Park, Cal.: Sage, 1992.

"The Struggle for Vietnam's Soul." *The Economist,* 24 June 1995, pp. 33-34.

United Nations Centre for Transnational Corporations. *International Accounting.* New York: United Nations, 1992.

United Nations Conference on Trade and Development, Programme on Transnational Corporations. *Accounting, Valuation, and Privatization.* New York: United Nations, 1993.

Wallace, R., S. Olesegun, John M. Samuels, and Richard J. Briston. *Research in Third World Accounting: A Research Annual,* vol. 1. London: Jai Press Ltd., 1990.

Winkle, Gary M., H. Fenwick Huss, and Chen Xi-Zhu. "Accounting Standards in the People's Republic of China: Responding to Economic Reforms." *Accounting Horizons,* September 1994, pp. 48-57.

Winkle, Gary M., H. Fenwick Huss, and Qiwen Tang. "Accounting Education in the People's Republic of China: An Update." *Issues in Accounting Education,* fall 1992, pp. 179-192.

Chapter 14

Eastern European Countries

With the disintegration of the U.S.S.R. and the reunification of Germany, the former countries of the Eastern bloc are beginning the process of moving to a free market economy. The transition to a market economy necessarily includes a high degree of privatization. **Privatization** involves the transfer of property from the state to individuals and private enterprises.

Accounting has a key role in the transition from a centrally planned economy to a market-based economy. Accounting, as the language of business, is crucial to a business enterprise. The effectiveness of privatization programs is dependent to a great extent on application of market-driven accounting concepts—especially managerial accounting concepts.

This chapter deals with the development of accounting standards in the Eastern bloc countries. This chapter begins with an overview of socialist accounting. Second, the topic of privatization is discussed. Third, four case studies of countries that have made political and economic progress in their move toward a market economy are presented: Hungary, Poland, the Czech Republic, and Russia. Reviewing these four countries will help us understand the challenges and opportunities faced by the region.

Choosing representative examples of transformations to capitalism in the former Eastern bloc countries is not an easy task. Wars and economic collapse have devastated several countries in the region. Wars in the former Yugoslavia (Bosnia-Herzegovina and parts of Croatia); economic ruin in Bulgaria and Romania; ethnic conflicts in Armenia, Azerbaijan, Georgia, Moldova, and Tajikistan—all have made economic progress difficult.

Socialist Accounting

Financial Accounting Systems

Certain commonalities with a capitalist system exist in socialist accounting. They include double-entry bookkeeping (in most cases), the calculation of profit in the case of a "khozraschet" (a self-supporting enterprise), periodic reporting of financial results, and use of the historical cost basis. However, under a non-market system the state has complete control over the volume and flow of goods and services. Prices of goods and services are set by the central planning authorities of the government, and not by market forces.

Since entrepreneurial activity was minimal in the former Eastern bloc and public ownership of enterprises was the rule, it is understandable why accounting systems were based on macroeconomics principles. In fact, there is a distinct similarity in the accounting for not-for-profit organizations, such as public universities, and socialist accounting systems. In essence, it was a fund-based accounting system. In such accounting systems, the main objective is to ensure that resources are used for the intended purposes. In socialist accounting, the main classifications of a balance sheet are as shown in Exhibit 14–1.

Exhibit 14–1   Sample Socialist Balance Sheet

A Socialist Enterprise
Balance Sheet
December 31, 19xx

Active		Passive	
Fixed and noncirculating assets	x	Sources of own and equivalent capital	x
Normal circulating means	x	Bank credits	x
Cash, settlements and other assets	x	Bank, credits and other liabilities	x
Balance	xx	Balance	xx

Working capital in a socialist entity consists of current assets only. Budgetary accounts are integrated with actual to determine whether working capital exceeds or is under the budgeted amount. A socialist system accounting is necessarily rigid and detailed. There is an account for each and every item because subsidiary ledgers are *not* used.

The distribution of profit is another area that is different in a socialist enterprise from a capitalist entity. Profits are used to pay for fixed assets, bank interest charges, and reserves. Any residual profit goes into the state budget. A simplified version of this distribution appears in Exhibit 14–2.

Exhibit 14–2   Sample Socialist Distribution of Profit Statement

A Socialist Enterprise
Distribution of Profit
For the Year Ended December 31, 19xx

Profit distribution:

- For productive assets
- Bank interest charges
- Other
- Macroeconomics measures (economic stimulation funds)

Cost Accounting Systems

Cost accounting systems in socialist countries are also different from those in capitalist countries. The objective of these systems is to provide information for calculating national income. Since there is no market system that dictates the prices of goods and services, the void is filled by standardized costs. Cost standards, however, are imposed rather than developed internally.

The intent of this overview is to give the student an appreciation of the problems in making the transition from a centrally planned economy to a market-based economy. This requires an entirely new orientation. Concepts such as profit, easily understood in free market economies, are alien to socialist economies. The next section discusses legal and accounting problems facing former Eastern bloc countries in making the transition to a free market economy.

Privatization

Conversion from a planned economy to a market economy takes place under laws dealing with business activities. Matters covered in a commercial code include issues such as property ownership and transfer, payment of creditors, bankruptcy, and employee rights. The purpose of these laws is to make it easier to operate under a market economy. *Thus, a prerequisite to privatization is a national legal framework.* Foreign capital is often invited to participate in the ownership of enterprises. In certain cases, the percentage owned by foreign investors may be restricted. Further, there may be a stipulation that ownership shares subsequently may be transferred only to nationals. The articles of incorporation may dictate the amount of profits that may be distributed to shareholders. Restrictions may be made as to who may be a member of the board of directors. Important to the survival of the enterprise is the infrastructure, licenses, and foreign exchange allotments. Negotiations with governments must be undertaken to ensure that these matters are handled efficiently.

For countries changing from a centrally planned economy to a market-based economy, legal structures—taken for granted in market-based economies—must be put into place. Constitutional changes may be required, such as amendments allowing individuals to own property. Accounting and reporting problems to be addressed while changing to a market economy include:

- Transition period problems
- Inflation
- Valuation
- Disclosure

Transition Period Problems

Since there is no record of previous enterprise performance, it is difficult to predict future performance. In most cases, there are no meaningful financial statements and certainly no marketing expertise. Thus, it is important to draw up accounting and auditing laws. As mentioned earlier, centrally planned economies use a fund accounting system. Since the focus on fund accounting is providing public services from appropriations, the thinking has to change so that financial reporting encompasses a profit orientation. One of the more vexing problems is how to account for equity in property when the state, individual, and/or enterprise may all claim ownership.

Although the inclination may be to set up accounting and auditing laws based on other countries' laws, these laws may not be well suited to a given country. Important environmental factors must be considered. A conscientious effort must be made to ensure that the accounting and reporting laws established do not create confusion or lend themselves to misinterpretation or misapplication.

Three elements essential to an effective transition to the market system are:

1. The adoption of a set of comprehensive accounting standards.
2. The development of an accounting profession.
3. The training of personnel to carry on the accounting function under a market-based economy.

An accounting framework is needed to determine the objectives of financial reporting and identification of the principal users. To this end, an independent accounting body should be set up to develop accounting standards. The development of an accounting profession is needed so that strides can be made in development of improved accounting theory and practice. Finally, personnel must be retrained so that they approach the discipline from a free-market perspective.

Accounting data. The accounting data used in a centrally planned economy is not geared to providing information on performance. Unrealistic depreciation rates, the lack of responsibility centers, the emphasis on production rather than profitability, and the lack of external accountability all make the accounting information meaningless for decision making. Concepts such as time value of money, discounted cash flow, and payback methods for investment decisions are largely foreign to accounting and financial personnel in countries with centrally planned economies.

Accounting personnel in such countries have been accustomed to a rigid and mandatory system. It is difficult for them to appreciate the accounting concepts embodied in a market-driven system that often calls for the exercise of professional judgment. To implement change, patience and education are important for success.

Inflation

Inflation has been a problem in different parts of the world at different times. The topic of inflation was discussed in Chapter 5. The former socialist countries have been grappling with inflation problems. Exhibit 14–3 shows annual inflation rates in Hungary, Poland, the Czech Republic, and Russia for a five-year period.

Exhibit 14–3 Comparative Inflation Rates				
	Hungary	**Poland**	**Czech Republic**	**Russia**
1988	15.5	60.2	0.2	—
1989	17.0	251.0	1.4	—
1990	29.0	585.0	10.8	—
1991	36.4	0.3	59.0	92.7
1992	23.0	43.0	11.0	1,353.0

Source: International Monetary Fund, *World Economic Outlook*, October 1993, p. 148.

Prior to privatization, inflation issues were not a major concern for Eastern bloc countries. But as the purchasing power of the monetary unit decreases through inflation, the resulting accounting issues require attention.

Valuation

Valuation of assets in formerly planned economies is often difficult. The fixed assets area is the most difficult for valuation purposes. For land, buildings, and equipment there are no established market values. In such cases, net profit may be a guide in estimating market value.

Example   Assume the following situation:

Net profit = 100,000 rubles
Current assets = 500,000 rubles
Rate of return on current assets = 10%
Rate of return on fixed assets = 20%
Therefore, the return on current assets is 50,000 rubles (10% × 500,000)
This leaves 50,000 rubles (net profit of 100,000 rubles less 50,000 rubles return on current assets) as the return on fixed assets
Thus, the total cost assigned to fixed assets is 250,000 rubles (50,000 ÷ 20%)

Other valuation issues concern receivables and inventories. In the case of receivables and inventories, an analysis must be made of potential losses. For receivables, a provision for bad debts must be made. Computation of net realizable values of inventory (estimated selling prices less disposal costs) may lead to write-downs.

To comply with market-driven accounting standards, classification of liabilities must be changed. The usual categories of liabilities, including trade payables, accruals, taxes payable, and long-term debt, must be presented in the balance sheet. Items such as pension and other related liabilities and contingencies are also important elements of the liability section of the balance sheet.

Disclosure

In offering capital stock and other securities for sale to the public in a market economy, it is necessary to disclose information that is needed by the user to make an informed judgment. Figure 14–1 shows the main steps in a public offering:

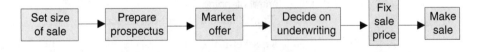

Figure 14–1   Main Steps in a Public Offering

Potential investors need information on the risks and rewards surrounding a security issue. In a market economy, it is necessary to supply users with audited financial statements of an entity. Investors assume that the financial statements present fairly the financial position and the results of operations of an enterprise in conformity with generally accepted accounting principles. The prospectus includes details of the financial information and also the issuer's past history. It presents comparative audited information as well as pro forma information. This information is deemed essential to investors in formulating opinions about the risks and rewards associated with the investment. No such system of disclosure exists in centrally planned economies because of the absence of a tradition of security offerings.

Training of Accounting Personnel

Under socialist accounting systems, the accounting function is limited to bookkeeping. Transformation to a free market economy requires that accounting personnel be retrained so that they understand underlying accounting assumptions and concepts such as accounting entity, periodicity, going concern, matching, full disclosure, and revenue recognition. The attendant conventions of conservatism and materiality also must be understood.

Accounting must be viewed as an information system providing relevant and timely information for decision making. This requires a completely new orientation for the accountants of former Eastern bloc countries. It has been estimated that about 2 million accountants must be retrained.

Besides the accounting assumptions and conventions mentioned above, the importance and content of a system of internal control also must be understood. The audit function, related to the internal control system, is a new phenomenon for accountants in formerly planned economies. The fundamentals of a market economy need to be taught to make market-driven accounting meaningful to the trainees. This requires that the instructor be knowledgeable in accounting systems both in a planned economy and in a free market economy.

Financial Statement Practices and Trends

The rest of this chapter is devoted to a review of financial statement practices and trends in Hungary, Poland, the Czech Republic, and Russia.

Hungary

History. From the 1800s to the present, the history of accounting principles in Hungary can be divided into three distinct periods:

1. 1800 to 1947   Western European influence
2. 1948 to 1988   Central planning
3. 1989 to present   Transition to a market-driven economy

Before the transition to a market-driven economy, the main task of the Hungarian economy was providing factual data to the government for purposes of controlling and measuring the economic activity of state enterprises. Since there were no market mechanisms, valuations of the firm were not needed. Accounting was a tool for assessing macro economic policies.

A key element in privatization was the 1990 opening of the Hungarian Stock Exchange, the first stock exchange to be opened in an Eastern bloc country. Opening the stock exchange necessitated development of accounting standards. In 1992, an accounting law, developed under the Accounting Department of the Ministry of Finance, was introduced. This law is in agreement with the IASC International Accounting Standards and the EU Directives. The law is designed for various users of accounting information such as the Union of Entrepreneurs, Chamber of Commerce, the World Bank, accounting professionals, academics, and others.

Form and content of financial statements. Besides the income statement and the balance sheet, notes to the financial statements and the board of directors report must be prepared. These should be adopted by the shareholders and filed with the registry court by May 31 of the following year. These statements, considered in the public domain, include the auditor's opinion and shareholders' resolution on distribution of profit.

Balance sheet. Previously, customers' advance payments were netted against accounts receivable. Now they are shown separately as liabilities in the balance sheet. For decision-making purposes, management can now focus on the efficient use of the entire asset base. Intangible assets are shown in a separate category. They are not included as part of fixed assets, as was the practice previously. Assets are shown according to liquidity and liabilities and are listed according to maturity. There is still no shareholders' equity section.

Income statement. The income statement includes revenues from sales and other sources. In Western Europe, two models of costs of sales can be used. They are the cost of sales model and the total cost model. Under the **cost of sales model,** the manufacturing costs are shown first, followed by distribution costs, and finally administrative costs. The cost of sales model is followed in Hungary with the refinement that manufacturing costs, marketing costs, and administrative costs are divided into the direct and indirect elements.

Accounting principles and practices. Before 1991, accounting regulations issued by the Ministry of Finance were geared toward tax reporting and statistical data for national economic planning. Since 1991, the law on accounting has been the source of generally accepted accounting principles. It has been heavily influenced by the Fourth and Seventh Directives of the EU and by the International Accounting Standards of the IASC.

Since the law has been in existence for a relatively short time, there is little information available on problems of its interpretation. Moreover, there is not enough history to determine how entities are complying with it. Among principles that are incorporated in the law are going concern, historical cost, conservatism, accrual accounting, truthfulness, consistency, comprehensives, clarity, and the use of the Hungarian language and currency.

Consolidation policy. According to the new law, if the entity owns 50 percent or less of another entity, the cost method of accounting should be used. If ownership is more than 50 percent or when there is a voting majority, the long-term investment should be consolidated. Any minority ownership appears in the balance sheet as a long-term investment. This requirement is effective in 1995.

Capital. Under the new law, owners' equity is divided into three sources:

1. Share capital
2. Capital reserves (share premium and other contributions not returnable)
3. Reserve for profit adjustment (retained earnings)

Treasury shares are shown as assets provided that such treasury shares are acquired from reserves. To this extent, then, it is not distributable as dividends and requires disclosure.

If there is a deficit, the deficit is shown as an asset if shareholders are obligated to fund it. Otherwise, it is shown as a negative item in the liability section.

Liabilities. The liability section is not very comprehensive. For example, it does not include all accrued liabilities. Although there may be differences between taxable income and accounting income, the balance sheet only reflects the liability for taxes payable. Also, there is no requirement to include any contingent liabilities. Two items that appear as liabilities are expected losses from accounts receivables and expected losses from obsolete inventories.

Foreign currency. Foreign currency transactions are recorded at the rate in effect at the date of the transaction. Assets and liabilities denominated in a foreign currency are translated at the rate in effect at the balance sheet date.

Property, plant, and equipment. Land used to be recorded without any assigned value. There are still some unsettled issues relating to the land account. Future legislation dealing with land is expected to resolve these issues.

Other items of property, plant, and equipment are valued using the historical cost basis only, and no other basis is acceptable. Although depreciation standards used to be fairly rigid, there is now some flexibility in this area. The depreciation method for book and tax purposes may be different. The law prescribes straight line depreciation, except that since 1994 accelerated depreciation methods have been allowed for certain types of assets.

Intangibles. Goodwill and other intangibles may be capitalized only if purchased from a third party. Intangibles other than goodwill may be written off over 6 years. Goodwill has an amortization period of 5 to 15 years.

Inventories. Under the new law, the actual cost or the weighted average methods are allowed for the valuation of purchased inventories.

Taxation. Reported income and taxable income amounts may not be the same. Certain adjustments are made to reported income to arrive at taxable income. The corporate income tax rate in 1995 is 18 percent.

Pensions. Pensions are handled through centralized planning. Contributions consist of contributions by both the employer and the employee. The portion paid by the employer is higher.

Trends. The new law goes a long way toward adopting the International Accounting Standards of the IASC. While certain areas are not yet in conformity, progress has been made in making financial statements more useful.

In a market economy, it is important for a firm to know its cash flow from operations, investing, and financing activities. Presently, there is no requirement for such a statement. Capitalization of leases is another area not covered by the law.

Accounting is essential to economic progress. It can be a powerful tool for facilitating the economic changes required in moving from a controlled economy to a market-driven economy. It appears that accounting principles will evolve naturally during the conversion to a market economy.

Poland

History. Accounting in Poland was influenced by Russia, Prussia, and Austria in the 1800s. However, the Napoleonic Code (1807) had the greatest impact on Polish standards. Later, when the Polish Commercial Code was enacted, and domestic law codified, accounting regulation was influenced by fiscal and tax considerations.

Polish accounting standards were supplanted during World War II when Germany occupied Poland. The Germans introduced a uniform German chart of accounts. When the Soviets took over, however, a centrally planned economy was instituted.

With the privatization moves of the late 1980s, the formation of foreign capital joint ventures, and the birth of commercial banking, accounting standards have necessarily been adapted to capture the new types of economic events. The majority of accounting standards are issued by the Ministry of Finance. Some accounting regulations are issued by the Polish Statistical Office.

Obstacles to change have arisen, however. There are multiple reasons for resistance to change.

> In a setback to the Polish Government's economic reform program, the Parliament in Warsaw defeated a bill today that would have converted 600 state companies into private enterprises at a single stroke. . . .

> After three years of delays, confusion and wrangling, the bill was regarded by experts as crucial in Poland's drive to adopt a market economy.

> Deputies who voted against the bill said they opposed the idea of foreigners having control over Polish companies, and many workers fear that privatization could cost them their jobs through layoffs.

> . . . In Poland, many workers favor privatization in theory, but they are also suspicious of it, especially when their own factory is at stake. Some fear being laid off, since companies that had turned private have often announced cutbacks as part of a restructuring to become competitive. . . .

> Damiam Damianos, the Warsaw representative of the International Finance Corporation, an affiliate of the World Bank that provides financing to private companies, found that workers had "no concept of depreciation."

> "They naturally assume that these huge plants with all that heavy machinery has to be worth millions of dollars," he said. "There's no such thing as the notion that something is worth a lot only if someone is willing to buy it."

> Mr. Damianos said the bill created an alliance between "the ideologues against the idea of foreign involvement and those who just felt it was too complicated."

> So far, privatization in Poland has been piecemeal. For three years, four governments prodded state companies and courted Western businessmen, but with few results. Foreign investment in Poland is less than in Hungary or the former Czechoslovakia.

Out of 3,500 companies previously owned by the state or local governments, only 54 had been sold to private investors as of December. Sixteen other were listed on the new Warsaw stock exchange, and several hundred companies, most of them small concerns, were taken over by their employees and managers.

"Three years ago there were high expectations that we would privatize some 50 percent of the state's assets after two or three years," Jerzy Thieme, an adviser to the Minister of Privatization, said in a recent interview in Warsaw. "It didn't happen."

He estimated that between 10 percent and 20 percent had been privatized.[1]

In January 1991, the Ministry of Finance issued a decree approving the current accounting standards. These standards are an adaptation of the EU Fourth Directive.

In line with the EU Eighth Directive, the auditing profession is changing. However, there are still State Authorized Accountants who are working mostly for large enterprises. They make sure that accounting reports meet the letter of the law. There are also accountants trained by the World Bank whose function is to audit enterprises that have received loans from the World Bank. International accounting firms are also present to audit joint ventures' business operations.

Form and content of financial statements. Since Polish companies are eager to get foreign investors, they realize the importance of having their financial statements comply with International Accounting Standards. The required financial statements include a balance sheet, an income statement, and notes to the financial statements.

Balance sheet. The balance sheet has the following categories: capital and reserves; liabilities and provisions; property, plant, and equipment; financial assets; and inventories. Manufactured inventory is shown at cost or net realizable values.

Income statement (profit and loss account). This statement is divided into two categories: costs and expenses, and income and profits.

Accounting principles and practices. The historical cost convention is followed except in cases where there has been hyperinflation.

Consolidation policy. If business enterprises are reported into divisions and prepare separate financial records, they must prepare consolidated financial statements. Intercompany receivables and payables must be eliminated.

Capital. There is a division between share capital and reserve capital. Statutes determine how to divide the former. In addition, the share premium account, revaluation reserves, and long-term reserves are all separately disclosed. Subscriptions receivable for unpaid shares are disclosed as an asset. The last item in this section is the profit and loss, which has been carried forward (retained earnings). Special reserves are shown as a liability at values determined under accounting regulations.

---

[1] "Polish Parliament Rejects Bill to Privatize Industries," *New York Times,* 19 March 1993, p. 3.

Liabilities. Trade creditors, taxes payable, and wages payable are some of the accounts that make up the short-term liabilities. Expenses can be accrued for up to three years. A distinction is made between long-term and short-term bank loans. The provision (allowance) for bad debts is considered a liability.

Foreign currency. The official rate of exchange at the year-end is used for monetary assets. Exchange gains and losses are shown in the income statement.

Property, plant, and equipment. Property, plant, and equipment are valued at historical cost. The straight line method of depreciation is used, although the accelerated method may be used in some cases.

Intangibles. Intangible assets are valued at historical cost, but are capitalized only if their value is more than the specified minimum amount. Goodwill is amortized over five years.

Inventories. Materials are valued at cost. First-in first-out, last-in first-out, or weighted average methods may be used for valuing inventories.

Taxation. The profit figure appearing on the financial statements is the basis for the tax liability. The corporate income tax in 1995 is at a rate of 40 percent. The general rate of value-added tax is 22 percent, although the rate of 7 percent applies to specified goods including food products, medicines, and various products for children.

Pensions. Social security comprises the pension system. In 1995, the contribution rate is 48.5 percent.

Trends. Harmonization of company law with the requirements of the European Union is an objective. For Poland to make a successful entry into the European market, it is important that improvements in financial reporting systems be made. The Securities Commission was established in 1991. It is influenced by the EU Fourth Directive. This should result in improvement in financial reporting.

Privatization, foreign investments, and democratization have created tremendous pressures on Poland to increase the number of trained accounting professionals and to improve accounting and reporting systems.

The Czech Republic

History. As in Hungary and Poland, accounting in the Czech Republic prior to Perestroika and Glasnost was essentially to comply with the directives of a centralized planned economy. Recent legislation has introduced many reforms. Audits of financial statements are designed to determine whether entities are in compliance with certain mandates.

Form and content of financial statements. For those companies using double-entry book-keeping, the financial statements consist of a balance sheet, profit and loss account (income statement), and notes to the financial statements. The notes detail the policies dealing with depreciation, valuation, etc. Enterprises not using double-entry bookkeeping must submit a statement of assets and liabilities and also a cash receipts and disbursements statement. The format for these is specified. An enterprise that is above a specified size must use a double-entry system.

Balance sheet. The Ministry of Finance recommends the format of financial statements. As of yet, there is no common format for a balance sheet.

Income statement. Results of company operations should be shown for the current year as well for the preceding five-year period. In addition, notes and comments should be included. Ratios and comments on recent developments are considered important disclosures.

Accounting principles and practices. According to the *Act on Accounting* and the Federal Finance Ministry decree "Chart of Accounts and Accounting Procedures," there is little flexibility in the use of accounting principles. Basically, these two pieces of legislation set forth the same principles that are contained in the EU Fourth Directive regarding historical cost, consistency, accrual accounting, the prudence concept, and limits on netting receivables and payables.

Consolidation policy. The Act states that if one entity owns 20 percent or more of another entity, consolidated financial statements must be prepared.

Capital. Companies created through the process of privatization are essentially share companies. They must disclose their shareholders' equity. The excess of par value is not part of capital, but is treated as revenue. A reserve is created from profit after tax at specified rate until the fund equals a specified percentage of shareholders' equity.

Liabilities. No distinction is made between current and noncurrent liabilities. Unlike other countries, bonds are measured at par value. The difference between market value and par value is shown as extraordinary revenue or extraordinary expense.

Foreign currency. Foreign currency transactions are converted at the rate on the date of the transaction. In translation, current assets and liabilities are translated at the rate in effect at date of the balance sheet. Provision is made for unrealized losses, but not for gains. The rate used is the one published by the Czech National Bank.

Property, plant, and equipment. Enterprises generally use the historical cost basis. Until 1991, land was not considered an asset since it was the property of the state. Property, plant, and equipment is valued at original cost. The straight line method or an accelerated method may be used for depreciation. Depreciation rates are based on the estimated life of the asset. A permanent decline in an asset's value requires a downward adjustment. Assets are not depreciated until placed in service.

Intangibles. Intangible assets consist of research and development costs related to patents, rights, royalties, and organizational costs.

Inventories. Materials are measured based on lower of cost or market. Since January 1991, the last-in first-out and first-in first-out methods are acceptable for inventory valuation.

Taxation. The corporate income tax rate is 41 percent. As of January 1995, the basic value-added tax rate is 22 percent, but a 5 percent rate applies to most services and various goods, including fuel and food items. Many goods and services are totally exempt from value-added tax.

Pensions. As in Hungary and Poland, social security takes care of the pension arrangements. The employers' social security contribution rate is higher than the employees' rate. As of January 1995, the rates were 26.25 percent for employers and 8.75 percent for employees.

Trends. Accounting and reporting standards and practice have been undergoing changes. Harmonization with the EU Directives and International Accounting Standards is the goal. Another goal is to have trained auditors in sufficient numbers to assume the duties that auditors assume in a market-driven economy. The Czech Republic has a relatively well-developed technology and a well-educated and skilled workforce.

Russia

History. Before the changes from a centralized economy to a market-driven economy, accounting was an end in itself rather than a tool for managing operations and providing information to users. The Russian economy is going through a period of rapid change as it struggles to adopt a free market system.

Form and content of financial statements. As in the case of the Czech Republic, the main financial statements are the balance sheet, the profit and loss account, and the accompanying notes to the statements. At present, financial statements consist of complicated forms.

Balance sheet. The Ministry of Finance mandated a balance sheet as of June 17, 1991. The sample balance sheet with classifications appears in Exhibit 14–4. Assets are not listed in order of liquidity. In category I of assets, fixed assets and other noncurrent assets are composed of tangible assets, intangible assets, and noncurrent investments. Under category I on the liability side are the sources of these assets: statutory fund, profit, and the depreciation of these assets. Under category II of assets are inventories and other costs. Category II on the liability side consists of claims, such as bank claims, on these assets. Finally, category III assets are monetary assets, securities, and settlements of assets converted into rubles. The sources of these assets appear in category III on the liability side—accounts payable, wages payable, and the like.

Exhibit 14–4   Russian Balance Sheet Format

Assets	Liabilities
I. Fixed assets and other noncurrent assets	I. Sources of assets (own resources)
II. Inventories and expenses relating to future periods	II. Bank credits for inventories and expenses relating to future periods
III. Monetary assets, settlements, and other assets	III. Bank loan payments and other liabilities

Source: Adapted from Adolf J. H. Enthoven, Jaroslav V. Sokolov, and Alexander M. Petrachkov, *Doing Business in Russia and the Other Former Soviet Republics: Accounting and Joint Venture Issues* (Montvale, New Jersey: Institute of Management Accountants, 1992), p. 27.

The balance sheet of a Russian entity provides balances at the beginning and end of the year. This presentation is comparable to the two-year comparative balance sheet common in Western countries.

Income statement. The main component of the profit and loss account consists of sales operations, general administrative costs, salary costs, and allocations to a reserve fund, which is required by law. Income is recognized at the time that cash is received rather than when there is a right to receive cash.

Accounting principles and practices. Russian accounting is still influenced by its heritage of a centrally controlled economy. Thus, accounting is mostly for tax reporting. Accounting principles are not developed to the extent that they have a noticeable impact on financial statements.

Capital. As in Western accounting, premium (or excess over stated value) is shown as a part of capital, but is included in the reserve fund.

Inflation accounting. Effects of inflation are a function of legislation.

Foreign currency. Monetary assets and liabilities denominated in foreign currencies are translated at the rate on the balance sheet date. The gain or loss appears in the profit and loss account and is taxable.

Taxation. The corporate income tax rate in 1995 is 35 percent, of which 22 percent is payable to regional authorities. The rate for contribution to regional authorities can be increased to 25 percent, thus making the overall tax rate 38 percent. The standard rate for value-added tax is 20 percent in 1995. A reduced 10 percent rate applies to certain food products and children's items. A special 3 percent value-added tax is charged in addition to the general value-added tax.

Pensions. Employers contribute to the pension fund at the rate of 28 percent and employees 1 percent of the gross payroll.

Inventories. The tax law is unclear as to inventory valuation. Recent legislation appears to allow only the weighted-average cost method for inventory valuation.

Property, plant, and equipment. The regulations generally allow only the straight line depreciation method. Accelerated depreciation may be used with specific approval of the tax authorities.

Trends. To facilitate the objectives of a market-driven economy, it is necessary that accounting and auditing be developed to such an extent that users of financial statements can make informed judgments about the risks and rewards of a particular investment option. Russia still does not have formal accounting standards. Existing accounting procedures do not conform to IASC standards, as is the case in several Eastern European countries.

Concluding Remarks

Political, economic, legal, and social systems in Eastern European countries are in a state of flux. The situation has not stabilized as quickly as many had expected, or at least hoped for, after the demise of communism. The whole area is going through a painful period of transition. Students should keep abreast of the developments in order to appreciate the current role of the region, and the individual countries of the region, in the global economy.

Note to Students

To keep abreast of privatization developments in Eastern Europe there is no better way than reading the current popular business press such as *The Wall Street Journal, Forbes, Business Week, Fortune, Financial Times, The Economist,* and publications of the "Big Six" accounting firms. Another good source of information is a newspaper with substantial coverage of world events, such as *The New York Times, The Christian Science Monitor,* or *The Los Angeles Times.*

To learn more on how accounting is changing in the former Soviet republics, consult the following journals: the *Journal of Accountancy,* the *IASC News,* the *Journal of International Financial Management and Accounting, Abacus,* the *Journal of International Accounting, Management Accounting,* and *The European Accounting Review.*

Other sources of information on accounting and related matters include the embassies of the various countries, the United Nations, the World Bank, the International Monetary Fund, and the U.S. Department of Commerce. To learn firsthand about financial reports, contact the stock exchanges—especially those in Poland and Hungary.

Chapter Summary

- The countries of Eastern Europe are presently in a state of transition. With the disintegration of the Soviet regime and the reunification of Germany, the transition to a market economy requires that infrastructures such as stock exchanges, banks, commercial laws, and accounting be in place.

- This chapter provided an overview of socialist accounting. The chapter also addressed the issue of privatization, together with the legal and accounting facets of such a move from a state-controlled economy to a market economy.

- Accounting problems involve the issues of transitioning, inflation, valuation, and disclosure to meet new challenges in the accounting function.

- Some progress has been made in countries such as Hungary, Poland, and the Czech Republic. After operating under a controlled economy for many decades, the necessary changes will take some time.

- Implementation of privatization is a complex undertaking. Human beings responsible for effecting change can have noticeable impact, as has been observed in Poland.
- To reach the goals of providing accounting information for a market-based economy, the three critical elements are a set of comprehensive accounting standards, development of an accounting profession, and training of accounting personnel.

Questions for Discussion

1. What is the objective of accounting in a state-controlled system?

2. How are prices set in a centrally controlled economy?

3. Why is a legal framework important in moving to a market-based economy?

4. What are the objectives of accounting in a market-oriented economy?

5. What are some of the problems in making the transition from a planned economy to a market-based economy?

6. "Valuation of assets can be a problem in the process of privatization." Explain.

7. Contrast accounting information needs in a planned economy versus a market-driven economy.

8. List the main steps of a public offering.

9. Why do potential investors need audited financial statements?

10. Why do accountants in Eastern bloc countries need to be retrained?

11. How do treasury shares appear in a Hungarian balance sheet?

12. Why are Polish companies interested in having their financial statements comply with IASC standards?

13. How is capital shown in a Polish balance sheet?

14. How are the requirements in the Czech Republic different for companies that do not use a double-entry system?

15. What are the sources of accounting principles in the Czech Republic?

16. What inventory valuation methods are acceptable in the Czech Republic?

17. What are the main elements of a profit and loss account in Russia?

18. Presently, what is the objective of accounting in Russia?

19. What is the accounting treatment of a gain or loss on foreign currency translation in Russia?

Exercises/Problems

14-1 Select the best available answer:

1. Which of the following is *not* a distinguishing characteristic of a unit of a centrally planned economy in contrast to a business enterprise in a market economy?
   a. Accounting systems are based on macroeconomics principles.
   b. A defined ownership cannot be sold or transferred.
   c. Cost accounting systems are less important.
   d. The profit motive is absent.

2. The financial reporting objectives of units in a centrally planned economy are:
   a. The same as the objectives of financial reporting by business enterprises.
   b. To ensure that resources are used for the intended purpose.
   c. Set forth in the International Accounting Standards.
   d. To assist governments to be publicly accountable in a socialist society.

3. The accounting system used by a unit of a centrally planned economy must make it possible to:
   a. Prepare a consolidated accrual basis statement for the unit.
   b. Prepare financial statements as required by the EU Fourth Directive.
   c. Present fairly the financial position of the units and results of its operation.
   d. Present the financial position of the funds.

4. A controlled economy reporting unit
   a. Publishes financial information the administration wants the public to have.
   b. Consolidates all financial data and publishes consolidated financial statements.
   c. Has an account for every item since subsidiary ledgers are not used.
   d. Publishes a comprehensive annual financial report.

14-2 Select the best available answer:

1. Which one of the following is *not* a requirement of the basic financial statements of a business enterprise in Hungary?
   a. Balance sheet.   c. Notes to the statements.
   b. Income statement.   d. Cash flow statement.

2. Which of the following organizations is the main influence on financial statement standards in Poland?
   a. International Accounting Standards Committee
   b. American Institute of Certified Public Accountants
   c. Financial Accounting Standards Board
   d. Government Accounting Standards Board

3. Which of the following is a working capital account under a socialist balance sheet?
   a. Cash   c. Accounts payable
   b. Equipment   d. Reserve for revenues

14-3 Select the best available answer:

1. Which of the following is an example of an intangible account in a Czech Republic balance sheet?
   a. Equipment   c. Patents
   b. Land   d. Receivables

2. Russian accounting principles are mostly for providing information for
   a. Creditors.   c. Taxation authorities.
   b. Shareholders.   d. Labor unions.
3. Which country was the first to open a stock exchange in the Eastern bloc?
   a. Russia   c. Hungary
   b. The Czech Republic   d. Poland
4. Which country had the most problems with inflation in 1991 and 1992?
   a. Russia   c. Hungary
   b. The Czech Republic   d. Poland
5. In moving from a controlled economy to a market economy, the most
   difficult area with respect to valuation is:
   a. Receivables.
   b. Payables.
   c. Tangible fixed assets (property, plant, and equipment).
   d. Cash.
6. In a market economy, it is not necessary to have
   a. An accounting profession.
   b. Generally accepted accounting principles.
   c. Trained accounting personnel.
   d. A national accounting board.
7. During periods of hyperinflation, which basis is the least relevant?
   a. Historical cost unadjusted
   b. Current cost
   c. Historical cost adjusted for changes in general price levels
   d. Fair market value

14-4   The Ludmila Co. decided to apply for a loan. It was requested to supply a balance sheet. Below are accounts with balances on December 31, 1996:

	Rubles
Intangible assets	25,000
Monetary assets	35,000
Bank credits secured by inventory	55,000
Inventory	40,000
Investments (short term)	50,000
Wages payable	10,000
Fixed assets	500,000
Investments (long term)	100,000

Required: Prepare an abbreviated balance sheet as mandated by the Russian Ministry of Finance. You will have to determine the amount for sources of assets.

14-5   The following are balances from selected accounts of Bakay Company, a Hungarian company:

	Forints
Share capital	100,000
Cash	50,000
Tangible assets	200,000
Capital reserves	145,000
Profit for the year	50,000
Wages payable	10,000
Reserve for profit adjustment (beginning of the year)	40,000

Required: Prepare the equity section of the Bakay Company balance sheet.

14-6 Jasinski Co., a company in Krakow, Poland, has goodwill on its books at a total cost of 126,000 zlotys. This is the first year of operation.

Required: Compute the amount of goodwill that should be amortized for the first year.

Case: Privatization Russian Style

Below are excerpts from a recent article from *The Wall Street Journal.*[2]

. . . Mr. Yeltsin had signed a privatization law in mid-1991, creating a state agency to oversee the unloading of state assets: the State Property Committee, known by its Russian initials, GKI. But little happened until—on the eve of the Soviet collapse—Mr. Gaidar appointed as head of the GKI a youthful politician from St. Petersburg, Anatoly Chubais.

. . . To help decide strategy, Mr. Chubais and his advisers compared plans for case-by-case privatization, such as Poland's, and mass privatization, such as the Czech Republic's. They debated how the models would translate to Russia. At that time, production in Russia was centrally controlled by ministries or subminitries, each running an entire industry. These organizations might not easily give up their authority. Reporting to the ministries were legions of so-called red directors, the apparatchiks spread across Russia who ran the actual factories, mines, oil fields and other state assets.

Mr. Chubais and his team concluded that in tackling this network, finesse would matter less than speed and scale. The only chance to reform Russia's economy and shore up the nation's new democracy was to start by quickly breaking the Soviet chains of central command.

In this divide-and-conquer strategy, the reformers aimed to entice the red directors into supporting privatization by offering them stakes in the enterprises

[2] Claudia Rosett and Steve Liesman, "Starting From Scratch: Much Has Gone Wrong With Russia's Privatization Efforts. But a Lot More Has Gone Right." *The Wall Street Journal,* 2 October 1995, pp. R14-R15.

they were already managing for the state. The industrial ministries, stripped of their assets, would be left to wither.

. . . A further aim was to create a broad base of property owners who would be opposed to reversing the changes. Matters such as raising revenue for the state and fine-tuning the distribution of state assets were secondary. For midsize and large enterprises, the GKI planners adopted a mass privatization strategy to be carried out largely by voucher auction, more like the high-speed Czech model than the deliberate Polish approach. The first step was for thousands of state enterprises to be "corporatized," or transformed into shareholding companies, with some portion of their shares slated for auction.

. . . To win over managers and workers of state businesses, as well as regional politicians, the GKI added a typically Russian touch of complexity: Each enterprise was allowed to choose from a menu of privatization plans.

In varying degrees, the plans allotted packets of shares—in many cases controlling stakes—to company insiders in exchange for cash or vouchers, or sometimes as straight giveaways. Another portion of the business would be auctioned to voucher holders generally. And in many cases a slice was reserved for the state—often for the regional GKI—to sell later for cash or so-called investment tenders, commitments to make substantial investments in companies in exchange for blocks of shares. When managers and workers could choose to keep a controlling interest in their privatized business, they usually did so.

Russian privatizers acknowledge that this tilt toward insider ownership was far from ideal for Russia's economy. Studies in recent years, including at least one on Russia, suggest that new owners and managers are more likely than old insiders to efficiently restructure a company. And restructuring of privatized businesses in Russia has indeed proved slow.

From a political standpoint, however, this approach offered incentives for both businesses and regional governments to go along with privatization in the first place.

. . . Since then, Russia has moved to the less systematic, more cumbersome process of selling yet more businesses, and remaining state stakes in companies, for investment tenders. Instead of spreading a company's shares among tens of thousands of little shareholders, as with vouchers, investment tenders allow big investors to put up the money needed for restructuring companies in exchange for big stakes.

But because investment-tender deals are generally decided on a case-by-case basis, not in an open auction, the opportunity for shady dealing is greater.

. . . Russian reformers are still grappling with some mighty hang-overs of central planning. One basic problem is the lack of property law—something privatizers in developed democracies can usually take for granted. Here, ambiguous property rights have deterred much-needed investment.

Russia's stock market, after an initial rally in 1994, went into a long slump from which it has only recently begun to recover. The slide was brought on when foreign investors discovered they couldn't be sure of owning stock they had paid for; company insiders could simply strike their names off the shareholder registers, most of which the companies themselves ran. As outlandish as it seems, there was no practical legal recourse. Only in the past few months has Russia begun crafting securities regulations to protect shareholders.

. . . Some shortcomings of Russia's initial blitz to create private property are also now making themselves felt. The special deals offered as inducements to insiders gave a big share of the pie to the old communist elite.

The resulting drag on restructuring means many ordinary Russians—those who didn't buy bread stores, but still work the nickel mines—have yet to feel big benefits from privatization. Meanwhile, they are resentfully watching the new nomenklatura enjoying the new perquisites of private ownership.

The greatest weakness of the program, says the World Bank's Mr. Blitzer, is that "The distribution of wealth which emerged was so unequal."

Required:
(1) Distinguish between the Polish and Czech privatization models.
(2) Discuss the strategy adopted by GKI to implement privatization. What were its strengths? Shortcomings?
(3) Referring to (2), what would you have done differently if you were in Mr. Chubais's position?
(4) Comment on the importance of legal framework for economic development.
(5) According to Mr. Blitzer of the World Bank, the greatest weakness of the Russian privatization program was that "the distribution of wealth which emerged was so unequal." Identify the reasons for this outcome of the program. What, if anything, could have been done differently to avoid this?

References

Alexander, David, and Simon Archer. *European Accounting Guide,* 2d ed. New York: Harcourt Brace & Company, 1995.

Allen, Michael. "Pro and Con." *The Wall Street Journal,* 2 October 1995, pp. R27-28.

———. "What Is Privatization, Anyway?" *The Wall Street Journal,* 2 October 1995, p. R4.

Anderson, Nancy. "The Globalization GAAP." *Management Accounting,* August 1993, pp. 52-54.

Becker, Gary S. "Rule No. 1 in Switching to Capitalism: Move Fast." *Business Week,* 29 May 1995, p. 18.

Belkaoui, Ahmed. *Multinational Financial Accounting.* New York: Quorum, 1991.

Catte, Pierto, Mastropasqua, and Cristina. "Financial Structure and Reforms in Central and Eastern Europe in the 1980's." *Journal of Banking and Finance,* vol.17, issue 5.

Center for International Education and Research in Accounting, Department of Accountancy. *The New Europe: Recent Political and Economic Implications for Accountants and Accounting.* Urbana, Ill.: University of Illinois, 1994.

Cheney, Glenn A. "Western Accounting Arrives in Eastern Europe," *Journal of Accountancy,* September 1990, pp. 41-43.

Clarke, P. "New Kids on the Bloc." *CA Magazine,* July 1990, pp. 17-22.

———. "The Eastern Front." *CA Magazine,* January 1993, pp. 30-37.

Doing Business in Hungary: Information Guide. New York: Price Waterhouse, February 1993.

Doing Business in Hungary. International Business Series. New York: Ernst & Young International, Ltd., 1993.

Doing Business in Poland: Information Guide. New York: Price Waterhouse, September 1992.

Doing Business in Poland: Supplement to the 1992 edition of the Information Guide. New York: Price Waterhouse, 1994.

Doing Business in the Czech and Slovak Republics: Information Guide. New York: Price Waterhouse, 1993.

Doing Business in the Czech Republic. International Business. New York: Ernst & Young International, Ltd., 1994.

Doing Business in the Russian Federation: Information Guide. New York: Price Waterhouse, April 1994.

Enthoven, Adolf, J. H. Jaroslav, V. Sokolov, and Alexander M. Petrachkov. *Doing Business in Russia and the Other Former Soviet Republics: Accounting and Joint Venture Issues.* Montvale, N.J.: Institute of Management Accountants, 1992.

Galuszka, Peter, Patricia Kranz, and Stanley Reed. "Russia's New Capitalism." *Business Week,* 10 October 1994, pp. 68-76.

Gupta, Parveen, P. "International Reciprocity in Accounting: Where in the World Are We Headed?" *Journal of Accountancy,* January 1992, pp. 45-54.

Hegarty, John. "Accounting Integration in Europe: Still on Track?" *Journal of Accountancy,* May 1993, pp. 92-95.

Hungary: International Tax and Business Guide Series. New York: Deloitte Touche Tohmatsu International, August 1994.

Jaruga, Alicja. Changing Rules of Accounting in Poland. *The European Accounting Review,* vol. 2, no. 1, 1993, pp. 115-126.

Kennett, David, and Marc Lieberman. *The Road to Capitalism: Economic Transformation in Eastern Europe and the Former Soviet Union.* Orlando, Fla.: The Dryden Press, 1992.

King, Neil Jr. "Faster, Faster." *The Wall Street Journal,* 2 October 1995, p. R6.

Krzywda, Danuta, Derek Bailey, and Marek Schroeder. "Financial Reporting by Polish Listed Companies for 1991." *The European Accounting Review,* vol. 3, no. 2, 1994, pp. 311-328.

Kvint, Vladimir. "Moscow Learns the Language of Business." *Journal of Accountancy,* November 1990, pp. 114-121.

Ling, Robert. "Valuation—The First Step." *Eastern Europe Bulletin. Deloitte Touche Tohmatsu,* June 1992, pp. 1-8.

Mandl, Dieter. "The New Austrian Financial Reporting Act." *The European Accounting Review,* vol. 2, no. 3, 1993, pp. 397-402.

Miller, Karen Lowry. "The Worst Is Finally Over in Eastern Germany." *Business Week,* 19 June 1995, p. 54.

Miller, Karen Lowry, Bill Javetski, Peggy Simpson, and Tim Smart. "Europe: The Push East." *Business Week,* 7 November 1994, pp. 48-49.

Rosett, Claudia, and Steve Liesman. "Starting from Scratch." *The Wall Street Journal,* 2 October 1995, p. R14-R15.

"Russia Leaps to Halt Bank System Paralysis," *Gulf News* (U.A.E.), 26 August 1995, p. 17.

Sherry, Gerald, and Russell Vinning. "Accounting for Perestroika." *Management Accounting,* April 1995, pp. 42-46.

Taxation in Eastern Europe, International Tax and Business Guide. New York: Deloitte Touche Tohmatsu International, February 1995.

United Nations Conference on Trade and Development Programme on Transnational Corporations. *Accounting, Valuation, and Privatization.* New York: United Nations, September 1993.

Glossary

Accounting Exposures. The transaction and translation risk exposures.

Accounting Principles. *See* Accounting Standards

Accounting Principles Board Opinion No. 8. The first attempt by the U.S. accounting profession to deal with the topic of pensions.

Accounting Principles Board Opinion No. 15. A standard issued by the Accounting Principles Board in the U.S. that outlines all the factors pertinent to the computation of earnings per common share.

Accounting Rate of Return (ARR). An accounting measure of income divided by an accounting measure of investment.

Accounting Rules. *See* Accounting Standards

Accounting Standards. The rules that govern the measuring and recording of economic activities and the reporting of accounting information to external users.

Accounting Standards Board (ASB). An organization in the United Kingdom that promulgates and issues accounting standards termed as Financial Reporting Standards.

Accounting Standards Committee (ASC). A committee in the United Kingdom that issued generally accepted accounting principles before being replaced by the Accounting Standards Board.

Accounting Standards Executive Committee (AcSEC). A committee formed by The American Institute of Certified Public Accountants. It issues standards (Statements of Position) on matters not covered by the Financial Accounting Standards Board.

Accrual Basis Accounting. An accounting basis that reflects transactions in the financial statements when they occur (and not as cash or its equivalent is received or paid).

Activity-Based Costing (ABC). An approach to costing that focuses on activities as the fundamental cost objects. It uses the cost of these activities as the basis for assigning costs to other cost objects such as products, services, or customers. It provides more accurate allocation of indirect costs than traditional methods.

Activity-Based Management. A discipline that focuses on the management of activities for improving the value received by the customer and the profit achieved by providing this value.

Activity Ratios. Ratios that measure how effectively the enterprise is using the assets employed.

Adequate Disclosure. Disclosure that is sufficient to meet information needs of the users of financial statements.

Advanced Determination Ruling (ADR).   A transfer pricing guideline in the U.S. that allows a company to get approval for a parent-subsidiary specific product pricing.

Alternative Minimum Tax (AMT).   A tax imposed in the U.S. that is equal to 20 percent of alternative mimimum taxable income.

Alternative Minimum Taxable Income (AMTI).   A U.S. corporation's taxable income that is modified by specified adjustments and tax preference items.

American Institute of Certified Public Accountants (AICPA).   An organization that issues the generally accepted auditing standards in the form of Statements on Auditing Standards in the United States.

American Institute of Certified Public Accountants' Statement on Auditing Standards No. 69.   According to this standard, the independent auditor's judgment concerning the "fairness" of the overall presentation of financial statements should be applied within the framework of generally accepted accounting principles.

Asia-Pacific Economic Cooperation (APEC).   An organization committed to the trade and investment concept of open regionalism. Its 18 member countries include Australia, Brunei, Canada, Chile, China, Hong Kong, Indonesia, Japan, Malaysia, Mexico, New Zealand, Papua New Guinea, Philippines, Singapore, South Korea, Taiwan, Thailand, and the U.S.

Associated Firms.   *See* Representative Firms

Association of Southeast Asian Nations (ASEAN).   The most important trading bloc in Southeast Asia. The member countries include Brunei, Indonesia, Malaysia, the Philippines, Singapore, Thailand, and Vietnam. The member countries plan to establish a free-trade area by 2003.

Auditor's Report.   A report that communicates the results of the external audit, and the format of the report is necessarily mandated by the nature of the audit. Since there are no worldwide uniform accounting and auditing standards, there is no worldwide uniform format of an auditor's report.

Australian Accounting Research Foundation (AARF).   An organization that issues the Australian Accounting Standards (AASs) on behalf of the Institute of Chartered Accountants in Australia and the Australian Society of Certified Practicing Accountants.

Australian Accounting Standards (AASBs).   Accounting standards issued in Australia by the Australian Accounting Standards Board. They are incorporated in the Corporation Law, and are designed either to give interpretation of certain standards or to deal with new issues.

Balance of Payments Deficit.   When a country's cumulative imports exceed its cumulative exports.

Balance of Payments Surplus.   When a country's cumulative exports exceed its cumulative imports.

Balance Sheet Recognition.   Information presented within the balance sheet.

Big Six.   Public accounting firms that have the capability to perform external audits in different parts of the world. The "Big Six" accounting firms include Arthur Andersen, KPMG Peat Marwick, Deloitte Touche Tohmatsu, Ernst & Young, Coopers & Lybrand, and Price Waterhouse.

Bilan Social (Social Report).   A required report in France. It contains mainly employee-related information covering topics such as pay structure, hiring policies, health and safety conditions, training, and industrial relations.

Budget.   The translation of corporate plans into financial terms.

Business Accounting Deliberation Council (BADC).   An organization in Japan that formulates and issues the financial accounting standards for business enterprises.

Canadian Institute of Chartered Accountants (CICA).   The only organization that issues accounting and auditing standards in Canada.

Cantador Publico.   An independent public accountant in Mexico.

Capital Budgeting.   The making of long-term planning decisions for investment.

Capital Leases.   Leases treated as a purchase of property by the lessee.

Capital Structure Ratios.   *See* Coverage Ratios

Center for International Financial Analysis & Research Inc. (CIFAR).   The organization that publishes *Global Company Handbook* and *Global Company News Digest.*

Centralized Internal Audit Model.   In this type of organization, there is only one central internal audit organization that is located at the headquarters of the parent company. The internal auditors travel to various parts of the world where operations are located to perform internal audit, and to perform other functions such as quality control, audit research, liaison with external auditors, training, and technical support.

Centralized Multinational Organizations.   Organizations that retain to a great extent the authority to make decisions at parent company headquarters.

Certified Internal Auditor (CIA).   A certification program sponsored by the Institute of Internal Auditors consisting of an examination and a mandatory two years of practical experience in internal auditing before certification.

Certified Public Accountant (CPA).   The professional designation for public accountants and independent (external) auditors in the United States.

Chief Financial Officer (CFO).   The senior officer empowered with oversight of the finance operations of an organization.

Classic System.   A national tax system that subjects income to taxes when income is received by the taxable entity.

Code de Commerce (Business Code). A source that provides the generally accepted accounting principles for business entities in France.

Codification of Standards for the Professional Practice of Internal Auditing. Pronouncements published by the Institute of Internal Auditors concerning general standards, specific standards, guidelines, statement of responsibilities, and a code of ethics.

Collectivism. The feeling that interests of the organization should have top priority.

Commissao de Valores Mobiliarios (CVM). The Securities Exchange Commission in Brazil that is responsible for accounting standards for publicly traded companies .

Commission des Operations de Bourse (Stock Exchange Commission). An organization in France that publishes recommendations, directed primarily toward public companies and their auditors, to adopt good accounting and auditing practices.

Committee of Sponsoring Organizations (COSO). A committee of the Treadway Commission that considers an effective internal audit function to be important for reliability and integrity of financial and operational information.

Companies and Allied Matters Decree (CAMD). In Nigeria, companies under the provision of the Companies and Allied Matters Decree of 1990 are required to appoint an independent auditor annually. The independent auditor is required to ascertain whether the information contained in the directors' report is consistent with the financial statements.

Consistency Principle. A requirement that accounting mentods be used consistenly from one period to the next unless conditions have changed that make it appropriate to switch to another method to provide more useful information.

Consolidated Financial Statements. The statements prepared by the parent company that essentially portray the financial position and results of operations of the parent and its subsidiaries as though they were one economic unit.

Constant Dollar Accounting. *See* Constant Monetary Unit Restatement

Constant Monetary Unit Restatement. A general term for restating historical cost basis financial statements for changes in general purchasing power of the monetary unit.

Control System. A system that compares the actual performance (results) with planned performance (goals) so that the management may take appropriate action as necessary.

Controlled Foreign Corporation (CFC). A U.S. multinational corporaion whose foreign subsidiaries' income and dividends are not subject to U.S. tax but instead are subject to the Sub-part F rule.

Convenience Translation. Translation of currency using the year-end exchange rates.

Conversion Value. The equivalent amount of another currency at a given exchange rate.

Copromotion Deal. A product that is promoted jointly by two companies under the same brand name and marketing plan. Generally, the manufacturing company handles receivables, inventory, and so on and pays a commission to the copromotor. Compensation is almost always based on the product sales level.

Correspondent Firms. *See* Representative Firms

Corridor Method. A method for the accounting of pensions that sets lower and upper limits on pension expense.

Cost-Based Transfer Pricing. The price one segment of a company charges another segment of the same company for the transfer of a good or a service based some type of cost. Examples include variable manufacturing costs, full manufacturing (absorption) costs, and full product costs.

Cost Center. A responsibility center in which a manager is accountable for costs only.

Cost Driver. Any factor that causes a change in the cost of an activity.

Cost Method. A method in which a subsidiary is retained at acquisition cost.

Cost Object. Any customer, product, service, project, or other work unit for which a separate cost measurement is desired.

Cost of Sales Model. Under this model for the presentation of costs of sales on the income statement in Western Europe, the manufacturing costs are shown first, followed by distribution costs, and finally administrative costs.

Coverage Ratios. Ratios that measure the degree of protection for long-term creditors and investors.

Current Cost Accounting. *See* Current Value Accounting

Current-Noncurrent Method. A translation method in which balance sheet items classified as "current" are translated at the current exchange rate on the balance sheet date and items classified as "noncurrent" are translated at appropriate historical rates.

Current Purchasing Power Accounting. *See* Constant Monetary Unit Restatement

Current Rate Method. A translation method that translates all assets and all liabilities at the current exchange rate—the rate at the balance sheet date, paid-in capital accounts at the applicable historical rates, dividends at the exchange rate on the date of declaration and on the income statement, and all revenue and expense items at the weighted average exchange rate for the period.

Current Value Accounting. Valuation systems designed to show the effects of changes in prices of individual items on financial statements.

Decentralized Internal Audit Model. In this type of organization, the internal auditors are on locations throughout the world, wherever international operations are located. Each international operation has its own internal audit organization.

Decentralized Multinational Organizations. Organizations that give managements of the subsidiaries considerable independence of action.

Declaration.   A declaration lacks an enforcement provision that binds parties. It can, however, be influential by getting commitment from the signatories.

Defined Benefit Plan.   A pension plan where the benefits to be received in the future are specified.

Defined Contribution Plans.   A pension plan where the assets in the pension fund determine the amount of retirement benefits.

Dependent Companies.   Companies under long-term control.

Direct-Financing Lease.   A lease where the lessor provides financing only, and assumes financial risks but does not assume inventory risk.

Discussion Document.   The second phase in the process of setting EU Directives. A document that is examined by the EU Commission working group and other interested parties.

Draft Directive.   The third phase in the process of setting EU Directives. Prepared for consideration by the European Parliament and the Union Economic and Social Committee.

Draft International Accounting Standard.   The final phase in the development of IASC's International Accounting Standards. Prepared by an IASC steering committee after its review of comments on the exposure draft. This draft is reviewed by the Board of the IASC and then published as an International Accounting Standard (IAS).

Draft Statement of Principles.   The second phase in the development of IASC's International Accounting Standards. A draft prepared by the Board of the IASC commenting on the point outline.

Dynamic Method.   A method of calculating pension liabilities in the Netherlands where the liabilities are related to annual wages.

Earnings Flexibility.   *See* Income Smoothing

Economic Exposure.   A condition that results from the impact of changes in exchange rates on future cash flows.

Economic Risk.   The uncertainty surrounding key elements of the investment process.

Efficiency Ratios.   *See* Activity Ratios

The Eighth Directive.   The EU Eighth Directive deals with auditing of financial statements of companies in EU countries, and specifies that they be consistent with EU law. It also sets qualifications for auditors and the firms conducting audits, including education and experience requirements. In addition, the Directive deals with ethical matters such as independence, and includes sanctions for cases in which audits are not conducted as prescribed by statute.

Environment-Specific.   An accounting system designed to provide information for making decisions in a given environment. Five major environmental influences on accounting consist of the economic system, political system, legal system, educational system, and religion.

Equity Method. A method in which income of a subsidiary is recognized by the parent company according to ownership percentage. The investment in subsidiary account balance is adajusted accordingly.

Equity Reserves. A general term to describe many different types of reserves that serve different purposes.

European Confederation of Institutes of Internal Auditing (ECIIA). This organization, comprised of 17 internal audit organizations representing 18 European nations plus Israel, helps in the development of internal auditing standards.

European Union (EU). A single trading block currently linking 15 European nations into a single market in order to eliminate tariff and custom restrictions. The 15 nations include Austria, Belgium, Denmark, Finland, France, Germany, Great Britain, Greece, Ireland, Italy, Luxembourg, Netherlands, Portugal, Spain, and Sweden.

European Union Directives. Rules issued by the European Union. These are binding on member countries.

Exchange Rate. The amount of one currency needed to obtain one unit of another currency.

Expense Liability Reserves. An equity reserve used to achieve income smoothing or to show a steady growth in income from year to year.

Expert Report. The first phase in the process of setting EU Directives. A report requested by the EU Commission on a selected project under consideration.

Exposure Draft. The fourth phase in the development of IASC International Accounting Standards. This draft is published after its approval by at least two-thirds of the Board of the IASC. Interested parties have six months to submit comments on the exposure draft.

Exposure Draft 53. A draft issued by the Australian Accounting Research Foundation that sets forth proposed standards for pensions in Australia.

External Expansion. Growth achieved when a company acquires one or more companies.

External Failure Costs. The costs of a defective product after it is shipped to the customer.

Facilitating Payments. Payments made to influence an official to take an action that the official must take anyway.

Factors of Production. A firm's inputs such as costs for labor, materials, machines, and buildings that are necessary for bringing the good to the market.

Femininity. The quality of life and nurturing.

Final Statement of Principles. The third phase in the development of the IASC International Accounting Standards. Submitted by the steering committee to the Board of the IASC after the Board's review of the comments on the draft statement.

Financial Accounting. A component of an organization's internal accounting system that provides information primarily for users outside the organization.

Financial Accounting Standards Board (FASB). The main body responsible for promulgating accounting standards in the United States.

Financial Ratio Analysis. An evaluation of financial performance and financial position between two or more firms.

Financial Reporting Disclosures. The information presented in financial statements. Such disclosures may be either within the statements or in the accompanying notes.

Financial Reporting Standard No. 3 (FRS3). An accounting standard in Great Britain that highlights a range of important components of financial performance to aid users in their understanding of accounts and to assist them in forming a basis for their assessment of future results and cash flows.

Financial Reporting Standards (FRSs). Standards issued by the Accounting Standards Board in the United Kingdom.

Financial Statement Analysis. The conversion of the data in financial statements into useful information.

Financing Leases. In the U.S., a type of capital lease where the lessor provides financing and earns interest revenue but earns no profit on the lease.

Footnote Disclosure. Information contained in a note accompanying the financial statements.

Foreign-Controlled Corporation (FCC). A corporation whose income from investment and businesses is subject to U.S. taxes.

Foreign Corrupt Practices Act (FCPA). An act passed by the U.S. Congress in 1977 and revised in 1988 intended to curb influence peddling.

Foreign Currency Forward Contract. An agreement with a currency trader, e.g., a bank, to deliver in the future one currency for another at an agreed-upon "forward" exchange rate.

Foreign Currency Transactions. Transactions denominated in a currency other than the reporting currency of the entity.

Foreign Currency Translation. A translation of amounts in accounts of subsidiaries recorded in a foreign currency to the currency used for consolidated financial statements.

Foreign Exchange Risk Management. The management of the risk of loss from currency exchange rate movements on transactions, translation, or remeasurement involving foreign currency.

Foreign Sales Corporation (FSC). A form of tax incentive designed to encourage exports by U.S. corporations.

Foreign Tax Credit. A means to avoid double taxation of foreign source income.

Forward Exchange Contract. An agreement to buy (or sell) a foreign currency in the future at a fixed rate called a forward rate.

Forward Rate. The fixed future rate used in a forward exchange contract.

The Fourth Directive. The EU Fourth Directive contains comprehensive accounting rules relevant to corporate accounting. It covers financial statements, their contents, methods of presentation, valuation methods, and disclosure of information.

Framework for the Preparation and Presentation of Financial Statements. This framework guides the IASC steering committees in their development of international standards.

Free Market Economic System. An economic concept used to denote the economic system of a country unimpeded by government restrictions, and ideally subject to the laws of supply and demand of the market.

Full Consolidation. The consolidation of dependent companies.

Functional Currency. The currency of the primary environment in which an entity operates.

Gearing Adjustment. A gearing adjustment equals average borrowing divided by average operating assets multiplied by total current value adjustment for cost of goods sold, depreciation, etc. It shows the benefit (or disadvantage) to shareholders from debt financing during a period of changing prices. The amount of gearing adjustment is added (deducted) to current cost income.

General Agreement on Tariffs and Trade (GATT). An international agreement designed to limit governmental intervention to restrict international trade.

General Price Index. An index used to estimate the amount of inflation or deflation in an economy.

General Price-level Accounting. *See* Constant Monetary Unit Restatement

General Reserve. An equity reserve that normally serves the same purpose as an appropriation of retained earnings, i.e., it temporarily restricts the maximum amount that can be declared for dividends.

Generally Accepted Accounting Principles (GAAP). Accounting principals in the U.S. that are recognized by a standard-setting body or by authoritative support.

Global.   International or worldwide.

Global Capital Markets.   Capital markets in a global economy that attract investors and investees from throughout the world.

Going Concern Concept.   The accounting concept that an economic entity will continue in operation for the foreseeable future.

Goodwill.   The amount paid by the buyer of a business for above-normal profits.

Governmental Accounting Standards Board (GASB).   In the United States, an organization responsible for establishing accounting principles for municipal and state government bodies, hospitals, universities, and other not-for-profit entities.

Harmonization.   Keeping the differences among national accounting standards to a minimum. Alternative accounting rules or practices may exist in different countries as long as they are "in harmony" with one another and can be reconciled

Hedging Strategies.   Measures taken to protect against risks associated with foreign exchange fluctuations.

High-Power-Distance Culture.   A state in which a person at a higher position in the organizational hierarchy makes the decision and the employees at the lower levels simply follow the instructions.

Historical Cost Convention.   A method of accounting using data in terms of the units of currency in which a transaction originally took place.

Imperfect Market.   A market where factors of production are relatively immobile

Imperfect Market Theory.   A firm engages in international trade to gain access to factors of production.

Income Leveling.   *See* Income Smoothing

Income Smoothing.   Use of reserves to transfer income between periods.

Individualism.   A state in which the employee attaches higher importance to personal and family interests than to the organization.

Inflation Accounting.   Accounting to cope with changing price levels.

Influence Peddling.   Providing monetary or nonmonetary benefits to a person in a position of authority in exchange for an action by that person that benefits the company—normally an action would not have been taken without the monetary or nonmonetary benefit.

Institute of Internal Auditors (IIA).   The most influential international organization in the development of internal auditing standards. It was established in 1941.

Instituto Brasileiro de Contadores (IBRACON).   The Brazilian Accountants' Institute that issues and codifies accounting standards.

Instituto Mexicano de Contadores Publicos (Mexican Institute of Public Accountants).
The accounting standard-setting body in Mexico.

Integrated Foreign Operation.   A foreign operation whose economic activities have a direct impact on the reporting (parent) entity.

Integrated System.   A national tax system that attempts to eliminate double taxation by taxing corporate income differently depending on whether it is distributed to shareholders or retained internally.

Intergovernmental Working Group of Experts on International Standards of Accounting and Reporting (ISAR). The ISAR group, consisting of 34 elected members representing governments around the globe, was established by the United Nations to focus on the development of international standards of accounting and reporting.

Internal Auditing.   An objective evaluation of operations and control systems of an organization to determine whether its policies and procedures are being followed and also whether its resources are safeguarded and used efficiently to achieve organizational objectives.

Internal Expansion.   Growth achieved by introducing new product lines, services, or capacity.

Internal Failure Costs.   The costs incurred when a defective product is detected before it is shipped to customers.

International.   *See* Global

International Accounting.   Accounting for international transactions, comparisons of accounting principles in different countries, and harmonization of diverse accounting standards worldwide.

International Accounting Standard (IAS).   An accounted rule developed by the International Accounting Standards Committee in order to harmonize accounting standards worldwide.

International Accounting Standard 19.   A standard issued by the International Accounting Standards Committee that guides companies that have set up pensions in a country where no accounting standards for pensions exist, such as Nigeria.

International Accounting Standard 21.   A standard issued by the International Accounting Standards Committee that requires the current rate method for translation of self-sustaining foreign operations. The translation gains or losses are transferred to reserves and reported in shareholders' equity. Income statement items of a self-sustaining foreign operation should be translated either at the actual rates or the average rate for the period, and the gains and losses are taken to a separate section of the shareholders' equity.

International Accounting Standard 29.   A standard issued by the International Accounting Standards Committee that requires that financial statements of a company reporting in a currency of a hyperinflationary economy be restated at balance sheet date for general purchasing power changes.

International Accounting Standards Committee (IASC). An organization engaged in efforts to harmonize accounting standards. In some countries, IASC standards are automatically adopted as national accounting standards.

International Accounting Standard Committee's Consultative Group. An international consultative group established by the International Accounting Standards Committee to expand the representation of organizations interested in financial reporting.

International Corporation. A company that exports its products overseas.

International Federation of Accountants (IFAC). An organization engaged in efforts to harmonize auditing standards worldwide.

International Monetary Fund (IMF). An agency of the United Nations established in 1994. Its major objectives include promoting stability in exchange rates, providing temporary funds to member countries to correct imbalances in international payments, promoting the free flow of funds across countries, promoting international cooperation in monetary issues, and promoting free trade.

International Organization of Securities Commission (IOSCO). A private organization of securities market regulators which promotes the integration of securities markets worldwide. Currently, it is working with the IASC to develop a core set of accounting standards by 1999 that will be acceptable for listing in securities markets worldwide.

International Resource Service Quick Reference Catalog. An annotated bibliography covering various aspects of international business developed by the State Committee on Global Opportunities of the California Society of Certified Public Accountants.

International Standard on Auditing 10 (Using the Work of an Internal Auditor). This pronouncement, issued by the International Federation of Accountants, requires the external auditor to evaluate the internal audit function. This standard also contains guidance regarding the procedures that should be considered by the external auditor in assessing the work of the internal auditor for the purpose of using that work.

International Standards of Accounting and Reporting for Transnational Corporations. A report issued by the Group of Experts on International Standards of Accounting and Reporting that included a list of financial and nonfinancial items that should be disclosed by multinational corporations to host governments.

International Standards on Auditing (ISA). A comprehensive set of auditing standards issued by the International Federation of Accountants. Audits conducted in accordance with these standards can be relied on by securities regulatory authorities for multinational reporting purposes.

Investment Center. A responsibility center where the manager is responsible for costs, revenues, profits, and investment in assets.

Japanese Institute of Certified Public Accountants (JICPA). The only professional accounting and auditing organization in Japan.

Just-In-Time (JIT) Production. A production system in which each component on a production line is produced immediately as needed by the next step in the production line.

Kabushiki Kaisha. Joint stock companies in Japan.

Kaizen Budgeting. A budgeting approach that projects costs on the basis of future improvements rather than current practices and methods.

Lease. A contract between a lessor and a lessee that gives the lessee the right to use specific property owned by the lessor, for a given time period, in exchange for cash or other consideration—typically a commitment to make future cash payments.

Leverage Ratios. *see* Coverage Ratios

Licensing Program. Proprietary information, such as patent rights or expertise, that is licensed by the owner (licensor) to another party (licensee). Compensation paid to the licensor usually includes license issuance fees, milestone payments, and/or royalties.

Limitadas (Ltda). Limited liability companies in Brazil whose owners are liable for the full amount of the company's legal capital until it has been paid.

Liquidity Ratios. Ratios that measure the enterprise's short-run ability to pay its maturing obligations.

Low-Power-Distance Culture. A state in which employees perceive few power differences and follow a superior's instructions only when either they agree or feel threatened.

Managerial Accounting (or Management Accounting). A component of an organization's internal accounting system that provides financial and nonfinancial information used by managers and others within the organization for use in planning, controlling, and decision making.

Market-Based Transfer Pricing. The price one segment of a company charges another segment of the same company for the transfer of a good or a service based on its current market price.

Marketing Quality Assurance (MQA). Quality specifications included in the British Standard 7850 Guide to total quality management.

Masculinity. The relative importance of the qualities associated with men such as assertiveness and materialism.

Master Operating Budget. A budget that summarizes corporate goals for a period of time (normally one year).

Material Segment. A segment of a company or group of companies whose revenue, profits, or assets represent a significant portion of the total revenue, profits, or assets of the company or a group of companies. The criteria vary from country to country, but usually a segment is considered material if it provides 10 percent of total assets, revenue, or income.

Materiality Concept. This concept, requiring use of professional judgement, describes information that must be included or disclosed to prevent financial statements from misleading their users.

Measurement. Recording economic transactions in the accounting system.

Merger relief. An exemption from accounting for the premium on shares used to acquire a subsidiary.

Monetary Items. All assets and liabilities expressed in fixed amounts of currency.

Monetary-Nonmonetary Method. A translation method that restates monetary items on the balance sheet at the current exchange rate on the balance sheet date and nonmonetary items at their historical exchange rates.

Multinational Corporation (MNC). A company that considers the globe as a single marketplace.

Multinational Enterprise (MNE). *see* Multinational Corporation

National Association of Security Dealers (NASDAQ). The automated quotation system for the over-the-counter market, showing current bid-ask prices for thousands of stocks.

National Consumer Index (NCR). The index used in Mexico to represent the excess (deficiency) due to the difference betreen current cost and holding gains in inventory and fixed assets.

National Institute of Statistics, Geography & Informatics (INEGI). A Mexican organization that provides foreign investors and multinational corporations that are interested in expanding their presence in developing countries with guideposts on wages, prices, and other critical variables.

National Trade Data Bank (NTDB). Data compiled by 15 U.S. government agencies for the U.S. Department of Commerce consisting of the latest census data on U.S. imports and exports by commodity and country, the complete CIA World Factbook, current market research, the Foreign Traders Index, and many other data series.

Negative Exposure. A condition that exists when a foreign subsidiary has more current liabilities than current assets.

Negotiated Transfer Pricing. A system that requires managers of selling and buying divisions to negotiate a mutually acceptable transfer price.

Net Present Value (NPV) Method. A discounted cash-flow method of calculating the expected net monetary gain or loss from a project by discounting all expected future cash inflows and outflows to the present point in time, using the required rate of return.

Nigerian Accounting Standards Board (NASB). The organization that issues the statement of the accountancy standards in Nigeria.

Nonmonetary Item. An item that does not represent a claim to, or for, a specified number of monetary units.

Nonroutine Reports.   Reports prepared for the purpose of providing information to managers to assist them formulate policies, prepare strategic plans, and prepare tactical (operational) plans.

North American Free Trade Agreement (NAFTA).   A trade agreement among Canada, Mexico, and the U.S. with the objective of creating a single market with no trade barriers.

One-Transaction Approach.   An approach used to translate foreign currency where the transaction is not considered to be completed until the final settlement. Any transaction gain or loss will be reflected on the settlement date in an adjustment to the value of the resource acquired.

Open Regionalism.   The use of declarations instead of treaties to combine an informal regional trading strategy with a commitment to global openness.

Operating Leases.   A lease where the lessor retains most of the risks and rewards of ownership.

Operational Plans.   *see* Tactical Plans

Ordre des Experts Comptables et des Comptables Agrees (Institute of Public Accountants and Authorized Accountants). An organization that issues recommendations to assist its members in the application of accounting standards in France.

Organization for Economic Cooperation and Development (OECD).   An organization that promotes worldwide economic development in general, and economic growth and stability of its member countries in particular. Its work focuses primarily on providing financial accounting and reporting guidelines to multinational corporations for disclosures to host countries.

Parent.   The company acquiring the stock of a subsidiary.

Parent/Subsidiary Relationship.   A combination of companies where control of other companies, known as subsidiaries, is achieved by a company, known as the parent, through acquisition of voting stock.

Payback Period (PBP) Method.   A capital budgeting method that measures the time it will take to recoup, in the form of net cash inflows, the net dollars invested in a project.

Performance Report.   A routine report that compares actual performance against budgetary goals.

Plan Compatable General (General Accounting Plan).   A chart of accounts that must be followed by all manufacturing and commercial entities in France.

Point Outline.   The first phase in the development of IASC International Accounting Standards. A review by an IASC steering committee of initial suggestions for new accounting standard topics proposed by any member of IASC or any other interested party.

Political Risk.   The actions and activities of foreign (host) governments directed at multinational corporations.

Pooling of Interests Method. An accounting method used for a business combination where the acquired entity's assets and equities are combined at book value. No goodwill is created in a pooling of interests.

Portfolio Approach. A method used to manage economic exposure of a company by offsetting negative exposure in one country with positive exposure in another.

Positive Exposure. A condition that exists when a foreign subsidiary has more current assets than current liabilities.

Power Distance. The extent of inequality between superiors and subordinates.

Principles of Professional Conduct. A section in the American Institute of Certified Public Accountants' Code of Professional Conduct that contains guidelines about the proper behavior of Certified Public Accountants in the United States.

Privatization. The transfer of property from the state to individuals and private enterprises.

Product Cycle Theory. A firm's progression from its domestic markets to international markets with exports being the entry point in international trade.

Productivity. The output per hour of workers' time.

Professional Organizations. An organization whose membership consists of individuals in a profession.

Profit Center. A responsibility center where the manager is responsible for both revenues and costs.

Profitability Ratios. Ratios that measure the degree of success or failure of a given enterprise or division for a given period of time.

Proportional Consolidation. The vehicle used for joint ventures where the percentage of shares held is applied to each line of the balance sheet and income statement.

Proportionate Consolidation. *see* Proportional Consolidation

Proposed Directive. The final phase in the process of setting EU Directives. Based on the comments received form the draft directive, this document is considered by the Union Council of Ministers. Adoption of a proposed directive or regulation requires a unanimous vote of the Council.

Prudence Concept. The concept that provision be made for all known liabilities and losses whether the amount is known with certainty or not.

Purchase Method. An accounting method used for a business combination where the acquired entity's assets and equities are combined at fair market value. Goodwill is created to the extent that cost exceeds the fair market value of the identifiable assets of the unit acquired.

Purchasing Power Gain. A gain that arises from holding monetary items during times when the general purchasing power of the monetary unit changes.

Purchasing Power Loss. A loss that that arises from holding monetary items during times when the general purchasing power of the monetary unit changes.

Qualified Business Unit (QBU). A self-contained foreign business operation whose functional currency is determined by the currency in which the unit keeps accounting records, borrows or lends money, and measures significant revenues and expenses.

Realization Concept. The concept that revenue should be recognized when goods or services have been transferred.

Realized Gains. Gains that are actually incurred.

Realized Losses. Losses that are actually incurred.

Regional Audit Staff Internal Audit Model. In this type of organization, the regional staff is responsible for performing audits in all of the operations in the region. This model has recently been gaining popularity among many multinationals.

Rental. A type of lease in which the lessor retains not only legal title, but most of the risks and rewards of ownership.

Representative Firms. Locally owned accounting firms that have agreements with a "Big Six" or some other accounting firm. The agreement covers areas such as standards of performance and standards of conduct.

Research and Development Costs. The direct and indirect outlays for exploring potential new products and developing new products.

Research Collaboration. Two or more companies that participate in a defined research program and benefit from the results. Research costs can be funded entirely by one of the parties, shared equally by the parties, or shared according to some other agreed-upon proportion.

Resident Staff and Central Reviewers Internal Audit Model. In this type of organization, the resident internal auditors located on site perform the audit work. Their work is periodically reviewed by the traveling members of the parent company's central internal audit staff.

Resident Staff and Regional and Central Reviewers Internal Auditing Model. In this type of organization, the resident staff conducts the internal audits. Regional reviewers, responsible for certain geographical areas, oversee their work to ensure compliance with the parent company policies. The central staff from headquarters makes periodic reviews to ensure reporting uniformity throughout all the regions.

Resident Staff and Regional Reviewers Internal Audit Model. In this type of organization, the work of the resident internal auditors is reviewed by the regional reviewers to ensure uniformity. Independent review from regional staff also enhances the degree of reliability of the reports.

Residual Income (RI). RI expresses performance in the form of a profit amount that is left after the cost of invested capital has been subtracted.

Return on Assets (ROA).   ROA equals net income divided by total assets.

Return on Investment (ROI).   ROI incorporates the investment base and profits to assess performance.

Revaluation Reserve.   An equity reserve used to value fixed assets at an appraised value or a replacement value. This is done by upward adjustment of the asset and correspondingly recording an equal amount in a revaluation reserve.

Revenue Center.   A responsibility center in which a manager is accountable for revenues only.

Routine Reporting.   Reports that enable managers to plan activities and control operations.

Rules of Professional Conduct.   A section in the American Institute of Certified Public Accountants' Code of Professional Conduct that contains rules that govern the performance of professional services and identify both acceptable and unacceptable behavior.

Sales-Type Leases.   In the U.S., a type of capital lease where a dealer's or manufacturer's profit or loss is a basic part of the transaction for the lessor.

San Francisco Declaration.   A declaration between 20 Pacific Rim nations that established five key goals: (1) The removal of barriers to trade, investment, and the flow of technology, (2) Nondiscriminatory commercial access for outside economies, (3) Strengthening efforts to keep the Pacific Rim region and the global economic system open, (4) Adherence to the principles of the General Agreement on Tariffs and Trade, and (5) Accommodation of subregional trade pacts.

Secondary Statements.   A complete set of financial statements including accompanying notes prepared according to the accounting standards of another country. Independent auditors express an opinion on secondary statements using the auditing standards of that country.

Selective Restatements.   Partial restatements of companies' reports used to help resolve the problems created by diversity in accounting standards throughout the world.

Self-Sustaining Foreign Operation.   A foreign operation whose activities generally have no direct impact on the reporting entity's operations.

The Seventh Directive.   The EU Seventh Directive addresses consolidated financial statement issues.

Shokentorihikiho (Securities and Exchange Law).   The set of requirements in Japan that applies to companies that have raised over 100 million yen publicly and are either listed on stock exchanges or trade in over-the-counter markets.

Sociedada Anonima (SA).   A corporate form of company organized to do business in Brazil. It is a required form for all public companies.

Solvency Ratios.   *see* Liquidity Ratios

Special Purpose Reports. Reports that help managers make resource allocation and pricing decisions.

Specific Price Index. An index that shows the price changes for a specific good or service over time.

Spot Rate. The rate quoted for current currency transactions.

Standardization. Full comparability of accounting information.

State Property Committee (GKI). A state agency in Russia created in 1991 to oversee the unloading of state assets.

Statement of Financial Accounting Standards No. 33. A standard issued by the Financial Accounting Standards Board in the U.S. in 1979 requiring general purchasing power information as well as current value information on supplementary basis from certain large companies. This standard was withdrawn in 1986.

Statement of Financial Accounting Standards No. 52. A U.S. foreign currency standard issued by the Financial Accounting Standard Board acknowledging that the functional currency of an entity is the currency of the primary environment in which the entity operates.

Statement of Financial Accounting Standards No. 87. A standard issued by the Financial Accounting Standards Board in the U.S. that requires firms to use the corridor method when accounting for pensions.

Statement of Financial Accounting Standards No. 89. A mandate issued by the Financial Accounting Standards Board in the U.S. to rescind SFAS No. 33 in the U.S.

Statement of Financial Accounting Standards No. 106. A standard issued by the Financial Accounting Standards Board in the U.S. that requires the use of accrual accounting for post-retirement benefits other than pensions and is effective for fiscal years beginning after December 15, 1992.

Statement of Financial Accounting Standards No. 115. A standard issued by the Financial Accounting Standards Board in the U.S. that requires valuation at current value (market-to-market) for equity securities with a readily determinable market value and for debt securities not intended to be held to maturity in the U.S.

Statement of Standard Accounting Practice (SSAP) 3. An accounting standard in the U.K. that requires listed companies to show earnings per share on the face of the income statement.

Statement of Standard Accounting Practice (SSAP) 16. A standard issued in the United Kingdom that requires current cost accounting either in supplementary statements or in the primary statements with historical cost also as a requirement. It was withdrawn in 1988 primarily due to criticism from business and a declining inflation rate in the U.K.

Statement of Standard Accounting Practice (SSAP) 24. The authority for pension accounting in the United Kingdom which sets forth the measurement and disclosure requirements.

Statement on Internal Audit Standard 5. A standard issued by the Institute of Internal Auditors that specifies that there should be maximum coordination between internal and external auditors.

Statements of Financial Accounting Concepts. Fundamental concepts on which accounting and reporting standards are based in the United States.

Statements of Recommended Practice (SORPs). Statements issued by the Accounting Standards Committee in the United Kingdom that are used when no specific guidelines exist for a specialized area.

Statements of Standard Accounting Practice (SSAPs). Statements issued by the Accounting Standards Committee before the Accounting Standards Board was formed in the United Kingdom.

Statements of Accountancy Standards. The accounting standards in Nigeria that are mostly based on International Accounting Standards issued by the International Accounting Standards Committee.

Statements on Auditing Standards (SAS). Standards issued by the American Institute of Certified Public Accountants in the U.S. concerning generally accepted auditing standards.

Static Method. A method used to calculate pension liabilities in the Netherlands where the liabilities are related to the years of service of the employee.

Statutory Consolidation. A transaction that consists of acquiring the net assets of another company or companies.

Statutory Merger. One company acquires the net assets of another company or companies.

Statutory (Legal) Reserve. An equity reserve required by several countries to provide additional protection to creditors.

Strategic Alliance. A firm's collaboration with companies in other countries to share rights and responsibilities as well as revenues and expenses as defined in a written agreement. Some common types of strategic alliances include research collaboration, a licensing program, and a copromotion deal.

Strategic Plan. A plan that integrates an organization's major goals, policies, and action sequences into a cohesive whole.

Strategic Planning. The process of deciding on the goals of the organization and the strategies for attaining these goals.

Sub-part F Rule. A tax provision in the U.S. that counters the widespread formation of business operations in the "tax-haven" foreign locations, places where U.S. corporations form a paper comapny for the purpose of shifting income to foreign jurisdictions that have no or low corporate tax rates.

Subsidiary.   The company whose voting stock is acquired by a parent company to exercise control over it.

Tactical Plans.   Nonroutine plans that are designed to implement strategic plans.

Target Costing.   A costing method that sets cost targets for new products based on market price.

Temporal Method.   A currency translation method in which translation is viewed as a restatement of the financial statements. The foreign currency amounts are translated at the exchange rates in effect at the dates when those items were measured in the foreign currency.

Territorial Approach.   A national tax system that only taxes domestic income.

Theory of Comparative Advantage.   Each country should produce only those goods and services that it can produce with relative efficiency.

Trading Blocs.   Free trade zones created by member countries through mutual agreements.

Transaction Risk Exposure.   A condition that is caused by the changes in the exchange rate between the transaction date and the settlement date.

Transfer Price.   The price one segment of a company charges another segment of the same company for the transfer of a good or a service.

Transnational Corporation (TNC).   The term favored by the United Nations as an alternative to the term *multinational corporation.*

Trend Analysis.   A financial analysis that provides intrafirm as well as interfirm comparisons for two or more periods or dates.

True and Fair View.   A British concept of what financial statements ought to convey and an important feature of the Fourth Directive. The implementation of this concept means that companies may be required to disclose additional or different information. Each country determines, based on its own circumstances, how its corporations should comply with the true and fair view concept.

Turnover Ratios.   *see* Activity Ratios

Two-Transaction Approach.   An approach used to translate foreign currency where any gains or losses are separately recorded as gains or losses from exchange rate exchanges.

U.S. Foreign Tax Credit (FTC).   A dollar-for-dollar reduction in the taxpayer's U.S. tax liability.

Uncertainty Avoidance.   The extent to which uncertainty is avoided in a culture.

Unconsolidated Financials.   Financial statements that are not "consolidated." This occurs when the parent and its subsidiaries are in such dissimilar businesses that presenting consolidated statements would not give the correct picture.

United Nations (UN).   An organization representing governments of all countries in the world.

United Nations' Children Fund (UNICEF). A program sponsored by the United Nations that provides developmental programs for needy children all around the world.

United Nations Economic and Social Council. A council empowered to make or initiate studies with respect to international economic matters and to make recommendations on such matters to UN members. It established the Commission on Transnational Corporations in 1974.

Universal. *see* Global

Unrealized Gains. Gains that are not yet actually incurred, for example, as a result of a foreign currency translation.

Unrealized Losses. Losses that are not yet actually incurred, for example, as a result of a foreign currency translation.

Value Added. Value added equals total revenue minus the cost of goods, materials, and services purchased externally.

Value Added Activities. Activities that customers perceive as increasing the utility (usefulness) of the products or services they purchase.

Value Added Statements. Primarily used in European countries for the purpose of showing, in financial terms, the contributions made by many participating groups in the creation of wealth in a company.

Value-Added Tax (VAT). An indirect corporate tax that is the major source of government revenues in Europe.

Zeiko (Income Tax Law). An income tax law in Japan that covers the determination of taxable income.

Index